HUMAN BEHAVIOR

An Inventory of Scientific Findings

BERNARD BERELSON

The Population Council

GARY A. STEINER

University of Chicago

HUMAN BEHAVIOR

An Inventory
of Scientific
Findings

HARCOURT, BRACE & WORLD, INC.
NEW YORK / BURLINGAME

CREDITS

ACOUSTICAL SOCIETY OF AMERICA For figure on page 356, from the *Journal of the Acoustical Society of America*, 22, 1950, p. 728, by Alex Bavelas. Published by the American Institute of Physics, Inc. Reprinted by permission of the Acoustical Society of America and the author.

AMERICAN ACADEMY OF POLITICAL AND SOCIAL SCIENCE For table on page 394, from the *Annals of the American Academy of Political and Social Science*, March, 1948, p. 86, by Liston Pope.

AMERICAN ASSOCIATION FOR THE ADVANCEMENT OF SCIENCE For figure and table on pages 42, 43, from *Science*, 130, July 17, 1959, pp. 134, 140, by Eckhard H. Hess. Reprinted by permission of *Science* magazine and the author.

For table on page 103, from *Science*, 132, August, 1960, p. 350, by Eckhard H. Hess and James Polt. Copyright 1960 by the American Association for the Advancement of Science. Reprinted by permission of *Science* magazine and the authors.

For table on page 176, from *Science*, 131, June 10, 1960, p. 1707, by William Dement. Copyright 1960 by the American Association for the Advancement of Science. Reprinted by permission of *Science* magazine and the author.

For figures on page 247, from *Science*, 130, August 21, 1959, p. 422, by Harry F. Harlow and Robert R. Zimmerman. Reprinted by permission of *Science* magazine and the authors.

For figures on page 248, from *Science*, 127, February 14, 1958, pp. 316, 317, by James Olds. Reprinted by permission of *Science* magazine and the author.

AMERICAN INSTITUTE OF PHYSICS For figure on page 93, from the *Journal of the Optical Society of America*, 28, 1938, p. 270, by Selig Hecht and Simon Shlaer.

AMERICAN LAW INSTITUTE For table on page 632, from *The Death Penalty*, by Thorsten Sellin, 1959. Copyright 1959. Reprinted with permission of The American Law Institute and the author.

AMERICAN PHILOSOPHICAL SOCIETY For table on page 191, from *Proceedings of the American Philosophical Society*, 96, 1952, p. 456, by Morris Swadesh. Reprinted by permission of the American Philosophical Society and the author.

AMERICAN POLITICAL SCIENCE ASSOCIATION For figures on page 420, from the *American Political Science Review*, 46, 1952, p. 1052, by Duncan MacRae, Jr.

AMERICAN PSYCHOLOGICAL ASSOCIATION For figures and tables from the following publications of the Association:

American Psychologist—figure on page 62, from 10, 1955, p. 811, by Nancy Bayley; graphs on page 98, from 17, 1962, p. 30, by S. S. Stevens; graph on page 134, from 11, 1956, p. 230, by B. F. Skinner.

Archives of Psychology—graph on page 510, from No. 194, January, 1936, p. 20, by E. L. Horowitz.

Journal of Abnormal and Social Psychology—table on page 94, from 57, 1958, p. 31, by N. F. Dixon; figure on page 117, from 42, 1947, p. 40, by J. S. Bruner and C. C. Goodman; figure on page 142, from 59, 1959, p. 269, by C. D. Williams; figure on page 145, from 51, 1955, p. 673, by W. S. Verplanck; table on page 147, from 59, 1959, p. 255, by H. C. Quay; figure and table on page 149, from 57, 1958, p. 14, by M. T. Mednick and O. R. Lindsley; table on page 154, from 59, 1959, p. 179, by Elliot Aronson and Judson Mills; figures on page 182, from 38, 1943, pp. 512, 513, by J. M. Levine and Gardner Murphy; figure on page 253, from 57, 1958, p. 169, by J. L. Gerwitz and D. M. Baer; table on page 255, from 65, 1962, p. 130, by S. W. Becker and Jean Carroll; figure on page 275, from 60, 1960, p. 55, by J. W. Atkinson and G. H. Litwin; graph on page 347, from 46, 1951, p. 96, by Leon Festinger and John Thibaut; figures on page 357, from 46, 1951, pp. 328, 330, by G. A. Heise and G. A. Miller; table on page 369, from 52, 1956, pp. 126–27, by Nancy Morse and E. Reimer; table on page 549, from 49, 1954, p. 213, by I. L. Janis and B. T. King; table on page 552, from 48, 1953, p. 84, by I. L. Janis and Seymour Feshbach.

Journal of Comparative and Physiological Psychology—figures on pages 273, 274, from 41, 1948, pp. 457, 459, by Judson S. Brown.

Journal of Consulting Psychology—table on page 288, from 16, 1952, p. 321, by H. J. Eysenck.

Journal of Experimental Psychology—figure on page 167, from 32, 1943, p. 514, by L. J. Briggs and H. B. Reed; table on page 175, from 53, 1957, p. 341, by William Dement and Nathaniel Kleitman; figure on page 179, from 51, 1956, p. 94, by C. W. Simon and W. H. Emmons; figure on page 183, from 12, 1929, pp. 15, 19, by J. J. Gibson; figure and table on page 184, from 15, 1932, pp. 80, 81, by L. Carmichael, H. P. Hogan, and A. A. Walter; table on page 203, from 44, 1952, p. 289, by R. E. Adamson; figure on page 204, from 47, 1954, p. 124, by R. E. Adamson and D. W. Taylor; figure on page 246, from 55, 1958, p. 291, by D. E. Berlyne.

Psychological Bulletin—table on page 144, from 55, 1958, p. 160, by Leonard Krasner; figures on page 200, from 49, 1952, p. 229, by Charles E. Osgood.

Psychological Monographs—figure on page 152, from 57, No. 3, 1944, p. 30, by W. K. Estes; figure on page 163, from 49, No. 4, 1937, p. 17, by L. B. Ward; figure on page 202, from 58, No. 5, 1945, p. 5, by Karl Duncker, trans. by Lynne S. Lees; table on page 205, from 54, No. 6, 1942, p. 1, by A. S. Luchins.

Psychological Review—graphs on pages 157, 158, from 4, 1897, p. 49, by W. L. Bryan and Noble Harter.

AMERICAN SOCIOLOGICAL ASSOCIATION   For the following graphs and tables from the *American Sociological Review*, reprinted by permission of the American Sociological Association and the authors: graph on page 306, from 10, 1945, p. 559, by Paul H. Landis and Katherine H. Day; graph on page 308, from 15, 1950, p. 524, by Paul C. Glick and Emanuel Landau; table on page 310, from 14, 1949, p. 403, by Judson T. Landis; table on page 315, from 16, 1951, p. 472, by Fred L. Strodtbeck; table on page 349, from 16, 1951, p. 463, by Robert F. Bales, Fred L. Strodtbeck, Theodore M. Mills and Mary Roseborough; table on page 360, from 18, 1953, p. 353, by Theodore M. Mills; table on page 482, from 16, 1951, p. 481, by Julius Roth and R. F. Peck; table on page 499, from 16, 1951, p. 231, by Everett S. Lee; table on page 511, from 15, 1950, p. 532, by W. S. M. Banks, II; table on page 540, from 17, 1952, p. 461, by Harold H. Kelley and E. H. Volkart; graph on page 592, from 5, 1940, p. 851, by S. A. Stouffer.

APPLETON-CENTURY-CROFTS   For table on page 80 and figure on page 81, from pp. 294, 300, of *The Achievement Motive* by David C. McClelland, John W. Atkinson, Russell A. Clark, and Edgar L. Lowell. Copyright, 1953, Appleton-Century-Crofts, Inc. Reproduced by permission of the publisher.

For graphs on pages 141, 153, from pp. 154, 288, of *The Behavior of Organisms: An Experimental Analysis* by B. F. Skinner. Copyright, 1938, D. Appleton-Century Company, Inc. Reproduced by permission.

For figure on page 152, from p. 112 of *Theories of Learning*, 2nd Edition, by Ernest R. Hilgard. Copyright, © 1956, Appleton-Century-Crofts, Inc. Reproduced by permission.

For figure on page 155, from p. 339 of *Schedules of Reinforcement* by C. B. Ferster and B. F. Skinner. Copyright © 1957, Appleton-Century-Crofts, Inc. Reproduced by permission of the publisher.

For table on page 263 by Hans-Werner Wendt, from p. 452 of *Studies in Motivation*, edited by David C. McClelland. Copyright, 1955, Appleton-Century-Crofts, Inc. Reprinted by permission of the publisher and the editor.

pages 223–24, from *Educational and Psychological Measurement,* 5, 1945, pp. 231–32, by Thomas W. Harrell and Margaret S. Harrell. Reprinted by permission of Educational and Psychological Measurement and the authors.

FOUNDATION FOR RESEARCH ON HUMAN BEHAVIOR, ANN ARBOR, MICHIGAN For table on page 230, from *Creativity and Conformity* by Frank Barron, Dorwin Cartwright, and Richard S. Crutchfield, 1958.

THE FREE PRESS OF GLENCOE, INC. For table on page 314, by Morris Zelditch, Jr. Reprinted with permission of the publisher from *Family, Socialization and Interaction Process* by Talcott Parsons, Robert F. Bales and others. Copyright 1955 by The Free Press, a corporation.

For table on page 318. Reprinted with permission of the publisher from *Marriage, Authority, and Final Causes* by George C. Homans and David M. Schneider. Copyright 1955 by The Free Press, a corporation.

For table on page 346, figure on page 350, and graph on page 351, by Robert F. Bales. Reprinted with permission of the publisher from *Working Papers in the Theory of Action* by Talcott Parsons, Robert F. Bales and Edward A. Shils. Copyright 1953 by The Free Press, a corporation.

For bar chart on page 327 and graph on page 442. Reprinted with permission of the publisher from *The Academic Mind* by Paul F. Lazarsfeld and Wagner Thielens, Jr. Copyright 1958 by The Free Press, a corporation.

For table on page 378, by Hans Speier. Reprinted with permission of the publisher from *Continuities in Social Research,* edited by Robert K. Merton and Paul F. Lazarsfeld. Copyright 1950 by The Free Press, a corporation.

For graph on page 412. Reprinted with permission of the publisher from *Union Democracy* by Seymour M. Lipset, Martin A. Trow, and James S. Coleman. Copyright 1956 by The Free Press, a corporation.

For graph on page 436, by V. O. Key, Jr., and Frank Munger. Reprinted with permission of the publisher from *American Voting Behavior,* edited by Eugene Burdick and Arthur J. Brodbeck. Copyright 1959 by The Free Press, a corporation.

For table on page 437, by Natalie Rogoff. Reprinted with permission of the publisher from *Education, Economy, and Society,* edited by A. H. Halsey, Jean Floud, and C. Arnold Anderson. Copyright 1961 by The Free Press, a corporation.

For table on page 441 by H. T. Himmelweit and table on page 475 by D. V. Glass and J. R. Hall. Reprinted with permission of the publisher from *Social Mobility in Britain* edited by D. V. Glass. First published in the U.S.A. in 1954 by The Free Press, a corporation. (See also Routledge and Kegan Paul, Ltd.)

For table on page 472 by Natalie Rogoff. Reprinted with permission of the publisher from *Reader in Urban Sociology,* edited by Paul K. Hatt and Albert J. Reiss, Jr. Copyright 1951 by The Free Press, a corporation.

For table on page 475. Reprinted with permission of the publisher from *Recent Trends in Occupational Mobility* by Natalie Rogoff. Copyright 1953 by The Free Press, a corporation.

For table on page 534. Reprinted with permission of the publisher from *The Adolescent Society* by James S. Coleman. Copyright 1961 by The Free Press, a corporation.

For tables on pages 563, 564. Reprinted by permission of the publisher from *Political Socialization* by Herbert Hyman. Copyright 1959 by The Free Press, a corporation.

For graphs on page 637. Reprinted with permission of the publisher from *Psychosis and Civilization* by Herbert Goldhamer and Andrew W. Marshall. Copyright 1953 by The Free Press, a corporation.

For table on page 638. Reprinted with permission of the publisher from *Culture and Mental Disorders* by Joseph W. Eaton. Copyright 1955 by The Free Press, a corporation.

HARCOURT, BRACE & WORLD, INC. For figure on page 165, table on page 166, and graph on page 221, from *Introduction to Psychology,* 3rd Edition, by Ernest R. Hilgard, 1962, Harcourt, Brace & World, Inc. (See also Rupert Hart-Davis, Ltd., and Methuen & Co., Ltd.)

For table on page 311 by W. J. Goode and quotation on page 449 by Morris Janowitz, from *Contemporary Social Problems,* edited by Robert W. Merton and Robert Nisbet, 1961, Harcourt, Brace & World, Inc.

For quotation on page 452 of the sixth stanza from the poem "Reflection from Anita Loos," from the *Collected Poems of William Empson,* 1949, Harcourt, Brace & World, Inc. (See also Chatto and Windus, Ltd.)

For figure on page 458, from *Black Metropolis* by St. Clair Drake and H. R. Clayton, 1945, Harcourt, Brace & World, Inc.

HOLT, RINEHART AND WINSTON, INC.   For table on page 311 by Paul H. Jacobson. Reprinted by permission of the author and publisher from Paul H. Jacobson, *American Marriage and Divorce*, Holt, Rinehart and Winston, Inc., copyright © 1959, p. 90.

   For table on page 335 by S. E. Asch and table on page 481 by Urie Bronfenbrenner. Reprinted by permission of the publisher from *Readings in Social Psychology*, 3rd Edition, Edited by E. E. Maccoby *et al.* New York, Holt, Rinehart and Winston, Inc., 1958, pp. 177, 421.

HOUGHTON MIFFLIN COMPANY   For graph on page 209 and table on page 225, from *The Revision of the Stanford-Binet Scale* by Quinn McNemar, 1942, Houghton Mifflin.

   For graph and table on page 210, from the *Stanford-Binet Intelligence Scale: Manual for the Third Revision Form L-M* by Lewis M. Terman and Maud A. Merrill, 1960, Houghton Mifflin.

INSTITUTE OF PERSONALITY ASSESSMENT AND RESEARCH   For table on page 230 by Donald W. McKinnon, from *The Creative Person*, 1961, Institute of Personality Assessment and Research, University of California and University Extension, Liberal Arts Department, Berkeley, California. Reprinted by permission of the author.

INTERNATIONAL UNIVERSITIES PRESS, INC.   For table on page 180, from *Memory and Hypnotic Age Regression* by Robert Reiff and Martin Scheerer, 1959, International Universities Press. Reprinted by permission of the publisher and Dr. Robert Reiff.

JOURNAL OF CLINICAL PSYCHOLOGY   For table on page 291, from the *Journal of Clinical Psychology*, 16, 1960, p. 94, by Stanley R. Graham.

THE JOURNAL OF COUNSELING PSYCHOLOGY   For graph on page 293, from *The Journal of Counseling Psychology*, 9, 1962, p. 32, by John M. Shlien, Harold H. Mosak, and Rudolf Dreikurs. Reprinted by permission of the Journal of Counseling Psychology and the authors.

THE JOURNAL PRESS   For figure on page 73, from *Genetic Psychology Monographs*, 47, 1953, p. 214, by Robert R. Sears, John W. M. Whiting, Vincent Nowlis, and Pauline S. Sears.

   For the following from the *Journal of General Psychology*: graph on p. 139, from 17, 1937, p. 136, by Carl I. Hovland; table on page 250, from 16, 1937, p. 184, by Maria Rickers-Ovsiankina.

   For illustration on page 187, from *Genetic Psychology Monographs*, 1, 1926, p. 139, by Heinrich Klüver.

   For the following from the *Journal of Genetic Psychology:* table on page 181, from 58, 1941, p. 437, by Harold E. Burtt; table on page 222, from 86, 1955, p. 355, by Dorothy I. Marquart and Lois L. Bailey.

   For the following from the *Journal of Psychology:* table on page 115, from 25, 1948, p. 212, by David C. McClelland and John W. Atkinson; figure and table on page 197, from 25, 1948, pp. 310, 311, 312, by Edna Heidbreder, Mary L. Bensley, and Margaret Ivy; table on page 267, from 25, 1948, p. 440, by Neal E. Miller and Richard Bugelski; graph and table on page 268, from 9, 1940, pp. 306, 307, by Carl I. Hovland and Robert R. Sears; table on page 342, from 25, 1948, p. 40, by Ralph M. Stogdill; table on page 502, from 22, 1946, p. 35, by Gordon Allport and Bernard M. Kramer.

   For graph on page 509, from the *Journal of Social Psychology*, 7, 1936, p. 194, by Verner Sims and James Patrick.

ALFRED A. KNOPF, INC.   For table on page 359 by Robert F. Bales and Edgar F. Borgatta. From *Small Groups: Studies in Social Interaction*, edited by A. Paul Hare and others, 1955, Alfred A. Knopf, Inc.

DAVID KRECH   For figures on pages 108, 118, and tables on pages 218, 219, from *Elements of Psychology* by David Krech and Richard S. Crutchfield, 1958, Alfred A. Knopf, Inc. (See also Richard S. Crutchfield.)

JUAN J. LINZ   For tables on pages 427, 573, from "The Social Bases of West German Politics" by Juan J. Linz, unpublished doctoral dissertation, Columbia University, 1959.

LITTLE, BROWN & COMPANY   For quotation on pages 618–19, from *The Emerging Nations*, edited by Max F. Millikan and Donald L. M. Blackmer, by permission of Little, Brown & Company. Copyright © 1961, Massachusetts Institute of Technology. Permission granted for United States, Canada, and the open market. (See also Asia Publishing Company.)

MC GRAW-HILL BOOK COMPANY, INC.   For figure on page 151, from *Introduction to Psychology* by Clifford T. Morgan. Copyright 1956, 2nd edition 1961. McGraw-Hill Book Company, Inc. Used by permission.

   For figure on page 272 by Roger G. Barker, from *Studies in Personality*, edited by Quinn McNemar and Maud A. Merrill. Copyright 1942. McGraw-Hill Book Company, Inc. Used by permission.

THE MACMILLAN COMPANY   For quotations on pages 65, 385, 388, 460, 466. Reprinted with permission of the publisher from *Human Society* by Kingsley Davis. Copyright 1940, 1949, by The Macmillan Company.

For quotation on page 156. Reprinted with permission of the publisher from *Science and Human Behavior* by Burrhus F. Skinner. Copyright 1953 by The Macmillan Company.

For illustration on page 170. Reprinted with permission of the publisher from *The Cerebral Cortex of Man* by Wilder Penfield and Theodore Rasmussen. Copyright 1950 by The Macmillan Company.

For quotations on pages 300, 313, 319, 321, 322, 650, and for the tables on pages 317, 651. Reprinted with permission of the publisher from *Social Structure* by George P. Murdock. Copyright 1949 by The Macmillan Company.

For quotation on page 391. Reprinted with permission of the publisher from *Our Primitive Contemporaries* by George P. Murdock. Copyright 1934 by The Macmillan Company.

For quotation on page 394. Reprinted with permission of the publisher from *Religion, Society and the Individual* by J. Milton Yinger. Copyright 1957 by The Macmillan Company.

ALBERT J. MAYER   For table on page 477 by A. J. Mayer and Philip Hauser, from *Class, Status and Power: A Reader in Social Stratification*, edited by Reinhard Bendix and Seymour M. Lipset, 1953, Free Press. Published originally in *La Revue de L'Institut International de Statistique*, Vol. 18, 1953. (See also Philip Hauser.)

MENTAL HEALTH RESEARCH INSTITUTE, UNIVERSITY OF MICHIGAN   For table on page 605, from *Behavioral Science*, 2, No. 4, 1957, p. 272, by Daniel Lerner.

METHUEN & COMPANY, LTD.   For United Kingdom rights for the figure on page 165, table on page 166, and graph on page 221, from *Introduction to Psychology*, 3rd Edition, by Ernest R. Hilgard, 1962, Harcourt, Brace & World, Inc. (See also Rupert Hart-Davis, Ltd.)

MILBANK MEMORIAL FUND   For graph on page 603, from the *Milbank Memorial Fund Quarterly*, 35, 1957, p. 211, by Francis C. Madigan.

NATIONAL PSYCHOLOGICAL ASSOCIATION FOR PSYCHOANALYSIS, INC.   For table on page 285 by Robert R. Sears, 1943, data from table by G. E. Gardner, 1931. Reprinted from *The Psychoanalytic Review*, 18, No. 1, Spring, 1931, through the courtesy of the Editors and the publisher, National Psychological Association for Psychoanalysis, Inc.

THE NEW YORK ACADEMY OF SCIENCES   For illustration on page 185 by Gordon W. Allport and Leo J. Postman, from *Transactions of the New York Academy of Sciences* (Series II), 8, No. 2, 1945, p. 66.

THEODORE M. NEWCOMB   For table on page 582, from *Personality and Social Change* by Theodore M. Newcomb, 1943, Dryden Press. Re-issued by Holt, Rinehart & Winston, 1957. Copyright 1943 by T. M. Newcomb.

OXFORD UNIVERSITY PRESS, INC.   For figures on pages 40 and 41, from *The Study of Instinct* by Nikolaas Tinbergen, 1951, Oxford University Press, Inc. Reprinted by permission. (See also John Wiley & Sons, Inc.)

For figure on page 109, from *Method and Theory in Experimental Psychology* by Charles E. Osgood, 1953, Oxford University Press, Inc. Reprinted by permission.

For quotation on pages 257 and 258, from *Explorations in Personality*, edited by Henry A. Murray. Copyright 1938 by Oxford University Press, Inc. Reprinted by permission.

For table on page 535, from *Television and the Child* by H. T. Himmelweit, A. N. Oppenheim, and Pamela Vince, 1958, Oxford University Press, Inc. Reprinted by permission.

THE PENNSYLVANIA STATE UNIVERSITY PRESS   For table on page 547, from *The Journal of General Education*, 7, No. 3, 1953, pp. 165–66, by B. S. Bloom.

PRINCETON UNIVERSITY PRESS   For table on page 373, bar graphs on page 376, table on page 445, and bar chart on page 512, by Samuel A. Stouffer *et al.* Reprinted from *The American Soldier: Adjustment During Army Life*, Vol. 1 of *Studies in Social Psychology in World War II* by Samuel A. Stouffer *et al.*, by permission of Princeton University Press. Copyright 1949 by Princeton University Press.

For table on page 447. Reprinted from *The American Soldier: Combat and Its Aftermath*, Vol. 2 of *Studies in Social Psychology in World War II* by Samuel A. Stouffer *et al.*, by permission of Princeton University Press. Copyright 1949 by Princeton University Press.

For graph on page 597 by Dudley Kirk. Reprinted from *Demographic and Economic Change in Developed Countries*, a Report of the National Bureau of Economic Re-

For table on page 312, reprinted from the *American Journal of Sociology*, 59, 1954, p. 463, by Thomas P. Monahan and William M. Kephart, by permission of The University of Chicago Press. Published 1954 by The University of Chicago.

For table on page 340, reprinted from the *American Journal of Sociology*, 62, 1957, p. 567, by John Johnstone and Elihu Katz, by permission of The University of Chicago Press. Copyright 1957 by The University of Chicago.

For figures on pages 419, 423, 544, 545, 551, 560, 567, 579, reprinted from *Voting: A Study of Opinion Formation in a Presidential Campaign* by Bernard Berelson, Paul F. Lazarsfeld, and William N. McPhee, by permission of The University of Chicago Press. Copyright 1954 by The University of Chicago. All rights reserved.

For figure on page 457, reprinted from *Deep South* by Allison Davis, Burleigh B. Gardner, and Mary R. Gardner, by permission of The University of Chicago Press. Copyright 1941 by The University of Chicago. All rights reserved.

For table on page 463, reprinted from the *American Journal of Sociology*, 61, 1956, p. 332, by Alex Inkeles and Peter H. Rossi, by permission of The University of Chicago Press. Copyright 1956 by The University of Chicago.

For table on page 609, reprinted from the *American Journal of Sociology*, 60, 1955, p. 497, by Otis D. Duncan and Beverly Duncan, by permission of The University of Chicago Press. Copyright 1955 by The University of Chicago.

For table on page 610, reprinted from the *American Journal of Sociology*, 57, Part 2, 1951, p. 14, by Robert Cooley Angell, by permission of The University of Chicago Press. Published 1951 by The University of Chicago.

THE UNIVERSITY OF MICHIGAN PRESS For table on page 269, from *Frustration: A Study of Behavior Without a Goal* by Norman R. F. Maier, University of Michigan Press, Ann Arbor Paperback Series. Copyright 1961 by The University of Michigan Press. Published originally by McGraw-Hill, 1949. Reprinted by permission of The University of Michigan Press and the author.

UNIVERSITY OF MINNESOTA PRESS For table on page 512, from *Interracial Housing: A Psychological Evaluation of a Social Experiment* by Morton Deutsch and Mary E. Collins. University of Minnesota Press, Minneapolis. Copyright 1951 by the University of Minnesota.

D. VAN NOSTRAND COMPANY, INC. For figures on pages 106, 107, 108, by Michael Wertheimer. From *Readings in Perception*, edited by David C. Beardslee and Michael Wertheimer, 1958, D. Van Nostrand Company, Inc.

For table on page 402 and graphs on pages 403, 612, from *The Achieving Society* by David C. McClelland, 1961, D. Van Nostrand Company, Inc.

For table on page 438 by Fred L. Strodtbeck. From *Talent and Society* by David C. McClelland, Alfred L. Baldwin, Urie Bronfenbrenner and Fred L. Strodtbeck, 1958, D. Van Nostrand Company, Inc.

DAVID WECHSLER For table on page 220 and graph on page 221, from *The Measurement and Appraisal of Adult Intelligence*, 4th Edition, by David Wechsler, 1958, Williams & Wilkins Company. Copyright by David Wechsler.

JOHN WILEY & SONS, INC., PUBLISHERS For figures on pages 40, 41, reprinted with permission from *Social Behavior in Animals* by Nikolaas Tinbergen, 1953, John Wiley & Sons, Inc. (See also Oxford University Press, Inc.)

For table on page 96 by S. S. Stevens, figures on page 105 by Edwin B. Newman, and graph on page 160 by Carl I. Hovland, reprinted with permission from *Foundations of Psychology*, edited by Edwin G. Boring, Herbert S. Langfeld, and Harry P. Weld, 1948, John Wiley & Sons, Inc.

For graph on page 137 by Ernest R. Hilgard. Reprinted with permission from *Handbook of Experimental Psychology*, edited by S. S. Stevens, 1951, John Wiley & Sons, Inc.

For graph on page 199, reprinted with permission from *A Study of Thinking* by Jerome S. Bruner, Jacqueline J. Goodnow, and George A. Austin, 1956, John Wiley & Sons, Inc.

For tables on pages 228, 234, and illustrations on pages 232, 233, reprinted with permission from *Creativity and Intelligence* by Jacob W. Getzels and Philip W. Jackson, 1962, John Wiley & Sons, Inc.

For tables on pages 413, 415, reprinted with permission from *Changing Patterns of Industrial Conflict* by Arthur M. Ross and Paul T. Hartman, 1960, John Wiley & Sons, Inc.

For graph on page 413, reprinted with permission from *Behavior of Industrial Work Groups* by Leonard R. Sayles, 1958, John Wiley & Sons, Inc.

For tables on pages 477, 639, reprinted with permission from *Social Class and Mental*

Illness: A Community Study by August B. Hollingshead and Frederick C. Redlich, 1958, John Wiley & Sons, Inc.

For bar charts on pages 479, 483, and table on page 485, reprinted with permission from *Elmtown's Youth: The Impact of Social Classes on Adolescents* by August B. Hollingshead, 1949, John Wiley & Sons, Inc.

WILLIAMS & WILKINS COMPANY   For the following selections from the *Journal of Comparative Psychology:* illustration on page 196, from 30, 1940, p. 462, by H. A. Witkin; graph on page 263, from 14, 1932, p. 433, by Orvis C. Irwin; tables on pages 264, 265, from 38, 1945, pp. 305, 312, by Herbert G. Birch.

WILLIAMSON MUSIC, INC.   For quotation on page 492 from the lyrics of *South Pacific,* "You've Got To Be Carefully Taught," by Oscar Hammerstein II. Reprinted by permission. Copyright © 1949 by Richard Rogers and Oscar Hammerstein II. Williamson Music, Inc., New York, New York, owner of publication and allied rights.

YALE UNIVERSITY PRESS   For table on page 78, from *Child Training and Personality: A Cross-Cultural Study* by John W. M. Whiting and Irvin L. Child, 1953, Yale University Press.

For table on page 129, from *ESP and Personality Patterns* by Gertrude R. Schmeidler and R. A. McConnell, 1958, Yale University Press.

For graph on page 160, from *Mathematico-deductive Theory of Rote Learning* by Clark L. Hull, Carl I. Hovland, Robert T. Ross *et al.*, 1940, Yale University Press. Reprinted in *Foundations of Psychology*, edited by Edwin G. Boring, Herbert S. Langfeld, and Harry P. Weld, 1948, John Wiley & Sons, Inc.

For figure and table on page 456, from *The Social Life of a Modern Community* (Yankee City Series, Vol. 1) by W. Lloyd Warner and Paul S. Lunt, 1941, Yale University Press.

For bar charts on pages 549, 553, from *Communication and Persuasion* by Carl I. Hovland, Irving L. Janis, and Harold H. Kelley, 1953, Yale University Press.

TO
WILLIAM MCPEAK

ACKNOWLEDGMENTS

We are indebted to a number of people and organizations for their assistance.

For financial help, direct and indirect, we owe thanks, in roughly chronological order, to Allen Wallis and James Lorie of the Graduate School of Business, University of Chicago; to Wilbur Schramm and his program for the utilization of the behavioral sciences, Stanford University; to John Gardner and his colleagues at the Carnegie Corporation of New York; to John Riley, Director of Social Research of the Equitable Life Assurance Society of America; to Lawrence Ferguson, Director of Behavioral Research Services of the General Electric Company; to Frank Notestein and other colleagues at the Population Council; and to John D. Rockefeller 3rd. They gave us the friendly encouragement that means so much in a pioneering project of this kind, where the outcome and even the effort contain a certain element of risk: can it be done at all? We remain most grateful for their support, moral as well as fiscal.

In the course of our work we have relied on many helpers and collaborators. This book would not have been as well done without their careful and loyal assistance in finding findings, checking references, verifying quotations, compiling the bibliography, keeping records, seeking permissions, doing the index, typing and retyping, and so on. As with the first group, their belief in the effort was important as well as their work. Mary Lynne Poole and Nan Reiss maintained effective control of the Chicago end of the work. Carol Bowman was remarkably efficient in managing the flow of work in New York, and contributed some editorial support as well. Donna Smith verified every quotation and citation in the book, secured all the permissions, compiled the bibliographical index, and helped with the subject index, and it is to her lasting credit that all the details were handled not only with professional competence but with good humor as well. Sarina Hirschfeld helped earlier by locating findings and later by working on the index, and both tasks were done with her exemplary reliability and skill. Without their good and friendly assistance, we can barely see how this book could have been completed at all, let alone now. We are and shall remain particularly grateful to them.

And for help in other ways we are indebted to Lee Cogan, Walter Graessle, Peter Graham, Sally Johns, Gail Kelly, Suzanne Popper, Sergio Tallachi, Peter Scalise, and Catherine Gallaway.

Among those who read and criticized parts of the manuscript at various stages and advised us on general questions as well as on materials for inclusion, particular thanks are due to Sam Becker, James Coleman, Amitai Etzioni, William Goode, Ernest Hilgard, Parker Mauldin, Robert Morison, and David Sills. Without their consultation we would have made more mistakes than in the end we did. We thank them for their comments and—the least we can do—absolve them of any responsibility for how it all turned out.

Irene Coltman and Ruth Berelson gave us a lesson in what humanistic learning can mean in such an effort, and particularly with regard to the concluding chapter.

To all, our deepest thanks for help and for encouragement. Both were needed to get this book done.

B. B.
G. A. S.

CONTENTS

HUMAN BEHAVIOR
An Inventory of Scientific Findings

This preparatory treatment consists in finding general propositions which express concisely what is common to large classes of observed facts: and these are called the empirical laws of the phenomena. We have, therefore, to inquire, whether any similar preparatory process can be performed on the facts of the social science: whether there are any empirical laws in history or statistics. . . . To collect, therefore, such empirical laws (which are never more than approximate generalizations) from direct observations, is an important part of the process of sociological inquiry.

JOHN STUART MILL

Let us settle the facts first and fight about the moral tendencies afterwards.

SAMUEL BUTLER
The Way of All Flesh

It is Facts that are needed; Facts, Facts, Facts. When facts have been supplied, each of us can try to reason from them.

JAMES BRYCE
Modern Democracies

Man is astonishingly good at dealing with the physical world, but he is just as astonishingly bad at dealing with human nature; therefore an inch gained in the understanding of and command over human nature is worth a mile gained in the understanding of and command over physical nature.

ARNOLD J. TOYNBEE
The Prospects of Western Civilization

Whatever his field of specialization, the scholar can be understood beyond the confines of his guild—but only if he is willing to raise his language above the jargon of his trade. The scholar must learn to speak to man.

RENÉ DUBOS
The Dreams of Reason

Much modern sociological theory seems to me to possess every virtue except that of explaining anything. Part of the trouble is that much of it consists of systems of categories, or pigeonholes, into which the theorist fits different aspects of social behavior. No science can proceed without its system of categories, or conceptual scheme, but this in itself is not enough to give it explanatory power. A conceptual scheme is not a theory. The science also needs a set of general propositions about the relations between the categories, for without such propositions explanation is impossible. No explanation without propositions! But much modern sociological theory seems quite satisfied with itself when it has set up its conceptual scheme. The theorist shoves different aspects of behavior into his pigeonhole, cries, "Ah-ha!" and stops. He has written the dictionary of a language that has no sentences. He would have done better to start with the sentences.

GEORGE C. HOMANS
Social Behavior: Its Elementary Forms

Chapter One

INTRODUCTION

This book is an inventory. Most inventories cover material objects, such as steel or automobiles or shoes or machines. This one is an inventory of knowledge: the present state of scientific knowledge about human behavior.

In a word, we consider ourselves reporters, and to some extent integrators, of the results of several decades of the scientific study of human behavior. Some years ago, a widely distributed report on the problems of the times, the Report of the Study Committee for the Ford Foundation on Policy and Program, observed that "our storehouse of verified knowledge of human behavior has a relatively low inventory." However that may be, we have attempted here to take an inventory of the behavioral sciences.

Our ambition in this book is to present, as fully and as accurately as possible, what the behavioral sciences now know about the behavior of human beings: what we really know, what we nearly know, what we think we know, what we claim to know. Our procedure is to do so in the form of important and verified generalizations (here called "findings"); in an ordered, 1–2–3–4 arrangement; and in plain English, with little of the terminology and few of the technicalities that are involved when specialists talk to specialists.

Now this is a large order. To begin with, human behavior itself is so enormously varied, so delicately complex, so obscurely motivated that many people despair of finding valid generalizations to explain and predict the actions, thoughts, and feelings of human beings—despair, that is, of the very possibility of constructing a science of human behavior. Furthermore, the literature of the behavioral sciences has grown so fast in recent years that the job of distilling its factual essentials is at best difficult and at worst foolhardy. The obstacles, indeed, are so formidable that we would not have attempted the task were we not so firmly convinced of the need for the product.

3

In our experience, there is a great deal of interest and curiosity about this field that is often frustrated or misinformed because of the difficulty of mastering the technicalities, penetrating the language, or simply finding one's way through the empirical detail. This book is our effort to present the substantive results to the nonspecialist: to the student, the layman, the academic colleague—even to the behavioral scientist in another corner of the field. We believe that the effort will be valuable to students of the liberal arts; we think that it will be useful to our colleagues in professional fields concerned with human behavior, in education or business or law or medicine or social work; we trust that it will help to inform the larger society about the behavioral sciences; and we even hope that it may be salutary for the field itself.

In recent years, distinguished scholars in the major disciplines of the behavioral sciences have called for something similar. Of his own field the late Clyde Kluckhohn observed that

> anthropologists of all branches have been so preoccupied with field work that the profession has not organized and assimilated what is in fact "known" [1957, p. 58].

At the same time, Ernest Hilgard said that

> the state [of factual knowledge] is not very satisfactory: neither is it very easy to remedy. The number of dependable "facts" in the various fields of psychology are not very impressive [1957, p. 7].

And Edward Shils argued that

> nothing is more necessary at present than the systematic collation and "shaking down" of American sociological research results to discover what they amount to, to weigh the evidence on crucial problems and to see what is really known on the basis of adequate evidence and what is still unsettled [1948, p. 43].

While we cannot claim that this book is what they had in mind, we are at least encouraged by the apparent correspondence in beliefs.*

* Also encouraging is a somewhat similar effort in a "harder" science, R. E. Peierls' *The Laws of Nature*, which came to our attention when we had nearly finished this book. Some of Mr. Peierls' introductory sentences serve equally well for us:

"This led to the idea of trying to set out the principles of modern physics in simple language and without assuming any previous knowledge. My experience led me to believe that it was possible to do this in a reasonable space, and that in doing so I would clarify my own ideas. Of these predictions I have already found the second one correct. Whether I was right in the first I must leave the reader to judge. . . .

"I would regard the effort of writing as well rewarded if I had succeeded in showing to some readers who have never been introduced to science at all, a little of the aims, the methods and the conclusions of the scientist. . . .

"I hope I have not allowed the reader to forget the way in which all the conclusions at which we have arrived depend on empirical knowledge and on experimentation" (1956, pp. 7-9).

In any case, other kinds of summaries of the behavioral sciences are already available—regular textbooks, theoretical statements, mathematical models, technical review articles, applied manuals, and the rest. Accordingly it seemed worthwhile to us to attempt this innovation, as a possible contribution both to the field itself and to the wider public.

The Nature of the Book

The task of constructing this book was fourfold: to select, to condense, to organize, to translate. We had to select findings from the large body of available literature. We had to condense the conclusions of various studies into a single generalization that would do them justice. We had to organize the findings into a sensible and coherent form. Finally, we had to translate the technical language, and often the jargon, of the behavioral sciences into reasonably plain English without corrupting meaning.

As the reader will quickly see, this book is made up of "findings." In the terminology of the behavioral sciences, what we here call findings might elsewhere be called propositions, generalizations, laws, or principles. The meaning of the term here will, we think, become most clear from the findings themselves; but as a capsule introduction, we refer to *important statements* of *proper generality* for which there is *some good amount of scientific evidence*.

By *importance* we mean theoretical importance to the disciplines themselves and/or practical importance to the society at large.

By *proper generality* we mean a middle ground. Highly specific or topical facts, on the one hand, and highly abstract statements, on the other, are both excluded in favor of findings that apply to a substantial range of human behavior and that make explicit the human content with which they deal. We have also omitted a considerable amount of rather specialized material at certain points—e.g., data on population studies, consumer behavior, or classroom learning of particular subjects. Our byword has been: enough generality to make the findings broadly relevant, not so much as to lose sight of human behavior as such.

By *scientific evidence* we mean data collected and analyzed according to the methods described in the next chapter. Just how much evidence is required to warrant inclusion here cannot be stated with much precision; the disciplines themselves have not settled what is "enough evidence," and in any event scientific standards vary from one segment of the field to another. But there must be some "hard" evidence for the finding, typically of a quantitative character, beyond simply an idea, a concept, a hypothesis, an insight, or a case history. As a general rule, we have tried to include the best-supported findings within each field, those we think most likely to be considered as established by a consensus of the professionals, and those where the behavioral sciences have made a distinctive contribution. But it is only fair to the behavioral sciences and to the reader—as well as to this book— to make it quite clear that not all the following findings have been "proved" to the satisfaction of all the qualified specialists. However, they presumably are among those for which more rather than less scientific evidence has been brought forward at the present time and those most credited by consensus of the experts.

There is, of course, more to the behavioral sciences than what appears here. Take as examples: methodological work that does not come within our purview; applied and practical work in which the ideas and techniques of the field are put to use in industry, government, and the professions; informed description of a wide variety of societies and situations; social commentary; conceptual definition; theoretical speculation. As anyone knows who has ever looked, the journals are filled with such material. Much of this work can lead to empirical generalizations of the sort contained here; but the work itself, however prestigious it is within the discipline and how- ever large it may bulk there, is not included here unless it has in fact led to such generalizations. This does not necessarily represent a judgment on our part as to the value of such efforts, but only our interest in doing a special kind of job. However, the reader should appreciate at the outset that what is contained here is by no means "all there is" to the behavioral sciences.

The best test of the value of this effort is in what follows. But since the book is itself the result of an empirical investigation, it seems to us only appropriate that we report on how we went about the experiment—for it was that!—of putting it together.

It would be nice to be able to say that the specifications and criteria were all clearly laid out at the start and that it was simply a job of following them out. But that was not the case. Rather, we began with a general idea of what we wanted to achieve: a distillation of the literature of the be- havioral sciences in order to communicate, with a minimum of misunder- standing, "what we really know" to nonspecialists. From then on, it was a matter of trial-and-error, of gradually clarifying what we meant by a "find- ing," determining the "right" level of generality, locating the boundaries of importance, deciding how much evidence was "enough," and so on. For example, we decided early on to dismiss speculation, impression, anecdotage, or insight as evidence, no matter how brilliant or stimulating, no matter how persuasive to us personally. Nor did we accept single case studies: we grant at the outset that any conceivable human behavior has in fact occurred, somewhere, sometime. We asked for something more, and we tried to be guided by what passes for evidence among the more highly reputed prac- titioners and journals in the several fields. At the margins, the decision as to whether a particular finding satisfied the criteria for inclusion was extremely difficult to make, perhaps impossible to make with full knowledge and consistency.

In building this inventory, we have relied to some extent on secondary summaries of the empirical literature. We did so for two reasons. The first is that it would be manifestly impossible to assemble this book from the original materials, simply because of their number if for no other reason. In 1960 alone, *Psychological Abstracts* listed about 8500 items and *Sociological Abstracts* about 2000. The second is that in the very nature of the case we wanted wherever possible to lean on the evaluation of a specialist in order to represent the rough consensus of particular fields. These days, no one can be an informed specialist in all the subjects covered here; certainly we are not, and hence there is bound to be some unevenness in coverage about which we can only warn the reader at the start. As a safeguard, we shall be quoting authorities throughout the book—which is, we think, as it should be.

In the very nature of the case, the findings presented here are simplified; how could any summary of such a large literature be otherwise? We hope they are not over- or unduly simplified, but the reader should also know at the outset that qualifications of various kinds are, or can be, attached to many, perhaps most, of the following findings. In the behavioral sciences, if not in human behavior, it is always "more complicated than that." The qualifications may derive from size of sample, composition of sample, level of proof, techniques of measurement, factors left uninvestigated, or other conditions, but they are usually there. Thus it seems only appropriate to warn that not all these findings are always operative just as stated, or rather that we do not yet know that they are. So not everything that follows can be certified as "absolutely true."

Accordingly, we have had to qualify a number of the findings by such phrases as "tends to" or "makes for" or "by and large," but that seems to us necessary at this stage in the development of the disciplines. Indeed, at one point early in the preparation of these materials, we considered semi-facetiously that every finding ought to be preceded by three sets of initials: UCC, OTE, and IOC, standing for "under certain circumstances," "other things equal," and "in our culture."

But only *semi*facetiously. For nothing is true in the behavioral sciences (or in life) except "under certain circumstances." As the great economist Alfred Marshall put it in his *Principles of Economics* (1890):

> The forces to be dealt with are so numerous that it is best to take a few at a time, and to work out a number of partial solutions as auxiliaries to our main study. . . . We reduce to inaction all other forces by the phrase "other things being equal": we do not suppose that they are inert, but for the time being we ignore their activity. This scientific device is a great deal older than science; it

is the method by which, consciously or unconsciously, sensible men have dealt from time immemorial with every difficult problem of ordinary life.

As for "in our culture," except for anthropological materials a large proportion of these findings are based upon data collected in the United States. The behavioral sciences are so much more active here than elsewhere that this is inevitable. We have tried always to be conscious of this limitation, and to note it wherever it was especially applicable, but the reader should know that a good deal of what follows is limited, strictly speaking, to Western culture and even to the American scene.

We have aimed at completeness, but we are under no illusion that we have achieved it. In a compilation of this kind, arbitrary decisions must continually be made in the course of applying the criteria for inclusion to the heterogeneous content of the field. As a result, some findings undoubtedly are here that should not be, and some are not here that should be. Our own uneven knowledge across the range of the behavioral sciences is partly responsible for that state of affairs; but, to repeat, we thought the job so important that it should be attempted even under that deficit. In short, it is only right to warn the reader that we have not been able to make all the judgments involved—on selection, on formulation, on evidence, on organization—to the satisfaction of all the specialists, perhaps not to the full satisfaction of any one of them, and sometimes not to our own satisfaction either. But at the same time we do claim that the book is at the very least illustrative of the kinds of empirically supported generalizations that the behavioral sciences are now producing. More than that, we believe that the book is representative of the field and, even further, that it contains a large proportion of all the eligible findings up to about the early 1960's.

Actually, the book probably contains both less and more than what other behavioral scientists might produce, given the same task: less, in that we have certainly missed some findings that would have qualified had they come to our attention; more, in that others might omit or modify many of the findings we have included. We are sure that individual specialists will object to particular findings on grounds of wrong formulation, doubtful validation, insufficient qualification, and so on. But of those who accept the rules of the game—to produce empirical findings of this kind—we trust that few will object to whole sections of material.* In any case, of course, the book is not meant for the specialist within his own specialty.

* According to a well-known philosopher of science:

"In no area of social inquiry has a body of general laws been established, comparable with outstanding theories in the natural sciences in scope of explanatory power or in capacity to yield precise and reliable predictions. . . . It is also generally acknowledged that in the social sciences there is nothing quite like the almost complete unanimity commonly found among competent workers in the natural sciences as to what are matters of established fact, what are the reasonably satisfactory explanations (if any)

The Plan of the Book

The next chapter provides a brief introduction to the scientific methods used in the study of human behavior. It is important for the reader, as background for what follows, to have in mind how studies in this field are designed and data collected. In addition, we have distributed throughout the book a number of tabulations and figures reporting the actual data of behavioral studies, again so that the reader can be constantly reminded of the character and form of the results. The intent, in short, is to give the reader a sense of the ways in which the knowledge reported here has been gathered and established.

The main chapters of the book deal with broad subjects covering the major aspects of human behavior to which scientific study has been devoted. Then follows a final chapter in which we review what has been done and present the image of man that seems to emerge from these pages.

Although the chapter headings are listed in the table of contents, it is perhaps worthwhile to repeat them here, in the order in which they appear:

The Individual
   Behavioral Development
   Perceiving
   Learning and Thinking
   Motivation
The Family
Face-to-Face Relations, in Small Groups
Organizations
Institutions
   Religious
   Economic
   Political
   Educational
   Military
Strata (social characteristics in common)
   Stratification
   Ethnic Relations
Publics (focus of attention in common)
   Mass Communication
   Opinions, Attitudes, and Beliefs

for the assumed facts, and what are some of the valid procedures in sound inquiry. Disagreement on such questions undoubtedly occurs in the natural sciences as well. But it is usually found at the advancing frontiers of knowledge. . . . In contrast, the social sciences often produce the impression that they are a battleground for interminably warring schools of thought, and that even subject matter which has been under intensive and prolonged study remains at the unsettled periphery of research" (Nagel, 1961, pp. 447–48).

The Society
  Social Demography
  Social Geography
  Social Change
  Social Conflict
  Social Disorganization
Culture

We wish to make two points about this scheme of organization. The first is that the topics are arranged roughly from the smallest unit of analysis to the largest—that is, from the individual, or elements within him, to societies and cultures as wholes. Naturally, nothing as complicated as human behavior can be neatly pigeonholed, but by and large this scheme does seem to provide not only a workable arrangement but also a more or less logical progression in the presentation.

The second is that although these topics appear on the page in linear form, we actually think of them as being circular. Thus, when we get to culture we shall be talking about its effects upon the individual and be closing the circle of what is, after all, not pieces and segments but whole human behavior. In other words, wherever one cuts into the circle, he has to go all the way around it in order to get the full picture.

In any such organization of complicated material there are sure to be numerous problems of arrangement. For example, the relationship between two factors might go under one heading or the other: Should a finding on the effect of the small group on opinions go with the former or the latter? Should political opinions be treated as opinion or for their political content? Should the intellectual differences between races be included with intelligence or with ethnic relations? We found it virtually impossible to maintain a single standard of classification and hence we confess to a certain arbitrariness in deciding just what went where. In general, we tried to put a finding where it seemed to us to contribute most to understanding, and for the rest to rely on the index.

Just as the book as a whole has an architecture, so has each chapter. First comes a brief section defining the key terms met for the first time in that chapter. Then follows the major section on the findings—which appear as numbered statements followed by illustrative material of various kinds. Finally, there is a small list of readings that leads back into the literature.

The Behavioral Sciences

We also want to say a word about the field itself—its scope, its history, its present state. In our usage here, we do not equate the behavioral sciences with the social sciences. The latter term is usually understood to cover six disciplines: anthropology, economics, history, political science, psychology, and sociology. By the behavioral sciences we mean the disciplines of anthropology, psychology, and sociology—minus and plus: *Minus* such specialized sectors as physiological psychology, archaeology, technical linguistics, and most of physical anthropology; *Plus* social geography, some psychiatry, and the behavioral parts of economics, political science, and law.

In short, we are concerned here with the scientific research that deals directly with human behavior. The definition of the field may become obscure or fuzzy at the edges, but it is reasonably clear at the center. As a general rule, whenever we came near the periphery, where the behavioral sciences shade off into another field, we have tended to draw back; it was often true that, the closer we came to such boundaries, the harder we found the task of identifying the findings. In any case, the list of topics covered in the book gives our notion of the scope of the field.

If there is one thing certain about this set of findings, it is that it will be different a generation hence, just as it would have been different a generation ago. A field of science, contrary to popular notions, is essentially a changing field; hence it may be useful to remark on the historical development of this particular branch of knowledge.

The first thing to be said is that the history of the behavioral sciences is a short one. There is, of course, a long history of study and thought about man in philosophy, literature, history, political theory, religion, law, and medicine—in many cases study and thought about the same kinds of problems now being investigated by behavioral scientists. However, it was not until the late nineteenth century that the empirical, experimental, systematic, operational, *scientific* investigation of human behavior really began.

We are thus dealing with a recently established field, as such things are measured. The laboratories of the European and American "founders" of modern psychology, Wilhelm Wundt and William James, were not set up until the 1870's. The British origins of anthropology date only from the mid-nineteenth century (Maine, Tylor, Frazer), and the first academic department in the United States was not organized until 1890. Sociology in its present state is younger still. Hence, just as the seventeenth and eighteenth centuries saw the maturing of the physical sciences, and the nineteenth that of the biological sciences, so the twentieth century marks the coming-of-age of the behavioral sciences.*

Despite the signs of growth and expansion, it would be wrong to assume that the behavioral sciences are in a state of secure self-confidence and undisturbed health. That is not the case. From both the outside and the inside, in recent years, have come critical comments and actions that reveal

---

* It would appear that the more intimate (to man) the subject matter, the younger the science. Astronomy before geography, physical science before biology, medicine before psychology—even though in each case the availability of data was in the reverse order.

skepticism and rejection from without, dissatisfaction and concern from within. Natural scientists and humanists within the universities, while usually sympathetic to the effort represented by the behavioral sciences, have been reserved in appreciation of their accomplishments; intellectuals outside the universities have often been dubious, when not downright contemptuous, of the whole enterprise. (What is required of them, as readers of this volume, is the willing suspension of disbelief—and similarly for specialists within the behavioral sciences, though for different reasons.)

Actually, one of us believes that the accumulated knowledge is quite impressive for only a few decades. (Did any science do much better in its first seventy-five years or so?) The other is a little disappointed that the record is not better. But we see no purpose in arguing the matter here; the following pages are themselves the best evidence on the point. To get our own position in the open, we think it only fair to make two observations.

First, we believe that there are some important things wrong with the behavioral sciences at this stage in their development: e.g., too much precision misplaced on trivial matters, too little respect for crucial facts as against grand theories, too much respect for insights that are commonplace, too much indication and too little proof, too little genuine cumulation of generalizations, too little regard for the learning of the past,* far too much jargon.

But second, we also believe that, despite all the faults of youth and immaturity, the behavioral sciences have already made important contributions to our understanding of man and will make many more; that they are an indispensable approach to that understanding; that they have already affected man's image of himself, and permanently so; in short, that they are a major intellectual invention of the twentieth century, and largely an American one.

To sum up, we try to say what is known about human behavior, by some rigorous requirements of evidence, as produced distinctively by the behavioral sciences: What does it all come down to? We state what is known in the form of propositions, and we try to organize them in a sensible way. We try to maintain a certain level of generality in which human behavior itself is visible, and we try to satisfy ourselves as to the importance and nontriviality of the findings as well as to their distinctive contribution as science.

We are responsible for the selection and evaluation of findings, for their formulation, and for their organization. But, of course, we have no responsibility for the original selection of problems to study, for the way the studies were set up, for the methods and techniques applied to them, for

---

* It is partly for this reason that we have included a few humanistic quotations at the head of each chapter, to suggest the continuity among intellectual activities.

the character of the data collected, or for the conclusions and interpretations that emerged—that is, for what the field now is. As Aristotle, the first great behavioral scientist, pointed out a long time ago, the man who puts the question should not be credited or blamed for the answer.

As the reader will see, the findings, which are the *raison d'être* of the book, are presented in an austere and perhaps stark form. They are simply set down, one after the other, without the elaboration, orientation, illustration, speculation, repetition, conceptualization, theorization, and transition that typically accompany such material. We consider that this treatment is required by our very effort to present the (more or less) hard knowledge of the field in this way. Accordingly, this may not be an easy book to read, but it is an easy book to study.

Finally, our experience in compiling this book has been that, like all other books but perhaps more than most, we could continue to refine, expand, clarify, make more consistent, find better illustrations, reorganize, restate, reevaluate—in short, to improve it. Especially in a pioneering work of this kind, that process is close to endless. But we prefer to put it forward now as, if nothing more, a first approximation. We hope that it will rate a better grade than Dr. Johnson gave to dogs walking on their hind legs and to lady preachers: he marveled not that it was done well but that it was done at all!

"For example" is no proof.

YIDDISH PROVERB

The natural sciences talk about their results. The social sciences talk about their methods.

Attributed to HENRI POINCARÉ

When you cannot measure it, when you cannot express it in numbers, your knowledge is of a meagre and unsatisfactory kind.

LORD KELVIN

When you can measure it, when you can express it in numbers, your knowledge is still of a meagre and unsatisfactory kind.

JACOB VINER

In discussions on method and scope, a man is nearly sure to be right when affirming the usefulness of his own procedure, and wrong when denying that of others.

ALFRED MARSHALL
Principles of Economics

The brooding imagination puzzling over a multivariate distribution which just came off the I.B.M. machine, and seeking order in apparent chaos, is creating as truly as the maker of a sonnet. Hence the dichotomy often suggested between the work of the scientist or artist is no more than a half truth; the goals may be different but the scientist's eyes, like the artist's, are oft in a fine frenzy rolling.

SAMUEL STOUFFER
*Some Comments on Research Techniques in Social Psychology,
Sociology, and Social Anthropology*

Chapter Two

METHODS OF INQUIRY

Behavioral scientists, someone has observed, can talk about methods with a capital *M* or with a small *m*. The capital *M* is used for the large questions: How are the scientist's values involved in the selection of problems or the interpretation of results? What is the proper relationship of observation to conceptualization? Do findings operate against their own further verification by changing the very actions to which they refer? Is man truly capable of being objective about himself? Is a science of human behavior possible at all?

The small *m,* on the other hand, is used for detailed questions of technique: How can a proper sample be selected? How can unwanted bias be reduced or eliminated from a questionnaire? How can proper experimental controls be set up? How can a valid measuring instrument be developed? How can a study be designed most economically?

In a book of this kind, devoted to findings, why give any attention at all to Method and method? There are two reasons.

The first is that the procedures by which the behavioral sciences work help to define the very nature of the field itself. Just as doctors or lawyers or engineers are defined by a set of techniques that they, and normally only they, are trained and even licensed to use, so are behavioral scientists. In the large, we have actually employed this criterion in deciding what to include as findings: that is, we have omitted many contributions to the understanding of human behavior made by novelists, historians, playwrights, biographers, and poets, not because their contributions are less true or less interesting than those included, but because they stem from techniques other than those used by the behavioral sciences.

The second reason is that an intelligent evaluation of these findings requires some acquaintance with the kinds of assumptions and evidence they are based on, as well as an awareness of the potentials and limitations of various types of data. Armed with such critical understanding, the reader should be better able to judge the validity of the findings, and hence to appraise their contribution without going overboard in either direction. To this end, we have deliberately sprinkled throughout the text a number of results—tabulations, charts, figures, correlations, and so on—adapted from the original research reports, so that the reader will constantly be reminded of the kind of data on which the findings rest, and hence of the character of this form of knowledge.

To begin with, we need to say a few words about the nature of science as applied to human behavior.

This is not the place to argue the Big Questions as to whether there can be a science of human behavior at all, or whether these disciplines are really sciences, or whether the assumptions and procedures of the natural sciences can properly be transferred to the study of human beings. It should be obvious that there are several ways other than the scientific by which men have come to an "understanding" of man (we use quotation marks because the meaning of the term changes with each method): common observation, intuition and self-inquiry, reflection and philosophizing, revelation, creative and artistic expression. By claiming that the scientific approach to understanding human beings is valuable, we do not necessarily mean to devalue any of the others. But we do claim that the scientific approach is distinctive and that scientific procedures in the behavioral sciences produce factual evidence that demands respect from men of reason, however skeptical they may initially be.

In any case, whatever the behavioral disciplines are—sciences or otherwise—they have more or less established the hard knowledge about human behavior that appears in the following pages, and that is a final test. By "established" we mean that they have produced evidence for these findings using the methods usually attributed to science. Only ideal science, of course, always lives up to all of the following; but real science, behavioral science included, strives to do so:

The procedures are public: The results and the methods are both communicable and communicated. The scientific report contains a detailed description of just what was done and how. The description is adequate if, and only if, another competent practitioner of the science can follow each step of the investigation as though he had been there. And scientific reports are, of course, honest: they are minutely true down to the finest detail. In addition:

The definitions are precise: Here again, the procedure must be crystal clear. As an example, the statement "aggressive subjects were found to have greater dependence on their fathers than nonaggressive subjects" is inadequate as a scientific report. How was aggression defined and measured? By what test or procedures and by what specific scores? Where was the cut-off point between aggressive and nonaggressive subjects? How was dependence on the father revealed?

The data-collecting is objective: Once the investigation is under way, the investigator is bound to follow the data, whatever way they may fall —for or against his hypothesis (however cherished), for or against his personal preferences as a man. Biased procedures in collecting data have no place in science, nor has biased perception of the results. As a result:

The findings must be replicable: Because of the openness of the inquiry, another scholar can test the finding by seeking to reproduce it. This is why "artistic sensitivity" or "clinical insight" is itself not sufficient, though it may of course suggest hypotheses for subsequent verification.

The approach is systematic and cumulative: Scientists strive to unify whole bodies of knowledge through the use of central concepts, and hence to build up an organized system of verified propositions, which is usually called a theory. Here is another important difference between scientific operations on the one hand and artistic ones on the other.

The purposes are explanation, understanding, and prediction: The scientist wants to know why and how, and to be able to prove it. If he can, then he can predict the conditions under which the specified behavior will occur. And if he can do that, then the question of control enters in as well. We have achieved a great deal of control over nature in the physical and biological sciences, and some in economic affairs; but the matter inevitably becomes more sensitive at the prospect that the behavioral sciences will enable us to control ourselves, i.e., one another.

Moreover, the outlook of the scientist is important. He assumes, first of all, that there is some order in nature—otherwise, why seek for uniformities? As a scientist, he tries to look at human behavior as part of the order of nature, along with animals, organisms, rocks, and galaxies. In short, he assumes no special causes in the case of man, no divine intervention, no capricious will.

Nor, as scientist, is he directly concerned with good and bad, right and wrong, moral and immoral, but only with what is true and false. Indirectly, he is concerned: moral considerations may lead him to study a certain subject, such as ethnic relations, but once engaged he is supposed to proceed in an impartial and dispassionate manner. This point of view is much harder to achieve in the behavioral sciences than it is in the physical or biological sciences, since it is much more difficult to view objectively such phenomena as murder, incest, personality, or love than it is to take a disinterested view of the finger, orbits of the stars, or an inclined plane. This is perhaps a principal reason for the belated development of the behavioral sciences and for much of the present resistance to some of their findings.

Finally, science is characterized by a certain point of view toward the

acceptance of new findings and ideas, involving both extreme openminded-
ness on the one hand and extreme skepticism on the other: that is, willingness to accept the possibility of everything but reluctance to accept anything
as fact until it is demonstrated. ("I am certainly willing to accept the
possibility that people have extrasensory perception, but I am not willing
to state that they *do* have it until I have definitive evidence.")

These few paragraphs, plus the details on various methods that follow,
must serve to suggest what is meant by the scientific study of human behavior
as presented in this book. We might say, by way of condensation, that in
our view the study of human behavior has made considerable progress
toward the status of a science in the past half-century or more, and in
several respects has achieved it. This is especially the case when one considers how extraordinarily difficult it is to establish sound, valid, objective
information on human affairs. The subject matter is itself highly complicated, often obscure if not hidden, hard to observe fully let alone control
experimentally. Consider the technical difficulties in observing the psychological development of a child; or in discovering how many people not in
mental hospitals act like those who are in; or in learning precisely what
effect campaign speeches have on a presidential election; or in validly
finding out what Negroes really think of white people; or in isolating the
causes of juvenile delinquency; or in establishing in fact just what relationship exists between childhood experience and adult personality. We are not
speaking here of having ideas or even convictions about such matters—that
is easy. We are speaking of having data, collected in a scientific manner
according to the criteria discussed above.

The reader would do well to keep this notion in mind in appraising the
results reported in this book: these findings have been reasonably well established despite the difficulties, often the intractabilities, involved in the
scientific study of human behavior.

As for methods with a small *m*, they can perhaps best be considered
under three headings: methods utilized in the design of studies, methods
of data collection, and methods of analysis. The last we shall try to suggest
throughout the book by presentations of data in the analytic forms in which
they initially appeared. The other two are discussed in this chapter, with
necessarily brief descriptions of the ways behavioral scientists proceed in
their empirical inquiries.

DESIGN

In the broadest terms, there are three designs used in the behavioral
sciences: the experiment, the sample survey, and the case study.

The Experiment

By *experiment* is meant any investigation that includes two elements: manipulation or control of some variable by the investigator and systematic observation or measurement * of the result. In short, it means active intervention on the phenomena of interest to see what, if any, effects are produced by the intervention.

The experiment has had a central place in the history of science. The importance of experimentation depends not so much on its precision, its objectivity, or its instruments as on the inherent efficiency of intervention in disentangling cause-and-effect relationships. Whenever its use is feasible, intentional intervention is the method that most readily exposes cause and effect; and if the behavioral sciences were able to experiment more widely on their materials they would be better equipped today with important findings. For example, we would know much more about the effects on personality of different ways of rearing children if experimentation were not precluded on moral and humanitarian grounds. And the field is currently making some progress on such basic problems as mental disease and emotional disturbance by means of physiological intervention in the nervous system accompanied by controlled observation of the behavioral results. The implantation of tiny electrodes in the brain has been used to induce fear, rage, joy, even "pleasure"; and ultimately such mapping of the brain centers that mediate emotions may have far-reaching clinical implications. Similarly, in human beings, chemical intervention has produced behavior that closely resembles certain manifestations of schizophrenia; and, in animals, certain parts of the brain have been systematically removed to see what effect that has on learned problem-solving.

THE CLASSICAL EXPERIMENT

The prototype of scientific experimentation, and in many ways its most foolproof form, is the classical experiment. The general question it answers is whether, and to what extent, one variable (called the experimental or independent variable) affects another variable (the dependent variable).

The logic is simple. Two groups are matched at the outset; one is given the experimental intervention (a piece of propaganda, a new drug that affects behavior, a French lesson taught in a new way, a special procedure that can introduce changes in working procedures in a factory); the result

---

* By *measurement* the behavioral scientist typically means something broader than what the term means to the layman. The behavioral scientist considers that an attitude has been measured if it can simply be distinguished as "for" or "against," "more" or "less." Finer quantitative distinctions, of course, are also measurements, but so are dichotomies or classificatory categories in general.

of the intervention is subsequently measured (i.e., its effect on attitudes, on personality, on the amount of French learned, on morale and productivity). The essentials of the classical experiment can be schematized as follows:

Experimental group, but not control group, exposed to intervention (the experimental or independent variable)

	Before	After
Experimental group or subject	B_e	A_e
Control group or subject	B_c	A_c

The figures represent measurements of the dependent variable, and the effect of the experimental variable is $(A_e - A_c) - (B_e - B_c)$.

Here is an illustration of a classical experiment concerned with the effects of a new tranquilizer pill on psychotic behavior:

(1) Define the population of subjects and draw a sample—e.g., a random sample of all the patients with a given diagnosis at a certain institution.

(2) Divide the sample at random into two groups. By definition the two groups will now be similar, within limits of sampling error, on *any* measurement. Thus there is no reason to expect one group to behave any differently in the future than the other. Flip a coin to decide which will be "experimental" and which "control."

(3) Define the dependent variable ("psychotic behavior"): How will it be measured or rated? Take a "before" measurement on each group.

(4) Define the experimental variable precisely—What doses of the tranquilizer over what period of time?—and administer it to the experimental group only. The control group will probably get a placebo—a pill that looks the same but has no active ingredients—to control for the effects of autosuggestion, and even for the effect of participating in the experiment at all (since that will involve some special attention, at the least). In some cases of this kind, for extra precaution, the experiment is "double blind": not only does the subject not know which pill he gets but, in order to control the expression of his own (conscious or unconscious) wishes in the matter, the experimenter does not know at the time either.

(5) Take "after" measurements of the dependent variable on each group.

(6) The difference between the two groups after the experiment, beyond any difference that may have existed before, is the effect of the ex-

perimental variable. In this case, it is the effect of the tranquilizer upon psychotic behavior.

The glory of the classical experiment is that its logic has no loophole. When all the conditions of the classical experiment have been met, and all four cells have been filled in, the final difference between control and experimental group *must* be due to the effect of the experimental or independent variable: both groups reflect the effects of any other variables not directly manipulated by the experimenter (such as time itself, atmospheric conditions, or the effects of having been selected to participate in the study). Thus the control group protects the experimenter against many of the common fallacies that plague less rigorous studies. Before-and-after observation of an experimental group alone is particularly vulnerable to the fallacy of *post hoc, ergo propter hoc.* Without a control group there is a temptation to attribute any subsequent change in the observed subjects to the experimental variable, whereas the change may have occurred without the experimenter's intervention.

Although there is a logical model for the classical experiment, in actual experiments the design is frequently modified for various reasons: costs, practical difficulties, and so on. In some cases, statistical approximations will do. For example, if the experimental and control groups are truly divided at random, the before-measurement may be omitted in the knowledge that the two groups will vary only within known limits of sampling error. The experiment simply consists of the administration of the experimental condition to one group and the subsequent after-measurements of both. If this after-measurement records a difference between the two groups that cannot be attributed to chance variation, it is taken to be the result of the experimental variable.*

Similarly, many experiments add onto the basic four-fold model. Some measure the effect of the experimental variable over time: propaganda may be effective right after its administration, but how long does it last? Others assess the effects of several experimental variables within a single investigation. The simplest form of this involves two or more experimental groups, each of which is measured against a single control group. For example, the

* It is sometimes hard to believe, but it is still true, that when a group has been divided at random into two groups, the groups will differ by no more than chance on *any* characteristic whatsoever. The proportion of blue-eyed people in the two groups, of redheads, of people over and under 5'7", of Catholics, of those who skipped breakfast this morning, of those opposed to capital punishment or in favor of a stronger United Nations—all will be roughly equivalent. There are statistical procedures that determine the probability of a given difference having arisen simply by such random division. Therefore, when a difference is greater than that which could reasonably be expected on the basis of random division, and the groups have in fact been randomly divided, the conclusion is that the difference is not due to their division but to something that happened to them afterward.

patients can be divided into three or more groups: one is the control, one gets tranquilizer A, one gets tranquilizer B, etc.

Moreover, modern statistical designs make it possible to evaluate the relative effects of a number of independent variables acting simultaneously and in combination. An investigation of classroom learning might vary the method of instruction, the sex of the teacher, the room lighting, and student motivation, all at one stage of observations; and then conclude which of these factors is the most important influence on learning, and how they act in combination.

So much for the general logic of experimental design: the principal point, worth repeating, is that the fundamental advantage of experimentation is not its precision or its instrumentation but its inherent logical rigor. Now let us apply the method to the settings and subjects of behavioral science experimentation. In our field, we can distinguish experiments in the laboratory and in natural settings.

The Laboratory Experiment—Animal

Behavioral scientists, notably psychologists, conduct intensive studies on animals in the laboratory: historically, the animals have usually been rats, pigeons, or apes. Why study lower animals when the objective is to understand people? The reasons are both practical and theoretical.

On the practical side, many experiments cannot be conducted on human subjects for legal and moral reasons—e.g., the behavioral effect of systematic destruction of various parts of the nervous system. In general, any experimental variable that involves bodily harm or undue pain, discomfort, embarrassment, or psychological or social damage is naturally excluded from experimental intervention with human subjects. In addition, animals are cheap, they cannot resist captivity, they are almost always available, and they do not have to be paid for their services.

On the theoretical side, the environment of animals, unlike that of human beings, can be completely and systematically controlled twenty-four hours a day. The lower animals reproduce more quickly and in greater numbers than human beings, and their mating can be controlled, thus making possible longitudinal studies of hereditary effects. With animals, far greater homogeneity of subjects can be attained by inbreeding, thus reducing sources of behavioral variation that are irrelevant and bothersome for some purposes. Animals are presumably simpler and thus more easily understood than people, hence some scientists argue that the study of human behavior must begin with the simpler forms (in the sense that arithmetic has to be mastered before the calculus). Finally, the acceptance of evolution as a biological fact leads to the assumption that, in principle, the processes underlying human behavior are an outgrowth of those represented in lower forms, and therefore the study of animals cannot be irrelevant. Findings from animal studies are not expected to be directly replicated in human behavior, but they may well provide the foundations on which the elaborations introduced at the human level must be built.

The Laboratory Experiment—Human

Human beings are also studied intensively in laboratory situations, both individually and in groups. Given the practicalities of the matter, the human beings involved are usually college students, and many of the practical advantages of using lower animals apply as well with students as subjects: they do not have to be paid, they are readily accessible, and they often cannot effectively resist the experimentation.*

We have reviewed the theoretical justification for studying rats and pigeons. What is the justification for using college sophomores or, more generally, representatives of any selected type of human subject for laboratory investigation?

The answer depends largely upon the expected variation of the phenomenon under study. There is little reason to suspect, for example, that the visual or auditory processes of college students vary considerably from those of other types of people; or that their eye movements, which signal dreams, are unique. Accordingly, the tendency to generalize to people at large on such issues is frequently supported by further studies, and college students turn out to be a reasonably good sample of human beings on such limited topics as those closely tied to physiological processes.

However, when the question deals with political attitudes, feelings toward the family, reactions to stress, life values, or such complicated or culturally determined matters, it is safest to assume, until proved otherwise, that there *are* important differences between college students and other categories of citizens. Hence, a priori generalizations of findings of this character must be avoided.

Another general problem of much experimental work done in the laboratory is that of "translation." Some laboratory experiments deal with phenomena that can be reproduced directly in the laboratory, such as depth perception, small-group problems, or the learning of certain skills. In these cases, the experimenter simply brings the behavior of interest into the laboratory for more careful scrutiny under experimental conditions. Many phenomena, however, cannot be transplanted to a laboratory either in principle or for such practical considerations as time, money, cooperation of subjects, and so on; or the phenomenon that interests the experimenter is a general one (motivation, love, hostility) that must be delineated to one

---

* In this connection, it is worth recalling an observation of the late Edward Tolman, a distinguished psychologist. He once noted how much of American psychology was based on two sets of subjects, rats and college sophomores, and enjoined his colleagues to remember that the former certainly are not people and the latter may not be!

specific instance for a given investigation. Such conditions require acts of "translation": before the experiment, translation of the phenomena of interest to the experimenter into the specific laboratory operations that will "tap" them; after the experiment, translation of the results of the specific operations performed back into the original concepts and phenomena.

An illustration will, we hope, make the point. The psychoanalytic notion of "repression" states that under certain circumstances individuals will force out of their awareness the memories of certain traumatic or psychologically damaging events. In addition, some impulses or desires that are unacceptable (e.g., killing or having sexual relations with one's father) may be repressed, that is, not be consciously acknowledged although they are actively present in the personality. When experimentally inclined psychologists wanted to test some of these notions in the laboratory, one design used was to show subjects a series of pictures—some pleasant, some unpleasant or gruesome—and at a later sitting ask them to describe the pictures seen. So the hypothesis that traumatic events get repressed is translated into the test: "Gruesome pictures will be accurately recalled less frequently than non-gruesome pictures."

Evaluation of such experimental results demands critical consideration of the translation involved and its validity. Students of repression might reject the experiment (as many of them did) not because it was poorly designed or failed to produce conclusive results but simply because they considered it irrelevant to their views of the concept of repression.

Note how this example illustrates the scientific requirement that results be reported operationally (what was done) as well as conceptually or theoretically (what they mean). When the experimenter reports that gruesome pictures were not described accurately with the same frequency as non-gruesome pictures, behavioral scientists can decide for themselves what relevance, if any, the finding has for issues in which they are interested.

THE NATURAL EXPERIMENT

Frequently the major elements of an experiment occur or are produced in the natural habitat of the behavior under study. Such experimentation avoids many of the problems of the laboratory situation discussed above, e.g., oversimplification and artificiality. In the natural experiment the subjects ordinarily do not know they are under investigation and hence do not modify their behavior as a result of being watched. On the other hand, natural experimentation is usually less precise, because the pertinent events are less fully under the experimenter's control.

The Planned Natural Experiment

In this type, as in the laboratory, the investigator intentionally manipulates the independent variable and then makes systematic measurements of the result. The tranquilizer study is an example; so is the illustrative study mentioned above dealing with classroom learning. A planned natural experiment often used in advertising research is the "split-run" technique: metropolitan newspapers frequently offer advertisers the opportunity to run two versions of an advertisement in the same issue, with coupons or other coded devices enabling "returns" from the two versions to be compared.

The Spontaneous Natural Experiment

Sometimes behavioral scientists are fortunate enough to come on a situation that happened by itself yet has most or all of the elements of a successful experiment. In such cases, an approximation of experimental results may be obtained.

For example, when television was being introduced, there was a period during which technical considerations were the principal determinants of which towns and cities would have stations. Thus it was possible to find a number of cities without TV and to know about when the medium would be introduced in them. This provided an opportunity to study "what television does" on a before-and-after basis, as compared with matched towns without TV (the controls). Similarly, studying the culture of a primitive community during and after the advent of technological developments provides an attenuated natural experiment under spontaneous conditions. Since, as noted above, the absence of a proper control is the technical failing of such studies, the investigator must often decide between naturalness and control, or compromise on some of each.

The Sample Survey

The sample survey, as a type of research design, does not refer simply to a public opinion poll, though a properly designed poll is certainly one example of a sample survey, and probably the most familiar one. In our sense, a sample survey is properly named in that it contains the indicated two elements:

(1) *A sample:* The investigator first decides what group or "population" he is interested in (American adults, voters, women of childbearing age, college students, etc.) and then selects a sample in the statistical sense. It may be "random," "representative," "quota," "weighted," or any of a number of technical types. The main point is that the sample is so chosen as to enable the experimenter to draw conclusions regarding the entire "population" and not simply those members of the population who happen to turn up in the sample.

(2) *A survey:* The investigator then collects some measures on the appropriate characteristics of the population being studied (number of tele-

vision sets or children in the household; how the members feel about Russia or religion; what they know about India or space; and so on).

Obviously there are certain questions that can be answered only by a sample survey. The question, "To what extent do American psychologists today believe that extrasensory perception exists?" can be answered by specifying a population and then asking a selected sample. No experiment will answer the question once and for all and neither will a case study. In general, whenever the investigator is interested in assessing or estimating the present state of affairs with regard to some variable that changes over time for a large group of subjects, a sample survey is the only practical way to get the answer. If the variable did not change over time, we could probably learn the answer once and for all by experiment; or if there were interest in only one or a few instances, case studies could provide the answer. These are certainly not the only conditions under which the sample survey is useful, but these are the conditions under which it is the imperative form of design.

In addition to simple measures of magnitude (How many people will vote?), sample surveys provide clues to relations between variables (and thus ultimately to cause and effect) by correlation of the various measures obtained. For example, a survey of number of children per family can provide a series of tables showing how fertility varies by families of differing class, race, rural-urban residence, religion, etc. This example, incidentally, illustrates another advantage of the sample survey in the study of relationships: many times the variables of interest are difficult or impossible to manipulate by experiment (years of schooling, race), so the only approach is to compare people who already differ on the characteristic in question and see how their behavior differs.

Such correlations are difficult to disentangle causally, because the direction of the influence is uncertain (and it is often reciprocal, which makes the matter more difficult still). To take a simple example, a correlation between reading an advertisement for a given make of car and buying the car could go either way—reading influenced purchase, purchase influenced reading. Even when the direction is clear, when one characteristic (e.g., race) antedates and is not affected by another (e.g., fertility), the nature of the causal relationship is quite complex, with several other factors usually involved (e.g., income, social position, religion, place of residence, age at marriage).

To handle change over time in certain investigations, a variant of the sample survey has been developed that is called the panel. This requires repeated measures of the appropriate characteristics on the same people, so that the investigation can study how changes were brought about over time. This method is particularly useful in campaigns that bring a variety of stimuli to the subjects' attention, and it is no accident that the method is used mainly in studies of marketing and voting. A major limitation of the panel technique is that, as the same people are queried repeatedly, they may change their behavior simply as a result of panel membership. As a control, panel responses are often checked against samples of "fresh" respondents.

The Case Study

The case study is complementary to the sample survey. The sample survey measures many people on few characteristics, usually at one point in time. The case study intensively examines many characteristics of one "unit" (person, work group, company, community, culture), usually over a long period of time. The goal of such investigations is to learn "all" about the area of interest for the one case involved. Typical case studies in the behavioral sciences might include: the life history of a psychotic; an intensive analysis of a patient's psychological disturbance; * an anthropological monograph describing in detail the technology and customs of a primitive culture; a detailed description and analysis of the socioeconomic classes existing in a small Southern town.

As the examples suggest, the detail and the depth of information over time that the case study provides makes this design particularly relevant for questions involving etiology and development: How does a particular neurotic manifestation emerge and change over time? What are the critical incidents that lead up to an industrial strike? How does the industrialization of a traditional society affect the family?

The chief limitation of this method is that the results are based on a sample of one, so that the degree of their generality is not known. Would another individual, another company, another community, another culture respond in the same way? In addition, the case study is often subject to the *post hoc, ergo propter hoc* fallacy, since neither a "control group" nor intervention by the investigator is provided as a safeguard.

Hence, case studies rarely *prove* anything, although they are frequently rich in clues and insights for further investigation. In many areas the case study is the idea-getting investigation par excellence. But since in this book we limit ourselves to what is more or less proved about human behavior, we shall bring in the results of case studies only when they have been verified in some way.

* In fact, case studies are one of the principal sources of data on many questions in clinical psychology, since the practicing clinician is interested in specific individuals and collects intensive data on his patients. The most important questions in this area revolve around such time-bound issues as how and when the various syndromes arise, develop, and change. Thus, clinical histories have practical significance for the therapist and stimulate many hypotheses in personality theory.

COLLECTION OF DATA

These research designs require that information about human behavior be gathered and recorded in some systematic fashion. We now discuss the potentials and problems of some of the major methods for collecting data that are used in the behavioral sciences: observation, report, records.

Direct Observation of Behavior

Frequently it is possible for the scientist to observe the behavior he is interested in as it occurs. He can do this either as a participant in the event or the community studied or as a nonparticipant. In either case, the fact that they are under observation may or may not be known to the subjects. This means that there are four types of direct observation, illustrated thus:

	Participant	*Nonparticipant*
Known to subjects	Social psychologist enrolls and goes through nurse's training program in order to learn how the recruits are taught. Identity is known.	Laboratory experiment in problem-solving in a small group. Psychologist sits in corner and takes notes, tape-records, or watches through a window. Anthropologist lives in primitive culture for a year, collects material on the religious life of the natives.
Not known to subjects	Sociologist gets job as laborer in order to study behavior of workers. Healthy psychologist has himself admitted to psychiatric hospital, with his identity and purpose unknown to the staff or to other patients.	Social psychologist on street corner observes and records behavior of drivers on approaching stop sign: how many stop completely, how many merely slow down, etc.

The relative efficiency of these methods depends, of course, on the character of the problem. A basic consideration is the extent to which the phenomenon under study is likely to be modified if the subjects know they are being studied.

Now in principle there probably is no problem in the behavioral sciences that is not affected at least potentially by the subject's knowledge that he is participating in the study. When people are observed by others, especially in behavior that is personally or socially significant, they frequently behave quite differently than they would otherwise. Tell a woman that she is going to be weighed every morning as part of a study and you run a high risk that she will change the very measurement at interest. Ask parents if you can observe how they treat their children under stress and you are not likely to see the full range of responses. In general, people, at least "in our culture," have a desire to please or impress, to be considered intelligent, acceptable, moral, or good, even (sometimes especially) by an impersonal scientific observer who does not judge their actions as such and who is a stranger unlikely ever to be encountered again.

This tendency on the part of a knowing subject may be irrelevant or insignificant in some studies; it can sometimes be controlled experimentally (as, for example, by a control group that also knows it is under study). But when the investigator wishes to describe behavior of a personally important or private nature, direct observation known to the subjects may be impossible. When the ethical problems of surreptitious observation are considered less weighty than the potential benefits to science, the investigator usually confesses his surreptitious observation subsequently and asks the subjects' permission to use the data so collected.

The actual means of recording direct observations vary from impressionistic field notes to precise and highly quantified ratings or precoded observations. For example, as we shall see later, one such method of quantitative recording and analysis utilizes a system of twelve categories into which all behavior that occurs in a face-to-face group can be classified. The observer, located behind a one-way mirror, can record on a moving belt the complete proceedings of a meeting, indicating who speaks to whom, in what order, and in which category each exchange falls.

Direct observation also includes records made on films, tapes, and other mechanical devices. In many instances, such records may yield quite accurate and comprehensive data since they can be studied at leisure by any number of observers (independently or in unison) and checked and rechecked as often as desired.

Verbal Report

Some phenomena are inherently out of the scope of direct scientific observation: behavior that is private (sexual behavior, arguments between husband and wife) or asocial (criminality and trickery) or protected by custom (certain religious matters) as well as the vast amount of behavior that simply does not exist in directly observable form (ideas, attitudes, feelings, beliefs). In addition, it is frequently not feasible on practical grounds to make direct observations of the number and scope that may be desired for a given study, even though it would be possible to do so.

Thus a great deal of behavioral science is based on (usually solicited) verbal reports of what has happened, what is expected to happen, how one felt, what one thought, and other conditions internal to the subject: "I voted Democratic"; "I was rarely spanked"; "The light is getting brighter"; "The blot reminds me of a turtle"; "I hate my wife"; "I want to get ahead"; "That's the way we do things around here"; "I thought it reasonable to go along with the others." Now there are a variety of techniques for obtaining and recording verbal reports, and they vary considerably in their advantages and disadvantages for particular problems. They can be roughly classified and ordered as follows, according to their characteristic contributions to the collection of behavioral data:

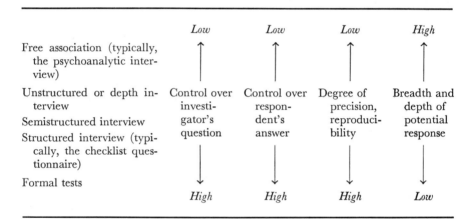

	Low	*Low*	*Low*	*High*
Free association (typically, the psychoanalytic interview)	↑	↑	↑	↑
Unstructured or depth interview	Control over investi-	Control over respon-	Degree of precision,	Breadth and depth of
Semistructured interview	gator's question	dent's answer	reproduci- bility	potential response
Structured interview (typically, the checklist questionnaire)				
Formal tests	↓	↓	↓	↓
	High	*High*	*High*	*Low*

Naturally, a great deal of data on human behavior comes directly from reports of these kinds. In general, as more and more constraint is placed upon both the interviewer and the respondent, the unknown biases introduced by the method of interrogation decrease while precision and reliability increase. Respondents confine themselves more and more closely to a specific topic and their answers typically become more directly comparable one to another.

At the same time, the potential range of responses decreases as constraint increases. The more structured the interview, the less "broad" the information obtained. Ideally, then, as a research project progresses from the initial exploratory or groping stage, through the middle range where the investigator begins to have specific hypotheses about his material, to the final step where he is concerned with pinning down or proving some point, the techniques would move from nonstructured through semistructured to totally structured. If totally structured techniques are applied in the initial stages, the risk is run of ruling out entire areas of response that did not occur to the investigator; applying nonstructured techniques in the final stages makes it less likely that any hypothesis will be rigorously confirmed or refuted. By and large, this general logic is observed in the field as a whole—over the long run in a series of studies of the same problem, as well as within a single inquiry.

FREE ASSOCIATION (THE PSYCHOANALYTIC INTERVIEW)

True free association represents the ultimate in freedom of response. Not only does the interviewer refrain from any direct questioning, but the subject himself is supposed to place no constraints whatever on what he says; he simply reports anything that comes into his mind. Ideally, even the ordinarily assumed constraints of speech are removed—logical sequence, rules of grammar, syntax, etc.—and the process approaches the freedom-from-rules characteristic of the content of dreams.

Verbal reports of true free association rarely occur, but they are approximated in some psychoanalytic interviews, where the length and the intimacy of the relationship, as well as the personal and social safeguards in the situation, make such behavior possible. The material in a transcript of such sessions over a period of several years is about as broad and deep a verbal report as can be secured in the form of data. The subject covers an exhaustive series of topics; each is treated at length and on repeated occasions; and the whole includes mention of behavior and feelings probably never before or again reported to anyone.

But the same factors that make such reports possible also restrict their accessibility as well as their controllability. When made, as they only rarely are, psychoanalytic transcripts are ordinarily restricted to the analyst or a small group of his colleagues and are not available for general publication or study.

THE UNSTRUCTURED OR DEPTH INTERVIEW

The unstructured or depth interview approximates complete freedom for the respondent in discussing a particular topic, but it does confine him to the area of major concern to the investigator; it frees the answers but limits the questions. The interviewer has no set list of queries but only an outline of topics he wants to cover. The wording, the sequence, and the intensity of questioning are left to the interviewer's discretion; ordinarily, they are tailored to each interview so as to produce the most meaningful material with the particular respondent.

Characteristic depth interviewing involves extensive use of the "non-directive probe," a query designed to produce further elaboration without influencing the content of the response in any way. Typical probes are: "Would you tell me a little more about that?", a nod of the head, a questioning repetition of the last few words spoken by the respondent, and "I don't quite understand," "Really?" or simply "Mmm."

The unstructured interview typically attempts to elicit all the respondent's information and attitudes related to the topic. In some cases, the discussion is recorded verbatim, and the interviewer also makes note of revealing facial expressions or gestures. So it allows analysis of the emotional flavor and the between-the-lines meaning communicated by the respondent's own language and subtle coloration of terms (that are not available when an answer must be given to specific questions in specific terms). It is these characteristics of the material that are appropriately referred to as "depth," and not the degree of consciousness of the attitudes tapped.

THE SEMISTRUCTURED INTERVIEW

This form gives greater control to the interviewer. It specifies not only the major topic to be stressed but also the questions to be asked and usually their order. Questions are of the "open-ended" type ("What do you think of Russia?"), in which the wording of the question is specified but the wording of the response is left to the respondent.

The semistructured interview is a compromise: as it acquires some of the advantages of reliability, precision, and control associated with the more structured techniques, it sacrifices some of the scope and depth of response obtainable by the less structured interviewing methods.

THE STRUCTURED INTERVIEW

In this case, the interviewer is entirely controlled in the wording and the sequence of questions; in addition, the respondent is confined to a precoded set of answers, made available to him by multiple choice or some other device: "When do you think men will reach the moon—this year, in one to five years, in five to ten years, or never? Or don't you know?" Or the familiar form: "How do you feel about the statement that it's more important to advance our knowledge of people than it is to reach the moon—strongly agree, mildly agree, can't say, mildly disagree, or strongly disagree?" Or the simple dichotomy: "Have you spanked a child of yours in the past two months—yes or no?"

TESTS AND INVENTORIES

The dividing line between tests and interviews is obscure, if indeed it exists. An ordinary paper-and-pencil, multiple-choice "attitude" test varies in no important respect from the characteristics of the structured interview; the questions merely happen to be printed instead of spoken. Such tests are in effect self-administered interviews and represent the extreme control on both questioner and respondent. The forms that ask the subject to answer fairly direct questions about himself (e.g., "How often do you have nightmares?") are usually called inventories. The term "test" usually refers to the subject's performance on a task as scored or evaluated by the investigator (as in an I.Q. or aptitude test).

Tests and inventories are typically concerned with measuring or evaluating the individual tested, whereas interviews (excluding psychiatric ones) are more generally interested in securing information on some event or topic. And tests are conducted on "subjects," whereas interviews are held with "respondents" (giving information about themselves) or with "informants" (giving information about others: the community, the society, the culture).*

Among the tests of personality are included both precoded paper-and-pencil tests and those in which the subject's free response is interpreted clinically. Illustrative of the latter category are the common "projective" tests, such as the Rorschach ink-blot test or the TAT (Thematic Apperception Test), which requires telling a story from a picture. The rationale for such tests is discussed in the chapter dealing with perception.

A useful distinction can be made between theoretical and practical tests. Theoretical tests are devised to answer basic questions about people and are judged by their contribution to basic understanding: What are the fundamental capacities? What is the nature of personality? How does an individual diagnosed as hysteric differ from an individual diagnosed as manic? Practical tests are devised to predict some events in the real world: Who will be a successful pilot? How much achievement can an individual expect in college? What is the probability of nervous breakdown? Which engaged couples will be happily married? Such tests are evaluated very simply, by seeing how much better they do than chance, and a test is as good or as bad as its proved ability to separate the ultimate "successes" from the "failures."

The methods of development and the basic characteristics of these two types differ considerably. For example, one of the principal objectives of theoretical tests is to become as "pure" as possible: to measure one thing and one thing only. If the score on a mathematical aptitude test is also influenced by the subject's reading ability, the test is considered "contaminated." On the other hand, very few of the practical criteria we wish to predict, like success in flying or in marriage, depend on "pure" abilities. Instead, they involve a combination of abilities and skills, with various combinations producing varying degrees of success. Therefore the most successful practical tests often contain a great jumble of items from a theoretical point of view.

Records

Sometimes the material at interest is simply not available for an original investigation—for instance, when it occurred a hundred years ago. At other

* The use of persons as informants is particularly common in anthropology, with a few members of a tribe or primitive society providing information on the life of the entire group. In sociology, the interviewee is usually a respondent, and the investigator (being a member of the society under study) is often his own informant.

times behavioral scientists are fortunate enough to have made available to them masses of interesting data that they had no part in collecting. Cases of the first type necessitate the use of secondary data; cases of the second type make analyzing the data inviting and frequently efficient.

Information recorded for other purposes but of great potential interest to students of human behavior comes from many sources: census statistics; life insurance records, medical histories; newspapers, magazines, novels, and autobiographies; admission and release records of psychiatric hospitals; records of prisons, churches, and schools; business transcripts of several kinds. In fact, it is hard to think of any recorded information regarding people and their behavior that could not be of potential value to behavioral science; the application is limited only by the ingenuity and energy of the investigator and the quality of the record. And much of such data is of a scope that no single scientific investigation could afford to collect.

In order to retrieve data from the volume of published material, the method of content analysis has been developed as a way of quantifying the characteristics of interest that appear in communications. This method is used quite extensively, especially for descriptive purposes. It consists, in effect, of classifying the content of books, newspapers, speeches, television shows, documents, or any other communication material into a set of categories so that their relative frequency can be determined. Is there more foreign news in magazines now than there was in the 1930's? How closely do television programs conform to stated standards? What shifts are made in adapting novels into films? How do international wars appear in the history texts of the contending powers? These are some questions to which content analysis has been applied.

The proof of the methods, however, is in the knowledge that they produce, to which the remainder of this book is devoted. This chapter described how behavioral scientists have secured empirical knowledge of human behavior. The following chapters set forth the results. The reader should keep in mind that the following findings have indeed been documented in one or another, or several, of these ways.

SELECTED READINGS

Collecting good data on human behavior is a hard task: the subject matter is highly complicated, it is difficult to control the material for scientific purposes without losing its very flavor, the fact of observation itself can change the behavior under study, recall and report are likely to be biased, and so on. As a result, behavioral scientists have given a great deal of attention to the methods of inquiry appropriate to the field. As a start, we note the following titles. They contain bibliographies so that the interested reader can follow through as far as he wishes.

Leon Festinger and Daniel Katz, eds. *Research Methods in the Behavioral Sciences.* Holt, Rinehart & Winston, 1953.

W. J. Goode and Paul Hatt. *Methods in Social Research.* McGraw-Hill, 1952.

Paul F. Lazarsfeld and Morris Rosenberg, eds. *The Language of Social Research: A Reader in the Methodology of Social Research.* Free Press, 1955.

Gardner Lindzey, ed. "Part 3. Research Methods," *Handbook of Social Psychology,* Vol. I: *Theory and Method.* Addison-Wesley, 1954.

Claire Selltiz *et al. Research Methods in Social Relations.* Rev. ed. Holt, Rinehart & Winston, 1959.

Those are rather general titles covering a range of research methods. For more particular treatments, see:

On the experiment:

W. G. Cochran and Gertrude M. Cox. *Experimental Designs.* 2nd ed. Wiley, 1950.

A. L. Edwards. *Experimental Design in Psychological Research.* Rev. ed. Holt, Rinehart & Winston, 1960.

R. A. Fisher. *The Design of Experiments.* 4th ed. Oliver & Boyd, 1947.

On the sample survey:

Herbert Hyman. *Survey Design and Analysis.* Free Press, 1955.

Herbert Hyman *et al. Interviewing in Social Research.* U. of Chicago Press, 1954.

Samuel A. Stouffer *et al. Measurement and Prediction.* Princeton U. Press, 1950.

On the case study:

R. G. Barker and H. F. Wright. *One Boy's Day: A Specimen Record of Behavior.* Harper, 1951.

John Dollard. *Criteria for the Life History.* Yale U. Press, 1935.

Henry Murray, ed. *Explorations in Personality: A Clinical and Experimental Study of Fifty Men of College Age.* Oxford U. Press, 1938.

On the analysis of the small group:

Robert F. Bales. *Interaction Process Analysis: A Method for the Study of Small Groups.* Addison-Wesley, 1950.

On testing procedures:

Lee Cronbach. *Essentials of Psychological Testing.* 2nd ed. Harper, 1960.

On content analysis:

Bernard Berelson. *Content Analysis in Communications Research.* Free Press, 1952.

On the analysis of accumulated ethnographic reports in anthropology:

George P. Murdock. *Social Structure.* Macmillan, 1949.

On the basic statistical background, including problems of sampling:

Allen Wallis and Harry J. Roberts. *Statistics: A New Approach.* Free Press, 1956.

Finally, as examples of comparative inquiry into the yield of different methods applied to the same problem, see:

Carl I. Hovland. "Reconciling Conflicting Results Derived from Experimental and Survey Studies of Attitude Change," *American Psychologist,* 14, 1959, pp. 8–17.

Paul Meehl. *Clinical vs. Statistical Prediction: A Theoretical Analysis and Review of the Evidence.* U. of Minnesota Press, 1954.

He hates his son who fails to ply the rod: the man who loves his son chastises him.

Proverbs 13:24

The childhood shows the man, as morning shows the day.

JOHN MILTON
Paradise Regained

The accent of one's birthplace persists in the mind and heart as much as in speech.

FRANÇOIS DE LA ROCHEFOUCAULD
Maxims

If people would but leave children to themselves; if teachers would cease to bully them; if parents would not insist upon directing their thoughts, and dominating their feelings—those feelings and thoughts which are a mystery to all (for how much do you and I know of each other, of our children, of our fathers, of our neighbour, and how far more beautiful and sacred are the thoughts of the poor lad or girl whom you govern likely to be, than those of the dull and world-corrupted person who rules him?)—if, I say, parents and masters would leave their children alone a little more,—small harm would accrue.

WILLIAM MAKEPEACE THACKERAY
Vanity Fair

Once roused, he opened his eyes to see his mother standing on the hearthrug with the hot iron near her cheeks, listening, as it were, to the heat. Her still face, with the mouth closed tight from suffering and disillusion and self-denial, and her nose in the smallest bit on one side, and her blue eyes so young, quick, and warm, made his heart contract with love. When she was quiet, so, she looked brave and rich with life, but as if she had been done out of her rights. It hurt the boy keenly, this feeling about her that she had never had her life's fulfilment: and his own incapability to make up to her hurt him with a sense of impotence, yet made him patiently dogged inside. It was his childish aim.

D. H. LAWRENCE
Sons and Lovers

Both the forcing of children and the fear of forcing them were inadequate substitutes for the long, careful watchfulness, the checking and balancing and reckoning of accounts, to the end that there should be no slip below a certain level of duty. . . . They had that wistful charm, almost sadness, peculiar to children who have learned early not to cry or laugh with abandon; they were apparently moved to no extremes of emotion, but content with a simple regimentation and the simple pleasures allowed them. They lived on the even tenor found advisable in the experience of old families of the Western world, brought up rather than brought out.

F. SCOTT FITZGERALD
Tender Is the Night

Chapter Three

BEHAVIORAL DEVELOPMENT

In the first part of the book, consisting of this and the next three chapters, we deal with the basic behavioral characteristics of the individual human being: capacities, limitations, and processes that underlie human behavior, in every form, wherever found. In that sense, the findings here will be the most general ones presented. The presumption is that most of the major propositions listed characterize human behavior per se, and not just particular groups or even particular societies. That presumption rests on two bases: first, that fundamental variations among human subjects have not in fact been observed on these matters; and second, that these aspects of human behavior are in the nature of basic processes and as such would reasonably be expected to hold throughout the species. In addition, as we shall see, a number of the cornerstone propositions also hold *across* species.

So we shall be speaking here of man, only later of men; and that distinction is responsible for the somewhat higher degree of abstraction in the findings reported at the outset. To a very large extent, as we shall see, human behavior is an outgrowth of social influences. By focusing first on "the individual" we do not mean to examine only those aspects of behavior that are unaffected by other people (if indeed there are any). We mean simply to stake out the range of behavioral fundamentals that would presumably hold for any individual from whatever social environment. In the remainder of the book we shall be building on, refining, and differentiating the general findings reported in these initial chapters.

DEFINITIONS

Adaptive behavior: Broadly, the ways in which an organism acts to satisfy its own needs and to meet the demands of the environment. In the case of lower animals, the term normally refers only, or certainly mainly, to the satisfaction of biological requirements (e.g., survival, physical well-being). In the case of man, it also includes the fulfillment of subjective desires (e.g., pleasure, personal satisfaction) that are not always directly related to physical demands.

Instinct, or instinctive behavior: Innate tendencies to respond in *particular,* usually adaptive, ways to *particular* internal and/or external conditions. Some illustrations, in context, will define this process more clearly.

Development: A very general term that refers to any and all of the orderly, progressive changes in behavior that accompany the growth of all normal human beings. In this chapter, the term refers only to the period from birth to maturity, though in more general usage "development" can be applied to the entire life cycle, from conception to death.

Maturation: Specifically, the biological development of the bodily machinery that does the behaving: the musculature, the nervous system, and so on. It is the underlying process necessary but not sufficient for normal behavioral development.

Socialization: The training or molding by which an individual is made a member of a particular society, i.e., how the infant becomes a child, the child an adult. Since the socializing is necessarily done by people who are already members of a society, the process provides continuity for the society's intangibles by passing on its traditions, customs, skills, mores, morals, etc.— that is, its culture—from one generation to another. In short, socialization means child-rearing in the broadest sense—not simply those actions deliberately taken by the parents to bring up the child properly, but all the ways in which all the people around him shape the child, consciously or not, from a newly born organism into a member of a particular society.

FINDINGS

Biological Background

As a starting point, we begin with the intriguing question: "How, if at all, does man's behavior differ from that of the rest of the animal kingdom, in degree and/or in kind?" The following answers draw from a broad overview of the animal kingdom as well as from direct findings of the behavioral sciences; in this introductory section we take the liberty of somewhat expanding our sights, at the inevitable cost in depth, in order to provide a larger perspective for the behavioral science materials that follow.

Any comparison between the behavior of man and that of all other animals reveals, first of all, that:

A1   Human behavior is far more variable, and therefore less predictable, than that of any other species. The repertoire and range of behavior available to any given man, as well as the range that exists across men, is far broader than anywhere else in the animal kingdom.

This is largely because

A1.1   Human behavior is more dependent upon learning and less regulated by instinct or other innate behavioral predispositions than the behavior of lower animals. In general, the lower the species, the more instinct-controlled, constant, and predictable the behavior.

Schematically:

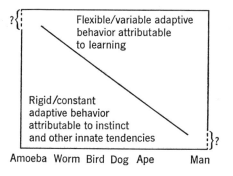

Innate, or "wired in," connections between fixed behavior patterns and certain environmental events (called innate releaser mechanisms) explain much of the adaptive behavior of even such relatively complex animals as fish and birds. For example, any normal male stickleback (a breed of fighting fish) will attack another male stickleback that approaches the nest, and attack it in the same way as any other stickleback; any female gray goose will retrieve her eggs if they are removed from the nest, will feed her young, and so on. But intelligent and purposive as these adaptive acts may appear, they do *not* depend on previous learning or on any understanding of their consequences. Instead, they are automatic, fixed responses released by certain fixed events; and the entire process goes blindly astray in a changed or unnatural environment:

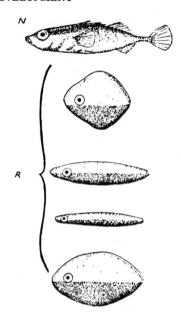

Models of sticklebacks were presented to a number of males. Some of the models were very crude imitations of sticklebacks, lacking many of the characteristics of the species or even of fish in general, but possessing a red belly (Series R). Others were accurate imitations of sticklebacks, but lacked the red (Series N). The males attacked the first group of models much more vigorously than they did the others. In this experiment the red colour was put into competition against all other morphological characters together. The results prove that the fish reacted essentially to the red and neglected the other characteristics. Yet its eyes are perfectly able to "see" these other details (Ter Pelkwijk and Tinbergen, 1937).

Much the same condition exists in the English robin. Lack (1943) discovered that a territory-holding male of this species would threaten a mere bundle of red feathers much more readily than a complete mounted young robin which showed all the characteristics of a robin except the red breast. Again, the red breast is the effective stimulus [Tinbergen, 1951, pp. 28–29].

The gray lag goose reacts to eggs that have rolled out of the nest by stretching the neck towards it, bringing the bill behind the egg and with careful balancing movements rolling it back into the nest. . . . The innate releasing mechanism of this response reacts to relatively few sign stimuli; objects of very different shape and size, provided they have a rounded contour, release it [*ibid.*, p. 84].

In short, experience is both unnecessary and irrelevant for this instinct-controlled mode of adaptation, and therein lies its chief advantage (no learning required) and its chief cost (lack of adaptability for the individual).

Gray lag goose retrieving egg

(*Ibid.*, p. 84, after Lorenz and Tinbergen, 1938)

Gray lag goose attempting to retrieve giant egg

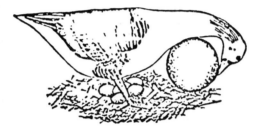

(*Ibid.*, p. 84, after Lorenz and Tinbergen, 1938)

Man has few if any specific, innate behavioral responses of that kind. Possible exceptions are the sucking pattern of the newborn infant, or his smiling; and perhaps some basic sexual responses.

>   **A1.1a**   An adaptive process that combines an innate behavioral pattern with the influence of experience is *imprinting:* the response is wired in and constant, but the specific object that will elicit it is established during one short but critical experience shortly after birth.

For example, all young geese or ducks follow the "mother," but it turns out that the response of following will become strongly attached to almost any object—within a quite broad range of physical characteristics, inanimate as well as alive—that happens to be present and followed during a critical period shortly after birth. Usually, of course, that object *is* the biological mother; but in the psychological laboratory it often is not, and various animals have been imprinted on decoys, spheres, and even human beings:

Laboratory imprinting apparatus

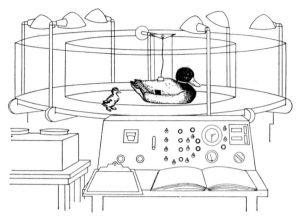

(Hess, 1959, p. 134)

Number and imprintability of different experimental animals *

Animal	Number †	Imprintability ‡
Ducks		
Wild mallard	3500	E+
Domesticated mallard	150	E
Peking	200	G
Rouen	100	F
Wood	50	P
Black	50	G
Total	4050	
Geese		
Canada	30	E+
Pilgrim	50	G
Total	80	
Chickens		
Jungle fowl	100	G
Cochin bantam	300	G
New Hampshire Red	100	G
Rhode Island Red	100	G
Barred Rock	200	G
Vantress broiler	500	G+
White Rock	100	F
Leghorn	200	P
Total	1600	

Animal	Number †	Imprintability ‡
Other fowl		
Pheasant	100	P
Eastern bobwhite quail	50	G
California valley quail	20	E
Turkey	30	F
Total	200	
Mammals		
Sheep	2	G
Guinea pig	12	G
Total	14	
Total	5944	

* Most of the animals were imprinted in runway and mallard decoy situations. Some of the Vantress broilers were imprinted on colored spheres, and the sheep were imprinted on human beings.
† Estimated for fowl, actual for mammals.
‡ E, excellent; G, good; F, fair; P, poor.

(*Ibid.*, p. 140)

Once animals have been imprinted on an artificial mother, they ignore the real one and remain loyal to the model (Hess, 1959). There is even some evidence that the objects of adult sexual behavior are partially determined by the nature of this first attachment.

A jungle fowl cock . . . was imprinted by me and kept away from his own species for the first month. This animal, even after 5 years—much of that time in association with his own species—courts human beings with typical behavior, but not females of his own species. This certainly is a far-reaching effect and is similar to the finding of Räber (1948), who reported on a male turkey whose behavior toward human beings was similar. An increased amount of homosexual courtship in mallards has been observed with some of our laboratory imprinted animals, which, while not a statistically valuable finding, perhaps points also to long-range, irreversible effects [Hess, 1959, p. 140].

There is no specific counterpart to the "following response" in human behavior; but, as we shall see, there is some evidence to support the proposition that critical periods in very early life exert a lasting influence on general social adjustment.

In contrast to these modes of adaptation is learning: *neither* the acts *nor* the environmental conditions that call them forth are specifically predictable across the species; *both* the acts and the conditions are tremendously variable as a result of experience. And so it is that human acts, abilities, interests, wishes, and even needs vary so greatly from man to man, group to group, culture to culture.

A2   Man achieves maximum flexibility in behavior, but the process requires prolonged childhood dependence—by far the longest in the animal world, as measured in portion of life span. In contrast to an insect, man not only can but must learn his fundamental repertoire of adaptive behavior if he is to survive.

From this one fact alone stem many of the most profound and far-reaching behavioral implications—from the universality of the family to the personality characteristics that derive from this period of dependency.

A3   Human learning, and thus human adaptive behavior, is communicated and therefore cumulative. Members of other species also learn, but only by immediate, personal experience.

No other animal goes to school or receives such symbolic instruction; as a result, each generation of a species starts from scratch. The best-informed trout, sparrow, or even ape today knows very little more, and does very little differently, than did his ancestors of three or three hundred generations ago. By contrast, the average college sophomore has more reliable knowledge of the physical universe than Aristotle had. This is possible because of man's *symbolic* capacity, which embodies two closely related, perhaps identical, facets:

First, human beings can think about things that are not present at the moment as well as things they have never actually experienced. Man can represent and manipulate objects, events, and relationships vicariously or internally—that is, symbolically—and not only through direct physical experience with them.

> From the psychological standpoint we may say that thinking is manipulation of the environment wholly or partially without overt activity. . . . In thinking, the environmental facts manipulated are either wholly or partially absent from present perception; i.e., there is always some symbolic activity involved. In short, thought processes intervene between sensory response and motor activity [Vinacke, 1952, p. 58].

There is serious question and argument about the extent to which lower animals can think in this sense. What scientific evidence there is suggests that they can do less than we ordinarily attribute to them on the basis of casual observation. Here is the type of evidence that suggests such limitations:

A hungry animal is first taught to go to whichever of three bulbs is lighted in order to get food—an easy matter for him after repeated trials in which food is always present behind the lighted bulb. In the critical "delayed response" test, the light is flashed and turned off while the subject is restrained; after a short delay he is released and permitted to choose. Under these conditions rats and cats can usually delay successfully for a matter of seconds, and dogs for a few minutes. A young child, of course, has no trouble finding the right light after half an hour, and an adult could choose correctly after many years. The critical aspect of this situation is that at the time of choice there is no external clue as to which is right—the information, if any, must survive and operate from within.

Similarly, although rats and some other lower animals can learn to run mazes involving twenty or thirty different choice points, they have a great deal of trouble with a type of maze that requires far fewer decisions—a maze in which the animal is simply required to run around the block twice to the left and then twice to the right. But apparently rats cannot symbolize this requirement, and the external cues remain the same: the same corner must elicit different responses at different times, i.e., to be followed by a right turn at one point and a left turn at another. Success at problems of this general character is usually related to the organism's position in the animal kingdom: racoons do better than rats, monkeys better than racoons. Human beings can of course extend the series indefinitely simply by counting. Except for boredom, they obviously have no difficulty going one hundred times one way and two hundred times the other.

Second, human beings communicate their thoughts (which stand for other things) by means of arbitrary and conventional noises, visual representations, and so on (which, in turn, stand for these thoughts). Only man has complex language and other such arbitrary symbol systems (mathematics, written music, and so on)—"arbitrary" in that there is no physical connection between the symbol (the sound or appearance of the word "cat") and what it stands for. Nor must the meaning be learned by repeated association, since one symbol can define another: "Let x stand for the neonatal mortality rate."

Other animals can "understand" or obey commands, but only by an immediate specific response to a specific sound after sound and action have been paired many times. No dog can comply with "Come here in two minutes," or "From now on, come whenever I say 'stay.'" And the most careful, childlike training fails to produce meaningful speech in chimpanzees, even though the vocal machinery is physically adequate.

In summary:

Unquestionably the behavioral characteristic which sets man apart from all other animals is the possession of language. Many other species *communicate* through vocalization and gestures, but none possesses anything approaching human language in modifiability and complexity.

As a matter of fact, the single diagnostic characteristic of language is sufficient in and of itself to identify an organism as a member of our species. . . .

Language depends upon and, at the same time, underlies another one of man's outstanding characteristics: namely, the capacity to establish a wide variety of exceedingly complex social interrelations. Language and the formation of social groups permit the transmission of information from one generation to the next and thus give rise to a new type of evolution, not seen in any other species [Beach, 1960, pp. 3–4].

A3.1   Although human languages have some features that are distinctive to man, they also have several features in common with animal systems of communication.

A recent summary of the factors differentiating human from animal systems of communication utilized thirteen "design-features," of which only a few were peculiar to man. It is shown in the table on the next page.

Here, briefly, are what the "design-features" mean:
    (1) vocal-auditory channel—as opposed to (e.g.) dance of bees
    (2) broadcast transmission and directional reception ⎤ stem from physics
    (3) rapid fading of the sound (transitoriness)   ⎦ of sound
    (4) interchangeability—"In general a speaker of a language can reproduce any linguistic message he can understand, whereas the characteristic motions of the male and female stickleback are different, and neither can act out those appropriate to the other."
    (5) total feedback—"The speaker of a language hears . . . everything of linguistic relevance in what he himself says. In contrast, the male stickleback does not see the colors of his own eyes and belly that are crucial in stimulating the female." This factor makes "thinking" possible.
    (6) specialization—"The bodily effort and spreading sound waves of speech serve no function except as signals [whereas] a dog, panting with his tongue hanging out, is performing a biologically essential activity"—cooling himself off—as well as "incidentally" making a sound which may be understood by other dogs.
    (7) semanticity—"A message triggers the particular result it does because there are relatively fixed associations between elements in messages (e.g., words) and recurrent features or situations of the world around us." Gibbons' calls of danger, for example, are characteristically semanticity.
    (8) arbitrariness—i.e., in choice of a word for a meaning; e.g., " 'Whale' is a small word for a large object; 'microorganism' is the reverse."
    (9) discreteness—of each sound—i.e., in contrast "with the use of sound effects by way of vocal gesture."
    (10) displacement—ability "to talk about things that are remote in space or time (or both)."
    (11) productivity—"the capacity to say things that have never been said or heard before and yet to be understood by other speakers of the language." On the other hand, "the gibbon call system can be characterized as closed" in this respect.
    (12) traditional transmission—i.e., "the detailed conventions of any one

The evolution of language *

Species	Design-features	Characteristics associated with communication
Man	Displacement Productivity Duality of patterning	Tool-making and carrying Larynx and soft palate separated Humor Vowel color Music
Hominoids	Discreteness Traditional transmission	Bipedal locomotion, not upright Occasional tool using
Primates	Specialization Semanticity Arbitrariness	Hands Hand-eye coordi- nation Binocular vision Mobile facial muscles Omnivorous?
Mammals (Land)	Broadcast transmission and directional reception Interchangeability Rapid fading Total feedback Vocal-auditory channel	Social behavior "Play" Warm bloodedness
Reptiles		Land egg Breathing with thoracic muscles
Amphibians		Legs Sleeping versus waking External ear
Vertebrates		Vision Hearing (internal ear)
Chordates		Motility Bilateral symmetry Front and rear ends

* The evolution of language and some related characteristics are suggested by this classification of chordates. The lowest form of animal in each classification exhibits the features listed at the right of the class. Brackets indicate that each group possesses or has evolved beyond the characteristics exhibited by all the groups below. The thirteen design-features of language appear in the second column. Some but by no means all of the characteristics associated with communication are presented in the column at right.

(Hockett, 1960, p. 93)

language are transmitted extragenetically by learning and teaching." Human genes carry only capacity to learn the language and "probably also a strong drive toward such acquisition." Uniformity of sounds made by some other species implies genetic source.

(13) duality of patterning—meaningful words are made up of relatively few meaningless sounds, which can be arranged in various orders to produce various words—e.g., "cat," "act" (*ibid.,* p. 90).

Finally, human beings, like animals, have physical needs that must be met if the individual and the species are to survive. But:

A4   Relatively little of what most people strive for most of the time is necessary for sheer survival, especially in societies where basic physical needs are amply provided for; and much of what many people want and do seems unrelated or even detrimental to their physical welfare.

Extreme examples are martyrdom, war, and suicide; more generally, there is smoking, drinking alcoholic beverages, dieting for appearance, and so on. Moreover:

A4.1   Even the behavior that does stem directly from the needs of the body and/or the species, such as eating, having sexual relations, or caring for the young, is not controlled nearly so directly by physiological needs as it is in the case of lower animals.

Food selection provides a good example. Rats, when allowed to choose cafeteria-style from fifteen to eighteen different substances, will select a wholesome, well-balanced diet. Similarly, if they have been kept on an unbalanced diet for a time, they will choose compensating foods when given the chance (Young, 1936, 1940). Human infants have also exhibited such sensible selection when allowed to: three newly weaned infants, ranging from six to twelve months in age, were allowed to select their own meals from trays of twelve to twenty different foodstuffs, two of them for six months and the other for a year. All three thrived and gained weight beyond the norms for their ages. One of the infants, who had rickets at the beginning of the experiment, ate large amounts of cod liver oil until the condition was relieved and then discontinued this regimen (Davis, 1928, 1935, 1943).

But except under extreme deprivations, or sometimes during pregnancy, the food selections of the human adult are not determined by biological need. A yen for lobster newburg; aversion to insects or horsemeat; the Indian refusal to eat sacred beef; the widespread practice of polishing rice and thereby removing food values, even among starving peoples—these certainly are not explained by physical needs. Here, again, learning not only directs the satisfaction of bodily needs but may override them. Furthermore, those human beings who do select a healthy diet do it largely by learning—"Remember the basic seven," "I need oranges for vitamin C"—and not by direct tastes for what they need.

Behavior arising out of the procreative need of the species is another case in point. In other mammals, but not in man, normal sexual behavior is dependent on and controlled almost entirely by the normal functioning of the testes and ovaries.

Receptiveness or "heat" in the female rat, for example, occurs only when the blood stream is rich with estrogen secreted by the ovaries during ovulation. At other times during the menstrual cycle, she is completely indifferent to the male. Neither of these statements holds for the human female, who is potentially receptive throughout the cycle and shows only slight temporal variations in sexual interest. Furthermore, a high percentage of women whose ovaries have been removed show little or no change in sexual desire.

Similarly, though the male rat's sexual behavior is affected less by the appropriate hormones than the female's, it is still under their control. Castrated rats may continue to mate for a short time thereafter, but then sexual behavior ceases unless hormones are artificially administered. By contrast, castrated men may lose some interest in sex, but the desire and the capacity for intercourse may continue for as long as several decades. Furthermore, artificially administered hormones have little effect on men whose sexual motivation is low; and even more revealing, when homosexuals are treated with hormones of their own biological sex, homosexual interest is likely to be increased rather than reversed if there is any effect at all. Thus:

> The principal difference between man and the lower mammals lies in the extent to which the sexual arousal mechanism is affected by symbolic factors. . . . Human sexual arousal is subject to extensive modification as a result of experience. Sexual values may become attached to a wide variety of biologically inappropriate stimulus objects or partners. Conversely, responsiveness in the usual heterosexual situation may be partly or completely blocked [Beach, 1956, p. 27].

A final, and closely related, example of human-animal differences in physical incentives is the strong motivation of the mother—both rat and human—to care for her young.

In the rat, the nature of maternal behavior is fixed and predictable, and triggered by the hormone (prolactin) that also stimulates the mammary glands. If this is injected into a virgin surrounded by young rats, she retrieves and cares for them in much the same way as does the actual mother (Ridde et al., 1935; McQueen-Williams, 1935).

Obviously, human mothers vary greatly in the degree and nature of maternal care they lavish on their young. A woman, even a virgin, may sometimes care for the young of another, but injections of prolactin are neither necessary nor sufficient to produce such behavior.

In summary, here is a recent comparison of the behavior of man's closest relative in the animal kingdom and primitive, preagricultural man:

	ECOLOGY			ECONOMIC SYSTEM		COMMUNICATION
	Group size, density and range	*Home base*	*Population structure*	*Food habits*	*Economic dependence*	
MEN	Groups of 50–60 common but vary widely. One individual per 5–10 square miles. Range 200–600 square miles. Territorial rights, defend boundaries against strangers.	Occupy improved sites for variable times where sick are cared for and stores kept.	Tribal organization of local, exogamous groups.	Omnivorous. Food sharing. Men specialize in hunting, women and children in gathering.	Infants are dependent on adults for many years. Maturity of male delayed biologically and culturally. Hunting, storage and sharing of food.	Linguistic community. Language crucial in the evolution of religion, art, technology and the cooperation of many individuals.
APES	10–200 in group. 10 individuals per square mile. Range 3–6 square miles. No territorial defense.	None. Sick and injured must keep up with troop.	Small, inbreeding groups.	Almost entirely vegetarian. No food sharing. No division of labor.	Infant economically independent after weaning. Full maturity biologically delayed. No hunting, storage or sharing of food.	Species-specific, largely gestural and concerned with immediate situations.

	SOCIAL SYSTEM				COMMUNICATION
	Organisation	*Social control*	*Sexual behavior*	*Mother-child relationship*	*Play*
MEN	Bands are dependent on and affiliated with one another in a semiopen system. Subgroups based on kinship.	Based on custom.	Female continuously receptive. Family based on prolonged male-female relationship and incest taboos.	Prolonged, infant helpless and entirely dependent on adults.	Interpersonal but also considerable use of inanimate objects.
APES	Troop self-sufficient, closed to outsiders. Temporary subgroups are formed based on age and individual preferences.	Based on physical dominance.	Female estrus. Multiple mates. No prolonged male-female relationship.	Intense but brief, infant well developed and in partial control.	Mainly interpersonal and exploratory.

Apes and men are contrasted in this chart, which indicates that although apes often seem remarkably "human," there are fundamental differences in behavior. Baboon characteristics, which may be taken as representative of ape and monkey behavior in general, are based on laboratory and field studies; human characteristics are what is known of preagricultural Homo sapiens. The chart suggests that there was a considerable gap between primate behavior and the behavior of the most primitive men known.

(Washburn and De Vore, 1961, pp. 70–71)

In general, then, human behavior is less static and stable than the behavior of lower animals; less directly under the control of specific physical
events inside or outside the skin; and more mediated by learned abstractions, carried around invisibly in the central nervous systems, by means of
which human beings affect each other's behavior. And it is precisely these
characteristics that make the empirical study of human behavior difficult,
yet necessary and possible.

Growth and Development

This section focuses on the changes that characterize the normal growth
and development of the human child. Although development or progressive
change (including deterioration) is a lifelong process, behavioral scientists
have stressed the beginning rather than the middle or end of the life cycle.
The early years have received most attention because of their practical
significance to parents and teachers; because they are considered particularly
important as the foundation years; and because they provide the most
rapid, obvious, and easily studied changes. In addition, children are a
plentiful form of human subject: they are found in large numbers in ma-
ternity hospitals, schools, and the homes of most psychologists, and they
are rarely in a position to refuse study.

We begin with the general principles that apply equally to the development of various aspects of behavior, and then move on to the specific findings that characterize motor or muscular development, speech, and finally
mental development, as examples of behavioral changes at different points
on the maturation-learning continuum.

DEVELOPMENT IN GENERAL

B1   By and large, the sequence of development is the same for all children;
i.e., it is general to the species.

Few healthy children run before they crawl or (less necessarily so) talk
well before they walk well. In addition:

B2   The age at which the various functions typically emerge is fairly
predictable; that is to say, the upper and lower limits of normality are not
far apart.

For example, normal American children can grasp and manipulate objects
by the end of the first year and learn to talk after the first but before the
third birthday. But within these rather narrow limits:

B3   There are individual differences in the rate (not the sequence) of
development; some children develop faster than others.

In addition, the nature of this difference is "undemocratic," in two ways:

B3.1   The faster child is likely to retain his advantage. There is no evidence that slower children are likely to catch up by compensating acceleration at a later date. Children who are taller, or smarter, or better at a variety of skills than are their contemporaries, are likely to remain superior at subsequent ages.

Similarly:

B3.2   The faster child is likely to be faster in many areas of development; that is, various functions are interdependent and correlated in their rates of development. The evidence again contradicts the common notion that a child who is above average in one respect will pay for it in another, or that the child slow at one skill makes up for it by being faster at another.

Especially misleading is the belief that exceptionally bright children are likely to be handicapped in other ways—in physical health, personality, or social adjustment. A major study followed a thousand exceptionally intelligent children as they grew up. They were, and remained, superior to the

Mental and physical traits of a thousand gifted children *

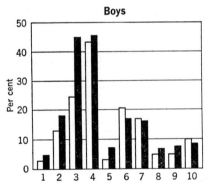
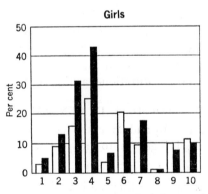

* Physical defects in gifted and control groups. Unshaded, gifted group; shaded, control group.
1. Per cent having frequent headaches.
2. Per cent with symptoms of general weakness.
3. Per cent of mouth breathers.
4. Per cent who have colds occasionally or often.
5. Per cent with poor or very poor hearing.
6. Per cent with vision somewhat defective or poor.
7. Per cent nervous.
8. Per cent with speech defects.
9. Per cent who are exceptionally timid.
10. Per cent who show tendency to worry.

(Terman *et al.*, 1925, p. 214)

average population in health and physique, in general personality and character traits, and in measures of academic and subsequent success. Maladjustment, instability, and psychosis occurred less frequently than in the general population.

> It is hoped that the superstitions so commonly accepted relative to intellectually superior children have been permanently swept away. . . . It is simply not true that such children are especially prone to be puny, overspecialized in their abilities and interests, emotionally unstable, psychotic, and morally undependable; nor is it true that they usually deteriorate to the level of mediocrity as adult life is approached [Terman, 1943, p. 305].

B4   As the child grows older, his behavior becomes successively more differentiated. The trend is from homogeneity to heterogeneity, from undifferentiated and global capacities and activities to ever more finely differentiated and specialized ones, from few-general to many-specific. This general finding can be illustrated in any of the behavioral processes typically abstracted for study.

As examples:

In perception: An infant, unable to discriminate toe from bedpost, mother from father, or day from night, becomes a child who can recognize and discriminate dozens of baseball players or automobiles, and finally an adult specialist who may be able to distinguish a Stradivarius from a copy or a vintage and a vineyard by taste.

In response: Physical responses become more specific and appropriate. The newly born child responds to almost everything—hunger, noise, an open diaper pin—with the same total eruption. Everything that can move moves, and loudly. But the child can take "scissors steps" or "giant steps," throw a fast ball or a curve. And the adult may have a vast enough repertoire of minutely distinguished responses to play a Chopin polonaise or pick up spares.

In thinking: What the world looks like to the neonate has fascinated psychologists just as the original state of man has occupied political philosophers. William James's classic assumption is familiar: "The baby, assailed by eyes, ears, nose, skin and entrails all at once, feels it all as one great blooming, buzzing confusion" (James, 1890, p. 488). Thus the mental world of the infant is thought to be divided into few parts—one of the first being the division into *me* and *not-me*. That of the child can be observed to contain many distinctions, and that of the adult many more still. We say that children "confuse" (i.e., classify together) events that are really different (i.e., differentiated by adults).

In motivation: Motives are not directly observable, so it is impossible to be sure that the infant's desires are as undifferentiated as they seem to be. He may feel the difference between hunger and thirst before he is able to respond differently to the two. But judging from what will satisfy, the infant is just plain hungry; the child wants a hamburger, with onions but without mustard; and the adult prefers a tossed green salad, with vinegar and oil and just a touch of garlic. This successive narrowing of the range of objects considered appropriate is known as "canalization."

In emotions: The newborn infant exhibits only one visible and general emotion—total excitement; by three or four months a positive outburst can be distinguished from a negative one; and in later years each of these is further differentiated into the innumerable and subtly distinguished sensitivities of the adult.

The approximate ages of differentiation of the various emotions during the first two years of life *

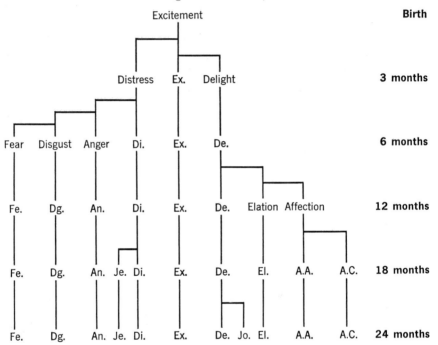

* A.A., affection for adults; A.C., affection for children; An., anger; De., delight; Dg., disgust; Di., distress; El., elation; Ex., excitement; Fe., fear; Je., jealousy; Jo., joy.

(Bridges, 1932, p. 340)

Two general things need to be said regarding the process of successive differentiation just discussed. First, regarding its nature, "successive differentiation" implies more (or less) than just getting better at things. True, finer distinctions in perception or response increase efficiency at the particular tasks that bred them, but they also decrease the potential range of other distinctions that can be easily learned: an unsliced cake can be cut in more ways than one already cut. Similarly, finely differentiated desires are more likely to be frustrated than general ones—a finicky eater more frequently goes hungry. This negative side of the coin is recognized in the common observation that older people are less flexible, more set in their ways than younger people.

Second, regarding its origin or source, development reflects the contributions of:

(a) inner changes in the machinery of the body and its capacities—the normal process of biological maturation, and

(b) accumulating experience in an environment that provides the opportunity to learn and/or perform.

Maturation, by definition, is always a necessary condition, but it is not always (strictly speaking, never) a sufficient condition; no child can do anything he is not biologically equipped to do, but no child can do everything he *is* biologically capable of. Thus behavioral development represents the interaction of a biologically ready child with an appropriate environment.

However, the relative contributions of these two sources of change vary. Some acts general to the species—such as grasping, walking, and standing—emerge with or without extended practice whenever the body is ready. In this sense it is misleading to call them "learned." Other behavior—playing tennis, speaking English, typing—is not universal; how, when, and whether it emerges depends upon the environment encountered. The skill must be learned. The following sections discuss motor development, the development of language, and mental growth in general; these provide examples of behavioral changes at different positions on this maturation-learning continuum.

DEVELOPMENT OF MOTOR CONTROL

The literature on when and how various muscular skills (grasping, skipping, eye movements) develop is vast and detailed. The hand is easier to see than the self; accordingly knowledge in the physical area is more thoroughly documented and virtually encyclopedic.

Here is one example of how detailed and thorough the study has become:

The stilling process of studying the motion film reveals eight types of grasp. . . . For the present purpose, however, these types may be conveniently grouped into three stages, which constitute the significant steps in the developments of grasping.

These are: *Simple palmar grasping, palmar grasping and thumb opposition, and finger-tip grasping.* In the first type, the fingers close on the cube and press it strongly against the heel of the palm with the thumb in line with the fingers. . . . In the next stage the cube is shifted toward the radial side of the hand, and the thumb begins to participate actively in grasping. In the final stage, thumb opposition is fully developed, and this permits the infant to balance the object between the tips of the fingers and the thumb [Halverson, 1943, p. 55].

Specifics of this order are naturally outside the scope of this book; comprehensive descriptions may be found in the Selected Readings.

The general findings concerning the development of motor control (beyond the over-all principles of development in the preceding pages) are:

B5   Control over the muscles develops from the head downward (the "cephalocaudal sequence") and from the inside outward (the "proximodistal sequence"). The muscles of the head are under control before those of the trunk; those of the trunk before those of the legs, and so on. At each "altitude," the muscles closer to the center develop coordination before those of the outposts (for example, arms before fingers).

B6   According to general developmental principles, the specific age at which the basic skills occur varies, but their sequence is predictable.

The following table summarizes the sequence of normal motor development, in a rough calendar.

Normative summary of motor development at various ages

One month	Lifts head when held to shoulder.
	Makes crawling movements when prone.
	Lifts head unsteadily when prone.
	Turns head laterally when prone.
Two months	Holds head erect for a short time when head is to shoulder.
	Lifts head when held horizontally on back.
	Lifts chest a short distance when prone.
	Makes vertical arm thrusts in random play when on back.
Three months	Holds head erect and steady when held to shoulder.
	Turns from back to side.
	Pushes or elevates self by arms in prone position.
Four months	Holds head steady when carried or when swayed.
	Tries to sit up when on back.
	Sits with resistant body pressure when supported by pillows.
	Hands frequently open.
Five months	Rolls from back to stomach.
	Sits with slight prop.
	Picks up cube from table on contact.
Six months	Sits momentarily without support if placed in a favorable leaning position.
	Grasps with simultaneous flexion of fingers.
	Retains transient hold of two cubes, one in either hand.
Seven months	Tends to unilateral reaching and manipulation.
	Rotates wrist freely in manipulation.
	Scoops or rakes hand to secure a pellet.
	Picks cube deftly and directly from table.
Eight months	Sits momentarily without support.
	Raises self to sitting position.
	Picks up pellet with partial finger prehension.
Nine months	Sits alone.
	Opposes thumb in seizing cube.
	Makes a locomotive reaction in prone position.
Ten months	Pulls self to standing position.
	Plucks pellet with precise pincer prehension.
Twelve months	Stands with support.
	Creeps or hitches alone.
	Walks with help.
	Shows a preference for one hand on reaching.
	Scribbles imitatively with a crayon.

Fifteen months	Stands alone.
	Walks alone.
Eighteen months	Climbs stairs or chair.
	Throws ball into box.
	Scribbles spontaneously and vigorously.
Twenty-one months	Walks attended on the street.
	Walks backward.
	Differentiates between stroking scribbles and circular scribbles.
Two years	Runs.
	Piles tower of six blocks with good coordination.
	Imitates vertical or horizontal strokes.
	Plays simple catch and toss with ball.
	Can operate a kiddy car around a chair.
Two and a half years	Goes up and down stairs alone.
	Piles seven or eight blocks with coordination.
	Tries to stand on one foot.
	Copies vertical line.
Three years	Draws a circle from copy.
	Creases a piece of paper neatly.
	Aligns a card to an edge.
Four years	Draws from copy.
	Traces diamond path.
Five years	Draws triangle from copy.
	Draws prism from copy.

(Gesell, 1925, pp. 378–84; Gesell, 1928, pp. 128–35)

B7   The ages at which the gross abilities (e.g., crawling, grasping, walking, climbing) first occur are determined almost entirely by maturational processes rather than by experience. Extended practice and encouragement before the critical age is reached do not accelerate their achievement, nor are they necessary once the time is ripe.

In one study, for example, one of a pair of identical twins was given extensive training in stair-climbing, creeping, walking, etc., starting at forty-six weeks of age and for a six-week period, while the control twin had no such training. No demonstrable superiority resulted: the untrained twin matched or exceeded the trained twin's performance at every chance. Indeed, the neglected twin scaled the stairs seven times on his very first trial (at fifty-three weeks), a record the other twin had not achieved until after four weeks of practice.

> It may well be that the relationships of learning and growth that are suggested by stair-climbing data are limited to gross motor functions such as locomotion which is common to the species. . . . But so limited . . . these findings . . . point consistently to the importance of maturational factors. . . . There is no conclusive evidence that practice and exercise even materially hasten the actual appearance of types of reaction such as stair-climbing [Gesell and Thompson, 1943, p. 216].

The same conclusion is supported by studies of cultures in which some parents severely restrict the practice opportunities of infants (e.g., by the use of cradle boards), but whose young walk at about the same time whether or not so restricted (Dennis and Dennis, 1940). Still more dramatically, salamanders raised in a state of suspended animation, via anesthesia, immediately swim as well, once thawed, as the normally reared and practiced controls (Carmichael, 1942). Furthermore:

B8   Encouraging the child to perform before the age of physical readiness may actually retard onset of the ability, by killing his taste and eagerness for it when he is physically ready. Thus:

B9   In the learning of complex skills or other abilities requiring training, practice is most effective at the point of maturation—not before, but also not long after, the period of biological readiness.

Similarly:

B10   Some animal studies find that interests or aversions toward certain environmental objects emerge at critical periods without previous experience with the objects, and thus seem to reflect underlying maturational processes.

> There is now a hard core of research evidence showing that animals acquire some of their interests and preferences for commerce with environmental objects in response to developmental processes. Animals born and reared under the restricted controls of laboratory conditions evidence preferences for activities with which they have had no prior experience. They persist in approaching and avoiding situations in the absence of either positive or negative reinforcements. Thus it appears that the development of neurophysiological structure is correlated with some approach-withdrawal tendencies which are independent of previous experience [Thompson, 1959, p. 11].

DEVELOPMENT OF SPEECH

B11   The tendency to speak is general to the human species (there is no known human population without speech), but the nature of the language is learned and largely arbitrary.

The development of language represents development at many levels. In the simplest sense, speech is a skill like typing. In concrete, instrumental use ("I want my mama"), certain responses are learned and linked with external stimuli. Speech, at this level, is acquired much as other physical skills are, through the processes of conditioning and habit formation taken up in detail in the chapter on learning.

But in a broader sense the development of speech parallels the development of thinking itself, because of the intimate association between language and thought. For example, when a child learns what "conditioning" means, or the distinction between "reference group" and "primary group," is he acquiring vocabulary or ideas? Similarly, what is a "great writer" great at—writing (language), or thinking? The answer to both questions, clearly, is "Both." Thus the development of the ability to manipulate the more abstract and symbolic aspects of language is indistinguishable from the general symbolic processes, and as such will be treated in the chapter on thinking.

Because of this close connection between language and thought, vocabulary and verbal ability are major components of all tests of general intelligence, and:

B12 There is a high correlation between verbal aptitude and other capacities (for example, mathematical and spatial abilities). General intelligence may be said both to stem (partly) from and to contribute to verbal ability.

B13 The characteristic sequence and time at which various aspects of speech typically appear, at least in Western cultures, are as follows:

AGE	FORM OF VOCALIZATION
One–two weeks	Irregular, intense, frequent (including during sleep), largely monotonic, frequently "no apparent reasons."
Mostly crying	Mostly "frontal vowels" a-e-i.
Two–four weeks	Begins to taper off; waking at night less frequent; different "cries" begin to be distinguishable.
Two–three months	"Instrumental crying" (begins and ends more predictably with a need and its satisfaction, respectively).
Three months	Babbling begins (simple vowel-consonant combinations, later become repetitive).
Four months	Shouts (as distinct from crying).
Six months	Most vowels, about half of the consonants produced ("back" consonants before "frontal" consonants, which require teeth and tongue control); simple sounds imitated orally but no ability to imitate words.
Eight months	"Babbling" at its peak.
Nine–twelve months	"Imitation readiness," successful attempts to imitate simple words, understands gestures.
Twelve months	Concrete meanings learned through association; responds to simple commands accompanied by gestures.
Twelve–fourteen months	The first five or six words mostly nouns—objects in environment—the "single word sentence."
Eighteen months	Verbs, adjectives and adverbs applied to familiar objects— "good," "hot," "give ball"; formation of simple phrases.
Twenty-four months	Simple sentences including pronouns, articles, conjunctions and prepositions.
Two–three years	Rapid increase in vocabulary, use of many descriptive adjectives, acquisition of fundamental grammar.
Four–five years	Complete sentences, all parts of speech.

(McCarthy, 1946, pp. 476–581; Hurlock, 1956, pp. 171–213)

B14   At all stages, the child's (like the adult's) latent, or passive, vocabulary (words understood) materially exceeds his spoken vocabulary.

B15   Other things equal, speech develops earlier and better:

.1   the *healthier* the child.

.2   the *more intelligent* the child.

A child who speaks early is almost surely bright; but one who does not is not necessarily dull, since other factors may delay the onset of speech. However, the age at onset of speech and the size of vocabulary at given ages are among the most reliable predictors of general intelligence.

.3   the greater the *opportunity* to learn.

Among the environmental factors found to be important are the number of adults in daily contact with the child (children who associate mainly with adults learn faster than those who associate mostly with children), the number of playmates, and the extent of exposure to verbal materials (books, magazines, radio, TV, etc.).

.4   the higher the *social class* of the family.

But differences do not appear until the end of the first year and a half, and they are probably due mainly to the two preceding factors.

.5   (after the first year) in *girls* than in boys, and the difference tends to expand with age.

In addition:

.5a   Except for lisping, speech defects are much more frequent in boys; again, the difference expands with age.

.6   in *normal homes* than in institutions.

Institutional children are slower than those of even the lowest socio-economic homes, and the speech handicap is likely to persist throughout life. This difference probably is an extreme case of the factors producing class differences in general (intelligence and opportunity) and, in addition, may reflect the deprivation with respect to close familial relationships.

.7   the fewer the number of *siblings*.

Again, probably because there is less individual stimulation in large families, and because of the relationship between family size and social class.

.7a   As a special case, twins and triplets tend to be retarded in speech development, as compared to single-birth children. The difference is most marked between two and five years of age; by nine, they have usually made up a good part of the difference.

.8   if the child is learning only one language.

Children taught two languages from the start are handicapped in both, as compared to the rate of a child learning either language alone. The difference becomes increasingly noticeable with age, to the extent that the child may have serious language difficulties upon entering school.

MENTAL DEVELOPMENT

Just as general physical development represents the combination of many specific body parts and functions not all growing at the same rate, so too general mental growth reflects the development of more specific mental abilities not all increasing at the same rate. Perhaps the two most important components, closely related to each other, are the mastery of language and the ability to form concepts.

While it may be possible to conceptualize the distinction between the development of the underlying mental capacities and the effects of learning, it is impossible to measure them separately. No test of any given child at a given point in time can measure the sheer capacity as distinct from the raw material the test itself provides as a task. This is why cross-cultural tests of "native intelligence" are so difficult to create. Furthermore, the measurement of "mental growth rates" depends largely on the specific tests employed—on how much weight they give to experience of various sorts. A survey of results from a wide variety of tests, however, supports these generalizations (see page 62).

B16   General mental growth from birth through adolescence shows about the same pattern as general physical growth during these years: it is very rapid at first, but then there is a decline in the rate of increase as puberty is reached.

B16.1   In all likelihood the decrease at puberty is more marked in the case of exceptionally bright children than in the case of those average or below average in intelligence: the latter maintain a steadier rate of increase throughout these years (although they do not catch up).

B16.2   While tests applied during infancy are not very reliable predictors of how intelligent the child and the adult will be, I.Q. measurements at age six or seven have stabilized, so that the relative standing of a child within a group of peers is not likely to change drastically in subsequent years.

There is a relatively high degree of consistency in intelligence-test ratings from year to year at the school age and beyond. Individuals tend to keep about the

Curves of means and standard deviations of intelligence

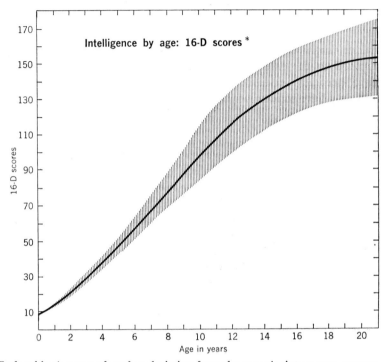

Intelligence by age: 16-D scores *

* Each subject's scores plotted as deviation from the group's sixteen-year average.

(Bayley, 1955, p. 811)

same rank or relative position from age to age. The correlations between intelligence-test ratings separated by an interval of one or more years are far from perfect, however. Fluctuations are likely to occur, but if the tests have been well administered and no outstanding changes in the child's circumstances have intervened (such as illness, emotional maladjustment, or transfer to a different environment), the upward or downward shift is likely to be relatively small in a majority of cases [Jersild, 1954, pp. 550–51].

B17   What happens in mental development from puberty to death is a subject of some controversy, because the factor of experience complicates adult tests of intelligence. In general, however, it appears that sheer cleverness, especially when coupled with speed, seems to reach its peak early in life (between puberty and the early twenties) and then declines slowly. On the other hand, understanding that builds on previous information and experience continues to increase with age (until senility), although very slowly as compared with the early years.

The subject of intelligence and its testing is taken up in detail later.

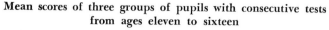

Mean scores of three groups of pupils with consecutive tests from ages eleven to sixteen

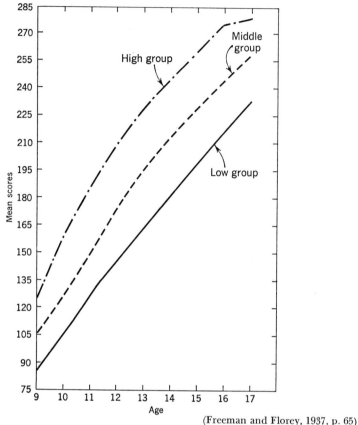

(Freeman and Florey, 1937, p. 65)

Socialization and Personality Development *

The state of current knowledge in this field is often contradictory and inconclusive, owing not only to the great complexity of the subject but

* Additional materials relating to personality appear in various places—for example, findings on conflict and adjustment in the Motivation chapter, on personality and class in Social Stratification, on personality and prejudice in Ethnic Relations, on personality and persuasion in Mass Communication, and on mental illness in the section on social disorganization. Within psychology now, except for the clinical literature, there is little concern with individual personalities or with personality per se as an independent category of study:

"The hoary tradition that treats personality as a distinct area of theory and research was further destroyed in 1957–58. Although the idea of an inclusive category of personality will continue to have appeal in parlor and poolroom, the same is not so true in systematic psychology. As an independent, isolated compartment, personality is on its way to oblivion" (Blake and Mouton, 1959, p. 203).

There are, of course, numerous tests and inventories on personality traits of one kind or another; where they have been correlated with significant behavior, the findings apto the difficulty of applying scientific procedures (since experimentation with human beings is all but ruled out in the nature of the case). As an expert in the field concluded, after reviewing the literature of the field:

> As yet this body of knowledge is not far advanced. There is no hard core of well-established and interrelated principles around which the study of socialization is focused. There are, rather, a large number of ill-assorted concepts and very tentative hypotheses [Child, 1954, pp. 656–57].

C1 Stimulation and contact—physical, mental, social—are necessary for normal human development (i.e., development into what the members of the society would consider a human being). This holds to some extent even at the biological level.

For example:

C1.1 Minimal physical stimulation is necessary for the normal maturation of the sensory machinery, and certainly for the proper training of its use.

For example, apes reared in darkness, or humans who gain sight late in life, must learn to see; weeks may pass before they can discriminate simple distinctions of shape—such as a triangle from a circle. Some retinal damage (that is, lack of normal maturation) usually results from such deprivation, and if the period has been long enough, permanent impairment or even blindness may result. As another example, dogs raised in isolation showed abnormalities such as strikingly slower sensitivity to pain. "It is concluded that early perceptual experience determines, in part at least, (a) the emergence of overt responses such as avoidance to noxious stimulation, and (b) the actual capacity to perceive pain normally" (Melzack and Scott, 1957, p. 160).

Further, some studies suggest that in addition to physical exercise a certain amount of fondling or mechanical stimulation is necessary for normal maturation of the muscles and nerves. Investigations of institutional children with minimal contact have shown some physical retardation in such populations. But the studies are rarely conclusive on this point, because other factors (the food, the type of children admitted, the psychological effects) cannot be segregated.

Another type of experimental evidence on the need for contact comes from recent studies of animal behavior. They show that in monkeys the skin texture of "artificial mothers" is a more important determinant of children's loyalty and love than whether or not they feed the young.

pear in the appropriate place, as, for example, with the "authoritarian personality" or "need-achievement." The specific details on each test are, naturally, beyond our scope.

In this ingenious experiment, newborn monkeys were raised with artificial models as "mothers." Through a variety of observations and tests, the monkeys appear to develop much the same love and affection for the models as normal monkeys do for the clinical animal. (This in itself suggests that the child's attachment to his mother is not entirely in reciprocation of mother love.) In one critical test, subjects were each reared with two ever-present mothers—a wire one that lactated and a terry-cloth counterpart that did not. The monkeys selected and snuggled with the terry-cloth model at all times, except when feeding; and in later tests of affection and dependence (e.g., which mother would he run to when frightened?), the monkeys demonstrated that they preferred the non-nurturant but soft mother.

Beyond the necessity of physical stimulation for normal maturation:

C1.2   Normal adult human behavior develops only through the stimulation of other people.

Beyond its biological base, human behavior is learned behavior—learned principally from others, since the newborn infant has no instinctive knowledge or ability that would enable it to survive in isolation. The nearest we can come to experimental evidence are occasional isolated children who were raised with a minimum of human contact for a period of up to six years (in verified cases); they showed few if any human capabilities or responses when discovered, but made some social and psychological recovery despite the early damage. For example, there is the case of Anna, an illegitimate child hidden away out of shame. She was left completely alone, except for feeding and enough minimal care to keep her alive, and with apparently next to no friendly contact. At the time she was discovered,

> Anna could not talk, walk, or do anything that showed intelligence. She was in an extremely emaciated and undernourished condition. . . . She was completely apathetic, lying in a limp, supine position and remaining immobile, expressionless, and indifferent to everything [Davis, 1949, pp. 204–05].

She appeared to be deaf and blind, and could do nothing for herself. When she died four and a half years later, she had progressed to the level of a normal two- or three-year old: she walked and ran, had some habits of cleanliness, knew some words and phrases and attempted conversation, played with a doll and blocks, etc.

> Isolation up to the age of six, with failure to acquire any form of speech and hence missing the whole world of cultural meaning, does not preclude the subsequent acquisition of these. . . . Most of the human behavior we regard as somehow given in the species does not occur apart from training and example by others. Most of the mental traits we think of as constituting the human mind are not present unless put there by communicative contact with others [ibid., pp. 207–08].

The people and groups that provide the stimulation and contact necessary for social development—the socializing agents—usually fall into two
classes: (1) those people with authority over the individual, such as parents
and teachers, and (2) those in positions of equality with him—age peers,
such as playmates or a circle of friends. Since the family is the socializing
agent during the critical first years of life, it naturally has great influence.
But because of the increased specialization of the functions of the family,
the rapidity of social change that tends to divide the generations, and the
high degree of mobility and social fluidity, the peer group is perhaps of
growing importance in modern urban life. In any event:

C2   Prolonged separation from the mother and a secure home environment (as in the case of hospitalized or institutionalized children)—beyond
the age of three months and up to about five years, but especially up to
about age thirty months or so—seems to lead to serious emotional and intellectual retardation: poor relations with people, inability to give or receive attention or affection for any prolonged periods, retarded speech,
curtailment of intellectual development, apathy and inaccessibility, even
some adverse effects on physical growth.

The deprivation can be of three kinds: no mother figure in the first
years, separation from the mother figure for a matter of months early in
life, or a shift from one mother figure to another.

C2.1   The more isolated and deprived the child or the longer the period
of separation, the greater the deterioration.

C2.2   In the earlier years, the better the child's relations with his
mother, the more he suffers from the separation; after age five or so,
the better his relations, the more he can tolerate the separation.

C2.3   People who have experienced such deprivation in childhood are
as parents less able than others to care properly for their own children.

The origin of adults being unable to make effective family relationships is not
infrequently itself the result of their having been deprived of a normal home
life in their own childhood. Thus the investigator is confronted with a self-
perpetuating social circle in which children who are deprived of a normal home
life grow up into parents unable to provide a normal home life for their children, thus leading to another generation of adults unable to do the same for
theirs. Most workers in child care regard this vicious circle as playing an important part in the total problem [Bowlby, 1952, pp. 82–83].

Here is an over-all summary by a leading investigator in this field.

[Studies, by direct observation, of the mental health and development of children
in institutions, hospitals, and foster-homes] make it plain that, when deprived

of maternal care, the child's development is almost always retarded—physically, intellectually, and socially—and that symptoms of physical and mental illness may appear. Such evidence is disquieting, but sceptics may question whether the retardation is permanent and whether the symptoms of illness may not easily be overcome. The retrospective and follow-up studies make it clear that such optimism is not always justified and that some children are gravely damaged for life. This is a sombre conclusion which must now be regarded as established [*ibid.*, p. 15].

It is only fair to add, however, that some specialists do not regard the evidence as sufficient for the conclusions reached, primarily on the grounds of incomplete controls and small numbers. A typical tabulation is presented below.

Differences between children who had spent their first three years in an institution and controls who had not (Goldfarb, 1943)

Function tested or rated	Test or rating method	Result expressed as	Results * Institution group	Control group
Intelligence	Wechsler	Mean I.Q.	72.4	95.4
Ability to conceptualize	Weigl	Mean score	2.4	6.8
	Vigotsky	Mean score	0.5	4.7
Reading	Standard tests	Mean score	5.1	6.8
Arithmetic	Standard tests	Mean score	4.7	6.7
Social maturity	Vineland Scale completed by caseworkers	Mean social quotient	79.0	98.8
Ability to keep rules	Frustration experiment	Number of children	3	12
Guilt on breaking rules		Number of children	2	11
Capacity for relationships	Caseworker's assessment	Number of children able to make normal relationships	2	15
Speech		Number of children up to average	3	14
Total number of children			15	15

* [In the case of all differences shown, p (which indicates the degree of probability that the observed differences are "due to chance") is less than .01; i.e., the probability that these differences are due to chance is less than one in a hundred.—Eds.]

(*Ibid.*, p. 37)

In order to bolster the case, those who claim major effects from early deprivation cite a few cases of maternal deprivation among animals, where experimental controls are possible. One such study dealt with

> twin goat kids, one of whom is separated from its mother for a brief spell each day and the other not. Except for the daily experimental period of 40 minutes, both kids live with and feed from their mother. During the experimental period the lights are periodically extinguished, a stimulus known to create anxiety in goats, and this produces very different behavior in the twins. The one which is with its mother is at ease and moves around freely; the isolated one is "psychologically frozen . . . and remains cowed in a corner. . . . This is ample demonstration of the adverse effects of maternal deprivation on the mammalian young and disposes finally of the argument that all the observed effects are due to heredity" [*ibid.*, p. 21, citing Liddell, personal communication].

More recent and more dramatic support comes from the previously mentioned studies of monkeys raised with surrogate mothers, and other monkeys in the same laboratory raised in varying conditions of isolation. For one thing, the conclusions support the notion that poorly mothered females become poor mothers:

> Four of our laboratory-raised females never had real mothers of their own, one being raised in a bare wire cage and three with cloth surrogates. The first week after the birth of the baby to the wire-cage-raised female, the mother sat fixedly at one side of the cage staring into space, almost unaware of her infant or of human beings, even when they barked at and threatened the baby. There was no sign of maternal responses, and when the infant approached and attempted contact, the mother rebuffed it, often with vigor. . . .
>
> The next two unmothered mothers constantly rebuffed the approaches of their infants, but, in addition, frequently engaged in cruel and unprovoked attacks. They struck and beat their babies, mouthed them roughly, and pushed their faces into the wire-mesh floor. These attacks seemed to be exaggerated in the presence of human beings, and for this reason all formal testing was abandoned for three days for the third unmothered mother because we feared for the life of the infant. The fourth unmothered mother ignored and rejected her infant but did not exhibit excessive cruelty [Harlow and Harlow, 1962a, pp. 222–23].

Beyond rejecting their offspring, monkeys raised in social deprivation show a variety of behavioral disturbances, such as "masochism" and "social insecurity." Masochistic animals may bite themselves or display other such self-punishing behavior when approached by human beings. "They defend themselves adequately, however, against other monkeys and are often extremely aggressive" (*ibid.*, p. 140). Perhaps most dramatic is the abnormal sexual behavior of these animals, especially the females. "With a single exception we have never seen normal appropriate sexual posturing in our wire-cage- or surrogate-raised females. The females do not approach the males, nor do they groom or present" (*ibid.*, p. 218).

Here are a summary graph and statement on the present state of observations in this intriguing series of animal experiments:

Experimental condition *	Present age	None †	Low	Almost normal	Probably normal	Normal
RAISED IN TOTAL ISOLATION						
Cage-raised for two years	4 years	P D S				
Cage-raised for six months	14 months	D S	P			
Cage-raised for eighty days	10.5 months			P D S		
RAISED IN PARTIAL ISOLATION						
Cage-raised for six months	5–8 years		P S	D		
Surrogate-raised for six months	3–5 years		P S	D		
RAISED WITH MOTHER						
Normal mother; no play with peers	1 year	S	P			D
Motherless mother; play in playpen	14 months			D	S	P
Normal mother; play in playpen	2 years					P D S
RAISED WITH PEERS						
Four raised in one cage; play in playroom	1 year				P	D S
Surrogate raised; play in playpen	2 years				S	P D
Surrogate-raised; play in playroom	21 months					P D S

* Results of experiments are summarized. The monkey's capacity to develop normally appears to be determined by the seventh month of life. Animals isolated for six months are aberrant in every respect. Play with peers seems even more necessary than mothering to the development of effective social relations.

† P, play; D, defense; S, sex.

(Harlow and Harlow, 1962b, p. 142)

Total isolation for two years resulted in failure to display social or sexual behavior in the next two years, spent in a joint living cage. Results on six months of such isolation are still being gathered and suggest severe, but not complete, social deficits. Only mild effects have been observed thus far in monkeys isolated through the first 80 days of life.

Partial isolation has produced behavioral aberrations in many monkeys and sexual inadequacy in all males and in all but one female. Four females were impregnated, in spite of inadequate posturing, and proved to be completely inadequate mothers.

Infants raised by live mothers were more advanced in social and sexual behavior than infants raised by surrogate mothers in a controlled playpen situation. The mother's role is not entirely clear, however, because in a more stimulating playroom situation, surrogate-mothered babies have shown normal social and sexual behavior.

Over all, it appears that the longer and the more complete the social deprivation, the more devastating are the behavioral effects. Further research is needed to evaluate the relative contributions of live mothers and infant companions to later adjustment [Harlow and Harlow, 1962a, p. 224].

However, according to at least one experiment in which a psychologist reared two infants with the barest human contact consistent with their physical well-being—but for only the first half-year of life—the experience seemed to have no effect on the children's social or emotional development. The experimenter concluded:

Two infants reared under conditions of minimum social stimulation and restricted practice for the first seven lunar months of life, and under less stringent conditions during the remainder of the first year, yielded during most of the first year a record of development not distinguishable from comparison records of infants in normal environments [Dennis, 1938, p. 157].

Some students consider the effects of early social deprivation to be related to the process of imprinting in animals, as discussed above. According to one of them, imprinting occurs in human beings, with the immutable bond probably being formed between the child and others of its kind between the ages of about six weeks and six months; hence, social deprivation in this period may have lasting and serious effects—"probably social apathy and emotional withdrawal." In addition, there is a critical period of fearfulness immediately following the period of imprinting. During this later period, the infant seems hypersensitive to strangers and more fearful in general. Frightening or otherwise traumatic events experienced at this time may have exaggerated and possibly permanent effects—"probably aggressiveness, and excessive demanding of attention, and moral delinquency" (Gray, 1958, p. 164).

We now turn to the fascinating topic of the effect of early socialization upon subsequent behavior, that is, the effect of child-rearing practices upon personality. But we pause once more to repeat our earlier warning that firm and clear evidence on this complex topic is definitely limited. Settled knowledge is hard to come by, of either a positive or a negative character, so in many instances we are left, in effect, with the Scotch verdict of "not proved." Two recent surveys of the field, one by a psychologist and the other by a sociologist, came to these similar conclusions:

Experiences of early infancy and childhood are alleged to be crucial in personality formation. Psychiatric observations, experimental work with animals, and systematic data on socialization in human subjects all point to the importance of early experience. The so-far available data do not, however, present un-equivocal evidence of the exact nature of the processes by which early life con-ditions are related to later development [Radke-Yarrow and Yarrow, 1955, p. 11].

The general tenor of the literature of the last decade . . . seems to be one of negative findings and of skepticism regarding readily demonstrable correlations between maternal behavior and general physiological and/or psychological de-velopment [Winch, 1957, p. 363].

We include here only those generalizations for which some hard data are available, and we call attention to contradictory evidence wherever that seems appropriate. But especially in view of the important practical impli-cations of these findings and the great difficulty in establishing them firmly, we wish to stress once more their tentative character—and probably the broader they are, the more tentative they are.

SOCIALIZATION PRACTICES IN GENERAL

C3   The closer the correspondence between socializing agencies (home vis-à-vis school or parents vis-à-vis peers), the more securely and the more rapidly the socialization takes place. The more the conflicts between them, the slower and the more uncertain the process.

If such conflict reaches a high degree of intensity, as felt by the subject, he will tend to renounce one agency in favor of the other, or renounce both, or become psychologically disturbed. In a study of Oriental Jews in Israel, for example, the gulf between the parents and the schools resulted in early school-leaving on the part of the children, poor grades, poor attendance, etc. (Eisenstadt, 1955, p. 99). At the same time, at least in the United States, part of the strain in the adolescent's relationship to his parents is relieved through membership in his peer group (Riley et al., 1961).

C4   Despite the extreme range in human cultures, certain similarities in socialization do exist across them.

It is hardly surprising that "some principles of personality development hold for mankind in general" (Whiting and Child, 1953). All human infants, regard-less of culture, know the psychological experience of helplessness and depend-ency. Sex differences in children and their parents lead to broad similarities in certain reactions. Situations making for competition for the affection of one or both parents and making for sibling rivalry are to some extent channeled dif-ferently by various cultures, but they cannot be eliminated—given the universal-ity of family life [Kluckhohn, 1953, p. 33].

C4.1   As between primitive and advanced societies (at least as the latter group is represented by the United States), the more primitive are gen-erally more lenient in their child-rearing practices.

They feed on demand more freely, wean much later, require control of body functions much later (Miller and Swanson, 1958, in comparisons with Whiting and Child, 1953).

C5   There is a tendency for parents to raise their children the way they were raised, although they may be unaware that they are doing so.

In a study of "sibling rivalry and social heredity," the investigator concludes:

> The mother's childhood rivalries persist in the present, so that the presence of children who are potential rivals to each other in a new generation reactivates in the mother the old feelings that have never been worked through. In these cases the complex identification of one of her children with herself, of another with her rival, and of herself with one or both of her parents, gives the dynamic background for re-enacting the old pattern [Hilgard, 1951b, p. 385].

C6   By and large, the pervasive emotional tone used by the parents in raising children (and especially the loving-rejecting tone) affects subsequent development more than either the particular techniques of child-rearing (e.g., permissiveness, restrictiveness, punishment, reward) or the cohesiveness of the marital unit (whether it is stable or broken by divorce or death).

> It is certain that one cannot infer directly from an objective description of cultural patterns for child training to their consequences in personality formation. It has been shown that roughly identical systems produce contrasting results in accord with the characteristic emotional tone in which they are administered by the mother and others, the different meanings which "the same" acts early acquire for children in different cultures, etc. [Kluckhohn, 1953, p. 17].

Here, again, it is worth repeating that it is the child's *perception* of the parents' attitudes that is important—more important than the objective attitudes themselves.

C7   The specific technique of punishment does seem to carry a boomerang effect, at least in the United States.

> The unhappy effects of punishment have run like a dismal thread through our findings. Mothers who punished toilet accidents severely ended up with bed-wetting children. Mothers who punished dependency to get rid of it had more dependent children than mothers who did not punish. Mothers who punished aggressive behavior severely had more aggressive children than mothers who punished lightly. . . . Harsh physical punishment was associated with high childhood aggressiveness and with the development of feeding problems [Sears *et al.*, 1957, p. 484].

For example, the following chart shows that "the more severely boys were punished for aggression by their mothers, the more aggressive they were in preschool" (Sears *et al.*, 1953, p. 214).

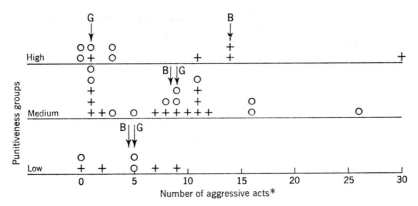

* Aggression: distribution of observed aggressive actions in the three subgroups that are distinguished from one another by amount of maternal punitiveness. Girls are represented by circles, boys by crosses. Medians are indicated by arrows.

(*Ibid.*, p. 214)

C8   The first-born child may differ from the later-born in being more serious, less carefree, more likely to be a problem-child.

We say "may" because the evidence here is far from conclusive. There are data that show a greater relative frequency of the first-born among delinquents and admissions to a child-guidance clinic (e.g., Rosenow, 1930), but that may be due to parental concern or to physiological factors associated with type of birth—the first birth being longer and more difficult, on the average, than later ones.

Evidence for deleterious effects of difficult births is fairly substantial. At the extreme, mechanical damage or temporary lack of oxygen during delivery can produce permanent neural impairment, with resulting motor disabilities, cerebral palsy, or low intelligence. Less drastically, instrument-born children seem to display the following characteristics more frequently than do other children: general hyperactivity, restlessness, irritability, distractibility, anxiety, speech defects, stuttering, and poor concentration (Wile and David, 1941; Despert, 1946; Boland, 1951). Conversely, "It is a well-known fact that Caesarean babies are the quietest" (Fries, 1941, p. 227).

The possibility of differential parental response to the child as a result of different types of birth must, however, be entered as a possible mediating mechanism by which type of birth could ultimately produce personality differences.

C8.1   First-born children, at least in our society, are probably more anxious; more dependent on others, especially in anxious situations; and more inclined to go along with the group than are other children.

This generalization is supported by a relatively small number of studies —but studies with remarkably consistent results, some of which we take up in detail later. Here are just two examples. The first table shows the number of "conformers" (those who changed expressed judgments from their original position to one closer to a group norm) among first- and later-borns. The other shows the greater tendency for first-borns to call off an experiment with increasing levels of electric shock before the maximum shock level is reached.

Influenceability and ordinal position

	Number of conformers	Number of nonconformers
First-born and only	32	22
Later-born	34	46

$\chi^2 = 3.62; p = .06.$

(Schachter, 1959, p. 87)

Ordinal position and tolerance of pain

	Number of subjects at maximum shock	Number of subjects below maximum shock
First-born and only	16	43
Later-born	28	28

$\chi^2 = 6.37 *; p < .02.$

* [χ^2, chi square, is a statistical measure used to compare observed sampling variations with expected variation from a standard population, and thus to determine how likely any observed differences are to arise from sampling variations in such empirical investigations. In this case, for example, the chi-square value leads to chance probabilities of less than two in one hundred.—Eds.]

(*Ibid.*, p. 49)

C9   Single critical or traumatic events in a person's life normally do not exercise major influence upon the development of personality.

In popular culture, the critical event is the personality determinant par excellence. "Psychological dramas" are ordinarily resolved with the sudden discovery of *the* traumatic event in a patient's history that is responsible for all the trouble. Psychiatric case studies suggest that specific traumatic events can be significant in the development of later neuroses but usually only against the background of existing neurotic tendencies. The same event that attains neurotic significance in one individual will be taken in stride by others. Incidentally, this illustrates the susceptibility of the case study to *ad hoc* fallacies. Any normal individual's development contains so many different events that a psychiatrist examining the record for any particular type of incident is likely to find it. It is difficult to find a case history of a psychotic or neurotic without some (usually childhood) traumatic experience; but it is equally difficult to find a case history of a normal person without such an experience. It is probably fair to say that among behavioral scientists today, there is little support for the notion that important differences in adult personalities reflect singular events in the life history.

DEVELOPMENT OF GENERAL PERSONALITY

C10   The less the affection, satisfaction of dependence, or warmth the infant and child receives (in other words, the more the reserve, neglect, or rejection), (1) the less developed is his subsequent personality likely to be and the less quickly he matures (in childhood)—i.e., the more he is apathetic, unresponsive, "vegetative," and incapable of independent action; and (2) the less strength of character and sense of self he is likely to have, leading even to the development of a psychopathic personality that feels no responsibility to others.

Similarly, the weaker the infant's or child's identification with his parents, the less developed and less strong his personality or ego is apt to be. For example, as we have seen, children raised under institutional conditions, with professional, part-time, and different "mothers," are much more likely to develop personality difficulties than children raised in their own homes by loving mothers. In general, the unloved child tends to be an unloving adult, with a high degree of self-hatred (i.e., unlovable).

[Terman's 1938] findings carry important suggestions about the probable influences of socialization variables on affiliative behavior. They suggest, for example, that a parent-child relationship which produces strong positive ties is an important influence on the general and life-long affiliative behavior of the child. Confirmation of the probable generality of this finding is provided by Sanford *et al.* (1943). They deal with affiliative tendencies in school children, as expressed primarily in relation to agemates, and find that these tendencies are positively correlated with the strength of affiliative and nurturant behavior of their parents toward them, and negatively correlated with parental rejection, capricious discipline, and lack of family support [Child, 1954, p. 676].

C11   Severity of socialization (i.e., highly rigid or highly critical practices by parents) seems to make for generalized anxiety in later life.

C12   The relation of early training practices—such as toilet training, demand or scheduled feeding, and weaning—to the development of personality is unclear.

Some studies find positive evidence, e.g., severe toilet training related to stinginess in adulthood. Others are negative, e.g., survey data showing no relation between "oral" traits and late weaning or demand feeding.

> The results of this investigation give no support to psychoanalytic thinking which maintains that breast feeding, demand schedules, and gradual weaning promote better adjustment than bottle feeding, regular scheduling, or abrupt weaning [Sewell and Mussen, 1952, p. 190].

Similar evidence comes from cross-cultural material showing that

> the Kaska personality norm is introvert and the Haitian extrovert, although in both societies babies are fed when they so desire, receive no pressure to control elimination, are comforted and handled when irritable or playful, and suffer no discipline for emotional willfulness [Underwood and Honigmann, 1947, p. 575].

The present state of the evidence seems inconclusive.

Efforts have been made, incidentally, to get at these important matters more precisely through studies of animal behavior. One study, for example, was designed to test the hypothesis that deprivation in infancy leads to greed in adults. Litter-mates of rats were divided into experimental and control groups. The control group was allowed unlimited feeding from birth while the experimental groups were food-deprived at different times during infancy. Tested as adults, the groups showed no differences when well fed; but after a period of hunger, when food was again available, those starved in infancy hoarded food whereas those previously well fed did not. Furthermore, those deprived earliest in infancy hoarded more than those deprived later (Hunt, 1941).

With regard to the human being, here is a summary statement from a thorough review of the empirical literature:

> We conclude that the rigidity of character structuring during the first year or two of life has been exaggerated by many authorities, and that the events of childhood and later years are of great importance in reinforcing or changing the character structure tentatively formed during infancy. . . . If one burns a die upon the infant's body, its stamp will endure throughout life. Perhaps there are intense and prolonged forms of experience during the first year which can similarly cast the infant's personality into a mold which cannot be reshaped by any subsequent events.

In the normal range of infant experience, however, we believe that events subsequent to the first year or two of life have the power to "confirm or deny" the personality of the growing infant, to perpetuate or remake it, depending upon whether the situation of later childhood perpetuates or alters the situation in which the infant was reared [Orlansky, 1949, pp. 38, 35].

DEVELOPMENT OF CONSCIENCE

C13   The more the control of the child is love-oriented, rather than based on physical punishment, the more effective is the parents' control over desired behavior and the stronger the development of the child's guilt feelings for improper behavior.

Here are the data from a recent major study showing that *both* warmth and withdrawal of love are effective in producing a strong conscience:

	Percentage of children with high score on measure of conscience	
	Mother relatively warm	*Mother relatively cold*
Mother uses withdrawal of love fairly often	42	18
Mother does not	24	25

(Sears *et al.*, 1957, p. 388)

C14   The earlier the socialization, the stronger the guilt feelings.

The table on page 78 contains a cross-cultural test of the generalization, in which "as a cultural index of the degree to which guilt feelings characterize the members of a society we have used a measure of the extent to which a person who gets sick blames himself for having gotten sick" (Whiting and Child, 1953, p. 227).

C15   The less the parental warmth and identification or the more the parental punishment, the slower the development of conscience.

The severity of the conscience is apparently determined less by the strictness of the child's treatment by the parents than by the related intensity of his feelings for the parents. The child's conscience reflects the parents' consciences more than their behavior, and socialization is effected through identification, first with the parents, then with others.

Relation between patient responsibility for illness and estimated age at onset of various aspects of socialization *

Age at onset	Weaning	Toilet training	Modesty training	Training in heterosexual inhibition	Independence training
Below 1.0	11.0 (2)	4.0 (2)			
1.0 to 1.9	11.6 (5)	11.9 (8)			
2.0 to 2.4	11.0 (10)	11.7 (7)			15.8 (4)
2.5 to 2.9	9.1 (9)	9.0 (1)			9.9 (8)
3.0 to 3.9	9.5 (4)	14.0 (1)	13.8 (4)		9.0 (9)
4.0 to 5.9	4.0 (2)	8.0 (1)	10.5 (3)		3.2 (11)
6.0 to 7.9			9.2 (5)	12.1 (7)	6.0 (1)
8.0 to 9.9				9.0 (3)	
10.0 and above			9.0 (1)	5.5 (4)	
Correlation coefficient	−0.42 ‡	+0.21	−0.50 †	−0.74 ‡	−0.34 †

ASPECT OF SOCIALIZATION

* The upper part of the table shows the mean index of patient responsibility for societies with various estimated ages at onset of each aspect of socialization; in parentheses after each mean is shown the number of societies on which it is based. The age intervals are not of uniform size, having been selected to avoid excessive bunching or spreading of cases in any of the five distributions. In the last line of the table are correlation coefficients expressing the closeness of relation between the index of patient responsibility and estimated age at onset of each aspect of socialization. Coefficients marked with a dagger are significant at the 5-per-cent point; those marked with a double dagger are significant at the 1-per-cent point.

(*Ibid.*, p. 256)

The superego is modelled upon the earliest parental images, when the parents were thought to be perfect and omnipotent. . . . Superego takes over the role of external authority figures and exacts conformity to society. The person is then said to be socialized [Hall and Lindzey, 1954, pp. 153, 165].

The stages in the development of the child's "moral judgment" (after Piaget, 1932) appear to be these: (1) nonrecognition of rules; (2) recognition of rules as absolute and morally correct, as given by authority; (3) recognition of the conventional (arbitrary, agreed-upon) character of rules; and (4) manipulation of and recognition of the changeability of rules.

C16   The less consistent the parents' teaching of moral values, or the more the perceived inconsistencies between their teaching and their behavior, the slower and weaker the development of conscience.

DEVELOPMENT OF INDEPENDENCE

C17   Rigidity and severity in the feeding and weaning of the infant make for dependency in early childhood years.

For example, one study constructed scores for "infant feeding frustration," based on measures of scheduled feeding and severity of weaning.

The best over-all statements of the relation between infant feeding frustration and dependency . . . are the correlations of .55 (girls) and .35 (boys) between the combined scales . . . and the total ranking on dependency [Sears *et al.*, 1953, p. 184].

C18   The more rejected the child feels, the more dependent he is likely to be.

**Relationship of child's current dependency to
maternal behavior threatening the love
relationship between mother and child**

	Per cent showing considerable dependency at kindergarten age
Use of withdrawal of love	
Seldom	20
Occasionally	24
Fairly often	46
Severity of punishment for aggression	
Little	14
Moderate	24
Severe	30
Amount of rejection	
No	20
Some	35

(Sears *et al.*, 1957, p. 525)

C19   The earlier and the more severely the infant or child is forced to be independent, the more concerned and even anxious he is about his independence in adult life.

C20   Very little satisfaction or nurturance during the period of infantile and childhood dependency (as in institutional cases) has been seen to have quite opposite consequences—little subsequent dependence in some, exaggerated dependence in others.

The former seem to have learned to do without (or in any case, they decline to submit their expectations to further disappointments) and the latter want what has been denied them.

C21   Very great nurturance during infantile and childhood dependency (as in the case of maternal over-protection and over-permissiveness) also seems to lead in opposite directions—continued need for dependency and hence lowered independence on the one hand, rebellious and defiant behavior on the other.

DEVELOPMENT OF AMBITION, DRIVE FOR ACHIEVEMENT

C22   Parental pressure for and reward of early achievement, when coupled with a high ratio of successes to failures, results in a high need for achievement (n Achievement) in later life, provided that the child has a good identification with his parents.

Apparently the mother is particularly important here (McClelland, 1961). The more reasonable such demands are upon the child (i.e., the more appropriate to his capacity), the more he will persist after achievement.

The general finding is supported, for example, by the following data from an inquiry to determine whether "stress on independence training by a culture [is] associated with higher achievement motivation for the culture as a whole" (McClelland *et al.,* 1953, p. 289).

Rank correlations *(tau)* between *n* **Achievement scores**
obtained from folk tales in eight cultures and ratings
of child training variables in those cultures

Culture	n Achievement Score	Rank	Independence training rank				Ranks for severity of training on other variables			
			Initial indulgence	Age	Severity	Age and severity	Nursing and weaning	Toilet	Sex	Aggression
Navaho	19	1	3.5	1	1	1	1	4.5	4.5	7
Central Apache	15	2	8	4	2	2	5	2.5	1	2.5
Hopi	13	3	7	2	6.5	4	5	4.5	6.5	2.5
Comanche	12	4	3.5	3	5	3	5	6.5	8	8
Sanpoil	9	5	6	5.5	3.5	5.5	3	1	3	5
Western Apache	5	6	3.5	5.5	3.5	5.5	2	8	2	6
Paiute	2	7	3.5	7	6.5	7	7	6.5	4.5	1
Flatheads	1	8	1	8	8	8	8	2.5	6.5	4
Tau *			−.56	.84	.64	.91	.42	.16	.16	−.18
p values			<.05	<.005	<.05	<.0005	<.15	.40	.40	.35

* *Tau* is a correlational measure of the joint variation of two characteristics, by rank, that can range from +1.00 (the ranks covary together) through 0.00 (change in one unrelated to change in the other, no covariation) to −1.00 (one increases as the other decreases, consistently).

(*Ibid.,* p. 294)

C23   The more the physical demonstration of affection as a reward for fulfilling parental demands for independence, the stronger the drive for achievement.

In one study, for example, the need-for-achievement score of sons receiving physical rewards (hugging and kissing) was 7.60 as compared with 3.64 for those who did not (McClelland *et al.,* 1953, p. 305).

C24   The earlier the parental demands for achievement, the stronger the subsequent drive for achievement.

In one study, the scores of eight- to ten-year-old boys on a measure of their need for achievement was charted against the ages by which their mothers wanted them to have learned certain demands, e.g., to stand up for their own rights with other children, to know their way around the city, to do well in school on their own, etc. Here is the result:

Need-achievement and demand *

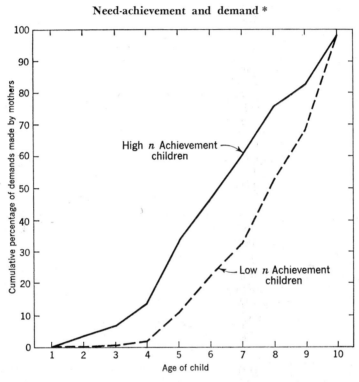

* Cumulative curves showing the proportion of total demands made up to each age level as reported by mothers of children scoring high and low on *n* Achievement (Achievement orientation).

(*Ibid.,* p. 300)

C25   The less restrictive and protective the parents, the more likely is the independent achievement of the children.

DEVELOPMENT OF AGGRESSIVENESS

C26   The more severe the punishment for aggression in infancy and childhood, the more direct or indirect expression of aggression later (indirect through fantasy), and the greater the subsequent anxiety about aggressive acts.

Some students seek to extrapolate such findings to broad political movements. For example, this line of thought is sometimes taken to explain the political revolts of young people in societies that firmly curb the growing youth—e.g., Germany with its authoritarian father, Latin America with its religious controls. The other side of the coin is the relative lack of such political concern among youth in the United States, with its freer family atmosphere. However, there are so many other factors involved in such a big picture, e.g., the better economic position of the United States, that others warn that it is not safe to draw such large inferences.

C27   The more parental rejection, over-protection, inconsistency, or conflict there is in rearing the child (and, inferentially, the more frustrating the child's home situation), the more marked are his aggressive tendencies.

This is consistent with the general frustration-aggression hypothesis (spelled out later), but the evidence so far seems somewhat contradictory and unclear.

DEVELOPMENT OF SOCIAL RELATIONS

C28   The more consistently warm the parents during infancy and childhood, and the less authoritative or overindulgent they are, the better the child's relations with his peers ("better" in being more responsive, open, friendly, etc.).

C29   The less use of physical punishment in childhood and the more use of reasoning, the less likely the child or adolescent to engage in delinquent behavior.

The table on the next page gives some data from a standard source (although the results may mask a difference in class).

C30   Every known society differentiates among several age groups and assigns certain appropriate behaviors to them.

These are called the age grades of the society. They vary in specifics from one society to another, but they are always present in some form as "a broad definition of human potentialities and obligations at a given stage of life" (Eisenstadt, 1956, p. 22).

Some age-grading is roughly tied to biological growth itself. As an anthropologist put it, in connection with relatively simple societies:

Though these phases do not invariably conform to stages of physiological growth, in relatively homogeneous social systems there is a close parallelism between them. For in such societies the basic educational tasks required to produce an adult person capable of playing a full part in maintaining and transmitting the

Methods of control of boy by parents *

Disciplinary methods	DELINQUENTS		NONDELINQUENTS		DIFFERENCE	
	Num- ber	Per cent	Num- ber	Per cent	Per cent	p
Mother						
Physical punishment	268	55.6	169	34.6	21.0	<.01
Reasoning	79	16.4	138	28.2	−11.8	<.01
Father						
Physical punishment	299	67.8	155	34.7	33.1	<.01
Reasoning	50	11.3	109	24.4	−13.1	<.01

* Percentages are based on known totals of 482 mothers and 441 fathers of the delinquents, and 489 mothers and 447 fathers of the nondelinquents.

(Glueck and Glueck, 1950, p. 132)

social capital seem to be complete at about the same time as the attainment of physical and sexual maturity and therewith the capacity for replacing the parental generation in productive and reproductive activities. But what I want particularly to emphasize is that the maturation of the individual and his proper passage through the life cycle is of paramount concern to society at large. This is shown in the widespread occurrence of institutionalized procedures for legitimizing each step in it, and especially for terminating the period of jural infancy, whether it ends with adolescence or extends into the stage of physical adulthood [Fortes, 1958, p. 10].

In a more complicated society, such as the United States, the factors of chronological age (years since birth), biological age (relative maturation), and social age (assigned roles) are sometimes out of synchronization. For example:

Modern medicine and diet have accelerated puberty by about three years over what it was in the beginning of the nineteenth century. On the other hand, social developments have tended to postpone the age at which people take responsible positions. For example, if puberty is at fifteen and a girl is married at seventeen there is a minimum delay between biology and society. However, if puberty is at twelve, and marriage at twenty, the situation is radically different. In terms of college entrance, people tend to enter older but to have grown up younger than formerly, and nothing in our system takes account of these facts [Washburn, 1961].

Perhaps the greatest age-divide in human life is between child and adult, and man has provided for this critical event in the individual's history:

C30.1   In most societies the transition from childhood to adulthood is marked by *rites de passage* that specifically signal the individual's responsibility for participating in the society as an adult.

This practice is relatively unclear in our own society, so that a certain ambiguity accompanies the period of adolescence. There is

> an ill-defined no-man's land that lies between the protected dependency of childhood, where the parent is dominant, and the independent world of the adult, where the person is relatively free from parental controls. This no-man's land is a place where the maturing person works out the extremely important developmental tasks of freeing himself from his family, making heterosexual adjustments, selecting a vocation, gaining an education and establishing a home of his own. . . . The adolescent's ambiguous position in the society may be a product of the loss of function for this age group in our culture [Hollingshead, 1949, p. 149].

There is some evidence, incidentally, that in many Western countries adolescence is the most idealistic period in life. The young person growing to maturity begins to see in adolescence the disparity between the moral precepts taught him as a child and the real conditions of life, and he often turns to a high moral and political altruism in reaction to his elders and in anticipation of his own imminent immersion in the actualities of life. This response includes rebellion against the parents, attachment to "causes," strong criticisms of the going order, etc. But note:

C30.2   The period of adolescence is not necessarily a period of intense emotional disturbance arising from the biological emergence of the sex drive or the psychological problem of becoming self-dependent.

The evidence across cultures indicates that adolescence is a period of *Sturm und Drang* only in those societies that make it so—e.g., by putting severe limitations on sexual behavior, or by providing sharp breaks between dependent childhood and responsible maturity, or by demanding so fast a change that a large gulf opens between the generations. In some non-Western societies that take a relaxed attitude toward growing up, the adolescents do not suffer particularly from the stress and strains that seem to us a natural, even biological, accompaniment of adolescence. Here, for example, is a quotation from one of the classic statements on the matter:

> Can we think of adolescence as a time in the life history of every girl child which carries with it symptoms of conflict and stress as surely as it implies a change in the girl's body?
>
>   Following the Samoan girls through every aspect of their lives . . . we found throughout that we had to answer . . . in the negative. [With few exceptions] adolescence represented no period of crisis or stress. . . . The diffused affection and the diffused authority of the large families, the ease of moving from one

family to another, the knowledge of sex and the freedom to experiment [were] a sufficient guarantee to all Samoan girls of a perfect adjustment [Mead, 1928, pp. 196, 157–58].

SELECTED READINGS

Here are two comprehensive texts that summarize the literature in the field:

E. B. Hurlock. *Child Development.* 3rd ed. McGraw-Hill, 1956.

W. E. Martin and C. B. Stendler. *Child Behavior and Development.* Rev. ed. Harcourt, Brace & World, 1959.

Two classic descriptive studies of child behavior in the early years are:

Arnold Gesell *et al. The Child from Five to Ten.* Harper, 1946.

Arnold Gesell *et al. The First Five Years of Life.* Harper, 1940.

For the kind of studies such texts are based on, see:

R. G. Barker *et al. Child Behavior and Development.* McGraw-Hill, 1943.

And for a detailed and thorough presentation of research findings of a more technical character, see:

Leonard Carmichael, ed. *Manual of Child Psychology.* 2nd ed. Wiley, 1954.

Here are some reviews of research on problems of early deprivation and critical periods during infancy:

F. A. Beach and J. Jaynes. "The Effects of Early Experience upon the Behavior of Animals," *Psychological Bulletin,* 54, 1951, pp. 239–63.

Philip H. Gray. "Theory and Evidence of Imprinting in Human Infants," *Journal of Psychology,* 46, 1958, pp. 155–66.

L. J. Yarrow. "Maternal Deprivation: Toward an Empirical and Conceptual Reevaluation," *Psychological Bulletin,* 58, 1961, pp. 459–90.

For material on socialization, see:

Irvin L. Child. "Socialization," in Gardner Lindzey, ed., *Handbook of Social Psychology,* Vol. II. Addison-Wesley, 1954, pp. 655–92.

David C. McClelland *et al. The Achievement Motive.* Appleton-Century-Crofts, 1953.

Harold Orlansky. "Infant Care and Personality," *Psychological Bulletin,* 46, 1949, pp. 1–48.

Robert R. Sears *et al. Patterns of Child Rearing.* Row, Peterson, 1957.

Robert R. Sears *et al.* "Some Child-Rearing Antecedents of Aggression and Dependency in Young Children," *Genetic Psychology Monographs,* 47, 1953, pp. 135–236.

J. W. M. Whiting and Irvin L. Child. *Child Training and Personality: A Cross-Cultural Study.* Yale U. Press, 1953.

There is no conception in a man's mind which hath not at first totally or in parts, been begotten upon the organs of sense. The rest are derived from the original.

THOMAS HOBBES
Leviathan

What thin partitions sense from thought divide!

ALEXANDER POPE
An Essay on Man

There are some philosophers who imagine we are every moment intimately conscious of what we call our *self;* that we feel its existence and its continuance in existence. . . . For my part, when I enter most intimately into what I call *myself* I always stumble on some particular perception or other, of heat or cold, light or shade, love or hatred, pain or pleasure. I never can catch *myself* at **any time** without a perception, and never can observe anything but the perception.

DAVID HUME

We can, at any time, double the true beauty of an actual landscape by half closing our eyes as we look at it. The naked senses sometimes see too little—but then always they see too much.

EDGAR ALLAN POE
Marginalia

What I have said about painting applies equally to novels and the intimate landscape of psychology. We exist on given premises, and readily acquire the habit of seeing the world, not so much as it actually is, but as we have been told and persuaded it is. How many diseases were non-existent, so to speak, until diagnosed and described! How many strange, pathological abnormal states we identify round us, aye, within us, once our eyes have been opened by reading Dostoevsky! Yes, I firmly believe he opens our eyes to certain phenomena;—I do not necessarily mean rare ones, but simply phenomena to which we had been so far blind.

Faced with the complexity almost every human being offers, the eye tends inevitably, spontaneously, unconsciously almost, to simplify to some extent.

ANDRÉ GIDE
Dostoevsky

Chapter Four

PERCEIVING

How people come to know and interpret their world is fundamental to the understanding of human behavior, since behavior, as distinct from sheer motion, is action that takes the environment into account.

Two basic starting points are: (1) all knowledge of the world depends on the senses and their stimulation, but (2) the facts of raw sensory data are insufficient to produce or to explain the coherent picture of the world as experienced by the normal adult. The first of these statements is axiomatic: a philosophical assumption not empirically verifiable but certainly not contradicted by any known facts. The second is an empirical finding that will be documented at length in these pages. Indeed, the study of perception is largely the study of what must be added to and subtracted from raw sensory input to produce our picture of the world.

Throughout the discussion we illustrate mainly by reference to vision, man's most important and most widely studied sense. But although the preponderance of evidence comes from visual experiments, the general propositions apply to the other senses as well.

DEFINITIONS

Stimulus: A key concept, or rather set of concepts, used in a great many ways in psychology and within the pages of this book. For purposes of this chapter, the term refers to a unit of sensory input—for example, some definable unit of light falling on and exciting the receptors in the retina of the eye. Even within this narrow definition, however, complexities inevitably arise in specifying the unit.

The unit of input may be defined by the environmental object that serves as the immediate source of the energy, as in the statement: "The stimulus was a red circle three inches in diameter." But defining the object clearly does not specify what happens in the eye, for any environmental object can project an infinite variety of patterns onto the retina, and various objects can produce identical projections. Furthermore, as we shall see, the unit as experienced by the observer is something else again, and cannot be inferred directly from the environmental object *or* the retinal pattern. (For example, a man may "see" his wife or "hear" footsteps when neither would be inferred by other observers.) A wide variety of technical designations has been elaborated to try to handle these distinctions. We will attempt to make do with the single term *stimulus,* relying on the context to convey whether we mean an environmental object, a sensory event, or something experienced as a unit.

Sensation: The immediate and direct apprehension of simple stimuli— the response of the sense organs to light, sound, pressure, and the like—or the experienced results of that process. So, for example, we sense or have sensations of color, brightness, shape, loudness, pitch, heat, and so on.

Perception: The more complex process by which people select, organize, and interpret sensory stimulation into a meaningful and coherent picture of the world. We perceive a friend in the crowd, or that a parking space is too small.

Ultimately, the neurological locus of the activity that translates and integrates sensory data into intelligible pictures of the world may be established. At present the distinction is helpful but hazy: sensation shades into perception as experience goes from the isolated and simple (a pinprick, a flash of light) to the complex interpretations characteristic of normal, ongoing awareness of the world.

Adaptation: In the field of perception this term has a technical meaning that refers specifically to "getting used to" certain sensations, becoming accommodated to a certain level of stimulation. The processes are discussed in detail later; we only note this special meaning here in order to forestall confusion with the broader term *adaptive behavior.*

FINDINGS

Sensation

Direct study of the sensory machinery has revealed a great deal about the ways in which the sensory apparatus of man works, in the physiological or neurological sense. But since we are concerned here with the behavior of the organism rather than with the behavior of neural pathways or sensory receptors, we shall not deal with that impressive body of literature.

We begin with some basic and general findings regarding the relationship between physical stimuli, as measured directly in the appropriate physical units, and the experience they produce in the human observer, as measured by observation or verbal report (or by direct experience, when the experimenter himself acts as subject). Technically, this is part of the field of *psychophysics,* one of the earliest concerns of scientific psychology, which attempts to establish quantitative relationships between the *psycho*logical dimensions of experience (loudness, pitch, color, etc.) and the *physic*al characteristics of stimuli (wave length, amplitude, intensity, etc.).

Perhaps the most general proposition on the mechanics of the sensory process is this:

A1   Sensation itself is fundamentally a matter of energy change or differentiation: a perfectly homogeneous environment or an absolutely unchanging one, regardless of the strength of its sensory input, is equivalent to none at all.

A perfectly homogeneous visual field, for example, is lost to the eye. A smooth surface of one color that completely surrounds the viewer loses it solidity and location: it may be six inches away, but all that appears is endless "film" or space. Even a simple differentiated shape quickly becomes imperceptible unless it plays continuously on different receptors in the retina. In one study, for example, an experimenter was able, by means of a mirror arrangement actually attached to the eye, to project an image on a given constant spot in the retina with no fluctuation whatsoever due to normal eye movements. Under such conditions the image disappears in a matter of seconds (Ditchburn *et al.,* 1959). More than that:

A1.1   A certain amount of differentiated input seems necessary for normal orientation and even for mental balance in the human being.

Experiments in sensory deprivation drastically reduce input and/or variability of input and in doing so produce marked deterioration in various capacities.

In a typical experimental situation, subjects were isolated in a cubicle; they wore translucent goggles to eliminate visual variability, and had their fingers separated by cotton and their hands cuffed in cardboard to reduce tactual stimulation.

Tests during and after the two- to three-day isolation period showed impaired effectiveness in diverse intellectual and problem-solving abilities, including verbal, mathematical, and spatial skills. In addition, subjects exhibited greater susceptibility to propaganda introduced while in isolation:

The experimental cubicle

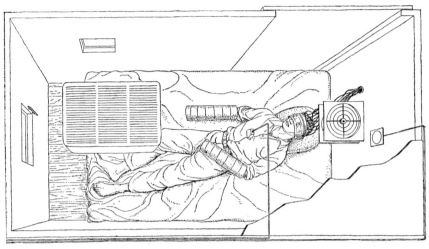

(Heron, 1961, p. 9)

Various degrees of "belief" in items at left, before and after listening to persuasive recorded lectures

Selections of attitude scale	Experimental group (exposed while in isolation)			Control group (exposed in ordinary laboratory setting)			Significance of (B-A)– (D-C)
	A Before	B After	Significance of differences	C Before	D After	Significance of differences	
1. Telepathy *	20.21	26.92	<.001	18.30	24.50	<.001	>.10
2. Clairvoyance *	16.08	25.10	<.001	16.26	22.09	<.001	<.07
3. Ghosts *	8.00	17.46	<.001	11.80	16.31	<.001	<.03
4. Poltergeists *	9.04	18.83	<.001	11.74	16.83	<.10	<.05
5. Psychical research †	15.42	18.53	<.001	15.23	16.51	<.001	>.10
Total scale	68.75	106.54	<.001	73.40	91.51	<.001	<.02
Interest Total	23.50	31.00	<.001	26.89	29.11	<.001	<.01
Important Scale	9.00	13.04	<.001	9.40	11.34	<.001	<.01

* Complete belief, 36; undecided, 15; disbelief, 0.
† Complete belief, 24.

(*Ibid.*, p. 15)

Furthermore:

Twenty-five of the 29 subjects reported some form of hallucinatory activity. Typically, the hallucinations progressed from simple to complex. The first symptom would be a lightening of the visual field. Dots of light or lines would then occur. Next would appear geometrical figures and patterns, generally composed of reduplicated figures, followed by isolated objects against a homogeneous background. Finally, full-blown scenes would appear. These seemed to be in front of the subjects. If they wanted to examine part of a scene more closely, they found that they could do so more easily by moving their eyes in the appropriate direction, as they would do if they were looking at a picture.

They had little control over the content of their hallucinations (one subject, for instance, could see nothing but eyeglasses, however hard he tried), nor were they able to start or stop them. They were often so vivid as to prevent the subject from sleeping, and one man left the experimental situation because he was disturbed by their persistence [*ibid.,* pp. 17–18].

Similarly, some pilots have reported weird and frightening sensations under the condition of extreme and prolonged isolation that is sometimes encountered in high-altitude flying:

A pilot on routine high altitude test flying was forced to descend by a "feeling of dissociation from earth and machine." He had the impression of being detached from the aircraft, of *looking at himself and the machine from outside* and of the aircraft itself being greatly diminished in size like a "toy suspended in space" [Jones, in Hebb, 1960, p. 741].

A report of a major symposium on the topic, reviewing various related studies, concludes:

The work reported in this volume supports the views of Hebb (1958) concerning the motivational effects of exteroceptive stimulation [i.e., input from the environment]. A variety of studies have demonstrated what he called "the immediate drive value of cognitive experience" (1955). These studies indicate that the absence of stimulation leads to the debilitation of behavior, making the individual less efficient and inducing strong affective states which are associated with marked changes in motivation. . . . As these studies suggest, the cognitive, perceptual, and emotional changes associated with and consequent to deprivation leave the subject less competent to meet the adaptational demands of his environment [Kubzansky and Leiderman, 1961, pp. 236–37].

Two other fundamental topics in perceptual investigation deal with the minimal stimulus values capable (1) of being sensed at *all* (the absolute threshold) and (2) of being told *apart* (the differential threshold). And as we shall see, the findings seem to have implications far beyond the psychological laboratory. The overriding generalization with respect to absolute and differentiated thresholds is this:

A2   Human sensitivity changes as it needs to: when there is abundant or superfluous input (e.g., brilliant illumination, very loud sound), the senses ignore—in fact, are incapable of detecting—small intensities or differences. As the available input decreases and becomes sparse, the sensitivity to detect intensity and difference increases tremendously, until man attains his maximum sensitivity under conditions of minimal stimulation.

This process not only provides more sensitivity when demanded but also protects the organism, via decreased sensitivity, from damaging, disruptive, or irrelevant bombardment when the input is high. Such accommodation in levels of sensitivity as external conditions vary is probably among the most general and far-reaching principles of human behavior, and we shall encounter it in various forms in subsequent chapters. Here, then, in somewhat greater specificity, are its foundations in the sensory thresholds.

THE ABSOLUTE THRESHOLD

Actually, there is some question as to whether an absolute threshold exists in a truly absolute sense—that is, whether a minimum value of energy can be established even under the most carefully controlled conditions. There is always some "noise" in the environment, i.e., stimulation unrelated to the input being measured; and there is always some unrelated activity in the sensory machinery being tested. Beyond that, it is necessary to distinguish *awareness* of stimulation ("I *see* it") from the ability to make better-than-chance guesses as to whether or not a "signal" is present. These and other technical considerations have given rise to a reformulation of the threshold notion in more statistical and probabilistic terms (known as "detection theory"). But at any rate:

A3   Up to the point of maximum sensitivity, the absolute threshold of a sense becomes progressively lower (that is, sensitivity, or the ability to detect stimuli, increases) with disuse or rest. The longer in total darkness, the more sensitive vision becomes ("sensory adaptation").

Just as a rough indication of the magnitude of this effect: the eye at its most sensitive, after a prolonged period in total darkness, will respond to a stimulus 1/100,000 as intense as that required when the eye is least sensitive, after sustained, strong exposure. As this suggests, under ideal conditions human receptors—especially in the case of vision—can be extremely sensitive.

> Measured under the best possible conditions, the absolute thresholds for various stimuli are amazingly low. . . . Thus, for example, it has been estimated that the physical energy equivalent to *one pin dropping one inch* would, if converted to light energy and properly distributed, be sufficient to stimulate *every one* of the more than four billion human eyes on earth! [Krech and Crutchfield, 1958, p. 51.]

Sensory adaptation stems directly from properties of the individual receptor cells that initiate sensory impulses—in the case of vision, the rods and cones in the retina. Within limits, the sensitivity of such neurons is directly related to the time since last fired. Immediately after firing, there is a brief period during which the cell is entirely incapable of being activated, regardless of the strength of bombardment; beyond this recovery period, stimuli of ever decreasing intensity will be adequate to fire the cell, until ultimate sensitivity is reached.

Here, for example, is a graph of the decrease in absolute visual threshold with time spent in the dark:

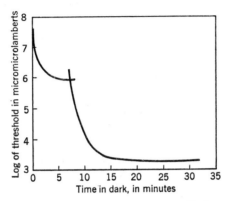

(Hecht and Shlaer, 1938, p. 270)

The two segments of the curve represent, respectively, the two types of receptors in the eye—the less sensitive cones (for color vision) and the more sensitive rods (for black and white vision), explaining why the world loses its color at night when there is only enough light to fire the rods.

A3.1   Under conditions of constant stimulation, receptors initially exhibit decreasing sensitivity; experience becomes less intense over time as input remains constant.

Hence the familiar experiences of "getting used to" a hot bath, a cold shower, the bright sun, the odor in a room.

A4   Conscious sensation is not always equivalent to the threshold as measured at the receptor end. Many stimuli strong enough to fire one or more receptor cells are too weak to create awareness, and some stimuli have measurable effects on behavior, not just on receptor cells, even though they are too weak or too brief to be consciously "seen" or "heard."

Thus, the threshold for awareness or conscious recognition may be higher than the threshold for effective perception as measured by more sensitive indicators. This process is called "subliminal perception" because the stimulus is beneath the threshold or "limen" of awareness, though obviously not beneath the absolute threshold of the receptors involved.

In one study, for example, subjects gave heightened involuntary responses of an emotional character (GSR, for "galvanic skin response") to nonsense syllables that had previously been paired with electric shock, when the syllables were later exposed at subthreshold speeds, i.e., at exposures too rapid for conscious recognition and report. Neutral syllables not previously shock-associated showed far smaller effects (Lazarus and McCleary, 1951). Similarly, emotionally loaded words, subliminally exposed, elicit higher galvanic skin responses than do neutral words.

Galvanic skin responses

Sub-ject	Mean GSR's		Means of maximum GSR's	
	"Emotional" items	"Neutral" items	"Emotional" items	"Neutral" items
MM	8.40	8.18	14.87	12.95
MT	15.35	14.05	23.98	21.22
MTp	2.73	1.88	5.28	3.90
MDp	2.52	1.99	4.78	3.68
FB	1.64	0.59	4.38	1.28
FSp	3.87	2.11	7.93	4.00
MBp	5.06	3.21	7.92	5.08

(Dixon, 1958, p. 31)

Other studies have demonstrated "appropriate" associations to words or drawings below the thresholds of recognition; or the ability to make better than chance discriminations or guesses about materials not consciously recognized or even "seen" at all. One experimenter, for example, flashed realistic or symbolic sex symbols (A-stimuli) just before briefly exposing ambiguous drawings of people who could be either male or female (B-stimuli). Under these conditions the A-stimuli are not consciously perceived, but they do influence responses to the perceived B-stimuli.

Effects of the subliminal figures were studied by comparing each S's [subject's] check-list rating of the B-figure with a group consensus of the appropriate A-figure. Drawings were rated for masculinity. Effects of the subliminal *genitals* were highly consistent on both check list and drawing, with S's tending either to incorporate or to exclude attributes of the subliminal A-figure in their impressions of the B-figure. Subliminal *symbols* were significantly effective in influencing S's drawing of the B-figure; but this effect was not correlated with response on the check list [Klein *et al.*, 1958, p. 265].

There is some theoretical controversy about the exact nature of the process and the measurements that demonstrate it, but the fact remains that subjects can give evidence that some stimulus material is getting through at thresholds beneath those required to produce the response "I see such-and-such," or even the response "I see something." In this sense, "unrecognized" stimuli do have effects—not just on the retina, but on feelings and thoughts as well.

A4.1   There is no scientific evidence that subliminal stimulation can initiate subsequent action, to say nothing of commercially or politically significant action. And there is nothing to suggest that such action can be produced "against the subject's will," or more effectively than through normal, recognized messages.

An important review of the matter recently concluded:

> One fact emerges from all of the above. Anyone who wishes to utilize subliminal stimulation for commercial or other purposes can be likened to a stranger entering into a misty, confused countryside where there are but few landmarks. Before this technique is used in the market place, if it is to be used at all, a tremendous amount of research should be done, and by competent experimenters [McConnell *et al.*, 1958, p. 237].

In short, while super hidden-persuasion may be something to fear, it is first something to document.

THE DIFFERENTIAL THRESHOLD

Next, with respect to the minimal difference that can be detected between stimuli, usually designated "differential threshold" or "jnd" (for "just noticeable difference"): the differential threshold varies not only with (a) the sensitivity of the receptor and with (b) the type of stimuli but also, and importantly, with (c) the absolute intensity of the stimuli being compared. This last introduces a fundamental principle:

A5   The size of the least detectable change or increment in intensity is a function of the initial intensity: the stronger the initial stimulus, the greater the difference needs to be. More specifically, where I is the intensity of the stimulus, ΔI the jnd, and k a constant for the particular type of stimuli:

$$\frac{\Delta I}{I} = k$$

This formulation is known as *Weber's law*.

Suppose the problem is to determine the differential threshold for unmarked weights, lifted by hand. What is the smallest difference that can be detected? If one weight is 300 grams, it may take an increment of 6 grams, or a comparison weight of 306 grams, before the subject detects a difference. But given a weight of 600 grams, a 6-gram increment is undetectable. According to Weber's law, it now takes a 12-gram increment, or a comparison weight of 612 grams, to produce a just noticeable difference:

$$\frac{6}{300} = \frac{1}{50} \quad \text{and} \quad \frac{12}{600} = \frac{1}{50}$$

Thus, k ("Weber's constant," or "Weber's fraction") in this case would equal $\frac{1}{50}$ or .02, and any two weights would be discriminable if they differed at least by the ratio 51:50.

Weber's law holds for all the senses, and for almost all intensities—in the case of vision and hearing, over more than 99.9 per cent of the usable stimulus range. When stimuli approach minimal intensity (the absolute threshold), the fraction may become considerably larger (discrimination is less acute); similarly, k may also increase for extremely intense stimuli. Thus, the relative power to discriminate is highest in the broad, normal range of intensities (although the general proposition holds for the extremes as well).

Here is a table of minimal Weber fractions for different sensory discriminations, obtained under ideal laboratory conditions. They provide a rough index as to the relative sensitivity and discriminating power of the various senses: the smaller the fraction, the greater the differential sensitivity.

	Weber ratio	Weber fraction
Deep pressure, from skin and subcutaneous tissue, at about 400 grams	0.013	$\frac{1}{77}$
Visual brightness, at about 1000 photons	0.016	$\frac{1}{62}$
Lifted weights, at about 300 grams	0.019	$\frac{1}{53}$
Tone, for 1000 cycles per second, at about 100 db above the absolute threshold	0.088	$\frac{1}{11}$
Smell, for rubber, at about 200 olfacties	0.104	$\frac{1}{10}$
Cutaneous pressure, on an isolated spot, at about 5 grams per mm	0.136	$\frac{1}{7}$
Taste, for saline solution, at about 3 moles per liter concentration	0.200	$\frac{1}{5}$

(Stevens, 1948, p. 268)

Weber's law stands as a milestone in psychological research. It is one of the first psychological laws worthy of the name, and it may prove to be of far greater and more general significance than the differential threshold problems that provided its initial formulation. In effect, it establishes a law of psychological relativity: subjective discriminations are not bound to absolute characteristics of stimuli but to relations between them.

This has been demonstrated in a number of diverse situations, from human judgments of aesthetic objects to the rat's ability to differentiate the length of two pathways in a maze (Yoshioka, 1929). Weber's law has also been applied in economic utility theory (Stigler, 1950), stock-market analysis (Osborne, 1959), and consumer attitudes towards prices (Webb, 1961). In addition, everyday observation lends credibility to the notion that Weber's law taps something quite general: a grocery store two blocks away seems much further than one around the corner, but Los Angeles seems about as far from Chicago as San Francisco does; the difference between one and two hours appears great, but the difference between a month and thirty-two days is negligible; a five-cent increase in the cost of a newspaper is quite noticeable, whereas one or two hundred dollars in the price of a house may be of little concern, and so on. As Thoreau once observed: "If you wish to give a man a sense of poverty, give him a thousand dollars— the next 100 he gets will not be worth more than the 10 he used to get."

More recently, continued psychophysical investigation has yielded still another and more general law, regarding the relationship between the magnitudes of the stimulus and the resulting sensation:

If you shine a faint light in your eye, you have a sensation of brightness—a weak sensation, to be sure. If you turn on a stronger light, the sensation becomes greater. . . . But how, precisely, does the output of the system (sensation) vary with the input (stimulus)? Suppose you double the stimulus, does it then look twice as bright?

The answer to that question happens to be no. It takes about nine times as much light to double the apparent brightness, but this specific question, interesting as it may be, is only one instance of a wider problem: what are the input-output characteristics of sensory systems in general? Is there a single, simple, pervasive psychophysical law?

Unlikely as it may seem, there appears to be such a law. . . . Within a first-order approximation, there appears to be no exception to the principle that equal stimulus *ratios* correspond to equal sensation *ratios*. . . .

The psychophysical power law relating the psychological magnitude ψ to the physical stimulus α can be written

$$\psi = k(\alpha - \alpha_0)^n$$

where k is a constant determined by the choice of units. The exponent n varies with the modality, and also with such parameters as adaptation and contrast. Generally speaking, each modality has its characteristic exponent, ranging from about 0.33 for brightness to about 3.5 for electric shock [Stevens, 1962, pp. 29–30].

These graphs illustrate the power functions for three different forms of stimulation.

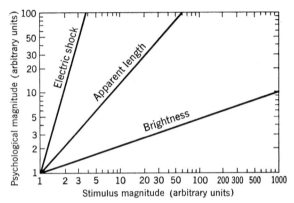

In log-log coordinates the power function plots as a straight line. The exponent determines the slope. These exponents are: electric current through the fingers, 3.5; apparent length of short lines, 1.1; brightness of luminous spot, 0.33.

(Ibid., p. 30)

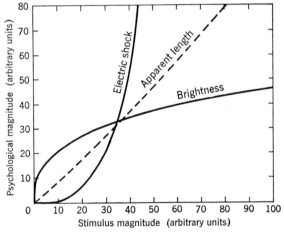

The straight lines in the above figure become curved in linear-linear coordinates. The curvature is upward or downward, depending on whether the exponent is greater or less than one.

(Ibid., p. 30)

Perception

Against the background of these findings on sensation, a basic—perhaps *the* basic—generalization on perception mentioned at the outset now takes on more meaning; the remainder of this section will elaborate it further.

B1   The facts of raw sensory data are themselves insufficient to produce or to explain the coherent picture of the world as the normal adult experiences it.

The raw units of sensory experience are bits of on-or-off information transmitted by discrete neural fibers, each originating in a specific receptor location and ending in a specific location in the brain. Literally, then, the sensory world consists of an almost infinite number of discrete impulses, in an ever changing pattern. In this sense, no man can have the same sensation twice.

But no one, fortunately, sees the world so fragmented. The perceived visual world, for example, contains many objects, not millions of discrete pinpoint impressions. In addition, the objects and the world they are in remain remarkably constant, even though the sensory input that represents them is always changing.

B1.1   There are some experiences with no corresponding sensory input.

Extreme and complicated examples are dreams and hallucinations. More simply, consider the apparent motion that occurs when two successive, slightly different stimuli are alternated (the so-called phi phenomenon, on which moving pictures are based). Lights *A* and *B* turned on and off at the appropriate rate are seen as one light moving back and forth between these points; the light actually appears at *C* and all other intermediate positions as it travels. There is corresponding retinal stimulation at *A* and *B*, but none whatsoever between them.

Note that phi is not due to movement of the eye—it can occur simultaneously in many directions, as in a motion picture. The phenomenon also appears in other senses: in touch, for example, two successive light pressures at nearby points produce a sensation of movement along the path.

B1.2   Many sensory stimuli normally fail to be represented in conscious experience.

For example, your nose: close the left eye and you see it with the right; close the right eye and you see it with the left; open both and where is it?

In short, sensory information does not correspond simply to the perception that it underlies. The fundamental reason for the difference between sensory data and perception is that sensory impulses do not act on an empty organism; they interact with certain predispositions and states already there, and immediate experience is the result of that interaction. The nature of experience, then, depends on two interacting sets of contributions: those of the environment, in the form of physical stimulation, and those of the observer himself, which we now review under the general headings of selection, organization, and interpretation.

SELECTION

First of all, the observer exercises selection regarding *what* aspects of the environment will be perceived.

B2   Of all possible stimuli—i.e., all bits of energy actually capable of firing receptors at any given moment—only a small portion become part of actual experience; and that portion is not a random sample of what is objectively available.

To begin with, the observer, of course, plays an active part in determining what will be allowed to stimulate the receptors at all: we look *at* some things, ignore others, and look *away* from still others ("selective exposure"). Beyond that, only a fraction of those stimuli that have gained effective entry to a receptor ever reach awareness ("selective awareness"). For example, at this moment you are mainly aware of the paragraph in front of you and, most of all, of this particular phrase. Yet the objects actually reflected in effective visual stimuli extend above, below, and well to the sides of the book. As this sentence calls them to your attention, objects on the periphery may enter awareness. Such selective awareness occurs between as well as within the various senses: you may also have been unaware of various noises, smells, pressures on the skin that have been present while you were reading.

B3   Which stimuli get selected depends upon three major factors: the nature of the stimuli involved; previous experience or learning as it affects the observer's expectations (what he is prepared or "set" to see); and the motives in play at the time, by which we mean his needs, desires, wishes, interests, and so on—in short, what the observer wants or needs to see and not to see. Each of these factors can act to heighten or to decrease the probability of perceiving, and each can act on both exposure and awareness.

B3.1   With regard to the stimulus factors, differential intensity or quality is a major determinant.

A cannon shot on a quiet street or sudden silence in the midst of a din gets attention whether or not anyone expects it or wants to hear it. Thus contrast, as illustrated by THIS word, is one of the most attention-compelling attributes of a stimulus.

B3.2   With regard to expectations, other things equal, people are more likely to attend to aspects of the environment they anticipate than to those they do not, and they are more likely to anticipate things they are familiar with.

Thus the difference between the trained observer and the layman is largely a matter of differential selectivity: the pathologist examining a microscope slide concentrates on the crucial (familiar and expected) microbe, while the novice sees an undifferentiated mass. Conversely, novel aspects of the environment—those that conflict sharply with expectations (e.g., a bearded lady)—will also get more notice than those unrelated to what is expected.

B3.3   With regard to motives, not only do people look for things they need or want; but the stronger the need, the greater the tendency to ignore irrelevant elements.

A hungry man looks for food and seeks out signs of it; but beyond that, at given levels of exposure, awareness of motive-relevant stimuli exceeds that for neutral ones. For example, words that have sexual as well as non-sexual connotation (e.g., fairy, screw) are more quickly identified in unclear carbon copies when they have recently been experienced in the sexual, rather than the neutral, context (Wiener, 1955).

In general, then, there is heightened awareness of relevant stimuli and depressed awareness of irrelevant ones. The adaptiveness of this mechanism is evident when it fails to operate, as in the case of the hypochondriac who is acutely aware of various inner sensations that most people ignore. The principle can also be applied to the so-called Art of Winning Games Without Actually Cheating:

> In a billiard room, your opponent has made a break of eight, and looks as if he may be going to make eight more. If two or more people are present they are likely not to be especially interested in the game, and quietly talking, perhaps. Or moving teacups. Or glasses. Simulate annoyance, *on your opponent's behalf*, with the onlookers. An occasional irritated glance will prepare the way; then stop your opponent and say:
> Gamesman (quietly): Are they worrying you?
> Layman: Who?
> Gamesman: Compton and Peters.
> Layman: It's all right.
> Or say to the whisperers, half, but only half, jokingly:
> "Hi, I say. This is a billiard room, you know. Dead silence, please!" [Potter, 1948, p. 60.]

Finally, pleasant or sympathetic scenes and messages are sought out, while painful or threatening ones are actively avoided; thus, the typical audience for partisan speeches or propaganda is weighted with those already sympathetic, as we shall see in the chapter on mass communication.

> **B3.3a**   There may also be decreased awareness of stimuli it is important *not* to see, once exposure has taken place ("perceptual defense"); that is, threatening or otherwise damaging materials may be *less* apt to reach consciousness than neutral materials at the same level of exposure.

In several experiments, threatening pictures or words are found to have higher thresholds of recognition and/or are described less accurately at given levels of exposure than are neutral materials. One such study used "Blacky Pictures," in which a small dog is found in a variety of situations, some rich in sexual significance. When two threatening scenes ("masturbation guilt," "oral sadism") and two neutral ones were flashed at near threshold speeds, the subjects took longer locating the threatening pictures than the neutral controls. Moreover, threatening pictures also made more of an impression (i.e., were reported to "stand out more") when exposure time was far beneath threshold.

Here is the author's summary and interpretation:

> This experiment was designed to test, within the framework of perceptual behavior, two psychoanalytic hypotheses: (a) the unconscious striving for expression of underlying psychosexual impulses (vigilance); and (b) the warding off of these threatening impulses as they begin to approach conscious awareness (defense). In the vigilance series, patterns of Blacky Pictures were flashed tachistoscopically *
> at .03 sec., and S's (seven men and seven women) were asked to indicate the position of the one picture "standing out the most." In the defense series, the ego was brought more into play by slowing the speed to .20 sec. and instructing S's to try to locate the correct positions of selected pictures.
>
>   The results were:
>
>   1. The vigilance hypothesis was supported in 11 of the 14 individual cases ($p < .05$). After a brief sensitization experience, most S's responded relatively more often to a traumatic psychosexual stimulus (Masturbation Guilt for men, Oral Sadism for women) than they had done in pre-sensitization trials, despite the absence of any conscious recognition of the pictures throughout.
>
>   2. The defense hypothesis was supported in 12 of the 14 cases ($p < .006$). At the close-to-conscious level, most S's experienced more difficulty in trying to locate a traumatic psychosexual stimulus picture than a relatively neutral one, in contrast to a previously greater sensitivity to the traumatic picture during the vigilance series [Blum, 1954, pp. 97–98].

A further study, carefully controlled to eliminate certain alternative explanations, corroborated the general finding by showing that

* The tachistoscope, encountered often in the perceptual laboratory, is simply a device for exposing visual materials for very brief, controlled periods.

subjects predisposed to use the mechanism of repression in conjunction with a given conflict will, when confronted subliminally with a conflict-relevant stimulus, show defensive behavior directly traceable to the perceptual process itself [Blum, 1955, p. 28].

For various technical reasons, interpretation of such experiments as perceptual defense is still not considered conclusive by some psychologists—mostly on the grounds that the subject's readiness or ability to *report,* rather than his ability to *perceive,* may be involved. But the findings themselves are as firm as those behind many other perceptual generalizations.

The tendency to be more open to some experiences and to shut out others seems to extend, literally, to the pupil of the eye.

B3.4   When looking at interesting or pleasant materials, as compared to neutral ones, the pupil dilates measurably. Conversely, looking at distasteful or disliked materials produces contraction.

Here are some illustrative results showing how men and women respond to various pictures:

Changes in mean pupil size, in terms of percentage of decrease or increase in area, from size during viewing of control patterns, in response to various pictures

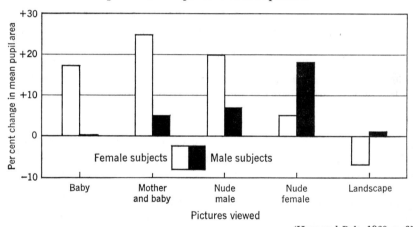

(Hess and Polt, 1960, p. 350)

Or, again, acknowledged homosexuals were discriminated from normals simply by their differential pupillary response to photographs of homosexuals versus female pin-ups:

Five normal males, five normal females, and five admitted homosexual males were shown three abstract paintings, six pictures of men and six pictures of women. Scores were obtained in terms of deviation from the mean change of the pupil in response to all twelve critical pictures. No normal male showed a total negative response to the six pictures of women. No homosexual or woman showed a positive response to the six pictures of women. There is no overlap between normal male and homosexual male subjects in their responses to the two categories of pictures. While the females and the homosexuals gave similar responses, the homosexuals showed a much greater rejection of pictures of women than did the female subjects [Hess, 1963].

The extent to which the response relates to the degree of interest versus the degree of liking has not yet been established. In addition, pupil dilation seems to signal sheer mental activity, e.g., working arithmetic problems mentally even when the materials thought about are not visually presented. Further:

> **B3.4a**   The response is not under conscious control or awareness. Subjects can neither report nor manipulate the pupillary response at will.

Thus, under certain circumstances, pupil reaction may be a more accurate index of subjective response to visual materials than verbal reports, e.g., when subjects might conceal or distort their real feelings. Thus this recent development may provide an objective measure of subjective state.

> Guillaume de Salluste once called the eyes "these windows of the soul." Even if the eyes are not the "windows of the soul," it has become increasingly apparent that the eyes, more specifically the pupil, register directly certain activities of the nervous system, including, but not restricted to, the effects of visual stimulation. Our evidence so far indicates that deeply rooted personal attitudes may be laid bare by the activities of the pupils [Hess, 1963].

ORGANIZATION

B4   Even the simplest experiences are organized by the perceiver; and the perceived characteristics of any part are a function of the whole to which it appears to belong.

The principles of organization, first developed and stressed by Gestalt psychologists (*Gestalt* is German for configuration or pattern), are best illustrated by visual demonstrations, but they apply to other senses as well. Here are some of the basic ones, as they become progressively more complex:

B4.1   *Figure and ground:* The simplest differentiated experience consists of a figure on a ground. The figure appears well defined, at a definite location, solid, and in front of the ground. In contrast, the ground appears amorphous, indefinite, and continuous behind the figure. The common contour of figure and ground appears to belong to the figure rather than to the ground:

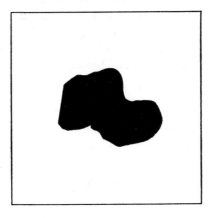

These distinctions are not inherent in the stimulus material, as is demonstrated by reversible figure-ground patterns:

A reversible cross

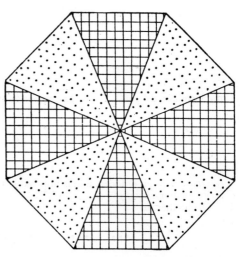

The Peter-Paul goblet

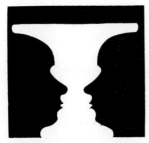

What do you see, the goblet or the famous twins? Whichever you see, try to find the other. Then, when you have found the other, try to turn the perception back to what it was at first.

Keep your eyes fixed near the center of the figure, and note whether you see an ✕ or a +. Maintain your fixation and see how long the cross at which you are looking lasts.

(Newman, 1948, p. 277)

In these figures the *same* stimuli serve alternately as figure and ground, changing their perceptual characteristics as they fluctuate. But the basic relationship between figure and ground remains.

The tendency for people to organize their perceptions into figure-ground is apparently innate, although learning affects what will be perceived as figure and what as ground. On gaining sight, congenitally blind adults exhibit figure-ground organization before many other visual abilities (Senden, 1932).

B4.2   *Grouping:* Elements in experience are automatically and almost irresistibly grouped—other things equal—according to proximity, similarity, and continuity.

Proximity

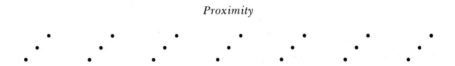

You see a row of small slanted groups $\left(\begin{smallmatrix} & \bullet \\ \bullet & \end{smallmatrix}\right)$ going from lower left to upper right.

That is, if we label the dots as follows, you see

$$\begin{array}{ccccc} & c & f & i & l \\ b & & e & h & k \quad \text{etc.,} \\ a & & d & g & j \end{array}$$

the form *abc/def/ghi/* . . . . The opposite organization,

ceg/fhj/ . . . , is not seen, and is impossible to achieve simultaneously in the entire series for most people.

Or, further, in

•••   •••   •••   •••   •••   •••

you see the triads *abc/def/* . . . and not one of many other theoretically possible groupings [Wertheimer, 1958, p. 117].

Similar grouping by proximity in hearing can be illustrated by the auditory stimuli of the Morse code.

Similarity

@	@	@	@	@	@
*	*	*	*	*	*
@	@	@	@	@	@
*	*	*	*	*	*

Here, greater horizontal similarity tends to overcome greater vertical proximity.

Continuity

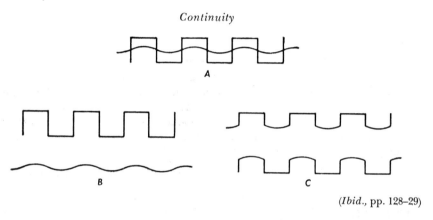

A

B

C

(Ibid., pp. 128–29)

A appears as composed of the elements in *B* rather than of those in *C;* the straight lines and arcs are grouped to produce the greater continuity.

B4.3   *Closure:* Experience tends to be organized into whole, continuous figures. If the stimulus pattern is incomplete, the perceiver tends to fill in missing elements.

For example, this is one dog, not twenty discrete blotches:

(Street, 1931, p. 41)

And here, closure tends to overcome proximity:

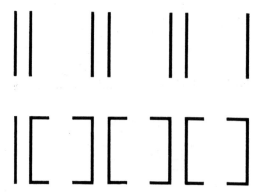

An example of the competition between grouping by proximity and grouping by closure. The seven lines above tend to fall "naturally" into three pairs and one isolate, by virtue of proximity relations. But the same lines below, with the addition of the short horizontal lines, tend to be grouped by closure with the more distant partner, overriding the influence of proximity.

(Krech and Crutchfield, 1958, p. 98)

B4.4   *"Good" figures:* When stimuli can be organized in various ways, the "best" one tends to win out perceptually—"best" in terms of similarity, continuity, proximity, closure, symmetry, and so on.

For example, note how difficult it is to find *A* in *B, C,* and *D:*

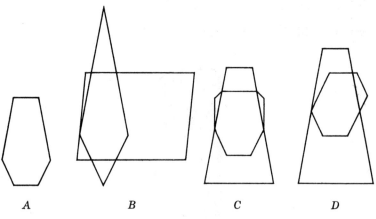

     A   *B*   *C*   *D*

(Wertheimer, 1958, p. 131)

or *E* in *F*

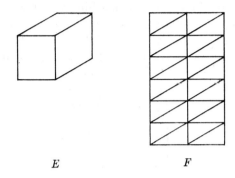

E   *F*

(Ellis, 1938, p. 118)

This principle is used in camouflage: a figure is destroyed, perceptually, by incorporation into a better one.

B5   People tend to perceive homogeneity in the internal characteristics of figures. Within the boundaries of a given figure, differences (up to a point) are ironed out ("assimilated").

For example, this circle, a "good" and whole figure, is a uniform shade of gray:

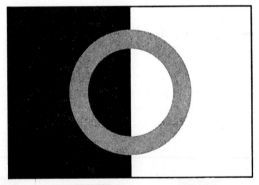

(Osgood, 1953, p. 235, citing Koffka, 1935)

Now dissect it vertically with a pencil, producing two figures: the right one is considerably darker than the left because of contrast effects with the respective backgrounds (discussed below). Slide the pencil slowly to one or the other side, and note how the appropriate shade is dragged into the other sector. Each portion, now a separate figure, tends to be perceived homogeneously within its boundaries.

Whether some of these organizational tendencies reflect learning or intrinsic properties of the perceptual machinery is a matter of theoretical dispute. For example, is grouping by continuity automatic, or does it come from the fact that experience with the real world has taught us that the figure $ is more likely to be composed of the elements in *A* than the elements in *B*?

S‖   ≬ ⁝ ♭

A   *B*

In any case, holding constant the characteristics of the stimulus:

B6   Perceptual organization, as well as perceptual selection, is affected by expectations based on experience and by motives.

For example, because of our experience, the word "jump" will be organized like this:

jump

and not like this (Wertheimer, 1958, p. 132):

ju in rp

And a more familiar stimulus pattern is likely to be seen as figure under conditions where a less familiar one would be ground—as when black figures such as these

become ground for this:

With regard to motives, how a reversible figure-ground pattern will be seen can be influenced by prior pleasant or painful associations with one or the other figure in isolation. The effect is such as to increase the likelihood that subjects will see the neutral or pleasant perceptual organization rather than the painful one. For example, when subjects have previously been shocked in association with one or the other figure in a reversible figure-ground pattern, they are more apt to report the nonshocked resolution than the shocked one when the reversible pattern is briefly exposed.

> In the present case, 164 unshocked and 101 shocked faces were reported for the A-B figure, and 98 unshocked and 81 shocked for the C-D figure, i.e., the same direction in both cases. In short, while purely "figural" factors were of importance, the shock procedure clearly had effect [Smith and Hochberg, 1954, p. 85].

Some of these principles of perceptual organization seem appropriate to more general and complex phenomena than the simple examples presented here for purposes of illustration. The need for "closure," for example, may apply to the tension that accompanies interruption of a task and the satisfaction and relief that come from its completion (i.e., attainment of the whole figure). Similarly, factors that impede creative problem-solving have been analyzed in terms of the "camouflage" of ideas, the necessary innovation being imperceptible by reason of its incorporation in a more familiar or "better" figure. Or again:

> The perception of individuals as belonging to a common group is achieved according to some of the principles made familiar by Gestalt psychology: similarity, proximity, good continuation, closure, etc. That is, we group together those of similar appearance, clothing, or mannerisms, assuming more congeniality, perhaps, than the similarity assures; we tend to see those who live near together or who associate together as sharing common values or beliefs (including "guilt by association"); we structure the social environment into figure and ground as we do the impersonal environment. When a figure appears, the boundaries are

sharpened, and the distinction between what belongs to the figure and what belongs to the ground becomes clear; we may thus structure the world into the "free world" and the "Communist world," ignoring many of the other differences between nations and governments [Hilgard, 1962, pp. 552–53].

Finally, these organizational demonstrations are perhaps the simplest instances of a highly general proposition applicable almost everywhere in human behavior: people respond neither to discrete elements one at a time nor to the sum total of discrete elements, they respond to the relationships between them. And this serves as an introduction to perceptual interpretation, where this proposition is further documented.

INTERPRETATION AND JUDGMENT

Stimuli, or patterns of stimuli, are often ambiguous; that is, there is no inherent or constant relationship between the sensory input and the stimulus objects it represents. Sometimes stimuli are physically weak or incomplete, as when something is dimly illuminated, partly obscured, briefly exposed, and so on. But even when the stimulus pattern is physically strong, the mechanics of sensation are such that no automatic, invariant conclusions about what is "out there" come from sensory input alone, because (1) even the simplest objects can produce an infinite variety of stimuli (e.g., a book held at varying distances, at different angles, under different conditions of illumination); and, conversely, (2) different objects can produce the same stimuli (e.g., a big disc far away and a small one nearby; an eighty-piece symphony orchestra and a twelve-inch hi-fi speaker). As a consequence, perception imposes the task of interpretation, of deciding what objects or events the sensory pattern actually does represent. Such interpretation is not usually a matter of conscious thinking-through but an instantaneous perceptual response. Accordingly:

B7   The greater the ambiguity of the stimulus, the more room and need for interpretation.

This is, in fact, the principle behind many diagnostic devices (projective tests) in which interpretations of ambiguous stimuli—for example, the ink blots of the Rorschach test—are taken to reveal something about the observer, on the basis that, again, the general determinants of interpretation (beyond the constant characteristics of the stimulus) are expectations from previous experience and motives, needs, and interests in play at the time.

B8   In interpreting ambiguous stimuli, the observer typically assumes that the most likely object(s) capable of producing the pattern are the ones actually involved. Further, the relative familiarity with alternatives is one of the strongest determinants of what will be considered likely. Thus:

B8.1   Familiar objects retain their perceived size, color, shape, etc., though their sensory projections fluctuate tremendously ("perceptual constancy").

This capacity to maintain constant perceptions in the face of widely and continually fluctuating sensations is highly adaptive because it is realistic: objects usually *do* remain the same size and shape as they change in angle of regard or in distance. But the same process will prove illusory when that is not the case.

For example, in an otherwise darkened room, when an oversized playing card is displayed considerably behind an undersized football, they are seen as the normal-sized objects in the reversed positions; each is perceived at the distance the normal-sized counterpart would have to be to project the observed pattern. The sensory pattern is interpreted as stemming from familiar objects at inverted distances rather than from the actual but unfamiliar objects at their true distances.

Or, again, rapidly exposed playing cards with reversed color-suit combinations (black hearts, red spades) will be distorted toward the familiar. The color or suit may be entirely misperceived as the expected one or, short of that, "compromised" with reality so that a black heart is seen as "purple" (Bruner and Postman, 1949).

Perhaps a more complex offshoot that may affect human relationships is the fact that people attribute some of the traits of familiar persons to strangers whose photographs resemble them ("parataxis"), whether or not they are aware of the connection. A recent review of studies in which subjects draw inferences from or interpret the photographs of others concluded that such generalization from the familiar is an important source of distortion:

> In the perception of strangers or the perception of photographic representations of them, two conflicting pressures concerning parataxis exist. On the one hand, there is not much involvement in the contemporary interpersonal situation; thus little pressure toward parataxic distortion is produced. On the other hand, the relative ambiguity of the perceptual situation tends to force the perceiver to utilize his past experience in forming impressions. Perhaps the crucial factor tending to produce parataxic distortion in particular situations is the degree of similarity of physiognomic, behavioral, or situational cues concerning the stranger to those concerning some significant other [Secord, 1958, p. 308].

B8.2   Familiarity with various possible alternatives is not the only determinant of "likelihood"; expectations regarding what is likely in the specific situation are also involved.

For example, on rapid exposure, ambiguous words (e.g., "chack") are interpreted in line with experimentally induced expectations: "chick," when subjects are led to expect names of animals; "check," when expecting travel-related terms (Siipola, 1935).

So, too, expectations or stereotypes regarding what specific people will be like are important determinants of how their subsequent behavior will actually be interpreted, at least on first impressions. Here, for example, is how student descriptions of the same instructor after the same class session varied, according to whether he had previously been described as "very warm" or "rather cold" in a brief written introduction:

Comparison of "warm" and "cold" observers in terms of average ratings given stimulus persons

Item	Low end of rating scale	High end of rating scale	Average rating		Level of signifi- cance of warm- cold differ- ence	Asch's data (1946): per cent of group assigning quality at low end of our rating scale *	
			Warm (N = 27)	Cold (N = 28)		Warm	Cold
1	Knows his stuff	Doesn't know his stuff	3.5	4.6			
2	Considerate of others	Self-centered	6.3	9.6	.01		
3 †	Informal	Formal	6.3	9.6	.01		
4 †	Modest	Proud	9.4	10.6			
5	Sociable	Unsociable	5.6	10.4	.01	91	38
6	Self-assured	Uncertain of himself	8.4	9.1			
7	High intelligence	Low intelligence	4.8	5.1			
8	Popular	Unpopular	4.0	7.4	.01	84	28
9 †	Good natured	Irritable	9.4	12.0	.05	94	17
10	Generous	Ungenerous	8.2	9.6		91	08
11	Humorous	Humorless	8.3	11.7	.01	77	13
12	Important	Insignificant	6.5	8.6		88	99
13 †	Humane	Ruthless	8.6	11.0	.05	86	31
14 †	Submissive	Dominant	13.2	14.5			
15	Will go far	Will not get ahead	4.2	5.8			

* Given for all qualities common to Asch's list and this set of rating scales.
† These scales were reversed when presented to the subjects.

(Kelley, 1950, p. 434)

B9   As the ambiguity of the stimulus increases and/or as the strength of motivation or subjective importance increases, people's interpretations will move in the "relevant" direction—that is, they will tend to see things as they want or need to see them.

For example, hungry subjects report more food objects in vague "pictures" (actually, just smudges) than do less hungry subjects:

Mean number of food-related responses per subject out of possible fourteen * for three degrees of strength of the hunger drive

Hours food depriva- tion	N	Average rated drive strength	σm	Strength of drive	Mean food related R's	σm	P_diff. occurring by chance with 4- hour	16- hour
1	44	3.30	.17	weak	2.14	.24	<.10	<.002
4	24	2.02	.17	medium	2.88	.36		<.42
16	40	1.90	.14	strong	3.22	.23		

* Counting three possible responses for the item which asked for three objects, any or all of which could be food-related.

(McClelland and Atkinson, 1948, p. 212)

When the goal is positive, the distinction between want and need collapses; when one is hungry, food is both necessary and pleasant to find. However, when a negative or threatening object is involved, e.g., an enemy sniper or the sound of an airplane engine faltering over the ocean, detection may be necessary—but it is certainly not pleasant. Does interpretation in such cases lean toward what is needed or toward what is wanted? The relationship and relative strength of the two tendencies is not clearly established. Sometimes protection against recognition of the threat seems to be dominant, as in the perceptual-defense studies. At other times, vigilance predominates—as when anxious people see threat everywhere. One hypothesis is that if the threat can realistically be averted, vigilance is a normal reaction; whereas perceptual defense comes into play when nothing could be done, even if the threat were recognized. In any case, as a complex example, anti-Semites as well as Jews rate a larger percentage of photographs as Jewish than do people not so concerned with the issue, in either direction:

Two groups of S's, 118 Jewish and 194 non-Jewish, labeled a group of 100 photographs as Jewish or non-Jewish. In addition, each S selected 30 of the 100 that appeared to be the most Jewish-looking. The photographs included 30 Jews and, in the non-Jewish group, 30 Americans, 20 Northern Europeans and 20 Southern Europeans. Each subject was also administered the California F scale.

In both groups high F scorers ["authoritarian," "ethnocentric"] labeled more photographs as Jewish than low F scorers, but in neither group was there a significant difference in accuracy between high and low scorers. There was no significant relationship in either group between response bias and accuracy. With respect to between-group differences Jews were more accurate than non-Jews and manifested a tendency to label more photographs as Jewish [Scodel and Austrin, 1957, p. 280].

Another study correlated ethnic prejudice with the tendency to cling to "familiar" interpretations when the sensory evidence begins to depart from the familiar: if a series of pictures gradually moves from dog to cat, people prejudiced against minority groups are slower than others to recognize the change and to switch their identification to the latter. Thus, people who tend to hold rigid social stereotypes are also more apt than others to cling to "stereotypic" perception in the laboratory, suggesting that the two processes do, in fact, have something in common. The author speculates that

it may well turn out upon further evidence that intolerance of perceptual ambiguity is related to a broader psychological disturbance of which prejudice —itself often a deviation from the prevalent code, especially in school—is but another manifestation [Frenkel-Brunswik, 1949, p. 128].

Judgment of Quantity

A special case of perceptual interpretation is the judgment of quantities: How big? How bright? How far? Often such judgments are equivalent to interpreting *what* the object is—midget or giant, model or real. Usually, however, they are independent of the designation of objects, at least to some extent: the perceived color, brightness, size, distance, and speed of a car do not affect its essential identification. A great deal of investigation has been given this matter, as a special case of perceptual interpretation. As in the more general finding:

B10   Interpretations of quantities are affected by expectations and motives.

For example, with reference to *expectations,* if a small wooden block weighs the same as a much larger one, the weight of the smaller will be grossly overestimated when subjects are told the correct weight of the larger and allowed to lift them both—apparently by contrast with the expected lighter weight of the smaller. Among one hundred military officers, the average overestimate was 2.5 times the correct weight, and in some cases the error reached sevenfold. And the illusion persists even after subjects are allowed to weigh both blocks, and know that they are identical in weight (Crutchfield *et al.,* 1955).

The operation of *motivation* or subjective importance is illustrated by a classic study which found that children overestimate the sizes of coins as compared with discs of the same size, and poor children by more than wealthy children—presumably because of the greater value the coins have for the former.

Size estimations of coins made by well-to-do and poor ten-year-olds
(Method of average error)

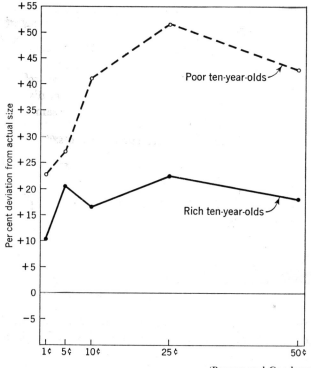

(Bruner and Goodman, 1947, p. 40)

This interpretation gains support from a later experiment where overestimation of the size of poker chips was experimentally induced in children by making the chips redeemable for candy (Lambert *et al.*, 1949).

In addition to, and interacting with, these effects of expectations and motives, judgments are made in accordance with the general proposition that perception is determined by relationships rather than absolutes:

B11 Judgments of magnitude are made within a frame of reference established by the total range of relevant stimuli.

For example, when the total range of luminosity varies from x to $2x$, a stimulus at $2x$ will be considered white. When the total range goes from $2x$ to $4x$, $2x$ will be seen as black and $4x$ as white. The facts that a white shirt appears white under all degrees of illumination ("brightness constancy"), that receding telephone poles are recognized as the same height ("size constancy"), that a book appears rectangular regardless of the angle of vision ("shape constancy")—all of these are due not only to familiarity with the objects involved but also to this principle. In each case, not only the specific object but the others surrounding it vary accordingly, so that the *relationship* between them remains constant. The black suit as well as the white shirt reflects less light at night: the luminosity relationship, and thus perceived whiteness, remains constant.

B11.1   The characteristic(s) differentiating a clearly defined figure from surrounding figures or from the background tend to be accentuated ("contrast").

Which is to say that figures are judged partially by reference to their surroundings. The question of whether this constitutes distortion is definitional. For example, all these heads are cut from the same gray paper.

(Krech and Crutchfield, 1958, p. 79)

Which of them represents the "real" appearance of this shade of gray? Cutting out the silhouette and holding it up "by itself" is no solution, since it will then also be against *some* background.

Again, the two center circles are the same size, though the surrounding circles suggest not, to our perception of them:

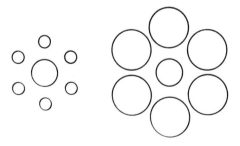

Contrast is thus the converse of assimilation, discussed above, in which differences within a figure are minimized. The relationship between the two processes is demonstrated in the following experiment.

A subject faces a blank wall that is differentially illuminated, gradually going from very bright to dim. It appears as a homogeneous, "average" brightness throughout (assimilation). If a very thin vertical line now separates the wall in two halves, one appears dark and the other light; each appears homogeneous within itself, but contrasts with the other. This shows the intimate relationship between organization (what will be perceived as "figure") and judgment (what characteristics will be attributed to the figure). In fact, the distinction between organization and interpretation or judgment, like many distinctions in this book, is one of convenience in analysis, and not one that can be rigorously maintained.

Experimentation with contrast and assimilation has been applied to behavior as complex as attitude formation. For example, information differing significantly from a stereotype tends either to be ignored or distorted to fit the stereotype (assimilation), or exaggerated and perceived as far more different than it really is (by contrast with the stereotype). As we shall see in a later chapter, differences in platform within a political party tend to be minimized by the partisan (assimilated), whereas differences between the party platforms are exaggerated (contrasted). So, also, if two people are perceived simultaneously, and both are liked but in unequal degrees, the difference tends to be leveled (assimilated). But if one is disliked and the other liked, both reactions become more extreme (contrast) (Peak, 1958).

Further, the comparison with "surrounding" characteristics can be temporal as well as spatial. An orange tastes sweet after a lemon but sour after sugar; a black silhouette (or negative after-image) appears before the eyes after exposure to a brilliant stimulus. Such contrasts are largely a matter of sensory adaptation: the sour receptors are relatively insensitive after heavy bombardment by the lemon, and the same is true for the sweet receptors after sugar. But more generally, and beyond the effects of purely sensory adaptation:

B11.2   People develop an "adaptation level" with respect to given stimulus magnitudes (e.g., temperature, light intensity, size of cars) based on the range of values that has been present in the relevant series.

That is, a stimulus will be judged in relation to the temporal series of which it is a recognized member; and values in the middle (not necessarily the arithmetic center or average) will appear to be "normal," "average," "neutral." Such values are said to be *at* the adaptation level. Values that depart from the adaptation level produce one-sided experiences: they feel or appear hot, large, bright, and so on.

For example, a subject is asked to rate each of a series of unmarked weights as "heavy" or "light." The first few judgments appear to be arbitrary, but soon an adaptation level develops such that some actually feel heavy and others light. The point at which judgments divide is normally not the center of the range nor the average of the series. A series ranging from 200 to 400 grams, for example, divides at about 250 grams (recall Weber's law). Adding new stimuli outside the previous range will shift the adaptation level and thus in turn will shift judgments of specific stimuli. A 300-gram weight that felt heavy in the original series becomes light when weights in the 600-gram range are added.

B11.3   Which stimuli become part of a series is partly a matter of organization, e.g., proximity, similarity, and so forth (as above), and partly a conceptual decision about the meaning attached to various stimuli through learning.

When an adaptation level has been established by a series of weights, as in the illustration just above, the surreptitious addition of another weight outside the series will shift it; but picking up an "irrelevant" object of equivalent weight (a tray, a cup of coffee) has no effect. This shows that something beyond sheer sensory adaptation is involved, since the muscles are subject to the same effects in either case.

The importance and implications of the notion of adaptation level rest on the fact that such judgments are not simply intellectual recognitions of relativity but matters of immediate perceptual experience. The weight *feels* heavy or light; cars *appear* large or small—but always depending on the rest of the series. The first warm day of spring feels much warmer than the first cool day of fall, though it may in fact be many degrees cooler, just as surely and directly as the heads on page 118 appear to be different shades of gray.

Thus, human perceptual judgments are inexorably under the control of the particular background brought to the judgment. Perceptually, as well as logically, there is no absolute correlate of any perceived magnitude. Even the distinction between black and white, which we normally take as the prototype of an absolute qualitative dichotomy, is perceptually a matter of degree. White immediately turns to black if and when the area surrounding it becomes more brilliantly illuminated—which is exactly how areas of black on a white movie screen are produced. Thus from the simplest sensory experiences, as we have seen, to the most complicated judgments of social norms and values, as we shall see, man responds relatively—by making comparisons that detect similarities and differences and little, perhaps nothing, more.

Finally, before leaving this section, we should say something about the question of how "realistic" perception is, given the observer's influences on interpretation. To what extent do the effects of learning and motives on interpretation "distort" perception?

With respect to learning, it is clear that these effects usually act to resolve stimulus ambiguity in a realistic way; in a normal environment, past experience ordinarily helps in the interpretation of the present. It is mainly when faced with "abnormal" (unusual or changing) stimulus conditions, as in illusions, that these learned assumptions produce erroneous interpretations.

Motives or subjective importance, however, may often "bend" interpretation, as when poor children overestimate the size of coins; there is no particular reason to expect a close match between what people need and/or want and the way the world actually is. But the distortion becomes pronounced only when stimulus ambiguity and/or motivation level is unusually high. The major effect of motives upon perception, under normal conditions, is through *what* will be seen—i.e., selection—rather than on *how* it will be seen—i.e., interpretation.

With regard to other than normal conditions, we conclude with two striking instances of human behavior, hypnosis and extrasensory perception. Both have been subjected to a good deal of scientific investigation. One has come through as well substantiated, the other is still controversial.

Hypnosis

Although this intriguing subject has only come into full scientific attention in the past few decades, it has been a matter of speculation and interest for centuries:

> The sleeping trance, which is a familiar part of hypnotism today, seems to have been discovered accidentally in 1784. . . . The discovery of the remaining major hypnotic phenomena followed rapidly, and by 1825 hypnotically induced positive hallucinations (seeing things which are not present), negative hallucinations (being functionally blind to things really present), hypnotic anaesthesias, hypnotic analgesias (insensibility to pain), and the action of post-hypnotic suggestion had all been clearly described [Hull, 1933, p. 9].

As this quotation suggests:

C1   Hypnotism works: that is, there is no question today that hypnotism can induce all of the following "unnatural" states:

.1   anesthesia and analgesia, local or general.

Demonstrations range from the familiar night club or vaudeville displays in which the hand is insensitive to fire or a pin, to the more serious applications in dentistry, obstetrics, and surgery.

> Hypnotic anesthesia, unlike chemical anesthesia, is in every respect harmless to the patient. It has all the prerequisites of the ideal anesthetic (Kroger and DeLee, 1943). . . . Where clinically applicable it seems completely without danger to

the patient and may be induced by the surgeon (and obstetrician) or his assistant. It has been used successfully in dentistry, obstetrics and surgery (Raginsky, 1948). It usually is induced by direct suggestion to the effect that the patient be relaxed, sleep deeply, feel nothing and be amnestic for the period of the operation or delivery [Rosen, 1959b, p. 61].

.2   positive and negative hallucinations.

Here is an example of the latter:

I say . . . , "You can now open your eyes, though without waking. Mr. X has gone home. Look around and tell me whether you can see him." The subject gazes around sleepily, apparently with some care, and replies that he cannot. I tell him to count the men present aloud, pointing to each with his finger. He does so. When he comes to Mr. X he passes him by without notice, and ends with a sum one less than the number of persons really present [Hull, 1933, p. 30].

.3   regression to an earlier age, along with recollection of otherwise forgotten experiences and skills.

The following experiment demonstrates regression in intellectual functioning as the result of the hypnotic regression.

The group selected for this study was composed of ten male undergraduate students in whom hypnosis could be induced rapidly, and who could maintain eye opening under hypnosis. The subjects were administered equivalent forms of the Otis Tests of Mental Ability first in the waking state and then in three hypnotically regressed states. All tests were administered in the same order and with the same instructions. . . .

Results from the testing under the various conditions mentioned above are as follows: In the waking state the mean score for the entire group was 59.2 with an equivalent IQ of 117. At the fifteen year age level the raw score was 54.2 with an IQ of 118. At the ten year level the score was 41.4, IQ 118, while at the final eight year level the mean score was 24.5 with an IQ of 118. The drop in raw score at each age level is consistent with what actually would be found at younger age levels with the IQ remaining constant.

The results of this experiment reveal that when an individual is regressed in age by hypnosis his mental functioning operates at a level consistent with the regressed age. These downward changes in intellectual functioning reflect losses in maturational power rather than losses in capacity or brightness [Haggerty, 1953, p. 35, reviewing Kline, 1950].

.4   unusual muscular strength, rigidity, resistance to fatigue.

In this category are demonstrations such as the "human plank":

The subject's body is rendered rigid by means of appropriate suggestions. He is then used to bridge the space between two chairs, and one or more individuals mount and stand on top of the unsupported portion of the body [Weitzenhoffer, 1953a, p. 123].

Others include marked increases in the maximum squeeze subjects can exert on a spring-loaded grip:

> In general, there are clear and definite indications that alterations of the motor functions are possible within limits but that these are not nearly so spectacular as popular belief would have them. The rule appears to be that, the less voluntary an activity is, the less easily and the less strongly it can be affected or controlled by suggestion [*ibid.*, p. 138].

.5   organic effects, normally entirely outside voluntary control.

Blisters and burned spots, possibly cold sores, can be produced by hypnotic suggestion; the former, by the simple suggestion that the subject has touched something hot. There is some debate as to whether cold sores can be suggested directly, or develop only as the result of a suggested emotional disturbance. A number of other studies report the reduction of warts as the result of hypnotic suggestion (McDowell, 1949).

.6   antisocial, repugnant, or dangerous acts.

Contrary to common belief, there is some evidence that people will do things under hypnosis that they would not normally do. One experimenter, for example, induced a hypnotized subject to put her hand into a box that apparently contained a rattlesnake and got another subject to throw acid in his face.

> The procedure was as follows: the subject, hypnotized, was brought into the presence of the stimulus box. Thereupon the experimenter poured sulphuric acid from a bottle into a glass, and in the presence of the subject, dipped a strip of zinc into the acid. The reaction was strong, with fumes steaming from the mouth of the glass. The subject was then asked, "Do you know what sulphuric acid is?" and regardless of the answer the explanation was given that "sulphuric acid is very dangerous. It will scar the skin and put out the eyes." The subject was then told to pick up the glass and throw the acid at the author's face, the author being protected, of course, by the invisible glass.
>
> Subject E picked up the glass and was very reluctant to throw the acid. She hesitated; the experimenter insisted and finally said, "I'm going to count three and when I finish you will throw the acid. One, two, three." The subject threw the acid, set down the glass, shuddered and covered her face with her hands She seemed very disturbed [Rowland, 1947, p. 43].

One experimenter induced subjects to "steal" money from the pocket of an overcoat and then lie about it when discovered (Wells, 1947). Another such study, however, failed to produce any such results and reached the following conclusions:

> To summarize this investigation, one may state briefly that a great variety of experimental procedures was employed upon a large number of well-trained hypnotic subjects to induce them, in trance states or in response to commands

and suggestions given during trance states, to perform acts of an unconventional, harmful, anti-social and even criminal nature, these acts to involve aggressions against both the self and others, as well as to permit direct abuse of the hypnotic subject by the hypnotist. Every effort was made to meet the need for control investigations covering the possibilities of waking behavior, for realism in the experimental situation, and for adequate and varied techniques of hypnotic suggestion. The findings disclosed consistently the failure of all experimental measures to induce hypnotic subjects, in response to hypnotic suggestion, to perform acts of an objectionable character, even though many of the suggested acts were acceptable to them under circumstances of waking consciousness [Erickson, 1939b, p. 414].

Here is a possible resolution of these contradictory findings:

In every instance where investigators have reported obtaining anti-social acts under hypnosis, the suggestions used were such as to alter the subject's awareness of the "true" situation by means of illusions, hallucinations, and paramnesias created in regard to both the imposed task and the environment in which it was to be carried out. On the contrary with few exceptions in those instances for which the subjects would not perform suggested anti-social acts no attempts were made to alter the subjects' awareness of the situation. They were merely told what to do and when to do it.

In the past there has been general agreement that subjects would carry out suggested anti-social acts if and when they (a) felt protected, (b) had latent criminal tendencies, (c) had an implicit trust in the hypnotist. . . . [There is] a fourth possible situation: the subject does not perceive the suggested act as being anti-social in nature. This can be brought about by altering his perceptions of the task and of his environment, as done in the investigations studied here [Weitzenhoffer, 1953b, pp. 49–50].

.7   posthypnotic suggestion, in which subjects, after coming out of a trance, carry out orders or suggestions made in the trance.

Here is an illustration:

A stenographer was told in the trance state that for the next week, while taking dictation she would change pencils on the 320th word, the 550th word and 725th word. These instructions limited the posthypnotic act to a very small aspect of the total task. During that time she took dictation from three psychiatrists, each of whom noted the phrases at which she changed pencils. Despite the fact that she used many combined word phrases (symbols combining two or more words) it was discovered by count later that she approximated the correct number closely, never exceeding an error of 10 and averaging an error of three words [Erickson and Erickson, 1941, p. 128].

Such posthypnotic techniques have been put to effective therapeutic use:

Posthypnotic suggestion, with or without analysis, is a powerful psychological device. It may be helpful in many types of complaint including insomnia, disturbing dreams, various fears and phobias, nervous headache, nervous habits such as nail-biting, excessive smoking, intemperate eating or drinking, functional speech disorders, and personality defects such as shyness, pugnacity, temper, awkwardness, dependency, and so forth [Rhodes, 1952, p. 11].

The general procedure is to suggest a posthypnotic aversion to the habit, or to suggest that the anxiety associated with a particular situation will be alleviated and that the subject will desire or enjoy the appropriate behavior.

C2   Some people are hypnotized more easily than others, and some cannot be hypnotized at all. In general, hypnotizability is related to age, sex, and intelligence, but not to any particular personality trait.

> In summary, it appears that we may say that suggestibility is highest at the ages of seven to eight, and that it is somewhat greater for women and girls than for men and boys, and greater for individuals of higher than of lower intelligence (these being measured on a Binet-type test). In regard to personality traits no general conclusions can be drawn [Weitzenhoffer, 1953a, p. 89].

C2.1   Although there is some relationship between a positive attitude toward hypnosis and hypnotizability, it is not an overriding or consistent one.

> On the whole, there is some evidence that a positive attitude favors suggestibility, and conversely expectation appears to be a negligible factor. Needs and motivation appear to be related in various ways to suggestibility. But whether they are to be considered as determinants of suggestibility is a debatable point [ibid., p. 86].

Not only is a cooperative attitude not necessary for hypnosis; some people can even be hypnotized against their will:

> A 21-yr.-old female subject was placed in deep trance in spite of a financial reward offered for her successful resistance. The subject kept her eyes closed, her ears stopped, and shouted continuously to drown out the experimenter's voice. . . .
> The particular subject in this case was a nurse, healthy and well-balanced, employed in a U.S. Veterans Administration psychiatric hospital. The experimenter was chief clinical psychologist there. The girl had been hypnotized before and was an excellent subject. . . . .
> The experimenter put his mouth close to her stopped ear and used a strong firm voice to suggest she would hear and heed his commands to be hypnotized, suggesting an excruciating headache whose pain could be escaped only by going into deep trance. After six minutes the subject went into a deep hypnotic state [Bordeaux, 1953, p. 49, reviewing Watkins, 1951].

While it is relatively simple to describe the kinds of effects hypnotism can produce, little is known about why hypnotism can produce them—i.e., about what hypnotism really is. There are various interpretations, ranging from the purely physiological to the purely social; and from those that view the hypnotic state as an extreme case of normal suggestibility to those that see it as a qualitatively distinct condition. At any rate:

C3   Brain waves and other physiological measures distinguish the hypnotic trance from normal sleep on the one hand and normal wakefulness on the other, although it appears closer to wakefulness.

But, indeed, it is not quite that simple:

> It would seem . . . that, although outwardly electroencephalograms show hypnosis to be more like wakefulness and less like sleep, a more refined study of the records shows hypnosis to be more like *light* sleep, and like neither waking nor deep sleep. In summary, thus far with a few minor exceptions it would appear that hypnosis is not at all like sleep, but resembles wakefulness in regard to a large variety of physiological phenomena [Weitzenhoffer, 1953a, p. 95].

Actually:

C4   The hypnotic trance, or something very close to it, can be induced by mechanical stimuli alone, as in highway hypnosis or trances produced by repetitive stimuli from certain machinery.

However, mechanical props are not necessary; hypnosis can be induced, as it usually is, simply by the hypnotist's verbal suggestions.

Finally, with respect to possible dangers:

C5   There is general agreement that while hypnosis per se has no harmful aftereffects, certain hypnotic or posthypnotic suggestions may produce or aggravate anxieties or other emotional disturbances.

It is this concern that leads to the caveat that hypnosis be used only by qualified professionals for legitimate purposes.

Extrasensory Perception, or "ESP"

The state of research in this controversial area can be summarized as follows:

A small number of investigators, roughly thirty to forty, who have done a large number of studies, are firmly convinced that there is such a thing as extrasensory perception or "awareness of or response to an external event or influence not apprehended by sensory means," e.g., telepathy, clairvoyance (Rhine & Pratt, 1957, p. 208). The majority of psychologists, most of whom have not studied the subject, are not convinced. Here are the summary results of four surveys among psychologists in the American Psychological Association, showing some increase, over the years, in the willingness to accept ESP as a possibility, but very little acceptance of the concept as an "established fact."

Comparison of results of four surveys

	Percentage of Respondents			
			Young psychologists	
Date of survey	Full members 1938	Fellows and life members 1952	Associates admitted in 1950	Associates admitted in 1955
	1938	1952	1955	1955
In your opinion, is "extrasensory perception"				
1. An established fact?	1.4	2.6	4.2	4.0
2. A likely possibility?	7.4	14.0	25.5	27.8
3. A remote possibility?	36.4	39.0	31.1	32.0
4. An impossibility?	14.5	10.3	7.8	6.5
5. Merely an unknown?	40.3	34.1	31.4	29.7
Total	100.0	100.0	100.0	100.0

(Warner, 1955, p. 233)

Judged by the scientific standards ordinarily applied in other areas of psychology, the evidence is often persuasive, although at the same time it is not as reproducible as one would wish in a scientific discipline. Furthermore, many psychologists argue that ordinary standards are in this case inapplicable, for one or both of two major reasons.

(1) The postulated phenomena are in themselves so implausible and depart so far from ordinary conceptions of what is physically possible that the evidence needs to be much more firm than evidence for more plausible hypotheses.

To demonstrate something highly implausible requires better evidence than to demonstrate something plausible. The reason is that supporting evidence for the plausible finding comes from many directions, while the implausible one must hang upon the slender thread of nonrandomness until certain systematic relationships are found that tie it firmly to what is known [Hilgard, 1962, p. 220].

(2) Even the effects claimed by those who *are* convinced are ordinarily very slight and the number of trials in each experiment is ordinarily very

large; and that raises certain statistical questions. The exact nature of such questions is varied and in any case highly technical; but they relate to the fact that when a large enough series of chance events is examined in enough different ways, "nonchance" characteristics are frequently observed.

There has even been some allegation of trickery or fraud in the conduct or reporting of ESP studies. But it is fair to say that there is no substantiating evidence for such criticism. In any case, *within* the body of scientific research on ESP, the following findings are probably considered to be best demonstrated. In view of the controversial character of this field, where the facts are still very much in doubt, we present some of the main findings claimed by investigators, but without the usual numbers signifying the acceptance of the proposition by most scholars.

. . .   Extrasensory perception (ESP) exists, in one form or another.

Four basic forms are usually distinguished, although they are related and some students think that there is a general factor uniting them (as with intelligence): (a) telepathy, or thought transference; (b) clairvoyance, or seeing distant objects or events; (c) precognition, or prophecy; (d) psychokinesis (PK), or influencing physical events through mental operations (e.g., influencing dice by "will").

The typical ESP study that has produced such findings involves a pack of twenty-five cards of five different types; the subject "calls" or guesses the identity of each in a series of runs through the pack. In telepathy, the cards are visible to a sender but not to the receiver; in clairvoyance the subject "reads" the cards as exposed or ordered by some mechanical device in another location; in precognition he predicts the fall of future cards, and so on. ESP, then, is indicated by a number of hits significantly above the chance expectancy of five per run. Most psychokinesis experiments have dealt with mental attempts to influence dice, thrown either by hand or by independent mechanical devices. A recent review of over two hundred studies of PK concludes that "evidence of PK as a psychological phenomenon is totally lacking" (Girden, 1962, p. 384).

. . .   People vary in their extrasensory capacities, and relatively few are highly sensitive.

Even the latter are "highly" sensitive only in that they consistently do somewhat, although not very much, better than chance. For example, the most highly sensitive subject may consistently guess only at the rate of seven correct out of twenty-five where five correct out of twenty-five is chance expectancy.

. . .   ESP seems to be related to the belief in its existence.

In one well-known study, subjects who reported for an experiment with the belief that ESP is possible did better than skeptics.

Subjects were required to make ESP responses under rigidly controlled conditions. Before making his first ESP response each subject was categorized as either a "sheep" or a "goat." The sheep were subjects who accepted (though sometimes with reservations) the possibility of paranormal success under the conditions of the experiment; the goats were subjects who rejected this possibility [Schmeidler and McConnell, 1958, p. 30].

The results:

ESP scores of subjects *

Acceptance ESP of	Series	Number of subjects	Number of runs (25 guesses)	Deviation from chance expectation	Mean hits per run †
Sheep	1	12	129	+56	5.43
	2	12	127	+33	5.26
	3	22	133	+31	5.23
	4	9	162	+34	5.21
	5	23	207	+45	5.22
	6	19	171	+27	5.16
	7	14	126	+16	5.13
Total		111	1055	+242	5.23
Goats	1	4	200	−10	4.95
	2	4	175	−13	4.93
	3	4	199	−11	4.94
	4	3	54	−41	4.24
	5	3	27	−23	4.15
	6	16	144	−26	4.82
	7	6	54	+8	5.15
Total		40	853	−116	4.86

* Subjects were tested individually. The study compares subjects who accepted the possibility of paranormal success under the conditions of the experiment (sheep) with subjects who rejected this possibility (goats).

† Chance expected value is 5.00.

(*Ibid.*, p. 33)

Some efforts to replicate this interesting finding, however, have been negative.

. . .   ESP performance is often better in the initial stages of an experiment, or under novel or spontaneous conditions. Psychokinesis, particularly, shows a striking and consistent decline from the early to the later trials in a series.

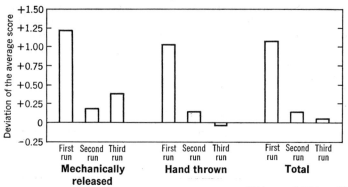

Decline in scoring rate within the set of three runs in the first series of dice-throwing tests of PK

(Rhine and Rhine, 1943, p. 36)

Finally, we should note that there are a large number of specific findings regarding the relative effectiveness of various sizes of cards or dice, distances between subject and sender, subjects with various personality patterns as measured by tests, and the like. But none of these, to date, is as well established or as general within the body of ESP research as are the above mainline findings.

SELECTED READINGS

The literature on sensory processes is quite thorough, detailed, and technical; in this area psychology and physiology merge. For a good overview of the sensory machinery, see:

F. A. Geldard. *The Human Senses.* Wiley, 1953.

Advanced and definitive articles on specialized questions—for example, time perception, basic correlates of the visual stimulus—appear in a major reference work:

S. S. Stevens, ed. *Handbook of Experimental Psychology.* Wiley, 1951.

The original, classic contributions of Gestalt psychologists can be sampled in:

Willis D. Ellis. *A Sourcebook of Gestalt Psychology.* Harcourt, Brace & World, 1938.
Kurt Koffka. *Principles of Gestalt Psychology.* Harcourt, Brace & World, 1935.
Wolfgang Köhler. *Gestalt Psychology.* Liveright, 1920.

A major review of various theories of perception is offered by:

Floyd H. Allport. *Theories of Perception and the Concept of Structure.* Wiley, 1955.

For theoretical and experimental application of principles of perception to the specific question of how people perceive people, see:

Renato Tagiuri and Luigi Petrullo, eds. *Person Perception and Interpersonal Behavior.* Stanford U. Press, 1958.

Finally, here are some recent technical summaries of the research literature dealing with special, more controversial, perceptual processes:

N. F. Dixon. "The Effect of Subliminal Stimulation upon Autonomic and Verbal Behavior," *Journal of Abnormal and Social Psychology,* 57, 1958, pp. 29–36.

Israel Goldiamond. "Indicators of Perception: Subliminal Perception, Subception, Unconscious Perception: An Analysis in Terms of Psychophysical Indicator Methodology," *Psychological Bulletin,* 55, 1958, pp. 373–407.

George S. Klein *et al.* "Cognition without Awareness: Subliminal Influences upon Conscious Thought," *Journal of Abnormal and Social Psychology,* 57, 1958, pp. 255–66.

J. C. Naylor and C. H. Lawshe. "An Analytical Review of the Experimental Basis of Subception," *Journal of Psychology,* 46, 1958, pp. 75–96.

J. B. Rhine and J. G. Pratt. *Parapsychology: Frontier Science of the Mind.* Thomas, 1957.

S. G. Soal and F. Bateman. *Modern Experiments in Telepathy.* Yale U. Press, 1954.

Thy wish was father, Harry, to that thought—
WILLIAM SHAKESPEARE
King Henry IV

But what then am I? A thing which thinks? It is a thing which doubts, understands [conceives], affirms, denies, wills, refuses, which also imagines and feels.

RENÉ DESCARTES
Meditations

Whatever withdraws us from the power of our senses; whatever marks the past, the distant or the future, predominate over the present, advances us in the dignity of thinking beings.

SAMUEL JOHNSON
Journey to the Western Islands

Nothing we ever do is, in the strict scientific literalness, wiped out. Of course, this has its good side as well as its bad one. As we become permanent drunkards by so many separate drinks, so we become saints in the moral, and authorities and experts in the practical and scientific spheres, by so many separate acts and hours of work.

WILLIAM JAMES
The Principles of Psychology

You cannot educate a man wholly out of the superstitious fears which were implanted in his imagination, no matter how utterly his reason may reject them.

OLIVER WENDELL HOLMES

Chapter Five

LEARNING AND THINKING

Most American psychologists, especially those of an experimental bent, regard learning as the fundamental process in the understanding of human behavior. And, as we have seen, the process of symbolic learning distinguishes man most sharply from the rest of the animal world.

Yet relatively little of what psychologists study under this heading deals with the kind of learning that occurs in the classroom or in reading for self-education—that is, with the kind of learning the layman usually has in mind when he uses the term. Actually, psychologists use a broad definition of learning that includes the special case of "study" but also incorporates all the other ways in which behavior changes over time as a result of experience.

The preponderance of systematic laboratory investigation deals with lower animals, chiefly the rat; and this concentration seems to be increasing: "If we count only the papers on learning [in a] broad sample of journals, . . . about 90% of our work with animal learning has been done on the rat" (Bitterman, 1960, p. 704). In addition to the practical and theoretical advantages of dealing with simpler animals, this practice stems in part from the Darwinian assumption that the learning process is continuous across species, i.e., basically the same wherever found. Here is the point as put by a leading scholar of animal and human learning:

[The figure on the next page] shows . . . three learning curves [indicating the rate of rewarded, hence "correct," responses over time. The small cross-marks show when rewards were administered]. Now, one of them was made by a *pigeon* in some experiments by Ferster and me, one was made by a *rat* in an experiment on anoxia by Lohr, and the third was made by a *monkey* in Karl Pribram's laboratory at the Hartford Institute.

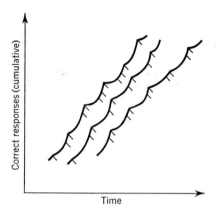

Pigeon, rat, monkey, which is which? It doesn't matter. Of course, these three species have behavioral repertoires which are as different as their anatomies. But once you have allowed for differences in the ways in which they make contact with the environment, and in the ways in which they act upon the environment, what remains of their behavior shows astonishingly similar properties. Mice, cats, dogs, and human children could have added other curves to this figure [Skinner, 1956, pp. 230–31].

Many psychologists, however, question the assumption, and argue that there are essential differences between species, or at least between other animals and man. But there is general agreement that much of what goes on in a rat can and does go on in a man, even if the converse does not hold: people do form habits, but rats are not able to read. Hence, extensive experimentation with simple, easily observable changes in animal behavior forms the basis for comprehensive theories of learning, in the hope that the theories will ultimately apply to some if not all human behavior. And in these pages we shall see some cases in which the transition seems to have been made successfully.

Moreover, laboratory studies of human learning have concentrated on the relatively simple and mechanical processes by which people acquire skills or memorize lists of items. The learning of ideas or the attainment of understanding, usually taken to be the highest or the most important form of human learning, has received less systematic attention than has simple learning—partly because of the great difficulties involved in studying it, partly because of the theoretical position that complex learning may reduce to principles extended from the analysis of simpler situations.

There is also an extensive literature in educational psychology that deals with classroom teaching and ways to increase its efficiency. This includes studies of how learning can best be managed in specific situations, and we list such findings here only insofar as they yield general principles of human learning.

DEFINITIONS

Learning: Changes in behavior that result from previous behavior in similar situations (as opposed to changes due to physiological variations such as growth, deterioration, hunger, fatigue, alcohol, or sleep). Mostly, but by no means always, behavior also becomes demonstrably more effective and more adaptive after the exercise than it was before. In the broadest terms, then, learning refers to the effects of experience, either direct or symbolic, on subsequent behavior.

Here, to illustrate the range of this definition, are a few examples of learning that will appear in the following pages:

the formation of conditioned responses (salivating at the sound of the dinner bell);

acquiring skill at typing, driving, receiving Morse code;

memorizing and reciting nonsense syllables;

remembering the substance or meaning of a written passage;

achieving understanding or sudden solutions of complex problems.

Response: The behavioral "output" counterpart of the "input" term *stimulus,* referring to any definable unit of behavior. The unit can be defined in various ways—for example, by its effects on some part of the environment, as in the learning curves on page 134, which simply report the number of times the subject depresses a lever, regardless of how it was pushed or pulled; by a specific anatomical or physiological event, e.g., salivation, a knee jerk, raising the left arm, doing a handspring; or, finally, by the meaning attributed to the behavior by the actor himself or by an observer, so that widely differing acts (extending the tongue, striking a blow, saying certain words) might all be classified together as "aggressive responses."

The term originally grew out of experiments and theories in which acts were considered to be elicited by particular stimuli (thus, stimulus–response); but the term is not so restricted in present usage, and a "response" does not necessarily imply a specific instigating stimulus.

Habit: As in common usage, this term refers to a connection between stimuli and/or responses that has become virtually automatic through experience, usually through repeated trials. So, for example, "1492" automatically elicits "Columbus" from most Americans; a printed word elicits certain manual responses in the skilled typist; a red traffic signal elicits braking in the motorist. Habits do not depend on thinking either for their formation or their execution; as a matter of fact, thinking sometimes interferes with their smooth performance.

Thinking: Like time, thinking is one of the immediate givens in human experience and, as St. Augustine observed about the former, we know exactly what we mean by the term until we try to define it. But formally it may help to point out that thinking is a representative process, dealing with events not necessarily present at the moment or even with objects and abstractions that have no physical reality (unicorn, God, $\sqrt{-1}$). Unlike perception, it is to some degree a spontaneous or self-sustaining activity not dependent upon immediate, continuous input from the environment. Heavy thinking can go on, sometimes more easily, in a dark and quiet room.

To oversimplify, it might be said that the formation of habits deals with the effects of direct experience; thinking, with symbolic experience. In actual behavior, of course, habit formation and thinking go on at the same time, and each affects the other in complex ways that are conceptualized quite differently by different schools of psychology. In this connection, we should add that an important but not established theoretical position holds that thoughts are themselves habits and are subject to the basic laws of habit formation.

FINDINGS

Habit Formation

SIMPLE ASSOCIATIONS

Perhaps the simplest case of habit formation is the process known as "classical conditioning":

A1 When a new stimulus is repeatedly paired with another stimulus that automatically elicits a certain response, the new one alone gradually becomes capable of eliciting the same or a similar response.

The original example was Pavlov's dog, who was taught to salivate in response to a variety of stimuli, such as a tone, a touch on the paw, the sound of a metronome (Pavlov, 1927). The general procedure and the terminology that goes with it are as follows:

A dog is harnessed so that he can be fed and his salivation measured accurately. Whenever he eats, saliva flows automatically as a normal physiological response to food in the mouth. (Food in the mouth is said to be an "unconditioned stimulus" that elicits the "unconditioned response" of salivation.) At first the sound of a bell produces no increase in saliva, but after a series of trials in which it rings just before food is delivered, the bell alone will produce salivation. The bell has become a "conditioned stimulus" capable of eliciting the "conditioned response" of salivation, and it will continue to do so over a number of trials—even if it is not accompanied or followed ("reinforced") by food.

A1.1   Association of the stimuli over a range of time intervals will produce some conditioning, but the most efficient procedure is usually for the conditioned stimulus to precede and/or overlap with the onset of the unconditioned stimulus.

Here, for example, are the results of various intervals in conditioning human eye-blinks:

The effect of stimulus separation upon simple eyelid conditioning *

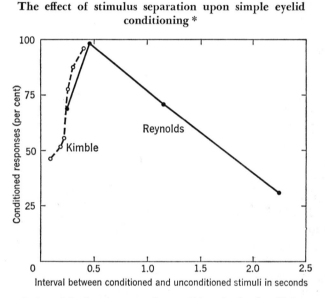

* The interval plotted is that between the conditioned stimulus (light or sound) and the unconditioned stimulus (an air-puff to the eye) with human adult subjects. The most favorable interval appears to be at or near 0.5 second. Backward intervals, in which the conditioned stimulus follows the unconditioned, are not shown.

(Hilgard, 1951a, p. 527, data from Reynolds, 1945, and Kimble, 1947)

A2   If the conditioned stimulus is presented repeatedly without the original unconditioned stimulus, it gradually loses its power to elicit the response ("extinction").

For example, if the bell is rung a number of times without any accompanying food, salivation subsides and finally ceases. Now this is not simply a matter of "forgetting," of passive decay with time. The conditioned response is unlearned or inhibited as a function of the number of "unreinforced" presentations of the conditioned stimulus. After a series of such extinction trials has reduced the response to zero, it may recover in some measure after a period of rest ("spontaneous recovery").

All this seems like a complicated way of saying that the dog initially learns that food follows the bell and salivates in anticipation, then gives up when he learns that food is no longer coming. However, the process is not nearly so simple—or more correctly, not nearly so complicated.

A3   Classical conditioning does not require conscious anticipation of the unconditioned stimulus, nor is extinction simply a matter of nonanticipation; both processes occur even in the absence of any such awareness.

For instance, it is possible to condition animals like worms, without a nervous system that enables conscious anticipation, or dogs in whom the cerebral cortex has been destroyed. One decorticate dog was conditioned to flex his leg at the sound of a whistle; this response was then extinguished and transferred to a light, by the standard procedure (Bromiley, 1948).

In human beings, conditioning can take place in the unborn fetus (Spelt, 1948), in the state of sleep, and in the waking state while the subject is entirely unaware of the fact that he is learning to respond to a conditioned stimulus. Conditioned responses will occur even though the subject knows that the unconditioned stimulus will *not* follow the conditioned stimulus. For example, subjects who had been conditioned to lift a finger at the sound of a tone that had been paired with shock, continued to do so when told that no more shock would be administered, and even when instructed to *avoid* making the response (Lindley and Moyer, 1961). Similarly, a hungry man salivates at pictures of food, although he doesn't expect to eat them; and in the theater one's heart rate quickens at sights and sounds associated with physical danger, or with sex, when one knows that he will not actually be involved.

The involuntary and automatic character of the conditioned response, which removes it from conscious control and sometimes even from awareness, has led some scholars to view the mechanism as basic to the formation of certain neurotic responses—for example, "groundless" fears or anxiety reactions to harmless stimuli, perhaps associated with threat in the past. This possibility is all the more plausible in the light of the fact that:

A4   Once a conditioned response has been established, it will be elicited not only by the conditioned stimulus actually used during training but also by a variety of similar stimuli ("stimulus generalization"); the magnitude of the response, however, decreases with the difference between the conditioned stimulus and the similar ones.

For example, here are the results of an experiment in which an emotional response ("GSR," galvanic skin response) was conditioned to a tone (Stimulus 1 on the graph). Stimuli 2, 3, and 4 represent tones of decreasing similarity in pitch. Such a curve is known as a "generalization gradient."

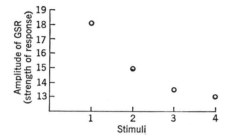

(Hovland, 1937, p. 136)

A4.1 Stimulus generalization occurs as an automatic part of the conditioning process, until the subject is specifically conditioned to discriminate between the conditioned stimulus and similar stimuli. Such "discrimination training" requires extinction of the response to the similar stimuli through a series of trials in which all the stimuli involved are presented, but only the appropriate one is followed by the unconditioned stimulus.

In these simple instances, as in more complex situations, stimulus generalization is a process of dual implications. The advantage, which usually outweighs the disadvantage, is that training in one situation enables people to respond appropriately in other similar situations—on various typewriters, in other cars, to differential pronunciations of the same language. On the negative side, there is the possibility of responding inappropriately when stimuli are similar but not the same, whenever the appropriate learning in discrimination has not occurred—as with the difficulty encountered in learning foreign words with familiar sounds but different meanings.

Examples of more serious and permanent misgeneralization may include a fear of all animals after being bitten by one; or perhaps, more symbolically, fear of all males or authority figures as a result of generalizing from a particular individual. One hypothesized explanation for the persistence of such generalizations is that once established, the fear may be strong enough to prevent the subject from exposing himself to the necessary discrimination or extinction experiences—as recognized in such clichés as: "If you don't go up again right after the near-crash [for an extinction trial], you'll never fly a plane again," or "I'll never let another man hurt me."

A5   One conditioned stimulus can be used to establish a further conditioned response ("second-order conditioning").

Once a dog salivates at the sound of a bell, he can be taught to salivate
to a whistle by pairing the whistle with the bell, and so on, as long as the
response lasts. But as we have seen, extinction occurs after a number of
trials if the unconditioned stimulus never follows.

This expands the implications of the conditioning process beyond stimuli
only one step removed from those that automatically evoke responses. So,
for example, the spoken word "bottle," through repeated association with
a certain object, comes to elicit some of the same reactions (images, thoughts,
even physical responses) as the object itself. Once established, this conditioned stimulus serves as reinforcement to establish similar responses to the
written form b-o-t-t-l-e, which in turn may be used to teach a foreign
equivalent, and so on.

Again, on the negative side, such chains of associations are thought to
underlie some remote fears—for example, fear of a color associated with
a garment associated with a person associated with threat. In practice such
chains may be rare because extinction occurs in the normal course of events:
the color is encountered in any number of unreinforced situations. The
learning would be expected to persist only when extinction conditions are
not encountered or submitted to.

In summary, then, classical conditioning is a process by which new stimuli
come to elicit responses essentially similar to those elicited by the original
stimuli. We turn now to a complementary basic process, a form of conditioning in which responses change in situations that are essentially similar to
one another.

INSTRUMENTAL BEHAVIOR

A child first calls an object "baba," then "badu," and finally "bottle";
a fisherman gradually gives up one lure in favor of another one that works
better. Systematic information on such trial-and-error learning comes from
a series of experiments in instrumental ("operant") conditioning that examine the process in its simplest form. Here is the basic experimental situation:

A hungry rat is put in a box that contains a lever connected to an automatic magazine that delivers food pellets whenever the lever is pressed.
The rat runs around restlessly, until somehow he presses the bar. A food
pellet ("reinforcement") follows, and he eats it. Soon he repeats the performance, and in a short time he is pressing the bar continuously. If the
magazine is now disconnected, the rate of bar-pressing decreases and finally

ceases, or almost ceases. Extinction has occurred, just as in classical conditioning. (The process is known as "operant" conditioning in that the response operates upon the environment.) The most general finding on instrumental conditioning, approaching the status of a law of behavior, is the following:

A6   When a response is followed by a reward (or "reinforcement"), the frequency or probability of its recurrence increases—where reward refers to any event that satisfies or "reduces" an existing need or motive, such as food to a hungry animal. When a reward no longer follows, the response rate tends to return to the preconditioning level ("extinction").

Conversely,

A7   When a response is followed by punishment, the frequency or probability of recurrence decreases—where punishment is any event that runs counter to the existing set of motives, e.g., pain. Again, when punishment is withdrawn, the rate tends to recover.

A7.1   Punishment, as compared with simple nonreinforcement, appears mainly to accelerate the decline in response rate rather than to deplete the reservoir of response.

When punishment is discontinued, subjects catch up, in total responses, to those subjects extinguished through nonreinforcement alone.

Effect of negative reinforcement upon extinction *

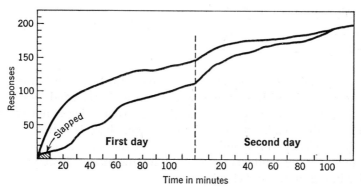

* The two curves are from groups of four rats each, with the same experimental history. All responses made by one group during the first ten minutes of extinction were slapped. The rate is depressed for some time, but eventually complete recovery is made.

(Skinner, 1938, p. 154)

In comparison, here is the course of extinction in a baby boy when rein-forcement (an adult entering the room) was simply withdrawn from a pre-viously reinforced response (tantrum at bedtime):

**Length of crying time in two extinction series as a function of
successive occasions of being put to bed ***

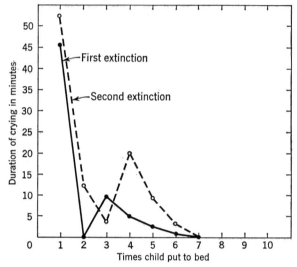

* Both curves are generally similar to extinction curves obtained with sub-human sub-jects. The second extinction series reached zero by the ninth occasion. No further tantrums at bedtime were reported during the next two years.

It should be emphasized that the treatment in this case did not involve aversive pun-ishment. All that was done was to remove the reinforcement. Extinction of the tyrant-like tantrum behavior then occurred.

No unfortunate side- or after-effects of this treatment were observed. At three and three quarters years of age, S appeared to be a friendly, expressive, outgoing child.

(Williams, 1959, p. 269)

Thus, depressing the frequency of response through punishment is not the same as extinguishing the response through repeated, *un*reinforced trials: slapping the child for approaching the cookie jar is not equivalent to removing the cookies. In punishment, then, there is active learning to avoid; the tendency to respond may persist at the same level, overcome for the moment by the tendency to avoid. This distinction is of practical sig-nificance in the control of behavior.

A8   Not only do direct rewards (as defined above) have such reinforcing properties, but so does any other stimulus that has led to reward in the past or has merely been associated with it. In short, neutral stimuli can acquire reinforcing properties by the laws of classical conditioning; and the same holds for negative reinforcement.

If, when the rat presses the bar, a light flashes an instant before the food is delivered, the light itself acquires reinforcing properties: the rat will learn new responses even if he is "rewarded" only by the light ("secondary reinforcement"). If the same light has been paired with electric shock, the rat will work merely to avoid the light. Again, if a secondary reinforcer is repeatedly presented without the original or primary reward, it loses its reinforcing properties through extinction. But:

A8.1   When stimuli lead to or are associated with not just one but a wide variety of rewards, they become powerful "generalized reinforcers," effective under a variety of motivational conditions and extremely resistant to extinction.

If light has been associated with food, and water, and sex, it will maintain its property as secondary reinforcer whether the rat is hungry, thirsty, or what have you—including motives with whose satisfaction it has *not* specifically been paired and over a large number of unreinforced trials.

At first glance, the central finding on the instrumental conditioning, like that of classical conditioning, appears to be an unnecessarily elaborate, roundabout statement of the obvious: animals and people will do things in order to get what they want. But again, the findings are not that simple, or that complicated:

A9   Instrumental conditioning, like classical conditioning, can occur automatically and without awareness. It does not depend on conscious striving for the reward, or even on awareness of any connection between the behavior and its consequences. In short, responses, including verbal ones, can be taught and extinguished by differential reinforcement without the knowledge of the subject himself.

For example, a number of studies illustrate that the content of ordinary conversation can be modified without the subject's awareness, by such secondary reinforcers as a nod, a smile, or expressed agreement regularly applied to arbitrarily selected classes of words or sentences.

It seems clear from Krasner's [1958a] review of 31 studies in this area that subjects may be trained by reinforcement to emit a particular kind of response without being "aware" that they have been "conditioned." The reinforcements may be either verbal or nonverbal ("That's good," or a nod). Two different examiners may also produce significant differences in the rate of conditioning [Rotter, 1960, p. 405].

Summary of results of "verbal conditioning" studies

Author	Reinforcing stimuli	Class of behavior reinforced
	POSITIVE RESULTS *	
Ball, 1952	"mmm-hmm"	"animal"
Greenspoon, 1955	"mmm-hmm"	plural nouns
Mandler & Kaplan, 1956	"mmm-hmm"	plural nouns
B. Sarason, 1957	"mmm-hmm"	verbs
I. Sarason, 1957	"mmm-hmm"	"verbal activity" verbs
Mock, 1957	"mmm-hmm," head nod	"mother"
Krasner, 1958b	"mmm-hmm," head nod, smile	"mother"
Salzinger & Pisoni, 1957	"mmm-hmm," "uh-ha," or "I see"	affect statements
Wilson & Verplanck, 1956	"mmm-hmm," "good," or writing	plural nouns, adverbs or travel verbs
Binder et al., 1957	"good"	"hostile" verbs
Cohen et al., 1954	"good"	"I," "we" pronouns
Cushing, 1957	"good"	"like" person in pictures
Grossberg, 1956	"good"	"I," "we" pronouns
Ekman, 1958	"good"	anti-capital-punishment response
Hartman, 1955	"good"	"I", "we" pronouns
Hildum and Brown, 1956	"good"	"attitudes"
Klein, 1954	"good"	"I," "we" pronouns
Nuthmann, 1957	"good"	"acceptance of self"
Taffel, 1955	"good"	"I," "we" pronouns
Tatz, 1956	"good"	a pair of digits
Fahmy, 1953	"good-one"	human responses
Spivak & Papajohn, 1957	"right"	autokinetic effect
Wickes, 1956	"fine," "good" or "all right"	movement responses
Wickes, 1956	head nod, smile, or lean forward	movement responses
Ekman, 1958	head nod, smile, and lean forward	movement responses
Greenspoon, 1954	light	plural nouns
Sidowski, 1954	light	plural nouns
Greenspoon, 1954	buzzer	plural nouns
McNair, 1957	bell tone	rate of verbalization
Verplanck, 1955	paraphrase, agreement, smile	opinions
Kanfer, 1954	"that's accurate," etc.	autokinetic effect
Hartman, 1955	head shake †	"I," "we" pronouns
Mock, 1957	head shake, "huh-uh" †	"mother"
Greenspoon, 1955	"huh-uh" †	plural nouns
	NEGATIVE RESULTS ‡	
Daily, 1953	"mmm-hmm"	"I," "we" pronouns
Hildum and Brown, 1956	"mmm-hmm"	"attitudes"
Cushing, 1957	"good"	"dislike" persons in pictures
Daily, 1953	"good"	"I," "we" pronouns
Marion, 1956	"good"	"I," "we" pronouns
Hartman, 1955	head nod	"I," "we" pronouns
Fahmy, 1953	repetition of response	human responses
Fahmy, 1953	"give another one, please"	human responses
Ball, 1952	light	"animal"
Nuthmann, 1957	light	"acceptance of self"
Taffel, 1955	light	"I," "we" pronouns
Ball, 1952	buzzer	"animal"

* The reinforced behavior changed significantly in the hypothesized direction during reinforcement sessions.
† Resulted in decrease; all others resulted in increase of reinforced behavior.
‡ The reinforced behavior either did not increase significantly or its increase was no more than in a control group.

(Krasner, 1958a, p. 160)

In one such study, seventeen different experimenters systematically applied such secondary reinforcers of agreement to any statement of opinion offered by unknowing subjects in the course of ordinary conversations. Here are some illustrative results:

Median cumulative frequency curves of opinion-statements and of all statements, for each ten-minute period of the experiment

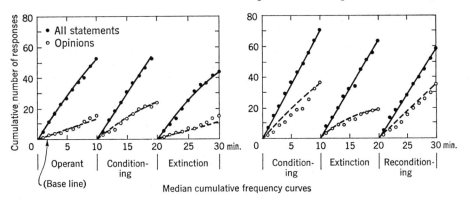

Median cumulative frequency curves

(Verplanck, 1955, p. 673)

The report concludes:

> The expected results appeared. Every S[ubject] increased in his rate of speaking opinions with reinforcement by paraphrase or agreement. Twenty-one [of twenty-four] S's decreased in rate with nonreinforcement. Over-all rates of speaking did not change significantly.
>
> In no case was the S aware that he was the subject of an experiment, or that the conversation was an unusual one [*ibid.*, pp. 675–76].

The author added, in a footnote,

> The writer, after having described the experiment to someone in casual conversation, had the illuminating experience of then being used as S by the person to whom he had described it. He showed the effect and, like, it would seem, *all S's* in this experiment, was quite unaware that he had been an S [*ibid.*, p. 676].

Such findings clearly speak to the question of how social conformity can occur without intentional compliance, or intentional influence, for that matter. Within the behavioral sciences, they have also provoked serious questions about how much significance can be placed on what people say and do not say in experimental, clinical, or other interview settings where the investigator himself may be influencing the subject's speech in the direction of his own hypothesis or bias, via such selective reinforcement. One common example is "interviewer bias." Poll takers have long recognized that opinionated interviewers are likely to bring back answers more favorable to their own attitudes. One recent investigation shows, for example, that expressed opinions can be influenced even in telephone interviews, and without reported awareness on the part of the respondent, simply by interviewer responses of "good" (Hildum and Brown, 1956).

The issue also touches on theories of personality development and disorder that are based in large measure on what patients say during therapy sessions:

> Quay [1959] examined the commonly held assumption that early family memories were just naturally imbedded in a subject's verbal productions. He carried out a study in which family recollections were reinforced for one group and non-family memories were reinforced for another group. The expected reinforcement effects appeared in virtually all subjects. One thus sees that the frequency of family recollections is a function of therapist behavior as well as subject behavior. It is only a short step further to recognize that therapists may be validating their own theories by selective reinforcement of the desired verbal productions [Seeman, 1961, p. 179].

Facing are the results of that study, which is the more significant in that

> the reinforcing stimulus chosen was a flat, noncommittal "uh-huh," spoken in a low conversational tone. Such minimal reinforcement was chosen because it is in keeping with a general psychotherapeutic type of response and because if a response this minimal could influence verbal behavior, then almost any remark of a psychotherapist would be reinforcing [Quay, 1959, p. 255].

Two more recent investigations, however, failed to find verbal conditioning without awareness and concluded that the case for it has been overstated. These studies found that verbal behavior could be conditioned by social reinforcers, but only, or mainly, when subjects were able to report the contingency:

> In these studies, a sentence-construction task was employed as the conditioning procedure and "Good" was the reinforcing stimulus. Awareness was inferred on the basis of subjects' responses to a detailed postconditioning interview conducted immediately following conditioning trials.
>
> The results of the four experiments were interpreted as supporting the hypothesis that "what is learned" in verbal-conditioning experiments is awareness of a response-reinforcement contingency. The extent to which subjects acted upon what they had learned seemed to depend upon how much they wanted to receive the reinforcement [Spielberger, 1962, p. 99].

And:

> In the research summarized here we repeatedly find no evidence of verbal operant conditioning without awareness—using report of a correct or correlated hypothesis as the indicator of awareness and a tone, "Umhmm," "Good," or avoidance of

Relative frequency of memories in the reinforced category
for the operant (Base Line) period and for the reinforcement period for the two experimental groups

| | "Family" group | | | | "Nonfamily" group | | |
S	Oper-ant	Rein-force-ment	Change	S	Oper-ant	Rein-force-ment	Change
1	.30	.43	+.13	1	.30	.47	+.17
2	.39	.41	+.02	2	.57	.32	+.25
3	.37	.29	−.08	3	.81	.89	+.08
4	.40	.48	+.08	4	.78	.80	+.02
5	.25	.12	−.13	5	.60	.70	+.10
6	.55	.58	+.03	6	.53	.84	+.31
7	.50	.56	+.06	7	.90	.73	−.17
8	.06	.26	+.20	8	.60	.63	+.03
9	.60	.70	+.10	9	.69	.70	+.01
10	.50	.46	+.04	10	.58	.64	+.06
11	.50	.62	+.12	11	.63	.70	+.07
12	.33	.47	+.14	12	.35	.58	+.23
13	.53	.62	+.08	13	.50	.58	+.08
14	.53	.70	+.17	14	.55	.80	+.25
15	.38	.43	+.05	15	.45	.61	+.16
16	.33	.48	+.15	16	.48	.54	+.06
				17	.18	.33	+.15
				18	.58	.57	−.01

(Quay, 1959, p. 255)

electric shock as the consequence. Certainly it is possible that with somewhat different conditions—perhaps longer series of trials, more potent reinforcers, or less figural response classes—we would have found it. But if this kind of learning or conditioning without awareness is to have the social generality commonly imputed to it (as by Dollard and Miller, 1950, for example) it seems likely that we would have found it in some of these experiments. Set against this is the repeated finding that subjects who report certain forms of awareness, or are informed in terms cognate with these forms, differ significantly—and usually dramatically—from controls [Dulany, 1962, p. 126].

At the moment, then, the role of awareness is an unresolved and lively issue in the theoretical literature. But many of the practical implications of verbal conditioning hold whether the process occurs with or without awareness—e.g., the possibility that psychotherapists confirm their own theories by reinforcing appropriate statements made by patients.

A10   Instrumental conditioning not only affects the relative frequency of acts already in the behavioral repertoire but, by simple extension of the above principles, produces or teaches new behavior through differential reinforcement of successively more effective approximations.

> In [a] demonstration, the bird is conditioned to strike a marble placed on the floor. . . . This may be done in a few minutes by reinforcing successive steps. Food is presented first when the bird is merely moving near the marble, later when it looks down in the direction of the marble, later still when it moves its head toward the marble, and finally when it pecks it [Hilgard, 1956, p. 88].

This is the procedure used to train animals in the wide variety of "unnatural" responses they exhibit in the circus and in various practical assignments. After reviewing some known wartime applications (for example, pigeons trained to guide a missile by pecking at the projection of the target), the principal investigator in this area cites this example:

> I cannot vouch for the authenticity of probably the most fantastic story of this sort, but it ought to be recorded. The Russians were said to have trained sea lions to cut mine cables. A complicated device attached to the sea lion included a motor driven cable-cutter, a tank full of small fish, and a device which released a few fish into a muzzle covering the sea lion's head. In order to eat, the sea lion had to find a mine cable and swim along side it so that the cutter was automatically triggered, at which point a few fish were released from the tank into the muzzle. When a given number of cables had been cut, both the energy of the cutting mechanism and the supply of fish were exhausted, and the sea lion received a special stimulus upon which it returned to its home base for special reinforcement and reloading [Skinner, 1960, p. 34].

No sea lion first cuts a mine cable by accident, and no human being first drives a car, recites a poem, or performs a concerto by accident. But each can and does approach the final skill gradually, through the ever more demanding contingencies of reinforcement—in the human case, normally secondary or social reinforcement ("right" versus "wrong," a gold star, or simply the desired feedback from the activity itself—"*That* looks, sounds, feels, more like it").

Investigators have applied these principles directly and systematically to human training through several lines of development. As one example, the overt behavior of psychotics has been subject to direct conditioning situations in the laboratory that replicate the simple animal conditioning apparatus, complete with a lever that delivers cigarettes, candy, or even glimpses of sexy pictures as reinforcement. The equipment looks very much like an ordinary vending machine. Here are illustrative results of a conditioning situation for two classes of psychotic patients and for normals. ("Testable" patients are those well enough to take standard clinical tests.)

Operant conditioning response measures for testable,
untestable, and normal subjects (median values)

	Responses	Number of pauses greater than ten seconds between responses	Total non-responding time (minutes)
Untestable	19	9	58
Testable	1421	44	41
Normals	9566	2	0

(Mednick and Lindsley, 1958, p. 14)

Some of such experiments, like the foregoing, are theoretical in nature, designed to detect differences between psychotics and normals or among various classes of psychotics; others are direct attempts to develop "healthy" responses by these methods. The latter have already produced some dramatic, if still few, results. For example, by the use of chewing gum as reinforcement for successive approximations, "verbal behavior was reinstated in two psychotics, classified as schizophrenics, who had been mute for 19 and 14 years. The procedures utilized involved application of operant conditioning" (Isaacs *et al.,* 1960, p. 12).

Another current offshoot of conditioning through successive approximation is programed instruction—a method that takes various forms, including the so-called teaching machine. All forms have the common characteristic that they elicit and systematically reinforce correct, and only correct, responses. To date, such programs have been successful in imparting various mechanical and technical skills, as well as academic subjects such as mathematics, psychology, logic, or interpretation of the Old Testament.

Porter (1959), using second and sixth graders in elementary school, reports that experimental groups taught spelling via teaching machines, performed significantly better on a standardized achievement test than the control groups (regular classroom instruction alone). . . .

Klaus & Lumsdaine (1960), in another part of their study, found that when their programmed textbook (physics—refraction of light) was used in lieu of normal instruction, the effect was substantially the same as that of students who had classroom instruction as well as programs. . . .

In general, it appears that instructional material which is programmed (involving short, easy steps, active responding by the student) is superior to instructional material presented in the usual textbook format, and superior to no instruction at all; while Porter's findings, along with those of Klaus & Lumsdaine, suggest that they can replace classroom instruction at the elementary and high school levels [Filby, 1961, pp. 237–38].

In addition, there is at least some evidence that students themselves react favorably to this method of instruction. Here are the results of a survey among college students after completing a one-semester course in psychology taught by machine:

If machines had not been used this year, I believe,	
I would have gotten less out of the course	84.3
it would have made no difference	12.1
I would have gotten more out of the course	3.4
In comparing work on the machine with studying the text, I felt that, *with the same amount of time and effort,*	
I learned much more on the machine	45.3
I learned somewhat more on the machine	33.0
there was no difference	0.9
I learned somewhat more from the text	16.9
I learned much more from the text	3.8
If I were to take another introductory course in a science or similar field, I would	
prefer to have machines used for part of the course	76.6
prefer not to have machines used	13.5
not care whether machines were used or not	9.9

(Holland, 1960, p. 6)

Basically, such programed instruction simply exposes bits of information of progressive difficulty and provides immediate reinforcement as each step is mastered by the student and evidenced in a correct response. Reinforcement is commonly secondary: "right" versus "wrong," or simply permission to go on. Such devices embody other pedagogic advantages in that the material must be carefully systematized before presentation and the machines allow each learner to proceed at his own pace. But presumably the chief factor behind their effectiveness is the immediate, systematic, and entirely nonarbitrary reinforcement they provide.

A11   The course and strength of conditioning is systematically related to the quantitative relationship between reinforcer and response (the "reinforcement schedule").

The relationships are as follows. In the simplest case, every correct response can be reinforced (a 100 per cent schedule). But there are several other possibilities under two general headings: *ratio* schedules, which reinforce every nth response; and *interval* schedules, which reinforce the first response after a given period of time. Some of the most significant findings in this field deal with the effects of different schedules.

A11.1 A 100 per cent schedule is usually the quickest way to establish new behavior or to increase the frequency of a response; that is, learning proceeds most rapidly when every correct response is reinforced.

But by the same token:

A11.2 Responses learned on such a schedule also extinguish most rapidly.

This graph, for example, compares extinction after 100 per cent and partial reinforcement in rats. The curves represent bar presses (cumulative) once reinforcement has been discontinued. Responses have ceased when the line becomes horizontal.

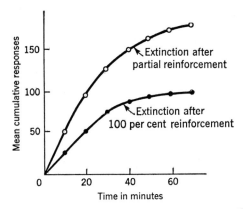

(Morgan, 1961, p. 204)

A review of thirty-five such comparisons, including both human and animal subjects in a wide variety of training situations, concludes:

> The most striking effects of partial reinforcement are apparent in response strength as measured by resistance to extinction. In almost every experiment, large and significant differences in extinction favoring the groups partially reinforced in conditioning over the 100% ones were found. The practical implication of this principle for maintaining behavior is obvious: Administer the reinforcing stimulus in conditioning according to a partial schedule, and the behavior will be maintained for long periods in the absence of external support from primary reward [Jenkins and Stanley, 1950, p. 231].

A11.3 Punishment on a 100 per cent schedule depresses the response rate more quickly than intermittent or partial punishment, but the effects of partial punishment last longer.

In this study, for example, when punishment was discontinued, animals trained on a 100 per cent punishment schedule made far more previously punished responses than did those discouraged on an intermittent schedule.

Evidence that periodic punishment is more effective than regular punishment *

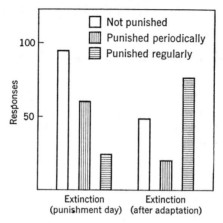

* The mean numbers of responses of three groups are shown, a control group extinguished in the usual manner, a group punished for responding whenever response occurred, and a group punished periodically, for responses occurring within every fourth minute of the forty-minute extinction period. Following the experimental day there were two adaptation days, when the animals were placed in the boxes with the levers retracted. The results for extinction are for the first day with the exposed lever, after these adaptation days. The adaptation period has almost completely eradicated the results of regular punishment, but the consequences of periodic punishment persist. Each group consisted of 6 rats. Data from Estes (1944), corrected for differences prior to extinction.

(Hilgard, 1956, p. 112)

It thus appears that partial reinforcement is more effective in stamping behavior either in or out. By the same token:

A11.4   Comparing the effects of various ratio schedules: the more frequent the reinforcement, the less frequent the response. (That is, the easier the payoff, the less the work.)

For example, one experiment compared response rates for rats that were reinforced every 16, 24, 32, 48, 64, 96, and 192 responses. (Such sparse reinforcement cannot be used in initial training but has to be approached gradually once the response is established.) The results are shown in the figure on page 153.

Note that in the third curve the rat on a 192-to-1 ratio is maintained at almost 1000 responses per hour, on a total of only five reinforcements during the hour.

These findings perhaps confirm folk wisdom on this topic. Every mother knows that one "yes" tends to undo many weeks of "no," that occasional acquiescence sustains requests at a high rate and through many unreinforced

Reinforcement at several fixed ratios *

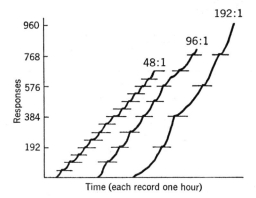

* The ratios are marked. Note the smooth accelerations between reinforcements (at horizontal lines).

(Skinner, 1938, p. 288)

trials. This principle may also underly the common observation that bad habits may be more difficult to break by cutting down than by quitting entirely.

There are two general lines of explanation for the greater strength of responses built on partial reinforcement. The first is the fact that fewer reinforcements during training make for greater similarity between the training series and the extinction situation. Following 100 per cent reinforcement, the extinction conditions of no reinforcement are easy to spot; but after a reinforcement ratio of 192 to 1, it takes at least 193 unreinforced responses before any difference actually occurs, and probably quite a few more before the difference becomes perceptible.

But beyond this there is the notion, now supported by experimental evidence as well as common observation, that a goal becomes more attractive as it becomes harder to attain or as more work has gone into it.

> Consider some person who is strongly attracted to some goal. It is quite reasonable for this person to be willing to expend more effort, or to endure more pain, in order to reach the goal than he would be if he were less attracted. . . . However, one finds the same process of reasoning in reverse. That is, if a person exerts a great deal of effort, or endures pain, in order to reach some ordinary objective, there is a strong tendency for him to persuade himself that the objective is especially valuable or especially desirable [Festinger, 1961, p. 2].

The author cites several experiments in evidence: in one of them, for example, girls who had endured embarrassment to gain admission to a group thought a tape-recorded meeting was more interesting and the girls more likable than did others who had gained easy access to the same group (Aronson and Mills, 1959).

Means of the sum of ratings for the different experimental conditions *

	Experimental conditions		
Rating scales	Control; no embarrassment (N = 21)	Mild embarrassment (N = 21)	Severe embarrassment (N = 21)
Discussion (9)			
M	80.2	81.8	97.6
Participants (8)			
M	89.9	89.3	97.7
Total (17)			
M	166.7	171.1	195.3

* The higher the rating, the higher the subject's evaluation of the group or the discussion.

(*Ibid.*, p. 179)

Or, again, rats required to press hard on a panel separating them from food made more unreinforced attempts once the food was removed than did those for whom the door had opened more easily (Aiken, 1957).

Furthermore, a study comparing extinction rates for animals trained on various reinforcement schedules found that the tenacity of response is much more closely related to the sheer number of unreinforced trials invested in training than to the reinforcement ratio per se.

> If one looks carefully at all the data, I think one finds reasonable evidence that insufficient reward does lead to the development of extra preference. . . . It seems clear that the inclination to engage in behavior after extrinsic rewards are removed is not so much a function of past rewards themselves. Rather, and paradoxically, such persistence in behavior is increased by a history of non-rewards or inadequate rewards. I sometimes like to summarize all this by saying that rats and people come to love things for which they have suffered [Festinger, 1961, p. 11].

None of this, of course, is to say that people—or rats, for that matter—prefer the hard to the easy way when both are available. The point is rather that when effort has been expended in the pursuit of a goal, that in itself can enhance its attractiveness. Another experiment clarifies the distinction. When rats are given their choice of two pathways to food, one easy and one difficult, they naturally choose the former. But rats trained only in the difficult pathway make more unreinforced trials once the food has been removed than do those who have run only the easier road.

A11.5   Response rates become even more stable, and behavior more resistant to extinction, if reinforcement is inconsistent; that is, if it varies in rate or in interval.

Instead of reinforcing on a fixed ratio, the experimenter may vary the ratio around an average value. Under such conditions, the dips immediately after reinforcement (as on page 153) flatten out, and an extremely high and consistent rate is maintained.

A11.5a   Extremely tenacious behavior is created by schedules with variable intervals—where reinforcement may be delivered one time after five minutes, the next time after twelve, then after two, and so on.

Here, for example, a pigeon pecks steadily at a rate of more than once per second during a nine-hour session with variable reinforcement, as shown by the small horizontal ticks. Each segment of the line represents a thousand responses, showing a total of almost forty thousand pecks for the nine-hour session.

Sustained performance on variable interval
during a nine-hour session

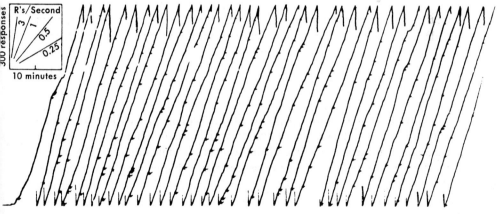

(Ferster and Skinner, 1957, p. 339)

As a matter of fact, pigeons have given as many as ten thousand *un*-reinforced responses after training on such a variable-interval schedule.

Probably not that effective is the slot machine, which is often cited as a device that utilizes a variable reinforcement schedule to produce human responses highly resistant to extinction, regardless of the over-all cost. In fact, a player may be especially hesitant to change machines after a losing streak ("the machine is due")—an interesting parallel between "thinking" human behavior and the behavior of rats and pigeons.

A11.6   The limiting case of inconsistent reinforcement is a schedule entirely unrelated to the subject's behavior—i.e., rewards introduced arbitrarily or at random.

By the same laws of instrumental conditioning, such schedules can produce what we would call superstitious behavior in lower animals as well as in human beings.

> Suppose we give a pigeon a small amount of food every fifteen seconds regardless of what it is doing. When the food is first given, the pigeon will be behaving in some way—if only standing still—and conditioning will take place. It is then more probable that the same behavior will be in progress when the food is given again. If this proves to be the case, the "operant" will be further strengthened. If not, some other behavior will be strengthened. Eventually, a given bit of behavior reaches a frequency at which it is often reinforced. It then becomes a permanent part of the repertoire of the bird even though the food has been given by a clock which is unrelated to the bird's behavior. Conspicuous responses which have been established in this way include turning sharply to one side, hopping from one foot to the other and back, bowing and scraping, turning around, strutting, and raising the head [Skinner, 1953, p. 85].

Note the conspicuous human responses perhaps established in the same way: rain dances, outfielders touching third base on the way to the dugout, men carrying "lucky" charms to the gambling table or on a bombing mission. This relation, more than analogy, illustrates the kind of connection the field hopes to develop between animal experiments and human behavior. Here, the results of simple experiments with rats and pigeons appear applicable to such a complex psychological phenomenon as human superstition. They suggest conditions under which such behavior develops: a reinforcer not under the control of the subject but dependent on the whims of the "experimenter" (in the human case, fate, chance, any unknown natural forces). They also seem to explain why superstitions last, why people do not "learn better" in the face of objective evidence that the superstitious ritual does not work. The more frequent the rain dance, the greater the chance that it *will* be reinforced some of the time. And according to the findings on reinforcement schedules, a single reinforcement is worth many unreinforced trials. Not only that, but the less frequently reinforcement occurs, the greater the tolerance for failure. According to this analysis, such superstitions persist largely *because* they work infrequently and sporadically, not in spite of that fact.

COMPLEX SKILLS

Although the preceding findings on conditioning may have far-reaching theoretical and practical implications, they deal directly with rather small and isolated units of behavior—saliva flow, bar pressing, and so on—mostly on the part of rats and pigeons. Now we move to studies of the acquisition of more complex human skills, such as riding a bicycle, typing, or reciting (but not necessarily understanding) a poem. These actions involve elaborate chains of habitual responses, and each of the links may be subject to the laws of classical and/or instrumental conditioning; hence, in principle, the entire process may ultimately be understood as conditioning. The following findings, however, speak more directly as to how and when, rather than why, skills develop.

With respect to the rate of acquisition, normally represented by a learning curve that plots success against the practice time or the number of trials:

A12   The most commonly observed rate of acquisition of complex skills is negatively accelerated: that is, learning is rapid at first but then the rate of improvement decreases and finally levels off.

Here is the classical example, a student's progress in learning to send telegraphic code.

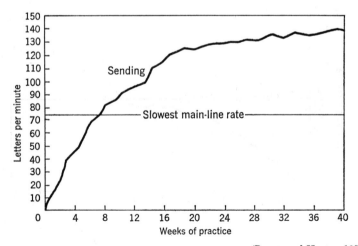

(Bryan and Harter, 1897, p. 49)

A12.1   Another common form of learning curve is S-shaped, with learning slow at first, then picking up in rate, and finally falling off in the typical way:

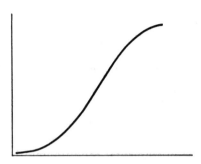

Such curves have been observed in classical conditioning and in memorizing as well as in the development of skills. Indeed, some psychologists believe that this is the *basic* learning curve, and that the preceding negatively accelerated curve represents merely the second half of an underlying S-shaped curve, the first part of which was missed by the experiment because the skill being taught drew on some previous skill.

A12.2   Learning curves often exhibit plateaus, or periods of relative standstill, before improvement resumes.

Here is an illustrative plateau in learning to receive telegraphic code, from the original study cited above:

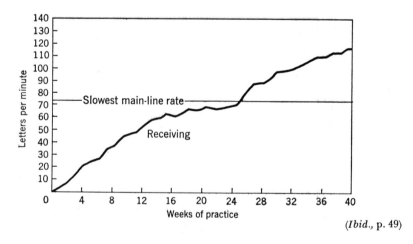

(*Ibid.*, p. 49)

There are two general explanations. First, a plateau may represent a pause between two successive stages of "sophistication" in the skill—so, for example, a plateau may occur when a subject reaches the limits of his ability to receive code or to type letter by letter but has not as yet begun to respond word by word. Further, the lower-order skill may actually conflict with—and therefore retard—learning of the higher-order skill. In such cases, then, plateaus are simply dividing points between two successive learning curves. Second, plateaus may reflect a temporary loss of motivation, when initial enthusiasm is dulled by the routine of practice.

Next, with respect to the most efficient allocation of practice time,

A13   Most generally, periods of practice separated by periods of rest achieve much more efficient learning than do longer periods of practice with few or no interruptions.

In other words, an hour of learning time divided into six ten-minute sessions will usually be more productive than a solid hour—with the qualification that each period of practice must be long enough to allow at least one or two complete trials, or runs, through the task. Practice periods cannot be so short as to break up the task into meaningless segments. For example, it is not efficient to learn to drive a car in a series of one-minute lessons.

Here is an illustration taken from a study of how people learn to trace a pattern when all they can observe is the mirror image of what they are doing:

An illustration from learning to trace a pattern by mirror image

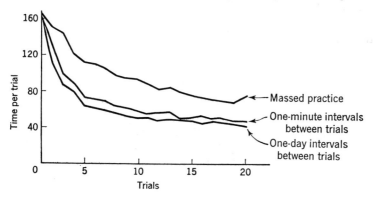

(Lorge, 1930, p. 16)

This superiority of distributed over massed practice is not confined to the learning of skills, but has been observed in a wide variety of learning situations, from simple instrumental conditioning through rote memorizing to the study of symbolic materials.

Memorizing lists of nonsense syllables: massed versus distributed practice in relation to length of list learned *

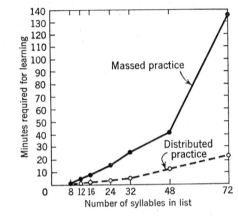

* Mean number of minutes required for learning by massed and distributed practice with varying lengths of lists of nonsense syllables. It is especially important to distribute practice with long lists. (Data from D. O. Lyon, as summarized by C. L. Hull *et al.*, *Mathematico-Deductive Theory of Rote Learning*, Yale U. Press, 1940, p. 131.)

(Hovland, 1948, p. 157)

TRANSFER OF TRAINING

To what extent does the learning of one skill help or hinder the learning of a subsequent one? If the old and new are identical, as in successive practice sessions with the same typing lesson, there is obviously a positive carry-over. At the other extreme, if the old and the new situation have nothing in common, there is obviously no effect in either direction. Many situations obviously fall somewhere in between, and it is to this middle range in which old and new are similar, in some, but only in some, respects that the concept of transfer of training refers.

As we have seen, habitual skills involve learned associations between a certain set of stimuli (e.g., a red traffic light, the letter "*a*") and the responses appropriate to them (foot on the brake, finger on the right typewriter key). Since old and new stimuli, as well as old and new responses, can be in varying degrees similar, the findings regarding transfer are in general consistent with simple conditioning principles.

A14   If the new skill presents stimuli that are similar or identical to those in a previous learning situation, and the stimuli demand similar or identical responses, high positive transfer usually results: i.e., learning of the new skill progresses more rapidly than it would if the situation were totally new (e.g., learning motorcycling after bicycling). However, if the new stimuli are identical with the old but require similar *but not* identical responses, then there is only slight positive transfer: the learning situation is so close to the old one that the previous response tends to persist.

A15   If the new situation presents stimuli that are similar or identical to those in a previous learning situation but demands dissimilar or opposite responses, negative transfer results; the previous response persists and retards acquisition of the new one. (For example, learning to type on a typewriter with a rearranged keyboard or to drive a car with brake and accelerator reversed.)

Furthermore, the old responses are likely to reappear even after the new ones have been mastered, and under the worst possible circumstances. Thus, in times of crisis or under stress, people may abandon present or new modes of coping with problems and revert to earlier patterns. For example, seasoned pilots have crashed when, in an emergency, they reverted to responses learned earlier and appropriate in former airplanes but disastrous with the present control system. (When a plane is landing dangerously "low and slow," left hand forward, on the throttle, and right hand back, on the stick, is the appropriate emergency response; but when the throttle is in the right hand, and the stick in the left, as in many aircraft, that response produces a power-off dive instead of a full-power climb.)

A16   If the new skill involves stimuli dissimilar to the old but requires similar responses, slight positive transfer results: learning is somewhat faster, but not much.

In this last case, the subject already knows what to do and how to do it —all he has to learn is where and when. Learning another meaning for a word or a new application of a principle is somewhat easier than learning the word or the initial application of the principle.

These findings have been documented systematically only with respect to learning associations between pairs of nonsense syllables (Bruce, 1933); but each, singly, has been observed in other learning situations, so that they probably constitute fairly general principles of transfer, at least within the realm of habitual skills. In brief summary, here are the basic findings:

| | *Stimuli* | |
Response	*Similar*	*Dissimilar*
Similar	High positive effect (except for identical/similar pairs, in which case effect is slight)	Slight positive effect
Dissimilar	Negative effect	No effect

In accordance with these general principles is the special case of transfer of training in academic disciplines. There is no evidence to confirm an old rationale for the study of subjects such as Latin or geometry. Apparently the study of formal disciplines does not develop general mental skills or faculties that are then automatically transferred to other subject areas. In a classical study, for example, with intelligence held constant, students of mathematics were not significantly more logical or reasonable in their approach to other problems than were students without mathematical training (Thorndike, 1924).

> The results . . . are in pronounced opposition to the traditional view that certain subjects produce much more general improvement in ability to think than others, and that among the subjects taught in high schools, languages and mathematics are the two that do this to the greatest degree.
>
> If we take, on the one hand, our Groups V (Algebra or Geometry or Trigonometry) and VI (Latin and French, which it will be remembered made the better showing of the two), and, on the other, our Group VIII (Cooking, Sewing, and Stenography), the best estimate of the greater gain in ability to think, due to spending a quarter of one's time during a high school year upon the former rather than the latter, is a little under 2½ points [composite score on tests of "general intelligence"]. This is only a quarter of the greater gain that one makes during a year by being white rather than colored, is less than the greater gain that one makes by being a high school boy rather than a high school girl in these cities, the subjects taken being identical! We find notable differences in gain in ability to think as measured by these tests but they do not seem to be due to what one studies [*ibid.*, pp. 94–95].

But if similarities between the content of one subject and another are explicitly taught, if the subjects contain identical elements (e.g., cognate words in several languages), or if general principles and their broad applicability are stressed in teaching, then the experience gained in study *is* more likely to be generalized to other appropriate subject areas. For example, stressing the derivation of English words in the study of Latin does increase English vocabulary (Haskell, 1923); and making explicit the principles behind the skill of shooting at underwater targets measurably improves the ability to transfer the skill when water depth is changed (Hendrickson and Schroeder, 1941).

In short, mental exercise in itself does not necessarily stretch mental capacities for automatic application to whatever tasks are encountered later, as does physical exercise.

RETENTION

Rote memorizing helps to bridge the gap between habit formation and thinking. In its simplest form, rote memorizing is simply the formation of chains of stimulus-response associations—and sometimes that is all or virtually all there is to the matter, as in the memorizing of nonsense syllables or a foreign lyric. When the content has no meaning for the subject, such recitiation is simply a habit of the vocal machinery, learned through repeated trials according to the laws of habit formation. More often, however, people have at least some understanding of what is being learned, and then memorization is affected, for better or worse, by the meaning of the material. Few people, for example, are likely to recall that Columbus discovered America in 1942. On the other hand, errors may actually be introduced if they "make more sense" than the original material, and conscious thought often interferes with the smooth operation of a habit chain. In reciting a poem or lyric, for example, a running start may carry a learner through a sticky or difficult passage more efficiently than thinking about what comes next.

Experiments with memorizing materials of varying degrees of meaning, from nonsense syllables to the richest symbolic material, yield these general findings:

A17 The amount of nonmeaningful materials memorized after successive learning trials increases according to the negatively accelerated curve typical for habitual skills.

Once learned, such material is forgotten according to the same pattern: much loss very quickly, with the rate of loss tapering off when most of the material has been forgotten.

A17.1 In some instances, however, there may actually be a slight gain in retention before the loss begins to set in; that is, more is remembered after a little while than immediately following the learning trials.

This phenomenon is known as "reminiscence" and can also occur in the acquisition of physical skills. Here is an example of reminiscence after rote memorization of nonsense syllables:

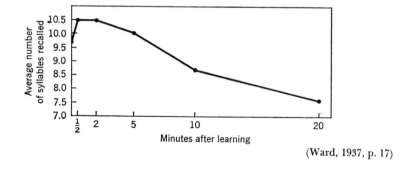

(Ward, 1937, p. 17)

A18   The beginning and the end of a series of items are memorized much more quickly than items in the middle (the "serial-position effect").

Here are the number of errors made by students in memorizing nonsense syllables and meaningful words:

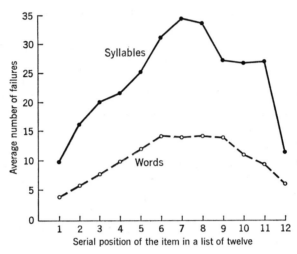

(Postman and Rau, 1957, p. 236)

This effect is probably a specific case of the more general finding:

A19   Materials that are isolated in memory—not followed or preceded by similar materials—are retained longer.

If *A* is originally learned to the same level of proficiency:

Time 1: Learning	*Time 2: Retention Test*
learns *A*	most recall for *A*
first learns *A'* learns *A*	less recall for *A* ("proactive inhibition")
learns *A*, then learns *A'*	least recall for *A* ("retroactive inhibition")

This is true for meaningful as well as nonmeaningful materials. And:

A19.1   The more similar in meaning the interposed materials are (short of identical), the more pronounced the inhibiting effects.

Recall the principles of negative transfer: similar responses may be "imported" inappropriately from one set of materials to the other. Says one summary:

If one of the determining conditions of proactive inhibition is transfer of training, our previous discussion of the conditions of negative transfer would lead us to expect that one of the most important conditions of proactive inhibition would be the similarity (formal or meaningful) of the stimuli involved in the two lists to be learned. This is corroborated by the results of a number of experiments (Blankenship and Whitely, 1941; Melton and Von Lackum, 1941; and, by inference, Bugelski, 1942; Underwood, 1944) [McGeoch and Irion, 1952, p. 396].

As an interesting, and significant, special case:

A19.2   Sleep immediately following learning results in more retention than when the subject stays awake after learning (even if he then gets the same amount of sleep before the retention test).

					Saving in relearning (per cent) *
Group I (N=26)	Learn	Sleep	Relearn		82
Group II (N=26)	Learn	Sleep	Waking activity	Relearn	86
Group III (N=18)	Learn	Waking activity	Relearn		64
Group IV (N=16)	Learn	Waking activity	Sleep	Relearn	59

|←——8 hours——→| |←——8 hours——→|

* When sleep follows immediately after learning, retention is high (82–86 per cent), regardless of whether the sleep is followed by waking activity before relearning. When learning is followed by waking activity, retention is less (64–59 per cent), regardless of whether sleep intervenes before the test of retention. The results show Group I to have higher savings (i.e., retention) than Group III, and Group II to have higher savings than Group IV, with equal elapsed time in each comparison. These results are statistically significant.

(Hilgard, 1962, p. 313, after McGaugh and Hostetter, 1961)

These findings, plus the general proposition that interspersed study periods produce more rapid memorization than do massed sessions, suggest that some sort of consolidation occurs after practice, and that other, similar learning interferes with it to some extent.

A20   With verbal materials, reading coupled with active recitation leads to much more efficient memorizing than reading only.

Given any amount of study time, it seems worthwhile to spend a large portion of it in recitation when the object is to memorize. A classical investigation reports that even if as much as 80 per cent of the total time for memorizing nonsense syllables is devoted to recitation, more learning occurs than if the entire time is devoted to reading:

Percent of time devoted to self-recitation (remainder to reading)	Percent of sixteen nonsense syllables recalled	
	Immediately	After four hours
0	35	15
20	50	26
40	54	28
60	57	37
80	74	48

(Gates, 1917, as adapted by Hilgard, 1962, p. 305)

Similar findings hold for memorizing meaningful passages (*ibid.*), foreign vocabulary (Seibert, 1932), and even spelling and arithmetic (Forlano, 1936). However, the advantage of recitation diminishes as the material becomes more meaningful and/or as the response involves comprehension.

This again documents, and probably partly depends on, the fact that much of what is learned in such rote memorization is mainly vocal habit rather than understanding of content. (Although we shall see later that simply reciting one side's arguments in a partisan debate tends to commit the reciter to that position.) And of course, memorizing also draws on understanding when there is meaning in the materials involved:

A21   Meaningful material is easier to memorize than nonmeaningful material; and once learned, it is retained longer.

For example, word lists are learned faster than lists of nonsense syllables; and nonsense syllables that approximate or suggest words are learned faster than those that do not (McGeoch, 1930). Similarly, as everyone knows, the essential meaning of a passage is retained long after the ability to recite it verbatim is lost.

Some representative curves comparing retention of general substance, specific facts, and nonsense are shown in the figure on page 167.

Two basic effects of meaning on memory can be distinguished, corresponding to the two basic meanings of "meaning":

Meaning as previous familiarity: The fact that words are easier to memorize than nonsense syllables says little more than that it is easier to learn something that is already known, or that resembles something already known, than it is to start from scratch.

Meaning as pattern: The series 2–7–12–17–22–27–32 is more easily learned than the series 2–8–4–7–6–14–3, not because of greater familiarity with the first set of digits, but because there is a pattern in the first that, in effect, re-

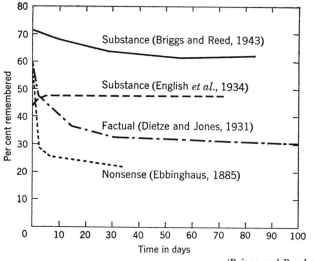

(Briggs and Reed, 1943, p. 514)

duces the amount of material that has to be retained. One need only remember: start with two and go up by fives, whereas in the second case nothing can substitute for actually memorizing all the digits. There is literally no limit to the number of digits in the patterned series that can be learned, i.e., reproduced at will; but how many digits in an unpatterned series can be reproduced?

Strictly speaking, of course, learning the first series by its pattern is not memorizing the series at all but only understanding the pattern and memorizing that. Such learning is not simply a matter of verbal habit formation—it depends on thinking: the pattern is not discerned gradually, by trial-and-error approximations, but in one step of understanding or not at all.

Habits, then, do not *require* understanding, either for their establishment or in their execution (although thinking may accompany both). They are learned gradually, through repeated trials, according to smooth and fairly predictable learning curves; and they deteriorate in the same way.

Some recent experiments do suggest that the primary unit of habit formation—the simple association between two stimuli or between a stimulus and a response—can be learned in one trial, in an all-or-nothing fashion. One important study showed that when subjects learned a series of paired associates (pairs of nonsense syllables or letter-number combinations), repeated exposure was not necessary for mastery. They either learned or failed to learn an association on any single given run through a series of such pairs. Thus:

Although repetition has long been regarded as essential in associative learning, there is some doubt as to how it achieves its beneficial effects. One possibility is that, in learning a list of items, the strength of association between each pair develops gradually, with each repetition adding an increment to the bond, until it is so strong that the first item produces recall of the second. According to this interpretation, repetition is a factor in the *formation* of associations. Another possibility is that repetition is essential because only a limited number of associations can be formed on any one trial. . . .

In two experiments, the learning of paired associates was studied. In each case, the traditional procedure was used for a control group, while for the experimental group unlearned pairs were removed and new ones submitted after each trial. No significant differences in rate of learning were found. This result suggests that repetition plays no role in the formation (as distinct from the strengthening) of associations, other than that of providing the occasion for new ones to be formed, each on a single trial [Rock, 1957, pp. 186, 193].

Nevertheless, important as this finding is for the theoretical analysis of the learning process, it does not deny the necessity for repetitive trials in the learning of more complex skills that involve chains of associations, nor the gradual acquisition pattern for such skills.

Thinking

By contrast, understanding or the attainment of meaning as it occurs in ordinary symbolic learning (reading a book or listening to a lecture) is not necessarily acquired gradually, through a series of ever closer approximations. And it does not require memorization (though again, some memorizing of the sentences in a passage may accompany the acquisition of its meaning). In thinking about a problem or a passage—or even in the perception of a complex or ambiguous figure—people frequently go from complete befuddlement to total solution, apparently in one invisible step (the "Aha!" phenomenon). Once attained, such understanding or insight does not degenerate gradually, as habits do.

That brings us to consideration of the symbolic thought process, certainly the most important form of human learning—and the hardest to study. Again, as in the preceding section, we go from the simpler or more measurable findings to the more complicated.

PHYSIOLOGICAL CORRELATES

The first and perhaps most direct question one can ask about the apparently invisible process of thinking is this: When people think, what movements or changes occur that are *visible* to the naked eye or to instruments? In other words, what is revealed by a close look at man thinking?

B1   In man, most forms of thinking depend upon the cerebral cortex; and damage to the cortex is invariably accompanied by corresponding deterioration or loss of various mental capacities.

The behavioral effects of total cortical loss are impossible to observe in man, since man cannot survive without the cortex. But partial damage produces partial loss of thought functions. For example, damage to the temporal (side) lobes frequently causes loss of memory for the meaning of familiar objects ("psychic blindness"). And speech seems to be centered unequally in one or the other half of the cortex (related to handedness), so that loss of certain functions of language and meaning (aphasia) is associated with temporal-lobe damage in the dominant hemisphere.

More specifically, with respect to the localization of various thought functions *within* the cerebral cortex:

B2   The higher the animal, the greater the cortical specificity. In man, specific thought functions are more likely to be dependent on particular cortical areas than in monkeys; in monkeys, more so than in rats; and so on.

A classical study found that in rats the degree of deterioration in learned skills and in the ability to reacquire them after brain damage corresponds mainly to the extent, not the location, of the injury. The evidence indicated that even if learning had previously resided in a now-damaged area, other portions could take over in the relearning (Lashley, 1929). In human beings, however, such substitutability is apparently far less extensive. Naturally, there is no experimental evidence on the effects of controlled, systematic brain destruction. The evidence comes from relatively few brain-injured persons, but it does suggest some specificities, as mentioned above.

In addition, some of the cortical areas that receive sensory impulses from various receptors have been "mapped," as have some centers that initiate orders to various muscles (although there is some evidence that such orders may at times originate from other places). Such a "cortical map" appears at the top of page 170.

Beyond cortical activity, thinking also involves and may depend upon a variety of lower nerve centers as well as some muscular activity:

B3   A general increase in muscle tone characteristically accompanies and even tends to facilitate thinking: the more concentrated the thought, the greater the general muscular tension.

Conversely:

With progressive muscular relaxation—not alone imagery, but also attention—recollection, thought-processes and emotion gradually diminish. . . . We find . . . the experience of muscular tenseness a *sine qua non* of imagery, attention and thought-process [Jacobson, 1938, pp. 188, 186].

B3.1   Tension has been recorded in specific muscles that are entirely unrelated to the content of the thought.

Cortical function *

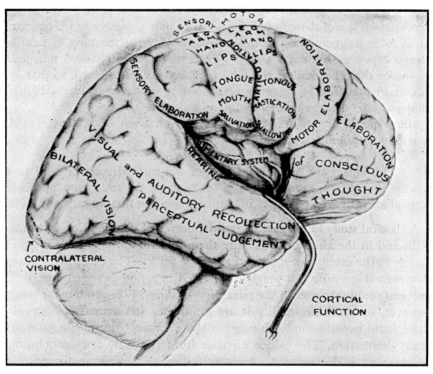

* This illustration serves as a summary restatement of conclusions, some hypothetical (e.g., the elaboration zones), others firmly established. The suggestion that the anterior portion of the occipital cortex is related to both fields of vision rather than to one alone is derived from the results of stimulation.

(Penfield and Rasmussen, 1950, p. 206)

For instance, an increase in muscular tension in the leg "almost invariably" accompanied elementary mental activity such as working arithmetic problems or jigsaw puzzles (Freeman, 1930).

More than that, there is even some evidence that:

B3.2   Artificially induced muscular tension facilitates some forms of learning.

Up to a point, subjects learned nonsense syllables more efficiently when muscular tension was induced by having them squeeze a spring-loaded grip; but when they were squeezing nearly as hard as they could, memorization performance fell below normal (Courts, 1939).

B4   Much thinking is accompanied by overt or latent movement in the specific muscles related to the thought content. ("Latent movement" refers to tiny muscular reactions not visible to the eye but revealed by electrical "action potentials" recorded via attached or implanted electrodes.)

B4.1 Action potentials and appropriate microscopic contractions occur in the muscles of body parts that subjects are told to imagine moving.

The location of the action potentials corresponds to the type of imagery. That is, if subjects are asked to *visualize* bending the right arm, potentials occur in the occular region; when asked to imagine *actually* bending it, the potential occurs in the arm (Jacobson, 1932).

Action potentials recorded in arm muscles involved in imagined activity

The subject, previously trained to relax, has been instructed, "Upon hearing the first signal, imagine lifting a ten-pound weight in the right forearm. Upon hearing the second signal, relax any muscular tensions, if present."

Conditions the same as for (other) figure. The instruction has been, "Imagine hitting a nail twice with a hammer held in your right hand." Between signal marks, two series of long vertical lines, indicating action potentials, are seen, separated by an interval of practically horizontal line, indicating relaxation.

(Jacobson, 1938, p. 330)

B4.2 Subvocal speech accompanies some but not all thinking.

Minute and rudimentary movements occur "in at least some of the muscles which would participate when the same words or numbers are actually whispered or uttered aloud" (Jacobson, 1938, as cited in Krech and Crutchfield, 1958, p. 474). This has been demonstrated with subjects thinking about poems, arithmetic problems, or even such abstract notions as "eternity." Similarly:

B4.3 Deaf subjects who talk with their hands produce action potentials in their arms and hands while dreaming. Much larger and more frequent action potentials of a manual nature are also recorded while such deaf people solve abstract intellectual problems—the harder the problem, the greater the potential—or even while making a "verbal" gesture such as nodding the head.

By way of control, there is little difference in manual potentials between deaf and hearing subjects when they imagine manual tasks. This result tends to confirm the verbal character of the potentials observed during dreams or thinking (Max, 1935).

There is even some evidence to the effect that, at least among children, observable speech movements during silent reading facilitate understanding of the material. Children of lower intelligence engage in this practice far more frequently than those who are bright; but at each level, those with speech movements achieved higher understanding than those without.

Silent reading and understanding, with and without speech movements (percentages)

Intelligence grade	Silent reading		Understanding	
	With speech movements	Without speech movements	With speech movements	Without speech movements
1	47.66	53.34	88.89	60.00
2	68.18	31.82	60.00	42.86
3	75.00	25.00	70.83	37.50
4	92.85	7.15	38.46	
5	100.00	0.00	7.69	

(Schilling, 1929, pp. 221–22)

The conclusion is that "the motor activity is a help in the understanding of what is read, a help of which the pupil makes more use, the lower his intelligence is" (*ibid.*, p. 222).

More recent studies, using sensitive electrical measures to discern silent or "subvocal" speech not visible to the eye, confirm this general interpretation. One experiment tested and supported these three propositions:

A. Good readers engage in less silent speech than do poor readers.
B. The reading of an easy text results in less silent speech than does the reading of a difficult one.
C. The reading of a clear text results in less silent speech than does the reading of a blurred one [Edfeldt, 1960, p. 153].

Following is a sample record from a related experiment showing the increase in silent speech as material becomes more difficult:

Electric activity in the vocal muscle during reading

Subject: Sixty-nine-year-old woman with an I.Q. of 95. *A,* action-potential pattern from the left vocal muscle; *B,* microphone recording.

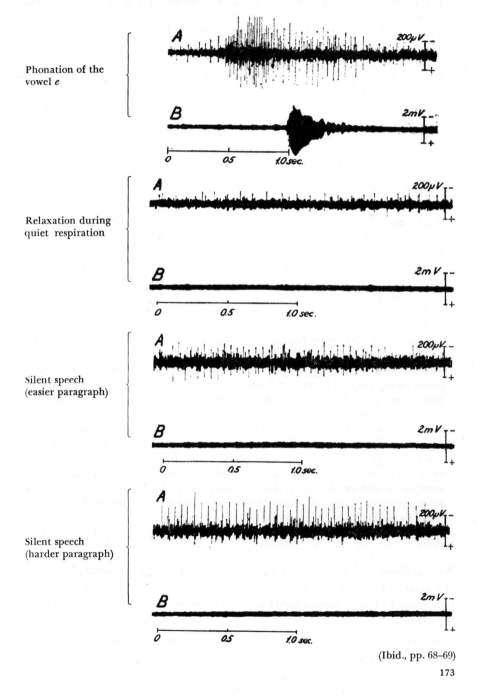

Phonation of the vowel *e*

Relaxation during quiet respiration

Silent speech (easier paragraph)

Silent speech (harder paragraph)

(Ibid., pp. 68–69)

173

The author concludes:

> It is evident that silent speech cannot be a habit which is, in itself, detrimental to the reading performance. It is a symptom of a reader's not being able to grasp the content of a text without difficulties. These difficulties may arise due to poor reading ability on the part of the reader or because the text has a low degree of understandability (i.e., is difficult in content) or of readability (i.e., is blurred, poor in typography or the like). Nothing definite can be said regarding whether silent speech actually constitutes an aid toward better reading comprehension, though it appears likely that it may do so. In any case, it seems quite clear that all kinds of training aimed at removing silent speech should be discarded. Although silent speech is a symptom of the fact that the reader is having difficulties in comprehending the text, the diagnostic value of this observation is still very doubtful (*ibid.,* p. 154).

By way of general summary on the role of muscular activity in thinking:

> It is fair to say that the picture is not yet clear. But from the mass of experiment which has been done to date on the relation of muscular activity to thinking, something like the following picture emerges. At the beginning of mental effort, there is in most people a widespread increase of muscular tension which rapidly drops to a level above that of rest. The resulting proprioceptive impulses [stimuli from the muscles] serve the function of general reinforcement to an increased cerebral activity. . . . During tasks which are difficult either *per se* or because of distraction, or during interruption of an accepted task, this tension is increased, thus providing the additional reinforcement necessary. This reinforcement apparently has an optimal range which varies from task to task and from individual to individual: if it rises above a certain stage, cerebral activity begins to be impeded by some mechanism as yet unknown. On the other hand, when the general bodily tonus falls below a certain stage, sleep may ensue, . . . although even during sleep there may apparently remain an irreducible minimum of general tonus. . . .
>
> Finally, there are conceivably still more specific changes of muscular tone, located in a part of the body specifically related to a particular thinking process. Possible examples are the changes observed by Jacobson during imagination or recollection of a manual activity; and also the changes occurring in the speech-musculature during verbal thinking which have been reported from many quarters. These, we have shown reason to believe, are probably facilitative in character also [Humphrey, 1951, pp. 214–15].

Finally, there are muscular correlates of mental activity even during sleep:

B5   Although dreams are *not* ordinarily "acted out" muscularly, rapid eye movements during sleep *are* associated with periods of dreaming; and they tend to reflect the dreamer's observation of the activity going on in the dream.

Subjects awakened during periods of observed eye movements report that they have been dreaming; those awakened while still-eyed do not.

Instances of dream recall after awakenings during periods of
rapid eye movements or periods of no rapid eye movements

Subject	Rapid eye movements		No rapid eye movements	
	Dream recall	No recall	Dream recall	No recall
DN	17	9	3	21
IR	26	8	2	29
KC	36	4	3	31
WD	37	5	1	34
PM	24	6	2	23
KK	4	1	0	5
SM	2	2	0	2
DM	2	1	0	1
MG	4	3	0	3
Total numbers	152	39	11	149

(Dement and Kleitman, 1957, p. 341)

The discovery of eye movements as a reliable indication of dreaming
paved the way for studies of dreaming itself. Such studies have produced
several interesting findings and upset some widespread beliefs.

B5.1   All the people studied dreamed every night—not just once, but
an average of four or five times.

B5.2   Dreams are not instantaneous but average twenty minutes each
and consume very close to 20 per cent of sleeping time; in fact, dream
time is usually realistic, i.e., the elapsed time within the dream roughly
matches the duration of the action itself.

A very much greater amount of dreaming occurs normally than had heretofore
been realized—greater both from the standpoint of frequency and duration in a
single night of sleep and in the invariability of its occurrence from night to
night. In other words, dreaming appears to be an intrinsic part of normal sleep
and, as such, . . . occurs every night in every sleeping person [Dement, 1960,
p. 1705].

If these findings are hard to believe, it is because:

B5.3   Most people do not recall all their dreams in the morning; when
a dream is remembered, it tends to be one that was dreamed later in the
night.

On the other hand, the notion that dreams serve some useful or even necessary function *is* supported:

B5.4   Subjects kept from dreaming by being awakened whenever eye movements signaled the onset of a dream became irritable and anxious in a matter of days, made progressively more frequent attempts to dream, and dreamed much longer during the first few nights of the recovery period, free of interference. The same subjects, awakened an equal number of times during nondreaming sleep, showed no such effects.

Subject	BASE-LINE NIGHTS *Per cent of time spent dreaming*	*Dream deprivation nights (number)*	FIRST DEPRIVATION RECOVERY NIGHT *Per cent of time spent dreaming*	FIRST CONTROL RECOVERY NIGHT *Per cent of time spent dreaming*
WT	10.5	8	34.0	18.0
HS	18.8	7	34.2	22.7
NW	19.5	5	17.8	20.2
BM	18.6	5	26.3	18.8
RG	19.3	5	29.5	26.3
WD	20.8	4	29.0	
SM	17.9	4	19.8	16.8
WG	20.8	3		

(Dement, 1960, p. 1707)

Psychological disturbances such as anxiety, irritability, and difficulty in concentrating developed during the period of dream deprivation, but these were not catastrophic. [However,] one subject . . . quit the study in an apparent panic, and two subjects insisted on stopping one night short of the goal of five nights of dream deprivation, presumably because the stress was too great. At least one subject exhibited serious anxiety and agitation. . . . The psychological changes disappeared as soon as the subjects were allowed to dream. The most important fact was that *none* of the observed changes were seen during the period of control awakenings.

The results have been tentatively interpreted as indicating that a certain amount of dreaming each night is a necessity. It is as though a pressure to dream builds up with the accruing dream deficit during successive dream-deprivation nights—a pressure which is first evident in the increasing frequency of attempts to dream and then, during the recovery period, in the marked increase in total dream time and percentage of dream time. The fact that this increase may be maintained over four or more successive recovery nights suggests that there is a more or less quantitative compensation for the deficit. It is possible that if the dream suppression were carried on long enough, a serious disruption of the personality would result [*ibid.*, p. 1707].

Another physical indicator of mental activity is the "brainwave." Electrodes attached to the surface of the scalp are able to record action potentials from the cerebral cortex that are then highly amplified and registered on a continuous graph to produce the electroencephalogram or EEG. Such records are particularly useful in diagnosing various types of brain damage, but they also provide information about the workings of the normal brain.

B6   As measured by EEG, the brain is constantly active—during relaxation, sleep, even moderate anesthesia.

A constant, underlying rhythm of about ten waves per second, characteristic of the normal EEG, is taken as the base-line measure of the spontaneous activity of the nerve cells in the cortex (termed the *alpha wave* or *alpha rhythm*—as on the "relaxed" record, below).

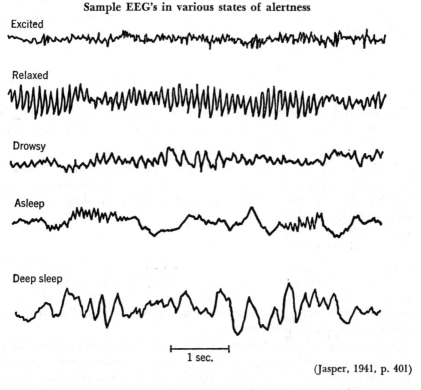

Sample EEG's in various states of alertness

Excited

Relaxed

Drowsy

Asleep

Deep sleep

1 sec.

(Jasper, 1941, p. 401)

B6.1   Conscious mental activity (such as mental arithmetic, or just attention or anticipation) reduces the amplitude of the alpha rhythm.

This is one reason why the alpha rhythm is assumed to represent spontaneous neural activity, which is interrupted or masked by external stimulation or selective brain activity.

B7   Some simple learning has been shown to be reflected in brain-wave changes.

An electrode attached to the visual area of the cortex records no noticeable effect of a sound stimulus. But after classical conditioning in which the onset of sound is repeatedly followed by a light, the sound alone produces the same EEG reaction from the visual cortex that the light previously elicited (Jasper and Shagass, 1941).

Thus EEG and measures of subvocal speech represent scientific approaches to "mind reading." Both register visible events that correlate to some extent with what is being thought, and thus they objectify—though still in a very rudimentary way—the study of the elusive but not metaphysical mind. Perhaps the most important nonclinical application of EEG records to date is in their use as reliable and objective indicators of varying states of consciousness, as illustrated above. This has made it possible, for example, to observe and record the stages of sleep without disturbing the subject. And experiments using this procedure have already yielded an important negative finding:

B8   Simple facts do not seem to be learned during sleep, when they are presented throughout the night by tape recording. Some learning does take place under these conditions, but EEG records reveal that all of it is attributable to the totally awake or drowsy period preceding sleep and not to the sleeping period itself.

In this case, for example, the only gain in knowledge from "sleep-learning," over a control group completely unexposed to the materials, occurred for those items presented *before* the real transition to sleep (see the chart on page 179).

SYMBOLIC MEMORY

Much thinking involves inner representations of the past—just *how* much depends on where the arbitrary line between present and past is drawn. This section deals with how experiences are "preserved" once the external stimuli are gone—how images and symbolic "traces" persist, change, and are manipulated over time.

As we saw, many associations and skills are learned and retained in ways that do not require symbolic representation: retention consists merely of the ability to duplicate or recite the correct habitual response. Here, we are concerned mainly with the retention of *meaning,* not of specific habitual responses; for example, the plot of a book or what happened last night.

B9   Other things equal, the longer since an experience, the harder it is to remember. But the rate of loss is not steady and continual (linear) with time.

As the following findings will document, there are periods of rapid loss and periods when memory "jells" and shows only slight deterioration; and

Percentage of answers recognized on multiple-choice test *

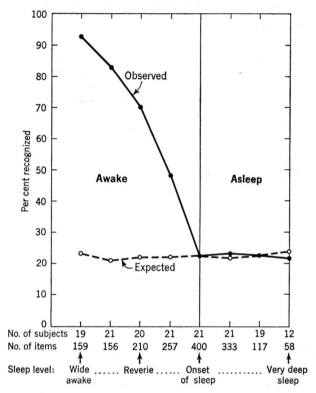

* Items were presented at varying levels along the continuum between a waking and deep sleep state. The expected value was that obtained from an untrained control group of comparable ability answering the same items.

(Simon and Emmons, 1956, p. 94)

the loss that does occur is not in the nature of passive decay but shows qualitative changes over time.

B10   Not all "forgotten" material is really gone; much of it can be and has been retrieved by various approaches.

B10.1   In hypnotic regression to an earlier age, subjects are able to recount the details of experiences long since "forgotten" in the normal state.

For example, in one study both control and experimental subjects were asked specific biographical facts associated with their school experiences at ages seven and ten: "What was the name of your second-grade teacher?" "Who sat in front of you in the fifth grade?" etc. The fifteen control subjects were asked again while simulating behavior at those ages, and the five experimental subjects were asked again while in the deep trance state of hypnosis and yet again after hypnotic regression to those ages. Here are data and conclusions:

Percentage scores of (credible) memories given by experimental subjects in the adult waking state and when regressed to ages ten and seven

| | Age ten | | Age seven | |
| | Adult | Re- | Adult | Re- |
Subject	waking	gressed	waking	gressed
A	14	57	0	86
B	14	57	0	86
C	21	86	14	100
D	57	71	43	100
E	29	64	29	100

Significance:
Age ten: t–4.89, $p < .01$ (4 degrees of freedom).
Age seven: t–13.4, $p < .01$.

(Reiff and Scheerer, 1959, p. 185)

Quantitatively the responses to our questionnaire indicate that when the experimental subjects were regressed to ages ten and seven, there was a statistically significant greater percentage score of memories than in the normal waking state. In contrast, there was no statistically significant increase in the percentage score of memories for the control subjects when they simulated ages ten and seven [*ibid.*, p. 186].

Similarly, people who left their country of birth at an early age and were reared in another can often speak, read, and write in the native tongue under hypnotic regression, although they have long ago "forgotten" it in the normal state. Even in the nonhypnotized subject, chains of associations started by some "clue" in the environment can often lead to the reconstruction of long "forgotten" experiences ("Where *did* I see that man before?"). The extensive free-association sessions of the psychoanalytic hour are an extreme case in point: the uninterrupted stream of associations may eventually bring back some very early (and presumably important) events. A less dramatic but more general demonstration is the simple fact that:

B10.2   Material previously learned and forgotten can be relearned with less effort than it took to learn it in the first place. This measure (the method of "savings") is the most sensitive indicator of retention, in that it will usually demonstrate some residual effects of earlier experiences even after other methods fail.

An extreme illustration was provided by a psychologist who read Greek passages to his baby every day for a three month period. When the boy was tested at the age of eight he was able to memorize those passages more quickly than others of equal length and difficulty (Burtt, 1941).*

Trials necessary for correct recitation, at age eight

Age in months at original reading (once daily, for three months)	Selection	Trials
15–18	III	382
18–21	VI	253
21–24	IX	385
24–27	XII	379
27–30	XV	328
30–33	XVIII	226
33–36	XXI	265
Average of control selections, learned new at age eight		435

(*Ibid.*, p. 437)

B11   In general, symbolic memory has the following life-span:

Shortest-lived "*hardest*"

(a) Unaided recollection (simply remembering what happened, without any external clues);

(b) Aided recall ("Remember what happened the night we went to so and so and X was there?");

(c) Recognition ("Haven't I seen you somewhere?");

Longest-lived "*easiest*"

(d) Savings ("I've forgotten what little bridge, calculus, etc., I ever knew, but I seem to be catching on faster this time.").

Most students, of course, are well aware that recognizing the right answer, as in multiple-choice tests, is easier than recalling it in response to an open-ended question. Actually, the first determinant of how well something is remembered is how strong the impression was in the first place. Formally:

B12   Other things equal, the better perceived and learned, according to the laws of perception and learning, the longer and/or more accurately material will be remembered.

But with initial impression constant, memory varies:

B12.1   Things important to remember are remembered better than things that do not make any difference ("importance" defined subjectively).

* This is perhaps a marginal case of "symbolic" retention, since the task at age eight was simply to learn by rote. Yet the infant did not recite the poetry—he just heard it—so whatever he retained must have been mental rather than vocal habit.

B12.2   Things pleasant or congenial to remember (not necessarily pleasant when they occurred) are remembered better than things unpleasant to remember (not necessarily unpleasant when they occurred).

Here is an illustration from the political scene. Pro- and anticommunist groups both learned congenial propaganda more rapidly, and forgot less of it, than was true of the equivalent counterpropaganda:

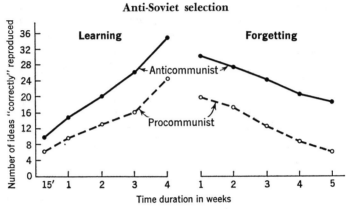

Anti-Soviet selection

(Levine and Murphy, 1943, p. 513)

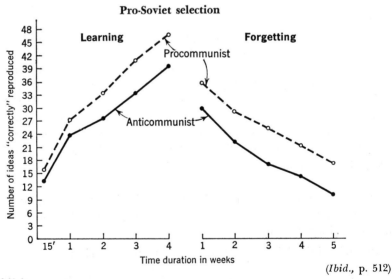

Pro-Soviet selection

(*Ibid.*, p. 512)

In addition:

B12.2a   There is some evidence that extremely unpleasant or "threatening" material is actively pushed *out* of conscious memory and is not recalled as well as neutral material.

This process, termed "repression," is discussed and documented later. Finally, as in the case of rote memorization:

B12.3   Events that stand in isolation are much better remembered than those followed by other events of a similar nature, and somewhat better remembered than events preceded by similar ones.

As noted above, memory typically becomes less accurate over time, but it does not exhibit regular, passive decay, like a fading photograph. When past experiences are recounted or reproduced at successive intervals:

B13   Remembered material undergoes systematic and meaningful changes reflecting, as in perception, tendencies to select, organize, and interpret in line with the determinants of these processes as outlined before.

Thus, for example, "meaningless" or "irrelevant" elements of the original material tend to be dropped out of reproductions; and, conversely, elements that would tend to make the material more meaningful or consistent may be invented and introduced in subsequent reproductions. Similarly, slightly incongruous or unusual elements may be eliminated or normalized in subsequent reproductions ("leveling") *or* they may be exaggerated ("sharpening").

Here is an illustration in the recall of simple figures:

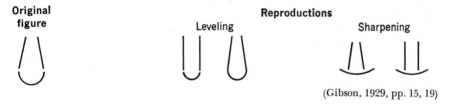

(Gibson, 1929, pp. 15, 19)

The same tendencies occur with respect to incongruous elements in remembering people, events, stories, and other more complex experiences. Sometimes a relatively minor, inconsistent aspect of the original scene is either eliminated in memory or becomes a main point of the story.

Along the same line, expectations introduced before original exposure to the material, as well as those that come into play subsequently, are often reflected in how material is remembered. In one study, for example, subjects were shown a series of simple yet ambiguous drawings, which they were asked to reproduce immediately after exposure. Each picture was preceded by a word announcing what was to be seen; labels were experimentally varied, as in the following table. The sample reproductions show that what was subsequently remembered moved in the direction of the induced expectation:

Reproduced figure	Word list I	Stimulus figures	Word list II	Reproduced figure

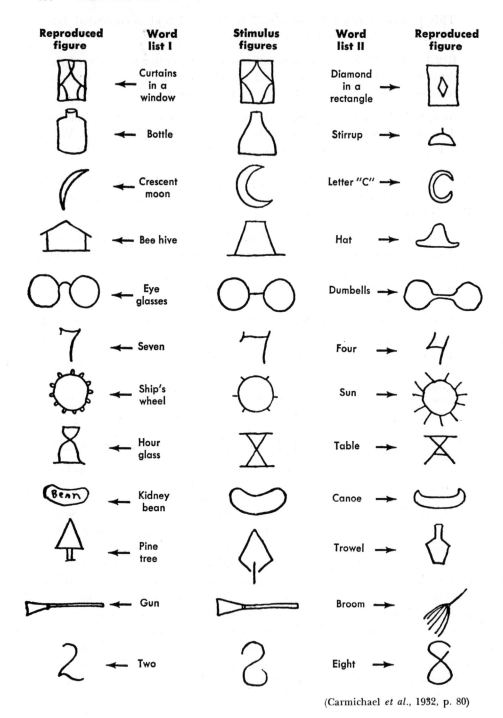

(Carmichael *et al.*, 1932, p. 80)

Figure	Per cent like figure named	
	LIST I	LIST II
1	47	78
2	100	69
3	65	48
4	69	75
5	45	81
6	87	94
7	54	47
8	83	100
9	90	63
10	86	100
11	76	85
12	87	40
Total per cent	74	73

(*Ibid.*, p. 81)

Finally, and by the same token, general social attitudes (e.g., stereotypes) influence memory, and the effects can by compounded by word-of-mouth communication, as in the spread of rumor. Here is an experimental demonstration using the familiar parlor-game design: one person describes a picture to another who passes on the information "as accurately as possible"

(Allport and Postman, 1945, p. 66)

to the next, and so on. A typical terminal report (the last in a chain of reproductions) was as follows: "This is a subway train in New York headed for Portland Street. There is a Jewish woman and a Negro who has a razor in his hand. The woman has a baby or a dog. The train is going to Deyer Street, and nothing much happened" (Allport and Postman, 1958, p. 57).

> What seems to occur in all our experiments and in all related studies is that each subject finds the outer stimulus-world far too hard to grasp and retain in its objective character. For his own personal uses, it must be recast to fit not only his span of comprehension and his span of retention, but, likewise, his own personal needs and interests. . . . Into the rumor, he projects the deficiencies of his retentive processes, as well as his own effort to engender meaning upon an ambiguous field, and the product reveals much of his own emotional needs, including his anxieties, hates, and wishes [Allport and Postman, 1945, p. 64].

In summary, then, qualitative changes in memory tend to comply with general perceptual principles: representations of the past, as of the present but even more so, tend to become more simple, more internally consistent, and more "stable figures" than they are in actuality; they also tend to conform to retroactive expectations and, to some extent, to the wishes of the subject.

Many such systematic changes in the "memory trace," and some others, were documented in a comprehensive and classic investigation of how British college students remembered a somewhat strange and therefore ambiguous story (an Indian folk tale), at successive times. The investigator's conclusions, now over thirty years old but still not obsolete, are worth quoting:

A Summary of the Main Conclusions Drawn from
The Method of Repeated Reproduction

1. It . . . appears that accuracy of reproduction, in a literal sense, is the rare exception and not the rule.

2. In a chain of reproductions obtained from a single individual, the general form, or outline, is remarkably persistent, once the first version has been given.

3. At the same time, style, rhythm, precise mode of construction, while they are apt to be immediately reacted to, are very rarely faithfully reproduced.

4. With frequent reproduction the form and items of remembered detail very quickly become stereotyped and thereafter suffer little change.

5. With infrequent reproduction, omission of detail, simplification of events and structure, and transformation of items into more familiar detail may go on almost indefinitely, or so long as unaided recall is possible.

6. At the same time, in long-distance remembering, elaboration becomes rather more common in some cases; and there may be increasing importation, or invention. . . .

7. Long-distance remembering is of two types at least:

    (a) The general setting, as expressed mainly through the subject's attitude to the material, continues to function, as also does outstanding detail.

The actual memory process is strongly and evidently constructive, and there is much use of inference.

(b) All that appears to function are one or two isolated but striking details.

8. Detail is outstanding when it fits in with a subject's pre-formed interests and tendencies. It is then remembered, though often transformed, and it tends to take a progressively earlier place in successive reproductions.

9. There is some indication . . . that, in some cases, the influence of affective attitude may be intensified with lapse of time.

10. In all successive remembering, rationalisation, the reduction of material to a form that can be readily and "satisfyingly" dealt with is very prominent [Bartlett, 1932, pp. 93–94].

The appearance of perceptual principles in memory is not accidental, since the dividing line between perception and memory is only a temporal one (that is, we perceive today and remember yesterday). It is, in fact, a moot question whether such qualitative changes actually occur "in" the memory trace itself (whether the picture changes, à la Dorian Grey) or whether the memory trace simply fades, with the changes noted in reproductions attributable to a perceptual process that scans these symbolic representations, finds them incomplete and ambiguous, and fills them in according to the ordinary perceptual assumptions.

Finally:

B14   Some people have a qualitatively different and quite remarkable capacity to retain literal, photographic images ("eidetic imagery").

Long after even a brief look at a picture or printed page, eidetic subjects can imagine it in minute detail. Here, for example, is a report of a woman's recount three months after she had seen this silhouette for sixty seconds:

(Klüver, 1926, p. 139)

S[ubject] sees the woman with the umbrella in her right hand. She is standing like that. (S indicates the position correctly.) "There is a fellow running with his car, his right foot in the air. There are some things on his car. The man at the right has lost his cigar; it has fallen nearly to the ground. There is a little man standing beside the woman. I do not see the white of his eye. To the right is a theatre. Above the door I see 'Entr.' At the left of the door there is a poster. Before the door there is a lantern pole. The globe appears to be in the form of a hexagon. I see the scissors very plainly. They point down to the ground. In the background there is a church. A row of trees can be seen to the left and in front of the church. There are three boys, playing marbles or something like that. (S indicates the position correctly.)" . . . (E[xperimenter] remarks: "Look at the woman!") "She looks like an old-fashioned woman. The skirt is running straight down. She has a kind of plume on her head. I see the pearl at her neck." ("Look at the man to the right!") "His stiff hat is falling down. The hat is entirely black." ("Draw this hat.") The drawing shows that S sees the opening of the hat in the same way as it is in the original picture [and so on for two more pages—*ibid.*, pp. 149–50].

As this instance shows, the eidetic's performance actually seems to scan a mental projection or photograph, rather than remember the picture in the ordinary sense. Hence, the term "photographic memory" may apply almost literally.

B14.1   Eidetic imagery is rare in adults—almost certainly less than 10 per cent—but it is more common among children.

Some students feel that such vivid and persistent images, in one form or another, are universal among children but are gradually lost with advancing age:

In Breslau, Fischer-Hirschberg (1924) found 99.3% (139 Eidetiker among 140). The acme of the eidetic gift was found to be between the twelfth and fourteenth year. In Vienna, H. Zeman (1925) found 88% (176 Eidetiker among 200). The acme was during the pre- and post-pubertal period. In Breslau as well as in Vienna a superiority of the female sex was discovered. The percentages, however, change considerably if the "latent" Eidetiker of Gottheil (1921) are excluded. In this case we have practically the same percentage in Vienna as found by Kroh in Marburg (1922): 61%; for Fischer-Hirschberg there remain 89.3% [Klüver, 1926, p. 79].

THE ELEMENTS AND VEHICLES OF THOUGHT

As we move toward the higher mental processes, we increasingly encounter the notion of images, symbols, and concepts as the elements of thought: inner representations of things, events, and relationships, or classes of them. The operational meaning of "inner representation" is best conveyed by the previous examples contrasting human symbolic behavior with the behavior of lower animals (p. 44). In essence, man can retain, organize, and manipulate the environment by reference to inner representations that stand for objects or events.

By way of introduction, the connection between the inner representation and what it stands for can be natural or arbitrary. An image is a natural representation, in that it embodies or recaptures some of the perceptual experiences actually associated with what it represents. Imagine a friend's face, a sunset, hot apple pie: the mind's eye (or nose) produces a more or less faithful account of what the physical eye and nose have experienced. On the other hand, the most important and most characteristically human form of thought employs symbolic representations that do not necessarily have anything in common with what they represent: the connection is purely arbitrary or conventional. Language is the single most important and most extensive such symbol system. When people think "in" words and sentences, as they often do when thinking alone (recall subvocal speech) and almost always do when thinking together, they manipulate representations ("cat," "x," "justice") that neither look, smell, or feel in any way like the things they stand for. (This form of manipulation actually involves two levels of symbolic representation. There is the inner thought "cat," which stands for the object, cat; and the printed or spoken word "cat," an *external* representation of that inner event. These levels are difficult to distinguish in ordinary language, and are often confounded in discourse. Our discussion of language as a system pertains to both levels in this representative process, as both steps require the same capacity to let one thing stand for another.)

Thus, most of the "higher" thought processes (e.g., reasoning as against recalling) employ arbitrary symbols as well as or instead of images and, most frequently, the language(s) of the thinker. In any case, even if the original thought is not symbolized in language, it must be verbalized before it can be communicated to others. (By language, we mean both the general language, e.g., English, and the specific language appropriate to the area of thought, e.g., mathematics, psychological terms, etc.) With regard to language:

B15   All races of men possess the physical, organic equipment needed to make the sounds used in any known language, so any normal person can learn to speak any language he is taught (especially if it is his first).

B15.1   All human languages, even those spoken by so-called primitive tribes, are complete, complex, and comparable.

Nowhere in the world has there been discovered a language that can validly and meaningfully be called "primitive." Edward Sapir wrote in 1921: "There is no more striking general fact about language than its universality. One may argue as to whether a particular tribe engages in activities that are worthy of the name of religion or of art, but we know of no people that is not possessed of a fully developed language. The lowliest South African Bushman speaks in the forms of a rich symbolic system that is in essence perfectly comparable to the speech of the cultivated Frenchman" [Hockett, 1960, p. 89].

But it is important to add that the comparability does not mean there is

> a set of pre-established universal ideas or meanings for which different languages merely have different tags. . . . [Note] Sapir's dictum that, "The worlds in which different societies live are distinct worlds, not merely the same world with different labels attached" [Hymes, 1960, p. 8, citing Sapir, 1929].

This is in line with the contention of some scholars that language affects man's very perception of his world.

One language, for example, makes no distinction between things and events, as we do via nouns and verbs (Whorf, 1956). Others do not distinguish our three tenses, but instead conjugate verbs on the basis of how certain or valid the action is. Speakers of these languages therefore order the world in ways strange to us, whereas they fail to express our most common-sense distinctions. In addition, cross-cultural studies and experiments both show that:

> **B15.1a**   People more readily discriminate between things they have different names for, and people have different names for things they can and do discriminate.

In an experimental demonstration, for example, the relative "ease of naming" was established for various colors on the basis of how quickly and by how short a word subjects could describe them. In the second step, another group of subjects was required to identify various colors out of 120 different colors mounted on a board. Ease of naming and ease of recognition were positively correlated (Brown and Lenneberg, 1954).

However, the causal nature and direction of this relationship is uncertain. Some believe that the nature of the language determines what can and therefore will be thought; others, that what is being thought about (for whatever reason) determines how language will be formulated and what it will include. Evidence suggests the possibility of effects in either direction, at least within the lifetime of any given individual. "After all, small boys interested in making snowballs distinguish 'good-packing' from 'poor-packing' snow. Skiers make still finer distinctions" (Brown, 1956, pp. 311–12). And among every subculture or social group with certain shared, unique experiences (soldiers, jazz musicians, other professional groups) we find a similarly shared and unique set of concepts and words.

As with most culture-individual relationships, the issue with respect to given individuals is different from the long-range question of how the culture got to be the way it is in the first place. Thus language is largely a "given" for any particular member of society, and, on the whole, more likely to influence than to be influenced by him. But specific languages are not given, and the student of culture faces the question of how the language developed into its particular form and content. Specific individuals largely inherit language; collectively, they have constructed and continue to modify it. Incidentally:

B15.2   Social distinctions among dialects are made not on linguistic grounds but on status considerations:

Before a single standard language has arisen in any given country, the local dialects are of equal social standing: in the early Middle Ages, the speech of Northeastern England, of Scotland, of Southern England were all equally acceptable, and each person spoke and wrote without hesitation in his own dialect. . . . But as soon as the dialect of any particular place or region comes to acquire special prestige for non-linguistic reasons such as political, economic or cultural dominance, then speakers of other dialects begin to have an inferiority complex concerning their normal native speech, and want to use instead the dialect whose use carries greater prestige. This situation then forces the local types of speech into an unfavorable position vis-à-vis the standard language, and use of a local dialect comes to have the connotation of lower social or cultural standing. . . . Francien became the basis of modern standard French because Paris became the capital of France; Castilian became the basis of standard Spanish, because Madrid became the capital of Spain; the English of London and Middlesex became likewise the basis of standard English [Hall, 1960, pp. 146–47].

B15.3   The "fundamental everyday vocabulary" of human languages appears to change at a roughly constant rate: an average of about 80 per cent retention of the vocabulary over a thousand years.

The application of this constant, by means of a technique called glottochronology, has enabled scholars to approximate the date of separation of two distinct yet related languages on the basis of the number of words they still have in common. Here are the rates of retention for a variety of languages:

	Per cent per 1000 years
Middle Egyptian 2100–1700 B.C. to Coptic 300–500 A.D.	76
Classic Latin 50 B.C. to present-day Romanian	77
Old High German 850 A.D. to present-day German	78
Classic Chinese 950 A.D. to modern colloquial North Chinese	79
Latin of Plautus 200 B.C. to French of Molière 1650 A.D.	79
Dominica Carib of 1650 to present day	80
Classic Latin 50 B.C. to present-day Portuguese	82
Koiné to present-day Cypriote	83
Koiné to present-day Athenian	84
Classic Latin 50 B.C. to present-day Italian	85
Old English 950 A.D. to present-day English	85
Latin of Plautus 200 B.C. to Spanish of 1600 A.D.	85

(Swadesh, 1952, p. 456)

For example:

> It has been shown that Eskimo and Aleut are modern divergent forms of an
> earlier single language. . . . To determine when the earlier single speech com-
> munity separated into two, we use lexicostatistic calculation based on the per-
> centage of like elements in test vocabularies of Eskimo and Aleut, and we find
> that about 2900 years have elapsed since the common period of these now dis-
> tinct languages. . . . Carbon samples obtained by Laughlin and Marsh from
> one of the earliest settlements on the Aleutians and subjected to laboratory tests
> of radioactivity were found to be about 3000 years old, practically coinciding with
> the independently obtained lexicostatistic date [ibid., pp. 452–53].

It also appears that

> words are borrowed, sometimes freely, almost always to some degree, between
> contiguous languages; sounds considerably less so; grammar least of all. That is,
> linguistic content lends itself to diffusion readily, linguistic pattern with more
> difficulty [Kroeber, 1948, p. 241].

For example, the French have borrowed the term "hamburger" but pro-
nounce it "omburzhay."

CONCEPT FORMATION

Most symbols stand not for a unique object or event but for a general
class linked by some common element or relationship. Such generalized
classes of meaning are called *concepts*. "Birthdays," "vegetables," "red objects," "boys," "books" are examples of concepts based on common elements
abstracted from a variety of particular experiences (and called "conjunctive
concepts"). "Oppositeness," "bigness," "sublety," "justice" are concepts
based on common relationships ("relational concepts"). Finally, a class may
be formed so as to include items that are either p or q ("disjunctive concepts"); for example: "To be a member of the class admissible to the
Altavista civic association, one must *either* reside legally in Altavista, *or*
own property there, *or* be engaged in business within the town's limits"
(Bruner et al., 1956, p. 158). Language is thus the repository and the vehicle
of concepts at various levels of generality—apple, fruit, food—and every
word in this sentence evokes one or more concepts in the English-speaking
adult.

How do people come to form their concepts? Many of the previous findings deal indirectly with concept formation, or at least can be reformulated
in such terms. For example, in the conditioning of ordinary conversation,
the subject unknowingly comes to respond in terms of the concept or class
of verbal responses arbitrarily reinforced by the experimenter: plural nouns,
family memories, statements of opinion, and so on. Similarly, the earlier
findings on stimulus generalization and discrimination, and subsequent

ones on problem-solving and on the acquisition of language, could also be placed under this heading.

The following findings, however, come principally from studies directly concerned with the process of concept formation and, for the most part, with how and under what conditions concepts are induced or attained from a series of specific instances.

B16   Neither the formation nor the application of a concept requires conscious recognition of the common elements or relationships involved in the specific instances.

> Several experiments show that concepts may be formed, retained, and used "unconsciously." This statement does not imply that the subjects are not conscious of the perceptual materials before them. It implies merely that sometimes the subjects do not consciously recognize what properties they use to group or classify the materials [Leeper, 1951, p. 743].

On the one hand:

B16.1   A concept can be induced from specific instances without awareness, and items can be classified according to a principle without recognition of the principle, or even without recognition that a principle is involved.

In a typical experiment, subjects are shown a series of symbols; for example, Chinese characters (Hull, 1920) or simple drawings simultaneously varying in color, nature, and the number of objects depicted (Heidbreder et al., 1948). The experimenter classifies the instances in advance on the basis of arbitrary but objective criteria and assigns various names to the different classes. The subject's task is to learn the correct name for each instance, either by memorizing the names as given by the experimenter or by guessing which of the names applies to each case. Eventually, of course, many subjects become aware of the principle involved, but the point is that they typically do far better than chance in guessing, or memorize more efficiently than memorization alone would allow, even when they cannot state the classifying principle.

> Some of the subjects . . . develop the ability to name new examples without being able to say how they do it, even when the necessary formulations lie well within the limits of their vocabularies. . . . These studies indicate . . . that complex guiding processes can be formed, retained, and used without the person's being aware of the process at any step. The subject is aware, of course, of the concrete materials and of his efforts to link names with concrete configurations. But he forms more generalized means of naming the figures without realizing that he is doing it [Leeper, 1951, pp. 731–32].

On the other hand:

B16.2   When subjects repeatedly apply a recognized principle, the conscious relationship gives way to rapid "unthinking" but correct responses. As with the task: "When given a part, name the whole."

When the same task had continued for a series of stimulus words, the conscious awareness of the task faded out even from the fore period and was reduced to a mere feeling of readiness. The preparation lost its specificity as a conscious state, but not as an adjustment, for it still insured correctness of response according to the task. With practice the set became at once less conscious and more efficient [Woodworth, 1938, p. 791].

Although concepts *can* be induced without awareness:

B17   Attaining concepts is not typically a matter of passive habit formation or gradual distillation from random guesses to the correct concept; human beings, as well as lower animals, often exhibit active search in which many "hypotheses" are formulated and tested before the correct concept is attained.

In the human case, such hypotheses are visible in introspective records of the conscious process attending the solution. For example, here is a transcript from an experiment in concept formation:

Trial 12   "I decided it can't be number of sides, because these have the same number of sides. I think I've tried everything I said I tried, but I feel now that I may have skipped one or made a mistake. I think I've tried upper into under and under into upper and curve into straight and straight into curve and left into right and right into left. Those two I had right were going in the same direction and I marked under into upper, so that's what I did here, but it can't be the right theory, because I've had some wrong that way I'm sure" [Heidbreder, 1924, p. 31].

In the case of the lower animals, there may or may not be such *conscious* hypotheses, but there are visible shifts from one to another persistent pattern of response (Krechevsky, 1932). Furthermore:

B18   Strategies or hypotheses in concept formation are not adopted and discarded simply as a consequence of differential reinforcement.

When reinforcement is only partial, but nevertheless the same for all strategies, rats as well as human beings will adopt first one and then another strategy for relatively long periods of time. Here, for example, is one rat's behavior in a discrimination apparatus where right-left and dark-light choices were equally correct (i.e., each was reinforced 50 per cent of the time). Thus there was no extrinsic "reason" to choose either dark or light, right or left. Yet, as the table shows, the animal developed consistent patterns in favor of one choice over another.

Day	Dark choice (per cent)	Right choice (per cent)	Combined habit * (per cent)
1	52	60	81
2	50	100	100
3	50	100	100
4	50	83	92
5	56	90	98
6	67	85	100
7	73	77	100
8	73	77	100
9	69	81	100
10	73	77	100
11	71	79	100
12	69	81	100
13	75	75	100
14	69	81	100

Total responses—672.
Choices to right—551.   Choices to dark—430.
Choices to left—121.†   Choices to light—242.

* One or the other of the two hypotheses dominant during the day.
† Of these 121, 14 or 11.5 per cent were light-left.

(*Ibid.*, p. 52)

In short, subjects will adopt various strategies even when no strategy at all—i.e., random behavior—works equally well; and they will give up one strategy in favor of another that works no better. Finally, note that such shifts are not simply a matter of attempting to improve the pay-off, because:

B18.1   Shifts in strategy will occur even when *all* strategies are fully reinforced, hence when it is impossible to make a "mistake."

In one such experiment, animals were allowed to run a maze of the type shown on page 196, with no "blind alleys," so that all approaches were equally and completely successful.

Every one of the 58 animals tested in these three free-choice situations repeated at least one type of choice to an extent beyond the 50 per cent +3α limit (i.e., departed from 50 per cent to a significant degree). Some animals showed as many as three different systematic responses, and one even showed four. The choices which were respected systematically included the following: (1) left-

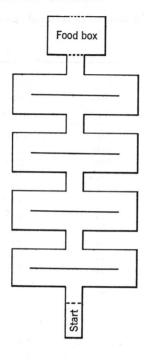

(Witkin, 1940, p. 462)

going (2) right-going (3) spatial alternation (making at one junction a choice opposite in direction to that made at the preceding junction) (4) spatial perseveration (repeating at the remaining three junctions the spatial choice made at the first junction. Thus, if on a given trial, the first choice was to the right, the three subsequent choices were to the right; if the first choice was to the left, the remaining choices on that trial were to the left.) (5) light-going (6) dark-going (7) striped-walls going (8) black-walls going, and (9) visual perseveration (repeating at the remaining three junctions the visual choice made at the first junction on that trial) [*ibid.*, p. 471].

These apparently spontaneous shifts in strategy suggest the matter of "curiosity" and "exploratory behavior" as a motive, discussed in the next chapter.

With respect to the relative ease of inducing various types of concepts, at least under the experimental conditions so far employed:

B19   The more concrete the concept, the more easily it is attained. Specifically, concepts based on similarity of object, of abstract form, of color, and of number, are, respectively, increasingly difficult to attain.

Here are some sample results from an experiment in the relative ease of inducing concepts of various types. The concept is considered attained when the subject applies the correct name in every instance.

Number of trials until concept is attained

Concepts	Mean	Concepts	Mean
Lorb (Shoe)	6.44	Pril (Red)	9.32
Telf (Bird)	6.60	Runc (Yellow)	9.92
Dwin (Book)	6.92	Kelm (Blue)	11.24
Lorb (Form)	6.76	Froj (Two)	14.28
Dwin (Form)	9.20	Blag (Four)	15.40
Telf (Form)	9.72	Nams (Five)	15.56

(Heidbreder *et al.*, 1948, pp. 311–12)

Course of events until concept is attained *

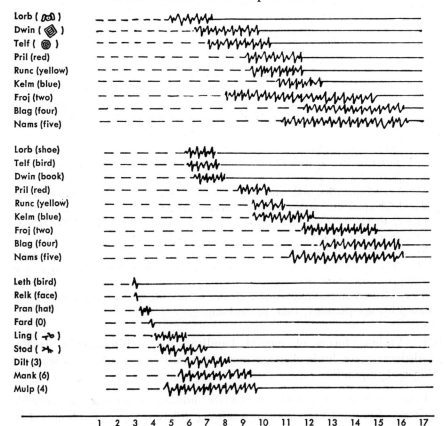

* The groups of nine lines represent the course of events during the attainment of the concepts in the experiment. The broken line indicates, in each case, the period before the First Correct Anticipation; the jagged line, the period between First Correct Anticipation and Concepts Attained; the smooth line, the period after Concepts Attained.

(*Ibid.*, p. 310)

By the same token:

B20   The growing child attains concepts in order of increasing abstractness and complexity.

The earliest concepts tend to be highly concrete: children classify on the
basis of sensory and often "irrelevant" characteristics.

> A pre-abstract period leads gradually to an ability to grasp first-hierarchy con-
> cepts, such as that "men" and "women" are all "people." This period begins
> at about the twenty-sixth month and is followed, by about the middle of the
> fourth year, by the ability to grasp second hierarchy concepts ("potatoes" are
> "vegetable," "apples" are "fruit," and both "vegetables" and "fruit" are "food").
> In turn, the child may develop an ability to grasp concepts of still higher
> hierarchies in later years (Welch and Long, 1940, Welch, 1940, Long and Welch,
> 1942) [Vinacke, 1951, pp. 16–17].

Here is a summary of the work of a distinguished worker in this field:

> In general, the findings of Piaget [1952, 1954], and Inhelder [Inhelder and Piaget,
> 1958], seem to be that intellectual development can be characterized as a series of
> stages in which each stage lays the foundation for its successor. There are four
> main stages. The first, which reaches from birth to two years, is characterized
> by sensorimotor development. During this stage the child learns that objects
> have permanency even when removed from his perceptual field. In the second
> stage, which covers from two to seven years, the child can use language and
> the internalization of actions becomes possible. Symbolic function appears but
> there is an absence of both "reversible operations" and of the concepts of con-
> servation of quantity, size, etc. (e.g., the child is apt to say that five checkers
> placed far apart are more than five checkers placed close together). In the third
> stage (7 to 11) the conceptual operations of the child include the ability to per-
> form concrete operations that belong to the logic of classes and relations but
> do not yet take into account their combinatorial possibilities. The fourth stage
> (11 to 15), which leads to adult logic, is now concerned with propositions as well
> as objects. Movement from one stage to another is determined by a combination
> of experiential and maturational variables, related to, but not exclusively deter-
> mined by, age [Kendler, 1961, pp. 464–65].

B21   Various forms of mental handicap—e.g., schizophrenia, feeble-
mindedness, some brain damage—can also result in a marked tendency to
think and respond in concrete rather than abstract terms.

There is a growing body of specific findings regarding the relative
efficiency of various stratagems in attaining different types of concepts. For
example:

B22   When subjects exposed to a series of symbols or instances are given
one positive example of the concept the experimenter has in mind and
asked to identify which of the others also belong, two general strategies

emerge: wholist and partist. In the wholist strategy, the subject assumes that *every* characteristic of the given positive instance is an essential defining characteristic of the class; he then eliminates whatever aspect is not present in the next positive instance, and so on until no further eliminations occur. In the partist strategy, he arbitrarily selects one aspect of the first positive instance as definitive and then modifies his hypothesis as either positive or negative instances prove inconsistent with it.

Individual subjects generally tend to one or the other strategy; and working against the pressure of time, the wholist strategy proves far superior to the other, for easier as well as more difficult problems (Bruner *et al.*, 1956). When there is no time pressure, the advantage of the wholist strategy disappears (Austin *et al.*, 1953).

Problems begun with whole and with part hypotheses *

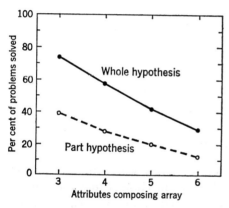

* Percentage solved as a function of the number of attributes represented in the problem.

(Bruner *et al.*, 1956, p. 146)

Finally, in the experimental situations studied to date:

B23   Positive instances (examples of what the concept is) generally contribute much more to the attainment of the concept than negative instances (examples of what the concept is not).

However,

Experimental studies by Smoke (1932, 1933) and others on the effectiveness of positive and negative instances in concept formation leave unanswered the extent to which the inefficiency of negative instances is due to S's difficulty in assimilating information presented in this form (in terms of what the concept "is not") and the extent to which it is due to the low efficiency of negative instances in transmitting the necessary information as to the characteristics of the concept. Further experimental work will have to hold the amount of information conveyed by the two types of instances constant in order to determine the relative difficulty of learning from the two types of instance [Hovland, 1952, p. 471].

As everyone knows, concepts can embody two layers of meaning. First, there is the literal, external referent—roughly, the dictionary definition of the word ("denotative meaning"). In addition, concepts can call forth a cluster of emotional and subjective associations not formally designated by the symbol but effectively aroused by it ("connotative meaning"). Scientific language is supposed to contain only the former; literary language is rich with the latter. A technique called the "semantic differential" has been developed for analyzing connotative meanings. In it terms are ranked on a scale between opposites, as illustrated below. Such analysis reveals that:

B24   Connotations are remarkably similar among similar people.

Here, for example, is how two groups of twenty people rate the word "polite" with respect to some characteristics that have no logical connection with it:

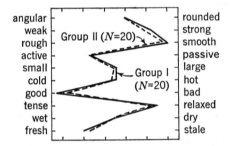

(Osgood, 1952, p. 229)

B24.1   Correlations among a variety of terms scored in this way by people from several cultures yield three main clusters that account for much of the variation in connotative meaning: evaluative (i.e., good-bad), strength (i.e., strong-weak), and activity (i.e., active-passive).

Almost any term can be described in these terms with consistency—which is to say that these are apparently general characteristics of connotative meaning, applicable to such diverse concepts as "leader," "hammer," "church," "Truman," "hot dogs," "color TV," "Marilyn Monroe," "elephant" (*ibid.*).

We now turn to the most subtle form of thinking as revealed in problem-solving and creativity. These processes are extremely difficult to trace, and it is fair to say that the behavioral sciences have made less progress here than in the study of habit formation.

PROBLEM-SOLVING AND CREATIVE THINKING

This section deals with what happens when people are faced with problems as opposed to tasks—that is, with situations where standard approaches either do not work or do not work well, where new or creative approaches must be developed.

A problem arises when a living creature has a goal but does not know how this goal is to be reached. Whenever one cannot go from the given situation to the desired situation simply by action, then there has to be recourse to thinking. (By action we here understand the performance of obvious operations) [Duncker, 1945, p. 1].

Thus, adding the integers from one to one thousand with no time limit is a task but not a problem for the normally schooled adult. Adding them within five minutes is a problem, soluble for most people only through a new or creative procedure. Obviously, the terms "new" and "creative" relate to the state of the particular thinker. A child solving a simple puzzle for the first time is creative; so is a scientist arriving at a conclusion not previously known to anybody, including himself.

Again, we begin with the simplest question: What are the overt, observable characteristics of the process that leads to creative solutions? Biographies of creative thinkers, experimental observations, and introspections by problem-solvers yield these descriptive findings:

B25   Novel solutions are rarely approached through overt, gradual, step-by-step approximation, with each step slightly closer than the preceding one; solutions seem to be attained or approached suddenly, or in spurts, after periods of futile attempt or even overt inactivity (again, the "Aha!" phenomenon).

As a matter of fact, solutions are frequently reported to occur at times of no conscious concern with the problem. For example:

> Just at this time I left Caen, where I was then living, to go on a geological excursion under the auspices of the school of mines. The changes of travel made me forget my mathematical work. Having reached Coutances, we entered an omnibus to go some place or other. At the moment when I put my foot on the step the idea came to me, without anything in my former thoughts seeming to have paved the way for it, that the transformations I had used to define the Fuchsian functions were identical with those of non-Euclidean geometry. I did not verify the idea; I should not have had time, as, upon taking my seat in the omnibus, I went on with a conversation already commenced, but I felt a perfect certainty. On my return to Caen, for conscience's sake I verified the result at my leisure [Poincaré, 1946, pp. 387–88].

Such observations have led to the statement that the "unconscious" solved the problem—which is valid description since it is literally true, but it is certainly no explanation of *how* the solution was achieved.

Some scholars believe that the conscious and/or observable approach characteristic of much problem-solving passes through phases that can be distinguished in a general way. Two such schemes, for example, are associated with distinguished scholars of the past:

Preparation	Suggestion
Incubation	Translation of a difficulty into a problem
Illumination	Framing of hypothesis
Verification	Reasoning
	Testing
(Wallas, 1921)	(Dewey, 1933)

In the case of problems that require more than one step or insight or that are soluble in a number of ways—for example, the typical engineering problem:

B26   The solution to a complex problem is generally approached via several increasingly specific considerations, starting with a general scanning of the class of possible approaches, moving to a selection of one or more "functional solutions," and then narrowing one or more of these into specific, operational solutions.

Here is the analysis of an actual problem in such terms, from a classical investigation:

> The practical problem whose solution was experimentally studied in greatest detail runs as follows: Given a human being with an inoperable stomach tumor, and rays which destroy organic tissue at sufficient intensity, by what procedure can one free him of the tumor by these rays and at the same time avoid destroying the healthy tissue which surrounds it? [Duncker, 1945, p. 1.]

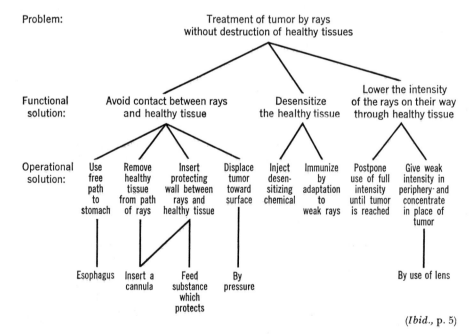

(Ibid., p. 5)

Throughout these pages, what in psychology is termed the adaptive importance of learned expectations has been apparent. The perceptual constancies, positive transfer of training, habit formation itself, and learning in general all represent and depend upon the over-all finding that people largely see and meet the world the way they have come to expect it to be as a result of previous experience. This expectation is of course useful, even necessary, for successful functioning in ordinary situations. But quite reasonably, familiar reactions made to familiar stimuli regarded in familiar ways will not (by definition) be creative very often. When the situation is not in fact ordinary, or when ordinary responses are inadequate, unordinary perceptions and reactions are required—just as ordinary perceptual responses prove illusory or erroneous in an unusual environment. Thus, most of the documented barriers to novelty can be seen as instances of interference *with* the novel *by* the familiar—in this sense, the retarding influence of learning. To begin with:

B27   Problems are difficult to solve when they require the use of the familiar in an unfamiliar way.

In one study, for example, subjects were asked to mount candles vertically on a soft wooden screen and were given a series of supplies including matches, eyedroppers, thumbtacks, small boxes, and so on. The solution required attaching the candle to a small box and then tacking the box to the screen. In the experimental group, the matches were placed inside the box; in the control group, the matches and the box were presented separately. The first group, regarding the box in its familiar function as match container, had a much lower rate of solution than the second group (Adamson, 1952).

Box problem

Group	Number of subjects	Number solving	Number below median of combined group
Experimental	29	12 (41) *	7 (24)
Control	28	24 (86)	22 (78)

* Numbers in parentheses are percentages.

(*Ibid.*, p. 289)

Similarly, people are unlikely to use a cord supporting a painting or a calendar to solve a problem, even though they are told that any object in the room can be used; and subjects find it difficult to solve a problem requiring the use of a pair of pliers as a pedestal rather than as a holding tool (Duncker, 1945). Furthermore:

B27.1   The more recently an object has been used in its familiar function, the greater the tendency to overlook the novel use.

In one experiment, subjects first constructed electrical circuits using *either* a microswitch or a relay. Both switch *and* relay were later available as items that could be used for weights in constructing a pendulum. Shortly after construction of the circuit, subjects tended to choose the other, nonfamiliar item for the novel application; but with increasing time, this tendency (functional fixedness) dissipated.

Functional fixedness as a function of log time

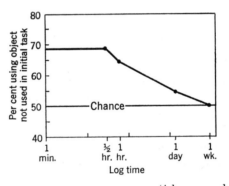

(Adamson and Taylor, 1954, p. 124)

B28   Specific solutions learned in one situation tend to impede or prevent the discovery of different approaches when a new situation demands them.

One of the simplest instances is what happens during the extinction trials in an ordinary experiment on instrumental conditioning. Pressing the bar has delivered food to the rat in the past, so it continues to press the bar long after the food magazine is disconnected, thus impeding discovery of a new solution that may be available. Similarly:

B29   General solutions or principles that have proven successful may stand in the way when they are not appropriate in a situation like those in which they have been effective.

In one study, for example, subjects were given a series of water-jug problems of this form: given empty jars holding *A, B,* and *C* quarts of water respectively, obtain *D* quarts:

Problem	Given the following empty jars as measures			Obtain the required amount of water
	(A)	(B)	(C)	(D)
1	29	3		20
2	21	127	3	100
3	14	163	25	99
4	18	43	10	5
5	9	42	6	21
6	20	59	4	31
7	23	49	3	20
8	15	39	3	18
9	28	76	3	25
10	18	48	4	22
11	14	36	8	6

(Luchins, 1942, p. 1)

The experiment began with a series of problems soluble by the same general solution (B-A-$2C$; problems 2–6). These were followed by simpler problems in which the correct amount could be obtained by one simple addition or subtraction (problems 7–11). Fully 81 per cent of the experimental subjects approached and solved the first simple case by the less efficient application of the complex general principle learned in the training trials whereas none of the control subjects took this detour—they all went directly to the simple solution.

B29.1   The interfering influence of the familiar extends even to situations where the subject is presumably confined to rigid rules of thought that should exclude it.

For example, the opinions or biases held by college students affect the conclusions they draw from a set of logical premises, so that they accept conclusions that are logically erroneous but consistent with previous learning. The conclusion, "Airplanes may be more effective than battleships," was erroneously accepted as following logically from a set of premises by 46 per cent of the students tested. None of the students in a control group given the same problem in symbolic terms (x, y, z) accepted the equivalent conclusion. Thus, previous belief in the effectiveness of airplanes overrode the logical constraints (Morgan and Morton, 1944).

The tone or language of premises also tends to spread to the conclusion drawn: i.e., if premises are stated in terms of universal positives ("*All* x's are y's, *all* y's are z's") correct conclusions that are negatively phrased ("All z's are not x's") will tend to be rejected (Sells, 1936). A logically irrelevant expectation, induced by the wording of the premises, interferes with the drawing of the logical conclusion.

B29.2   Solutions can be impeded or prevented by erroneous and unconscious perceptual assumptions regarding the "inherent" limitations of a problem.

For example: draw four straight lines that pass through all of these dots without lifting the pencil.

.   .   .

.   .   .

.   .   .

Most people complicate the problem by assuming that all the lines have to stay inside the "square"—an assumption based on the familiarity and/or goodness of the square as a figure. Most of the familiar table puzzles and games—"Make a certain figure out of so many matches or coins"—are based on this barrier; e.g., "Make four equilateral triangles out of six matches," where subjects unnecessarily assume the limitation of two dimensions. Conversely:

B29.3   Solutions can be suggested by perceptual clues, even when the clues are not consciously recognized.

One classical problem, for example, requires subjects to connect two strings hanging from the ceiling, far enough apart so they cannot be reached simultaneously. One solution is to tie a weight to one of them and swing it like a pendulum, so it can be reached when it approaches the other. This solution was rapidly attained by many previously stumped subjects when the experimenter brushed against the string and set it swinging; yet a minority were unable to report, even after direct questioning, that they had received a clue from this movement (Maier, 1931).

In general then, the more general and abstract the previous learning, the more help and the less barrier it is likely to prove in future problems. A general principle—by the usual principles of transfer of training—is appropriate to more situations than a specific, mechanical procedure; and a principle that is understood is more easily modified to fit new situations than a formula learned only by rote.

Thus, mechanical learning of skills, procedures, or formulas is less effective in preparing the student for different situations than learning the principle or abstraction underlying the procedure; and although such learning may at times produce more immediate mastery ("Never mind 'why,' just tell me 'how' "), the mastery is not as easily retained ("I've forgotten how and don't know why").

Most of these points are illustrated in a classic Gestalt treatise on productive thinking (Wertheimer, 1959). The author considers the case of grade-school children who had been taught to determine the area of a rectangle and were then given the problem of finding the area of a parallelogram. The book discusses many ramifications of the problem, but among the salient observations are these:

The characteristic response to the assignment among children who have not as yet "had parallelograms" is rejection of the problem on that basis. "How can I do that? We haven't learned that yet." (You may be experiencing the adult equivalent: "Let me see—what *was* that formula?") This response itself attests to the child's adherence to specific procedures, rather than to understanding; it does not occur to him that the rectangle solution may be relevant because it was learned as a mechanical set of operations to be applied under specific circumstances. Alternately, some students blindly generalize or transfer the now inappropriate procedure for rectangles ($l \times w$).

Once the student is taught the correct procedure, "Drop a perpendicular from the corner, call it 'altitude' and then take $l \times a$,"

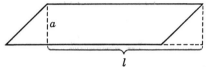

(Wertheimer, 1959, p. 14)

he may still be at a loss with even a slight apparent modification, such as the same figure on its side:

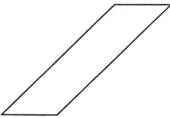

(*Ibid.*, p. 16)

And his parallelogram training is of no use in calculating the area of other figures, such as

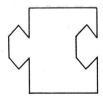 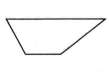

(*Ibid.*, pp. 18–19)

But if instead of learning just the procedure he attains insight into the *why;* if he perceives the underlying relationship or principle—that a parallelogram is "really" just a rectangle with a triangle cut from one side and stuck on the other, and vice versa—

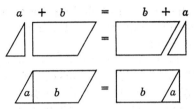

$$a \quad + \quad b \qquad = \qquad b \quad + \quad a$$

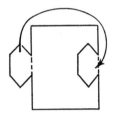 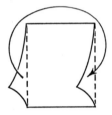

(*Ibid.*, p. 70)

then the reason for the formula is apparent—in a basic sense of that word. The student now has no problem with any parallelogram regardless of size or position and can figure the area of the above different figures by the same approach: take the disturbing protrusion and use it to fill the disturbing hole:

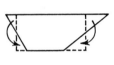

As an appropriate summary to this section, as well as to the larger issue of the relationship between habit formation on the one hand and thinking on the other, here is the conclusion reached by the investigator of the water-jug problem cited above:

> This study should not be taken to controvert the values of habits. Exercise and even drill have their values. Mechanized responses have a place in one's behavior. They possess the advantages of releasing one from the bother of finding anew responses to recurring everyday situations, they equip one with precise, ready, and speedy responses to certain aspects of his environment; and they free the mind so that it can more adequately deal with complicated tasks. What the study has shown is that in mechanization there are certain dangers. When the individual does not adequately deal with problems but views them merely from the frame of reference of a habit; when he applies a certain habituated behavior to situations which have a better solution or which, in fact, are not even solvable by the just working habit; when a habit ceases to be a tool discriminantly applied but becomes a procrustean bed to which the situation must conform; when, in a word, instead of the individual mastering the habit, the habit masters the individual—then mechanization is indeed a dangerous thing [Luchins, 1942, p. 93].

INDIVIDUAL DIFFERENCES

It is clear to common observation that there are marked and persistent differences in how well different people can learn and can solve problems. The common as well as the psychological term to cover such differences is "intelligence." This section deals with the nature and measurement of intelligence and some other differences relevant to problem-solving ability:

with what is known about the determinants of differences in intelligence; and with the distribution of intelligence throughout the population.

General Intelligence

Although the only fully precise definition of intelligence is "what the intelligence tests measure," the theory underlying the construction of such tests closely matches the ordinary concept of intelligence as general mental ability. Raw native capacity, unaffected by learning, is as impossible to measure as it is to observe (since there are no people without experience). Yet the concept of general intelligence, as well as its measurement, is intended to exclude those skills that are closely associated with specific training: for example, the differences between a mathematician and a musician in their ability to integrate equations is not attributable to intelligence. What is meant, and what the tests try to measure, are differences in the capacity to respond effectively in totally new situations or in situations that are equally familiar to all.

Thus, for example, some items presumably are completely novel to the taker of the test, while others assume familiarity of content, or at least equal opportunity to have become familiar—as in a task to assemble blocks into a familiar object without being told what they are meant to form.

Intelligence measurements of children are usually reported in terms of the well-known I.Q. (Intelligence Quotient) score, developed as follows.

The fact that mental ability grows from infancy to the age of fifteen or sixteen (and perhaps thereafter) gives rise to the concept of mental age and makes it possible to develop some empirical measures thereof. The procedure is to find those test items that increasing percentages of children at successive ages answer correctly, and then to score each item for age level according to the age at which most children first master it. For example, this item, of the general form "Brother is a boy; sister is a _____" is placed at age seven:

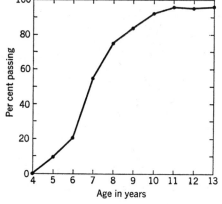

(McNemar, 1942, p. 93)

A subject's mental age is defined as the highest age level for which he answers all items correctly, with additional credit for the percentage of correct answers at higher levels. The original meaning of I.Q. was simply this mental age divided by the chronological age, multiplied by 100 to eliminate decimals. Scores of over 100 thus indicated more rapid develop- ment than average, and vice versa (as described in Terman and Merrill, 1937).

Since a 1960 revision of the test and scoring procedure, designed to make I.Q.'s at various ages more directly comparable, I.Q. is no longer calculated in this way, but its interpretation remains essentially the same. At present, the I.Q. is a relative score comparing the child's mental ability to others of his age, with 100 as the average.

Here is how I.Q. scores are distributed (in the standardizing sample of 3184 native-born white American children):

I.Q.	Per cent	Classification
160–169	0.03	
150–159	0.2	Very superior
140–149	1.1	
130–139	3.1	Superior
120–129	8.2	
110–119	18.1	High average
100–109	23.5	Normal or average
90–99	23.0	
80–89	14.5	Low average
70–79	5.6	Borderline defective
60–69	2.0	
50–59	0.4	Mentally defective
40–49	0.2	
30–39	0.03	

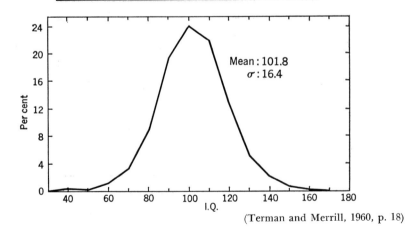

Mean: 101.8
σ: 16.4

(Terman and Merrill, 1960, p. 18)

The following findings deal with intelligence only as defined and measured by such tests—principally, by various forms of the Stanford-Binet (I.Q.), Wechsler-Bellevue, and Wechsler Adult Intelligence Scale, or WAIS. But such measures are by no means unrelated to behavior in the real world. In the first place, the tests are designed to measure what most people mean by "intelligence" or "mental ability"—quickness of mind, ability to "see through" a problem and solve it, verbal and numerical aptitudes, capacity to see relationships and to reason, etc. Furthermore, measured intelligence among children and adults is by no means an artifact of the particular test employed or of testing in general. Actually the major tests of general intelligence have high positive correlations with each other, so an individual's position in a group is not likely to vary greatly with the particular test used. The Stanford-Binet and the Wechsler-Bellevue, for example, correlate about .85; and the same figure holds between the WAIS and the Army General Classification Test (Wechsler, 1958, p. 105).

Moreover, measured intelligence shows substantial correlation with success in important activities that are normally considered intellectual. For example:

Expectancies at various levels of mental ability *

I.Q.

130	Mean of persons receiving Ph.D.
120	Mean of college graduates
115	Mean of freshmen in typical four-year college
	Mean of children from white-collar and skilled-labor homes
110	Mean of high-school graduates
	Has 50–50 chance of graduating from college
105	About 50–50 chance of passing in academic high-school curriculum
100	Average for total population
90	Mean of children from low-income city homes or rural homes
	Adult can perform jobs requiring some judgment (operate sewing machine, assemble parts)
75	About 50–50 chance of reaching high school
	Adult can keep small store, perform in orchestra
60	Adult can repair furniture, harvest vegetables, assist electrician
50	Adult can do simple carpentry, domestic work
40	Adult can mow lawns, do simple laundry

* From Beckham, 1930; Havighurst and Janke, 1944; Plant and Richardson, 1958; Wolfle, 1954; *Guide to the Use of GATB*, 1958; and others.

(Cronbach, 1960, p. 174)

And here are some correlations between I.Q. and achievement in various high school subjects the following year:

With reading comprehension	.73
With reading speed	.43
With English usage	.59
With history	.59
With biology	.54
With geometry	.48

(Bond, 1940, p. 29)

So, in short, it does appear that the tests do measure something and that that something is close to what is normally meant by intelligence. Now for the important findings:

C1   Intelligence is not a single, unitary trait. It is composed of a series of specific abilities, but they are positively correlated with each other—that is to say, they have something in common and hence there is such a thing as general intelligence.

As early as 1904, an English psychologist began to develop the notion of a general intelligence factor. By the mid-1920's he had concluded that "the G [general factor] proved to be a factor which enters into the measurements of ability of all kinds, and which is throughout constant for any individual, although varying greatly for different individuals" (Spearman, 1927, p. 411). This specific formulation has been challenged, but the basic notion of a general intelligence factor remains. Most intelligence tests include both verbal and nonverbal items. The two scores typically intercorrelate about .50, and performance on each set correlates with academic achievement to about the same extent.

An extensive classical investigation (Thurstone and Thurstone, 1941) analyzed people's performance on some sixty different tests and found that the results could be distilled to, or accounted for by, seven general factors (or "primary mental abilities," as they were then designated). These abilities, along with illustrative items from a test subsequently developed to measure each of them in the "pure" state, are:

V
Verbal Comprehension

Today much of our clothing is designed to make a fashionable appearance rather than for
style   protection   children   sale   dresses

Synonyms: quiet   blue   still   tense   watery

N
Number

Is this addition right or wrong?   42
61
<u>83</u>
176

Mark every number that is exactly three more than the number just before it:

4   11   14   10   9   12   16   8   10   3

S
Spatial Perception

Put a mark under every figure which is like the first figure in the row.

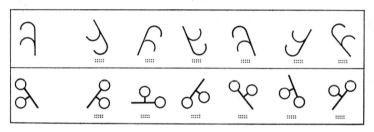

M
Memory

Study associations such as "chair-21" and "box-44." Mark the correct number on a later test.

R
Reasoning

Letter series (Which letter comes next?)   abxcdxefxghx . . .

Letter groupings (Which group is different?)   AAAB   AAAM   AAAR   AATV

W
Word Fluency

List as many four-letter words beginning with C as you can.

P
Perceptual Speed

Look at the pictures and find those that are *exactly* like the first one in the row.

In each column of words below, mark the word printed backward which is the same as the first word.

lamp	book	purse	horse	most
look	bond	purse	hunch	more
lake	bent	pedal	honey	meat
lamp	bank	phase	hedge	moat
lens	book	pulley	horse	milk

(Cronbach, 1960, p. 257; Thurstone and Thurstone, 1941, pp. 49, 63)

And here are the intercorrelations found between six of these abilities and "general intelligence":

Correlations between six primaries

	N	W	V	S	M	R
N	1.000					
W	.466	1.000				
V	.385	.512	1.000			
S	.256	.174	.167	1.000		
M	.187	.390	.393	.149	1.000	
R	.540	.480	.548	.386	.389	1.000
g *	.603	.686	.676	.339	.474	.843

* g, general factor. Its interpretation here would be that the primary mental abilities are correlated by a general factor which operates through each of the primaries. Each of the primary factors can be regarded as a composite of an independent primary factor and a general factor that it shares with other primary factors.

(Thurstone and Thurstone, 1941, pp. 37–38)

These particular factors are not absolutely final or "primary"; they depend to some extent on the specific tests and the method of analysis. But the general finding that they illustrate still stands: regardless of instrument, various mental abilities can be differentiated but they are positively correlated rather than compensatory, as sometimes supposed. That is:

C1.1   People superior in mathematical aptitude are also likely to be superior in verbal and other mental skills, and vice-versa.

Here, for example, are the correlations among various subtests of the Wechsler Adult Intelligence Scale:

Intercorrelation of the tests—WAIS,
ages twenty-five–thirty-four *

Test	Information	Comprehension	Arithmetic	Similarities	Digit span	Vocabulary	Digit symbol	Picture completion	Block design	Picture arrangement
Comprehension	0.70									
Arithmetic	0.66	0.49								
Similarities	0.70	0.62	0.55							
Digit Span	0.53	0.40	0.49	0.46						
Vocabulary	0.81	0.73	0.59	0.74	0.51					
Digit Symbol	0.57	0.44	0.43	0.53	0.41	0.60				
Picture Completion	0.67	0.56	0.50	0.56	0.39	0.61	0.48			
Block Design	0.58	0.49	0.51	0.52	0.39	0.53	0.47	0.62		
Picture Arrangement	0.62	0.57	0.49	0.52	0.47	0.62	0.51	0.57	0.58	
Object Assembly	0.45	0.43	0.37	0.39	0.30	0.43	0.44	0.54	0.61	0.52

* 150 male and 150 female subjects.

(Wechsler, 1955, p. 16)

C2   I.Q. scores are quite stable after the age of six or seven. Fluctuations occur but they are small compared to the range of scores; so the relative standing of a child within this group is not likely to change much.

Here are some illustrative data:

Correlation of mental test with test at a later age *

Approximate age at first test	Name of first test	Years elapsed between first and second test			
		1	3	6	12
3 months	California First-Year	.10 (CFY)	.05 (CP)	−.13	.02
1 year	California First-Year	.47 (CP)	.23	.13	.00
2 years	California Preschool	.74 (CP)	.55	.50	.42
3 years	California Preschool	.64		.55	.33
4 years	Stanford-Binet		.71	.73	.70
6 years	Stanford-Binet	.86	.84	.81	.77 (W)
7 years	Stanford-Binet	.88	.87	.78	.80 (W)
9 years	Stanford-Binet	.88	.82	.87	
11 years	Stanford-Binet	.93	.93	.92	

* Data from Bayley, 1949. Some entries have been estimated from closely related data in Bayley's report. Initials indicate second test; W, Wechsler-Bellevue. Where no initial is given, the Stanford-Binet is the second test.

(Cronbach, 1960, p. 176)

As for change or fluctuation in an individual's scores, the average difference from test to retest (15 months later) is only 5 I.Q. points, although a few cases show far greater deviations (up to 25 or 30 points).

Hence, if the concern is with the measurement of a particular child,

to say that the average change is about five points does not help a great deal, because in dealing with clinical cases one can never be sure that the particular case under observation may not be one that will show a large amount of change. It would seem advisable therefore to secure at least two ratings wherever an intelligence rating is especially important in disposing of the case or in making recommendation [Brown, 1930, p. 348].

Perhaps fortunately and unfortunately, respectively:

C2.1   The stability of the I.Q. score holds at both the upper and the lower extremes.

Bright children remain bright, dull children remain dull—although a bright child may not fulfill his potentials and a dull one may be trained to utilize his capacities more fully. More specifically:

C2.1a   An exceptionally bright child can expect, on the average, an exceptionally bright future by almost any measure—including physical and mental health, social adjustment, and occupational success.

This finding comes largely from the elaborate investigations of gifted children discussed earlier (Terman and Oden, 1947, 1959).

C2.1b   To date, no known treatment will substantially elevate the mental prospects of the severely retarded.

Of the 4,200,000 children born annually in the United States 3 per cent (126,000) will never achieve the intellect of a 12-year-old child, 0.3 per cent (12,600) will remain below the 7-year intellectual level, and 0.1 per cent (4200) if they survive, will spend their lives as completely helpless imbeciles, unable even to care for their own creature needs [Masland et al., 1958, p. 3].

There are, however, a few recorded cases of feeble-minded subjects with outstanding or "trick" abilities in specific, narrow areas ("idiot savants"). For example, one subject with an I.Q. of 50 exhibited remarkable memory, could spell words forward and backwards, and could play complex musical compositions by ear—but by ear only (Scheerer et al., 1945). Others have been known to play excellent chess.

Now for a crucial question, leading into the determinants of intelligence: To what extent are such differences in measured intelligence attributable to native endowment and to what extent are they a result of varying educational experiences?

C3   Large differences in intelligence, as measured by the standard intelligence tests, are due principally to heredity.

Here is one expert's review of studies on

how much difference in ability results from the types of environmental difference usually found among homes and communities. One summary, with which most others agree fairly closely, is that the variation in tested intelligence among school children is accounted for

> 75 per cent by heredity
> 21 per cent by environment
> 4 per cent by accidental factors

Environment has an effect, but not so great as to wipe out hereditary advantages and disadvantages [Cronbach, 1954, p. 210, citing Shuttleworth, 1935].

The major evidence on this point comes from studies that compare test scores of persons with different degrees of genetic similarity. A classical study examined nineteen pairs of identical twins separated early in life and reared in significantly different surroundings. (Identical twins, of course, originate in the same cell and therefore have identical genetic endowment.) Tested in adolescence or as adults, the twins showed an average difference of only eight I.Q. points, barely greater than that observed for the same individuals tested on repeated occasions. The greatest single difference was twenty-four points—compared to an over-all population range of about 140 I.Q. points—and again, this is no larger than the largest fluctuations observed for single individuals.

Judges also rated the educational opportunities of each member of the pair. The contribution of differential educational advantages was positive, although small in I.Q. differences; and in some cases, a higher "educational advantage" actually went with a lower I.Q. score (Newman *et al.*, 1937). The data appear on page 218.

Other studies have compared correlations between family members of varying relationship. The findings conform with what would be expected on the basis of certain statistical assumptions regarding the genetic structures involved, and are quite close to correlations established for physical stature (see table on page 219).

In addition, the I.Q. of adopted children correlates positively with that of their true parents, from whom they have been separated, not with that of their foster parents (Skodak and Skeels, 1949). Furthermore, in lower animals such as rats, where systematic breeding experiments are feasible, the intelligence of strains can be raised or lowered at will by selective

Comparative adult I.Q. of identical twins
separated in infancy or childhood

Sex	Age at separation	Age at testing	Differences in educational advantages *	Differences in I.Q. between twins †
f	18 mo.	35	37	24
f	18 mo.	27	32	12
m	1 yr.	27	28	19
f	5 mo.	29	22	17
f	18 mo.	29	19	7
f	18 mo.	19	15	12
m	2 yr.	14	15	10
f	3 mo.	15	14	15
m	2 mo.	23	12	−2
f	6 mo.	39	12	−1
f	14 mo.	38	11	4
m	1 mo.	19	11	1
f	1 yr.	12	10	5
m	1 yr.	26	9	1
m	1 mo.	13	9	−1
f	6 yr.	41	9	−9
f	2 yr.	11	8	2
f	3 yr.	59	7	8
m	1 mo.	19	7	6

* As rated by five judges; maximum possible difference was 50 points.
† Negative entries indicate that the I.Q. difference ran counter to the rated difference in educational opportunity.

(Krech and Crutchfield, 1958, p. 575, data from Newman et al., 1937)

mating. Within nine rat generations, one experimenter was able to produce decidedly "bright" and "dull" groups (in maze learning) by selective breeding from an original, unselected population (Tryon, 1940). Finally, as another suggestion of biological factors behind differences in tested mental ability, a recent study of two groups of children differing in ascorbic acid concentration showed a mean difference of 3 I.Q. points in favor of the high group, but when the diets were supplemented with orange juice the previously low group caught up (Kubala and Katz, 1960). The importance of this finding lies not in the three I.Q. points that might be gained by drinking orange juice before a test, but in the suggestion that more general and pervasive dietary differences may be partly responsible for observed I.Q. differences between groups, such as those discussed below.

None of these biological differences precludes the fact that:

Correlations among relatives

	Stature	Intelligence
Between siblings	.54	.51
Between parents and children	.51	.49
Between grandparents and grandchildren	.32	.34
Between uncles (or aunts) and nephews (or nieces)	.29	.35
Between first cousins	.24	.29

(Burt and Howard, 1956, as adapted by Krech and Crutchfield, 1958, p. 576)

C4   Consistent, though relatively small, average differences in measured intelligence result from environmental differences in learning opportunities and pressures.

So, for example (as we shall see in more detail in the chapter on ethnic relations), the I.Q. of Negro children moving from the South to the North shows an average improvement, which increases with time (Lee, 1951). Probably in part for the same general reasons, children in rural areas show lower average scores than those from cities—in America (McNemar, 1942) as well as in Europe (Klineberg, 1931).

Both genetic and environmental factors, then, can contribute to observed differences in average intelligence among various groups.

C5   Measured intelligence in the United States, at present and in the recent past, varies with:

.1   race.

The findings on this characteristic are presented and discussed at length in Chapter 12.

.2   sex.

Over-all scores show consistent but negligible average differences in favor of males, but substantial differences exist with respect to the more specific abilities that make up the total score.

Such differences are, in general, consistent with popular stereotypes: males are usually superior in mathematical reasoning, judgment and manipulation of spatial relationships, and mechanical aptitude, while

females exceed males in vocabulary, verbal fluency, and straight memory.
Here are some illustrative, specific comparisons:

**Male and female performance on subtests of the WAIS,
ages sixteen–sixty-four ***

Test	Sex	Mean
Information	M	10.18
	F	9.64
Comprehension	M	10.04
	F	9.71
Arithmetic	M	10.35
	F	9.25
Similarities	M	9.32
	F	9.66
Digit Span	M	9.43
	F	9.43
Vocabulary	M	9.65
	F	10.02
Digit Symbol	M	8.25
	F	9.37
Picture Completion	M	9.72
	F	9.04
Block Design	M	9.50
	F	9.09
Picture Arrangement	M	9.21
	F	9.22
Object Assembly	M	9.33
	F	9.26

* Total number, 1700; 850 male, 850 female.

(Wechsler, 1958, p. 147)

The findings on the WAIS suggest that women seemingly call upon different
resources or different degrees of like abilities in exercising whatever it is we
call intelligence. For the moment one need not be concerned as to which approach is better or "superior." But our findings do confirm what poets and
novelists have often asserted, and the average layman long believed, namely,
that men not only behave but "think" differently from women [Wechsler, 1958,
p. 148].

.3   age.

In terms of absolute, not relative, test performance, mental ability grows
rapidly from birth through puberty, somewhat more slowly from then until
the early twenties, at which point slow but steady decline sets in, with rather
rapid deterioration beginning at about age sixty-five (not shown).

Changes in full-scale scores of the Wechsler-Bellevue Form I, ages seven–sixty-five

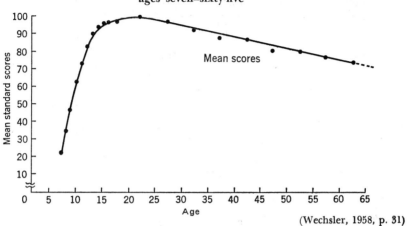

Mean scores

(Wechsler, 1958, p. 31)

But there are two serious qualifications:

.3a   The decline after early adulthood is not uniform but holds mostly for those abilities most heavily dependent upon speed of

Decline of adult intelligence over the years *

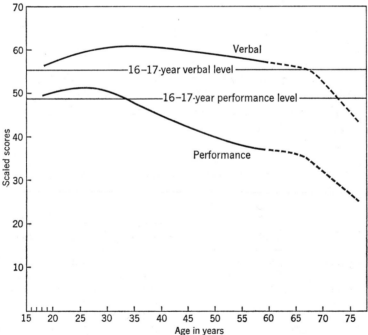

* Age changes in intelligence-test scores. Data for subjects from age sixty and over are taken from a different sample.

(Wechsler, 1955, as adapted by Hilgard, 1962, p. 413)

performance and sheer abstract "cleverness." Measures more dependent on verbal skills and on judgment, as well as those drawing
more heavily on experience, show a slower decline.

.3b   Though such decline in intelligence is almost always observed
in cross-sectional studies (i.e., simultaneous tests of people in various
age groups), it has *not* been found in longitudinal investigations in
which the same people are tested repeatedly.

However, the longitudinal studies have so far been confined largely to
exceptionally bright subjects—who, incidentally, show continual increase
in intelligence until their fifties (cf. Bayley and Oden, 1955). Thus, differences in the results may be due either to methodology or to some difference
between the normal and the exceptional case.

.4   occupation and social class.

Substantially higher average I.Q.'s are consistently found among members
of the higher social strata.

There is some disagreement in interpretation: Is this selection or effect?
That is, to what extent does higher intelligence contribute to success and
to what extent does social position contribute to higher I.Q. scores via
educational opportunity, pressures to perform, or class bias in test items?
But there is no disagreement on the facts, as a major review concludes:
"The relationship of I.Q. to socioeconomic level is one of the best documented facts in mental test history" (Tyler, 1956, p. 317).

A good deal of scientific effort has been devoted in recent years to attempting to develop so-called culture-free or culture-fair tests—tests that
presumably do not contain a middle- or upper-class bias in their very construction. Even with them, however, class differences remain in substantial
form, though occasionally somewhat diminished. Here are some illustrative
data:

**Average scores for the group as a whole and for
each of the three socioeconomic classes**

Test	Socioeconomic status		
	High	*Middle*	*Low*
Culture-free IPAT (4–8 years)	117.7	107.0	97.0
Culture-free IPAT (8–12 years)	100.3	105.9	97.7
Culture-free IPAT (total)	107.3	109.7	97.5
Binet (4–7 years)	116.0	115.9	100.2
Binet (8–15 years)	94.9	103.9	85.7
Binet (total)	103.3	108.3	89.8

(Marquart and Bailey, 1955, p. 355)

The following table, for example, compares intelligence scores for various occupational groups among Air Force enlisted men. (Bear in mind that occupations with still higher average I.Q. scores, e.g., nuclear physicists, are not represented here because they are not usually found among enlisted men.) Note also that while the average and the lowest I.Q.'s decline steadily, the top I.Q. in every group is very high. Thus there are no dull accountants or lawyers but there are some very bright shipping clerks, riveters, and lumberjacks. The distribution of bright people throughout social classes can have important effects upon a system of social stratification (see Young, 1959).

Mean GCT standard scores, standard deviations, and range of scores of 18,782 AAF white enlisted men by civilian occupation

Occupation	N	M	Me-dian	Standard deviation	Range
Accountant	172	128.1	128.1	11.7	94–157
Lawyer	94	127.6	126.8	10.9	96–157
Engineer	39	126.6	125.8	11.7	100–151
Public-relations man	42	126.0	125.5	11.4	100–149
Auditor	62	125.9	125.5	11.2	98–151
Chemist	21	124.8	124.5	13.8	102–153
Reporter	45	124.5	125.7	11.7	100–157
Chief clerk	165	124.2	124.5	11.7	88–153
Teacher	256	122.8	123.7	12.8	76–155
Draftsman	153	122.0	121.7	12.8	74–155
Stenographer	147	121.0	121.4	12.5	66–151
Pharmacist	58	120.5	124.0	15.2	76–149
Tabulating-machine operator	140	120.1	119.8	13.3	80–151
Bookkeeper	272	120.0	119.7	13.1	70–157
Manager, sales	42	119.0	120.7	11.5	90–137
Purchasing agent	98	118.7	119.2	12.9	82–153
Manager, production	34	118.1	117.0	16.0	82–153
Photographer	95	117.6	119.8	13.9	66–147
Clerk, general	496	117.5	117.9	13.0	68–155
Clerk-typist	468	116.8	117.3	12.0	80–147
Manager, miscellaneous	235	116.0	117.5	14.8	60–151
Installer-repairman, tel. & tel.	96	115.8	116.8	13.1	76–149
Cashier	111	115.8	116.8	11.9	80–145
Instrument repairman	47	115.5	115.8	11.9	82–141
Radio repairman	267	115.3	116.5	14.5	56–151
Printer, job pressman, lithographic pressman	132	115.1	116.7	14.3	60–149
Salesman	494	115.1	116.2	15.7	60–153
Artist	48	114.9	115.4	11.2	82–139
Manager, retail store	420	114.0	116.2	15.7	52–151

Occupation	N	M	Me-dian	Standard deviation	Range
Laboratory assistant	128	113.4	114.0	14.6	76–147
Tool-maker	60	112.5	111.6	12.5	76–143
Inspector	358	112.3	113.1	15.7	54–147
Stock clerk	490	111.8	113.0	16.3	54–151
Receiving and shipping clerk	486	111.3	113.4	16.4	58–155
Musician	157	110.9	112.8	15.9	56–147
Machinist	456	110.1	110.8	16.1	38–153
Foreman	298	109.8	111.4	16.7	60–151
Watchmaker	56	109.8	113.0	14.7	68–147
Airplane mechanic	235	109.3	110.5	14.9	66–147
Sales clerk	492	109.2	110.4	16.3	42–149
Electrician	289	109.0	110.6	15.2	64–149
Lathe operator	172	108.5	109.4	15.5	64–147
Receiving and shipping checker	281	107.6	108.9	15.8	52–151
Sheet-metal worker	498	107.5	108.1	15.3	62–153
Lineman, power and tel. & tel.	77	107.1	108.8	15.5	70–133
Assembler	498	106.3	106.6	14.6	48–145
Mechanic	421	106.3	108.3	16.0	60–155
Machine-operator	486	104.8	105.7	17.1	42–151
Auto serviceman	539	104.2	105.9	16.7	30–141
Riveter	239	104.1	105.3	15.1	50–141
Cabinetmaker	48	103.5	104.7	15.9	66–127
Upholsterer	59	103.3	105.8	14.5	68–131
Butcher	259	102.9	104.8	17.1	42–147
Plumber	128	102.7	104.8	16.0	56–139
Bartender	98	102.2	105.0	16.6	56–137
Carpenter, construction	451	102.1	104.1	19.5	42–147
Pipe-fitter	72	101.9	105.2	18.0	56–139
Welder	493	101.8	103.7	16.1	48–147
Auto mechanic	466	101.3	101.8	17.0	48–151
Molder	79	101.1	105.5	20.2	48–137
Chauffeur	194	100.8	103.0	18.4	46–143
Tractor driver	354	99.5	101.6	19.1	42–147
Painter, general	440	98.3	100.1	18.7	38–147
Crane-hoist operator	99	97.9	99.1	16.6	58–147
Cook and baker	436	97.2	99.5	20.8	20–147
Weaver	56	97.0	97.3	17.7	50–135
Truck driver	817	96.2	97.8	19.7	16–149
Laborer	856	95.8	97.7	20.1	26–145
Barber	103	95.3	98.1	20.5	42–141
Lumberjack	59	94.7	96.5	19.8	46–137
Farmer	700	92.7	93.4	21.8	24–147
Farmhand	817	91.4	94.0	20.7	24–141
Miner	156	90.6	92.0	20.1	42–139
Teamster	77	87.7	89.0	19.6	46–145

(Harrell and Harrell, 1945, pp. 231–32)

And here are data for children of various occupational classes:

Mean I.Q.'s of children according to fathers' occupations

Fathers' occupational classification	Chronological ages			
	2–5½	6–9	10–14	15–18
I Professional	114.8	114.9	117.5	116.4
II Semiprofessional and managerial	112.4	107.3	112.2	116.7
III Clerical, skilled trades, and retail business	108.0	104.9	107.4	109.6
IV Rural owners	97.8	94.6	92.4	94.3
V Semiskilled, minor clerical and business	104.3	104.6	103.4	106.7
VI Slightly skilled	97.2	100.0	100.6	96.2
VII Day labor, urban and rural	93.8	96.0	97.2	97.6

(McNemar, 1942, p. 38)

.5   national origin.

In general, Jews, Scandinavians, Germans, English, and Americans attain higher average scores than Southern Europeans of various nationalities.

Such differences are documented in several investigations (e.g., Hirsch, 1926), but they do not hold up when the various nationalities are tested in their country of origin—which suggests that the differences among immigrant groups and their progeny are due to selective migration and/or to educational differences in the home environment typical of the various immigrant groups.

All of these differences are subject to environmental and genetic influences, in unknown degree, and cannot be assigned to one or the other factor on the basis of present evidence. Before leaving these generalizations, however, we should reiterate that small differences in average I.Q. may be of scientific interest but are of virtually no practical value in predicting the capabilities of individuals, since the differences within groups so far exceed and overlap the differences between them.

Finally, these interesting and unexpected findings:

.6   birth order.

Within families, there is a consistent increase in average intelligence from first-born to last-born.

This finding holds only *within* families. Across the population at large, later-born children have lower average I.Q.'s because larger families are more prevalent among groups with lower I.Q.'s in general. Here are the data from a carefully controlled study of several hundred children each compared only to his or her own siblings. The average advantage over the first-born rises to eighteen I.Q. points for those born eighth or later.

I.Q. and birth order

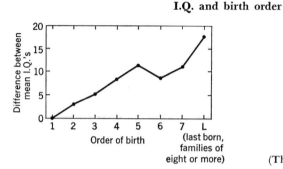

(Thurstone and Jenkins, 1931, p. 14)

There are two suggested interpretations: (1) that younger children have more opportunity to learn test-related skills from older siblings, and (2) that duration of labor shortens with successive births, and that intelligence is negatively related to birth difficulty.

.7   slightly higher average intelligence and scholastic achievement is associated with summer and fall births.

There is nothing . . . that denies a slight I.Q. advantage for cold weather conceptions. On the other hand, there is nothing that would warrant long vacations for the country's obstetricians for the first half of each year [Gordon and Novak, 1950, p. 63].

A frequent interpretation of this relationship is that summer- and fall-born children enjoy a general health advantage that is reflected in tested intelligence.

Creativity

In recent years a number of studies have tried to isolate the distinguishing characteristics of highly creative and original people. The studies are not directly comparable or additive because they employ different definitions of creativity, they study people in different lines of work (ranging from fine arts to industrial chemistry), and they apply different tests and measures.

To begin with, here are two examples to illustrate the wide range of subject matter and conclusions. First, here are several findings on the psychological characteristics of more and less creative groups of industrial chemists. Creativity was established by ratings of peers and superiors, and the "highs" and "lows" were then subjected to a wide variety of tests:

1. The more and less creative men do not differ significantly from each other in a test of verbal intelligence.
2. The more creative men are less anxious than the less creative men.
3. The more creative men are more autonomous, more dynamic, and more integrative than their less creative colleagues.
4. The more creative men see their own attitudes as being more different from others.
5. The less creative man has more authoritarian attitudes than does his more creative colleague.
6. The more creative men place higher value on practical matters and utility; more emphasis on harmony and form and less emphasis on mystical values and the acceptance of the church as an institution in comparison to their less creative colleagues.
7. In describing themselves the two groups differ in that while the more creative men are more oriented to achievement and acceptance of their own inner impulses, the less creative men are more oriented to avoiding situations in which they might be blamed for their activities or in which they might feel inferior.
8. The more creative men give more evidence of psychological well-being than do the less creative men.
9. The less creative man appears to take risks where they are less warranted, more than is true of his more creative colleague.
10. In a problem-solving situation, the more creative man works slowly and cautiously while he is analyzing his problem and gathering his data. Once he obtains the basic data and approaches the point of synthesis, he works rapidly. The less creative man spends less time in analyzing the problem but more time in attempting to synthesize his material [Stein, 1957, pp. 18–19].

For contrast and comparison, here is a summary of the distinguishing characteristics of a group of forty of the most creative architects in the country, as nominated by a panel of experts and compared with two control groups of architects not selected for creativity.

If I were to summarize what is most generally characteristic of the creative architect as we have seen him, it is his high level of effective intelligence, his openness to experience, his freedom from petty restraints and impoverishing inhibitions, his aesthetic sensitivity, his cognitive flexibility, his independence in thought and action, his high level of energy, his unquestioning commitment to creative endeavor, and his unceasing striving for creative solutions to the ever more difficult architectural problems which he constantly sets for himself [McKinnon, 1961, p. V-24].

Here are some generalizations that seem to be emerging:

C6   Creativity is not simply a matter of intelligence. A high I.Q. is necessary for creativity in some fields (e.g., nuclear physics), not necessary in others (graphic arts), and is never sufficient. Highly intelligent subjects are found in the low creativity groups in virtually every study.

Here, for example, is an illustration of the low relationship between creativity, as measured in paper and pencil tests, and I.Q. among a sample of adolescents.

Intercorrelations between creativity and intelligence tests

	Variable number	Test	Boys (above diagonal) N = 292					
			Variable number					
			Tests of creativity					
			1	2	3	4	5	6
Tests of crea- tivity	1	Word association		.369	.344	.303	.420	.378
	2	Uses	.371		.206	.222	.175	.186
	3	Hidden shapes	.351	.197		.159	.414	.366
	4	Fables	.320	.276	.153		.220	.131
	5	Make-up problems	.488	.279	.525	.269		.246
	6	Intelligence quotient	.371	.147	.303	.115	.393	

Girls (below diagonal) N = 241

(Getzels and Jackson, 1962, p. 20)

Noteworthy in the table are the relatively low correlations between IQ and performance on tests requiring the indicated creative thinking abilities. It must be remembered that this is a sample with a very high mean IQ, and some of the attenuation may be due to this factor. But, as we shall see, there are replications of these findings with other, less extreme groups [*ibid.*, p. 20].

Another investigator finds virtually no relationship between on-the-job creativity of research scientists and their performance on intelligence tests, or for that matter, on tests of engineering ability.

Perhaps the most striking of the omissions from the criterion-correlated variables are the ability measures. The correlation for the Terman *Concept Mastery Test* was −.07, for the *Minnesota Engineering Analogies Test* +.13, and for the *General Information Survey* +.07. None of these values is significant, and one is in the negative direction! [Gough, 1961, p. III-8.]

In short:

The relationship between intelligence and creativity . . . is . . . by no means a simple one. Where the subject-matter itself requires high intelligence for the mastery of its fundamentals, as in mathematics or physics, the correlation of measured intelligence with originality in problem-solving within the discipline tends to be positive but quite low. Among artists such as painters, sculptors, and designers, the correlation between rated quality of work and measured intelligence is zero or slightly negative. Again, however, it must be remembered that commitment to such endeavours is already selective for intelligence, so that the average IQ is already a superior one. A generalization which I would suggest, based not only on my own studies and those of my colleagues at the Institute but upon a number of other researches during the past three years at the University of Minnesota, the University of Chicago, and the National Merit Scholarship Corporation is this: Over the total range of intelligence and creativity a low positive correlation, probably in the neighborhood of .40, obtains; beyond an IQ of about 120, however, measured intelligence is a negligible factor in creativity, and the motivational and stylistic variables upon which our own research has laid such stress are the major determiners of creativity [Barron, 1961, p. II-10].

C7   Highly creative people show a preference for, and interest in, complexity and novelty; they have intrinsic interest in situations that require some resolution, rather than those that are cut-and-dried.

Perhaps the single most well-established conclusion to which our work has led, not only with writers but with other artists and with scientists as well, concerns the creative individual's response to apparent disorder and his own need to find a subtle ordering principle. . . . In preferences for paintings, as in line drawings, the more original subjects were inclined to like best the apparently unbalanced. . . . The same tendencies were apparent in the tests which require active expression rather than mere preference—the completion of line drawings and the construction of mosaics. Original individuals were disposed to introduce asymmetry and complexity into their drawings and mosaics [ibid., pp. II-4, II-6].

The first table on page 230 documents the greater preference for complexity among the more creative architects and among all the creative groups studied as compared with a control sample of normal adults.

There is a pronounced difference in mean score between creative architects (Architects I) and the comparison samples of architects unselected with respect to creativity (Architects II and III) in their liking of the rich, complex and asymmetrical. Similarly, in the total sample of architects, scores on an Institute scale which measures the preference for perceptual complexity correlate +.48 with rated creativity [McKinnon, 1961, p. V-17].

Behind this inclination to like and to construct what is not too simply ordered there appears to be a very strong need to achieve the most difficult and far-reaching ordering. When confronted, for instance, with the Rorschach inkblot test, original individuals insist to a most uncommon degree upon giving an interpretation of the blot which takes account of all details in one comprehensive, synthesizing image [Barron, 1961, p. II-6].

Barron-Welsh art scale *

Mean scores and standard deviations for various groups

	N	Mean	S.D.
Artists (standardization group)	80	40.3	12.9
Artists (first cross-validation group)	30	39.1	13.8
Architects I [40 "most creative"]	40	37.1	9.8
Writers I	20	31.5	12.5
Architects II	43	29.5	10.1
Women mathematicians I	16	28.1	12.5
Women mathematicians II	28	26.9	15.4
Men mathematicians I	26	26.9	12.7
Architects III	41	26.1	12.1
Research scientists	45	24.0	12.3
Student engineers	40	21.5	11.8
Men mathematicians II	21	19.4	10.1
Normal adults (original standardization group)	300	13.9	7.6

* Measuring preference for complexity and asymmetry.

(McKinnon, 1961, p. V-16)

With regard to the personality characteristics of creative people, relative to others:

C8   Highly creative people are more likely than others to view authority as conventional rather than absolute; to make fewer black-and-white distinctions; to have a less dogmatic and more relativistic view of life; to show more independence of judgment and less conventionality and conformity, both intellectual and social; to be more willing to entertain, and sometimes express, their own "irrational" impulses; to place a greater value on humor and in fact to have a better sense of humor; in short, to be somewhat freer and less rigidly controlled.

Here are some illustrative data:

Times conforming to unanimous but wrong group answers to simple questions (percentages)

	High on originality	*Low on originality*
Air Force captains	24	40
Mills College seniors	23	41
Research scientists	12	20

(Barron *et al.*, 1958, p. 16)

As another indication, the previously mentioned study of high-school students who were highly creative but not highly intelligent, and vice-versa, found far greater unconventionality in the occupations being considered by the creative group.

> When the occupations mentioned are analyzed into conventional (lawyer, doctor, professor) and unconventional (adventurer, inventor, writer) categories, it is found that the high creatives give a significantly greater proportion of unconventional occupations than do the high IQ's [Getzels and Jackson, 1962, pp. 57–58].

Quantity and quality of occupations mentioned by the experimental groups on direct and indirect sentence-completion tests

Group	Number of occupations mentioned			Unusual occupations	
	Total	$\overline{X}$	s	Number mentioned	Number of subjects mentioning
		DIRECT TEST			
High I.Q. (N = 28)	51	1.82 *	1.09	6	5 †
High creative (N = 26)	68	2.61 *	1.41	24	16 †
		INDIRECT TEST			
High I.Q. (N = 28)	100	3.57 †	1.81	12	10 *
High creative (N = 26)	130	5.00 †	1.80	29	17 *

t used to test differences between means in column 2.
χ^2 used to test differences between frequencies in column 5.
* Significant at .10 level.
† Significant at .01 level.

(*Ibid.*, pp. 57–58)

In the same study, when asked to tell stories about stimulus pictures:

> The high creatives tend to free themselves from the stimulus, using it largely as a point of departure for self-expression. . . . The picture stimulus may be of a man in an airplane, but the story he wants to tell is about a divorce; the picture stimulus may be of a man alone in an office, but the story he wants to tell is of a private eye in a cereal factory. . . . The high creativity adolescent has a more playful—or if you will, more experimental—attitude toward conventional ideas, objects, and qualities [*ibid.*, p. 42].

The more creative adolescents, when asked to draw pictures, respond with freer and more humorous productions. Here are contrasting examples:

232

High I.Q.

NAME _____

GRADE _____ DATE _____

Directions: In the space below, draw a picture appropriate to the title, "Playing Tag in the School Yard." You may draw any picture you like — whatever you may imagine for this theme.

"PLAYING TAG IN THE SCHOOL YARD"

High creative

NAME _____ GRADE _____ DATE _____

Directions: In the space below, draw a picture appropriate to the title, "Playing Tag in the School Yard." You may draw any picture you like — whatever you may imagine for this theme.

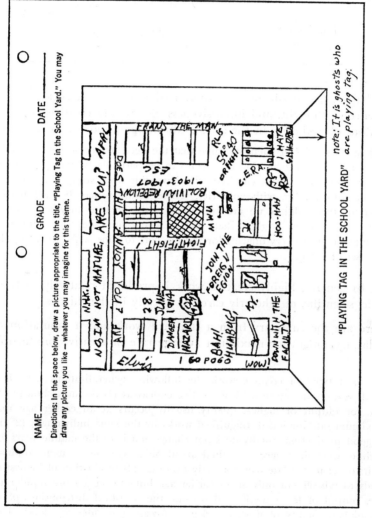

"PLAYING TAG IN THE SCHOOL YARD"   note: It is ghosts who are playing tag.

(Ibid., pp. 48, 46)

Humor-present versus humor-absent in the drawings of the high I.Q. and the high creative groups

	High I.Q. ($N = 28$)	High creative ($N = 26$)	χ^2	P
Humor-present	5	14	6.6	.02
Humor-absent	23	12		

(*Ibid.*, p. 49)

Perhaps as a result of this combination of unconventionality, independence of thought, and impulsiveness, potentially creative people often run afoul of authority in the social, educational, and occupational realm:

> Almost all studies of scientists agree that the need for autonomy, for independence of action, is something that seems to be particularly strong in this group. Under adolescent stress, children who have this need strongly are most likely to get into conflict with authority. These conflicts may become particularly acute in the children we are concerned with, because they are very bright. Many of them are brighter than their teachers, and they can think up a lot of things that are very difficult for the teachers to cope with [Roe, unpublished manuscript, 1963].

C9   In general, highly creative work is produced relatively early in the artistic, scientific, or scholarly career—typically in the thirties.

Here are the summary from a standard work and a tabulation of the "modal age ranges for maximum average rate of creative production" by field:

> For most types of creative work the following generalizations have been derived. Within any given field of creative endeavor: (1) the maximum production rate for output of highest quality usually occurs at an earlier age than the maximum rate for less distinguished works by the same individuals; (2) the rate of good production usually does not change much in the middle years and the decline, when it comes, is gradual at all older ages—much more gradual than in its onset in the late teens or early twenties; (3) production of highest quality tends to fall off not only at an earlier age but also at a more rapid rate than does output of lesser merit, and because the statistical distributions of age for the highest quality of work are skewed toward the older age levels, both the mean and median ages are higher than the modal values [Lehman, 1953, p. 326].

Before age thirty	*Thirty–thirty-four*	*Thirty-five–thirty-nine*	*Forty and over*
Chemistry	Mathematics	Astronomy	Novels
Poetry	Physics	Physiology	Architecture
	Botany	Opera	
	Symphonies	Philosophy	

And:

C9.1   Within any field, the large majority of creative contributions is made by a small minority of contributors.

In one study of seven diverse fields (e.g., music, geology, chemistry, gerontology), the top 10 per cent of contributors produced about 50 per cent of the work. "If the men in the bottom 50 per cent of each group are combined, their total contribution is, in every instance, less than the contribution of the highest decile" (Dennis, 1955, p. 278).

SELECTED READINGS

For systematic summaries of findings and theories in conditioning and learning in general, see:

Ernest R. Hilgard and D. G. Marquis. *Conditioning and Learning.* 2nd ed. Appleton-Century-Crofts, 1960.
S. S. Stevens, ed. *Handbook of Experimental Psychology.* Wiley, 1951.
Ernest R. Hilgard. *Theories of Learning.* 2nd ed. Appleton-Century-Crofts, 1956.

With respect to the practical issues of educational psychology, some standard references are:

John A. McGeoch. *The Psychology of Human Learning.* Rev. by Arthur L. Irion. 2nd ed. McKay, 1958.
Lee J. Cronbach. *Educational Psychology.* 2nd ed. Harcourt, Brace & World, 1963.
J. M. Stephens. *Educational Psychology.* Rev. ed. Holt, Rinehart & Winston, 1956.

A good illustration of how principles of stimulus-response associations can be systematically elaborated to apply to complex behavior appears in:

Charles E. Osgood. *Method and Theory in Experimental Psychology.* Oxford U. Press, 1953.

For examples of attempts to formulate principles of learning in precise mathematical terms, see:

Clark L. Hull. *A Behavior System.* Yale U. Press, 1952.
R. R. Bush and W. K. Estes, eds. *Studies in Mathematical Learning Theory.* Stanford U. Press, 1959.

The original work in rote memorization of nonsense syllables is:

H. Ebbinghaus. *Memory.* Trans. by H. A. Ruger and C. E. Bussenius. Teachers College, Columbia U., 1913.

The counterpart in the area of qualitative changes produced in meaningful material is:

Frederick C. Bartlett. *Remembering*. Cambridge U. Press, 1932.

Extensive explorations in inductive concept formation are reported in:

Jerome S. Bruner *et al. A Study of Thinking*. Wiley, 1956.
W. Edgar Vinacke. "The Investigation of Concept Formation," *Psychological Bulletin*, 48, 1951, pp. 1–31.

For various approaches to creative or productive thinking and problem-solving, see:

Max Wertheimer. *Productive Thinking*. Rev. by Michael Wertheimer. Harper, 1959.
Milton Rokeach. *The Open and Closed Mind*. Basic Books, 1960.
N. R. F. Maier. "An Aspect of Human Reasoning," *British Journal of Psychology*, 24, 1933, pp. 144–55.
Karl Duncker. "On Problem Solving," trans. by Lynne S. Lees, *Psychological Monograph*, 58, No. 5, 1945.

There is also a comprehensive, annotated bibliography of research and theory regarding creativity and creative people:

Morris I. Stein and Shirley J. Heinze. *Creativity and the Individual*. Free Press, 1960.

The literature on intelligence and its testing is highly technical and detailed; the following present and discuss the latest revisions in the major intelligence tests:

David Wechsler. *The Measurement and Appraisal of Adult Intelligence*. 4th ed. Williams & Wilkins, 1958.
Lewis M. Terman and Maud A. Merrill. *Stanford-Binet Intelligence Scale: Manual for the Third Revision Form L-M*. Houghton Mifflin, 1960.

The findings regarding the distribution of intelligence are summarized in:

Leona E. Tyler. *The Psychology of Human Differences*. 2nd ed. Appleton-Century-Crofts, 1956.
A. Anastasi. *Differential Psychology*. 3rd ed. Macmillan, 1958.

By way of contrast to learning as a mode of adaptation, there is a most interesting analysis of animal behavior under instinctive control:

Nikolaas Tinbergen. *The Study of Instinct*. Oxford U. Press, 1951.

The classic in classical conditioning is:

I. P. Pavlov. *Conditioned Reflexes.* Trans. and ed. by G. V. Anrep. Oxford U. Press, 1927.

In instrumental conditioning:

B. F. Skinner. *The Behavior of Organisms.* Appleton-Century-Crofts, 1938.

Attention is called to the cognitive functions in infrahuman species by:

Wolfgang Köhler. *The Mentality of Apes.* Harcourt, Brace & World, 1926.

Pleasure and nobility between them supply the motives of all actions whatsoever.

A R I S T O T L E
The Nicomachean Ethics

Man doth not live by bread only.

Deuteronomy, 8:3

In vain the sage, with retrospective eye,
Would from the apparent what conclude the why,
Infer the motive from the deed, and show
That what we chanced was what we meant to do.

A L E X A N D E R   P O P E
Moral Essays

The truth was that he died from solitude, the enemy known but to few on this earth, and whom only the simplest of us are fit to withstand. . . . The brilliant "Son Decoud," the spoiled darling of the family, the lover of Antonia and journalist of Sulaco, was not fit to grapple with himself single-handed. Solitude from mere outward condition of existence becomes very swiftly a state of soul in which the affectations of irony and scepticism have no place. It takes possession of the mind, and drives forth the thought into the exile of utter unbelief. After three days of waiting for the sight of some human face, Decoud caught himself entertaining a doubt of his own individuality. It had merged into the world of cloud and water, of natural forces and forms of nature. In our activity alone do we find the sustaining illusion of an independent existence as against the whole scheme of things of which we form a helpless part.

J O S E P H   C O N R A D
Nostromo

In this world there are only two tragedies. One is not getting what one wants, and the other is getting it. The last is the real tragedy.

O S C A R   W I L D E
Lady Windemere's Fan

Chapter Six
MOTIVATION

So far in these pages, man is capable of perceiving, learning, and thinking —ways in which he meets problems and satisfies needs. But, so far, he has no problems, no needs to satisfy. This chapter deals with the objects and nature of human striving: the things man needs, wants, or fears, and how he seeks to attain or avoid them, insofar as they have been empirically documented. In the following pages, then, behavioral-science man begins to approach the whole striving human being as we see him in real life.

In ordinary discourse, complex behavior is almost never explained in terms of specific responses to specific stimuli. For example, an entire series of diverse acts—looking for money and car keys, driving to the corner, parking, entering a store, and buying a cigar—is normally recognized as one coherent behavioral unit, held together and identified by the goal or end result. The sequence appears to be initiated, directed, and maintained by the underlying motive.

We take such needs or desires for granted as underlying causes of behavior because we experience them; everyone feels that there are things he wants and that he takes steps to get them. The behavioral sciences, too, find motivation a key concept in explaining behavior, but, as we shall see, on somewhat different grounds. Conscious striving is neither necessary nor sufficient to establish motivation, as the term is used in these pages.

DEFINITIONS

Motivation: The general term that we will use to refer to all those inner striving conditions variously described as wishes, desires, needs, drives, and the like. Theoretical distinctions are often maintained among these more specific labels, but for our purposes the more general notion is adequate.

Formally, then, a motive is an inner state that energizes, activates, or moves (hence "motivation"), and that directs or channels behavior toward goals. In short, a motive results in and hence can be inferred from purposive, means-ends behavior. Hunger, the quest for power or status, the desire to land on the moon or to own a new car—all these are motives according to this definition, though obviously motives of varying generality and duration.

Goal: The object, condition, or activity toward which the motive is directed; in short, that which will satisfy or reduce the striving. We use all three words—object, condition, and activity—to take account of the fact that "ends" can usually be stated in such alternative terms. For example, a hungry man can be said to seek: (a) food, (b) to eat, (c) satiation. In part, the distinction is empirical as well as semantic. For example, is a thirsty dog satisfied by drinking if the water never reaches his stomach? Or, conversely, is he satisfied if the water enters his stomach directly? Is a power-hungry man satisfied by power, per se; by engaging in those activities that increase his power; or by some inner security that can stem from power as well as from other sources?

Physiological motives: Those motives that stem directly from the physical needs of the organism, whose satisfaction is essential to the survival or physical well-being of the individual or the species: hunger, thirst, elimination, pain-avoidance, mating, and so on. Since such motives would take us far into the field of physiology, we deal with them summarily here.

Secondary, learned, social, or psychogenic motives: Terms used to designate those motives not demonstrably in the direct service of physical needs. To strive for social acceptance or status, to work to write a symphony or climb a mountain, to try to keep the schools segregated or to integrate them, to want to complete college or understand human behavior—these are examples.

It is difficult to frame a label for such motives without implying a theory of their origin: thus, the word "secondary" grows out of learning theory, which postulates that these goals develop from association with, or as instruments to, primary physiological ones. Similarly, the designation "social" implies both an origin and a further goal behind the motive. We shall take up what is known regarding origins in the following pages; but to anticipate the fact that the issue is not settled, and to keep that fact in view, we use these terms interchangeably throughout the chapter.

One note of caution needs to be stressed before we move on to the findings. Since motives are both inferred from and taken to account for purposive behavior, there is always the danger of accepting circular reasoning—of taking a motive as an explanation of the very behavior from which it was inferred. When the conditions that produce or arouse a motive are known, or when there are independent measures of it, motives help to explain behavior. When such conditions are not met, motives may serve to describe behavior, but they do not explain it.

Motive as description: A man works hard and long hours, talks about the importance of "getting ahead," and asks his wife to invite important people to dinner. This behavior is conveniently summarized by the observation that he is ambitious or has so-called achievement motivation. That inductive statement is descriptive, and may be predictive of other acts; for example, the probability that he will volunteer for a Sunday work assignment.

But the statement is in no sense *explanatory*. It is seductive, but fallacious, to say that he works hard because he is ambitious; we know no more about the causes of the observed behavior than we did before we applied the term. Incidentally, there is instructive historical precedent for this fallacy in the physical sciences. Intrinsic tendencies have often been used to explain the very things from which they were inferred, as when Aristotle "explained" why stones fall and smoke rises by granting them intrinsic or essential tendencies to fall and rise, respectively.

Motive as explanation: Hunger, inferred from food seeking and eating, *is* legitimate as an explanatory concept because it can be related to events other than the behavior from which it is inferred. The conditions that arouse it can be exactly specified, and so can indicators of the state other than food-seeking behavior (e.g., stomach contractions).

In short, anyone can make a child hungry, but not anyone can make him ambitious—and therein lies the essential distinction. Being able, truly able, to explain the former, we can predict and control in line with the explanation.

FINDINGS

The Physiological Motives

There is a great amount of physiological literature on the mechanics of the primary motives: what chemical imbalances act as a trigger for what bodily reactions and how the entire system is regulated. As in the case of sensory physiology, we omit such findings on the ground that they stem from biological science more than from behavioral studies. However, it does seem appropriate to say a few words about the kind of work that goes on at or near the borderline, where the primary motives are very much involved in human behavior.

To begin with, the primary motives are usually classified according to some such scheme as this:

(a) Positive or supply motives: These result from deficiency and produce seeking and consumption of needed substance (e.g., hunger, thirst).

(b) Negative or avoidance motives: These result from the presence of harmful or potentially harmful stimulation and produce flight or avoidance (e.g., pain or fear).

(c) Species-maintaining motives: These result from the nature of the reproductive system and produce mating, children, and nurturant behavior (e.g., sex).

This classification is clearly based on biological function or consequence, not on subjective goal. A hungry man is not necessarily concerned with restoring the blood level of x or y, nor a sexually aroused one with contributing to the species. In the latter case, indeed, subjective concern may actually be in the opposite direction, thus illustrating a most general finding to the effect that subjective concern and real purpose ("real" in some objective sense) do not always match.

Here are a few findings that indicate the kind of knowledge that is produced near the borderline of the biological and behavioral sciences, with regard to primary motives:

. . . Hunger pangs disappear almost entirely after several days without food; but in cases of prolonged semistarvation, subjects report increasingly severe hunger sensations, to the point where food virtually dominates behavior, thoughts, and wishes.

> Preoccupation with thoughts of food is mentioned repeatedly in the field reports from semi-starvation areas. Characteristically, in a hospital for Germans who became Russian prisoners of war, eating (and bowel movements), not sex, was the principal topic of conversation, and heated arguments revolved around recipes [Friedrich, 1950; quoted in Keys *et al.*, 1950, p. 833].

. . . Continued intake of some nonessential substances, such as alcohol or narcotics, can produce a continuing need for them; hence, supply motives can be acquired through addiction.

Regardless of any psychological factors that may be involved, once a person is addicted he has a physiological need that acts in essential respects like hunger or thirst. That narcotics addiction is not just a social phenomenon is demonstrated by experimentally induced morphine addiction in chimpanzees. Like their human counterparts, addicted chimps exhibit a striving for the drug that may exceed that for food: when food and syringe were both withheld for eighteen hours, the chimps directed most of their efforts toward the latter (Spragg, 1940).

. . .   The longest recorded sleepless siege, nine days, produced marked although temporary deterioration.

The effect of sleep deprivation on behavior, thinking, motor performance, and biological energy transfer systems was studied in a single subject who remained awake without drugs for 220 hours. . . . Behavioral changes included irritability, paranoid thinking, expansiveness, grandiosity, hypnagogic states, visual hallucinations, and episodic rage. . . . Deficits in thinking and visual-motor performance occurred cyclically across days of wakefulness, with gradual deterioration finally resulting in virtual untestability on the ninth day [Luby *et al.,* 1960, p. 191].

. . .   Characteristically, behavior that reduces or avoids pain is physiologically adaptive, but fear of pain may also prove nonadaptive. Avoiding the real or imagined pain of certain medical procedures, for example, may keep people from needed treatment, especially when the treatment-pain is acute and the disease-pain mild or nonexistent.

. . .   The acts that satisfy hunger, thirst, and sex take on important social significance. That is, they become the focal point for significant rites and rituals with symbolic meaning that transcends their biological functions: e.g., the family meal, the business lunch, the puberty rite, the marriage ceremony, the corner pub.

. . .   In general, and most significant for what follows, although primary motives stem from innately determined physical needs of the species, human learning markedly influences the selection of goals and the methods of attaining them. For the primary motives are not primary in the sense that they always take priority.

Gratification is often postponed and sometimes renounced entirely in favor of the secondary or social motives—even at the point where survival itself is at stake. In order to achieve some nonbiological goal, people will starve in the presence of appropriate food (Gandhi, the volunteers in the starvation experiment); they will starve rather than eat food they have come to consider inappropriate; they will renounce sex for the cloth, and renounce life itself for any number of causes. In short, as we recall from an earlier chapter, human behavior is far less subject to the direct control of physiological regulators than is animal behavior; it is far more variable as a result of learning; and social and psychological factors often determine the specific form in which the primary motives get expressed—*what* will be eaten; *how often, by whom,* and *in what way* sexual activity will be engaged in; *at what point* honor takes over from sheer survival. With regard to this last, here is one scholar's estimate of the situation:

Proportions of the total population manifesting various forms of deviate behavior in starvation

Activities induced by starvation	Percentage of the population succumbing to the pressure of starvation
Cannibalism (in noncannibalistic societies)	Less than one third of 1 per cent
Murder of members of the family and friends	Less than 1 per cent
Murder of other members of one's group	Not more than 1 per cent
Murder of strangers who are not enemies	Not more than 2 to 5 per cent
Infliction of various bodily and other injuries on members of one's social group	Not more than 5 to 10 per cent
Theft, larceny, robbery, forgery, and other crimes against property which have a clear-cut criminal character	Hardly more than 7 to 10 per cent
Prostitution and other highly dishonorable sex activities	Hardly more than 10 per cent
Violation of fundamental religious and moral principles	Hardly more than 10 to 20 per cent
Violation of various rules of strict honesty and fairness in pursuit of food, such as misuse of rationing cards, hoarding, and taking unfair advantage of others	From 20 to 99 per cent, depending upon the nature of the violation
Violation of less important religious, moral, juridical, conventional, and similar norms	From 50 to 99 per cent
Surrender or weakening of most of the aesthetic activities irreconcilable with food-seeking activities	From 50 to 99 per cent
Weakening of sex activities, especially coitus	From 70 to 90 per cent during prolonged and intense starvation

(Sorokin, 1942, p. 81)

With this brief treatment of the primary motives—no more than a hint of the great amount of scientific work done in this field—we now turn to the influential secondary, or social, motives.

Secondary, Learned, Social, or Psychogenic Motives

Relatively little day-to-day behavior is directly instrumental in satisfying physical needs. Saving for a trip abroad, working to get ahead, buying a new car, or reading a book are not in themselves biologically adaptive. Still further removed from physical satisfaction, for example, are heroism or martyrdom, artistic production or religious asceticism. Yet such behavior is purposive and goal-directed. What motives are to be inferred, and how do they relate to biological needs?

There are several possibilities. In the first place, we have seen that people learn to pursue some such goals by the principles of secondary reinforcement, as discussed under classical and instrumental conditioning.

A1 Anything instrumental in attaining primary gratification, or simply associated with primary gratification in the past, takes on reinforcing or rewarding properties and hence can become a goal.

Whether or not this is always or necessarily the explanation, human striving for money, acceptance, or affection *can* be produced on this basis: each has been redeemed for, or associated with, physical gratification. Similarly, intellectual or aesthetic activities and skills can be associated with and lead to greater efficiency in satisfying physical needs.

On the other hand, many psychologists hold that some such nonphysiological motives are just as basic or "primary" as physiological ones—in the sense that they are universal and are not dependent on learned associations with other gratifications. For example:

A2 Striving for stimulation, information, knowledge, or understanding —*which* depends on the level of animal and the level of activity—appears to be a universal motive among the primates, and especially man.

Lower animals as well as people actively seek stimulation of various kinds. Sights, sounds, smells, and other sensations that have not led to nor been associated with physical satisfaction, seem to be interesting, attractive, and sometimes demonstrably rewarding in themselves. Perhaps the simplest instance is the so-called orientation response:

A2.1 Other things equal, novel or changing stimuli command more attention and examination than familiar ones.

It is this reflex which brings about the immediate response in man and animals to the slightest changes in the world around them, so that they immediately orientate their appropriate receptor organ in accordance with the perceptible quality in the agent bringing about the change, making full investigation of it. The biological significance of this reflex is obvious. If the animal were not provided with such a reflex its life would hang at every moment by a thread. In man this reflex has been greatly developed with far-reaching results, being represented in its highest form by inquisitiveness—the parent of that scientific method through which we hope one day to come to a true orientation in knowledge of the world around us [Pavlov, 1927, p. 12].

A2.2 Complex, variegated stimuli attract more attention than do simple ones.

Human infants, for example, look first at the more complex (right hand) figures when arrays such as these are presented:

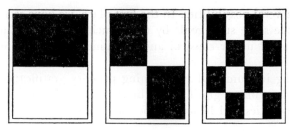

(Berlyne, 1958b, p. 316)

And in the following pairs, adults spend more time examining the right-hand figures than they do with the corresponding simpler or more regular or more familiar versions.

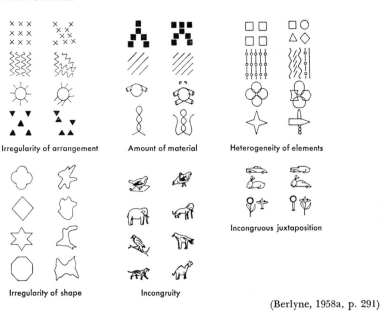

(Berlyne, 1958a, p. 291)

A2.3 Animals will expend energy to introduce variability into an otherwise constant or consistent situation, even when there is no extrinsic reward.

Recall, for example, the spontaneous "hypotheses" or changes in patterns of response by rats in situations where the pay-off remains the same, regardless of response. In fact, rats will cross an electric grid just to get to the other side—that is, simply to explore a new environment—when not under the influence of any other known motives or rewards (Warden, 1931).

A2.4 Sheer physical contact and cuddling appears to be intrinsically gratifying to and sought by the infant, and even necessary for normal physical and personality development. And, at least in monkeys, there is also evidence that an inanimate source of "contact comfort" *alone* can attract something closely resembling the affection that offspring normally attach to the mother.

In the recent but already classical studies mentioned above, monkeys were raised with artificial models as surrogate "mothers." In a critical test, they came to love their terry-cloth mothers, and in preference to a wire alternate that had nursed them since birth. "Love" was evident in all the strivings that are normally taken as indicators: clinging, fleeing to her when afraid, grief when separated, strenuous efforts to return, and the like.

Time spent on cloth and wire mother surrogates
(Both Equally Available)

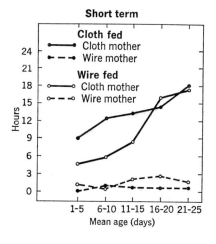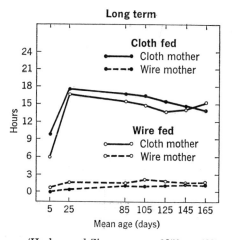

(Harlow and Zimmermann, 1959, p. 422)

These data make it obvious that contact comfort is a variable of critical importance in the development of affectional responsiveness to the surrogate mother, and that nursing appears to play a negligible role. With increasing age and opportunity to learn, an infant fed from a lactating wire mother does not become more responsive to her, as would be predicted from a derived-drive theory, but, instead becomes increasingly more responsive to its nonlactating cloth mother. These findings are at complete variance with a drive-reduction theory of affectional development [*Ibid.*, p. 423].

A2.5   Not only sensory stimulation, but direct electrical stimulation of "pleasure centers" in the brain is rewarding, as indicated by its ability to reinforce responses in line with the ordinary instrumental conditioning situation.

Rats learn to push levers when reinforced only by such stimulation, just as hungry rats do when rewarded by food.

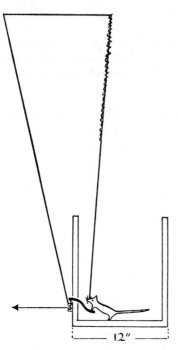

Diagram of apparatus by means of which a rat delivers electric shocks to its own brain *

* When the rat steps on the pedal, the electric circuit is closed and current is transmitted to its brain by means of implanted electrodes.

(Olds, 1958, p. 316)

Electric-current functions *

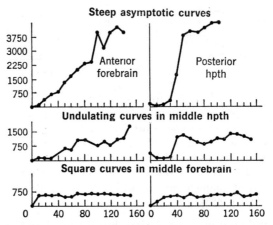

* The hourly self-stimulation rate (plotted along the ordinate) tends to rise as current (on the abscissa) increases from 0 to 160 microamperes in steps of ten. In the middle hypothalamus the curve shows a temporary decline when the electric field invades an area where electric stimulation has a negative motivational effect. In the middle forebrain there is an abrupt rise to five hundred responses an hour and then no further increase, because there is a very small field in which positive motivational effects are obtained, surrounded by a larger neutral area.

(Ibid., p. 317)

The areas in which the stimulation produces the approach or rewarding effect occupy a larger proportion of the brain than do the areas in which the avoidance or punishing effect is produced. Therefore, the brain cannot be thought of as tending mainly to produce behaviors which *decrease* its own excitation, for a large portion causes behaviors which *increase* excitation (*ibid.*, p. 318).

A more recent review of research into the motivational aspects of electrical stimulation of the brain concludes:

> Electrical stimulation in a very broad set of brain areas yields effects on behavior tantamount to those of primary reward. The areas involved are largely in hypothalamus and rhinencephalon.
>
> With current correctly adjusted and the electrodes correctly placed, it is possible to generate more motive force with this type of reward than with any other reward used in animal experimentation. With current set lower, or electrodes differently placed, far milder effects are achieved, effects comparable in every way with conventional rewards. With telencephalic electrodes, satiation occurs so that animals will self-stimulate daily for fixed periods of time but not indefinitely. With some hypothalamic electrodes, there is no satiation so that animals self-stimulate to the point of exhaustion [Olds, 1962, p. 595].

A2.6   Lower animals as well as human beings exhibit intrinsic interest in puzzles, problems, and other mental or physical exercises.

So, for example, monkeys presented with a latch-type lock learned to open it, and opened it repeatedly with no visible reinforcement other than the results of the act itself.

> A manipulation drive, strong and extremely persistent, is postulated to account for learning and maintenance of the puzzle performance. It is further postulated that drives of this class represent a form of motivation which may be as primary and as important as the homeostatic drives [Harlow *et al.*, 1950, p. 234].

The human satisfaction in problem solving is apparent in the variety of games, puzzles, and other such mental gymnastics often pursued simply "for fun"—or at least without any demonstrable extrinsic reward. Furthermore:

> **A2.6a**   There is a tendency to resume interrupted mental tasks that are being done without extrinsic reward, and, under certain conditions, to remember the interrupted tasks better than completed control problems.

Here, for example, are the results of an experiment that documents people's spontaneous tendency to complete tasks that are arbitrarily assigned and in no known way instrumental to a further goal:

The primary tasks which were interrupted were as follows:
1. Putting together a six-piece jig-saw picture puzzle.
2. Building a toy log cabin.
3. Copying a multicolored pegboard design.
4. Making human or animal figures by fitting together wooden pegs of different shapes ("Krazy-ikes").
5. Reassembling a door lock which had been taken apart. . . .

The upper row of [the table] shows how . . . different forms of reaction to the interruption distribute themselves in the normal group. In the great majority of cases (72.5 per cent of all interrupted tasks) the subjects returned to the interrupted task and finished it at the first opportunity, i.e., generally as soon as the interposed task was completed [Rickers-Ovsiankina, 1937, pp. 182, 184].

Relative incidence of different forms of reaction to interruption in normal and schizophrenic subjects (in percentage of interrupted tasks)

Subjects	Number of interrupted tasks	Reaction to interruption (percentages)			
		R	R?	DR	NR
Normal (108)	309	72.5	3.5	9.0	15.0
Schizophrenic (61)	220	41.8	15.5	0.5	42.3

R: Resumption and completion.   DR: Desire for resumption.
R?: Resumption without completion.   NR: Non-resumption.

(*Ibid.*, p. 184)

In addition, from another study:

The proof that the resumption (or as the case may be, a repetition of the activity) fails to occur as soon as the tension system is discharged by the attainment of the goal is important for the character of the quasi-needs as tension systems. It is shown that a substitute satisfaction can have the same effect and, further, that the presentation of the half-finished work of another person does not, as a rule, cause a tendency to completion [Lewin, 1935, p. 243].

The following results show relative recall for interrupted versus successfully completed tasks, under conditions where the subjects were not personally or emotionally involved in the task. (As we shall soon see, when feelings of personal adequacy are at stake, the opposite effect has been observed.) In this case, each subject was assigned an assortment of twenty tasks—e.g., arithmetic problems, puzzles, making clay models—and was then interrupted before completing some of them. Note that all but six of the thirty-two subjects recalled more of the tasks that were interrupted than of those they were allowed to complete successfully. This effect, incidentally, is greater for more involving tasks and for those individuals interrupted just before completion.

The ratio of the retained uncompleted to the retained completed activities $\dfrac{RU}{RC}$ *

		Rank Order of Subjects			
		Activities			
Rank $\dfrac{RU}{RC}$	Subject	ΣR	RU	RC	$\dfrac{RU}{RC}$
1	Wd.	7	6	1	6
2	Be.	9	7	2	3.5
3	St.	13	10	3	3.3
5	Jf.	8	6	2	3.0
	M.	8	6	2	3.0
	Eu.	12	9	3	3.0
7	Pl.	7	5	2	2.5
10	Paj.	9	6	3	2.0
	Gin.	9	6	3	2.0
	Hf.	6	4	2	2.0
	Pt.	15	10	5	2.0
	Ml.	12	8	4	2.0
14	Dm.	11	7	4	1.75
	V.	11	7	4	1.75
	Git.	11	7	4	1.75
16	Dm. E.	13	8	5	1.6
19	Ml. R.	15	9	6	1.5
	Jn.	10	6	4	1.5
	Rm.	15	9	6	1.5
	Gld.	10	6	4	1.5
	Jic.	10	6	4	1.5
23	Ml. E.	12	7	5	1.4
	Kür.	19	11	8	1.4
	Hn.	12	7	5	1.4
25.5	Glk.	16	9	7	1.3
	Jnk.	14	8	6	1.3
28	Gl.	12	6	6	1.0
	Wlt.	12	6	6	1.0
	Schn.	10	5	5	1.0
30.5	Sim.	11	5	6	0.8
	Fr.	9	4	5	0.8
32	Sim. H.	7	3	4	0.75
Arithmetic mean		11.1	6.8	4.25	1.9

* ΣR, number of retained activities; RU, number of retained uncompleted activities; RC, number of retained completed activities; RU/RC, ratio of retained uncompleted to retained completed activities.

(Lewin, 1935, p. 245, adapted from Zeigarnik, 1927)

In summary, then, curiosity, in the most general sense of that term, acts as a motive; that is, it induces purposive behavior which leads either to its satisfaction or to tensions when frustrated.

As mentioned earlier, those goals and sources of satisfaction related to interpersonal relationships are also subject to two general interpretations. On the one hand, desires to master or be mastered, to love and nurture or to attack, or simply to be with others can originate as learned means to physiological ends. Rats, for example, have been taught to fight each other to avoid electric shock; and when the fighting partner was removed the subject transferred or displaced his aggression to the innocent bystander, a doll (Miller, 1948). Fighting in self-defense, the killing of prey for food, or the battle between males for mates have even more direct physiological functions. On the other hand, certain social manifestations, even among lower animals, appear to be basic and primary—i.e., only indirectly if at all related to physiological needs.

A3   Affiliation per se is exhibited in all primates; as we have seen, some form of social contact appears necessary for the normal physical and personality development of the human infant; and total isolation is virtually always an intolerable situation for the human adult—even when physical needs are provided for.

If such evidence is needed, an examination of the consequences of social isolation shows convincingly that the social needs are indeed powerful ones. Autobiographical reports of such people as religious hermits, prisoners of war, and castaways make it clear that the effects of isolation can be devastating. For example, a prisoner (Weissberg, 1951) writes, "Gradually the loneliness closed in. Later on I was to experience situations which amounted almost to physical torture, but even that seemed preferable to absolute isolation." Such reports are extremely common and seem to be as typical of those who have gone into voluntary isolation as those forced into solitary confinement. . . .

Aside from these reports of profound disturbance, anxiety, and pain, the condition of absolute social deprivation as described in these autobiographical reminiscences seems responsible for many other dramatic effects. Most prominently, the following three trends characterize many of these reports:

First, the reported "pain" of the isolation experience seems typically to bear a nonmonotonic relationship to time—increasing to a maximum and then, in many cases, decreasing sharply. . . .

Second, there seems to be a strong tendency for those in isolation to think, dream, and occasionally hallucinate about people. Indeed, comparison of the anchoritic or hermit saints with the cenobitic saints indicates greater frequency of visions and hallucinatory experiences for the religious solitaries.

And third, those isolates who are able to keep themselves occupied with distracting activities appear to suffer less and be less prone to the state of apathy (Schachter, 1959, pp. 6–8).

A4   Status or dominance hierarchies are exhibited in every known human society, and are even observed in lower animals such as dogs, goats, cows, and hens.

For example, definite and consistent pecking orders are established among hens (Schjelderup-Ebbe, 1935); and a herd of cows will establish a dominance hierarchy and march in that order returning from pasture.

Differentiation in status sometimes, and in our society often, leads to the desire to rise within the social system. In some groups there is particular emphasis on upward mobility to the point where getting ahead becomes a dominant and pervasive motive for members. The importance of social stratification in human affairs is documented in a later chapter devoted entirely to this matter. That chapter details the conditions and implications of striving for status; we merely note it here as a widespread and important human motive.

A5   As in the case of hunger, thirst, and other physiological needs, some social motives appear to increase with deprivation. For example, agreement or approval is a more effective reinforcer with subjects who have been deprived in that respect than it is with satiated subjects.

One experiment employed a simple instrumental conditioning situation: children could drop marbles into either of two holes in a "game," with one of the two responses reinforced by "hm hm," "good," "fine." Some of the subjects were first "socially deprived" (they spent twenty minutes alone); the controls went directly into the experiment, while the third group was "satiated" on the way to the laboratory by extremely solicitous and approving reactions on the part of the experimenter. Here are the results in the subsequent experiment:

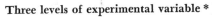
Three levels of experimental variable *

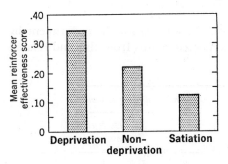

* There were thirty-four subjects in each group.

(Gerwitz and Baer, 1958, p. 169)

Thus, a reinforcer appearing to be typical of those involved in children's social drives appears responsive to deprivation and satiation operations of a similar order as those controlling the effectiveness of reinforcers of a number of the primary appetitive drives [*ibid.*, p. 172].

A5.1   The presence of others appears to be more eagerly sought in anxious situations than in calm ones; and in anxious situations, by first-born and only children more often than by the later-born.

In one study, for example, when subjects reported to participate in a psychological experiment, anxiety was aroused as follows:

In the high-anxiety condition, the subjects, all college girls, strangers to one another, entered a room to find facing them a gentleman of serious mien, horn-rimmed glasses, dressed in a white laboratory coat, stethoscope dribbling out of his pocket, behind him an array of formidable electrical junk. After a few preliminaries, the experimenter began:

"Allow me to introduce myself. I am Dr. Gregor Zilstein of the Medical School's Departments of Neurology and Psychiatry. I have asked you all to come today in order to serve as subjects in an experiment concerned with the effects of electrical shock."

Zilstein paused ominously, then continued with a seven- or eight-minute recital of the importance of research in this area, citing electroshock therapy, the increasing number of accidents due to electricity, and so on. He concluded in this vein:

"What we will ask each of you to do is very simple. We would like to give each of you a series of electric shocks. Now, I feel I must be completely honest with you and tell you exactly what you are in for. These shocks will hurt, they will be painful. As you can guess, if, in research of this sort, we're to learn anything at all that will really help humanity, it is necessary that our shocks be intense. What we will do is put an electrode on your hand, hook you into apparatus such as this (Zilstein points to the electrical-looking gadgetry behind him), give you a series of electric shocks, and take various measures such as your pulse rate, blood pressure, and so on. Again, I do want to be honest with you and tell you that these shocks will be quite painful but, of course, they will do no permanent damage" [Schachter, 1959, pp. 12–13].

The subjects were then given their choice of waiting for the experiment by themselves or with others. Here are the pooled results from this and related experiments:

	Number choosing to wait	
	Together	*Don't care and alone*
First-born and only	32	16
Later-born	21	39

$$\chi^2 = 10.70 \qquad p = .01$$

(Ibid., p. 44)

Under low-anxiety conditions—where subjects were assured the "shock" would be quite mild—the difference disappeared.

> Clearly, then, these results are specific to anxiety, and it may be concluded that anxiety produces considerably stronger manifestations of affiliative needs in first-born and only children than in later-born children [*ibid.*, p. 46].

Perhaps related to this is the fact that:

> **A5.1a**   First-born children show a greater tendency than later-born to conform or comply with the judgments expressed unanimously by members of a group.

The procedure is one used in several of the classical experiments that are reported in detail later. Subjects, in a group setting, are asked to announce their perceptual judgments—e.g., to select which of two lines matches a third one in length. They then find the evidence of their senses in direct contradiction with the unanimous judgment of the other members (who are accomplices of the experimenter). Do they "go along" and make the wrong but popular judgment? Here are the results by birth order.

Birth order	Number of subjects	Number of errors	Percentage yielding	p
First-born	24	117	40.6	
Later-born	24	85	29.5	$< .01$

(Becker and Carroll, 1962, p. 130)

Whether or not some such needs for affiliation, approval, status, curiosity, and perhaps other nonphysiological motives are innate and general to all men (rather than learned as means to other ends), there is no doubt that many of the most important human strivings *are* learned. Landing on the moon, writing textbooks, or getting academic degrees are certainly not goals general to all men at all times. Yet each constitutes a source of general, pervasive, and dominant motivation for some people, so that it would be difficult to understand their behavior without taking these longings into account.

Such strivings, and their innumerable counterparts in various occupations and life situations are not simple offshoots or elaborations of physiological needs, as are learned food preferences and appetites. They reflect the effect of learning in a more basic way: the goals themselves are acquired and bear no intrinsic relationship to biological needs, with which they may actually conflict.

There is much theoretical controversy—but little evidence—on the relationship between such motives and the physiological ones. One position is that all nonphysiological goals are acquired as means to biological ends; or through simple association with them, via secondary reinforcement.

Even a chimpanzee, for example, can be made acquisitive or avaricious of poker chips once he has learned that they can be redeemed for food in a vending machine (Wolfe, 1936). Another position is that even if such goals acquire their original attraction as means to other ends, they may then persist in their own right (e.g., greed may persist beyond the need for money). Still another school of thought views complex social strivings as transmutations or elaborations of the physiological needs (e.g., the infant's need for food and physical succor flowers into general social dependence—the need and search for social and symbolic approval and support). And, finally, nonphysiological needs may be entirely independent of physiological functions; they may be innate or arise out of social interaction, but in either case may exist without any present or historical roots in physiological satisfactions.

This theoretical issue is basic to the scientific understanding of behavior, but it is not of great importance at the practical level. Regardless of which one or combination of these fundamental relationships between physiological and learned motives is found to be correct, we know that people strive for objects and conditions not essential to their physical well-being and occasionally detrimental or even fatal to them; that many (and perhaps all) of these strivings are learned, not innate, and arise principally out of social interaction; that some of the most important learned motives stem from primary face-to-face associations—with the family, close friends, the occupational group. The process by which motives arise in social interaction is basic to the study of behavior. It is treated directly in the chapters on socialization, small groups, social stratification, and the family; and, although less directly, the topic is included in almost every other chapter to follow.

Listing and Classifying Learned Motives

Since learned motives arise out of infinitely variable experience, lists of such motives must either be specific to particular cultures at certain points in time or so general as to lose much of their explanatory value.

Furthermore, even within a given social situation, motives can be listed and classified at several levels of generality. For example, the moon-reaching motive can be subsumed under one or another more basic motive, such as the need to achieve recognition, or to master the environment, or to increase national security. But each of these, in turn, can be reduced to a still more basic motive, until the universal—and tautological—quest for "happiness" is reached. So it is difficult to maintain any particular level of generality as "basic"; the number and breadth of motives listed is arbitrary and depends upon the purpose of the classification.

Accordingly, various writers have constructed lists of motives ranging from very short and highly general lists to more specific ones containing as many as fifty or sixty social motives. One classical scheme reduced social motives to four basic "wishes"—for security, recognition, response from others, and new experience (Thomas, 1923). On the other hand, one of the classifications underlying much current research lists twenty-eight social (psychogenic) "needs," as follows:

—Need Acquisition (Acquisitive attitude). To gain possessions and property. To grasp, snatch or steal things. To bargain or gamble. To work for money or goods.
—Need Conservance (Conserving attitude). To collect, repair, clean and preserve things. To protect against damage.
—Need Order (Orderly attitude). To arrange, organize, put away objects. To be tidy and clean. To be scrupulously precise.
—Need Retention (Retentive attitude). To retain possession of things. To refuse to give or lend. To hoard. To be frugal, economical and miserly.
—Need Construction (Constructive attitude). To organize and build. . . .
—Need Superiority (Ambitious attitude). This has been broken up into two needs: the need Achievement (will to power over things, people and ideas) and the need Recognition (efforts to gain approval and high social status).
—Need Achievement (Achievant attitude). To overcome obstacles, to exercise power, to strive to do something difficult as well and as quickly as possible. (This is an elementary Ego need which alone may prompt any action or be fused with any other need.)
—Need Recognition (Self-forwarding attitude). To excite praise and commendation. To demand respect. To boast and exhibit one's accomplishments. To seek distinction, social prestige, honours or high office. . . .
—Need Exhibition (Exhibitionistic attitude). To attract attention to one's person. To excite, amuse, stir, shock, thrill others. Self-dramatization. . . .
—Need Inviolacy (Inviolate attitude). This includes desires and attempts to prevent a depreciation of self-respect, to preserve one's "good name," to be immune from criticism, to maintain psychological "distance." It is based on pride and personal sensitiveness. . . .
—Need Infavoidance (Infavoidant attitude). To avoid failure, shame, humiliation, ridicule. To refrain from attempting to do something that is beyond one's powers. To conceal a disfigurement.
—Need Defendance (Defensive attitude). To defend oneself against blame or belittlement. To justify one's actions. To offer extenuations, explanations and excuses. To resist "probing."
—Need Counteraction (Counteractive attitude). Proudly to overcome defeat by restriving and retaliating. To select the hardest tasks. To defend one's honour in action.
—Need Dominance (Dominative attitude). To influence or control others. To persuade, prohibit, dictate. To lead and direct. To restrain. To organize the behaviour of a group.
—Need Deference (Deferent attitude). To admire and willingly follow a superior. To co-operate with a leader. To serve gladly.

—Need Similance (Suggestible attitude). To empathize. To imitate or emulate. To identify oneself with others. To agree and believe.

—Need Autonomy (Autonomous attitude). To resist influence or coercion. To defy an authority or seek freedom in a new place. To strive for independence.

—Need Contrarience (Contrarient attitude). To act differently from others. To be unique. To take the opposite side. To hold unconventional views. . . .

—Need Aggression (Aggressive attitude). To assault or injure. To murder. To belittle, harm, blame, accuse or maliciously ridicule a person. To punish severely. Sadism.

—Need Abasement (Abasive attitude). To surrender. To comply and accept punishment. To apologize, confess, atone. Self-depreciation. Masochism. . . .

—Need Blamavoidance (Blamavoidance attitude). To avoid blame, ostracism or punishment by inhibiting asocial or unconventional impulses. To be well-behaved and obey the law. . . .

—Need Affiliation (Affiliative attitude). To form friendships and associations. To greet, join, and live with others. To co-operate and converse sociably with others. To love. To join groups.

—Need Rejection (Rejective attitude). To snub, ignore or exclude. To remain aloof and indifferent. To be discriminating.

—Need Nurturance (Nuturant attitude). To nourish, aid or protect the helpless. To express sympathy. To "mother" a child.

—Need Succorance (Succorant attitude). To seek aid, protection or sympathy. To cry for help. To plead for mercy. To adhere to an affectionate, nurturant parent. To be dependent. . . .

—Need Play (Playful attitude). To relax, amuse oneself, seek diversion and entertainment. To "have fun," to play games. To laugh, joke and be merry. To avoid serious tension. . . .

—Need Cognizance (Inquiring attitude). To explore (moving and touching). To ask questions. To satisfy curiosity. To look, listen, inspect. To read and seek knowledge.

—Need Exposition (Expositive attitude). To point and demonstrate. To relate facts. To give information, explain, interpret, lecture [Murray, 1938, pp. 80–83].

We present these two well-known instances simply to illustrate the long and short of classifying motives. There are, of course, numerous other schemes, but there is no single accepted way of classifying motives.

Personality Typologies

Closely related to the problem of designating and classifying social motives is the matter of designating and classifying "personality types." Here also, the number and nature of categories is largely arbitrary and depends mainly on the use to which the scheme will be put.

For example, when fascism and World War II aroused interest in the matter of blind allegiance to dictators, tests were developed to distinguish between "susceptible" and "nonsusceptible" personalities. The studies found that the following traits—designated "authoritarianism"—tend to occur in combination: great concern with authority, involving deference to superiors and assertion over underlings; little personal regard for others; tendency to "manipulate and exploit" and the expectation of being similarly treated; conventionality, conformity, lack of "individuality"; strict "morality," self-righteousness, moral indignation; failure to accept one's own "immoral" impulses coupled with the tendency to attribute evil intent and actions to other groups, particularly minorities; stereotyped, inflexible "black-and-white" thinking; intolerance, bigotry, superstition; general hostility, destructiveness, cynicism; exaggerated concern with sex.

Case studies suggest that severe disciplinary treatment by parents, with undue emphasis on morality, unquestioning obedience, and harsh punishment, tends to produce such "authoritarian personalities," but the evidence on this score is by no means firm.

The major test of "authoritarianism" (the so-called F-scale—F for fascism) has been seriously questioned on methodological grounds. It consists of a series of statements such as these:

Obedience and respect for authority are the most important virtues children should learn.

No sane, normal, decent person could ever think of hurting a close friend or relative.

An insult to honor should always be punished.

Every person should have complete faith in some supernatural power whose decisions he obeys without question.

In each case, agreement contributes positively to the "authoritarian" score. But all of the items are worded positively, and other studies show that people differ simply in their tendency to agree with such statements, regardless of content. To what extent, then, are high-F subjects "authoritarian" and to what extent "acquiescent"? And to complicate the issue further, is acquiescence itself an aspect of authoritarianism? At any rate, the acquiescence element in F-scale scores has been demonstrated by "reversing" the content of some of the items. When this is done, the same subjects agree to statements that contradict each other in content.

But whether the scale measures authoritarianism, acquiescence, or both, high scores have been found to correlate with a number of tendencies, such as:

preference for conventional versus deviant graphic designs (Rosenberg and Zimet, 1957);

intolerance of ambiguity, high-F subjects making a quicker "commitment" than others in situations of uncertainty (Milton, 1957);

greater conformity to the group by high-F subjects under conditions of experimentally stimulated social pressure (Beloff, 1958).

The complete list of measures found to correlate significantly with the F-scale includes: prejudice, political preferences, family ideology, teachers' attitudes, rigidity, anxiety, xenophobia, reenlistment intent, cooperation in experimentation (Titus and Hollander, 1957).

Another extended research program has focused on the achievement motive, dividing people according to how much emphasis they place on getting ahead, making good, accomplishment in general. In this case, the personality typology is based entirely on the strength of a given social motive, though the motive varies with the situation as well as with the individual, and can be experimentally manipulated.

In this case, measurement is done through "projective" fantasy: subjects tell stories about pictures of various situations—a boy seated at a desk, two men working at a machine, and the like. The task is to write a brief story about each picture, indicating what is happening and what will happen as a result. The stories are then scored for frequency and importance of themes dealing with success and achievement; the degree of agreement between independent scorers is usually high enough to consider the measure an objective one.* Measured by this procedure, as examples, high need-achievement has been found to be correlated positively with: sustained effort in a laboratory task (Wendt, 1955); maintenance of independence in a situation that tends to evoke conformity (Krebs, 1958); ability to perceive camouflaged, or embedded, figures (Wertheim and Mednick, 1958); endurance and probability of reaching correct solutions to problems (French and Thomas, 1958); and, on the other hand, high need-achievers have been shown to try less hard than others once having failed (Vogel et al., 1958).

As in the authoritarianism literature, there are some reservations that center on the method of measurement and its validity. Evidence from a variety of sources suggests that there is far from a one-to-one correspondence between themes in fantasy stories and other measures of motivation; that what the subject says about a picture and what his overt behavior says about him may be quite different, if not unrelated. Furthermore, one investigation found a disturbingly low correlation between need-achievement scores of the same subjects tested nine weeks apart (Krumboltz and Farquhar, 1957).

A recent annual review of work in this field concludes:

> The impression is that the measurement of [need-achievement] is in less trouble than are the anxiety or authoritarianism measures. . . . But you can never be

---

* Here is an example of a story indicating high need-achievement:

"A young boy is daydreaming about the past wars in which doctors have participated. He is not sure of the course to follow. He cannot decide whether or not to become a doctor. He is thinking about John Drake, the great surgeon of World War I, and his great feats in it. He was certainly a remarkable man. The boy will finally become a famous surgeon himself and in turn will be an incentive to the future doctors of the world to work hard and be interested only in the welfare of mankind" (McClelland *et al.*, 1953, p. 187).

sure. Indeed, a prediction here is that n-achievement and other needs assessed from fantasy materials will increasingly be under attack at the methodological level. . . .

As far as the year is concerned, [the achievement motive] is not on the critical list, but its health is by no means improving. Embarrassing questions are being asked as to whether it's a dimension that varies directly with other items of behavior, and disturbing evidences of low reliability are offered. For need achievement as with anxiety and authoritarianism, it is almost as though for every study which reports findings in one direction, there is another with opposite results [Blake and Mouton, 1959, pp. 215, 218].

Finally, the practical problems of diagnosis and prediction in the psychiatric clinic have given rise to two of the most widely used personality tests, the Rorschach, or ink-blot test, and the Minnesota Multiphasic Personality Inventory, with their consequent classification schemes. Any test, of course, can produce personality classifications based on differential scores or profiles, just as a priori typologies of personality produce tests designed to distinguish the various types hypothesized. The empirical research relating results of such tests to clinical as well as other behavior, among neurotics, psychotics, and "normals," is staggering in amount, highly detailed, and beyond our scope.

Characteristics of the Motivated State

By definition, the general result of motivation is purposive goal-directed behavior that leads to satisfaction. But this comprises a variety of more specific changes—in activity level, physical and emotional tension, perception, even thought processes. Here, for example, are the general effects of motivation on the learning process as summarized in a review:

The motivating conditions of the individual have three readily discriminable functions in the learning process:

1. They *energize* the organism—make it active—and in this sense support the variable and persistent activity of the organism when relief of the motivating condition is not immediately obtained. . . . Accumulating evidence favors the view that this energizing function of the motive is mediated by increases in the general level of activity (static and phasic muscular activity) which in turn facilitate and inhibit perceptual, ideational, and motor activities. . . .

2. The motivating condition *directs* the variable and persistent activity of the organism. . . . The behavior gives many evidences of organization and directedness. In a "new" situation all responses in the repertoire of the individual are not equally probable of occurrence; some are more likely to occur than others. In part at least this is attributable to the motive. . . .

3. The third function of the motivating condition in the learning process may

be termed its *emphasizing* or *selective* function. The motivating condition defines the consequences of responses, and these consequences . . . determine the later performance of the individual [Melton, 1950, pp. 672–73].

The following findings deal in somewhat more detail with such components of purposive goal-directed behavior.

B1   In the simplest case, as deprivation and intensity of motivation increase, behavior goes from passivity to vague restlessness or uneasiness, and then to directed, purposive acts.

B1.1   Even in the absence of any external goal or stimuli related to the goal, gross bodily activity can change markedly with changes in the strength of physiological motives.

Here, for example, is the relationship between sheer treadmill activity and periods of heat in the female rat.

Activity level and oestrous cycle in rats *

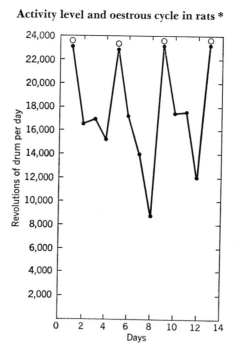

* Activity in rats tends to be at its maximum near the peak of the oestrous cycle.

(Wang, 1923, p. 12)

Similarly, the general bodily activity of human infants increases steadily between feedings:

Motility of seventy-three infants between two consecutive nursings

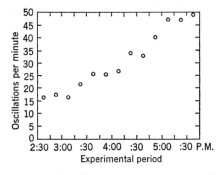

Experimental period

(Irwin, 1932, p. 433)

With more complex human motives operating in more complex environments, general bodily activity is not closely related to the level of any
particular motive. But, of course:

B1.2   In the absence of external constraints, energy expended on specific
tasks is positively related to the strength of the appropriate motive.

Here is an instance: this table shows the number of arithmetic tasks attempted by subjects with low, medium, and high "achievement motivation"
(as independently assessed), during a period when the assigned tasks were

Relationship between *n* achievement and other variables

(High-School Sample, $N = 38$)

	Need-for-achievement scores			
	Low (N = *10*)	*Medium* (N = *18*)	*High* (N = *10*)	*p Low-high (approximate)*
Performance output in unscheduled period: mean number of tasks attempted	49.5	61.2	70.9	.01
Performance output in scheduled period: mean number of tasks attempted	69.6	77.3	84.5	(.1)
Performance quality in unscheduled period: mean error per cent	15.4	12.1	8.2	.05
Performance quality in scheduled period: mean error per cent	22.4	11.6	9.8	.05
Combination measure: number of tasks correct, in unscheduled period	41.9	53.8	65.1	.001
Improvement in output scheduled over unscheduled period, per cent	40.4	26.2	19.0	(.05)

(Wendt, 1955, p. 452)

scheduled for speedy performance and during an unscheduled period when the rate of performance was left to the student's own initiative. Note the greater difference among the groups under the latter condition:

B1.3   As intensity of motivation increases, there is also a general increase in tension—both muscular, as measured by ordinary physical indicators of muscle tone, and emotional or "psychological."

B2   While a moderate level of tension is normally adaptive—i.e., it improves the chances of attaining the goal—tension in the extreme proves disruptive and incapacitating. In general, performance is most efficient when motivation is high but not too high; behavior deteriorates when motivation reaches "panic" levels (as in freezing or blowing up under pressure).

An experiment with chimpanzees who had to solve a problem in order to get at food illustrates the major aspects of this rise and fall in efficiency with increasing motivation. Here are the data, showing the initial increase and later decrease in efficiency as deprivation progresses. (The experimenter attributes the departure of the twelve-hour results to the fact that the twelve-hour test occurred in the morning, after the normal night's sleep during which period there would ordinarily be no meal.)

Time required to solve stick and hooked-rope problems *

Prob- lems	Length of food deprivation in hours					
	2	6	12	24	36	48
1	.430	.019	.008	.190	.036	.017
2	1.00(F) †	.077	.078	.000	1.00(F)	1.00(F)
3	.014	.200	.160	.110	.004	.002
4	.009	.070	.018	.046	.060	.072
5	1.00(F)	.013	.017	.036	.099	.048
6	.016	.017	1.00(F)	.145	.053	1.00(F)
7	1.00(F)	.170	.050	.092	.051	.178
8	.500	.047	1.00(F)	.013	.025	.120
9	1.00(F)	.117	1.00(F)	.202	1.00(F)	.128
10	.270	1.00(F)	.078	.122	.590	1.00(F)
11	1.00(F)	.210	.137	1.00(F)	1.00(F)	.083
Total	6.240	1.940	3.544	1.956	3.918	3.648
Means	.567	.176	.322	.178	.356	.332

* Time scores are given in decimal fractions of one hour.
† (F) designates failure, or nonsolution of the problem.

(Birch, 1945, p. 305)

When motivation is very low the animals are easily diverted from the problem by extraneous factors and behavior tends to deteriorate into a series of non-goal-directed acts. Under conditions of very intense motivation, the animals concentrated upon the goal to the relative exclusion of other features of the situation which were essential to the solution of the problem. Also, the frequent occurrence of frustration responses, such as tantrums and screaming, when a given stereotyped pattern of response proved to be inadequate, hindered the animals in their problem-solving efforts. Those animals who worked at the problems under the intermediate conditions of motivational intensity behaved in a manner which indicated that, although the food acted as a central factor in determining the direction in which they organized new patterns of response, they were not so dominated by a desire to obtain the food that they were incapable of responding to other relevant features of the problem situation. Their behavior was characterized by both direction and flexibility in response [*ibid.*, p. 316].

This statement suggests the reason behind the inverted U-shaped relationship, on a graph, between motivation and performance.

B3   Motivation focuses attention and behavior on goal-related aspects of the situation. At first this increases the likelihood of satisfaction by eliminating irrelevant acts and considerations; but as additional motivation focuses attention still further on the goal itself, and restricts behavior to attempts at immediate gratification, tangential but necessary acts may be excluded.

The following table, from the above experiment, shows the chimpanzees' increasing tendency to make direct, futile attempts to reach the food as deprivation increased.

Frequency of noninstrumental reaching under different motivational conditions

Hours deprivation	Reaches	Time	R/T * (approx.)
2 hours	25	6.240	4
6 hours	10	1.940	5
12 hours	43	3.544	12
24 hours	20	1.956	10
36 hours	76	3.918	20
48 hours	117	3.648	32

* R, total number of direct, noninstrumental reaches in all ten stick-using problems; T, total time in hours spent at the ten stick-problems under each condition.

(*Ibid.*, p. 312)

Literally as well as metaphorically, when the fear of fire is strong enough, people jump from the window rather than look for the fire escape.

In earlier chapters we have already noted the effects of motivation on perception and thinking. To summarize briefly, people tend to select, organize, and interpret stimuli in line with existing motives; their thoughts and memories are similarly channeled and modified according to what it is important or gratifying to think and remember. These effects of motivation, on perception and on thinking, are normally adaptive, within the bounds imposed by reality. But both perception and thinking can become distortive or self-deceptive when the situation is sufficiently unclear and/or the motives sufficiently intense. In general, and as an over-all summary statement:

B4 When the real world and the motives of the subject are at odds, behavior is first designed to bring the real world into line with the motives. But when this is impossible, for external or internal reasons, the discrepancy (or dissonance, as it is now called) can be reduced by appropriate changes in the perception of reality.

Here is a simple and timely example: the fear attached to smoking, when not actually avoided by abstinence, can be reduced by appropriate skepticism about its harmful effects:

Opinions of respondents concerning the linkage between cigarette smoking and lung cancer (percentages)

Group	Per cent who thought linkage was		
	Proved	Not proved	No opinion
Nonsmokers ($N = 348$)	29	55	16
Light smokers ($N = 59$)	20	68	12
Moderate smokers ($N = 105$)	16	75	9
Heavy smokers ($N = 41$)	7	86	7

(Festinger, 1957, p. 155, data from Minneapolis *Sunday Tribune*, March 21, 1954)

Frustration, Conflict, and Adjustment

So far we have looked at motives one at a time and under conditions where purposive goal-directed behavior is possible. But in the real world things are rarely that simple. Behavior is not normally under the control of one isolated motive at a time; several, often inconsistent, motives are normally in play. Beyond that, internal and external barriers stand between people and their goals even when the goals are perfectly clear and consistent. Thus, some of the most important implications and consequences of motives lie not in their direct satisfaction but rather in the adjustments and resolutions required when direct satisfaction is impossible.

FRUSTRATION

When an external barrier stands between a motivated subject and his goal, he normally tries to circumvent, remove, or otherwise master it. (The rat may learn to run the maze or push the bar; the man, to solve the problem.) But when the barrier is not mastered and/or the motivation increases in intensity, the resulting frustration of the goal-directed behavior produces a number of less adaptive results:

C1   The barrier itself may be attacked, physically or symbolically.

The man kicks or curses the broken lawnmower; the child strikes the table corner that has caused him pain, at the cost of incurring some more; and the speeding motorist has appropriate feelings and comments about the policeman who stops him.

In part, this transformation of frustration into aggression probably stems from the state of nature where physical attack was often necessary and successful in removing the barrier. Within the human context, however, where direct physical assault is not normally required or adaptive, this mechanism rarely helps attain the initial goal. Further, and still less realistically adaptive:

C1.1   When the actual barrier is physically, psychologically, or socially invulnerable to attack, aggression may be displaced to an innocent but more vulnerable bystander ("displaced aggression").

So, for example, boys at camp showed significantly increased hostility toward minority groups (Mexicans, Japanese) after they had been subjected

The effect of a frustration imposed by the in-group upon attitudes expressed toward out-groups *

| | Traits attributed to minority | | | |
| | Favorable | | Unfavorable | |
	BEFORE	AFTER	BEFORE	AFTER
Mean	5.71	4.11	2.93	3.26
After minus before	−1.60		+.33	

* Half of the subjects rated Japanese on favorable and unfavorable traits before the frustration of having arduous tests substituted for accustomed recreation and then rated Mexicans afterwards; the other half rated Mexicans first and Japanese afterwards. Since the results of both groups were similar, they have been combined.

(Miller and Bugelski, 1948, p. 440)

to a long and frustrating testing session that deprived them of their weekly night at the movies. The frustrating agent—the tester—was neither Mexican nor Japanese.

> To the extent that the less favorable attitude toward the foreigners may be termed aggression, the results suggest that the frustrations imposed on the young men by the experimenters elicited aggression which was generalized somewhat to the far away foreigners who could not possibly have been to blame for the situation [*ibid.*, p. 441].

Similarly, historical data reveal that lynchings used to increase when economic indices, and especially the farm value of cotton, went down. The chart shows the historical pattern; the following table, the correlation coefficients:

Relation of total lynchings to a composite economic index *

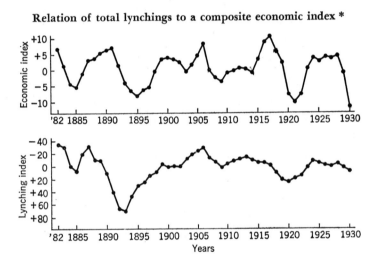

* Both curves represent deviations from a trend line.

(Hovland and Sears, 1940, p. 307)

Correlations between economic indices and lynching data *

Variables	
Economic index—Total lynchings	.65
Per-acre value of cotton—Negro lynchings	.63
Farm value of cotton—Negro lynchings	.72

* Data based on deviations from trend lines.

(*Ibid.*, p. 306)

A later study reduced these correlations somewhat, but they still remained in effect.

> In the present instance the frustrating agent is not an object; one cannot be aggressive against a condition represented by index numbers. It is true, however, that certain individuals probably *represent* the condition symbolically, e.g., merchants, landlords, wealthy persons. These are individuals in a preferred and protected situation in society, however, and aggression directed toward them would elicit a relatively great amount of retribution (punishment). Hence, following the principle that anticipation of punishment inhibits acts of direct aggression (Dollard *et al.*, 1939), the aggression is directed toward persons in a less favorable and protected position who are unable to mobilize adequate retribution [*ibid.*, p. 308].

Here is still another example that suggests long-lasting aggressive consequences of extended frustration in childhood. (In this case, childhood frustration was not observed directly but based on the subjects' descriptions in adulthood of their home life as children—and hence the association may be a spurious one.)

Differences in aggressive behavior in persons having different degrees of childhood frustration

	Home situation	
Behavior traits	*Group 1 (most frustrated) per cent*	*Group 4 (least frustrated) per cent*
Rude answering to parents	76	29
Irritated by parents	98	72
Feeling that teachers are unfair	36	12
Carry grudges	55	26
Frequent quarreling with friends	93	71
Broken engagements	26	7
Average	64.0	36.2

(Maier, 1949, p. 117, data from Watson, 1934)

Apparently such frustration-based attacks are not confined to human beings:

> Cole taught raccoons (a) to climb their cage for food at the sight of a card representing an appropriate "invitation"—and (b) to refrain from doing so when a different card was shown. Significantly, if the animals did not receive the anticipated reward after responding to the proper "sign," they tore up the card with a

displaced fury comparable to a maiden's attack on the previously cherished letters of a newly faithless lover [Masserman, 1961, p. 168].

In summary, as stated in the classical "frustration-aggression hypothesis":

The proposition is that the occurrence of aggressive behavior always presupposes the existence of frustration and, contrariwise, that the existence of frustration always leads to some form of aggression [Dollard *et al.,* 1939, p. 1].

Whether or not this is always and invariably the case, the evidence suggests that there is often such a relationship.

C2   Under conditions of frustration, behavior may revert to earlier, less adaptive modes; and it may show general deterioration, even in areas unrelated to the frustrating event.

In one study, for example, preschool children were happy and played productively with incomplete toys—boat with no pond, ironing board without iron—until a screen was lifted to reveal the missing but still inaccessible pieces on the other side of a barrier. Their play then deteriorated markedly, with twenty-five of the thirty subjects regressing to play typical of younger children (e.g., kicking over the ironing board, scribbling instead of drawing). The average regression in mental age, as rated by observers, was seventeen months (Barker *et al.,* 1941). Or, again, after frustration was experimentally induced by a physical task that looked easy but proved difficult, those who failed showed a decline in performance on an intelligence test immediately thereafter, whereas those who succeeded showed no such effect (Lantz, 1945).

C3   Frustration, especially when produced by or coupled with punishment, may produce extremely rigid and nonadaptive behavior, which may endure even when the barrier is removed to make the goal directly accessible.

For example, in one experiment, rats were first taught to jump one of two stimulus cards by the standard procedure: the correct jump only, and always, led to food. When this discrimination had been learned, frustration was introduced by rewarding and punishing either response 50 per cent of the time, on a random basis. Regardless of which card was selected, the rat now stood a fifty-fifty chance of being fed or shocked. Under these conditions animals developed extremely rigid responses, such as always jumping to the right. This stereotyped response persisted even when it was made *more* frustrating—i.e., when they were shocked 100 per cent of the time and, still more striking, even when the other card was entirely removed, to reveal directly accessible food (Maier, 1949).

C4 Sometimes prolonged or intense frustration produces flight rather than further fight for the goal. When survival is not at stake—and sometimes even then—people may give up and leave the situation, physically or psychologically.

For example, some of the children in the frustrating play experiment mentioned above tried to leave the room altogether; and it is a matter of common observation that people will leave jobs, sports, clubs, or other activities toward which they have demonstrated strong interest and motivation if these situations become sufficiently frustrating.

CONFLICT

The previous findings hold, in principle, for one motive blocked by an inner or outer barrier. Now we take up the more complex case of conflict: situations in which two or more motives block each other, at least in part —in which there are mutually exclusive motives, goals, or means to goals. Such situations vary in intensity and duration from momentary and trivial decisions (what to order for lunch); to more serious and long-term choices (whom or whether to marry); to still more basic and long-lived clashes between behavioral predispositions (to be independent from but dependent upon; to love and to hate).

For purposes of analysis, the simplest forms of conflict and their behavioral outcome can be schematized as follows:

(1) The choice between two or more mutually exclusive positive goals ("approach-approach" conflict).
(2) Ambivalence with respect to a goal that embodies both positive and negative characteristics ("approach-avoidance" conflict).
(3) The dilemma between two or more threats ("avoidance-avoidance" conflict).

C5 The choice between two positive goals naturally becomes more difficult and takes longer when they are seen as of equal value, but in any case it remains relatively easy to make a selection. Choices are ordinarily made quickly and without much vacillation ("approach-approach").

Experiments as well as common sense demonstrate that the donkey does not starve between two haystacks. The conflict is said to be "unstable," since the situation tends to resolve itself. The following graph shows the average number of seconds young boys took to decide which of two drinks they would prefer, when making actual and hypothetical choices, according to the degree of difference in preference between the two drinks. There were six drinks in all, each compared with every other.

Resolution of conflicts between alternatives *

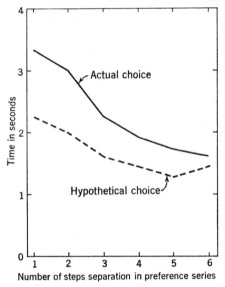

* Measured in time elapsing during the resolution of conflicts between alternatives separated by different "distances" in the preference series; mean scores.

(Barker, 1942, p. 18)

By contrast:

C6   When goals are at once satisfying and threatening, pleasant and painful, attractive and anxiety-arousing, people's behavior vacillates at a point near but not too near the goal: at a distance the tendency to approach predominates, near the goal the tendency to avoid is greater. The result is a stable or self-maintaining conflict that tends to keep the organism at the point where the two tendencies cross (approach-avoidance).

This finding and its interpretation are demonstrated in simple physical terms by the following animal experiment. Rats first taught to approach food at the end of an alley are then shocked while feeding there. When subsequently placed in the alley at a point far from the food, the rat approaches to a certain point and then stops. If put down nearer the food box, he retreats to approximately this same point. Furthermore, the point to which he retreats corresponds to the intersection of the approach and avoidance tendencies as independently measured with different subjects, again in simple physical terms: rats are harnessed and the tug on the harness is measured at various points while approaching food or while avoiding shock. The resulting gradients show that:

C6.1   The pull toward a positive goal increases with nearness, but only slightly; while the tendency to retreat from a negative goal rises very steeply as it is approached.

Approach and avoidance gradients *

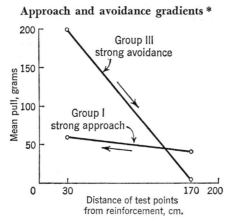

* The approach gradient represents the mean force exerted by forty-six-hour motivated rats when restrained at two points in the alley. The avoidance gradient reveals the force exerted by rats in their efforts to avoid a region where strong shock has been given. Although the experimental points in this figure have been joined by straight lines, no assumption is intended with respect to the linearity of the gradients.

(Brown, 1948, p. 457)

Thus, the point of vacillation can be moved toward the goal either by increasing the approach gradient *or* by decreasing the avoidance tendency, and vice-versa. Here are the theoretical results of the two procedures:

Approach-avoidance conflicts *

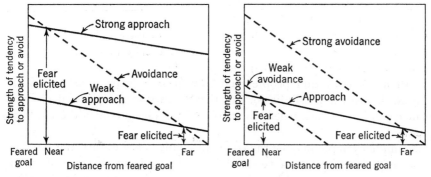

* From Neal E. Miller, "Experimental Studies of Conflict," in *Personality and the Behavior Disorders,* edited by J. McV. Hunt. Copyright 1944, The Ronald Press Company, New York. Reprinted by permission.

The figure on the left is a graphic representation of how an approach-avoidance conflict is affected by increasing the strength of approach; the figure on the right, of how the conflict is affected by decreasing the strength of avoidance.

(Miller, 1944, p. 440)

And here are some actual data showing shifts in gradients as a result of changes in motivation:

Effect of reduced shock and reduced drive upon the strengths of the avoidance and approach responses *

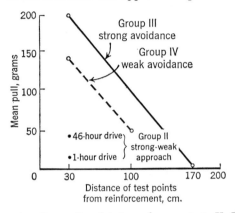

* This figure summarizes the results of tests made on groups II, III, and IV, and illustrates the effect of reduced shock and reduced drive.

(Brown, 1948, p. 459)

Note the differential psychological and practical consequences of these curves. For example, if a closer approach is induced by an increase in the value of the goal (e.g., by bribery), it is at the cost of sharply increased fear or anxiety, whereas reducing the avoidance gradient produces a closer approach with a much smaller increment in associated fear.

So far these findings can be generalized to complex human behavior mainly by analogy. The process does seem directly comparable to the behavior often associated with goals that are at once attractive and frightening (e.g., physically dangerous sports, certain forms of social relationships, some illicit activities). At a distance (measured, in the human case, in psychological as well as physical units) the attractions often seem far more apparent than the risks, and people tend to approach (make plans, read brochures, discuss the possibilities). But they often stop at the point of imminent commitment—i.e., where the avoidance gradient crosses the approach gradient.

A simple example may be the common ambivalence toward the purchase of an expensive item (cost versus desire), especially in the case of luxury items. Repeated approaches (window shopping, inquiries, price haggling) often stop just short of purchase—perhaps because the pain or guilt associated with the expenditure rises more sharply as the point of commitment is approached than does the attractiveness of the item.

The setting of level of aspiration—the income, status, or grades that people subjectively shoot for—has also been analyzed in approach-avoidance terms. The notion is that people set their sights on that level of achievement where the approach gradient, associated with increasing attractiveness of goals, crosses the avoidance gradient, associated with the increasing fear of failure.

For example, subjects rated, by independent measures, as high in achievement motivation and low in test anxiety tend to select tasks that are challenging—not so easy that success is assured nor so difficult that failure is not experienced as such. Those with low achievement motivation and high test anxiety showed a smaller concentration of challenging choices, and relatively more of these choices were in the psychologically safer extremes of difficulty. Here are the data (subjects were allowed to choose their own distance from the target in a ring-toss game):

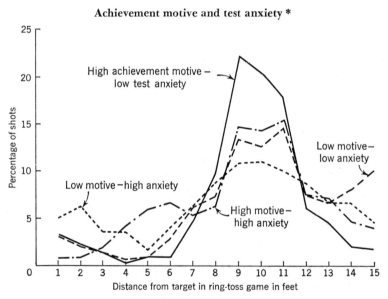

Achievement motive and test anxiety *

* Percentage of shots taken from each line. Graph is smoothed according to the method of running averages, for subjects classified as high or low simultaneously in n Achievement and test anxiety, H-L ($N = 13$), H-H ($N = 10$), L-L ($N = 9$), L-H ($N = 13$).

(Atkinson and Litwin, 1960, p. 55)

When, and only when, there are barriers or constraints that keep the subject in the situation and tend to force a choice between two negative goals, a dilemma or avoidance-avoidance conflict exists. (Without some physical or psychological barrier the subject simply leaves the situation and avoids both.)

C7   Avoidance-avoidance conflicts are stable and tend to stay unresolved: approach toward one of the horns of the dilemma increases the tendency to retreat toward the other one, since fear or anxiety is minimal when the distances from both are maximized.

A word about the practical implications of the barrier may be in order. Whenever people try to induce others to do something disagreeable or threatening by imposing punishment as an alternative, the procedure can be only as effective as the strength of the barrier. The threat of excommunication can be used only to the extent that church members hesitate to leave; and the upper limits of prison brutality are set by the difficulties of escape. So, also, industrial supervision today cannot utilize the same negative sanctions and controls that are possible in principle and often in practice when there is a high cost attached to leaving a job.

When intense fear attaches to all alternatives and physical or psychological distance is small, such conflicts produce acute anxiety; ultimately, even when the physical barriers are impenetrable, people may escape psychologically. In the extreme case there may be complete loss of contact with reality, as in some forms of psychosis; but short of that, there is often an overriding sense of unreality about the situation even though there is intellectual awareness of what is happening. For example, 69 per cent of World War II combat flyers reported sometimes or often feeling a "sense of unreality, that this couldn't be happening to you" (Shaffer, 1947, p. 139). And here is a noted clinical psychologist's account of his own reactions in a Nazi concentration camp:

> The writer feels that he was able to endure the transportation and what followed, because he convinced himself that these horrible and degrading experiences somehow did not happen to "him" as a subject, but only to "him" as an object. . . . It was as if he watched things happening in which he only vaguely participated. Later he learned that many prisoners developed this same feeling of detachment, as if what happened really did not matter to oneself. It was strangely mixed with a conviction that "this cannot be true, such things do not happen." Not only during the transportation but all through the time spent in camp, the prisoners had to convince themselves that this was real and not just a nightmare. They were never wholly successful. The feeling of detachment which rejected the reality of the situation might be considered a mechanism safeguarding the integrity of the prisoners' personalities. They behaved in the camp as if their life there could have no connection with their "real" life [Bettelheim, 1958, p. 304].

EXPERIMENTAL "NEUROSES"

From two bodies of literature comes the suggestion that neurotic disturbances among human beings, or at least some disturbances, stem from conflict. On the one hand, psychoanalytic theory, supported by case studies, holds that unresolved and repressed conflicts originating in infancy are the primary determinants of neuroses. On the other, far removed in theory and in research design, are experiments in which certain simple conditioning procedures produce something approximating neurotic behavior in lower animals.

The psychoanalytic hypotheses are still largely untested in the laboratory. Securing experimental evidence on human beings is clearly limited by ethical as well as practical considerations, so most of the evidence that deals directly with human beings comes from case studies. Hence our documentation in this section will draw more heavily on clinical case history than do the other sections in this book, but we shall confine ourselves to generalizations that have some corroboration in animal experiments.

C8 Neurotic behavior can be produced by ambiguous stimulation such that the same or very similar stimuli are sometimes rewarded and sometimes not, or sometimes rewarded and sometimes punished.

The original, classical demonstration was provided by Pavlov as early as 1927. After a series of trials in which food always followed the presentation of a circle but never an ellipse,

the shape of the ellipse was now approximated by stages to that of the circle (ratios of semiaxes of 3:2, 4:3 and so on) and the development of differentiation continued . . . with some fluctuation, progressing at first more and more quickly, and then again slower, until an ellipse with ratio of semiaxes 9:8 was reached. In this case, although a considerable degree of discrimination did develop, it was far from being complete. After three weeks of work upon this differentiation not only did the discrimination fail to improve, but it became considerably worse, and finally disappeared altogether. At the same time the whole behavior of the animal underwent an abrupt change. The hitherto quiet dog began to squeal in its stand, kept wriggling about, tore off with its teeth the apparatus for mechanical stimulation of the skin, and bit through the tubes connecting the animal's room with the observer, a behavior which never happened before. On being taken into the experimental room the dog now barked violently [Wolpe, 1958, p. 38].

Similarly, cats who have been first fed, and later shocked, immediately following the same buzzer exhibit the following behavior:

Three manifestations were constant and common to all animals: (1) resistance to being put into the experimental cage; (2) signs of anxiety when inside the cage (muscular tension and mydriasis [dilation of the pupil of the eye] were invariable); (3) *refusal to eat meat pellets anywhere in the cage even after 1, 2, or 3 days' starvation.*

Quantitative change in general activity was almost invariable. An increase or decrease was usually constant for an individual animal. Increased activity took the forms of restless roving, clawing at the wire netting, butting the roof with the head, and ceaseless vocalizing. Decreased activity varied between tense infrequent movements in the standing posture and very intense immobile crouching.

Symptoms that were observed intermittently in all animals were hypersensitivity to "indifferent" stimuli, piloerection [hair standing on end], howling, crouching, and rapid respiration.

Certain cats displayed special symptoms in addition to those that were common to all. The respiratory rate of Cat 9 always rose from about 30 to about 60 as soon as he was put into the cage. Cat 15, who had micturated while being shocked, invariably micturated a few seconds after being placed in the cage. Cat 6 manifested almost continuous trembling. Cat 8 developed a symptom that it seems permissible to call hysterical. He jerked his shoulders strongly every few seconds in the experimental cage, and also in his living cage *if I entered it.* This jerking suggested an abortive jumping movement, and may well have had its origin in the fact that on the first occasion on which this animal was shocked he jumped through a hatch in the roof of the cage that had been left open inadvertently. All but the first-mentioned of these four cats had been through Schedule I.

Whatever symptoms an animal showed in the experimental cage were invariably *intensified by presentation of the auditory stimulus* that had been contiguous with the occurrence of the shock [Wolpe, 1958, p. 52].

Cats with such experimentally induced neuroses, incidentally, find relief in alcohol—the neurotic symptoms disappear under its influence. In addition:

Half the experimental animals eventually learned that alcohol relieved some of their neurotic tensions and inhibitions, and thereafter chose to empty the cocktail-shaped glass that held milk spiked with 5 per cent alcohol in preference to the plain milk in the eared mug. This preference was not affected by any variations in the position of the two glasses on the rotary stand, and remained statistically significant as long as the animals remained neurotic (Masserman and Yum, 1946) [Masserman, 1961, p. 155].

C9   Approach-avoidance conflicts can also produce neurotic symptoms, including psychosomatic ailments. (Such conflicts differ from the above case in that no punishment or reward is administered except at the subject's own initiative; but in order to get the reward, he must stand the punishment.)

The rigorous experimental evidence is still confined to lower animals, but there the findings are clear. For example, gastric ulcers were produced in rats who spent one month in a standard approach-avoidance situation: animals had to endure electric shock at the food box or water hole during forty-seven of every forty-eight hours. Control animals, simply deprived of food and water for forty-seven of each forty-eight hours for the same period of time, developed no ulcers.

That is the basic situation postulated to account for some similar human complaints:

Mrs. A. suffered from two conflicts which produced her misery. The first might be described as a sex-fear conflict. Thanks to childhood circumstances she had developed strong sex appetites. At the same time strong anxieties were created in her and attached to the cues produced by sex excitement. However, she saw no connection between these remembered circumstances and the miserable life she was leading. The connective thoughts had been knocked out and the conflict was thus unconscious. The presence of the sexual appetites showed up in a kind of driven behavior in which she seemed to court seduction. Her fear was exhibited in her revulsion from sexual acts and thoughts and in her inability to take responsibility for a reasonable sexual expressiveness with her husband. The conflict was greatly intensified after her marriage because of her wish to be a dutiful wife. Guilt about the prospect of adultery was added to fear about sex motives [Dollard and Miller, 1950, p. 19].

Unconscious Motives and Indirect Expression

As we have said, the simple human motives are usually accompanied by a conscious sense of striving as well as by awareness of the object that will satisfy them. A hungry man knows that he is hungry, that what he wants is food, and that he is taking steps to get it. Thus, his behavior in this regard can be predicted with a fair degree of accuracy on the basis of his own feelings and reports.

With the more complex social motives, however, this direct and consistent relationship between purposive behavior and subjective experience does not always hold. People often act in consistent ways that produce consistent results—and under conditions where they seem to have a choice in the matter. Thus their behavior bears all the external signs of being purposive and goal-directed. Yet they themselves often vehemently deny the motive that would be inferred, or even report the opposite motivation.

For example, a young woman may confine her relationships to married men, to unlikely prospects, or to those otherwise ineligible. She may have had several broken engagements, always at her initiative and just before the wedding day. By simple inference, these consistencies seem to point to a motive: "avoidance or fear of marriage" or "desire to stay single." Yet she herself might protest vigorously and sincerely believe that she wants nothing more than to get married.

D1 The goals and the motives inferred from consistent, purposive behavior do not always match the goals and the motives experienced or reported by the actor, and the discrepancy is not necessarily a matter of intentional misstatement. In short, motives can operate and find expression entirely outside of awareness: some motivation is unconscious.

In the simplest case:

D1.1   The goal sought, and the means employed, can be so habitual or automatic as to escape awareness.

A good illustration is provided by the previously cited experiments in the instrumental conditioning of ordinary conversation (see the chapter on learning and thinking). Recall that the subject clearly acted so as to gratify a social motive—i.e., he changed his conversation to increase the number of times the listener approved by nodding or agreeing, yet he was completely unable to state *that* or *how* he was doing so. Such motives, of course, can be brought to awareness simply by calling the subject's attention to what is happening. But beyond such simple nonawareness, there is evidence that people actively press some motives out of consciousness ("repression").

D1.2   Some motives are so unacceptable, threatening, or repugnant that they are unrecognized or unacknowledged; conscience or the need to maintain self-esteem act as internal barriers that block direct expression and awareness. And in such cases, people may express the motive in any number of devious or disguised ways, i.e., in indirect expressions that do not seem to be related to it.

The documentation here comes principally from clinical experience and hypnotic studies. The clinical evidence is summarized as follows:

> The observed clinical facts are (a) that conscious process can be rendered unconscious (repressed), and (b) that as an inherent part of repression, resistances form which make it impossible for the repressed processes either to become conscious spontaneously or to be unveiled by direct self-inspection, with the result (c) that energetic forces which originally were part of the previously conscious processes become detached from them when they are repressed ("primary dissociation"), and then (d) become manifest in the various disguised forms (of which displacements are one example), which we encounter in the psychopathology of everyday life (Freud, 1913), in personality structure, and in neurotic symptoms. Each step of this has been reproduced in experimental hypnosis to the satisfaction of the most exacting skeptic (Erickson, 1939a) [Kubie, 1962, p. 92].

Here is an illustration of just one such hypnotic demonstration, in which the motive and the barrier to its direct expression were both induced by hypnosis:

> The subject was brought into a state of profound hypnosis, during which he was instructed that after awakening he would (1) notice Dr. D. searching vainly through his pockets for a package of cigarettes; (2) that he then would proffer his own pack, and (3) that Dr. D. absent-mindedly would forget to return the cigarettes whereupon the subject would feel very eager to recover them because he had no others. He was further told that (4) he would be too courteous to ask for the cigarettes either directly or indirectly but that (5) he would engage in a conversation that would cover any topic except cigarettes although at the

time his desire for the return of the cigarettes would be on his mind constantly.

When he was awakened the subject saw that Dr. D. was looking for cigarettes. He thereupon courteously offered his own and at the same time became involved in a conversation during which Dr. D., after lighting the cigarette, absent-mindedly placed the pack in his own pocket. The subject noted this with a quick glance, felt of his own pockets in a somewhat furtive manner as if to see whether or not he had another pack, and showed by his facial expression that he had no others. He then began chatting casually, wandering from one topic to another, always mentioning in some indirect but relevant fashion the word "smoking." For example, he talked about a boat on the bay at New Haven, commenting on the fact that the sight of water always made him thirsty, as did smoking. He then told a story about how the dromedary got one hump and the *camel* two. When the question of travel was raised he immediately pictured the pleasure he would derive from crossing the Sahara Desert rocking back and forth comfortably on a *camel*. Next he told a tale of Syrian folklore in which again a camel played a role. When he was asked to tell something interesting about patients he told of taking a patient to see a marathon dance which the latter enjoyed immensely while he himself was reminded by the antics of the dancers of a circus where one would see elephants, hippopotami and *camels*. Asked what he would like to do, he commented on the pleasant weather and said there was nothing more glorious than paddling in a canoe or floating at ease on the water, smoking [Erickson, 1939a, pp. 339–40].

In this demonstration, both the wish and its unacceptability are trivial; the repression process occurs only because of the hypnotic suggestion. In the real-world counterpart, however, such nonconscious motives are powerful and pervasive in themselves, and they become seriously unacceptable as a result of the primary and consistent socialization through which the child acquires his initial sense of right and wrong.

In our society, the two most generally recognized instances of repression are motives relating to aggression and to sex. Expression in both of these areas is severely restricted and regulated, being subject to strong and consistent taboos. As a result, many aggressive and sexual impulses are denied—not just before others but even to oneself. For example, we shall see that there is no known human society without some form of prohibition against incest. Accordingly, few normal adults recognize erotic attraction toward those family members covered by the taboo—in fact, the thought of sexual relations with close family members is often repugnant. Yet there is no biological reason to suppose that such attractions do not exist; and instances of human incest in less restricted social groups suggest that they do, to some degree. Similarly, there are few forms of legitimate direct aggression against other people—at least against other members of one's own group. But there are a variety of institutions that permit acceptable forms of less-direct aggressiveness: prize fights, football games, television quiz shows, keen competition in various spheres.

D2   Acts or impulses that provoke anxiety, damage self-esteem, or are otherwise disturbing, are often explained away—that is, attributed to "good" reasons rather than to the less acceptable but "real" ones ("rationalization").

Here are some everyday examples: "Sour grapes"; "I'll be able to learn more if I take a break now"; an alcoholic taking a drink "Just to get rid of the hangover"; "I left her [for another woman], but it's for her own good in the long run." As the examples illustrate, rationalizations may be objectively true—maybe the grapes *are* sour, maybe it *is* to her advantage. The point is that they involve self-deception as to the reason for the act.

Here is a summary of one experimental demonstration:

> A subject under hypnosis is told that when he wakes from the trance he will watch the pocket of the hypnotist. When the hypnotist removes a handkerchief from the pocket, the subject will raise the window. The subject is told that he will not remember the hypnotist's telling him to do this.
>
> Aroused from the trance, the subject feels a little drowsy, but presently circulates among the people in the room and carries on a normal conversation, all the while furtively watching the hypnotist's pocket. When the hypnotist in a casual manner removes his handkerchief, the subject feels an impulse to open the window, takes a step in that direction, but hesitates.
>
> Unconsciously he mobilizes his wishes to be a reasonable person; so, seeking for a reason for his impulse to open the window, he says, "Isn't it a little stuffy in here?" Having found the needed excuse, he opens the window and feels more comfortable [Hilgard, 1962, p. 513].

D3   Repressed motives or other unacceptable and unrecognized aspects of one's own personality may be attributed to others ("projection").

Everyday examples: supermoral, sexually frustrated spinster sees most other women as "evil," "prostitutes," "promiscuous"; father thinks all of his favorite daughter's suitors are out for no good. This mechanism has been documented in several areas of research. For example, girls who scored high on tests of anti-Semitism showed overt moral strictness and lack of emotionality, but a greater-than-average tendency to attribute licentiousness and aggression to others—especially minority groups—in stories they were asked to make up.

> The high extremes show a certain *aversion against emotionality* or at least against the expression of certain basic needs. These needs are then often projected onto others, especially certain outgroups. In the stories of the high extremes, aggression and sex often appear in infantile forms, isolated from the life of the heroine with whom the girls identify. As was pointed out above, aggression in these cases is not manifested by the heroine, but is projected into the environment, or destiny, or "lower" people such as proletarians, Jews, Mexicans, etc. These "inferior" people are seen not only as aggressive, but generally as uninhibited. . . . Examples are: "It is a young girl and her boy

friend. They are lower class people, and don't know any better than to do this sort of thing. I have an aversion for the things such people do. They are thinking of getting married and are looking forward to a bright future; though I don't believe such people can ever make much of themselves. I don't believe in holding hands in public." . . .

These sentences express contempt and at the same time envy for the "lower class sexuality." An important tendency of the girls high on anti-Semitism is thus to keep one's basic impulses repressed, to keep oneself pure and reputable. Primitive needs are rendered ego-alien and projected onto an alien group. The constant repression leads to a distortion of reality, which is chiefly manifested in the projective evaluation of minority groups [Frenkel-Brunswik and Sanford, 1945, pp. 280–81].

Projection occurs mainly with respect to those negative traits that are self-applicable but unrecognized. For example, here are the major conclusions from a study comparing self-descriptions with descriptions by and of others among ninety-seven fraternity brothers:

1. Those subjects who lacked insight into the amount of a given trait they themselves possessed tended, on the average, to attribute a greater amount of that trait to other people than did those subjects who possessed an equal amount of the trait but had insight. This fact is in accord with the principle of projection. . . .
2. Subjects lacking insight into their own possession of a trait assigned more extreme ratings to others on that trait than did subjects possessing insight. This difference was in the same direction from the mean as was the subject's own deviation in that trait.
3. Projection was not operative in influencing the judgments of all subjects on any given trait; its occurrence was apparently confined to those who lacked insight. . . .
6. Those subjects who lacked insight into their own possession of reprehensible traits considered the reprehensibility of those traits greater than did those subjects who had insight.
7. There was no evidence that lack of insight was a general tendency influencing a given subject's judgments on all traits; it seemed to be specific to one trait rather than to be a general "personality trait" in itself [Sears, 1936, pp. 161–62].

Two other defense mechanisms were discussed in earlier sections: displacement, in which aggression toward one person or object is expressed toward an innocent bystander when the real object is invulnerable or unknown; and the repression of unpleasant or threatening experiences, reaching extremes in some cases of amnesia. Here is a summary statement regarding the state of evidence on the latter mechanism:

There is abundant clinical evidence for repression as a mechanism of defense. Perhaps the most convincing evidence to the outsider is that from amnesia, when a person loses his personal memories, often to recover them later without relearning. Amnesias show that memories may be unavailable even though they are not really lost. . . .

Despite the crudity of the experiments, nearly all of them have shown that pleasant items or experiences are more readily recalled than unpleasant ones, and that memories that reduce self-esteem are recalled with greater difficulty than those that enhance self-esteem. Thus the experimental results in general agree with psychoanalytic theory, though few of the experiments have been very helpful in moving us forward in our understanding of the phenomena [Hilgard, 1952, pp. 7–8].

Finally, as perhaps the most dramatic form of indirect expression:

D4   Repression of strong unacceptable motives is sometimes accompanied by overt behavior and conscious feelings that are *opposite* to the repressed tendencies ("reaction-formation").

For example, the mother of an "unwanted child" may be overprotective, solicitous, superloving—proving to herself and the world that she never had and does not have any negative feelings toward the child; or, as often recognized, "Methinks the lady doth protest too much."

Clinical evidence for such transformations between underlying motive and overt behavior is widespread. The following excerpts from a letter received by a psychiatrist from an antivivisectionist clearly show the overt and recognized "humanity" of the correspondent masking a base of tremendous hostility and sadism.

> I read [a magazine article] . . . on your work on alcoholism . . . I am surprised that anyone who is as well educated as you must be to hold the position that you do would stoop to such a depth as to torture helpless little cats in the pursuit of a cure for alcoholics. . . . A drunkard does not want to be cured —a drunkard is just a weakminded idiot who belongs in the gutter and should be left there. Instead of torturing helpless little cats why not torture the drunks or better still exert your would-be noble effort toward getting a bill passed to *exterminate* the drunks. . . . My greatest wish is that you have brought home to you a torture that will be a thousand fold greater than what you have, and are doing to the little animals. . . . If you are an example of what a noted psychiatrist should be I'm glad I am just an ordinary human being without letters after my name. I'd rather be just myself with a clear conscience, *knowing I have not hurt any living creature,* and can sleep without seeing frightened, terrified dying cats—because I know they must die after you have finished with them. No punishment is too great for you and I hope I live to read about your mangled body and long suffering before you finally die—and I'll laugh long and loud [Masserman, 1961, p. 38].

The foregoing are simple illustrations of a variety of forms of indirect expression that can be given to motives when they are repressed or otherwise frustrated from direct expression. Such forms are often called "defense mechanisms"—because they protect against the anxiety and the loss of self-esteem that come with awareness of "repugnant" motives or of failure. Defense mechanisms, like learned motives themselves, have been classified in various ways.

Though many instances of indirect expression are reported from the clinic, the quantitative evidence is rather sketchy—yet it is consistent with the basic formulation. Following are two illustrations of the tenuous but positive connection between theory and evidence in this field. Freud attributed paranoia, or persecution complex, to a very complex series of transformations, summarized as follows:

> Since homosexual impulses are highly disapproved and a person who manifests them ordinarily suffers serious social punishment, such impulses are usually hidden as much as possible. It is presumed that the great majority of people who feel themselves to be somewhat homosexual avoid recognition of the fact themselves. This repression is not always entirely successful, however, and the constant breaking through into consciousness of the forbidden tendency may be accompanied by severe feelings of guilt and anxiety.
>
> Freud (1911) pointed to a not uncommon mechanism by which such anxieties might be eliminated; this was through the medium of denying that the impulses came from the self (projection) and by converting the love emotion into its opposite (reaction-formation). The homosexual reaction was converted from "I love him" to "I hate him," and when this defense proved insufficient, the latter was converted by projection to "He hates me." This final stage of the defensive process is the full blown paranoia [Sears, 1943, p. 71].

Farfetched as these connections may seem, homosexuality, both overt and symbolic, is far more often observed in paranoid patients than in the psychiatric population as a whole.

Incidence of homosexual behavior and symbolism in a paranoid population of both sexes (from Gardner, 1931, p. 60) and in an ordinary psychopathic sample of females (from Strakosch, 1934, p. 57) (percentages)

Type of practice of homosexuality	Paranoid and paranoid precox: Gardner		General psychopathic: Strakosch
	Male (N = 60)	Female (N = 60)	Female (N = 700)
POSITIVE	51.7	38.7	6.4
Symbolic	30.0	20.0	4.7
Overt	21.7	18.7	1.7

(Sears, 1943, p. 72)

Similarly, those adult personality characteristics summarized as the "anal character" (stinginess, orderliness, obstinancy), are presumed to arise in reaction against the child's early anal eroticism. One study found small but definitely positive correlations among these characteristics in a sample of thirty-seven college men each rating every other (Sears, 1936), and another found some evidence that stinginess and several other theoretically related personality characteristics are more frequently observed among persons who are able to recall early anal eroticism than among those without such history.

Frequency of occurrence of anal traits in persons who could
and could not recall childhood anal erotism or constipation
(from Hamilton, 1929, pp. 467–468)
(percentages)

	Frequency of occurrence			
	MEN		WOMEN	
Anal-erotic trait	Anal (N = 35)	Nonanal (N = 65)	Anal (N = 24)	Nonanal (N = 76)
Stinginess or extravagance	46	37	42	22
Sadism	77	37	54	25
Masochism	74	18	54	21
Fetichism	28	14	33	22
Concern for clothes	87	66	75	70

(Sears, 1943, p. 68)

In summary, and in general, behavior, attitudes, and feelings are not always what they seem to be—not what they seem to be to an observer and not even what they seem to be to the actor himself. What a man does, why he does it, and what he thinks or feels at the time he is doing it are related, but not always in a simple, straightforward, conscious way. Because direct satisfaction is not always possible, "solutions" to intra- and interpersonal problems are frequently characterized by devious and complicated connections between underlying motives, conscious states, and overt behavior. As a result, the conscious or apparent reasons for an act may not be the "real" reasons; the conscious or apparent feelings or attitudes toward a person or event may not be the "real" ones; and the conscious or apparent objects of attitudes and feelings may not be their "real" objects.

Although the following findings do not deal, strictly speaking, with motivation, we include them here because the general discussion of neuroses, conflicts, unconscious motives, and indirect expression serves as appropriate background.

Effects of Psychotherapy

What is known about the effects, especially the effectiveness, of psychotherapy? Psychotherapy refers to any treatment in which the patient or client (the designation varies among different schools of therapy) talks to the doctor, therapist, or counsellor (again, the label varies) during a series of sessions ranging in number from several to several hundred. In psychotherapy, mental or emotional disturbances are treated only through communication between patient and therapist. Direct physiological intervention (such as drugs or electric shock) is not included in psychotherapy per se, although such treatment is sometimes administered concurrently. Other personal relationships—minister-parishioner, parent-child, social worker-client, teacher-student, friend-friend—may embody many of the elements involved in formal psychotherapy. But by definition, and in many cases by law, they are not called psychotherapy, and their therapeutic value has not been studied systematically from this point of view. To begin with the most important practical issue:

E1   There is no conclusive evidence that psychotherapy is more effective than general medical counseling or advice in treating neurosis or psychosis. Strictly speaking, it cannot even be considered established that psychotherapy, on the average, improves a patient's chances of recovery beyond what they would be without any formal therapy whatsoever.

A decade ago an important review examined twenty-four so-called outcome studies involving over eight thousand patients who had received some form of psychotherapy, either psychoanalytic or eclectic (miscellaneous or mixed forms). The results are summarized in the table on page 288.

Those encouraging figures were then compared with two baselines: (1) the rate of recovery among five hundred neurotics treated only "by their own physicians, with sedatives, tonics, suggestion, and reassurances" (Eysenck, 1952, p. 320). The cases represented insurance claims in which the company verified "total disability," defined as inability to carry on an occupation for remuneration or profit for at least a three-month period. The multiple criterion of recovery included return to work, lack of further serious complaints, and successful social adjustment; and (2) the discharge rate for patients diagnosed as neurotic in New York State hospitals between the years 1917 and 1934. The patients received little and in most cases no psychotherapy.

The results: slightly more than two-thirds of the patients visiting general practitioners were rated as "recovered" within two years; and the same

Summary of reports of the results of psychotherapy

	Number of cases	Cured; much improved	Improved	Slightly improved	Not improved; died; left treatment	Percentage cured; much improved; improved
PSYCHOANALYTIC						
1. Fenichel [1930, pp. 28–40]	484	104	84	99	197	39
2. Kessel & Hyman [1933]	34	16	5	4	9	62
3. Jones [1936, pp. 12–14]	59	20	8	28	3	47
4. Alexander [1937, pp. 30–43]	141	28	42	23	48	50
5. Knight [1941]	42	8	20	7	7	67
Total cases	760		335		425	44
ECLECTIC						
1. Huddleson [1927]	200	19	74	80	27	46
2. Matz [1929]	775	10	310	310	145	41
3. Maudsley Hospital Report [1931]	1721	288	900		533	69
4. Maudsley Hospital Report [1935]	1711	371	765		575	64
5. Neustatter [1935]	46	9	14	8	15	50
6. Luff & Garrod [1935]	500	140	135	26	199	55
7. Luff & Garrod [1935]	210	38	84	54	34	58
8. Ross [1936]	1089	547	306		236	77
9. Yaskin [1936]	100	29	29		42	58
10. Curran [1937]	83		51		32	61
11. Masserman & Carmichael [1938]	50	7	20	5	18	54
12. Carmichael & Masserman [1939]	77	16	25	14	22	53
13. Schilder [1939]	35	11	11	6	7	63
14. Hamilton & Wall [1941]	100	32	34	17	17	66
15. Hamilton et al. [1942]	100	46	5	17	32	51
16. Landis [1938]	119	40	47		32	73
17. Institute Med. Psychol. (quoted Neustatter)	270	58	132	55	25	70
18. Wilder [1945]	54	3	24	16	11	50
19. Miles et al. [1951]	53	13	18	13	9	58
Total cases	7293		4661		2632	64

(Eysenck, 1952, p. 321)

percentage of neurotics were discharged annually from New York State hospitals with little or no psychotherapy. The writer concluded:

> These data . . . fail to prove that psychotherapy, Freudian or otherwise, facilitates the recovery of neurotic patients. They show that roughly two-thirds of a group of neurotic patients will recover or improve to a marked extent within about two years of the onset of their illness, whether they are treated by means of psychotherapy or not. This figure appears to be remarkably stable from one investigation to another, regardless of type of patient treated, standard of recovery employed, or method of therapy used. From the point of view of the neurotic these figures are encouraging; from the point of view of the psychotherapist, they can hardly be called very favorable to his claims [*ibid.,* pp. 322–23].

As to the relative rate of improvement in psychoanalysis as against other forms of psychotherapy, when patients who failed to complete analysis were excluded from the tabulation, psychoanalysis fared no better and no worse than the eclectic therapies: both reflected the average, two-thirds improvement rate. When drop-outs were included, the improvement rate among analysands fell to an average of only 44 per cent.

It is fair to add that this study met with some criticism from the advocates of psychotherapy. As the author himself said:

> The figures quoted do not necessarily disprove the possibility of therapeutic effectiveness. There are obvious shortcomings in any actuarial comparison and these shortcomings are particularly serious when there is so little agreement among psychiatrists relating even to the most fundamental concepts and definitions. Definite proof would require a special investigation, carefully planned and methodologically more adequate than these *ad hoc* comparisons [*ibid.,* p. 323].

Over the intervening years, the "definite proof" has still not materialized. A recent reviewer of the then-current studies of outcomes similarly concluded:

> Most of these outcome studies leave a great deal to be desired. Many times the criteria of success are the most subjective sorts of judgments—sometimes by the therapists themselves! Occasionally the criteria are more objective, and the factor analytic studies show much promise. But we may say that in general the more rigorous the criteria the less encouraging are the reported results [Snyder, 1958, pp. 366–67].

Even a critic of the earlier investigation and its conclusion said:

> We feel that the only conclusion which can be made at this point is that we have as yet *no data* on the basis of which to evaluate the therapeutic effects of psychotherapy [De Charms *et al.,* 1954, p. 233].

And again in 1960:

> The kind of generalization which seems the most difficult to make is that which applies to the efficiency, value, or relative superiority of any specific method

of treatment. Rubinstein & Parloff (1959, p. 277), in their summary of the American Psychological Association-sponsored conference on psychotherapy, had the following to say on the subject of outcome research:

"Although one of the prime purposes of the conference, as described in the original plan, was to provide 'a comprehensive picture of the status of research on the effects of psychotherapy,' as if by some tacit agreement the issue of outcome was skirted by the conference" [Rotter, 1960, p. 403].

Finally, a 1962 review still finds no definitive investigations, just promising future lines of research:

From the standpoint of the researcher, the most heartening development is not the publication of definitive investigations—there are none—but rather the emergence of a number of thoughtful and searching analyses of what is needed in psychotherapy research, what is not needed, how researchers might go about advancing the field, and what obstacles need to be overcome [Strupp, 1962, p. 469].

In light of the methodological difficulties and the negative results surrounding the investigation of over-all effectiveness, the emphasis in recent years has switched to more specific and tangible measures of change during psychotherapy. The measures of change range from scores on particular diagnostic tests to specific forms of behavior such as frequency of coitus. Each school of therapy naturally concentrates on those tests or acts that are central to its own theory and accepts change in the appropriate direction as evidence of "improvement." While such interpretations are open to debate—does a particular score or a Rorschach response really indicate greater health than the previous one?—the findings themselves are beginning to provide substantial evidence that some measurable changes do occur during therapy.

For example, sexual behavior and attitudes are recognized as important in most schools of therapy, and:

E2   Changes toward a more positive attitude regarding sexual activity and toward freer, more enjoyable sexual activity than the patient was previously capable of having are reported as correlates of psychotherapy from several camps.

The table on page 291, for instance, shows that the reported frequency and enjoyment of coitus increases with length of psychoanalytic treatment. Similar improvements in sexual relationships are noted in a recent report on the practice and results of an entirely different approach to psychotherapy—one that views neurosis and its treatment in terms of conditioning and extinction principles:

[The] patient is instructed to expose himself only to sexual situations in which pleasurable feelings are felt exclusively or very predominantly. . . . If he is able to act according to plan, he experiences a gradual increase in sexual responsiveness to the kind of situation of which he has made use, with generalization to

Coital behavior at various points in psychoanalytic treatment

Length of treatment	Number of subjects	Percentage enjoying satisfactory coitus	Percentage having coitus twice a week or more
MEN			
Before treatment	25	40	44
0–5 months	16	69 *	56 *
6–11 months	16	76 *	38
12 months or more	15	67 *	67 *
WOMEN			
Before treatment	39	34	24
0–5 months	30	57 *	40 *
6–11 months	27	44	41 *
12 months or more	38	63 *	50 *

* Significant at 0.1 level.

(Graham, 1960, p. 94)

sexual situations of other kinds. The range of situations in which love-making may occur is thus progressively extended as the anxiety potentials of stimuli diminish, and at each extension these potentials diminish further. This may well be called a *virtuous circle* [Wolpe, 1958, pp. 130–31].

Another important school of psychotherapy, known as "nondirective" or "client-centered," stresses the importance of self-worth and self-esteem. One of the most extensive investigations of this type of counselling focuses on the discrepancy between how the client sees himself and how he would like to be (self-ideal).

E3 Discrepancies between self-concept and self-ideal are greater among people who present themselves for therapy than in normal controls; and over the course of client-centered therapy, the discrepancy tends to decrease: self and ideal come closer together.

Here is a statement from the leader of that school:

The characteristic person who enters therapy has a picture of himself which is far removed from—or even negatively correlated with—the concept of the person he would like to be. This seems to indicate a considerable degree of inner distress or tension. . . . During the process of therapy sufficient change occurs so that at the conclusion of therapy, and at the follow-up point, there is a significantly greater congruence of self and ideal. . . . In other words, the client has come to be—in his own eyes—a person who is much more similar to the person he would like to be. This change is especially marked in those clients rated as showing considerable therapeutic movement. . . . During the follow-up period there may be some falling-away from this achievement, some small degree of regression in the direction of the previous state [Rogers, 1954, pp. 416–17].

In a major study, a hundred self-referring statements were sorted into nine piles on a continuum from "like me" to "unlike me," separately for self and ideal according to these instructions:

1. *Self-sort.* Sort these cards to describe yourself as you see yourself today, from those that are least like you to those that are most like you.
2. *Ideal sort.* Now sort these cards to describe your ideal person—the person you would most like within yourself to be [Butler and Haigh, 1954, p. 57].

Here are some illustrative results, obtained when the two sorts are correlated to measure their correspondence:

Self-ideal correlations in the client group

Client	Precounseling r	Postcounseling r	Follow-up r
Oak	.21	.69	.71
Babi	.05	.54	.45
Bacc	−.31	.04	−.19
Bame	.14	.61	.61
Bana	−.38	.36	.44
Barr	−.34	−.13	.02
Bayu	−.47	−.04	.42
Bebb	.06	.26	.21
Beda	.59	.80	.69
Beel	.28	.52	−.04
Beke	.27	.69	−.56
Bene	.38	.80	.78
Bens	−.30	−.04	.39
Beri	.33	.43	.64
Beso	.32	.41	.47
Bett	−.37	.39	.61
Bico	−.11	.51	.72
Bifu	−.12	−.17	−.26
Bime	−.33	.05	.00
Bina	−.30	.59	.71
Bink	−.08	.30	−.20
Bira	.26	−.08	−.16
Bixy	−.39	−.39	.05
Blen	.23	.33	−.36
Bajo	.16	.29	.47
Mean z	−.01	.36	.32
Corresponding r	−.01	.34	.31

Further studies have elaborated and refined these self-ideal correlations. Following, for example, is the pattern of convergence between self and ideal over time, for two groups of patients in client-centered therapy and for one group under Adlerian treatment (a form of psychoanalysis that emphasizes the importance of feelings of inferiority). The chart also shows the differential effects of limiting the sessions to twenty interviews as against allowing an unlimited course of treatment.

Mean correlation chart

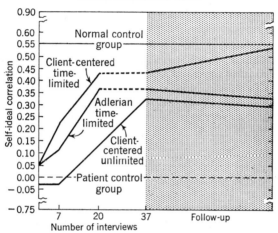

(Shlien *et al.*, 1962, p. 32)

It is seen that the passage of time had no effect on the normal and patient control groups as far as mean self-ideal . . . correlations were concerned. Second, all therapy groups showed marked improvement, particularly between the seventh and twentieth interviews. Gains were maintained on follow-up. Finally, the two time-limited groups improved more rapidly than the unlimited group, although the level at termination was about the same [Strupp, 1962, pp. 454–55].

Finally, some information is accumulating on the relationship between personal characteristics of patients (beyond the diagnostic labels) and prognosis in psychotherapy.

E4   In general, the higher the social class and level of education, the more psychologically sophisticated, the younger, and the less seriously sick the patient, the better the chances that he will finish and benefit from psychotherapy.

In other words, the more like the therapist and the less in need of help, the better the prospects for the patient. Whether this is because therapists prefer such patients and are more effective in dealing with them, or because these characteristics are necessary or helpful for psychotherapy, is unknown; but the findings themselves are consistent.

A recent review of several important studies has this to say:

These studies, viewed in the light of research previously published as well as work dealing with the clinical evaluations of therapists, yield a rather consistent picture. First, the prospects for successful psychotherapy seem to be enhanced when there is a certain congruency between the patient's expectations and the therapist's notions of what is to be accomplished. Second, therapists appear to have fairly definite, and probably valid, ideas of what constitutes a promising patient. . . . Patients considered good prognostic risks are described as young, attractive, well-educated members of the upper middle class, possessing a high degree of ego-strength, some anxiety which impels them to seek help, no seriously disabling neurotic symptoms, relative absence of deep characterological distortions and strong secondary gains, a willingness to talk about their difficulties, an ability to communicate well, some skill in the social-vocational area, and a value system relatively congruent with that of the therapist's. Such patients also tend to remain in therapy, profit from it, and evoke the therapist's best efforts. By superficial behavioristic criteria, such patients may not appear very "sick"; however, neither our culture nor our psychological tests are very sensitive to unhappiness, silent suffering, and despair.

From the above it is evident that only a relatively restricted band of the population meets these criteria, which, incidentally, are not very different from the ones originally postulated by Freud [*ibid.*, pp. 459–60, 470–71].

SELECTED READINGS

A good elementary treatment of the various physiological motives appears in:

Clifford T. Morgan and E. Stellar. *Physiological Psychology.* McGraw-Hill, 1950.

For more specific and detailed accounts of the physiological foundations and behavioral results of basic biological needs, see:

E. W. Dempsey. "Homeostasis," in S. S. Stevens, ed., *Handbook of Experimental Psychology.* Wiley, 1951.
Clellan S. Ford and Frank A. Beach. *Patterns of Sexual Behavior.* Hoeber, 1951.
Harry F. Harlow. "The Nature of Love," *American Psychologist,* 13, 1958, pp. 673–85.

Curiosity as a general motive is documented and discussed in:

Daniel Berlyne. "The Arousal and Satiation of Perceptual Curiosity in the Rat," *Journal of Comparative Physiology and Psychology,* 48, 1955, pp. 328–46.

More specifically still, the rewarding aspects of electrical stimulation of the brain are described in:

James S. Olds and P. Milner. "Positive Reinforcement Produced by Electrical Stimulation of Septal Area and Other Regions of Rat Brain," *Journal of Comparative Physiology and Psychology,* 47, 1954, pp. 419–27.

For diversified treatment of a wide variety of topics related to motivation, a good reader is:

David C. McClelland, ed. *Studies in Motivation*. Appleton-Century-Crofts, 1955.

A yearly symposium, in which major current trends are presented and discussed in depth, is reported in the annual:

Marshall R. Jones, ed. *Nebraska Symposium on Motivation*. U. of Nebraska Press, published annually from 1953.

Two important and classical examples of theoretical attempts to integrate the study of human motivation are:

A. H. Maslow. *Motivation and Personality*. Harper, 1954.
Kurt Lewin. *A Dynamic Theory of Personality*. Trans. by Donald K. Adams and Karl E. Zener. McGraw-Hill, 1935.

Experimental approaches to the matter of frustration and conflict can be sampled in:

John Dollard *et al*. *Frustration and Aggression*. Yale U. Press, 1939.
N. R. F. Maier. *Frustration*. McGraw-Hill, 1949.
Neal E. Miller. "Theory and Experiment Relating Psychoanalytic Displacement to Stimulus-Response Generalization," *Journal of Abnormal and Social Psychology*, 43, 1948, pp. 155–78.
Orval H. Mowrer. "A Stimulus-Response Analysis of Anxiety and Its Role as a Reinforcing Agent," *Psychological Review*, 46, 1939, pp. 553–66.

The first contains the original statement of the frustration-aggression hypothesis.

The following two selections by Freud serve as good introductions to quite another frame of reference:

Sigmund Freud. *The Interpretation of Dreams*. Trans. by A. A. Brill. Macmillan, 1933.
Sigmund Freud. *The Psychopathology of Everyday Life*. Macmillan, 1917.

Finally, here are some recent books that exemplify an emerging trend in the study of social motives. Each isolates an important and carefully delineated motive, or set of motives, and presents rather extensive research literature along with discussion and interpretation of its implications:

Leon Festinger. *A Theory of Cognitive Dissonance*. Row, Peterson, 1957.
David McClelland *et al*. *The Achievement Motive*. Appleton-Century-Crofts, 1953.
Stanley Schachter. *Psychology of Affiliation*. Stanford U. Press, 1959.

Better a dish of vegetables, with love, than the best of beef stewed with hatred.

Proverbs 15:17

Before fathers and mothers, uncles and aunts, itch as you may, you dare not scratch.

Chinese Proverb

When you have all done, saith Avicenna, there is no speedier or safer course, than to join the parties together according to their desires and wishes, the custom and form of law; and so we have seen him quickly restored to his former health, that was languished away to skin and bones; after his desire was satisfied, his discontent ceased, and we thought it strange; our opinion is therefore, that in such cases nature is to be obeyed.

ROBERT BURTON
The Anatomy of Melancholy

Mr. Knightley and Harriet Smith!—It was an union to distance every wonder of the kind. The attachment of Frank Churchill and Jane Fairfax became commonplace, threadbare, stale in the comparison, exciting no surprize, presenting no disparity, affording nothing to be said or thought. Mr. Knightley and Harriet Smith! Such an elevation on her side! Such a debasement on his! It was horrible to Emma to think how it must sink him in the general opinion, to foresee the smiles, the sneers, the merriment it would prompt at his expense; the mortification and disdain of his brother, the thousand inconveniences to himself. Could it be? No; it was impossible. And yet it was far, very far, from impossible.—Was it a new circumstance for a man of first-rate abilities to be captivated by very inferior powers? Was it new for one, perhaps too busy to seek, to be the prize of a girl who would seek him? Was it new for anything in this world to be unequal, inconsistent, incongruous—or for chance and circumstance (as second causes) to direct the human fate?

JANE AUSTEN
Emma

The family is a survival of the principle which is more logically embodied in the compound animal—and the compound animal is a form of life which has been found incompatible with high development. I would do with the family among mankind what nature has done with the compound animal, and confine it to the lower and less progressive races. Certainly there is no inherent love for the family system on the part of nature herself. Poll the forms of life and you will find it in a ridiculously small minority. The fishes know it not, and they get along quite nicely. The ants and the bees, who far outnumber man, sting their fathers to death as a matter of course, and are given to the atrocious mutilation of nine-tenths of the offspring committed to their charge, yet where shall we find communities more universally respected? Take the cuckoo again—is there any bird which we like better?

SAMUEL BUTLER
The Way of All Flesh

Chapter Seven
THE FAMILY

In a preceding chapter we dealt with the ways in which the newborn human being develops and is made into a member of some human society, largely through the influence of the family. We now continue our consideration of human behavior as it is associated with and affected by the family.

Since almost everyone has direct, intimate, and continuous knowledge of at least one family, and usually two (his parents' and his own), everyone knows something about the substantial ways in which the family has affected him, and hence affects human behavior. But it is perhaps worth adding that this institution has received constant attention from every kind of behavioral scientist. The psychologist studies child-rearing in the family; the sociologist studies courtship and marriage practices; the anthropologist studies kinship patterns.

DEFINITIONS

Family: Nuclear family means the immediate group of father, mother, and child(ren) living together. The *extended* family includes other relatives: grandparents, uncles and aunts, cousins, in-laws, and so on. Together they make up *kinship.* By *family of orientation* is meant the family you were born into; by *family of procreation* is meant the one you establish by marriage.

FINDINGS

For convenience, we organize the findings into three sections: those dealing with sexual behavior, those dealing with courtship, marriage, and divorce, and those dealing directly with the family and the kinship system.

297

Sexual Behavior

A1   Although the basis for sexual motivation is physiological, there is no known society in which the frequency or the form of human sexual behavior is determined solely by physiological factors.

To quote a major source:

> Frequency of human sexual relations is rarely determined solely by the physiological condition of the participants. . . . In human beings frequency [of sexual relations] is rarely a simple function of the degree of readiness, desire, or potency of the two partners. On the contrary, every society imposes restrictions upon a couple's sexual activity and enforces various periods of abstinence which have nothing to do with the man's or woman's capacity for erotic responsiveness or sexual performance [Ford and Beach, 1951, pp. 83, 75].

Here, as an example, is the situation with regard to marital intercourse during pregnancy:

Attitudes of sixty societies toward the occurrence of marital intercourse during the wife's pregnancy *

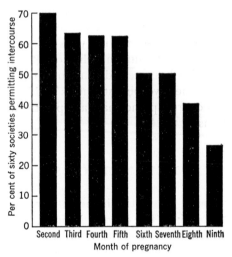

* Since pregnancy is not detected until at least the second month, there are no prohibitions until that time. Thenceforth coitus is subject to taboo in some societies. However, even during the final month of gestation one-fourth of the societies permit continuation of sexual relations.

(Ibid., p. 216)

A1.1   The physical gratification in sexual behavior is intimately bound up with deep psychological gratifications: the need for security, feelings of personal worth, feelings of power, the assurance of being loved and lovable.

A2   In general, human sexual behavior has both important similarities to and differences from animal (chiefly mammalian) sexual behavior. Among the important similarities are: the prevalence of male-female intercourse; the presence of homosexuality (mainly among males and adolescents); the presence of masturbation; the use of foreplay and sensory stimulation; and the presence of sex play at a young age. Among the important differences are: the greater control exercised by the cerebral cortex in human behavior (as contrasted with the role of the sex hormones in animal behavior—probably an evolutionary shift); the greater variability of sexual practices in the human being; the prevalence of indirect stimulation in the human being, as compared with genital stimulation in the animal; human-animal differences in positions during intercourse; the apparent infrequency of orgasm among female mammals below man; and the tying of human sexual activity to the period of the day least active in other respects.

Such comparisons are documented and detailed in Ford and Beach, 1951.

A3   Interest and activity in sexual matters are first evidenced in human beings at a very early age and are then and thereafter conditioned by the surrounding society (parents, family, peers, and the wider community).

After reviewing the cross-species and cross-cultural evidence, we are convinced that tendencies toward sexual behavior before maturity and even before puberty are genetically determined in many primates, including human beings. The degree to which such tendencies find overt expression is in part a function of the rules of the society in which the individual grows up, but some expression is very likely to occur under any circumstances. . . . As long as the adult members of a society permit them to do so, immature males and females engage in practically every type of sexual behavior found in grown men and women [Ford and Beach, 1951, pp. 197, 198].

A3.1   Sexual practices in human societies differ widely in a variety of ways that are directly attributed to cultural learning during the period of growing up: the frequency, the occasions, and the positions of intercourse; the activity-passivity of males and females; autoerotic behavior; infliction of pain; the amount and kind of foreplay; and so on.

It might be expected that in our own species learning would have the most marked and far-reaching effects upon sexual activities. This expectation is amply verified by the facts. Human sexuality is affected by experience in two ways: First, the kinds of stimulation and the types of situations that become capable of evoking sexual excitement are determined in a large measure by learning. Second, the overt behavior through which this excitement is expressed depends largely upon the individual's previous experience. . . . To a certain degree, unguided trial-and-error learning may influence the development of the individual's sexual patterns. But this is exceptional. By far most of what people learn to feel and to do in the realm of sex is learned from or with other individuals [*ibid.*, p. 262].

A3.2   Premarital sexual relations are allowed in a clear majority of human societies, but extramarital relations are almost universally condemned.

Premarital license prevails in 70 per cent of our cases [158 societies]. In the rest, the taboo . . . appears to be largely a precaution against childbearing out of wedlock rather than a moral requirement [Murdock, 1949, p. 265].

Only five societies out of 148 "freely allowed" adultery.

A4   The more severely a society controls sex training in childhood, the more restricted its own sexual practices are likely to be in adult life.

For example, "the societies with high sex anxiety are more likely to have long postpartum taboos [on coitus] than those with low sex anxiety," as shown in the following table (Whiting, 1954, p. 530).

Relation between the degree of sex anxiety induced during socialization and the duration of the pospartum taboo restricting coitus *

Duration of the postpartum taboo restricting coitus		
A few weeks to a month	*A month to a year*	*One year to three years*
HIGH SEX ANXIETY		
		Abipone
		Azande
		Chiricahua
		Dahomeans
		Dobuans
Manus	Chagga	Kwoma
Sanpoil	Chamorro	Tiv
Tanala	Riffians	Wogeo
LOW SEX ANXIETY		
Chenchu	Kwakiutl	Bena
Chewa	Hopi	Lesu
Lamba	Thonga	Trobrianders
Lepcha		
Marshallese		
Marquesans		
Murngin		
Siriono		
Witoto		

* From Gardner Lindzey, *Handbook of Social Psychology*, 1954, Addison-Wesley, Reading, Mass. Reprinted by permission.

(*Ibid.,* p. 530)

A4.1   At least in the United States, and probably in many other societies, the young learn sexual practices and sexual mores from their peers more than they do from adults.

A4.2   In all likelihood, a certain amount of experience in sexual play during adolescence contributes to satisfactory sexual relations during adult life.

This finding is based primarily on mammalian studies. For example:

> Males and females of several subhuman primate species are known to indulge in a great deal of sexual play which leads eventually to the perfection of adult patterns of heterosexual coitus. There is some reason to believe that the practice thus acquired is essential to the performance of biologically effective intercourse in adult life. The contribution of sexual experimentation and learning in human sexual relations is unknown. But the zoological data suggest that personal experience in coitus may be very important [Ford and Beach, 1951, pp. 197–98, citing Yerkes and Elder, 1936].

Some scholars believe that this finding is applicable to man as well as to mammalian species. Here is the statement of findings from the original citation:

> Our data justify the following statements of fact. Prior to sexual maturation, the female chimpanzee, if with other members of her species of comparable age and both sexes, learns from social contacts all that is necessary to enable her to behave wholly appropriately and effectively in the mating situation, and even to encourage, direct, or definitely to aid the male in copulation. By contrast, and this seems strange indeed, the recently matured male who is inexperienced in mating with a mature and receptive female commonly acts initially as does the sexually immature male, somewhat playfully, puzzled, and as if at a loss how to meet the situation. Even if, with the cooperation of the female, he attempts to copulate, he usually fails. . . . Our data indicate that the role of the sexually competent male is not taken by reason of maturation solely, but instead that experience and practice are essential to biological adequacy of performance and still more to perfection and skill. Seemingly it requires months for the mating pattern of the male chimpanzee to become so far perfected that it is satisfactory to the experienced female and in highest degree efficient as reproductive function [Yerkes and Elder, 1936, pp. 12–13].

A5   Sexual behavior varies (at least in the United States but probably in other countries too) according to the following characteristics:

.1   *Socioeconomic status:* For U.S. men, the highest total sexual outlet occurs among those who have only some high-school education and are in semiskilled occupations. For U.S. women, there is a slightly higher outlet for those with high-school education and beyond.

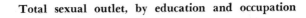

Total sexual outlet, by education and occupation

(Kinsey *et al.*, 1948, pp. 336, 420–21)

Patterns of sexual behavior may be strikingly different for the different social levels that exist in the same city or town, and sometimes in immediately adjacent sections of a single community. The data show that divergencies in the sexual patterns of such social groups may be as great as those which anthropologists have found between the sexual patterns of different racial groups in remote parts of the world. There is no American pattern of sexual behavior, but scores of patterns, each of which is confined to a particular segment of our society [*ibid.*, p. 329].

.1a   The higher a person's education or socioeconomic status, the greater the diversity of his sexual practices (i.e., the more experimental they are).

.1b   Differences in sexual behavior by socioeconomic status begin to appear very early in life.

Some of the most fundamental distinctions between the social levels are already discernible in pre-adolescents as young as 3 and 4. The ease or embarrassment with which such a child discusses [numerous sexual acts] indicate in practically every instance that the 3- or 4-year-old child has already acquired something of the social attitudes on at least some of these issues [*ibid.*, p. 441].

.1c   Differences in sexual behavior related to socioeconomic status seem to be correlated with the social position eventually acquired, rather than with the actual social position held at the time.

In general, it will be seen that the sexual history of the individual accords with the pattern of the social group into which he ultimately moves, rather than with the pattern of the social group to which the parent belongs and in which the subject was placed when he lived in the parental home [*ibid.*, p. 419].

This finding, however interesting, is subject to the technical caution that it results from retrospective interviewing, so that the recall of early practice may be contaminated by the present situation.

.2   *Sex:* On the average, men engage in sexual activity earlier than women and more often than women; are more responsive to psychological and symbolic materials associated with sex; and are more likely to engage in self-stimulation. *But* men and women do not appear to differ in the initiative taken for sexual activity (across cultures generally, although not in our own) or in the speed of achieving orgasm.

Here, for example, are some data from a standard source:

Comparison of aging patterns among single females and males

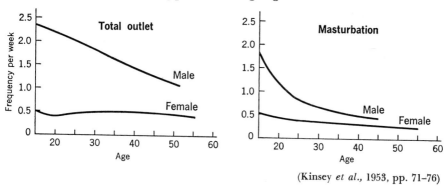

(Kinsey *et al.*, 1953, pp. 71–76)

As for the matter of initiative in sexual matters:

Whatever the methods of solicitation employed, the evidence indicates that initiative is more or less evenly distributed between the sexes in most mammalian species. From the cross-cultural evidence it seems clear that unless specific pressures are brought to bear against such behavior (as in our society), women initiate sexual advances as often as do men [Ford and Beach, 1951, p. 105].

.3   *Age:* In the United States, at least, the general pattern of sexual behavior is pretty well established in men by age sixteen (later for women), and by time of marriage most men have already passed the peak of their sexual capacity, which occurs in late adolescence.

As for generational differences, some students of the subject believe that there is little difference in sexual activity between one generation and the next:

In general, the sexual patterns of the younger generation are so nearly identical with the sexual patterns of the older generation in regard to so many types of sexual activity that there seems to be no sound basis for the widespread opinion that the younger generation has become more active in its socio-sexual contacts. The only instances in which a larger number of the younger generation is involved at an earlier age apply to such activities (masturbation, nocturnal emissions, and petting) as are not ordinarily considered when the charge is made that the younger generation is becoming increasingly immoral [Kinsey, *et al.*, 1948, p. 397].

Where differences do appear, it is at the lower socioeconomic level, presumably because of recent improvements in nutrition and hence maturation.

.4   *Religion:* At least in the United States, the more devout people, both men and women but especially the latter, begin sexual activities at a later age and engage in them less frequently and more conservatively; but once sexual activity is begun, the differences are small.

The differences between religiously devout persons and religiously inactive persons of the same faith are much greater than the differences between two equally devout groups of different faiths. In regard to total sexual outlet the religiously inactive groups may have frequencies that are 25 to 75 per cent higher than the frequencies of the religiously devout groups [*ibid.*, p. 486].

.5   *Place of residence:* At least in the United States, there are relatively minor differences in sexual behavior between rural and urban residents.

Courtship, Marriage, and Divorce

B1   The large majority of adults in all societies are married.

It is mainly in urban-industrial societies that the proportion of women never marrying by the end of the reproductive span exceeds 10% [Davis and Blake, 1956, p. 219].

Here are some comparative figures:

Percentage of women never married

India, 1931	0.8	Ireland, 1946	26.3
Ceylon, 1946	3.4	Sweden, 1945	20.9
Malaya, 1947	3.3	Switzerland, 1941	20.1

(*Ibid.*, pp. 218–19)

Of course, the form of marriage differs from society to society, among the (only) four possibilities: monogamy, polygyny (one male, more than one female), polyandry (one female, more than one male), group marriage.

Nowhere is the individual allowed to decide the matter for himself. In all societies there is a particular marriage form that is well ingrained in the culture, and most frequently there is only one form that meets with high social approval [Kenkel, 1960, p. 28].

B2   Economic factors tend to determine certain marriage practices, such as age at marriage, rate of marriages, remarriage of widows, etc.

For example:

.1   Marriage rates increase during prosperity, decrease during depression.

.2   In general, the rates of delayed marriage and nonmarriage are higher in urban, industrial societies.

Perhaps non-marriage occurs more often in industrial societies because these societies depend less upon kinship and the family as bases of social organization. The fact of being or not being married affects less the individual's economic chances. In pre-industrial societies, where the family is a productive unit, marriage has a high value for the individual. Also, where the partners to marriage are self-selected by a competitive process of courtship, as in modern countries, there tends to be a substantial proportion who are not successful in attracting a suitable mate [Davis and Blake, 1956, p. 222].

.3   Early marriage is encouraged in agrarian societies based on clans or joint households.

In such cases, economic independence is less likely to be a prerequisite for marriage, and at the same time the marriage adds economic strength to the household. In addition, early marriage is variously motivated: there is pressure to marry off daughters (since they would not have a permanent place in their parents' households), and women are most marketable when very young (it is then that they are most attractive and most likely to bear children); the younger the bride, the more docile she is in adjusting to the household she joins; joint households or clans usually have parental arrangement of marriages, and this makes for early marriage; parents are motivated to marry off their daughters young in societies with brideprices, since the money can be used to secure wives for their sons. Societies in which the young couple lives apart from the parents tend to have later age of marriage (*ibid.*, 1956).

As for the matter of romantic love, so important to Western marriage:

.4   Even in primitive societies, in which marriages are often arranged by the elders or by social custom, sentiment and affection typically enter into the match before or after the event itself.

B3   People tend to marry people who are in various social ways like themselves, rather than to marry people with differing characteristics. The similarities include, in rough order of importance (mainly in the United States), these social characteristics:

.1   race.

A series of studies in the United States, usually in cities, has consistently shown that less than 1 per cent of marriages are interracial (for a summary, see Barron, 1946). The intermarriage rate for the non-Negro nonwhite population (Chinese, Japanese, Indians, Mexicans) is higher than for the Negro population.

.2   religion.

"Next to race, religion is the most decisive factor in the segregation of males and females into categories that are approved or disapproved with respect to nuptiality" (Hollingshead, 1950, p. 622). Cross-religious marriages are more common when one of the groups is small, and hence has less opportunity for matches within the group. For example:

Percentage of all Catholic marriages that are mixed

In dioceses where the Catholic population is 2 per cent or less of the total	60–70
In dioceses where the Catholic population is 50–70 per cent of the total	less than 20

(Thomas, 1956, p. 155)

Although the rates vary considerably, as a rough order of magnitude it appears that in the United States about 10–15 per cent of all Catholic marriages are interfaith and less than 5 per cent of all Jewish marriages are interfaith.

Even where religious intermarriages occur, our study has shown they lead increasingly to the conversion of one partner or the other, and hence the re-establishment of socio-religious unity within the family [Lenski, 1961, p. 327].

.3   socioeconomic and educational status.

"Women are likely to marry above themselves in education and men to marry below themselves" (Landis and Day, 1945, p. 558).

Proportions of college youth who married youth of higher, equal, or lower educational status

	Higher	Equal	Lower
Men (132 cases)	8.3	9.1	82.6
Women (123 cases)	25.2	22.8	52.0

(*Ibid.*, p. 559)

In another study of marriage, in Madison, Wisconsin, from 1937 to 1943, 67 per cent of the college-educated grooms married brides with some college education as against 87 per cent the other way around (Sundal and McCormick, 1951). In the United States there is a reversal of marriage rates by class: upper-class men are more likely to marry than lower-class men, and upper-class women less likely than lower-class women.

.4   age.

Without any systematic evidence it would be almost anyone's impression that the wives of old men are older on the average than the wives of young men. But since things are not always as they seem, it is in order to note some studies which corroborate this impression [Winch, 1957, p. 351].

This finding has to do with age at marriage and it actually requires some qualification: after reaching middle age, men tend to marry younger women (e.g., a fifty-year-old man might marry a twenty-five-year-old woman); and in remarriages the wife is relatively younger, as indicated in the chart on page 308.

.5   previous marital status.

"Those who are marrying for the second or subsequent time tend to marry persons who have also been married before" (Winch, 1957, p. 351). And again, there is "a greater age spread in remarriage than in first marriages." Actually, there is a strong tendency to remarry within a particular marital status: divorced to marry divorced, widowed to marry widowed.

.6   residential propinquity.

Numerous studies of choice of marriage partners which have been made by sociologists over the years . . . indicate that even in our largest cities . . . where modern transportation facilities make possible quick and easy movement, approximately one-quarter of all marriages are contracted by persons living within five blocks of one another and half are contracted by persons living within twenty blocks of one another [Freedman *et al.*, 1956, p. 81].

The selection of a wife was once for most persons a selection from a small set of eligible girls. One might think that urbanization alone radically increases the number of eligibles. Yet this is not so, as at least one study has shown: in a class-bound and residence-bound society (France, before World War II) the effective range of selection of marriage partners was as low in Paris as in the most isolated hill communities, and lower than in middle-sized towns [Coleman, 1958, citing Sutter and Tabah, 1951].

In general, then, "the more than a hundred studies of homogamy have shown that the likelihood of husband and wife sharing almost any characteristic is greater than chance expectation, whether this characteristic is a physical one, such as height or color of eyes, or an economic factor such as occupational background" (Goode, 1961, p. 428). There is a summary table on page 309.

At the same time, choice of a marital partner is not altogether a matter

Years wife was younger or older than her husband, United States, 1948

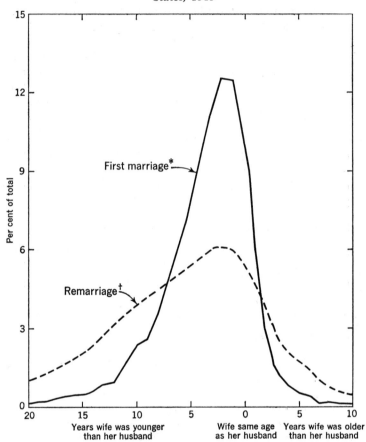

* Both spouses married once.

† One or both spouses remarried. Four point moving average.

(Glick and Landau, 1950, p. 524)

of similarities; rather, it seems to some extent to be a matter of *social* similarities and *psychological* differences. For there is some evidence to the effect that:

B3a   In a society allowing free selection of marriage mates, each partner tends to seek within the field of eligible partners that person who most nearly satisfies his own psychological needs *and* who is most nearly satisfied by his own personality.

This is called the "theory of complementary needs": "In mate-selection each individual seeks within his or her field of eligibles for that person who gives the greatest promise of providing him or her with maximum need

Assortative mating for physical, psychological, and sociological characteristics

Characteristic	Population	Number of pairs	Authors	
Age	U.S.	2500	Lutz '03	.76 ± .01
Stature	English	1000	Pearson and Lee '03	.28 ± .02
Eye color	English	774	Pearson '06	.26 ± .03
Weight	U.S.	989	Burgess and Wallin '44	.21 ± .03
Cephalic index	U.S.	319	Harris and Govaerts '22	.02 ± .04
Memory	U.S.	80	Schooley '36	.57 ± .05
Intelligence (Stanford)	U.S.	174	Burks '28	.47 ± .04
Association (Kent-Rosanott)	U.S.	80	Schooley '36	.47 ± .08
Neurotic tendency (Thurstone)	U.S.	80	Schooley '36	.30 ± .07
Dominance (Bernreuter)	U.S.	100	Hoeffeditz '34	.15 ± .07
Religious affiliation	U.S.	941	Burgess and Wallin '44	.75 *
Drinking habits	U.S.	989	Burgess and Wallin '44	.55 *
Number of children desired	U.S.	951	Burgess and Wallin '44	.51 *
Years of education	U.S.	1000	Burgess and Wallin '44	.40 *
Number of siblings	U.S.	988	Burgess and Wallin '44	.10 *

* Tetrachoric correlations.

(Spuhler, 1959, p. 736)

gratification." For example, "a highly hostile individual would seek to mate with a highly abasing person [i.e.], 'one who enjoys receiving expressions of hostility.' " Two needs (X + Y) in two people (A + B) "are complementary when A's behavior in acting out A's need X is gratifying to B's need Y and B's behavior in acting out B's need Y is gratifying to A's need X" (Winch, 1958, pp. 88–89, 91, 93). In a detailed analysis of a number of variables, out of 388 correlations, 256 came out in accordance with the theory. And four types of complementary needs emerged from the data:

Mother-son	dominant wife, dependent husband
Ibsenian	dominant and nurturant husband, dependent wife
Master-servant girl	husband overtly dominant and covertly dependent; wife subservient, strong, traditional
Thurberian	husband inhibited in expression of feelings, wife highly expressive

(*Ibid.*, pp. 333–34)

As the author of the theory recently put it: "Husbands and wives tend to be unlike and complementary with respect to the intensity of their needs" (Winch, 1957, p. 354).

B4   Marital adjustment and happiness are more likely:

.1   the more alike the marriage partners.

"A consistent finding from several studies is the correlation between diversity of cultural background of husband and wife and marital maladjustment" (Broom and Selznick, 1957, p. 382), especially with regard to ethnic differences. For example:

Rate of divorce or separation by religious faith of husband and wife (percentages)

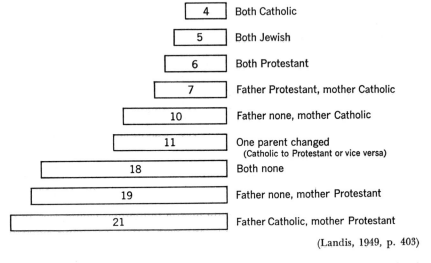

4	Both Catholic
5	Both Jewish
6	Both Protestant
7	Father Protestant, mother Catholic
10	Father none, mother Catholic
11	One parent changed (Catholic to Protestant or vice versa)
18	Both none
19	Father none, mother Protestant
21	Father Catholic, mother Protestant

(Landis, 1949, p. 403)

.2   the better the adjustment of the partners during the period of courtship.

Life is continuous and what seems right and proper and comfortable at one point is likely to feel so a short time later, or even over a longer period.

.3   the happier the partners perceive their own parents' marriage to be.

.4   the higher the level of education of the partners, or their socioeconomic status.

.5   the more religious they are.

.6   the less psychologically disturbed or anxious they are.

B5   In virtually every society, preliterate and pre-industrial as well as advanced, there is a recognized procedure for dissolving marriages and releasing the partners (that is, for "divorce"). At the same time, in virtually every society, divorce is subject to some social disapproval.

From these cases [forty non-European societies] it emerges, as a first conclusion, that practically all societies make some cultural provision for the termination of marriage through divorce. The Incas stand isolated as the solitary exception; among them a marriage, once contracted in the presence of a high official representing the emperor, could not subsequently be dissolved for any reason. None of the other thirty-nine societies in our sample compels a couple to maintain their matrimonial relationship where there are reasons for separation that would impress most contemporary Americans as genuinely cogent [Murdock, 1950, pp. 195–96].

Furthermore, in general, men and women have roughly equivalent rights to terminate an unsatisfactory marriage; and "a few basic reasons [for divorce] recur repeatedly as those considered justifiable in a wide range of societies. These are incompatibility, adultery, barrenness or sterility, impotence or frigidity, economic incapacity or non-support, cruelty, and quarrelsomeness or nagging" (ibid., p. 199).

The rate of marital dissolution is greater among many preindustrial or "primitive" societies than it is, for example, in the United States—which has a relatively high rate among Western nations.

In addition to the Incas [no divorce], the stability of marital unions is noticeably greater than in our society among Atayal, Aztecs, Creeks, Dahomeans, Ganda, Hopi, Hottentot, Jukun, Kazak, Lakher, Lango, Murngin, Ona, Sirioni, and Witoto. In the remaining twenty-four societies, constituting 60 per cent of the total, the divorce rate manifestly exceeds that among ourselves. Despite the widespread alarm about increasing "family disorganization" in our own society, the comparative evidence makes it clear that we still remain well within the limits which human experience has shown that societies can tolerate with safety [ibid., p. 197].

B5.1   The long-run trend in divorce rates, at least in Western countries, is upward; and it fluctuates with the business cycle (up in prosperity, down in depression).

Number of United States divorces per 1000 existing marriages, 1860-1956 *

Year	Number
1860	1.2
1880	2.2
1900	4.0
1920	7.7
1940	8.7
1956	9.3

* Based on data from Paul H. Jacobson, American Marriage and Divorce, Holt, Rinehart & Winston, 1959, p. 90. The data from 1920 on contain annulments, and all these data are partly estimated, since not all states are included in the divorce registration system. The earlier rates are, of course, even more open to question than the later.

(Goode, 1961, p. 411)

Partly, of course, the long-run increase is tied to the emancipation and the equalitarian status of women, as well as to the rise of the urban industrial society. For when women are not solely or mainly dependent on their husbands for their subsistence, separation or divorce is relatively easy and frequent.

B5.2   At least in the United States, the timing of marital dissolution reaches a peak around the third year.

After the first few months of marriage, the risk quickly rises, to reach a maximum during the third year. For example, in 1955, the rate per 1000 existing marriages was 18 during the first year, 25.1 in the second (i.e., less than two years), 25.4 during the third, and 22.1 during the fourth. Thus, after the third, the rate begins to drop [Goode, 1961, pp. 411–12].

B5.3   At least in the United States, the breakup of families, through divorce, desertion, or separation, is highest among:

.3a   the lower socioeconomic strata.

.3b   no-faith or mixed-faith marriages.

The divorce rate itself is higher among Protestants than Catholics; but if desertion and separation are included, the religious groups are nearly the same in rate of marriage dissolution. In this sense, desertion and separation are sometimes called the functional equivalents of divorce for those groups that strongly disapprove of divorce itself. For example:

Desertion cases by religious group
Philadelphia whites only, 1950
(percentages)

Religious group	1950 white population	Philadelphia white desertions		
		Both same religion	Husband's religion	Wife's religion
Jewish	16	9.6	10.5	10.5
Catholic	40	44.4	54.9	55.8
Protestant	44	22.9	33.9	33.0

(Monahan and Kephart, 1954, p. 463)

.3c   nonwhites, especially Negroes.

However, as the Negro becomes more and more assimilated into American society, his marriage and divorce rates come closer to those of the whites.

.3d   urban residents.

But here, too, the differences are diminishing.

.3e   marriages characterized by premarital pregnancies.

In addition, an authority in this field lists the following "background characteristics associated with a greater or lesser proneness to divorce":

Greater proneness to divorce	*Lesser proneness*
Marriage at very young age (15–19 years)	Marriage at average age (males, 23; females, 20)
Short acquaintanceship before marriage	Acquaintanceship of two years or more prior to marriage
Short engagement, or none	Engagement of six months or more
Couples whose parents had unhappy marriages	Couples with happily married parents
Nonattendance at church, or mixed faith	Regular church attendance, Catholics and adherence to the same church
Disapproval by kin and friends of the marriage	Approval of kin and friends
General *dis*similarity of background	Similarity ("homogamy") of background
Different definitions of husband and wife as to their mutual role obligations	Agreement of husband and wife as to the role obligations

(Goode, 1961, pp. 425–26)

It appears, incidentally, from

refined statistical calculations . . . that children have only a small effect on the maintenance of a marriage. . . . Unfortunately for those who seek easy solutions of family disorganization, it also seems likely that a family in which there is continued marital conflict, or separation, is more likely to produce children with problems of personal adjustment than a family in which there is divorce or death. . . . [The] choice usually has to be between a continuing conflict or a divorce. And the evidence so far suggests that it is the *conflict of divorce,* not the divorce itself, that has an impact on children [*ibid.,* pp. 454–56].

The Family and Kinship Systems

C1   The family and the institution of marriage exist in every known human society.

In a diverse sample of 250 societies, there is not a single exception:

Whatever larger familial forms may exist, and to whatever extent the greater unit may assume some of the burdens of the lesser, the nuclear family is always recognizable. . . . One fact stands out beyond all others, that everywhere the husband, wife, and immature children constitute a unit apart from the remainder of the community [Murdock, 1949, p. 3].

The family has this universal importance in human society, presumably, because it performs major social functions without which a society could not be maintained: provision for economic support, channeling of sexual behavior, reproduction, child-rearing (including some educational and religious upbringing), placement in the class system, emotional support.

Furthermore, in all societies marriage is the preferred arrangement for having children. Even where illegitimacy occurs frequently, it is disapproved: in general, both the parents and the child are socially punished. Illegitimacy occurs most frequently among lower-class and marginal groups, and it decreases as such groups become integrated into the larger society.

Marriage and the family, or something like them, also exist in animal species below man. In general, the more stable family units are found among the larger, the more intelligent, the slower maturing, the longer-lived animals—that is, those most like human beings in these respects. One big difference is that within a given primate species, family life seems to be much the same, whereas it varies widely among human beings.

> From the data available, it appears that more or less stable mateships are formed in all societies, among several species of subhuman primates, and in some lower animals. The most prevalent pattern of mateship among all primates . . . is a multiple one in which two or more females are attached to a single male [Ford and Beach, 1951, p. 122].

C1.1   Although the form of the family and associated kinship arrangements vary widely, there is no direct relationship between the family form and the economic or technological society in which the family exists.

> For example, the Eskimo type of kinship is the closest to that of the U.S. Indeed, . . . no theorist has been able to state, let alone prove, any set of systematic propositions about the relations between the family and other institutions [Goode, 1959, p. 180].

C2   Across societies, the husband is more likely to provide material support and at least *de jure* authority within the family and the wife is more likely to provide affection and moral support.

This is in essence a distinction that we shall be dealing with again. It deals with the so-called instrumental and expressive needs of all small groups (here including the family)—the need for leadership and fulfillment of the task on the one hand, the need for morale and cohesion on the other. Here are the data, from a cross-cultural survey of fifty-six societies:

	Instrumental	*Expressive*
Father	48	8
Mother	6	50

(Zelditch, 1955, pp. 347–48)

C2.1   In virtually all societies, children and women are subject to the authority of the man who lives with them (typically, although by no means always, the biological father; he can also be a grandfather or maternal uncle).

There is a general qualification:

C2.2   That spouse will dominate family decisions who is most closely tied to the prestige of kinship or to the material support of the family.

For example, women are not the dominant figures in societies with matrilineal descent, but they do have more influence within the family there than in patrilineal societies. From an experimental study of domestic problem-solving situations: "That husband or wife whose role is most strongly supported by kinship or economic considerations in the culture will tend to dominate in the discussion" (Strodtbeck, 1952, cited in Chapin, 1957, p. 276). In an inquiry into husband-wife disagreements, here were the results:

	Decisions won by	
Cultural group	Husband	Wife
Navaho (matrilineal)	34	46
Mormon (patrilineal)	42	29

(Strodtbeck, 1951, p. 472)

C3   The greater the social heterogeneity to which the family is subjected, the weaker its own internal integration, especially with regard to the extended family.

In a society in transition from an agricultural to an urban civilization characterized by heterogeneity and cultural conflicts, there is not the same uniformity in family integration as found in a homogeneous society [Burgess and Locke, 1953, p. 312].

C3.1   The more social movement by family members—geographical, occupational, socioeconomic, educational, religious—the weaker the family ties and the less the family's contribution to the maintenance of social positions.

The tie to the nuclear family may still be emotionally strong, but not so strong as if the family still lived and thought together.

The son may move to superior position, or the daughter marry into one, thus subordinating the parent and placing the family's superior adult in an inferior position of rank. . . . Open systems with free competition disperse the members of many families over distant parts of the rank order. . . . In a closed system the older generations are more likely to be related to the younger ones. The two families often form into a *grosse* family, held together in primary interaction biologically, territorially, and socially. They provide the hard core of fixed position for their members and closure for movement beyond their limits [Warner, 1957, p. 243].

C3.2   Those family members whose own aspirations (occupational and social) are out of line with the remainder of the family—being either quite high or quite low—are typically involved in tension within the family and in unsatisfactory personal relations.

C3.3   Over a long period, the family in Western society has come to have a different place in the individual's life, largely through the transfer of economic activities away from the home.

In the simpler society, kinship is the major channel for a range of social activities. In the modern industrial society, new institutions come to take over various economic, educational, and religious functions. But the emotional intensity within the family is probably as great now as it always was.

C3.4   The weaker the integration of the family, the more likely the members are to join in general political or social movements of a deviant character (such as juvenile delinquency).

When family integration weakens, the individual becomes more available for participation in some kinds of collective behavior. This availability has two aspects: (1) the individual can be more self-centered psychologically, more conscious of and concerned with his own needs and problems; and (2) his actions do not have direct, inescapable consequences for the lives of others who are dependent on him [Broom and Selznick, 1957, p. 406].

C3.5   Psychological disturbance in one member of the nuclear family will disturb the psychological equilibrium of the entire family.

Many psychiatrists believe, for example, that there cannot be just one mentally ill person in a family or, indeed, that the sickest member is necessarily the one who finds his way to a doctor or clinic. They feel that certain types of mental disturbance require treatment of the family as a whole, not just the individual.

C4   In every known human society, there is a prohibition against incest— i.e., against sexual relations or marriage with *any* member of the nuclear family and with *some* members of the extended family.

The very few known exceptions within the nuclear family involve ritualistic permissions before a hunt or battle, royal or sacred prerogatives, etc. The exceptions are so rare and so special that it is fair to say that this is a genuine universal in human behavior (for others, see the chapter on culture).

In no known society is it conventional or even permissible for father and daughter, mother and son, or brother and sister to have sexual intercourse or to marry. . . . The evidence from our 250 societies . . . is conclusive:

Relative (of man)	Premarital intercourse		Postmarital intercourse		Marriage	
	For- bidden	Per- mitted	For- bidden	Per- mitted	For- bidden	Per- mitted
Mother	76	0	74	0	184	0
Sister	109	0	106	0	237	0
Daughter	—	—	81	0	198	0

(Murdock, 1949, p. 12)

Nor is the prohibition against incest unknown among animals. Some animals—mainly those with both family and wider social groups, which, as we have seen, tend to be the larger, the more intelligent, the slower maturing, and the longer-lived among their species—do restrict sexual behavior within the nuclear family, although none, so far as we know, do so beyond that family.

The origins of the prohibition are so ancient that we cannot say with any scientific assurance just how it began. But among behavioral scientists, the reasons for the universality and the intensity of the incest taboo are believed to be mainly these:

(a) The belief, and in certain circumstances the fact, that intrafamily relations produce deteriorated offspring—the genetic reason.

(b) The need to defend the nuclear family, and to a lesser extent the extended family, from the intense strain that would arise from sexual rivalries, passions, and jealousies—the maintenance-of-the-family reason.

(c) The original need to develop a social group larger than the family for purposes of protection and sustenance, and the consequent desirability of pushing family members outward in order to broaden alliances—the mutual-assistance reason. (One of the major consequences of the prohibition is the discontinuity of the nuclear family, which typically contains only two generations.)

(d) The need to preserve the parents' authority over the rearing of the children by clearly separating the parental and the sexual roles, and the need to encourage adjustment to the larger society outside the family—the socialization and social-integration reasons.

(e) To account for intensity of maintenance, the fact that the taboo is taught early and severely.

C4.1   When the taboo within the nuclear family is broken, incest is much more likely to involve the daughter-sister than the mother; and at least in Western society, it is likely to involve people of low intelligence, of low social-economic status, and of low association with the larger society—highly marginal groups not attached to the norms of the larger society. Tennyson, incidentally, spoke of "the crowded couch of incest in the warrens of the poor," in *Locksley Hall, Sixty Years After.*

C4.2   With regard to the extended family, the incest prohibition ranges widely in the specific relatives it puts out of bounds in various societies: it does not apply universally to any one relative; it does not correlate with nearness of blood tie; it does correlate with kinship terminology similar to that used within the nuclear family (e.g., to any relative called "mother").

C5   In all known societies there are customary, but differing, arrangements for determining behavior among people who are related to one another through descent or marriage.

That is, there is everywhere recognition of the extended family—those kinsmen who are not members of one's own family of father, mother, child(ren)—and beyond that there are everywhere formalized ways of treating such people: grandparents, in-laws, uncles and aunts, cousins of differing degree, and so on. The ways are not the same from one society to another and, indeed, neither are the definitions of just *who* is a relative, or which one he is. But whatever the rules are, they help to regulate such behavior as deference among kin, ceremonial practices, intermarriage and preferential mating, sexual relations, economic responsibilities, etc. Here, for example, is an instance in one case of bereavement:

> One effect of the kinship systems in a great many societies is to formalize the replacement of the lost person, often by offering as close as possible a substitute—for practical and emotional reasons—as in the levirate (marriage to husband's brother) and sororate (marriage to wife's sister). As Murdock [1949] has shown in an analysis of 250 societies, these forms are preferred in 127 groups, occasional or absent in 58, and no data are available on 65 others [Caudill, 1958, pp. 14–15].

And here are some data on the preferred marriage in patrilineal as against matrilineal societies:

	Kin group	
Preferred marriage	*Patrilineal*	*Matrilineal*
Mother's brother's daughter	22	4
Father's sister's daughter	2	5

(Homans and Schneider, 1955, p. 34)

The rationale is

> that the locus of jural authority in father or mother's brother would be an important determinant of ego's sentimental ties with kinsfolk. In the former case, father and father's sister would be sentimentally "distant" from ego, mother's brother "close." And in the latter case, mother's brother would be "distant," father and father's sister "close" [*ibid.*, p. 58].

> All societies are faced with the problem of establishing priorities, as it were, i.e., of defining for individuals a particular group of kinsmen to whom they are privileged to turn first for material aid, support, or ceremonial services. All cultures meet this problem by adopting a rule of *descent* [Murdock, 1949, p. 14].

Descent is figured in one of three main ways: through the father's line (patrilineal); through the mother's line (matrilineal); or, as in our society, through both (bilateral). Descent controls succession and inheritance and even influences residence, so that, for example, matrilocal residence (with wife's family) is associated with matrilineal descent. In general, among primitive societies, descent is a more potent factor in determining kinship relations than is residence. But regardless of how descent is traced, nearly all human beings recognize their relations to both father's and mother's families.

In a way, the extended family can be seen (as some scholars believe) to be a necessary element for the operation of society, even our own, since it stands between the clan or community (too big for some purposes) and the nuclear family (too small). For example, the extended family takes on some welfare provisions for its members (helping Cousin Clara when she has a baby, finding Aunt Alice a job, taking care of Grandma).

C5a The total network of a group of intermarrying people is about the same size in modern Western society as is found in primitive society (from about 1000 to 2800 people).

Within France, for example, the average size in some large urban centers was about the same as in remote mountain areas:

> Even in a modern society, the network of people united by kinship ties is much smaller than might be expected, of about the same size as in primitive groups. The inference is that, while the absolute size of the intermarrying group remains approximately on the same scale in all human societies . . . , a complex society becomes such not so much because of an expansion of the isolate itself [i.e., the intermarrying group] as on account of an expansion of other types of social links (economic, political, intellectual); and these are used to connect a great number of isolates which, by themselves, remain relatively static [Levi-Strauss, 1953, p. 535].

In modern Western society, close kinship ties and frequent personal inter-action have been thought to be greater in the upper and the lower classes than in the middle class. At the top of the social pyramid, the aristocratic family hangs together out of tradition, self-respect, self-interest, and "posi-tion." At the bottom, it is more a matter of mutual help, although there is a good deal of that in the U.S. middle class too, e.g., helping the married son or daughter to maintain class position. Until recent years, scholars tended to think that kinship relations had fallen off in the modern indus-trial society, but some studies have shown that they are strong even in the city (e.g., Sussman, 1953; Young and Willmott, 1957).

> We were surprised to discover that the wider family, far from having disappeared, was still very much alive in the middle of London. This finding seemed to us of more interest than anything we had been led to expect, all the more so when it transpired that the absence of relatives seemed to be as significant on the estate [suburb] as their presence in the borough. . . . If we are to pick out one conclu-sion, it is the importance of residence. The Bethnal Greeners whom we have been describing did not change their residence just because they got married. They have remained in their district, and consequently in their families of origin. The wife stays close to her mother because she already shares so many common interests and associations, and since she stays nearby, she keeps them alive and renews them. The wife's relationship most of all with her mother, but also with her other female relatives, is firmer than the husband's relationship with his men relatives, unless indeed he works with them. But the husband, while he may move toward his wife's home, does not usually move far from his own parents [Young and Willmott, 1957, pp. xvi, 93].

C5.1   In all known societies, even quite poor ones, provisions are made for the feeding and care of aged relatives.

> In summary, then, individuals everywhere seem to have become progressively de-pendent upon others for their food with the onset of old age. The assurance of food from a group or communal source has not been entirely lacking in the simplest known societies. In fact, it appears that customs of sharing food with the aged have been strongest in very harsh and difficult environments, when the food supply has been less constant, and where types of maintenance have been less well developed, as among collectors, fishers, and hunters. With advance to herding and agriculture, and the development of cultural traits characteristic of "higher" civi-lization, such as grain supplies, property, trade, debt-relations, and slavery, sup-port of the aged through communal sharing of food appears to have declined in importance or to have taken on features more characteristic of "organized charity" [Simmons, 1945, pp. 34–35].

Actually, the arrangements differ somewhat for men and women:

> Considerable prestige has been accorded to the aged in primitive societies, but only under culturally determined circumstances and for a limited age period which rarely extended into decrepitude. Sexual differences have been significant.

The more favorable cultural milieu for aged men has been found to be within a patriarchal type of family organization; where herding or agriculture has been the chief means of maintenance; where there have been more or less permanent residence, a constant food supply, and a well-regulated political system; and where property rights in land, crops, herds, goods, and even women have been deeply entrenched. Aged women seem to have gained relatively more prestige in simpler societies characterized by collection, hunting, and fishing; and particularly in matriarchal forms of family organization. Their position also seems to have been better among farmers than herders. Aged men have been able to achieve considerable prestige even under circumstances normally conducive to elevating the rights of women; but old women have often been at very great disadvantage where cultural factors have been weighted in favor of aged men. Wherever aged women have been respected, old men have rarely been without honor; but prestige for aged men has offered no assurance of the same status for women. If either sex has lost respect in old age, it has been more likely to be the women than the men [*ibid.*, p. 81].

C5.2   To some extent (not great), the kinship line followed by a primitive society is probably associated with its economic and technological situation: e.g., societies that depend on hunting or herding for subsistence will tend toward patrilineal organization; those that depend on stable agriculture will tend more toward matrilineal.

C5.3   In general, the historical development is from the matrilineal organization to the patrilineal and then to the bilateral (i.e., from unilateral to bilateral).

Patrilineal and matrilineal peoples are found side by side and in restricted areas with culture showing unmistakable evidence of historical connections. It should now be clear that wherever such a situation exists, if the two types of structure are in fact genetically related, the patrilineal tribes must have evolved from a matrilineal organization, and not vice versa. It must likewise be true that in all societies with full-fledged double descent the matrilineal kingroups were the first to be evolved, the rule of patrilineal descent representing a secondary development [Murdock, 1949, p. 218].

C6   Differentiation among relatives is reflected in greater variety and complication of kinship terminology—who in the extended family is called what.

Anthropologists have assembled a great body of data from a large number of societies throughout the world that describes who is called by what term and how the kinship relations are handled. People are usually expected to behave the same way toward all kin designated by the same term. For example, American society calls father's brother and mother's brother both "uncle"—and in principle people behave similarly toward both—but that is by no means universal. Indeed, in some societies several women are called "mother"—e.g., mother, mother's sister (our "aunt"), even mother's mother's sister's daughter (a form of cousin or aunt to us). In some cases, kinship terminology mainly follows generational lines, with the degree of relationship subordinate; in other cases, relationship takes precedence over generation.

This whole field of study is highly developed, highly sophisticated, and highly technical; and it is not necessary for our purposes to follow out all the elaborations. But to give some flavor of the matter, here are some typical findings:

> When secondary or tertiary relatives of any kin-type are called by a kinship term used to denote a primary relative, the daughters of such secondary or tertiary relatives tend to be called by the same kinship term as the daughter of the primary relative [Murdock, 1949, p. 139].

> In the absence of exogamous matrilineal or patrilineal lineages, sibs, phratries, or moieties, separate kinship terms tend to be applied to comparable relatives of the same generation who are linked to Ego by connecting relatives of different sex [ibid., p. 163].

> In societies with endogamous demes, sibling terms tend to be extended to both cross and parallel cousins [ibid., p. 160].

> In the absence of clans and of polygamous and extended families, the isolated nuclear family tends to be associated with kinship terminology of the lineal type. . . . Bilateral kindred tend to be associated with kinship terminology of the generation type [ibid., pp. 157–58].

SELECTED READINGS

In the field of sexual behavior the three standard sources are probably these:

Clellan S. Ford and Frank A. Beach. *Patterns of Sexual Behavior.* Harper, 1951.
Alfred C. Kinsey *et al. Sexual Behavior in the Human Female.* Saunders, 1953.
Alfred C. Kinsey *et al. Sexual Behavior in the Human Male.* Saunders, 1948.

There is a large literature on marriage and divorce. A good starting summary for marital and family problems is:

William J. Goode. "Family Disorganization," in Robert K. Merton and Robert A. Nisbet, eds., *Contemporary Social Problems.* Harcourt, Brace & World, 1961, pp. 390–458.

An overview of the American scene is contained in:

Paul H. Jacobson. *American Marriage and Divorce.* Holt, Rinehart & Winston, 1959.

And on the selection of marital partners and the incidence of marital happiness, see:

Ernest W. Burgess and Harvey J. Locke. *The Family: From Institution to Companionship*. 2nd ed. American Book Company, 1953. Chaps. 14–15, pp. 375–447.
Robert F. Winch. *Mate Selection*. Harper, 1958.

On the family and kinship systems, see:

William J. Goode. *World Revolution and Family Patterns*. Free Press, 1963.
George P. Murdock. *Social Structure*. Macmillan, 1949.

Mutual confidence is the pillar of friendship.

Chinese Proverb

> For o thing, sires, saufly dar I seye,
> That frendes everich other moot obeye,
> If they wol longe holden companye.
> Love wol nat ben constreyned by maistrye;
> Whan maistrie comth, the god of love anon
> Beteth his winges, and farewel! he is gon!

GEOFFREY CHAUCER
The Franklin's Tale

He was welded into a common personality which was dominated by a single desire. For some moments he could not flee, no more than a little finger can commit a revolution from a hand. . . . There was a consciousness always of the presence of his comrades about him. He felt the subtle battle brotherhood more potent even than the cause for which they were fighting. It was a mysterious fraternity born of the smoke and danger of death. . . . He suddenly lost concern for himself, and forgot to look at a menacing fate. He became not a man but a member.

STEPHEN CRANE
The Red Badge of Courage

> Much madness is divinest sense
> To a discerning eye;
> Much sense the starkest madness.
> 'Tis the majority
> In this, as all, prevails.
> Assent, and you are sane;
> Demur,—you're straightway dangerous,
> And handled with a chain.

EMILY DICKINSON
Poems of Life, XI

". . . At a time like this there's no room for—well—personal views. The man who doesn't toe the line is lost."

"I see what you mean."

"No, you don't see entirely. He not only loses himself, he weakens his friends. If you leave the line, you leave a gap in the line."

E. M. FORSTER
A Passage to India

Chapter Eight

FACE-TO-FACE RELATIONS,
IN SMALL GROUPS

What is distinctively human comes from the primary fact that man lives his life in groups, with other people. Behavioral scientists have given a great deal of attention to this subject: earlier in the form of theoretical analysis of the "primary group," recently more in the form of empirical experimentation on the small group. As we move out from the individual to larger and larger social units, it is appropriate that we follow the section on the family with this one on the small, cohesive, solidary group. Indeed, as we shall see, the family itself can be viewed as just such a group.

DEFINITIONS

Small group: By this term is meant an aggregate of people, from two up to an unspecified but not too large number, who associate together in face-to-face relations over an extended period of time, who differentiate themselves in some regard from others around them, who are mutually aware of their membership in the group, and whose personal relations are taken as an end in itself. It is impossible to specify a strict upper limit on the size of the informal group, except for the limitation imposed by the requirement that all the members be able to engage in direct personal relations at one time—which means, roughly, an upper limit of around fifteen to twenty. If the aggregate gets much larger than that, it begins to lose some of the quality of a small group or, indeed, begins to break up into small subgroups.

For our purposes, the term covers a number of different kinds of small groups, and we shall try to note the application of particular findings wherever appropriate. In order to exemplify the variety of small groups, we can identify here (1) the autonomous group, e.g., a circle of close friends built on free choice and voluntary association; (2) the institutionalized small group, e.g., the family; (3) the small group within a large organization, often called a mediating group because of its linking position between the individual and the organization, e.g., the work group in a factory or office, a group of soldiers (buddies) in the army; and (4) the problem-solving group, e.g., a committee with a task to perform.

Taken as a whole, these categories come down to two broad types—those small groups with specific tasks to do and those, like the family, with more diffuse purposes. Another way to look at them is to think of those groups mainly oriented to the task (such as a work group), those mainly oriented to social and emotional satisfactions (such as a bridge club), and those oriented to achieving roughly equivalent amounts of each objective (such as some voluntary associations involved in charitable activity). As the definition quickly suggests, a society is full of small groups, and everyone spends a good deal of his life in them.

In sum, the essential elements in the definition are: small size, personal relations, some duration, identification of the members with the group and hence some solidarity, differentiation from others, genuine goals, common symbols, and autonomy in setting up procedures.

Interaction: This is a generic term for the exchange of meanings between people. Usually interaction is direct communication—mainly talking and listening, often writing and reading—but it can also include gestures, glances, nods or shakes of the head, pats on the back, frowns, caresses or slaps, and any other way in which meanings can be transmitted from one person to another and back again: the simultaneous effect is usually central. Simply being present in a small group and being taken into account involves interaction too. The term is somewhat awkward, but some single word is required to cover all the various ways in which people can and do express themselves in face-to-face meetings; "interaction" refers to communication in its broadest sense.

FINDINGS

The findings are organized here into three main sections. The first deals with how small groups are formed, the second with how they influence their individual members, and the third with how they operate internally. A fourth topic, the relation of small groups to the larger organizations in which they often operate, is covered in the following chapter on complex organizations.

Formation

A1   The more people associate with one another under conditions of equality, the more they come to share values and norms and the more they come to like one another.

In other words, small groups rest on shared values and shared contact. The free-forming groups mentioned above are constituted on these bases. The forced-choice groups, such as families and fellow workers, have frequency of contact built into them, and that itself tends to effect a convergence of values and norms.

The shared values include not only those associated with such social positions as educational status, age, class, or ethnicity, but beyond that they reflect such matters as attitudes, tastes, beliefs, and behavioral norms. Apparently, "friendship is more frequently based on similarity of ideals than on similarity of personality," in the narrower sense of that term (Klein, 1956, p. 106). And, as data from a study of college and university faculties indicates, homogeneity of outlook leads to satisfaction:

Homogeneous faculties have better social relations than faculties divided on permissiveness

Permissiveness of the faculty	Proportion of respondents who are highly satisfied with faculty relations (Percentages)	Number of colleges
Mainly permissive	43 (631)	21
Divided: majority permissive	32 (664)	27
Divided: majority conservative	31 (362)	18
Mainly conservative	48 (197)	11

Several studies have shown that the sharing of beliefs which are relevant to a group facilitates friendships among that group and that, inversely, close personal contacts lead to a similarity of relevant attitudes.

(Lazarsfeld and Thielens, 1958, p. 147)

As one authority in the field puts the general point:

Interaction between persons leads to sentiments of liking, which express themselves in new activities, and these in turn mean further interaction. . . . The more frequently persons interact with one another, the stronger their sentiments of friendship for one another are apt to be. . . . The more frequently persons interact with one another, the more alike in some respects both their activities and sentiments tend to become [Homans, 1950, pp. 119, 120, 133].

In most cases, then, the more interaction there is within the group, the more positive are the feelings of the members toward the group, and particularly among those members directly engaged in the interaction. And the more interaction among the members of a group—i.e., the more they share opinions among themselves—the more they tend to converge in their judgments of the topics under consideration.

As a corollary of the effect of interaction, people tend to choose others as friends on the basis of the physical distance between them. For example, in a study of housing projects there was

> a strong relationship between sociometric choice and physical distance. In both projects the greatest number of choices were made to people living closest to the person choosing and the choices decreased continuously as distance from the home of the chooser increased. The actual measured distances involved were quite small, in no case being larger than 180 feet. Yet the effect of even these small distances is . . . marked. . . . This same relationship holds for choices outside of the court or building. The greater the physical separation between any two points in these communities, the fewer the friendships [Festinger *et al.*, 1950, pp. 431–44].

Here is one set of illustrative data:

The relationship between sociometric choice and physical distance on one floor of a Westgate West building

1 *Units of approximate physical distance*	2 *Total number of choices given*	3 *Total number of possible choices*	4 *Choices given* (2) ——————— *Possible choices* (3)
1	112	8 × 34	.412
2	46	6 × 34	.225
3	22	4 × 34	.162
4	7	2 × 34	.103

(*Ibid.*, p. 38)

A1.1   There is a tendency for people to gravitate into groups or subgroups with the effect of maximizing their shared values.

We say "with the effect of" rather than "in order to" because the gravitation is not always rational and deliberate. But if the group is insufficiently comfortable, in a psychological sense, the individual will be on the lookout for a more congenial set of associates, either within or outside of the group—for congeniality he must find in order to feel assured of the correctness of his own behavior. This tendency leads some scholars to speak of a human need in this regard—"the need for consensus."

The one way in which it is possible for a population to satisfy both the individual-autistic demands and the demands of social reality is to sort itself into subgroups which are in fact characterized by this kind of consensus [Newcomb, 1959, p. 288].

Incidentally, such groups often distinguish themselves by the use of a special language—the jargons of jazz fans and hot-rodders, the secret lingoes of social clubs, even the unique endearments of lovers.

These group languages possess an expressive and an emotion-laden quality which is conducive to group conviviality and consensus. . . . The specialized vocabulary of a deviant group helps to open the gates to full-fledged membership, serves as a symbol of self-identification with the group, and provides an easy way of creating the psychological climate peculiar to the nature of the group [Bram, 1955, p. 44].

Thus people tend to belong to small groups with uniform or consistent standards that reduce confusion over what is the right behavior, hence increase the favorable reaction of their fellows. But such simplification is not always possible—life is too complicated. In a complex society individuals are often caught between, or even among, informal groups with conflicting standards. Hence:

> **A1.1a**   When caught in cross-pressures between the norms of different groups of which he is simultaneously a member, the individual will suffer some emotional strain and will move to reduce or eliminate it by resolving the conflict in the direction of the strongest felt of his group ties.

The stronger the ties which bind the individual to one of the overlapping groups, the more he will be influenced by the norms of that group. . . . One would expect that the looser the boy's family ties, the more readily he would be guided by the norms of gang loyalty. There are several studies which suggest that the relative hold of conflicting norms depends to some extent on the intimacy of the supporting group ties [Freedman *et al.,* 1956, p. 178].

In line with the earlier finding on the importance of sheer frequency of contact, the individual will go along with the group with which he has most active interaction. Hence, immediate relatives are more likely to be effective than remote ones, and the small, intimate group more influential than the large, less personal association (when the two are in conflict).

The avoidance of cross-pressures is valuable to most people, because they prefer a harmonious state. Here a related point is made in formal language by a leader in this field:

As a practical matter, distributive justice is realized when each of the various features of his investments and his activities, put into rank-order in comparison with those of other men, fall in the same place in all the different rank-orders. This condition, which we call status congruence, is . . . [the condition] of social certitude: the status of a man in this condition is secure, established, unambiguous in the eyes of his fellows. To attain status congruence is a reward to men, and to forego it, a cost; and they have learned various means by which they may attain the reward or avoid the cost. Congruence facilitates social ease in the interaction among men, and so when they are working together as a team, a congruent relationship between them, by removing one possible source of friction, should encourage their joint efficiency. Up at least to middle levels of congruence, the evidence shows that it does do so [Homans, 1961, p. 264].

A2   The larger the proportion of new members joining an established group within a given period of time (short of actually taking it over), the greater will be the resistance of the group to their assimilation.

Whereas a few newcomers will be welcomed, to stimulate or to strengthen, a larger number will generate the fear that the group is being overwhelmed or inundated. New members, when sufficiently large in number, tend to be disliked and distrusted because they form "their own group" within the original one, or at least threaten to; or because their members lead to a splitting up of the original group.

A2.1   New personal relations tend to conform to established relations. Thus if A and B are friendly and B is cool to C, then A will tend to develop a cool relationship toward C too.

A2.2   New members of a small group are likely to feel inferior to established members.

For example:

On the whole the replacements [in a military unit] seemed to feel inferior *vis-à-vis* the established primary group into which they are not yet accepted and which had a dual source of prestige in their eyes—both as combat veterans and as an established primary group sharing intimacies and "knowing the ropes" [Shils, 1950, p. 30].

A2.3   The less change there is in a group's membership, the higher the group's morale will be.

A "tightly knit group" significantly means both a group difficult to enter and one whose members closely identify with one another. The less permeable the group, the more value attaches to membership and, in turn, the more intense the adherence to group perspectives [Lasswell and Kaplan, 1950, p. 35].

A2.4   The more eager an individual is to become a member of a small group, the more he will conform to its norms of behavior.

This is part of a broader finding that applies not just to small groups but to organizations, institutions, and strata as well. That is, people tend to take on the behavior of the group or the class they aspire to join—for example, people wanting to get ahead in the world begin to learn upper-class etiquette.

A3   The more interaction or overlap there is between related groups, the more similar they become in their norms and values; the less communication or interaction between them, the more tendency there is for conflict to arise between them. And vice versa: the more conflict, the less interaction.

> Communication between conflicting groups tends to be suspended. The sense of threat and the increased concern for internal solidarity leads to a blocking of communication channels. For example, when labor-management conflict is intense, union leaders avoid all except the most official and circumscribed contact with the employers, partly because they would be exposed to criticism from their own members [Broom and Selznick, 1957, p. 33].

A3.1   The less contact between members of different groups, the less will there be a mutually recognized, proper behavior for their relations. If such contact sharply increases, there will tend to be increased tension until the proper behavior is defined and established.

Today's example, perhaps, is Negro-white relations in the South.

A4   Small groups of a free-forming character tend to be particularly numerous and influential in those modern, advanced societies that are open and liberal in their social and political organization.

> In societies with a high degree of political equality, there is a high orientation to the approval of other members of [the] primary group. Each being equal, people are less inclined to assert themselves against the "tyranny of the majority," and equality dissolves those traditional standards in the name of which one can stand up against group pressures. The individual is thus without support. With their constitutional guarantee of freedom of association for peaceable purposes, such societies secure the existence of a network of private, primary groups in a way which would be impossible in a dictatorship. For example, primary group membership can serve as a substitute for political office, and private primary groups can even to a great extent be the main vehicles of standards and tastes in the society [Brotz, 1959].

Influence

B1   The small group strongly influences the behavior of its members by setting and/or enforcing standards (norms) for proper behavior by its members—including standards for a variety of situations not directly involved in the activities of the group itself.

The small group is where a great deal of human behavior, including the "right" way to behave, is learned and enforced. The group can set standards for a range of behaviors beyond its own jurisdiction. For example, how the members of his primary group are going to vote is important in bringing the individual member to his own "decision" in general elections (Lazarsfeld *et al.*, 1948); how the prestigious members of the surrounding community feel about politics is influential in changing the minds of the new members (Newcomb, 1943); how workers respond to official standards of productivity often depends on group relations on the job (e.g., the group can set lower standards for production than those officially set). Even pairs of workers can "control" one another's output, when output is visible; and such correspondence disappears when the individuals are isolated from one another (Hughes, 1946b).

The influence of even a very small, experimentally organized group on the setting of a norm was demonstrated in a well-known study in which the subjects estimated the movement of a light in a darkened room—a light that did not move at all. The experimenter started with individuals who then joined into groups and with groups that were later separated into individuals, with the results shown on page 333.

> When the individual, in whom a range and a norm within that range are first developed in the individual situation, is put into a group situation, together with other individuals who also come into the situation with their own ranges and norms established in their own individual sessions, the ranges and norms tend to converge. But the convergence is not so close as when they first work in the group situation, having less opportunity to set up stable individual norms [Sherif, 1952, p. 255].

B1.1   The more stable and cohesive the group is, and the more attached the members are to it, the more influential it is in setting standards for their behavior.

For example, in the study of housing projects mentioned above, the people living in the relatively cohesive courts of the projects were most likely to conform with regard to activities of the community council. On page 334 is the correlation between the proportion of deviants on that issue and the choices of friendships in the courts. In short, "if a person wants to stay in a group, he will be susceptible to influences coming from the group, and he will be willing to conform to the rules which the group sets up" (Festinger *et al.*, 1950, p. 91).

> **B1.1a**   The deviant members of the group are more likely to change their behavior to meet the standards of the modal members of the group than the other way around.

The modal members are more numerous and hence can exert more pressure. In addition, they are more moderate than the deviants (extremists) on either side; hence they can both represent compromise on the issues involved and claim the virtue of holding the group together.

Medians in groups of two subjects

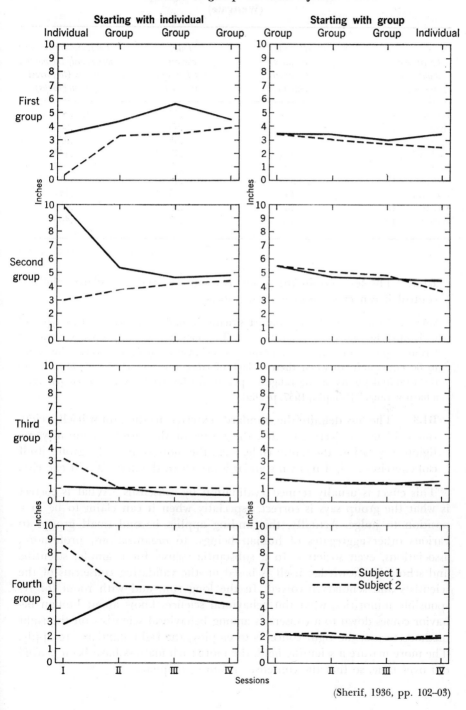

(Sherif, 1936, pp. 102–03)

Cohesiveness of court and strength of group standards
(Westgate)

Court and number of residents		Per cent deviates (to court pattern)	Total choices (of friends) in court	Total choices in court minus half the mutual choices (to correct for subgroups)
Tolman	13	23	.62	.529
Howe	13	23	.63	.500
Rotch	8	25	.55	.523
Richards	7	29	.47	.433
Main	7	29	.67	.527
Freeman	13	38	.48	.419
Williams	13	46	.53	.447
Miller	13	46	.56	.485
Carson	13	54	.48	.403

(Festinger *et al.*, 1950, p. 92)

B1.2   The less certain the group is about the right standards, the less control it can exercise over its members.

Stouffer, in a study of role conflict situations, finds evidence for two types of variability in role expectations: "(a) When members of a group agree on the terminal points of a *range* of permissive behavior, but also perceive the range to be large, and (b) when there is lack of consensus among the members as to the terminal points of the range of permissive behavior, even if each perceives a narrow range" [Chapin, 1957, p. 269].

B1.3   The less definite the standards external to the group itself (scientific evidence, objective reality, the norms of the larger community, religious revelation, the moral code, etc.), the more control the group itself can exercise—and, if its own standards are clear, the more it will exercise.

This effect is usually termed "validation by consensus." What is correct is what the group says is correct, especially when it can claim to be in a position to judge. Actually, this finding applies beyond small groups to various other aggregates of human beings: to organizations, professions, associations, even societies. In a substantial sense, for example, scientific and scholarly knowledge itself is based on the validating consensus of the scientists and scholars involved. In the long run, and with room for responsible minorities, what the behavioral sciences know about human behavior comes down to a consensus among behavioral scientists on the right methods to use, the right concepts to employ, the right standards to apply. The more mature a scientific field, the more such matters have been proved out over time, so that the consensus is more complete.

B1.3a   When neither an objective nor a group basis of judgment exists, and when divine revelation is not accepted, judgments tend to be unstable; as a consequence there is an increase in interaction within the group in order to reduce the ambiguity.

Studies of pressures toward conformity found that "reactions are evoked more easily when pressures are exerted on attitudes towards social issues; factual matters and personal preferences seem to be most resistant to change" (Blake and Mouton, 1961, p. 231).

B1.3b   As a special case: a single individual tends not to hold out against the weight of an otherwise unanimous group judgment, even on matters in which the group is clearly in error.

In one dramatic series of experiments, "a group of eight individuals (male college students) was instructed to judge a series of simple, clearly structural perceptual relations—to match the length of a given line with one of three unequal lines. Each member of the group announced his judgments publicly" (Asch, 1958, p. 175). In a series of eighteen trials, an uninstructed minority member of the group, who responded after the other seven, was faced with purposely incorrect judgments by the others in twelve trials. Here are the results:

Distribution of errors in experimental and control groups

Number of critical errors	Critical group * (N = 50)	Control group (N = 37)
0	13	35
1	4	1
2	5	1
3	6	
4	3	
5	4	
6	1	
7	2	
8	5	
9	3	
10	1	
11	3	
12	0	
Mean	3.84	0.08

* All errors in the critical group were in the direction of the majority estimates.

(*Ibid.*, p. 177)

In short, "one third of all the estimates in the critical group were errors identical with or in the direction of the distorted estimates of the majority" (*ibid.*, pp. 176–77). Only one-fourth of the subjects were completely independent of the majority view. With just one partner in judgment, however, most subjects held firm against the rest of the group. Thus a subgroup of at least two, each reinforcing the other, was required for firm independence from the group judgment—even when the latter was clearly mistaken. The full distorting effect occurred in as small a group as four—three against one—and the proportion that "goes along with the group" is presumably much higher in the absence of an objective standard of what is correct. A similar study using school children as subjects came up with a similar conclusion (Berenda, 1950).

B1.4   If the small group's activities are imposed from outside, the norms set by the group are likely to be limited in character; if they are determined from within, they are more likely to take on the character of ideal goals, to be constantly enlarged and striven for.

For example, when management sets the general work load, the work group on the job will tend to set the appropriate norm for output (and it will tend not to be maximum). If a group sets its own goals, they will typically be ideals realizable only in stages, so that the group goes from one to the next under its own power.

B1.5   Members of a group typically perceive the group's opinion to be closer to their own opinions than it actually is.

Whether this is due to association with a biased sample of like-minded individuals in the group or to an attempt to allay anxiety about nonconformity by minimizing deviation from the group standard remains a problem for further research [Kelley and Thibaut, 1954, p. 768].

By virtue of the informality in the operations of most small groups, issues may be kept from being put to a clear test. People advance their opinions; and even though there may be an immediate reaction, it is difficult for them at times to estimate the degree to which they can count on firm support. In consequence:

B1.5a   The more frequent the interaction among the members of a group, the more correctly they can judge the opinion of the group, i.e., the more predictable the group's behavior becomes to them and hence the more reliable as a guide to proper behavior.

B1.6   People in a group tend to agree with the opinions of people they like (i.e., they judge the opinion by judging the advocate); and they tend to think that the people they like agree with them and that those they dislike do not.

B2   The group strongly influences the behavior of its members by providing them with support, reinforcement, security, encouragement, protection, rationale, rationalization, etc., for their "proper" behavior; and by punishing them for deviations through the use of ridicule, dislike, shame, threat of expulsion, etc.

When an individual is genuinely attached to a group, and in close and continuous contact with it, his group-anchored behaviors and beliefs are extremely resistant to change; in such circumstances the group can exercise firm "control" over him.

> When a group member accepts and conforms to the standards or norms of a group, his security is enhanced by virtue of the supportive power that the group is capable of mobilizing to enforce these standards. Hence, a group in which norms or standards have become well "institutionalized" will be able to present a secure front to the outside world [*ibid.*, p. 764].

For example, in studies of the United States Army in World War II there is evidence to the effect that those soldiers closely tied to cohesive groups in the Army were more responsible in carrying out their soldierly duties, more confident of being able to perform well as soldiers, less fearful in battle, less likely to resort to prayer under danger, and less likely to capitulate or surrender under stress (Stouffer *et al.*, 1949, Vol. II).

B2.1   Within a group, a network of communication tends to develop in which one's friends reward one's conformity while one's enemies punish deviance from group norms.

For example, a study of adolescents found that when some people like and others dislike the same individual, the likers are apt to select conformist characteristics in describing him while the dislikers are apt to describe him in deviant terms. Moreover, the more approval an individual receives for his conformity, the more likely he is to receive some disapproval as well (Riley and Cohn, 1958).

B2.2   The response of the group to deviation from its norms for behavior is, first, discussion and persuasion to bring the dissenting minority into line; second, disapproval of the dissenters; third, lowered ranking for the dissenters; and fourth, their expulsion or induced resignation from the group.

The last extremity, which amounts to changing the composition of the group in order to retain the initial consensus, is employed particularly in those cases where the issue is seen as highly important for the group, where cohesiveness is highly valued, where the disagreement is of sizable magnitude, and where the group is small enough for the disagreement to be keenly felt. As an authority recently put it:

Men give social approval, as a generalized reinforcer, to others that have given them activity they value, and so make it more likely that the others will go on giving the activity. One of the kinds of activity some men find valuable is that their own behavior and that of others they are associated with in a group should be similar in conforming to a norm. . . . People that find conformity valuable reward conformers with social approval, but they withhold approval from those that will not conform, or even express positive dislike for nonconformists as having denied them a reward they had the right to expect.

Some members of a group conform for the norm's sake, . . . and some for the approval's sake, but both will come to say that they do it for the norm's. The more a member values an activity incompatible with conformity . . . and the more valuable are his sources of social approval other than the conformers in his group, the less likely he is to conform: a companion in misery is still a companion [Homans, 1961, p. 129].

As a result, then, of both the individual's selection of which group to belong to and the influence and pressure of the group upon its members, including the withdrawal or the expulsion of the deviants (nonconformers), most informal groups come to achieve a certain harmony of outlook. Here is a summary statement:

B3 Small groups tend toward uniformity in attitudes and actions, in values and behavioral norms—i.e., in the "right" way to think and act— under the following conditions:

.1   The greater the attractiveness of the group for its members, as compared to other groups, the more important its goals or other properties (e.g., provision of companionship) are for the individuals in it, and the stronger is the member's desire to remain in the group or his dependence on it.

In such cases the members are likely to change their own minds so as to conform to the group's position or, especially with those members at or close to the modal position of the group, to try to change others into conformity with the group.

.2   The more pressures for uniformity there are within the group, especially when it is united by a broad ideology (like a cell of the Communist party).

.3   The more important the issue at hand is for the group, or the members' perception of its importance.

.4   The more homogeneous the group is in social composition or in personal status, any initial range of opinion notwithstanding.

.5   The more visible the member's opinion or action is to the group, or theirs to him (in which case "corrections" can be seen and made more readily).

As a corollary, the more centrally located the member as a source of communication within the group or the more influential he is, the greater his conformity to group norms (Hopkins, 1959).

.6   The more frequent the personal interaction among the members is, within or outside the group itself.

.7   The more personal interaction there is within the group on the basis of equality, with no one exercising much authority over anyone else, and the less personal competition there is within the group.

.8   The more directly and fully the members participate in the determination of the group's standards.

.9   The more favorably the members are regarded by one another.

   B3a   Small groups in established, elite strata tend to be more tolerant of deviation from norms than such groups in socially mobile strata.

In the former case (e.g., the British aristocracy) there are certain fixed standards for behavior, but in other spheres the individual is free to "be himself." In mobile strata there are few fixed standards and, as a result, much behavior becomes subject to the authority of the group itself, thus discouraging extremes of behavior.

Internal Operations

RANKING

C1   In most groups, there is a rough ranking of members, implicit or explicit, depending on the extent to which the members represent or realize the norms and values of the group: the more they do, the higher they rank.

One leader in this field considers that such groups, as well as other aggregates within society, can be divided into three "levels of status"—upper, middle, and lower—and that conformity to and deviation from norms varies accordingly. In his view, the middle status persons are the ones most likely to conform to norms: compared to the lower stratum, they have more to lose by risky deviation; compared to the upper stratum, they have more to gain by conformity. Compared to the lower, they are more likely to have assimilated optimistic, striving norms and are more likely to have the opportunity to rise. Compared to the upper and lower strata, they are more likely to be criticized by other group members for deviation from norms. Compared to the lower, they are more likely to be ostracized and therefore are under more continuous and stricter social controls; they are more likely to put a high premium on group membership and, as we have seen, such a premium correlates with conformity in empirical studies. Nonconformist behavior is likely to be more innovative among upper status persons than among lower status persons; it is the recognized responsibility of upper status persons to be innovative (since this is a recognized function of leadership); and upper status persons stand to gain further esteem and authority through successful innovations; lower status persons' nonconformity is more likely to be apathetic or deviant than innovative behavior. Upper status persons have more freedom from group control than the others (Homans, 1961, pp. 338 ff.).

He goes on to elaborate the basic finding, as follows:

> It is not just conformity that gets a man high esteem (rank) in a group, so long as many members conform to more or less the same degree. He must also provide services for the others that are in short supply, services that they cannot easily get elsewhere, including not just conformity but a high degree of conformity [Homans, 1961, p. 163].

C1.1   The closer an individual conforms to the accepted norms of the group, the better liked he will be; the better liked he is, the closer he conforms; the less he conforms, the more disliked he will be.

"Deviates are rejected while conformers become popular" (Argyle, 1957, p. 155). People like to be liked, so they tend to engage in actions that will maintain or increase the esteem they receive from those around them. This means, as we have said, that there is always a tendency to go along with the group—a tendency that is realized unless there are strong countervailing influences, such as science or faith or the norm of another group to which the individual belongs.

As an example, even the preference in popular music among teen-age girls varies, within neighborhoods, according to popularity among peers.

> Highly popular girls are shown to conform more closely than the less popular to the prevailing neighborhood norms in popular music. Musical tastes and preferences for particular songs and for particular disk jockeys are found to be anchored in relatively small groups of friends, suggesting that personal relations play an important role in musical fads and fashions [Johnstone and Katz, 1957, p. 563].

Sociometric status and conformity to neighborhood norm

Number of sociometric choices received	Hyde Park girls prefer "blues" songs		South Shore girls prefer "happy" songs	
	NUMBER	PER CENT	NUMBER	PER CENT
Three or more	16	88	15	87
Two	9	56	23	78
One or less	24	38	39	64

(*Ibid.*, p. 567)

There is, however, this qualification, as noted above:

> Very high ranking members, . . . who have a secure social position, do not conform as strictly to some group norms as do individuals of middle rank [and are not] subjected to serious pressure to conform. Rather, a certain tolerance of "eccentricity" among high-ranking members is the rule in many groups [Riecken and Homans, 1954, p. 793].

C1.2   To the extent that the group's objectives are vague, undirected toward any special interest, and purely "social," the ranking of the members will be based on such personal characteristics as amiability, good-naturedness, charm, and, in general, "personality."

For this reason, one's standing in an informal group need not parallel the more impersonally determined rank that one has in the society as a whole. Such rank can be "dropped," or there can be equality among the members that does not exist outside the group.

C1.3   As the group's norms are or become poorly defined, the ranking of the members will be less clear or definite.

C1.4   Conformity to the group's norms for behavior is related to prestige and security within the group in the following way: the highest ranked and most secure members feel most free to express their disagreement with the group, both privately and in public; the lowest ranked members are more likely to disagree privately but conform in public; and the average members are most likely to agree both privately and in public.

C1.5   The higher the rank of the member within the group, the more central he will be in the group's interaction and the more influential he will be.

> The corner boys as well as members of formal organizations observe channels; that is, the same suggestion that will be rejected or ignored if made by a low-status member may be acted upon if made by a high-status member. Many earlier experiments have been devoted to showing that subjects perceive and judge content differently according to their assumptions about the character of the source [Bales, 1959, p. 299, referring to Whyte, 1943].

LEADERSHIP

C2   The following personal characteristics are associated with the exercise of leadership in voluntary groups (as well as in some larger and more formal associations):

size (height and weight)
physical appearance and dress
self-confidence, self-assurance

sociability, friendliness
will and determination, energy
intelligence (where information and mental skill are required)

"But [leaders] must not exceed the followers by too large a margin, for great discrepancies between the intelligence of leaders and followers militates against the emergence of the leadership relation" (Gibb, 1954, p. 886). For example, a discrepancy of over thirty points in I.Q. score makes for difficult or even impossible relations (*ibid.,* citing Hollingworth, 1942, a study of children).

Here is a summary tabulation of the personal factors correlated with leadership (mainly, note, among students):

Author	*I.Q.*	*Grades*	*Age*	*Height*	*Weight*
Ackerson (boys)	.18		−.01		
(girls)	.32		−.11		
Bellengrath (boys)	−.139 *	.05 *	.27	.17	.25
(girls)			−.32	.44	.42
Drake	.47				
Eichler	.0614	.1155	.2067		
Flemming	.44				
Garrison (School 1)		.30	−.12	−.02	−.02
(School 2)		.36	−.25	−.13	−.04
Goodenough	.10		.71	.71	.52
Howell	.08	.39			
Levi (Elem.)	.259	−.274			
(Jr. H.S.)	.255	−.0005			
Newstetter	.17		.45		
Nutting	.90	.11	.20		
Parten	.34		.67	.67	
Partridge	.54		.55	.43	.46
Reynolds	.22	.27			
Sheldon	.060	.190		.049	.024
Zeleny	.44		.487	.346	.204

* Total scores of boys and girls combined.

(Stogdill, 1948, p. 40)

As a general cautionary comment, the following appraisal must be added:

Much effort, both scientific and otherwise, has been invested in the attempt to select young men who will turn out to be good military leaders. It is fair to say that, in contrast to the obvious success scored in recent years in the selection of people for various kinds of specific jobs, no one has yet devised a method of proven validity for selecting either military or non-military leaders [Sanford, 1952, pp. 20–21].

However:

C3   In general, the "style" of the leader is determined more by the expectations of the membership and the requirements of the situation than by the personal traits of the leader himself.

C3.1   The leadership of the group tends to be vested in the member who most closely conforms to the standards of the group on the matter in question, or who has the most information and skill related to the activities of the group.

C3.2   Normally, the leader is better able to affect the group's means than its goals.

In one well-known experiment, for example, leaders were introduced into groups of children who had previously met sufficiently to "institutionalize group traditions." The leaders were slightly older than the other children and were judged to show initiative and directing ability whereas the ordinary members were not. Nevertheless,

> the leader takes over the habits and traditions of children who are younger than himself and who in the day nursery had been his underlings following his guidance. Now he engages in those activities which the group had developed before he entered it. His own undertakings remain unsuccessful or gain acceptance only in a modified form suiting the traditions of the group. . . . In the overwhelming majority of our cases the leader was forced to accept the group's traditions—that is, he proved weaker than the group but still managed to play the role of the leader [Merei, 1958, pp. 524, 526].

C3.3   When groups have established norms, it is extremely difficult for a new leader, however capable, to shift the group's activities.

If he tries very hard, he won't be a leader very long.

C3.4   Leaders of small groups tend to direct the group's activities along lines at which they themselves are proficient and away from those areas where they are less competent.

C3.5   The longer the life of the leadership, the less open and free the communication within the group and probably the less efficient the group in the solution of new problems.

C3.6   The leader will be followed the more faithfully the more he makes it possible for the members to achieve their private goals, along with the group's goals.

C4   Active leadership is characteristic of groups that determine their own activities, passive leadership of groups whose activities are externally imposed.

Active leaders guide, persuade, direct, coerce. Passive leaders mediate or serve as models. If the group's activities are determined within the group, the leader is likely to act as guide and director. If the activities are determined externally, the leader is likely to act as agent or coordinator. But once selected, the same leader deals with both the "domestic" and the "foreign" relations of the group.

C5   In a small group, authoritarian leadership is less effective than democratic leadership in holding the group together and getting its work done. Democratic leadership is more effective with respect to the durability of the group, the members' satisfaction with it, their independence vis-à-vis the leader, and their productivity on the task.

This finding is based on a famous series of experiments, but it must quickly be added that they had as subjects young American boys in contrived situations—and students from an experimental university-connected school at that—so it is not clear just how generalizable this important result might be. The boys were organized into groups with three kinds of leaders —autocratic, democratic, and laissez-faire. A typical result is shown on page 345.

> The chief differences to be noted . . . are: (1) the large number of leader-dependent actions in both reactions to autocracy; (2) the large extent of critical discontent and of aggressive behavior in the aggressive reaction to autocracy; (3) the frequency of "friendly, confiding" conversation and of group-minded suggestions in democracy; and (4) the contrast between democracy and laissez-faire in work-minded conversation [White and Lippitt, 1960, p. 84].

The matter is further complicated by personality differences:

> Authoritarian personalities prefer status-laden leadership, accept strongly directive leadership, and regard the authoritarian leader as "better" than his more democratic counterpart. In fact, they tend to express open hostility towards a leader as soon as he reveals any signs of "weakness." Equalitarian personalities, on the other hand, accept authoritarian leadership only as the circumstances demand it [Gibb, 1954, p. 910].

C6   The leadership of small groups must simultaneously satisfy two necessary but often conflicting needs of the group: the need for initiative, guidance, contribution of ideas, etc. (the intellectual leader) and the need for harmony, liking, mutual acceptance, etc. (the social leader). These two demands on leadership are rarely combined in the same person.

An individual may begin by fulfilling both requirements, but before long they are differentiated. In one experimental series, for example, the top position on both "Liking" and "Ideas" was held by the same person in

Boys' behavior toward their leaders

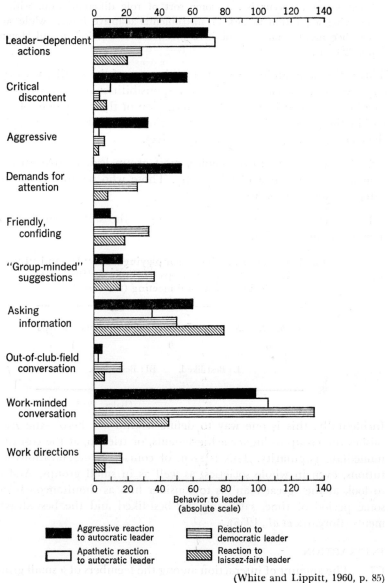

(White and Lippitt, 1960, p. 85)

56 per cent of the cases at the first session but that fell to 12 per cent at the second and was down to 8 per cent by the fourth (Slater, 1955, p. 504).

> What seems to occur is . . . some sort of role differentiation, with one man achieving a position as task or instrumental-adaptive leader, while some other man becomes the target of positive affective choice [Riecken and Homans, 1954, pp. 823–24].

This is the same finding we noted in the case of the family, with the father and the mother dividing these two responsibilities. It is also closely related to a finding noted below on the alternation of the two modes of expression within the group—advancing the task (instrumental-adaptive) and keeping the members happy (integrative-expressive).

C6.1   When put to the choice, most group leaders give up the instrumental role in favor of popularity. Those who try to control the group tend to lose popularity.

In one experimental series, for example, the shift from first to second meeting went like this:

Number of cases in which man playing both "BI" and "L" roles in first meeting drops "L" role or "BI" role or both in second meeting (ten cases)

Drops "L" role	Drops "BI" role	Drops both roles
0	9	1

L: Best liked.   BI: Best ideas.

(Bales, 1953, p. 160)

Incidentally, this is one way to define a kind of "hero"—the leader who pushes the group to higher achievements, or tries to, at the cost of his own immediate popularity. This is seen, of course, in organizations and institutions, even in whole societies, as well as in small groups. And one way to look at the "great man" is to consider him as simultaneously, and over some period of time, satisfying the best-liked and the best-ideas requirements (Borgatta *et al.,* 1955).

INTERACTION

C7   The amount of interaction among the members of a small group varies with the following conditions:

.1   Interaction increases as the cohesiveness of the group grows (and, as we have seen, the increase of interaction itself tends to lead to still further cohesiveness).

.2   Interaction decreases as internal dissension rises in a small group of high emotional attachment, and particularly so on topics producing dissension; once the block is lifted, there is typically a quick increase in hostile communications.

It is easy to see, for example, how this operates within the family—even between husband and wife.

.3   Interaction increases in small groups of little emotional attachment as the members perceive that there is disagreement within the group on a particular subject.

.3a   The more relevant the subject is for the group or the sharper the disagreement, the more interaction there will be on the matter.

.3b   Communications will be addressed primarily to the members perceived as the minority (the deviants) within the group, so long as the members in the majority feel that there is a chance to change minority opinions into harmony with the rest. When the majority feels there is no longer any such chance, communications to the deviants fall off sharply and in effect they are expelled from the group. Both the rise and the fall of such communications to deviants are sharper in groups that are comparatively cohesive.

The farther the member deviates from the group norms, provided that he still remains within the group, the more communications are directed to him. But the less the deviant is wanted in the group, the fewer the communications directed to hold him within the fold.

In one experiment, for example, here was the distribution of communications to people holding different positions on the issues:

Patterns of communication (first ten minutes)

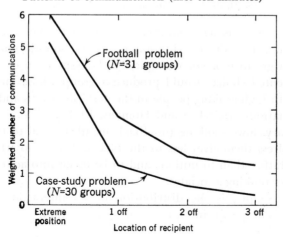

(Festinger and Thibaut, 1951, p. 96)

A word of caution: Such findings, and those that immediately follow, have emerged mainly from studies of small groups brought together under experimental conditions. Although there is some real-life validation, it is well to keep that limitation in mind.

C8   The distribution of interaction within a group is not random but is governed by the following considerations:

.1   Given enough time and freedom of communication (e.g., a testing or feeling-out period), a small group will typically establish working lines of communication, which can then be more or less formalized within the group.

.2   Communication within a task-oriented small group is most nearly equal among the members when no one of them possesses special competence and when there is no clear answer to the question at hand.

.3   Any person within a small group receives roughly the same proportion of the communications made by each of the other members.

This does not mean that communications are distributed equally around the group, either on the giving or receiving end, but rather that if, say, 25 per cent of the remarks made by B are directed to A, about 25 per cent of those made by C, D, E . . . are also made to A. In other words, the "pull" of a particular member in a small group, whether that pull is strong or weak, is roughly the same throughout the membership.

.4   Communications within a small group are more likely to be directed from equal to equal and from the higher-ranking members to the lower-ranking members than from the lower-ranking to the higher-ranking.

In total, the high-ranking members interact more than do the low-ranking within a group. But the distribution of interaction depends upon the character of a group too. For example, "a differentiation of task-oriented and social-oriented choices would produce a group whose members interacted most with high-ranking people in the 'task' situations and with equals in 'social' situations" (Riecken and Homans, 1954, p. 798).

As a corollary, lower-ranking (less-liked) members tend to talk less altogether, to address themselves less to the task and more to irrelevant matters, to react rather than to initiate, and to be taken into account less than are their higher-ranking associates.

Here, for example, is the distribution of all interaction in eighteen sessions of six-man groups in an experimental situation:

Person originating act	To individuals						Total to individuals	To group as a whole	Total initiated
	1	2	3	4	5	6			
1		1238	961	545	445	317	3506	5661	9167
2	1748		443	310	175	102	2278	1211	3989
3	1371	415		305	125	69	2285	742	3027
4	952	310	282		83	49	1676	676	2352
5	662	224	144	83		28	1141	443	1584
6	470	126	114	65	44		819	373	1192
Total received	5203	2313	1944	1308	872	565	12205	9106	21311

(Bales *et al.*, 1951, p. 463)

The findings indicate that if participants in a small group are ranked by the total number of acts they initiate, they will also tend to be ranked:

(1) by the number of acts they receive,
(2) by the number of acts they address to specific other individuals, and
(3) by the number of acts they address to the group as a whole

[Bales *et al.*, 1951, p. 468].

.5 Communications increase when members are in physical proximity to one another.

As a real-life example, in studies of interracial housing projects it was found that

of *all* the women, regardless of degree of physical proximity, those mostly likely to hold Negroes in high esteem were the ones who both engaged in extended street conversation or in neighborhood associations with Negroes *and* perceived the social climate as favorable to interracial association. The proportion of such women was twice as great among those living near Negroes as among those living farther away [Wilner *et al.*, 1952, pp. 68–69].

C9 In general, there is an alternation within groups, especially those having tasks to perform, between communications (interactions) dealing directly with the task and communications dealing with emotional or social relations among the members—the former tending to create tensions within the group and the latter tending to reduce them and achieve harmony.

This is related to the so-called instrumental-expressive dichotomy involved in the leadership of a small group. Both tendencies apparently need to be satisfied in all small groups engaged in some task—and in some larger aggregates as well. Here is one prominent set of categories used in the observation and analysis of the "interaction process" within a small group:

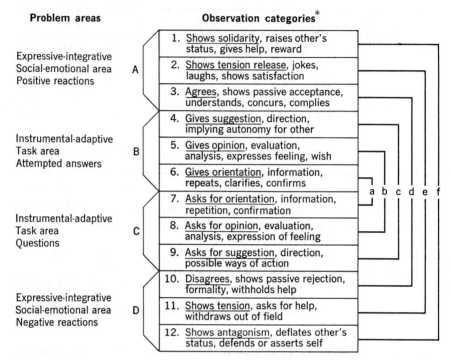

Problem areas   **Observation categories** [*]

Expressive-integrative
Social-emotional area   A
Positive reactions

1. Shows solidarity, raises other's status, gives help, reward
2. Shows tension release, jokes, laughs, shows satisfaction
3. Agrees, shows passive acceptance, understands, concurs, complies

Instrumental-adaptive
Task area   B
Attempted answers

4. Gives suggestion, direction, implying autonomy for other
5. Gives opinion, evaluation, analysis, expresses feeling, wish
6. Gives orientation, information, repeats, clarifies, confirms

Instrumental-adaptive
Task area   C
Questions

7. Asks for orientation, information, repetition, confirmation
8. Asks for opinion, evaluation, analysis, expression of feeling
9. Asks for suggestion, direction, possible ways of action

Expressive-integrative
Social-emotional area   D
Negative reactions

10. Disagrees, shows passive rejection, formality, withholds help
11. Shows tension, asks for help, withdraws out of field
12. Shows antagonism, deflates other's status, defends or asserts self

a b c d e f

[*] A subclassification of system problems to which each pair of categories is most relevant:

a. Problems of orientation.
b. Problems of evaluation.
c. Problems of control.

d. Problems of decision.
e. Problems of tension-management.
f. Problems of integration.

(Bales, 1953, p. 112)

And on page 351 is an illustration of its application through the phases of a group discussion. According to the author,

> an increase of task-oriented activities in the early parts of a meeting, that is, Questions and Attempted Answers, seems to constitute a disturbance of a system equilibrium which is later redressed by an increase in social-emotional activities, that is, both Positive and Negative Reactions. . . . Those groups dealing with full-fledged problems tended to show a typical phase movement through the meeting: the process tended to move qualitatively from *relative* emphasis on attempts to solve problems of *orientation* ("what is it") to attempts to solve problems of *evaluation* ("how do we feel about it") and subsequently to attempts to solve problems of *control* ("what shall we do about it") [*ibid.*, pp. 140–41].

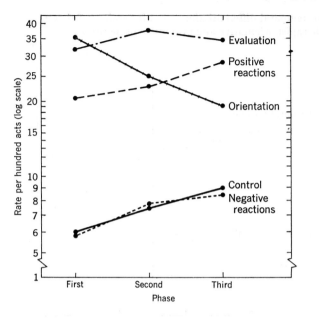

Another study, an intensive analysis of psychotherapy data (see page 352),

revealed that the patterning of therapist behavior over the life (or early life) of therapy was indeed similar to that of the participants in the problem-solving groups studied by Bales. . . . Therapist behavior characterized as orientation (asking for and giving repetitions, clarifications, and confirmations) decreases through the first fifty hours of therapy, while evaluative behavior (asking for and giving opinions, evaluations, analyses, and expression of feeling) increases and then appears to reach a plateau [Lennard and Bernstein, 1960, p. 65].

C9.1   In the course of time, as the group goes on with the task, somewhat less of the communication within the group is devoted to the task itself, and somewhat more to the personal relations of the members and to their control of one another.

Riecken and Homans (1954, p. 823) interpret this as indicating that a more permissive atmosphere develops in which explicit agreement is unnecessary. An alternative explanation might be that these laboratory groups got bored with the task in later meetings [Argyle, 1957, p. 159].

Over a longer period of time, as a group exhausts items for discussion, it still needs to maintain communication for its own stability and vitality—even if interaction becomes ritualistic, as in some forms of griping, complaining, or horseplay.

Patterns of temporal differentiation over fifty sessions of therapy: therapist orientative and evaluative propositions

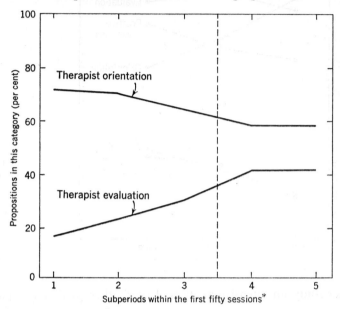

* $N = 101$ sessions, 9282 therapist propositions. The five subperiods are (1) sessions 1–3; (2) sessions 4–6; (3) sessions 7–8; (4) sessions from the third and fourth months of therapy; and (5) sessions from the fourth through the seventh months of therapy. The vertical broken line on the graph calls attention to the fact that the later two groups of sessions are not consecutive with the earlier sessions.

(Lennard and Bernstein, 1960, p. 65)

OUTCOMES

C10   Both the effectiveness of the group and the satisfaction of its members are increased when the members see their personal goals as being advanced by the group's goals, i.e., when the two are perceived as being in harmony. When members push their own needs, both satisfaction and effectiveness decline.

> If self-oriented needs are allowed full expression, neither productivity nor member satisfaction is achieved, because of the effects of task failure (and consequent dearth of external rewards) upon member satisfaction. Thus, it would seem that suppression of self-oriented need behavior is in some degree necessary in order for the group to achieve its external goals [Riecken and Homans, 1954, p. 810].

This kind of consideration gives rise to the notion of the "hidden agenda" in group meetings—what each, or at least many, of the members is *really* after. The open agenda is what the group is supposed to be doing—solving a problem, planning a campaign, organizing itself for action, etc. The hidden agenda consists of what is basically motivating its members—relative power, increase in prestige, desire for promotion or recognition, etc. Some scholars believe that every group meeting has its hidden agenda—and that a wise leader will guide himself by it as well as by the open agenda.

C11   The more threatened the individual members feel (i.e., the more they think they will personally lose something by the group's performance), the more concerned they become about being accepted in the group and the less effective the group as a whole becomes, with regard to both efficiency of performance and satisfaction of the members.

C12   The more compatible the members are, in norms, skills, personality, status, etc., and the more the procedures of the group are accepted and understood, the more effective and satisfying is the performance of the group in its tasks.

> A badly organized or unorganized group, or a group with status conflict, resembles a competitive group:
> the attainment of aims by one member hinders other members in the performance of their own work;
> members withhold information from one another;
> members communicate hostile feelings and criticisms;
> members communicate a great deal of material unrelated to the task [Klein, 1956, p. 39].

At least in American studies, and on tasks requiring collaborative activity, cooperative groups are more cohesive and more personally satisfying than internally competitive ones, and their performance is more homogeneous and usually more effective.

> In the cooperative group situation, where rewards were equal for all members in solving problems, there was evidence of more coordination of effort, attentiveness to fellow members, mutual understanding, willingness to accept and to agree, orientation to the goal and orderliness of procedure, productivity, better quality of product, quality and friendliness in discussion, favorable evaluation of the group products, and sense of obligation to others to win their respect [Chapin, 1957, p. 273].

C13   Active discussion by a small group to determine goals, to choose methods of work, to reshape operations, or to solve other problems is more effective in changing group practice than is separate instruction of the individual members, external requests, or the imposition of new practices by superior authority—more effective, that is, in bringing about better motivation and support for the change and better implementation and productivity of the new practice.

Here are the results of a well-known experimental study within a factory, with a group participating in discussion about a change in work practices after it previously had not done so. (Note, however, that small numbers were involved and that the subjects were young, inexperienced girls and not hard-bitten "veterans of the line").

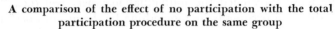

A comparison of the effect of no participation with the total participation procedure on the same group

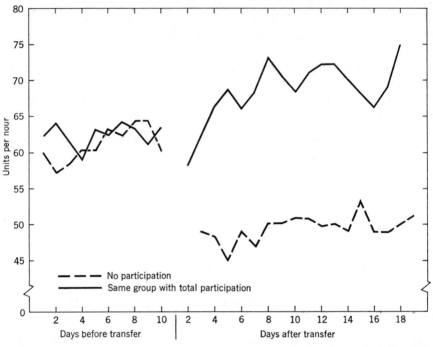

(Coch and French, 1948, p. 523)

C13.1   When change is desired, it is typically more effective to influence people as group members than to do so in an isolated, individual-by-individual manner.

Sometimes, as we have suggested, this involves breaking up the parent group into a number of supporting subgroups. For example:

When an individual or small group was to be changed away from a standard of a larger group (e.g., when delinquent adolescents or chronic alcoholics are to be "reformed" or "cured") it was necessary to insulate the individual from the larger group (the delinquent neighborhood or the social circles the alcoholic frequents) in order to reduce the efficacy of the forces that maintain the individual's level of behavior at the "old level" and to maximize the possibility of "unfreezing" and "moving the level" in the retraining or therapeutic sub-group [Riecken and Homans, 1954, p. 827].

The paradox is that it is easier to change people as group members than as isolated individuals, but hard to change the group itself because of the very support members receive from one another.

C14   Under the following conditions the solution given to a problem by a small group, after discussion, is more satisfactory than the average or composite solution of the individuals making up the group:

.1   When the problem has a definite and identifiable solution, i.e., when it is technical rather than attitudinal.

.2   when the initial judgments of the individuals in the group are not homogeneous, so that a range of possible solutions is initially available to the group for its consideration.

.3   when the task requires that each member make a judgment about the same matter.

.4   when rewards and punishments are given to the group as a whole rather than to individuals within the group.

.5   when the information or skills needed for the solution are additive.

.6   when the task can be subdivided.

.7   when the task includes "traps" that single individuals might miss.

The collective judgment of a group is superior to the judgment of most of the individuals. Two distinct processes are involved—firstly, discussion leads to the improvement of individual judgments, and secondly, the combination of individual judgments is advantageous [Argyle, 1957, p. 119].

This is a highly complicated matter, and there are numerous qualifications involving, among other things, the kind of people concerned (most of the experimental subjects have been students), their motivation, the type of task, the criteria for performance, and the artificiality of some experiments. A thorough review of the literature, nevertheless, recently concluded that

in general, in the evaluation of the relative quality of the products produced by groups in contrast to those produced by individuals, the group is superior. The superiority of the group, however, all too frequently, is not as great as would be expected from an interactional theory. In many studies, the product of the "best" individual is superior to that of the "best" group [Lorge et al., 1958, p. 369].

However, some experts believe that the alleged gain by the group over the individual is only that of an averaging effect.

Four judgments are better than one for the same nonsocial reason that four thermometers are better than one. The only consistent finding . . . is the trend toward homogeneity or reduction of variance [Johnson, 1955, p. 471, cited in Bales *et al.*, 1957, p. 398].

C15   The communication network within a task-oriented group affects the group's performance and the members' satisfaction in the following ways:

One-way communication (as against mutual communication) makes for less accuracy in performance and less confidence on the part of the members.

Centralized communication (through a single point) makes for satisfaction at the center of the group but not at the periphery; for efficiency on the task when that requires coordination of the members' contributions as against simply their addition; for clear identification of the leader; for less adaptability; for greater chance of falling into errors and less chance of correcting them; and for more restraint in members' criticisms of group procedures or outcomes.

A number of small-group experiments have been carried out in order to test the qualities of different ways of organizing internal communications. Here, for example, are data showing that the leader emerges at the position of highest centrality:

Frequency of occurrence of recognized leaders at the different positions in patterns *A*, *B*, *C*, and *D*

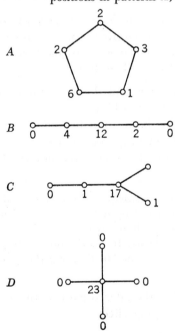

(Bavelas, 1950, p. 728, quoting Leavitt, 1949)

And here is the effect of different communication networks, as they are called, on the efficiency of three-man groups set experimentally to complete a set of words when each of the three was working from a partial list:

The five nets *

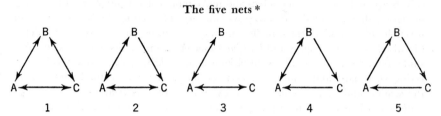

1   2   3   4   5

* The arrows indicate the direction of communication from talker to listener.

(Heise and Miller, 1951, p. 328)

Performance of the group on the word problems as a function of the communication net

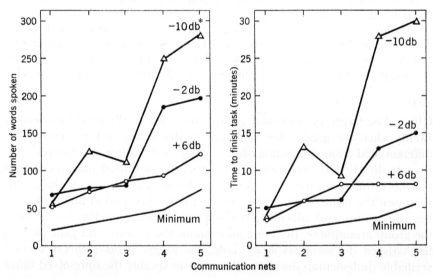

* The *db* refers to the amount of "white noise" introduced by the experimenter as a masking device; −10db is the largest amount.

(*Ibid.*, p. 330)

A closed chain in which only one-way communication was possible between any two persons was by far the least efficient; an open chain, which allowed two-way communication between any two adjacent individuals, was intermediate; a closed chain where all members talked and listened to all other members was most efficient [*ibid.*, p. 366].

With other tasks, however, the results changed.

An expert in this field summarizes the matter this way:

(1) One-way communication is considerably *faster* than two-way communication. (2) Two-way communication is *more accurate* than one-way. . . . (3) The receivers are more sure of themselves and make more correct judgments of how right or wrong they are in the two-way system. (4) The sender finds himself feeling psychologically under attack in the two-way system, because his receivers pick up his mistakes and oversights and *let him know about them.* The receivers may make snide remarks about sender's intelligence and skill, and, if the receivers are trying very hard and taking the task seriously, they may actually get angry at the sender, and he at them. (5) The two-way method is relatively noisy and disorderly—with people interrupting the sender and one another, with the slowest man holding up the rest, and so on. The one-way method, on the other hand, appears neat and efficient to an outside observer, but the communication is less accurate. . . .

Groups whose problems require the collation of information from all members work faster when one position is highly centralized and the others relatively peripheral. But the morale, the self-correctiveness, and perhaps the creativity of such groups may be better when the communication network is more equalitarian and when each member has more than one source of information.

Highly centralized groups may often be used for their consistency with general organizational designs, their speed, and their controllability; but they are also used as psychological defense devices to protect superiors' "weaknesses" from being exposed to subordinates, and vice versa [Leavitt, 1958, pp. 123, 205].

SIZE

C16   The larger the informal group, from two or three up to fifteen or twenty, then the greater the demands on the leader and the more he is differentiated from the membership at large; the greater the group's tolerance of direction by the leader and the more centralized the proceedings; the more the active members dominate the interaction within the group; the more the ordinary members inhibit their participation and hence the less exploratory and adventurous the group's discussion; the less intimate the group atmosphere, the more anonymous the actions, and generally the less satisfied the members as a whole; the longer it takes to get to nonverifiable (judgmental) decisions; the more acceptable the unresolved differences; the more the subgroups formed within the membership; and the more formalized the rules and procedures of the group.

For most of these tendencies, the watershed seems to be around size 5–7. That is about the number of people, apparently, that can be taken into account at one time, as individuals: the council of the Indian village is called the *panchayat*—group of five, and the correct number for a dinner party, according to an English adage (from Disraeli?), is "more than the graces and fewer than the muses."

Formality in leadership emerges rapidly beyond that number and so do subgroups (which can in turn be taken into account as units, thus increasing the number of persons who can be taken account of personally). The picture changes somewhat with age:

> Increasing maturity of the personality associated with age permits effective participation in larger groups. In the early stages of growth the number of children observed in play groups varies with the age of the child. Preschool children tend to play first individually, although in parallel, then in pairs, then in larger groups [Bales *et al.*, 1957, p. 394].

Here is a representative analysis of interaction within the (experimental) small group of different sizes, according to the categories of analysis presented on page 350:

Mean profile of *N* individuals, by group size *

Category	Group size 2 *N* 8	3 12	4 16	5 20	6 18	7 28
1. Shows solidarity	9.2	9.1	10.3	9.7	11.2	10.5
2. Shows tension release	11.2	11.4	12.8	14.2	18.4	16.6
3. Agrees	27.2	27.0	22.3	23.1	21.6	21.3
4. Gives suggestion	14.3	13.5	13.7	15.9	18.4	19.2
5. Gives opinion	31.7	34.0	35.0	32.0	32.1	31.2
6. Gives orientation	25.3	23.3	23.7	26.6	24.1	25.7
7. Asks for orientation	12.0	10.2	10.5	10.2	10.2	10.1
8. Asks for opinion	9.8	8.5	8.2	8.5	7.4	7.1
9. Asks for suggestion	5.2	5.9	5.0	6.4	4.6	5.9
10. Disagrees	10.2	15.6	19.9	14.5	17.7	16.4
11. Shows tension	12.4	8.6	10.0	9.1	6.3	6.6
12. Shows antagonism	1.0	3.5	5.2	3.3	3.9	3.8

* The profile of each individual is the sum over four sessions of his raw profile in each session, converted to a percentage profile and transformed to arcsine equivalents.

(Bales and Borgatta, 1955, p. 400

The mean profile of initiated behavior for individuals by group size is indicated. . . . When the size of the group increases, showing tension release (category 2) and giving suggestion (category 4) show emphatic increases. Showing solidarity (category 1) appears to increase somewhat with group size, and if groups of size two are excluded from consideration, giving information (category 6) also appears to increase. Showing tension (category 11) shows an emphatic decrease with increase in group size, and decreases are also visible in showing agreement (category 3) and asking for opinion (category 8). Again, if groups of size two are disregarded, giving opinion (category 5) shows a decrease when the group size increases.

Most of the trends observed appear to be results of two gross factors. The first is that the relative talking time available per member decreases as size increases. The second is that each person is confronted with an absolutely larger number of persons as size increases. Each is under pressure to maintain a more or less adequate relationship with each other. Thus as size increases, each member has more relationships to maintain, and less time to do so [*ibid*, pp. 400–01].

C17   Some sizes of small groups appear to have particular properties, as follows:

Groups of two: High tension and emotion, tendency to avoid disagreement, high exchange of information, high potential of deadlock and instability, high differentiation of role with one person the active initiator, the other the passive controller (with veto). These properties characterize the delicate balance involved in a situation where there is no other support within the group for either participant in case of disagreement, and where mutual tolerance is necessary for survival of the group (e.g., husband-wife).

Groups of three: Power of the majority over the minority of one, usually the two stronger over the weakest member; most stable, with shifting coalitions.

Here, for example, are the results of an experimental series of forty-eight problem-solving sessions of three-man groups that confirm Simmel's proposition that the primary tendency in the threesome is segregation into a pair and another: "The two more active members form the pair and the least active member is the relatively isolated third party" (Mills, 1953, p. 353).

Median rates of support according to rank order of contributions of members ($N = 48$)

As initiator	As recipient			Rate of total support output
	Most active	Medium active	Least active	
Most active	—	12.0	7.0	9.7
Medium active	11.1	—	3.8	8.9
Least active	4.0	2.5	—	3.5
Rate of total support intake	15.2	15.0	12.4	—

(*Ibid.*, p. 353)

Odd versus even groups: More disagreement in even groups (4, 6, 8) than in odd (3, 5, 7), due to the formation of subgroups of equal size. The personally most satisfying size seems to be five—ease of movement within; 2:3 division provides support for the minority members; large enough for stimulation, small enough for participation and personal recognition.

SELECTED READINGS

The literature on small groups is particularly large, as this field has been among the most active in sociology and social psychology since the war. For orientation, see:

Robert F. Bales. "Small Group Theory and Research," in Robert K. Merton *et al.*, eds., *Sociology Today: Problems and Prospects*. Basic Books, 1959, pp. 293–305.

Robert F. Bales *et al.* "Structure and Dynamics of Small Groups: A Review of Four Variables," in Joseph B. Gittler, ed., *Review of Sociology: Analysis of a Decade*. Wiley, 1957, pp. 391–422.

Leon Festinger. "Informal Social Communication," *Psychological Review*, 57, 1950, pp. 271–92.

George C. Homans. *The Human Group*. Harcourt, Brace & World, 1950.

George C. Homans. *Social Behavior: Its Elementary Forms*. Harcourt, Brace & World, 1961.

Harold H. Kelley and John W. Thibaut. "Experimental Studies of Group Problem-Solving and Process," in Gardner Lindzey, ed., *Handbook of Social Psychology*, Vol. II. Addison-Wesley, 1954, pp. 735–85.

Henry W. Riecken and George C. Homans. "Psychological Aspects of Social Structure," in Gardner Lindzey, ed., *Handbook of Social Psychology*, Vol II. Addison-Wesley, 1954, pp. 786–832.

Edward Shils. "The Study of the Primary Group," in Daniel Lerner and Harold D. Lasswell, eds., *The Policy Sciences: Recent Developments in Scope and Method*. Stanford U. Press, 1951, pp. 44–69.

Two major collections of readings in this field are:

Dorwin Cartwright and Alvin Zander, eds. *Group Dynamics: Research and Theory*. 2nd ed. Row, Peterson, 1960.

A. Paul Hare *et al. Small Groups: Studies in Social Interaction*. Knopf, 1955. (This contains a full, annotated bibliography of studies.)

Summarizing a variety of literature on leadership is:

Bernard M. Bass. *Leadership, Psychology, and Organizational Behavior*. Harper, 1959.

Many of the important empirical inquiries are cited in the chapter itself. Those by Asch, Bales, Bavelas, Festinger, Lippitt and White, and Sherif might be cited as among the better known or most representative.

On the methodological side, the following authors and titles have been influential:

Robert F. Bales. *Interaction Process Analysis: A Method for the Study of Small Groups*. Addison-Wesley, 1950.

Kurt Lewin. *Resolving Social Conflicts: Selected Papers on Group Dynamics,* ed. by Gertrude Weiss Lewin. Harper, 1948.

J. L. Moreno. *Sociometry, Experimental Method and the Science of Society*. Beacon House, 1951.

The first impression that one gets of a ruler and of his brains is from seeing the men that he has about him. When they are competent and faithful one can always consider him wise, as he has been able to recognize their ability and keep them faithful. But when they are the reverse, one can always form an unfavorable opinion of him, because the first mistake that he makes is in making this choice. . . . When you see the minister think more of himself than of you, and in all his actions seek his own profit, such a man will never be a good minister, and you can never rely on him.

NICCOLÒ MACHIAVELLI
The Prince

One must lie low, no matter how much it went against the grain, and try to understand that this great organization remained, so to speak, in a state of delicate balance, and that if someone took it upon himself to alter the disposition of things around him, he ran the risk of losing his footing and falling to destruction, while the organization would simply right itself by some compensating reaction in another part of its machinery—since everything interlocked—and remain unchanged, unless, indeed, which was very probable, it became still more rigid, more vigilant, severer, and more ruthless.

FRANZ KAFKA
The Trial

Somehow, somewhere among his seniors, a decision had been come to that he was not going to be one of the successes. . . . The word must have gone round the reaches above him: "He'll go a lot further," or "He won't." In a way it was not difficult to explain. . . . The number of bosses was small enough for them all to know each other well, and so for the judgment to get around easily. Secondly, the bosses (a) were clever men, and (b) took to this kind of assessing and judging with enthusiasm. There was nothing to show that they made many mistakes either. Mind you, they were not without the power to help their own prophecies along: the man who was tipped for success got the more exciting jobs, while the man who was tipped for failure was headed towards some backwater. . . . Remember that in this particular sphere, men's perceptions have a notable record of letting them down: it is very hard indeed to perceive that you are tipped for un-success.

WILLIAM COOPER
Scenes from Married Life

Chapter Nine

ORGANIZATIONS

In recent years sociologists have become more and more interested in the study of organizations. But however active the work, it is perhaps fair to say that the concern has been expressed primarily in conceptualizations, theoretical formulations, and a few case studies; it has not yet eventuated in a major body of findings established by hard scientific evidence. This explains, in part, why such a burgeoning field is represented here by a relatively small set of findings. Another reason is that material dealing with behavior in certain types of organizations, notably economic and industrial, will be found in the following chapter.

As for the importance of the topic itself, it is perhaps necessary only to quote the introductory words of a recent book by two authorities in the field:

> Organizations are important because people spend so much of their time in them. . . . In our society, preschool children and nonworking housewives are the only large groups of persons whose behavior is not substantially "organizational" [March and Simon, 1958, p. 2].

In daily life, of course, organizational behavior is interwoven with face-to-face and institutional relations; for our purposes, however, it can be treated separately in this way.

DEFINITIONS

Organizations: A standard book in this field begins by saying that "it is easier, and probably more useful, to give examples of formal organizations than to define the term. The United States Steel Corporation is a formal organization; so is the Red Cross, the corner grocery store, the New York

State Highway Department" (March and Simon, 1958, p. 1). According to another specialist, "an organization consists of a number of people, formally joined together and usually assigned specific functions, for the purpose of achieving a stated goal" (Sills, 1962).

Among the types of (formal or complex) organizations that might be cited by way of exemplification are business firms, military units, churches, hospitals, clubs and lodges, colleges and universities, political parties, prisons, and labor unions. Besides their specialization by field of activity, what do such organizations have in common? The major characteristics are these:

Formality: An organization typically has an explicitly formulated set of goals, policies, procedures, rules, and regulations that define appropriate behaviors for its members.

Hierarchy: An organization typically has a pyramidal arrangement of power and authority with more or less clearly demarcated levels. Some people are higher in the organization than others and hence have some authority over what the others do as members of the organization. As a rough rule of thumb, an organization has at least three levels of authority.

Size and/or complexity: An organization usually contains more than just a few people; usually the membership is large enough so that close personal relations among all are impossible. (Strictly speaking, some small and simple groups can be called organizations—the corner grocery store cited above or the doctor's office with a medical technician, nurse, and stenographer—but usually something more substantial than that is meant.) Hence, there is a certain impersonality about the organization's actions or dealings with its public, and this is where the normal connotation of bureaucracy comes in. As a matter of fact, in much of the sociological literature the terms "bureaucracy" and "organization" are synonymous, or virtually so (and "bureaucracy" is by no means limited to governmental organizations).

Duration: An organization typically exists longer than the lifetime or the affiliation of any particular member or leader. Thus a business firm, a university, a political party, a particular church will still be there fifty or a hundred years from now—with, of course, a completely new set of members. In most cases, organizations have some physical property to mark them off—a plant, an office, a campus, an army base, a hospital, and so on.

Voluntary associations: This term usually refers to those organizations that people belong to part time and without pay, such as clubs, lodges, good-works agencies, and the like: the Rotary, the volunteer unit of the March of Dimes, the local PTA, the Boy Scouts, the auxiliary of the local church, the American Legion chapter, the university alumni association, the neighborhood unit of the Republican party, and so on. Typically such associations have a different legal status from other organizations. Voluntary associations often have small, full-time professional staffs to serve the membership and to guide and coordinate their activities.

FINDINGS

The findings are presented in two sections: (1) the organization itself (its place in society, over-all operation, internal arrangements); and (2) leaders and members. Note that many of the findings deal with the two broad purposes or consequences of organizational activity: (1) productivity (i.e., output, efficiency, "getting things done") and (2) satisfaction of the members (i.e., morale, participation, identification with the organization, etc.). Roughly speaking, the first is material and tangible (work), the second is attitudinal (feelings).

The Organization

A1   The larger, the more complex, and the more heterogeneous the society, the greater the number of organizations and associations that exist in it.

The more differentiated the members of a community are, the more associations they tend to have—differentiated by occupation, place of residence, race, religion, class, interest, way of life. Modern industrialized society, with its variety of social groupings, is more highly organized in this sense than a peasant society or a primitive society or simply a small society, where kinship or occupational or other traditional ties are sufficient.

> Since American society is differentiated, people seek associations with others like themselves; since differentiation is so extensive, and organizations tend to attract people of similar backgrounds, large numbers of associations exist [Sills, 1960, p. 75].

In addition, as has often been observed, there are historical conditions beyond size or complexity that call forth the development of organizations: for example, the need to administer waterways in ancient Egypt or the need to run large standing armies in European countries with sizable land frontiers. Furthermore:

> One of the historical conditions that favors the development of bureaucracy is a money economy. . . . Generally, a money economy permits the payment of regular salaries, which, in turn, creates the combination of dependence and independence that is most conducive to the faithful performance of bureau-

cratic duties. Unpaid volunteers are too independent of the organization to submit unfailingly to its discipline. Slaves, on the other hand, are too dependent on their masters to have the incentive to assume responsibilities and carry them out on their own initiative. . . . Consequently, there were few bureaucracies prior to the development of a monetary system and the abolition of slavery [Blau, 1956, pp. 36–37].

A1.1   Organizations tend to call forth organizations: if people organize on one side of an issue, their opponents will organize on the other side.

This can be seen on the national level (Big Labor, Big Business, Big Agriculture, Big Education), on the local level (as in a school-board controversy), and within an industry (e.g., the industrial relations departments that are formed in response to unionization).

A1.2   There is a tendency for voluntary associations to become more formal.

Voluntary organizations having once started on their life career, grow and gain momentum toward formalization of structure. As growth in size of membership proceeds, structure subdivides into subgroups of smaller size and with different functions. . . . An increasing emphasis upon conformity and status develops, and the voluntary organization begins to have traditions. In short, the process of growth and formalization has run its course and the original "voluntary" organization has become a full-fledged institution [Chapin, 1957, pp. 263–64].

A2   There is always a tendency for organizations (of a nonprofit character) to turn away, at least partially, from their original goals.

In the literature, this is usually called "goal-displacement," and it is at the core of Michels' famous "iron law of oligarchy."

This phenomenon of goal-displacement is perhaps the most frequently noted pathological aspect of large-scale organizations. . . . Practically every serious observer of large-scale organizations has noted instances of this tendency [Sills, 1957, p. 62].

Typically it occurs through putting means in the place of ends, procedures in the place of goals. A study of the French civil service showed how goals were averted or changed through the routinization of procedures (Sharp, 1931), and a study of the American navy showed the same result from over-adherence to regulations (Davis, 1952).

But goal-displacement can also arise from getting a number of people involved who then want to follow their own ends, as in the case of the TVA (Selznick, 1953): this is sometimes viewed as the central dilemma of organizational life—in order to get some things done, you have to organize others to do them; as soon as you do, they want to get into the act of deciding what is to be done and how. Goal-displacement can arise from other roots as well: having to collaborate with people of different ideological persuasion, as in the case of the bureaucracy in Saskatchewan when the Canadian Commonwealth Federation came to power (Lipset, 1950); or from failing to respond to broad social changes, as in the case of the WCTU (Gusfield, 1955).

In some cases, of course, such adaptation of the original goals to the requirements of the new situation is necessary—or at least, seems to the participants to be necessary—for the strengthening or even the survival of the organization. An oversimplified way to put this is to say that most organizations will adjust rather than die: after all, they are made up of human beings most of whom will do the same.

But there is a related tendency for organizations to move from one goal to another in order both to survive and to realize general ends. According to one specialist, speaking of American labor unions:

> The main development was not the one stressed by Michels: unions did not relinquish their original objectives. Quite the contrary, they achieved them in large part and strove for new, further-reaching reforms. Thus, the right of collective bargaining supplied a basis for the fight for workers' pensions, a social innovation far surpassing the aspirations of union members a few decades ago. This process, the reverse of displacement of goals, can be called "succession of goals"; as earlier objectives are attained, they become stepping stones for new ones. . . . Once a union has achieved its major objectives, the enthusiasm of its members tends to wane. Many withdraw their support, financially and otherwise, and thereby threaten the persistence of the organization. The very fact that union officials are interested in maintaining their job and power constrains them to seek new ways of stimulating membership support. An effective method for recreating vigorous interest in union affairs is to establish new objectives for which workers are willing to fight. Hence, new goals often emerge in organizations as old ones have been reached. This is the case not only in unions but also in other organizations marked by bureaucracy's stamp [Blau, 1956, p. 95].

Although there is always some pressure for leaders to be responsive to the wishes and expectations of members, there are frequently occasions when leaders put other values well ahead of immediate representativeness (e.g., "progress," "long-run interests," or the organization's or their own survival). Accordingly, at any given time, there are numerous organizations in which the members do not approve the policies of the leaders but do little if anything to oppose them.

A2.1   The day-to-day decisions of an organization tend to be taken as commitments and precedents, often beyond the scope for which they were initially intended, and thus come to affect the character of the organization.

This development has been documented, for example, with reference to two such different organizations as the TVA and the National Foundation for Infantile Paralysis. Here are summary statements from each of them:

> Day-to-day decisions, relevant to the actual problems met in the translation of policy into action, create precedents, alliances, effective symbols, and personal loyalties which transform the organization from a profane, manipulable instrument into something having a sacred status and thus resistant to treatment simply as a means to some external goal [Selznick, 1953, pp. 258–59].

> Decisions made for the purpose of solving immediate problems often determine the ultimate character of an organization. . . . The Foundation's almost total dependence upon a fund-raising strategy based upon obtaining small gifts from large numbers of people emerged from two decisions made in the Depression year 1933: to solicit gifts from the people of Georgia in order to finance the construction of a new building at Georgia Warm Springs, and to raise funds nationally by sponsoring President's Birthday Balls; the characteristically middle-class composition of the Foundation's Volunteer membership may be traced in large part to the decision to ask postmasters, Democrats, and persons of civic prominence generally to organize these Birthday Balls; and the patient care program is a direct outgrowth of the decision to permit local Committees for the Celebration of the President's Birthday to retain for use in their own communities a portion of the funds raised in 1935. This brief listing of examples suggests the general applicability to the Foundation of this aspect of Selznick's thesis: the Foundation's "character" today is clearly in many respects the result of decisions made with other ends in view [Sills, 1957, pp. 255–56].

As a special case of note:

> **A2.1a**   The very effort to measure organizational efficiency, as well as the nature of the yardstick used, tends to determine organizational procedures.

For example, a study of a state employment agency showed how the "statistical records of performance" that were used not only "made major contributions to operations" but also had indirect consequences in channeling work among the agents, in favoring some types of clients over others, in stressing some types of tasks over others, and so on (Blau, 1955).

A3   The larger the organization becomes, the more ranks of personnel there will tend to be within it.

A modern university, for example, now has a variety of ranks—lecturers, fellows, research associates, tutors, etc.—besides the traditional professorial divisions. The United States Army has more kinds of sergeants than it used to have and even has a rank beyond general. The top man in a big business firm used to be the president, but he has now moved up to be chairman of the board in order to make more room below. This is especially the case in organizations in which skill and achievement are the key criteria for advancement.

A4   The more physically decentralized the organization, with administrative autonomy given to the units, the more different and often discordant understandings and points of view there will be within the organization, and the more they will be tolerated.

Similarly, the more channels of communication there are within an organization, the greater will be the discrepancy among the members' understandings and points of view. Actually, decentralization is one means of containing deviance within a single over-all organization, and this makes for the survival of the whole.

A4.1   The more decentralized the organization, with lower units autonomous yet visible to higher ones, the better the identification of the members with the organization is likely to be.

One reason for this is the individual's better chance to be taken into account in a decentralized situation: smaller pond, bigger frog.

In one well-known experiment in industry the degree of centralization was systematically varied. In two offices there was close supervision over subordinates, in two similar offices there was delegation of authority. After a year, the more centralized office had higher productivity, but the decentralized one had better morale. Here are some illustrative data and the conclusions:

	"Autonomous" program (decentralized)		*"Hierarchically-controlled" program (centralized)*	
	Average before	*Average after*	*Average before*	*Average after*
Index of satisfaction with company	4.01	4.18	4.15	3.88
Index of productivity (per cent)	48.6	58.6	48.5	62.6

(Morse and Reimer, 1956, pp. 126, 127)

The individual satisfactions of the members of the work groups increased significantly in the Autonomous program and decreased significantly in the Hierarchically-controlled program. Using one measure of productivity, both decision-making systems increased productivity, with the Hierarchically-controlled program resulting in a greater increase [*ibid.*, p. 129].

And in a study of a national health organization, decentralized control over the spending of funds helped to keep up the vitality of the local units (Sills, 1957).

A4.2 An organization is more likely to be strongly centralized during external crises than during normal periods.

Thus military organizations are more centralized than most other types, and they are closer to crisis conditions:

> The greater the imponderables and uncertainties that military command has to face, the more emphasis is placed on explicit orders, elaborate directives, and contingency plans [Janowitz, 1959, p. 83].

A5 A period of innovation and change affecting an organization is likely to produce a heightened amount of communication among the members, communication oriented both toward the task and toward mutual emotional support.

A6 The communications down the organizational hierarchy are likely to be critical, and the communications up the hierarchy are likely to be commendatory.

> Bad relations in the line of command will result in poor communication. Gardner (1944) has described the way in which members of social organizations are nervously looking upwards while their superiors assess them, and how bad news is held up or distorted in order to keep the good opinion of those higher up. . . . In a laboratory experiment on groups with status divisions, Kelley (1951) found low-status members more ready to communicate upwards about irrelevant matters, and unwilling to criticise high-status members [Argyle, 1957, pp. 190–91].

A6.1 The more rigidly or formally organized the hierarchy, the less the upward flow of informal communications.

For example, this is particularly evident in the military, because of its sharp distinctions by rank. In a governmental agency, one study showed, subordinates consulted with one another about difficult decisions rather than with their supervisor, lest he interpret such consultation as indecisiveness or weakness (Blau, 1955).

A7 The efficiency of a large formal organization is sizably enhanced when its own chain of command or decision or communication is tied into the informal network of groups within the organization, so that the network can be used to support the organization's goals.

Members are often tied to an organization by their membership in primary groups that mediate between the individual and the organization. As a sensitive observer of organizational functioning once put it: "Informal organizations are necessary to the operation of formal organizations as a means of communication, of cohesion, and of protecting the integrity of the individual" (Barnard, 1950, p. 123). The individual's feeling that he is a part of a respected group which is in effective contact with a symbol or agent of the organization and which has its views taken into account—that feeling is highly desirable, sometimes indispensable, from the standpoint of both the group and the organization, as well as the individual's own morale.

In short, the informal group is extremely effective in translating, interpreting, and supporting the organization's norms and practices. For example, absenteeism, turnover in personnel, and work productivity have been found to be directly based on the existence of close personal relations within the formally organized work group. "Primary-group identification within the working team and primary-group relations with representatives of the management are very important variables in the determination of the output rate in industrial work" (Shils, 1951, p. 48, on Mayo, 1933). In some experimental studies, the self-selection of job partners resulted in an increase of productivity and morale as well as in a lessening of turnover.

> Output control is a basic objective of group action as well as an essential element in maintaining group stability. . . . The durability of the worker's relation to his job depends on the efficiency of this process. Again we need to note that the resultant is not always unfavorable to management. We have many instances on record where the work group has sanctioned increasingly high productivity. . . . [And] there are many instances when the management seeks to *reduce* quality but the workmanship norm resists such changes [Sayles, 1958, pp. 152–53].

Communication from a central authority to a community works much better if conducted through the informally selected leaders of the "basic social units" set up by the residents (Leighton, 1945). The American soldier's efficiency in combat and his morale in general are traceable directly to his membership in primary groups within the army:

> Studies have shown the relative unimportance of direct identification with the total symbols of the military organization as a whole, of the state, or of the political cause in the name of which a war is fought, as contrasted with the feelings of strength and security in the military primary group and of loyalty to one's immediate comrades. . . . The effective transmission and execution of commands along the formal lines of authority can be successful only when it coincides with this system of informal groups [Shils, 1951, p. 64, on Stouffer *et al.*, 1949, I].

Toward the end of World War II, the motivation of German soldiers to continue in battle derived directly from their loyalty to a primary group, rather than to a higher authority or the "system." The more closely people were tied to a primary group, the greater their resistance to the enemy:

> For the ordinary German soldier the decisive fact was that he was a member of a . . . *social* unit which satisfied some of his major primary needs. He was likely to go on fighting, provided he had the necessary weapons, as long as the group possessed leadership with which he could identify himself, and as long as he gave affection to and received affection from the other members [Shils and Janowitz, 1948, p. 284].

At the same time, and for the same reasons:

A7a   Strong informal groups within an organization, when hostile to its goals or methods, can effectively oppose the organization.

A study of production workers in a large factory compared the average productivity of work groups which were highly cohesive with that of those which were not highly cohesive and found that work group cohesion could result in productivity which was either higher or lower than the plant norm [Seashore, 1957, p. 66, citing Seashore, 1954].

Where the formal controls . . . are not supported by the informal social pressures of one's fellows, not to mention internalization which operates even in the absence of one's fellows, there is almost certain to be widespread violation of the rules. One of the most celebrated examples in American history was the case of the prohibition of intoxicating liquor; an American Army example in World War II was the case of the prohibition of fraternization with German civilians in the early days of occupation of enemy territory [Stouffer *et al.,* 1949, I, 411].

A7.1   In consequence of this relationship between the organization and the informal groups within it, plus the presence of hierarchical levels within any organization, the intermediate leaders are subject to differing demands and expectations from above and below—typically, demands for productivity from above, demands for human consideration from below—and hence to actual or potential conflict in their behavior.

This is the classical cross-pressure situation for foremen, middle managers, chief nurses, committee chairmen, deans, school superintendents, noncommissioned officers, and people in similar positions. For example, an industrial study found that the ratings of foremen by superiors and subordinates were inversely correlated: there was a tendency for those well thought of by one group to be ill thought of by the other (Fleishman *et al.,* 1955). In the United States Army the noncommissioned officer is valued from below for "being a good fellow" and from above for "being a strong military leader":

If an intermediate-level officer is to be a real leader, he has a dual role to play. He must accept the norms and values of superior authority, thus serving as an agent of the impersonal and coercive organization of which he is a part. To the extent that he does this effectively his superiors regard him highly. At the same time, he must win the willing followership of the men under him, so that he wields over them authority which they have themselves given him [Gibb, 1954, p. 894].

Here are some data that show the noncom in the middle:

Comparison of privates, noncoms, and officers on attitudes toward noncom behavior

	Per cent who agree with each statement		
	Privates (384)	Noncoms (195)	Officers (31)
SOCIAL RELATIONS			
"A noncom will lose some of the respect of his men if he pals around with them off-duty."	13	16	39
"A noncom should not let the men in his squad forget that he is a noncom even when off-duty."	39	54	81
DISCIPLINARIAN			
"A noncom has to be very strict with his men or else they will take advantage of him."	45	52	68
"A noncom should teach his men to obey all rules and regulations without questioning them."	63	81	90
WORK SUPERVISOR			
"A noncom should always keep his men busy during duty hours even if he has to make them do unnecessary work."	16	22	39
"The harder a noncom works his men the more respect they will have for him."	10	18	42
"On a fatigue detail, a noncom should see that the men under him get the work done, but should not help them do it."	36	37	68

(Stouffer et al., 1949, I, 408)

[There is a] tendency for the officers to approve a more "official" point of view on the part of the noncom, and the opposite tendency for the enlisted man to approve informal cooperation from the noncom in escaping official regulations [ibid., I, 408].

Leaders and Members

The literature on organizational leadership is largely concerned with the effect of different styles of leadership. Various ways of characterizing such styles have been used, but essentially they seem to come down to a dichotomy represented by these distinctions taken from organizational studies:

Employee-oriented	*as against*	Production-oriented
Participatory		Autocratic (or ultrapermissive)
Considerate		Initiatory
Loose		Close
Integrative		Dominative
Persuasive		Arbitrary
Self-defined as group leader		Not so defined

The flavor comes through: call it the friendly, helpful boss as against the tough, impersonal one. (Actually, the characteristics above tend to correlate with one another; that is, the participatory leader is also likely to be employee-oriented, persuasive, integrative, etc.) On this basis, then:

B1   The more friendly-helpful the boss,

.1   the less the absenteeism.

.2   the more the productivity (if that is a goal of the organization and the unit).

.3   the more likely the subordinates are to feel that the organization's requirements are reasonable, and the more willingly they accept changes in organizational practices.

.4   the better liked the leader is.

.5   the more strongly the subordinates identify with the organization.

.6   the less tension there is within the organizational unit, and the more the internal cohesion.

.7   the higher the subordinates' morale (and this is especially so).

The general rationale goes something like this. Participatory leadership means that the leader is seen to some extent as another member of the group, not as an outsider with authority. Pressure for production means neglect of personal factors, thus more strain. Close supervision is likely to mean no real leadership at the top and no independence or responsibility below, plus little personal consideration; the harder the task, however, the more such supervision is likely to be welcomed. In short, it appears that the best organizational leader firmly keeps the goal before his subordinates and urges them to meet it; at the same time, he treats them like human beings. Here, for example, are some data on closeness of supervision from a study of different sections within an insurance company:

Relation of section productivity to closeness of supervision of employees *

	Close supervision	General supervision	Not ascertained
Heads of high-producing sections	6	5	1
Heads of low-producing sections	11	1	0

* The findings are based upon an over-all code that defines closeness of of supervision as the degree to which the supervisor checks up on his employees, gives them detailed and frequent instructions and, in general, limits the employees' freedom to do the work in their own way. This over-all code is derived from the supervisors' discussions of their jobs.

(Kahn and Katz, 1953, p. 617)

Relation of section productivity to closeness of supervision of section head by superior *

	Close or fairly close supervision	Fairly general or quite general supervision	Not ascertained
On high section heads	2	9	1
On low section heads	8	4	0

* Closeness of supervision is based on an over-all code, and was defined for coding purposes as the degree to which the section head was given freedom to handle his own problems by his superiors, as compared with the degree to which the superior was directly involved in running the section.

(*Ibid.*, p. 619)

B2   The leader's style of leadership tends to be influenced by the style in which he himself is led.

This finding is consistent with the one noted in the chapter on small groups, namely, that people take as their models those who have higher prestige and rank. As a related matter:

B3   The more closely the member holds to the organization's professed values, the more likely he is to be promoted within the organization.

For example, here are some data from the American army:

Promotion of recruits as related to previously expressed attitudes forming a scale of conformity to Army

Score on conformity scale	Percentage becoming NCO's by March, 1944, among PFC's making indicated score in November, 1943	Percentage becoming NCO's by March, 1944, among privates making indicated score in November, 1943	Percentage becoming PFC's by January, 1944, among privates making indicated score in September, 1943
Relatively high score (5–6)	27 (144)	31 (68)	87 (32)
Medium score (3–4)	22 (100)	28 (130)	82 (44)
Relatively low score (0–2)	13 (84)	17 (112)	62 (26)

(Stouffer *et al.*, 1949, I, 265)

Within the Army, as in perhaps any institution and especially any authoritarian institution, the price of advancement was at least a minimum conformity with the system, in mind as well as in action [*ibid.*, p. 264].

B4   The requirements for organizational leadership change with the life of the organization: at the start the leader is characterized more by doctrinal loyalty, aggressiveness, and personal quality ("the charismatic leader"); later, when the organization is well established, by administrative skills ("the bureaucratic leader").

Within sociology, this change is termed the "routinization of charisma." As stated by its formulator:

In its pure form charismatic authority may be said to exist only in the process of originating. It cannot remain stable, but becomes either traditionalized or rationalized, or a combination of both. . . . With the process of routinization the charismatic group tends to develop into one of the forms of everday authority, particularly the patrimonial form and its decentralized variant or the bureaucratic [Weber, 1947, pp. 364, 369].

Here is a description of this process in the United Automobile Workers, by an organizational sociologist:

> This union was founded in 1935, in a situation of severe economic distress. Militance was the keynote during its early years. The problem of leadership was largely one of conducting a struggle for power and recognition, in which techniques of mobilization necessarily played a large role. . . . After the union achieved its initial aims, the older methods of direct strike action, associated with a class-struggle out-look, became inappropriate and sometimes even harmful. . . . There began a movement away from militance, toward more astute negotiating techniques. To implement this change, a widespread turnover of personnel was required [Selznick, 1957, pp. 108–09].

B5   When authority and responsibility within an organization do not at least roughly correspond to the (perceived) contributions of the members, there is likely to be more than the normal amount of tension within the organization.

For example, if lower ranks unduly originate or suggest changes for their superiors, that makes for some strain. In a broad sense, this is the problem of keeping authority and ability (skills) in proper balance in the modern technological and complex organization. Furthermore:

B5.1   Within an organization, conflict between leaders and subordinates tends to increase the number and the concreteness of the organization's regulations, and vice versa—i.e., regulations go along with conflict.

Conflict can refer here not only to overt disagreements but even to differing perceptions of what various people are supposed to do (Gouldner, 1954).

B5.2   Correspondence in attitude toward the organization is closest between ranks in organizations with a strong ideological flavor (such as religious or political organizations), medium in occupational organizations, and least in coercive organizations (such as the army or custodial institutions).

This is partly due, of course, to the facts of recruitment: one chooses the first, must engage in the second, and is forced into the third. For an extended analysis of other characteristics of these types of organization—there called normative, utilitarian, and coercive—see Etzioni, 1961a.

With regard to coercive organizations, officers and enlisted men in the

American army agreed on certain general issues of World War II but disagreed increasingly on questions involving the status system or hierarchy within the army:

Social perspectivism according to rank order of subject matter

| | Average difference between officers and enlisted men | |
	Ratio	*Percentage points*
Opinions about reality not involving army as a whole, self, or relations between officers and enlisted men	1.2	8.2
Opinions about the individual self, not involving hierarchical relations: feelings of officers and enlisted men in combat	1.2	11.0
Opinions, not involving moral judgment, about the behavior of enlisted men	1.3	10.2
Opinions about the army as a whole	1.8	24.9
Opinions, involving moral judgments, about the behavior of enlisted men	2.9	20.6
Opinions about relations between enlisted men and officers	2.9	44.4

(Speier, 1950, pp. 125–27)

B6   The closer the requirements of organizational membership are to the member's interests, training, ambition, goals, or self-image generally, the better he likes the organization and the more likely he is to stay in it.

For example, disparity between the task and the member's education will lead to his dissatisfaction. So will disparity between the member's desire for innovation and the routine character of the task. So will an unfavorable disparity between the prestige of the member's organization and that of other organizations to which his family and friends belong.

B7   The higher the post, with regard to requirements of technical skill or responsibility, the stronger the member's identification with and devotion to the task, the greater his independent motivation for the task, and the less his concern for "human relations" as a need on the job.

For example, professionals like their jobs better than people in other occupations like theirs.

B8   Members closely identified with the organization are more likely to conform to its norms (after all, they largely set them). They are also more likely to be critical of the organization (they care enough to want it to be better), but the criticism is more likely to deal with means or arrangements than with ends or objectives.

B9   Members of organizations consistently tend to overestimate the prestige of their own organization relative to others of similar character.

This is perhaps a special case of selective perception, or of ethnocentrism. For example, members of academic departments tend to place their own department higher in the scale of prestige or quality than outsiders place it. But,

> the Aggrandizement Effect is by no means unique to academic departments. It appears to be a general characteristic of sets of intercommunicating similarly structured organizations. The senior author, in a study of fifty-five sets of six organizations of varied types, found that raters overestimated the prestige of their own organization eight times as frequently as they underestimated it, and that net overestimation of the prestige of the raters' own organizations could be discerned in every one of the sets. [The organizations included] fraternities, sororities, teen-age clubs, Protestant churches, Catholic parishes, public high schools, private colleges, dance studios, nursing schools, hospital services, chain hamburger stands, savings and loan associations, pest-control firms, community centers, country clubs, dress shops, advertising agencies, Campfire Girl groups, branch Y.M.C.A.'s, photographic studios, Young Judea clubs, banks, chain supermarkets, printing firms, employment agencies, architectural firms, insurance agencies, foreign-student clubs, Skid Row missions, trucking firms, department stores, religious youth organizations, and social science departments [Caplow and McGee, 1958, p. 105].

B10   When physical withdrawal from membership is not permitted (as in the case of the army or other so-called total institutions), there is likely to be a high rate of private rejection of membership and a high rate of neurotic behavior.

With regard to voluntary associations:

B11   Participation in voluntary associations (in the United States) is greater among urban residents, among those in the prime of life, among the married-with-children, among those moving up in the class system, among those with residential stability, and especially among people of more education and high socioeconomic status.

In addition, there is a little evidence to the effect that men who were active in formal organizations [the term refers here to social and athletic clubs, veterans' and fraternal groups—what we call voluntary associations] . . . tended to have a relatively low marital integration. . . . High participation . . . probably resulted from a desire of the men to be away from home and, in turn, aggravated difficulties in their marriage [Farber, 1959, p. 80].

B11.1   Members tend to participate most when the association does not have a large salaried staff; when the members have considerable power relative to the officers; when the association is not large; when it is not highly specialized internally; and when the membership is homogeneous in character or has few competing attractions.

The broad effects of voluntary associations within the society are usually considered to be these: (a) to promote participation in the social life, by providing frequent and attractive opportunities for personal contacts; (b) to increase personal freedom, by increasing the choice of appropriate modes of behavior; (c) to promote social change, by increasing pressures from particular organized segments of the society; (d) both to sharpen and to soften class distinctions, depending on the extent to which the associations are limited to "one's own kind" as against bringing diverse groups together in a common cause—i.e., the extent to which people's memberships are homogeneous or heterogeneous in character.

SELECTED READINGS

The literature of the field has recently been reviewed by:

Allen H. Barton. *Organizational Measurement and Its Bearing on the Study of College Environments*. College Entrance Examination Board, 1961.
Amitai Etzioni. *A Comparative Analysis of Complex Organizations: On Power, Involvement, and Their Correlates*. Free Press, 1961.
James G. March and Herbert Simon. *Organizations*. Wiley, 1958.

Two collections of articles dealing with organizations are:

Amitai Etzioni, ed. *Complex Organizations: A Sociological Reader*. Holt, Rinehart & Winston, 1961.
Robert K. Merton *et al.*, eds. *Reader in Bureaucracy*. Free Press, 1952.

For major examples of empirical work in this field, see:

Peter Blau. *The Dynamics of Bureaucracy*. U. of Chicago Press, 1955.

Alvin W. Gouldner. *Patterns of Industrial Bureaucracy.* Free Press, 1954.

Robert Kahn *et al. A Study of the League of Women Voters of the United States.* Survey Research Center, 1956.

Seymour M. Lipset. *Agrarian Socialism: The Cooperative Commonwealth Federation in Saskatchewan.* U. of California Press, 1950.

Philip Selznick. *TVA and the Grass Roots.* U. of California Press, 1953.

David L. Sills. *The Volunteers.* Free Press, 1957.

Samuel A. Stouffer *et al. The American Soldier.* Princeton U. Press, 1949. Vols. I, II.

Individuals may do without religion, societies cannot.

Attributed to **HILAIRE BELLOC**

The England of today . . . was producing a new race of mankind, over-conscious in the money and social and political side, on the spontaneous, intuitive side dead. . . . This is history. One England blots out another. The mines had made the halls wealthy. Now they were blotting them out, as they had already blotted out the cottages. The industrial England blots out the agricultural England. One meaning blots out another. The new England blots out the old England. And the continuity is not organic, but mechanical.

D. H. LAWRENCE
Lady Chatterley's Lover

Orthodox democratic theory assumes that every citizen has, or ought to have, thought out for himself certain opinions, i.e., ought to have a definite view, defensible by arguments, of what the country needs, of what principles ought to be applied in governing it, of the men to whose hands the government ought to be entrusted. There are persons who talk, though certainly very few who act, as if they believed this theory, which may be compared to the theory of some ultra-Protestants that every good Christian has or ought to have . . . worked out for himself from the Bible a system of theology.

JAMES BRYCE
The American Commonwealth

For generation after generation, Adamses and Brookses and Boylstons and Gorhams had gone to Harvard College, and although none of them, as far as known, had ever done any good there, or thought himself the better for it, custom, social ties, convenience, and, above all, economy, kept each generation in the trade. Any other education would have required a serious effort, but no one took Harvard College seriously. All went there because their friends went there, and the College was their ideal of social self-respect. . . . The chief wonder of education is that it does not ruin everybody concerned with it, teachers and taught.

HENRY ADAMS
The Education of Henry Adams

The spirit of an army is the factor which multiplied by the mass gives the resulting force. To define and express the significance of this unknown factor—the spirit of an army—is a problem for science.

Ten men, battalions, or divisions fighting fifteen men, battalions, or divisions, conquer—that is, kill or take captive—all the others, while themselves losing four. . . . Consequently, the four were equal to the fifteen, and therefore $4x = 15y$. Consequently $x/y = 15/4$. This equation does not give us the value of the unknown factor but gives us a ratio between two unknowns. And by bringing variously selected historic units (battles, campaigns, periods of war) into such equations, a series of numbers could be obtained in which certain laws should exist and might be discovered.

LEO TOLSTOY
War and Peace

Chapter Ten
INSTITUTIONS

In order to handle the business of living, man has invented and developed a range of social institutions. Although many needs find their expression in organizations, voluntary associations, and small groups, as spelled out above, there remains a good deal of behavior influenced by the complex and long-lasting systems called institutions.

Their pervasiveness is suggested by a quick review of how people spend their time. On weekdays, adults work and children go to school. On Sundays, people go to church. On certain Tuesdays, in the United States, they vote; on other days they have to pay taxes; and on all days they must obey the law and, as good citizens, keep informed on the activities of their government. If the country gets into war, men may have to go into the army. If one commits a crime, he may have to go to jail. In all these instances, people are behaving in ways influenced or even regulated by institutions set up for the purpose.

Two warnings must be sounded with regard to what is and is not included in this chapter. First, the very subject matter shades off into history, philosophy, political science, and economics. As a general rule, we have tried to stop on the clearly behavioral-scientific side of such arbitrary boundary lines; but it is only fair to say that the division is a particularly hard one to make in this chapter. Second, there is for some of these sections a large applied literature—for example, marketing studies and personnel psychology in the case of industrial institutions, classroom experiments on the teaching of particular subjects such as reading or arithmetic, and selection tests for military personnel. In line with our purpose to cover only the general behavioral material, we do not include detailed findings of that nature. What these two warnings come down to, in a way, is that both the broadest and the narrowest materials are omitted.

DEFINITIONS

Institution: This term, like several others in the behavioral sciences, is given different definitions by scholars of different proclivities. Essentially, the differences come down to this: an institution as a "complex normative pattern" governing behavior in certain fundamental and recurring situations, as against an institution as the organized aggregate to which the norms are applied. Roughly speaking, the distinction is between the procedures and the system. The former is the more technical definition, the latter the more popular. According to the former, marriage and communion are examples of institutions; according to the latter, the family and the church are.

For our purposes, the idea is perhaps best conveyed simply by naming some of the more important institutions in modern life—those with which we shall deal here:

religious institutions, for relations with the supernatural;
economic institutions, for producing and consuming;
political institutions, for distributing power, administering the government, selecting officials;
educational institutions, for training the young, transmitting skills and culture from one generation to the next;
military institutions, for defense of the nation

Most scholars consider the family itself as a basic social institution, for reproduction and child-rearing, but since we have already considered that in a separate chapter, we need not deal with it here. Nor do we need to get into definitional niceties or controversies. The plain fact is that a great deal of life is spent in connection with one or another institution, as common usage of the term makes clear, and it is convenient for our purposes to organize a number of findings under the institutions through which human affairs are centered—the institutions, that is, which guide and control behavior. This arrangement is based on the type or subject matter of the institutional behavior.

FINDINGS

Religious Institutions

The behavioral sciences typically define religion as man's relation to the supernatural—to something superempirical, described by the society as sacred or holy, requiring or involving worship. In studying the subject across a wide range of societies, the behavioral scientist makes a distinction between religion (typically in more advanced societies) and magic (in more primitive ones), although no sharp line is drawn.

> We should not think of the difference between magic and religion as a rigid dichotomy but rather as a wide gradation involving several rather independent variables. What they have in common is the reference to a supernatural realm, but they differ with respect to (a) the kind of ends pursued, (b) the type of attitudes involved, (c) the particular kind of supernaturalism required, and (d) the pattern of behavior exhibited [Davis, 1949, p. 537].

> Magic and religion are not dichotomies, but make up a *continuum* along several identifiable dimensions, and are distinguished only ideal-typically. Some of these dimensions are: specificity of goal desired, manipulative vs. cajoling attitude, type of professional-client relationship, collective vs. private ends, etc. [Goode, 1955, p. 128].

The libraries are filled with writings on religion of a philosophical, theological, and historical character; here we deal only with scientific studies, with that small portion of the literature in which something approximating scientific evidence has been put forward.

AS INSTITUTION AND ORGANIZATION

A1 All known human societies have religion(s).

Inasmuch as it is anchored in men's attitudes, the supernatural is as real as the natural or the human; men apparently have to come to terms with all three.

> There are no peoples however primitive without religion and magic, . . . nor . . . the scientific attitude [nor] science. . . . In every primitive community, . . . there have been found two clearly distinguishable domains, the Sacred and the Profane; in other words, the domain of Magic and Religion and that of Science. On the one hand there are the traditional acts and observances, regarded by the natives as sacred. . . . On the other hand, . . . the careful observation of natural process and a firm belief in its regularity [Malinowski, 1948, p. 1].

As a matter of fact, the two are often in conflict, particularly at the extremes: strong religion tends to drive out strong science, and vice versa.

Precisely because its values are invested with sacred sanction, religion is a powerful force in any society—for integration within religious communities, as well as for potential conflict between them and the larger society.

> The very fact that a religion so powerfully binds together its own group of worshippers means that if a religion is not shared by all or most members of a society, it may be sharply divisive and disruptive, even a destructive, force. Furthermore, religion does not invariably play a conservative, stabilizing role. Particularly in times of cataclysmic social and economic change religion has often

played a creative, innovating—and even revolutionary—part [Nottingham, 1954, p. 16].

The authoritative claim that the gods want man to behave in a certain way (or that society's ideas or abstract ethical values require certain behavior) has more influence than a simple assertion of how other men want him to behave.

As a case of religious development, take this example:

> What is expressed by the primitive mind as myth is conceived of in terms of doctrine at a more advanced level of civilization. . . . In the course of historical development, definite tendencies toward *systematization* may be discerned. . . . The way is now prepared for the establishment of an over-all *authority* to decide and define doctrine. A more or less unified system of a normative character ("doctrine") is thus substituted for a variety of independent mythological traditions, associated only by chance. This marks the origin of "theology" proper. . . . The written tradition now replaces the oral tradition in the form of sacred writings. In order to rationalize the fundamental conceptions which are the expressions of particular religious experiences, theologians develop normative systems of faith bolstered with appropriate apologetic defenses. . . . Theology eventually produces philosophy [Wach, 1944, pp. 20–22].

A1.1   Across societies, the range in religious behavior is extreme.

There is little point here in going into the voluminous literature on the range in religious practices from primitive to complex societies. The sacred objects themselves vary widely, as does the organization of the religion; its practice, individual and collective; its relation to other aspects of the society (such as the economy, politics, or science); the elaboration of its ritual; the incorporation of its beliefs into daily life; the aspects of life that it covers; the quality of its ethical system; the degree to which it is involved in good works of a social character; and indeed everything else connected with it. Religion is always there, but is seldom the same: that can be considered a basic summary statement. For example:

> *When* do men worship? In every cult there are times, sacred times, which are better fitted than others for the performance of an act of worship. Hours, days, months, seasons, or years are set aside as dedicated to the deity, to be observed with care. . . . Morning or evening hours, the *horae* (of prayer), the *dies dominica*, the Sabbath, Eastertide, Holy Week, the month of Ramadan, and the jubilee year are examples of special periods reserved for worship. . . .
>
> *How* do men worship? By silently concentrating and meditating upon the divine presence, or by acknowledging it in sound or word, we render homage to a power which invites adoration. It is moving to see how a simple sound—a whistle, noise, or the ejaculation of a word or two—suffice for the most primitive men to dispel evil spirits and to attract the attention of, as as well as establish communion with, the deity. . . . Gestures are used, such as the kiss and folding of hands; body positions such as standing and kneeling are also known. . . .

[These] are employed either independently or as accompaniment to the spoken or sung word. . . . Silence, or the use of a numinous word, may be the profoundest acknowledgment of the divine presence. Gestures, postures, and movements contribute to the development of the pantomime and the sacred dance, universally used as a major part of the ritual. . . . The sacred dance is found among Amerinds, and in Australia, Polynesia, Africa, Southeastern Asia, Northern Asia, the Near and Far East [Wach, 1958, p. 104–06].

A1.2   For the more elaborate development of religious beliefs and practices, societies require neither too high nor too low a sense of security and well-being.

Marked excess or deficiency of security is prejudicial to the development of belief in the supernatural. The optimum condition for religion and magic would be a middle one, in which the total environment and social situation gave people some uneasiness but not too much. This rather tame conclusion at least derives support from the undoubted facts that most cultures are religious, and that most of them have recurrent worries but not crushing ones [Kroeber, 1948, p. 604].

A1.2a   Religious belief and practice is most likely to be brought into play by individuals and societies in connection with important but uncertain matters (e.g., birth and death, war, accidents, danger, etc.).

From his studies of the Trobriand Islanders, for example,

Malinowski [1948] came to the conclusion that when great uncertainty about the outcome is associated with activities vital to human societies, the use of magicoreligious or other comparable techniques as means for allaying tension and promoting adjustment is inevitable [Nottingham, 1954, p. 34].

Malinowski himself offers as "an interesting and crucial test" the practices associated with fishing there:

While in the villages on the inner lagoon fishing is done in an easy and absolutely reliable manner by the method of poisoning, yielding abundant results without danger and uncertainty, there are on the shores of the open sea dangerous modes of fishing and also certain types in which the yield greatly varies according to whether shoals of fish appear beforehand or not. It is most significant that in the lagoon fishing, where man can rely completely upon his knowledge and skill, magic does not exist, while in the open-sea fishing, full of danger and uncertainty, there is extensive magical ritual to secure safety and good results [Malinowski, 1948, p. 14].

A1.3   Supernatural beings in all religions respond like man, with the higher moral values of the society raised to sacred status. They have control over the real world, including man, and/or they stand in judgment over man.

The supernatural entities, or gods, are not always held to have bodies like men, but their values, attitudes, perception, and thoughts are "anthroposocial." That is, their "personalities" are like those of members of the society. This is evidenced by these facts:

(a) The deities take notice of man's actions;

(b) The deities act broadly to further man's welfare, such welfare conforming closely to the society's desires;

(c) The deities desire human attention. . . .

(d) The deities usually punish men for not acting in accordance with the rules of the society, such punishment usually occurring in *this* world;

(e) The deities are not invariably "good," for they may also have "moods," and some are whimsical or destructive at times;

(f) The relationships between deities and men, and among deities, are also conceived in such social terms, in that there will be communication, promises, reminders, approval, and perhaps even threats [Goode, 1955, p. 127].

A1.4   On the average, the more complex the society, the more varied the institutional forms of religious belief and practice.

As humanity moves from small isolated societies in the direction of huge, complex, urbanized ones, the following changes can be noted: *First,* the gods tend to be gradually withdrawn from the local scene. . . . *Second,* anthropomorphism tends to diminish. . . . *Third,* religion tends to be increasingly separated from everyday affairs. . . . *Fourth,* religious homogeneity tends to diminish. . . . *Fifth,* the religious system tends to become fragmented . . . [and] the stage is set for church-state conflict. . . . All of these tendencies can be summed up under the heading of secularization [Davis, 1949, pp. 542–43].

A2   Religion in primitive societies (as with life in general there) appears to be more of a collective experience than it is in advanced societies, which tend to be more individualistic.

The savage depends upon the group with whom he is in direct contact both for practical co-operation and mental solidarity to a far larger extent than does civilized man. . . . [The] principle that primitive religion "was essentially an affair of the community rather than of individuals" has become a *Leitmotiv* of modern research [Malinowski, 1948, p. 5].

A2.1   The primitive society is likely to constitute a natural religious group, i.e., one in which the whole society or community shares a single religion. As society becomes increasingly complex, it moves more toward the formation of groups that are specifically religious.

The religion of the natural group is less changeable and more likely to be taken for granted than that of the complex society, since it is reinforced by other aspects of the common society and is hence less subject to challenge. With the rise of specifically religious groups come religious individualism and secularization.

The more advanced the process of social and cultural differentiation, the more diversified are the forms of religious expression. Christianity, Mohammedanism, Buddhism, Hinduism, and Confucianism, each of them forming one great religious community, are highly diversified economically, socially, and culturally. Yet there is an important difference. Hinduism is ethnically heterogeneous but politically—now—united; Confucianism is ethnically and politically rather homogeneous. Hindu and Confucian societies are also national units, whereas Islam, Buddhism, and Christianity extend over a vast conglomeration of peoples and nations [Wach, 1944, p. 268].

At the same time, it is true that religious practice varies within a primitive society just as it does in a complex one.

The field anthropologist knows . . . that the primitive religious belief is not homogeneous. There are atheists and believers, religious traditionalists and creators, in any primitive society. . . . Although there is considerable integration between religious and political power in most primitive societies, as there is in our own, there is also conflict [Goode, 1955, p. 124].

A3   Whatever its origins, religion almost always becomes organized in the society (that is, it comes to be expressed through an organization or several organizations, beyond its expression in sentiment or devotion alone).

The major exception is a lack of organization in mystical religions, at least at their outset, although later it often occurs as a way to oppose the traditional religious forms or even to proselytize for the mystique. It is customary in the sociology of religion to speak of a natural movement from sect to church—from religious ideology and ritual to religious organization:

The two stand in dynamic relationship to each other in two principal respects: over time, the sect slowly accrues to itself more and more of the attributes of the church, losing its sectlike qualities in the process. In turn, as a religious institution becomes more churchlike in character, the likelihood increases that dissenting groups will form which in protest may break away to form new sects [Glock, 1959, p. 158].

One study related this movement to the shift from agriculture to industry in a Southern community,

to show how the two types of institution contributed to the process of change but in radically different ways; the churches through direct and often open cooperation with the mill owners, the sects through sublimating latent resentments of the mill workers by redirecting their concerns from this world to the next [*ibid.*, p. 158, on Pope, 1942].

A4   The internal formation of dissenting groups is the more likely, (a) the more highly organized the religious institution into a church with dogma, ritual, literature, personnel, hierarchy, etc.; (b) the greater the expansion of the institution, with accompanying modifications and compromises; and (c) the more complacent the leadership is, or is seen to be.

There is a tendency for such groups to break away to form their own religion, but there is also a countertendency for the parent religion to accommodate them with special internal dispensations.

A4.1   Religious sects and prophetic leaders are more likely to arise in periods of social disorganization and rapid social change than in periods of tranquillity.

According to a summary on the sociology of religion:

> The religious leader known as a prophet typically appears when the established values of a social group seem to be threatened by contact with alien cultures. Thus the prophet usually appears among minority groups whose values are threatened by invaders, by assimilation, or by migration. . . . It would not be correct to say that prophets invariably arise among minority peoples subjected to value conflict. Such a condition is necessary but not sufficient for the successful work of this type of religious leader. Also important are a people who are willing to admit the possibility of charismatic insight and who feel a degree of uneasiness concerning their own and others' behavior and beliefs. . . .
>   There are numerous well-known examples of the prophet type. Moses, for instance, became prominent when the wandering Israelites experimented with worship of the golden bull. Almost all of the major Jewish prophets arose to condemn the uneasy accommodation between Israelite and Canaanite customs and institutions. . . . Patheseske, Kanakuk, and Smohalla were famous American Indian prophets, a religious type unknown to the Indians before their cultures were threatened by invading Europeans. . . . Until recently a man known as Prophet Jones gained a wide following among Negroes in Detroit. Unsystematic but strongly convincing evidence suggests that he appealed especially to the transplanted Southern Negro whose traditional rural Baptist religious values came into conflict with the values of secularized Northern urbanism [Hoult, 1958, pp. 122–23].

A4.2   The more revealed or intense the claims of the religious organization, the more likely the corresponding religious affiliation is to be divisive within the society.

The more strongly people feel about such an important matter, the less likely they are to compromise with regard to it.

A5   The basic values and organization of the society both affect and are affected by the religious values and organization.

With respect to basic values, American pragmatism and stress-to-action means that the churches are highly valued for their social utility and their stand on social questions, as against their theological positions. More broadly, the rise of secularization has meant that religion has lost its former controls over education, welfare, legal practices, etc.; and the development of a complex system of stratification means that religious practices begin to vary within the strata. Here are two examples:

> We find in religious philosophy a reflection of the real world; the theology of a people will echo a dominant note in their terrestrial mode of life. A pastoral culture may find its image in a Good Shepherd and his flock; an era of cathedral building sees God as a Great Architect; an age of commerce finds Him with a ledger, jotting down moral debits and credits; emphasis upon the profit system and the high-pressure salesmanship that is required to make it function, picture Jesus as a super-salesman; and, in an age of science, God "is a god of law and order" (Millikan, 1931), a Great Scientist, moving about in his cosmic laboratory, his experiments to perform.
>
> In ancient Egypt, . . . in the very early period, there were numerous deities, many of which were *local* gods, or patrons of little kingdoms. As the political unification of Egypt progressed, a few of the greater gods emerged as *national* deities. As the nation became more and more integrated under the rule of a powerful single head, there was a tendency for one god to become supreme. [Thus], the ascendancy of Re, the sun-god [White, 1948, pp. 101–02].

> An agricultural people inhabiting a cool and arid region needs, above all things, warmth and rain for the growth of its crops. It is understandable, consequently, that Hopi should worship a Sky God who brings rain, an Earth Goddess who nourishes the seed, and a Sun God who matures the crops, as well as a special Corn Mother and a God of Growth or Germination [Murdock, 1934, p. 348].

With respect to organization, there is Max Weber's famous thesis on the effect of Calvinism on the rise of modern capitalism:

> A specifically bourgeois economic ethic had grown up. With the consciousness of standing in the fullness of God's grace and being visibly blessed by Him, the bourgeois businessman, as long as he remained within the bounds of formal correctness, as long as his moral conduct was spotless and the use to which he put his wealth was not objectionable, could follow his pecuniary interests as he would and feel that he was fulfilling a duty in doing so. The power of religious asceticism provided him in addition with sober, conscientious, and unusually industrious workmen, who clung to their work as to a life purpose willed by God [Weber, 1958, p. 177].

The relationship between Puritanism and the rise of science provides a similar illustration:

> The Puritan ethic, as an ideal-typical expression of the value-attitudes basic to ascetic Protestantism generally, so canalized the interests of seventeenth-century Englishmen as to constitute one important *element* in the enhanced cultivation

of science. The deep-rooted religious *interests* of the day demanded in their forceful implications the systematic, rational, and empirical study of nature for the glorification of God in His works and for the control of the corrupt world [Merton, 1957, pp. 574–75].

For example, although in the mid-seventeenth century, "the Puritans constituted a relatively small minority in the English population, . . . they constituted sixty-two per cent of the initial membership of the [Royal] Society" (*ibid.*, p. 585). Even in modern America, incidentally, Catholics are underrepresented among scientists (Knapp and Goodrich, 1952).

AS INDIVIDUAL AND GROUP BEHAVIOR

A6   At least in the United States, participation in organized religious activity is higher:

.1   among women, especially widows.

Ringer . . . finds, for example, that parishioners who are both spouseless and childless are much more likely to be deeply involved in church life than those who are in a core family with both a spouse and a child. Finding that the relationship holds when other possibly explanatory variables are held constant, he infers that for some individuals, at least, involvement in the church functions as a family substitute. His finding also shows that women parishioners of low social status are more deeply involved than those of higher social status. The differences are magnified in parishes located in wealthy neighborhoods. He concludes that the church provides status security for lower-status women members, particularly those living in high-status communities, where class discrimination is more likely to limit their access to secular organizations [Glock, 1959, pp. 171–72].

This study found that 70 per cent of the single, widowed, or divorced women over thirty were "highly involved" in the church as against 52 per cent of the married without children and 42 per cent of the married with children thirteen years of age or more (Ringer, 1956, p. 44).

.2   among older people (those closer to death).

Here is a summary of the place of religion in the life cycle:

(3–10) Children are considerably religious, at first holding fairy tale beliefs, later accepting the standard ideas of their group. (10–18) Intellectual doubts start at a mental age of 12, followed by emotional stress; these conflicts are often resolved at about the age of 16 either by conversion to religion or by a decision to abandon the religion of childhood. About 20 per cent of those converted to religion experience a sudden crisis, the rest are "graduals." There is no general increase in religious activity during these years. (18–30) There is a sharp decline in all aspects of religious activity, the years 30–35 being the lowest point in the life-cycle. (35 onwards) There is a steady increase from about 35 until old age, which is marked by a widespread belief in God and the afterlife [Argyle, 1958, pp. 69–70].

The disparity in church involvement between men and women also increases throughout the life cycle. In a recent study of the values held by American college students, it was found that there was considerable disagreement over various theological doctrines:

> Student opinion was much more likely to converge on the characteristics that they felt were most important to seek in an "ideal mate," or the guarantees which they would expect from an "ideal democracy." They were more likely, too, to find areas of agreement about the most important aims of college education or even about the characteristics of an "ideal job." . . . It appears that the norms for religious belief among these college students may be much less fixed and much less patterned than they are in these other institutional areas [Goldsen et al., 1960, p. 164].

.3   in the middle class. (Differences by education are slight, except that the most highly educated appear to engage less in religious activities than do others).

.4   among those whose parents were religious or whose spouses are members of the same religion or denomination.

A6a   The more strongly religious the member, the more he thinks the church should engage in the "salvation of souls," as against social action.

Permissiveness toward church participation in political affairs is inversely correlated with degree of involvement in church life

	Index of general church involvement			
	High	Fairly high	Moderate	Low or none
Per cent who endorse an active political role for the church	39	56	56	60
Total number of cases	(99)	(171)	(528)	(393)

(Ringer, 1956, p. 123)

A7   Church affiliation is tied to social class.

For example, in the United States, within Protestantism, the Episcopalians tend to be upper class, the fundamentalist sects lower class. And upper-class denominations are more formal in their religious observance, lower-class denominations more emotional.

Class composition of religious bodies, 1945–46 (percentages) *

	Upper class	Middle class	Lower class
Congregational	24	43	33
Episcopalian	24	34	42
Presbyterian	22	40	38
Methodist	13	35	52
Lutheran	11	36	53
Baptist	8	24	68
Jewish	22	32	46
Catholic	9	25	66

* Derived from a breakdown of four polls taken by the American Institute of Public Opinion in 1945–46, covering approximately 12,000 cases. Each poll covered a "voting sample" of approximately 3000 cases.

(Pope, 1948, p. 86)

A7.1   The most deprived groups in the society are the most likely to engage in salvationist religions.

Such religions are attractive to such people because they promise rewards in other worlds, to soften the deprivations of this one.

There is evidence that religion, particularly in the form of sects, has served as a functional alternative to political extremism. During the Depression, when organized radicalism made little headway in this country, small religious sects grew rapidly [Lipset, 1960, pp. 39–40].

At the same time, some minority groups develop strongly aggressive religions to help them get more of the world's rewards. For example:

The more a minority group does share and wants to share in the dominant culture of a society, the greater its power, the stronger its hope, the more its religious tradition encourages an emphasis on the values of this life, the more aggressive its leadership, the more the personality tendencies of the members encourage them to confront life directly, rather than inventing symbolic solutions—under these circumstances, the farther the religious response to its status will move down the road of acceptance-avoidance-aggression, and the more it will develop secular themes to supplement or replace the religious sectarian movements [Yinger, 1957, pp. 178–79].

A number of findings involving religion appear in other sections. In order to recall their general character, we repeat that religious affiliation has consequences in a wide range of nonreligious forms of behavior. For example:

In political attitudes: The Catholics and Jews in this country vote more consistently Democratic.

In marital relations: The religious report greater happiness; Catholics divorce less but desert more than do non-Catholics; "the differences between nonattenders and those who attend church regularly are often greater than the differences among people affiliated with different churches" (Goode, 1961, p. 424).

In deviant behavior: There is less crime by church attendants; "Catholics have a particularly high rate for crimes of violence, while Protestants have a slightly above-average rate for sexual offenses and Jews for fraud" (Argyle, 1958, p. 100).

In sexual behavior: There is less activity among religious people.

In ethnic prejudice: The devout tend to be less prejudiced.

A recent study of the "religious factor" in a large urban center in the United States summarized the matter as follows, in "the central finding of our study":

From our evidence it is clear that religion in various ways is constantly influencing the daily lives of the masses of men and women in the modern American metropolis. More than that: through its impact on individuals, religion makes an impact on all the other institutional systems of the community in which these individuals participate. Hence the influence of religion operates at the social level as well as at the personal level.

Depending on the socio-religious group to which a person belongs, the probabilities are increased or decreased that he will:

	Order of groups on each item
"enjoy his occupation"	Jews, white Protestants, white Catholics, Negro Protestants
"indulge in installment buying"	Negro Protestants, white Catholics, white Protestants, Jews
"save to achieve objectives far in the future"	Jews, others
"believe in the American Dream"	white Protestants, Jews, white Catholics and Negro Protestants
"vote Republican"	white Protestants, white Catholics, Negro Protestants, Jews
"favor the welfare state"	Jews, Negro Protestants, white Catholics, white Protestants
"take a liberal point of view on the issue of freedom of speech"	white Protestants, white Catholics and Jews, Negro Protestants
"oppose racial integration in the schools"	white Protestants and white Catholics, Jews
"migrate to another community"	Negro Protestants, white Protestants, white Catholics and Jews

Order of groups on each item

"maintain close ties with his family"	Jews, white Catholics, Negro Protestants, white Protestants
"develop a commitment to the principle of intellectual autonomy"	Jews, white Protestants, white Catholics, Negro Protestants
"have a large family"	Negro Protestants, white Catholics, Jews, white Protestants
"complete a given unit of education" (rather than drop out)	Jews, white Protestants, white Catholics, Negro Protestants
"rise in the class system"	Jews, white Protestants, white Catholics, Negro Protestants

[Lenski, 1961, p. 289]

According to this study,

it seems clear that the differences associated with religion are substantial. In general they are of a magnitude comparable to the differences associated with class on the same questions. What is even more important, the *range* of variables affected by religion seems to be fully as great as that affected by class. . . . The main point seems clear: *socio-religious group membership is a variable comparable in importance to class, both with respect to its potency and with respect to the range, or extent, of its influence* [*ibid.*, pp. 293, 295].

Here are a few illustrations of the comparative differences. From a list of thirty-five items, we have selected a few that show no difference in discrimination and others that show differences each way (white Protestants and Catholics only):

Dependent variable	*Mean percentage difference between classes* *	*Mean percentage difference between socioreligious groups* †
Chances for upward mobility good	11	11
Public officials not interested in average man	8.5	8.5
Republican preference	37.5	22.5
Expects CIO members to agree with him re controversial issues	37	17
Gambling wrong	13.5	24.5
Birth control wrong	3.5	44.5
Mean difference (total list)	11.3	12.3
Median difference (total list)	9.0	11.0

* With socioreligious group held constant.   † With class held constant.

(Lenski, 1961, pp. 293–94)

Economic Institutions

INDUSTRIALIZATION

B1   The rise of industrialization affects the family: it undermines and finally disintegrates relatively tight and large kinship groupings in simple societies, shifts the distribution of power within the nuclear family, and changes marital patterns.

According to a British anthropologist:

The experience of anthropologists has indicated that general patterns such as the following tend to be observed as social implications of technical change in small-scale "primitive" or peasant communities:

1. Large-scale descent groups tend to give way to smaller kin units centering on the nuclear family.
2. Linked with this is the tendency for a shift of authority to occur from one income-controlling category of persons to another—e.g. (a) From elders controlling income from land to younger people, usually males, controlling income from external wage-labour, trade and other enterprise. (b) From one type of kin authority to another, e.g., mother's brother to father in a matrilineally oriented society. (c) From traditional leaders to *novi homines* [Firth *et al.*, 1959, p. 282].

And according to an American sociologist:

Each high or low rate in the pre-industrializing or early industrializing phase was the product of specific family patterns. . . . The major [changes] seem to be the following:

1. Freedom of marital choice, with these accompanying changes.
    a. Marital bargaining is taken from the hands of elders;
    b. The young couple must be economically independent;
    c. The age of females at marriage is likely to drop; that of males depends on several additional variables; at a minimum, there develops the notion of a "proper maturity at marriage";
    d. The pattern of class homogamy does not change;
    e. In cultures where there was nearly universal marriage (India, Japan, China), there may be a slight diminution in the percentage ever married;
    f. There is a diminution of age-discrepant marriages, i.e., between spouses of very different ages.
2. Marriages between kin diminish.
3. The dowry or bride price begins to disappear.
4. Illegitimacy rates increase in systems where most marriages were consummated between children (e.g., India, but *not* China and Japan). Since most civilizations seem to have various forms of marital unions which are not fully legitimate, the movement toward a conjugal system (as in Japan) may actually reduce the illegitimacy rate.

5. Concubinage and polygamy decline.

6. Theory cannot state whether fertility in a conjugal system will be high or low, but it will be at least controlled in the interests of the couple not the kin group. Under industrialization, of course, in general the rate falls. And any movement toward a conjugal system reduces the *size* of *household;* e.g., even in Africa, where possibly marital fertility may be increasing.

7. Infanticide decreases, though here we have no firm numerical data with which to measure its rate in the past in those countries where it has been supposed to exist (India, Japan, China, and the Arab world).

8. Matriliny weakens, although here our Western bias may exaggerate changes in lower caste Indian or Central African systems; i.e., the system seems strange, and thus we are more alert to changes in it.

9. The divorce rate will be high, but the *trend* in any given culture will depend on its prior level. As noted before, it may drop if the rate was already high, and the new system yields some new elements of stability (e.g., the removal of the Japanese mother-in-law's right to send the bride back to her parents).

10. Where remarriage of divorcées or of the widowered or widowed was unlikely, it becomes common. Here, stereotypes confuse somewhat, since divorce was certainly more common in some countries (e.g., China) than commonly supposed, and remarriage of the widow or widower more common as well (China, Japan) [Goode, 1960, pp. 13–15].

Those are general summaries. Here is the conclusion of a specific investigation:

Recent growth in the social structure, though initiated at first by certain forcible modifications in the political system from without, appears in Malabar to have issued mainly from change in the society's methods of exploiting the material world. In the traditional economy of Malabar, there was little capital accumulation and scarcely any cumulative development. This allowed for, though it did not determine, a social system whose principal forms of grouping (caste and unilineal descent group) were based on birth, and between whose territorial segments (kingdom, district and village) there was little mobility. Principal features of the present economy, by contrast, are the accumulation of capital and the progressive development of a machine technology, entailing urbanization, occupational specialization by individuals, and a market economy. Such an economy necessitates social and spatial mobility, which are incompatible with primitive groupings based on birth. The change from a matrilineal to a bilateral kinship system, the emergence of the elementary family at the expense of the unilineal group, and the decrease in range and functions of the kinship system, appear therefore as part of the over-all change from a feudal to a semi-industrial economic and social system [Gough, 1952, pp. 86–87].

B1.1   The family patterns of the lower classes change more rapidly under industrialization than do those of the upper classes.

In an industrializing process both the peasant and primitive proletarians are forced to adjust their family patterns more swiftly to the industrial system, and find at least more immediate opportunities in it. By contrast, the middle and upper strata can best use these new opportunities by loosening their kin ties more slowly. Thus, we would expect that changes in the latter family system are more likely to occur on a general basis only later in the system [Goode, 1960, p. 9].

B2   Industrialization undermines the traditional forms of social organization and substitutes a system of stratification in which (a) there are more social roles to be filled than there were before and (b) achievement on the job becomes increasingly important (as against, for example, a traditional factor such as age).

The mobility promoted by industrialization is the effective force: geographical mobility, social mobility, occupational mobility. Such movement of people, taking them away from traditional ways of life and putting them in touch with new ways, is both a dissolving and a reorganizing agent. Here is a general summary:

> In general, and with deference to the variety of specific forms that modernization has taken historically and in the contemporary scene, the central tendency of sociological change appears to be the multiplication of key social roles, in part new roles, in part adaptations of old ones. As life becomes more technically oriented, power and prestige shift away from the few dominant men in the traditional structure—the wealthy pasha, the wise priest, the village elder—toward men equipped to perform more specific functions in the modern division of labor. Professional and technical skills are required for the roles associated with the growth of cities and the spread of industries, the technical advances and monetization of agriculture, the growing dependence of public policy upon an informed and participant citizenry. The banker and the economist tend to replace the landowner and moneylender as sources of cash and managers of credit; the industrialist and manager replace the merchant and trader; the civil servant, the engineer, the agronomist, and others take over special functions that earlier were concentrated in village elders and other men of hereditary wealth or wisdom [Millikan and Blackmer, 1961, p. 30].

B2.1   In general, the faster the rate of industrialization, the more difficult the adjustment of the newly recruited workers.

B3   Industrialization increases the number of voluntary associations connected with work: during the transitional period, they tend to have special purposes (mainly to promote a commitment to the new kind of work); when the labor situation has become stabilized, they tend to be more personalized and smaller.

B4   The amount and kind of technology employed in the economic system is the single most important factor determining the behavior associated with the system: the nature of the job, the definition of the working day, the recruitment and selection of workers, their training and retraining, the development of informal groups on the job, the relations of superiors and subordinates, and even several non-job matters in the family, the community, or the society generally.

With regard to this last, for example,

> both Negro and white farm workers will be increasingly affected by farm mechanization. Landlord-tenant relations, Negro-white population ratios in the rural South, migration rates and goals, relief and other policies unquestionably will undergo considerable modification [Simpson and Yinger, 1953, p. 362].

And more generally:

> Upon reflection it appears as though all of our relevant variables are related to the technological system designed by the company to organize the work process. The degree of independence or dependence among workers in the flow of work, the number and similarity of jobs concentrated in any one location, the indispensability of any part to the whole, the extent to which work loads and output standards can be accurately defined, and even the promotional ladders (and status relationships) are determined to a large extent by the kinds and quantity of equipment, skills, and plant layout utilized. . . . The social system erected by the technological process is also a basic and continuing determinant of work group attitudes and actions [Sayles, 1958, p. 93].

B4.1   The greater and more complicated the technology, (a) the greater the bureaucratization of the economy; (b) the more the skills needed in the labor force; (c) the greater the disparity between the skills needed at the top and the skills needed at the bottom; (d) the fewer the resources devoted to the agricultural segment; (e) the greater the proportion of the labor force in service occupations as against primary production; (f) the more productive the system; (g) the less important the place of individually owned property and hence the more important the organizational rules; (h) the greater the reliance on industrial innovation (i.e., the spiral contained in the "faith in technological progress").

With regard to this last,

> emphasis on innovation is historically unique. The history of technological advance makes clear that innovation tended to be resisted rather than welcomed. Only since the Industrial Revolution has the reverse been generally true [Dubin, 1958, p. 117].

B4.2   Technological growth tends to have the following broad effects on social life: increase of population; commercialization of the economy, and an attendant increase in contractual relations among men as against status relations; urbanization; stratification into working and middle classes; emergence of organizations and associations; increased division of labor, and hence interdependence of occupations, regions, etc.; and increased rationalism in human affairs.

Such tendencies of movement from status to contract, organic to mechanical solidarity, Gemeinschaft to Gesellschaft, sacred to secular, etc., are, of course, only probable. In such cases as the introduction of a single new item—tool, crop, or animal—nothing of the sort may happen—*Cf.* the gun in barbarous, the potato in peasant, or the horse in Amerindian society. Only when several items or a complex are involved are the probabilities high [Firth *et al.,* 1959, p. 293].

Note that the technology introduced may be quite different in each instance, but the social effects tend to be similar, particularly in countries of similar stages of industrial development. As a corollary:

B4.3   The social consequences of technological change are typically much more substantial in less developed societies than in advanced ones (partly due to the "ceiling effect").

Experience suggests that societies which already possess an advanced technology can absorb a substantial amount of technical innovation without profound social changes. . . . In less advanced economies, however, the social consequences of technical change have often been profound [*ibid,* p. 270].

B4.4   Technological equivalence between societies tends to be accompanied by equivalences in the system of communication, in socialization and education, in sexual and marital relations, and in demographic rates; but not in political control, religion, or art and leisure.

B5   Within a society, a stress on achievement in certain kinds of imaginative literature appears to be associated with the subsequent rate of economic development.

An ingenious and large-scale study of the "achieving society," from a psychological point of view, concludes that

a concern for achievement as expressed in imaginative literature—folk tales and stories for children—is associated in modern times with a more rapid rate of economic development. The generalization is confirmed not only for Western, free-enterprise democracies like England and the United States but also for Communist countries like Russia, Bulgaria or Hungary [McClelland, 1961, p. 105].

The following table indicates the relationship of need-achievement and economic expansion:

Rate of growth in electrical output (1952–58) and national *n* Achievement levels in 1950

(*Deviations from Expected Growth Rate* * *in Standard Score Units*)

	National n Achieve-ment levels (1950) †		Above ex-pec-ta-tion	National n Achieve-ment levels (1950) †		Be-low ex-pec-ta-tion
	3.62	Turkey	+1.38			
	2.71	India	+1.12			
	2.38	Australia	+.42			
	2.33	Israel	+1.18			
	2.33	Spain	+.01			
High *n*	2.29	Pakistan	+2.75			
Achievement	2.29	Greece	+1.18	3.38	Argentina	−.56
	2.29	Canada	+.06	2.71	Lebanon	−.67
	2.24	Bulgaria	+1.37	2.38	France	−.24
	2.24	United States	+.47	2.33	Union of South Africa	−.06
	2.14	West Germany	+.53	2.29	Ireland	−.41
	2.10	U.S.S.R.	+1.62	2.14	Tunisia	−1.87
	2.10	Portugal	+.76	2.10	Syria	−.25
	1.95	Iraq	+.29	2.05	New Zealand	−.29
	1.86	Austria	+.38	1.86	Uruguay	−.75
	1.67	United Kingdom	+.17	1.81	Hungary	−.62
	1.57	Mexico	+.12	1.71	Norway	−.77
	.86	Poland	+1.26	1.62	Sweden	−.64
				1.52	Finland	−.08
Low *n*				1.48	Netherlands	−.15
Achievement				1.33	Italy	−.57
				1.29	Japan	−.04
				1.20	Switzerland	−1.92
				1.19	Chile	−1.81
				1.05	Denmark	−.89
	Correlation of *n* Achievement level (1950) *x* deviations			.57	Algeria	−.83
	from expected growth rate = .43, *p* <.01			.43	Belgium	−1.65

* The estimates are computed from the monthly average electrical production figures, in millions of kilowatt-hours, for 1952 and 1958, from the United Nations' *Monthly Bulletin of Statistics* (January, 1960), and "Statistical Papers, Series J," *World Energy Supplies* (1951–54 and 1955–58).
† Based on twenty-one children's stories from second-, third-, and fourth-grade readers in each country.

(*Ibid.*, p. 100)

A similar conclusion is reached for a number of achieving societies in the past as well: ancient Greece, Spain in the late Middle Ages, England from Tudor times to the Industrial Revolution, the Wesleyanites, and pre-Incan Peru. As for the long-range trend in the United States, here is the relationship between the "mean frequency of achievement imagery in children's readers and the patent index, 1800–1950":

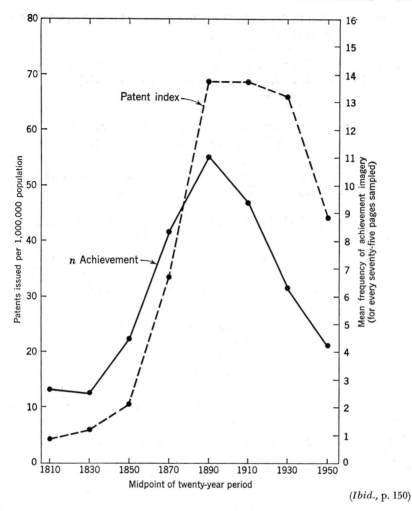

(*Ibid.*, p. 150)

B6 Prolonged unemployment typically leads to a deterioration of personality: passivity, apathy, anomie, listlessness, dissociation, lack of interest and of caring.

An early, pioneering study of the unemployed in an Austrian village found this pattern with respect to use of leisure time, activity-passivity, sense of time, ability to cope, etc. (Lazarsfeld-Jahoda and Zeisel, 1933). From the summary of another study:

> In short, prolonged unemployment operates as a severe depressant on the individual's relations to his society and himself. This would appear to be particularly true for those who lacked strong social ties prior to the depression (Komarovsky,

1940, p. 129). But it also holds, if to a lesser extent, for workers with a long history of collective activity and social solidarity; for example, a study of unemployed Polish workers disclosed their "disassociation of feelings of solidarity . . . [leaving] only scattered, loose, perplexed and hopeless individuals (Zawadski and Lazarsfeld, 1935, p. 245) " [Kornhauser, 1959, p. 165].

OCCUPATIONAL CHOICE

B7   At least in the United States, a person's occupational choice is less a single decision than a (partly irreversible) series of decisions made mainly during his teens. In general, the choice is made earlier by the brighter young people than by the less bright, and the choice tends to follow the father's occupation, especially in the upper classes.

B8   Occupational choice is much more restricted in the lower classes than in the upper—because of fewer opportunities for education and training, lowered expectations, ignorance of alternatives, need for early income, probably a greater stress on the immediate gratification of desires, the lack of informed and sympathetic adult advice, and the greater operation of chance.

> The process of occupational choice determination among the lower income group suggests that with a few notable exceptions it can be characterized by two terms: passive and stunted. These adolescents convey the impression that although they have considerable concern about entering the job market, they believe that there is little they can do about it in advance beyond selecting a high school where they can pursue an appropriate vocational course [Ginzberg et al., 1951, pp. 155, 178].

One study of people twenty-five years and over in six cities found that "accidental circumstances were largely responsible for the occupations held in 1950 by 23 per cent of all men and 37 per cent of all women"; most of the men held manual jobs (Palmer, 1954, p. 135). In short, "the socially underprivileged young person has seen less, read less, heard about less, has experienced less variety in his environment in general, and is simply less aware of the world's possibilities than is the socially privileged young person" (Lazarsfeld, n.d., pp. 20–21).

B9   The higher the status of the occupation, the more voluntary are the entrants to it and the more stable their occupational decision.

The lower occupations are more likely to be entered reluctantly, as a last resort. From a study of American college students:

> The fields in which career-shoppers are few, are principally the established professions which require intensive specialized training beginning even at the undergraduate level. On the psychological side, this sort of early and constant

specialization can build up the feelings of involvement, investment, and identification that tend to anchor the student to his field. His regular interaction with other people who are likewise becoming specialists reinforces this process. In sociological terms, one would predict that the student who has selected one of these fields and stayed with it throughout his college career has been more successfully socialized to the values, standards, and subculture of his profession than has his counterpart who has shopped around for a career during his early college years [Goldsen *et al.*, 1960, pp. 41–42].

B10   Given a reasonably free choice, people maintain some correspondence between their career plans and their occupational values.

For example, in the study of American college students, it was found that there is a close relationship between people's career plans and their occupational values. Those college students planning to go into business have the largest proportions who say they want to "earn a great deal of money" during their lives. Those students going into artistic fields, journalism, the sciences, teaching, and certain other professions are particularly likely to say they desire creative outlets for their personal capacities as a principal goal during their lives. Those students planning to enter medicine, teaching, personnel work, and hotel administration have the highest proportion saying that "opportunity to be helpful to others" is a principal goal in their future lives (Goldsen *et al.*, 1960, pp. 42–46).

This notion can even be broadened to take account of choices of women's occupations by women.

Women in American society, more than men, think of themselves as sensitive to the nuances of interpersonal relations; they are more interested in being socially useful, in dealing with people and touching their lives in a direct and personal way. If they enter "appropriate" occupations, it is not only because these are the ones accessible to women, but also because they are the occupations that the women feel will permit them to put to good use their special talents for interpersonal relations and interests in people [*ibid.*, p. 49].

Thus the American social system teaches women to have the appropriate occupational motivations for the work they are most likely to enter.

THE WORKING FORCE

There is, of course, a large descriptive literature on the characteristics of the working force throughout the world that we do not cover here.

B11   In virtually all societies, almost all males in their middle years (say, twenty to fifty-five) are in the labor force. Below and above these ages, however, there are differences between the industrialized and nonindustrialized countries: in the former, somewhat fewer of the young and old men are in the labor force.

Here are the summary data:

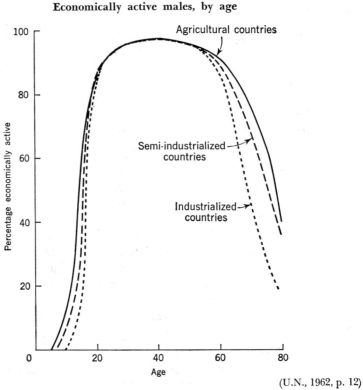

Economically active males, by age

(U.N., 1962, p. 12)

The decline in the importance of agriculture as a means of earning a living has curtailed employment opportunities for marginal workers such as young boys and elderly men. . . . In addition, economic advancement has made it both possible and necessary for young persons to continue their schooling to a later age, and larger numbers have gone on to acquire university degrees. This period has seen much progress in the development of social legislation concerned with pension schemes and other welfare measures which have encouraged earlier retirement. All of these factors have operated to bring down the activity rates among young persons and among the elderly in the industrialized countries [*ibid.*, pp. 16–17].

As a result, a smaller proportion of a man's lifetime is spent in the labor force in industrial as against nonindustrial countries: roughly "about 65 per cent of the total expectation of life for the industrialized countries, 67 per cent for the semi-industrialized countries, and 70 per cent for the agricultural countries" (*ibid.*, p. 19). And in the industrialized countries, the less skilled workers spend more years of their lives at work than the more skilled.

B11.1   Job changes occur more frequently in the less skilled occupations than in the highly skilled ones, and more frequently in the early years of the working career than in the later ones.

B11.2   The countries, the industries, and the companies with higher rates of industrial innovation are more likely to be staffed with skilled personnel than are those with lower rates.

As any industrial society advances, it becomes increasingly dependent upon the brains and much less dependent upon the brawn of its working forces. In other words, managers, administrators, scientists, engineers, and skilled technicians are bound to increase as a percentage of total employment, while the proportion of manual workers and other less skilled employees tends inevitably to diminish. Experience in the United States, as the most advanced industrial society in the modern world, has been consistent with this pattern. . . . The development of innovations has apparently affected the occupational structure of entire industries. For example, between 1947 and 1955 the ratio of non-production workers increased sharply in aircraft, electronics, chemicals, ordnance, and petroleum. Each of these industries developed innovations for its own use, or for use by others. The proportion of highly skilled personnel increased less rapidly in the textile, apparel, lumber, railroad, and utility industries, which adopted, for the most part, innovations developed by others [Hill and Harbison, 1959, pp. 3, 54–55].

B12   Among women, participation in the labor force rises in the industrialized countries to about age twenty and then drops sharply (single women working until marriage); in the nonindustrialized countries, participation is relatively steady from the late teens to about age fifty.

[But] in most of these countries, a labour market in the sense that it is known in industrialized countries is not highly developed. Much of production is carried out in household enterprises, and changes in a woman's marital status or in her responsibilities for the care of children do not have the same implications for her continuation in employment that they have in the industrialized countries where most economic activity is centered outside the home [U.N., 1962, pp. 21–23].

As in the case of men, participation in the labor force is higher for both the young and the old in the nonindustrialized countries.

Marital status is a central factor: single women are in the labor force more than married women, with the divorced and widowed in between; married women without small children more than those with; women with few children more than those with several.

Widowed, divorced and separated women occupy a special position in all communities, and a certain degree of economic security is often provided for them either by custom or by legislation. Social security pensions for widows may be provided in industrially developed countries, while in some less developed countries the extended family may be required by tradition to assure their maintenance. . . . The legal provision of alimony or maintenance allowances may also have the same effect for divorced or separated women. These institutional and cultural factors may be expected to influence the activity rates for widowed, divorced, and separated women. . . . The activity curves for widowed and divorced women are remarkably similar in shape for nearly all countries; they show declining rates with advancing age [*ibid.*, pp. 44–45].

Some scholars believe that in modern Western society the loss of working talent due to the low participation of women in the labor force is greater than the losses due to class or ethnic inequality.

ON THE JOB

B13   Absenteeism and labor turnover, in the modern industrial establishment, are greater in times of full employment, among recently employed workers, among disaffected workers, and in situations of low vitality of informal work groups.

With regard to the last factor:

Research indicates that employees who have no opportunity for close social contact find their work less satisfying, and this lack of satisfaction often reflects itself in lower production and higher turnover and absenteeism. Many years ago Elton Mayo observed that employees in a textile plant who worked at isolated jobs were highly dissatisfied and consistently failed to meet production standards. Staggered rest periods helped a little. But when the company permitted these workers to take rest periods *as a group*, production and satisfaction both increased. Another company, where the girls worked in small, isolated booths, had the same experience. When management put glass partitions between the booths, the rate of turnover and the number of grievances both dropped sharply. Similarly, researchers in hospitals have discovered that maids feel uncomfortable when they work only in the company of high-status personnel (doctors, nurses, etc.) with whom they cannot associate with ease. Several hospitals have found that when three or four maids are grouped together as a team, turnover falls and a much better job is done [Strauss and Sayles, 1960, p. 57].

B14   With regard to work incentives:

.1   In many nonindustrialized countries, money wages are in themselves not a sufficient incentive for a worker's continuous application to his job.

.2   In the advanced industrial society of the United States, piece-rate systems

.2a   do not achieve maximum production and they often lead to worker-management conflict, especially under conditions of mutual distrust.

It is one of the best demonstrated propositions in social science that, in general, workers do not respond to the incentive to the full extent of their physical and mental capacities. In most instances, they reach a point which they come to consider "a fair day's work" and do not go beyond that point. . . . If worker attitudes toward management are hostile and suspicious, we can predict that, no matter how highly developed the time study techniques, the incentive system will be a focal point of conflict. If workers react toward management with a degree of good will and an expectation of good faith, then there will still be incentive problems, but the parties will develop ways for resolving those problems to mutual satisfaction [Whyte and Miller, 1957, pp. 310, 314].

.2b   are least effective for the lowest levels of workers.

.2c   are more effective as group piece work, and in smaller groups.

And there:

In work groups paid on a piece-rate basis we find that norms prescribing restriction of output, and norms prescribing secrecy about earnings and production records may be functional equivalents in one specific sense: both are likely to reduce interpersonal tensions resulting from invidious comparisons of work achievement [Zetterberg, 1961, p. 83].

Another example of the same tendency is the informal transformation of an individual incentive system into a group one, through the pooling of sales (Babchuck and Goode, 1951).

A reminder: There is a very large and detailed literature in applied psychology and industrial relations on this subject and the following one, with varying and often contradictory results arising from the range of circumstances that can affect such matters. We have not attempted to represent it here in all its detailed complexity.

B15   With regard to satisfaction on the job:

.1   The better (perceived) the monetary returns and fringe benefits of the job, the higher the job satisfaction.

.2   The greater the responsibility, authority, prestige, or importance associated with the position, the higher the job satisfaction.

In general:

Work satisfaction varies greatly by occupation. Highest percentages of satisfied workers are usually found among professionals and businessmen. In a given plant, the proportion satisfied is higher among clerical workers than among factory workers, just as in general labor force samples it is higher among middle-class than among manual working-class occupations. Within the manual working-class, job satisfaction is highest among skilled workers, lowest among unskilled laborers and workers on assembly lines [Blauner, 1960, p. 341].

.3   The fuller or the more congenial the organization of informal groups on the job, or the association of coworkers off the job, the higher the job satisfaction.

This is one of the liabilities of the assembly line—its thin, stretched-out arrangement works against the formation of informal work groups (Walker and Guest, 1952). A similar result was found with the introduction of "long-wall" mining practices in England (Trist and Bamforth, 1951). Incidentally, these findings "seem surprisingly similar to the findings of the urban sociologists . . . [with regard to] the change in social organization flowing from the change from the wheel-spoke towns of the railroad days to the modern strip-towns growing up along the highways" (Haire, in Dahl *et al.*, 1959, p. 74).

The power of strong informal groups to reduce turnover and absenteeism has also been remarked upon: in a study of the fast-growing American aircraft industry in World War II, it was found that

> the irregular attendance group were not a group at all, but a collection of unrelated individuals; it is in this collection that one finds the greater part of absenteeism and turnover [Mayo and Lombard, 1944, p. 24].

.4   The less routinized and fragmented the work, the higher the job satisfaction.

For example, in a study of the "man on the assembly line," it was found that "nearly twice as many workers left the jobs with extreme mass production characteristics as left jobs with moderate mass production characteristics"—i.e., repetitiveness, mechanical pacing, frequency of breaks in routine, infrequency of social interaction, etc. (Walker and Guest, 1952, p. 122). Here is one set of illustrative data:

Repetitive and nonrepetitive work as factors in liking or not liking previous jobs

	Repetitive job	*Nonrepetitive job*	*Total*
Liked	13	109	122
No difference	6	6	12
Disliked	28	6	34
Total	47	121	168

$$\chi^2 = 70.93 \qquad p < .001$$

(*Ibid.*, p. 53)

The people who seem to adjust best to monotonous, routine work are those whose basic satisfactions are not tied to the job (e.g., married women devoted to their families).

.5   The more experienced people become in their work careers or the longer they have to "fit" the job, the higher their job satisfaction (after an initial period of high morale at the start).

Morale is high when people start their first jobs; it goes down during the next few years, and remains at a relatively low level; when workers are in their late twenties or early thirties morale begins to rise. This rise continues through the remainder of the working career in most cases [Herzberg et al., 1957, p. 11].

.6   The more flexible, better adjusted, and energetic the worker, the higher the job satisfaction.

The worker dissatisfied with his job . . . is often rigid, inflexible, unrealistic in his choice of goals, unable to overcome environmental obstacles, generally unhappy and dissatisfied. It must be emphasized that not all workers with these psychological characteristics are dissatisfied with their jobs. The data do show that workers dissatisfied with their jobs often show these characteristics [ibid., p. 20].

The relationship between satisfaction with the job and performance on it is complicated and conditional: at any rate, there is no direct, positive correlation. Actually, the over-all finding is still in some dispute. Two recent reviews of the literature came to these conclusions:

In 54 per cent of the reported surveys high morale was associated with *high* productivity; in 35 per cent morale and productivity were *not* found to be related; in 11 per cent high morale was associated with *low* productivity. . . . The correlations obtained in many of the positive studies were low. . . . That positive job attitudes are a tremendous asset to industry is supported by much of the experimental evidence now available [Herzberg et al., pp. 103, 112].

There is little evidence in the available literature that employee attitudes of the type usually measured in morale surveys bear any simple or, for that matter, appreciable relationship to performance on the job [Brayfield and Crockett, 1955, p. 408].

EMPLOYER-EMPLOYEE RELATIONS

B16   The first labor unions in a country are more likely to be formed by skilled than by unskilled workers.

This is presumably the case because of the greater amount of education, ambition, self-consciousness, and self-realization on the part of the skilled workers. In a way, this can be seen as a special case of the general finding that strong moves toward a better life come not from people in the lowest strata but from those who have emerged enough to appreciate what they might get and to have the energy and will to fight for it.

B16.1   White-collar workers are more difficult to organize into unions than blue-collar workers. White-collar unions tend to be most successful when organized alongside strong unions of manual workers (e.g., railway clerks or clerical personnel in the printing industry).

White-collar people are harder to organize, among other reasons, because of their upward ideology, their training outside the factory, and the greater proportion of women in such jobs.

B17   Participation in the union is greater the more homogeneous the groups being represented (e.g., among workers with common ethnic backgrounds, close residences, similar jobs) and the more favorable the attitude toward the union in the immediate social groups to which the worker belongs.

Here, for example, is an illustration of the effect of personal relations off the job, from a study of union printers:

Relationship between informal social relations with other printers and interest in union politics *

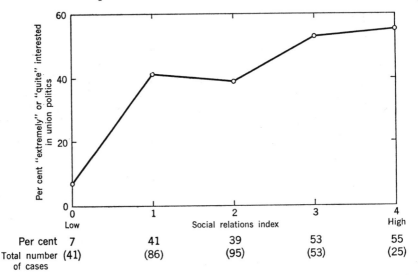

	Low			High
Per cent	7	41	39	53	55
Total number of cases	(41)	(86)	(95)	(53)	(25)

* The social relations index is a measure of the printer's informal contacts with other printers outside the shop.

(Lipset *et al.*, 1956, p. 72)

It has even been found, for example, that "the skilled sons of skilled workers and the unskilled sons of unskilled workers were more likely to be active unionists than the skilled sons of the unskilled, or the unskilled sons of the skilled" (Lipset and Linz, 1956, p. 63). On the broader scene, this is seen as one reason for the recruitment of a small proportion of the potential union members in the United States, where unions "have been handicapped by their slightly illegitimate position relative to the American value system. 'Union' connotes 'class' organization" (Lipset, 1961, p. 82).

Here are the figures on union membership in Europe and the United States in recent years:

Union membership as a percentage of nonagricultural
employment, 1948–56 (annual averages
for three-year periods)

	1948–50	1951–53	1954–56
Denmark	56.0	56.9	57.3
Netherlands	42.5	42.8	40.4
United Kingdom	48.1	47.8	46.8
Germany	41.5	45.0	41.3
Norway	55.4	57.5	57.5
Sweden	57.7	61.0	62.7
France	55.4	36.8	26.5
Italy	90.1	80.3	74.5
United States	32.1	33.2	33.9

(Ross and Hartman, 1960, p. 17)

B17.1   On the whole, the higher the status of the members and the more satisfied they are, the more actively they participate in union affairs.

Our own studies of grievance behavior confirm the over-representation of the more prestigeful members of the plant community (Sayles & Strauss, *The Local Union*, 1953). Recently an investigator of unofficial strikes in the coal mining industry in Great Britain found that the highest paid production workers (taking into account incentive earnings) contributed most of the stoppages and the lowest paid workers the least, with the craft workers presumably falling somewhere in the middle (Baldwin, 1955) [Sayles, 1958, pp. 43–44].

In one intensive industrial study, the level of participation as well as other activities involving employer-employee relations were found to vary markedly according to type of work group:

Summary of work-group differences

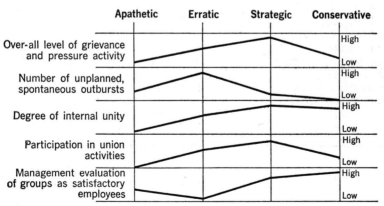

(Sayles, 1958, p. 39, *q.v.* for detailed definition of the types)

B17.2   Participation itself makes for more involvement in union affairs.

Whatever the reason an individual joins the union and participates in its functions, the participation tends to pull him more strongly into union life. There is evidence indicating that most union members become participants either more or less involuntarily or for limited special reasons, but that participation results ultimately in much deeper involvements (Sayles & Strauss, 1953; Rose, 1952) [March and Simon, 1958, pp. 72–73].

B18   Favorable attitudes toward the union are not automatically correlated with unfavorable attitudes toward the company: rather the contrary.

If the member is for the union, does this mean he must be against management? That this picture of one-sided loyalty is a misconception is one of the best demonstrated propositions in industrial relations research today. . . . Statistically, we find substantial correlations indicating that prounionists tend to be promanagement too, while antiunionists tend to be antimanagement also [Whyte and Miller, 1957, p. 326].

In one study of a large plant, for example, it was found that 57 per cent of the foremen, 73 per cent of the workers, and 88 per cent of the stewards expressed "dual allegiance," i.e., were favorable to both union and management (Purcell, 1953, p. 263). Here are the data:

Dual Allegiance in Chicago Swift-UPWA Plant Community
(random, stratified sample of 192 employees,
by sex, race, and service: 1950; percentages)

Employees	Men	Women	Negro	White	Short service	Middle service	Long service
Unfavorable to both	0	0	0	0	0	0	0
Neutral to both	.5	0	0	1	0	2	0
Neutral to company, favorable to union	4	0	4	2	5	4	2
Neutral to union, favorable to company	8	4	3	10	5	5	11
Neutral to union, unfavorable to company	.5	0	1	0	2	0	0
Favorable to company, unfavorable to union	12	24	10	20	7	10	27
Favorable to union, unfavorable to company	.5	0	1	0	2	0	0
Dual allegiance	74	71	80	67	79	79	60

(*Ibid.*, p. 264)

B19   The longer the history of union-management relations, the shorter the duration of the strikes that do occur.

We should note the remarkable abbreviation of strikes as a whole during the twentieth century. This trend has operated almost everywhere. The decline has not come about quickly or spasmodically, but steadily and gradually. . . . [There are] two reasons for the general trend. First, the modern strike is less frequently a trial of economic strength, and more often a demonstration of protest, than the strike of previous decades. Second, even the classical collective-bargaining strike is settled more rapidly than it previously was [Ross and Hartman, 1960, pp. 24–25].

Here are the data:

Average duration of strikes

	1900–29 (days)	1948–56 (days)	1948–56 as per cent of 1900–29
Denmark	28.7	4.3	15
Netherlands	32.7	7.5	23
United Kingdom	23.0	4.3	19
Germany	15.6	9.9	63
Norway	33.6	15.2	45
Sweden	37.1	22.6	61
France	14.4	2.9	20
India	26.6	8.8	33
Canada	27.1	19.3	71
Australia	14.2	3.2	23
Finland	36.0	15.8	44
South Africa	15.8	2.6	16

(*Ibid.*, p. 24)

B19.1   There is greater propensity to strike in industries that by their nature tend to insulate the workers from the larger community (such as mining or lumbering).

Here are the hypothesis and the data from a central study:

(a) Industries will be highly strike prone when the workers (i) form a relatively homogeneous group which (ii) is unusually isolated from the general community and which (iii) is capable of cohesion; and (b) industries will be comparatively strike free when their workers (i) are individually integrated into the larger society, (ii) are members of trade groups which are coerced by government or the market to avoid strikes, or (iii) are so individually isolated that strike action is impossible. . . .

The members of these groups [the isolated industries] not only have the same grievances, but they have them at the same time, at the same place, and against the same people. In the more peaceful industries, their inevitable grievances are dispersed—by stratification of the workers (as in steel), by scattering of the employees (as in agriculture), by absorption of the workers into a mixed community (as in trade), by scattering of the targets (the employer, the landlord, the grocer, and the policemen being quite different people). . . . Industrial tranquillity depends on keeping grievances dispersed so that they may be handled one at a time. Proponents of social unrest are most successful in those places where, and at those times when, grievances are highly concentrated [Kerr and Siegel, 1954, pp. 195, 192].

General pattern of strike propensities *

Propensity to Strike	Industry
High	Mining
	Maritime and longshore
Medium high	Lumber
	Textile
Medium	Chemical
	Printing
	Leather
	Manufacturing (general)
	Construction
	Food and kindred products
Medium low	Clothing
	Gas, water, and electricity
	Services (hotels, restaurants, etc.)
Low	Railroad
	Agriculture
	Trade

* From Clark Kerr and Abraham Siegel, "The Interindustry Propensity to Strike: An International Comparison," in *Industrial Conflict*, edited by A. Kornhauser, R. Dubin, and A. M. Ross. Copyright 1954. McGraw-Hill Book Company, Inc. Used by permission.

(*Ibid.*, p. 190)

B20   The typical development of labor-management negotiations is from the single firm to the industry and then to the national economy via political action.

B20.1   Bargaining is more characteristic of prosperity, political action more characteristic of depression or the threat thereof.

B21   As a union becomes established, it tends: (a) to take over some management functions (such as recruitment, discipline, promotion); (b) to take over management points of view and practices (such as concern for production and professionalization of its own staff); (c) to develop a bureaucracy of its own (for example, its leadership changes from "social movement" to "organization"); (d) to centralize its own practices; (e) to lessen its demands upon management; (f) to have a decrease in active participation from its own members.

An intensive analysis of the two-party system in a single union concluded with a list of about twenty-five conditions making for greater chances of democratic processes within a union: see Lipset *et al.*, 1956, pp. 414–17.

Political Institutions

PARTIES, GOVERNMENTS, SYSTEMS *

C1 In a modern democratic industrial country, with substantial social heterogeneity, political parties must appeal to a range of social groups in order to secure a majority.

As a matter of fact, this seems to have been the case even in the earliest days of the United States:

> Using ecological techniques, Dauer (1953) showed that the Federalists disappeared as a party because they were oriented toward the urban middle-class part of their social base, and antagonized the rural part of their initial support. He suggests that even at the beginning of American political history, parties had to include a variety of strata among their supporters to get a majority, that the tendency of Hamilton and other right-wing Federalist leaders to build a one class party led to the collapse of their party [Lipset, 1957a, p. 6].

This finding means, for example, that conservative parties must stress issues which do not divide people along class lines in order to extend their support down the social pyramid; that radical parties in democratic countries must soften their doctrine to extend their appeal upward; that agrarian parties must extend their appeal to urban groups; and so on. Partly as a corollary, business groups in democratic countries tend to maintain ties with all major political parties, for the obvious reasons.

C2   The more rigid the stratification of the society, the more likely it is that class-oriented parties will emerge.

C3   Religious parties are most likely to emerge when the church considers itself God-ordained; when it considers itself opposed on church rights by a significant political group; when it is a substantial and concentrated

* This section is bound up with traditional political science and hence is especially hard to define sharply. Although the boundaries seem to be fuzzier here, and the determination of what is not behavioral-science knowledge particularly difficult, the section can, we hope, be viewed as indicative of the available generalizations.

minority within the country; and when the political system of the country is multiparty rather than two-party in nature. Upon establishment, the religious party is likely to take a central position in opposition to class-oriented politics; and it is likely to be welcomed as a coalition partner by secular parties, because of the difference in what each side considers the salient issues.

C4   Agrarian parties are more likely to emerge when a large proportion of the population is dependent on agriculture; when the urban-rural differences are great or sharply growing (as under conditions of rapid industrialization); when there is a sizable peasant society of the traditional kind; and when there is no strong religious party as an alternative.

C5   Regional parties can emerge on economic, social, or historical grounds, but they typically require additional differences of an ethnic, religious, linguistic, or cultural character to sustain themselves.

   C5.1   Regional parties, across countries, tend to be conservative in their political leanings and hence a form of modified class politics; and regional interests within national parties, being more or less permanent minorities, tend to be opportunistic in political alignments for regional benefits.

C6   In a system or region dominated by a monopolistic party, political activity is more likely to be directed to change within the party itself than to its overthrow and supplanting.

   Partly this is due simply to the greater opportunity for personal and social gain that exists within the party (an effort from outside is likely to be quixotic); and partly because a long period of political control will so interweave the political institution with other institutions in the community that it will tend to be supported lest all lose together.

C7   Despite the concentration on party differences, especially during political campaigns, supporters of opposing national parties in democratic societies agree on a wide range of political matters important to the security of the society.

   In a study of an American community, for example, it was found that "even in the heat of a presidential campaign there are only minor disagreements between Republicans and Democrats on a wide range of political considerations"—what the important issues were, the criteria to judge by, the expectations about the political future, the importance of the election, even on certain political issues (Berelson *et al.*, 1954, p. 185). Here are some examples of partisan agreement:

On such style issues as internationalism and civil rights, there is either general consensus or nonpartisan dispute

International opinions	Percentages		Civil rights opinions	Percentages

International opinions	Percentages (Rep / Dem)
Country better off if not so many foreigners here	35 / 29
Approve the admission of 200,000 refugees	39 / 39
In the present trouble in Palestine, the Jews are more in the right than the Arabs	45 / 44
Communist spies are a threat to this country	75 / 66
The United States should be firmer with Russia	83 / 77

Civil rights opinions	Percentages (Rep / Dem)
America must be on guard against the power of the Catholic Church	16 / 8
Jews are generally dishonest in business dealings	26 / 32
Negroes are generally lazy and ignorant	43 / 31
There is a "very great need" to improve the position of Negroes and other minority groups	46 / 47

■ Republicans
□ Democrats

(Berelson *et al.*, 1954, p. 190)

It is this sort of agreement that makes for the successful operation of a pluralist political system. As the authors state:

Such organizing agreements, though "needed," are not always built into the system by rational and purposive design. They arise from diverse sources: from the pressure of commonly experienced events and the uniform interpretation given them by the mass media; from objective reality itself; from a myriad of small-scale factors inducing disagreement within but agreement between the lines of larger social organization on which parties are based; from the giant weight of the American cultural and political tradition that blankets all segments of society. From such sources may (or may not) come the elements of consensus that permit a reasonably orderly and peaceable debate on political issues. For a democratic political system to survive as an institution organizing and containing the social struggle, the partisans must hold positions in common as well as in opposition [*ibid.*, p. 193–94].

C8   In the United States, the weaker the two-party system in a state, the more pressure groups are likely to influence the state government.

C9   The more heterogeneous the background of the civil service, the more likely it is to take a mediating or professional position with regard to contending political parties, and thus over time to shift issues from political to bureaucratic decisions.

Those interested in furthering social change have viewed this norm as a conservative force, since it operates to force reformist administrations to retain in office civil servants whose social background and training disposes them to object to many reformist policies (as documented in Lipset, 1950, ch. 12). The same norm, viewed from the perspective of the requisites of a democratic political system, operates to make possible the continuity of democratic government during a turnover in political offices. By permitting a separation between the personnel of the government and the personalities and policies of politicians temporarily in office, bureaucracy in government decreases the strains of party strife [Lipset, 1959, p. 102].

C10   In the legislature, in the United States, those representatives whose margin of election was narrow tend to follow their constituencies in legislative voting; those whose districts are most typical of their party's constituency tend to follow the party's position and are least likely to cross party lines; and those whose own opinions are extreme relative to their state are more likely to seek their political careers in the legislature than in state-wide office.

Here is an instance of the first two findings in a state legislature.

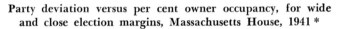

Party deviation versus per cent owner occupancy, for wide and close election margins, Massachusetts House, 1941 *

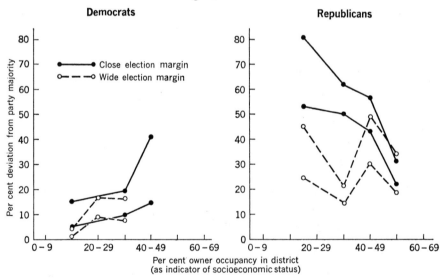

* The upper line of each pair shows the most deviant quartile; only one-fourth of the representatives from a given type of district deviated from their party majority more than this. The lower line of each pair shows the median per-cent deviation; half the representatives of a given type of district deviated more, and half less, than this value.

(MacRae, 1952, p. 1052)

The general tendency of the curves is the same: toward greater deviation in districts less characteristic of the party. The Republican representatives with wide election margins were more "regular" . . . than were those with close margins, especially in atypical districts. The same is true of the Democrats in this session, though to a lesser degree [*ibid.*, p. 1052].

C11   Democratic political institutions are likely to be stable over a long period when the following social conditions are present:

   a   some, but not great, differences in culture or standard of living among classes.

Nondemocratic governments appear to be more likely under conditions of extreme social similarity or extreme social disparity (for example, when there is a small ruling elite with a large mass far removed in social interaction).

   b   few sharp discontinuities due to such major historical movements as industrialization, urbanization, war, depression, or a shift out of feudalism or colonialism.

   c   open leadership, accessible to various groups within the society (or at least perceived to be), and diversity of background of leaders.

   d   substantial numbers of intermediate organizations, between the primary group or the family on the one hand and the society on the other, that tie the individual to the national scene, provide representation of his interests, and limit the power of the national government and of other organizations. Those sections of major social strata (e.g., classes) that are poorly integrated tend to support mass movements in disproportionate numbers.

The first-named social category in each of the following pairs possesses the fewer social ties and is more responsive to mass movements.
   (a) free-lance intellectuals vs. intellectuals in corporate bodies (e.g., universities);
   (b) new business vs. old business;
   (c) small business vs. big business;
   (d) unskilled workers vs. skilled workers;
   (e) mining and maritime workers vs. workers in other kinds of industry;
   (f) poor farmers and farm laborers vs. small farmers vs. wealthier farmers;
   (g) youth (especially students) vs. adults;
   (h) politically apathetic vs. politically involved;
   (i) unemployed vs. employed [Kornhauser, 1959, p. 223].

   e   cross-cutting, overlapping, pluralistic identifications among parties and political positions, rather than sharply clear and distinct associations.

When people are pulled in different directions by their personal allegiances, political minorities are better protected and political conflict lessened.

    f   predominantly secular ideologies.

C11.1   The more stable the democratic system, the more the different groups within it will respond similarly to the same major events.

> If conditions facilitate the growth of leftist opinion, then the Socialists should gain votes among the well-to-do and among the workers, although they remain relatively weaker in the upper strata. And Conservatives should grow among the poorer groups during a period of right-wing ascendancy. Conversely, an indicator of low consensus would be a situation in which a political tendency grows only among the groups to whom it primarily appeals—for example, the left gaining among the workers, while an opposite trend grows in other strata—i.e., the right gaining among the middle classes. This is precisely the situation which Marxists call revolutionary, and which . . . occurred in Germany before 1933 and in Moscow and Petrograd in 1917 [Lipset, 1960, p. 33].

INDIVIDUALS AND GROUPS *

Political Participation

C12   People who participate in politics in one way are likely to do so in another; and there is roughly an increasing order of participation from active campaigning for one's candidate, to reading about and talking politics, to "being interested," to voting.

That is, relatively few work for their party, but those who do are relatively high on each succeeding measure of participation. Thus, many people who vote are not really interested in the election but do so simply out of social pressure, as is illustrated on page 423. It also appears that, on the whole, fewer people think an election affects them personally than think it makes a difference to the nation—in one study, 30 per cent and 72 per cent respectively (Saenger, 1945).

C12.1   Activists within political parties are likely to come from ethnic groups that sanction gregarious activities and/or seek political advancement; from occupations free of regular work schedules and directly benefiting from political activity (e.g., lawyers, real estate and insurance salesmen) ; and from the dominant social group within the locality being represented.

---

* There is some similarity in subject matter between the following material and that in the chapter on opinions, attitudes, and beliefs, and the reader is referred there for further information.

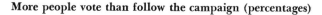

More people vote than follow the campaign (percentages)

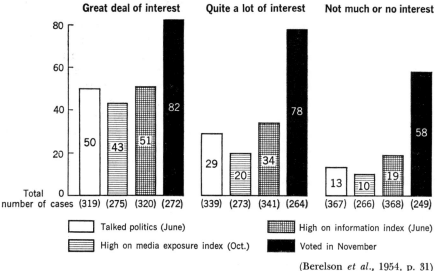

(Berelson *et al.*, 1954, p. 31)

With regard to this last:

An inquiry carried out amongst Parisian branches of the Socialist party seems to reveal a fairly close correspondence between the quality of militants and the social environment of the branch; it may be expressed in the following formula: the nature of the militants tends to coincide with the dominant social category. In a branch with a working-class majority, the militants are chiefly workmen, the proportion of workmen amongst them being higher than their proportion amongst the members. On the other hand, in a branch situated in a middle-class quarter, of which the majority of members are civil servants, tradesmen, lawyers, teachers, and so on, the proportion of militants of middle-class origin exceeds their proportion of the membership. . . . The explanation seems to be fairly clear; in a branch that is predominantly middle class, the workmen feel isolated amongst people who share their political opinions but not their mentality, their daily preoccupations or their instinctive reactions; the same is true for the middle-class members of a predominantly working-class branch. Social differences among members seem therefore to provide an obstacle to the development of militancy. One is tempted to say that the more homogeneous the milieu, the higher the index of militancy. Herein lies the superiority of techniques of organization by separate and homogeneous milieux, such as are to be found in Communist cells [Duverger, 1959, pp. 112–13].

C13 The higher a person's socioeconomic and educational level—especially the latter—the higher his political interest, participation, and voting turnout.

Studies done in several countries all show a clear correlation between social status and political activity of various kinds.

The higher one is in the social structure, the more likely one is to be sophisticated about politics. This assumption flows from a number of attributes: 1) the higher status individuals are better educated, and presumably the more education one has the more likely he is to understand and perceive the consequences of politics; 2) in general, the higher one's economic position, the more directly does government action impinge on his welfare, and consequently the more likely is he to understand the need for political theory; 3) the higher one is in the social structure the more likely is he to interact with persons who are politically knowledgeable and active, for the higher his status the more likely is he to receive information about politics from exposure to various media [Lipset and Linz, 1956, pp. 17–18].

As we just saw, the major exception is that political action is relatively high among lower socioeconomic groups in communities in which they dominate the political and/or social spheres.

C14   Men are more active politically than women.

In addition:

A moralized political orientation characteristic of women, arising from maternal responsibilities, exclusion from more socially valued areas of activity, and narrower orbits, tends to focus female political attention upon persons and peripheral "reform" issues [Lane, 1959, p. 216].

C15   Middle-age groups are more active politically than young adults or the old.

Life conditions associated with middle age, including property ownership, family responsibilities, acceptance of group status, and more homogeneous social environment, tend to promote greater political interests and participation [*ibid.,* p. 219].

C16   Urban residents are somewhat more active politically than rural residents, especially with regard to national affairs.

In addition, it is probable that

the greater the sense of differences between group members of a voting district and surrounding populations, the greater the participation of group members in politics (enclave effect) [*ibid.,* p. 264].

C17   Wherever they are permitted to participate, minority ethnic groups are at least as active politically as the community at large.

In fact, a little more can be said:

> The greater the ethnic conflict in a community (where all may vote) the greater the rates of participation of the conflicting groups. . . . [And] the less impartial and "bureaucratized" the administration of justice and services, the more ethnic (and other socially identifiable) groups will be drawn into politics. The conduct of American municipal administration is unusually sensitive to the relative voting strength of ethnic groups, [and hence] ethnics usually participate more in local politics than non-ethnics [Lane, 1959, p. 243].

C18   People who tend to be involved in social affairs generally—community residents of some duration, those active in voluntary associations and other organized activity and closely tied to the broader society—tend to be active politically as well; and they are the first to respond to broad changes affecting the group with which they are identified.

For example, a study of the growth of "agrarian socialism" in Saskatchewan, via the Cooperative Commonwealth Federation, found that

> when the attitudes of a class are in flux, because of changing social and economic pressures, those who are most thoroughly integrated in the class through formal organization are the first to change. . . . The unorganized mass became C.C.F. supporters only gradually, following the organizationally active members of their class [Lipset, 1950, pp. 197–98].

C19   People with well-adjusted personalities are likely to be active politically (in nonextremist politics, that is).

C20   The more cross-pressures the individual is subject to, from conflicting political attitudes or social positions or group affiliations or personal environments, the less his political interest, participation, and voting turnout; the later he makes up his mind on political issues; and the more changeable his political preference.

Data from an early voting study are presented in the chart on page 426.

C21   At least in the United States, political participation is greater in periods of crisis than in quiescent periods; greater in national than in local elections; greater on domestic "class" issues than on foreign policy (though this may now be softening); and greater on sectional issues than on class issues.

> Slavery, reconstruction, free land, monetary policies, including the monetization of silver, tariff, control of trusts, labor, social security, relief, all seem to have been historically more salient than foreign policy. . . . Historically, periods of sectional conflict in the United States (North against South, East against West)

Both cross-pressures and lack of interest delay the final voting decision. (Their joint effect is especially strong. Separately, they show about equal strength.)

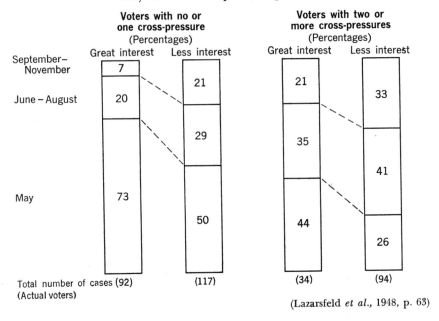

(Lazarsfeld *et al.*, 1948, p. 63)

have experienced greater electoral turnout than periods of class conflict [Lane, 1959, pp. 25–26].

C21.1   Depression and unemployment lead to political apathy on the part of the lower socioeconomic strata more readily than to radical political action. Political action by the lower socioeconomic strata is more likely in the upturn than in the trough of the depression.

Political Preferences

C22   The higher the socioeconomic status, the greater the conservative vote.

This is the omnibus finding. Socioeconomic status is variously indicated by income, occupation, class identification, education, and so on; and conservatism-liberalism is usually defined with reference to the broader distribution of income or power.

Every study of the social basis of political movements in the several countries of Western civilization indicates that the parties represent distinctive strata. Despite the great and complex diversity of historical conditions among the "Western" countries, three main political tendencies stand out in all of them: the left, based on the working class; the conservative right, based on the more privileged strata and institutions; and the center, based on the middle classes, especially the self-employed [Bendix and Lipset, 1957, p. 91].

Here is just one among many possible illustrations:

Party preference of the major divisions of the German nonfarm population (men and women) (percentages)

	Working class	Urban middle class		
		Salaried middle class	Inde-pendents	Total
Socialist and Communist	50	25	15	21
Christian Democrat	32	51	49	49
Bourgeois	9	16	29	21
Other	9	8	8	8
Total number of cases	(1172)	(669)	(414)	(1083)

(Linz, 1959, p. 200)

In effect, the finding is explained in the obvious way: the top layers of a society have more to conserve so they vote conservative, the lower layers want more so they vote to change the going arrangements. This general finding can be qualified and elaborated in a number of ways, as follows:

C22.1   Class is the single most important differentiator of political preferences across societies; it is more important in urban than in rural areas.

Actually, although concern is often voiced about the "labor vote," there is probably a more solidary "business vote," in the sense that there is less deviation from the class vote among upper status groups—who, being better educated and better informed as well as more homogeneously supported in personal contacts, are more likely to recognize and express their class interest.

C22.2   Within each social class, the upper strata are more likely than the lower to hold conservative views.

In countries in which workers are faced with a choice between two large labor-oriented parties, the skilled and better paid section of the working class is more likely to support the moderate left (Socialists) while the unskilled and less-well paid are more prone to back the extreme left (Communists) [Lipset and Linz, 1956, p. 6].

Similarly, owners of large farms are more conservative in political preferences than the owners of small farms, farm tenants, or farm laborers.

C22.3   The more the upward mobility, the greater the conservative political preferences, to the extent that those moving up are accepted as "belonging" by those already at the top.

This last phrase distinguishes the normal situation in the United States from that in some European countries where the newly arrived, economically, are not accepted socially and react by not conforming to upper-class practices politically. In Germany and Sweden, for example, skilled workers tend to be more radical than unskilled. And in the United States, the better-off radicals tend to be members of ethnic or religious minorities.

C22.3a   The greater the (perceived) opportunity for upward mobility, the less radical the political preferences.

In general, it seems true that the greater the emphasis which the values of a society place on the possibility of upward mobility, the less radical in the sense of favoring major changes in the stratification order are its lower classes [Lipset and Linz, 1956, p. 13].

This is often cited as an explanation for the reformist views of American labor, as compared with the radical and revolutionary views of European labor.

C22.4   The difference in political preferences between high and low socioeconomic strata is likely to be greater (a) the more "closed" the society (i.e., the less the chance of upward mobility by the lower groups) and (b) the more divergent their respective satisfactions with the going order.

At the same time, and as a major qualifier of the main finding:

C23   The higher a person's socioeconomic status, and especially his education, the more liberal his political preferences, when these do not deal directly with class (rich-poor) distinctions—i.e., the more liberal his democratic values, such as civil liberties, freedom of speech, and so on.

This is a significant point in two ways. First, it means that the leaders of the society are more advanced on such matters than are the rank and file. Second, it means that the romantic-radical notion of the working class as the repository of political virtue is false.

Here, for example, are some data from an American study made during the McCarthy period (the community leaders are on the average better educated than the cross-sections):

Community leaders are more willing than the rank and file to give nonconformists the right to speak

Question: If a person wanted to make a speech in your community favoring government ownership of all the railroads and big industries, should he be allowed to speak, or not?

Percentage answering

	No	No opinion	Yes	
Selected community leaders	14		84	(1500)
Cross-section in same cities as leaders	29	10	61	(897)
National cross-section, rural and urban	31	11	58	(4953)

■ No   ▤ No opinion   ☐ Yes

Question: If a person wanted to make a speech in your community against churches and religion, should he be allowed to speak, or not?

	No	Yes
Selected community leaders	34	64
Cross-section in same cities as leaders	58	39
National cross-section, rural and urban	60	37

Question: Consider a man whose loyalty has been questioned before a Congressional committee, but who swears under oath he has never been a Communist. Should he be allowed to make a speech in your community, or not?

	No	Yes
Selected community leaders	11	87
Cross-section in same cities as leaders	21	71
National cross-section, rural and urban	21	70

Question: Suppose an admitted Communist wants to make a speech in your community. Should he be allowed to speak, or not?

	No	Yes
Selected community leaders	47	51
Cross-section in same cities as leaders	66	29
National cross-section, rural and urban	68	27

(Stouffer, 1955, pp. 29, 33, 36, 41)

C24   Within socioeconomic status, occupation appears to be more important than income in determining political preference; the basic split is between white-collar and manual workers.

There are a number of additional findings that cover specific occupations. A large amount of detailed data in support of them, from studies in various countries, appears in Lipset and Linz, 1956.

PROFESSIONALS

C24.1   By and large, in Western democracies, professionals are about as conservative in political preference as business groups.

Given the fact that professionals are among the most privileged groups in income and prestige, and that they rank their social class position high and are perhaps the most satisfied occupational group in terms of job satisfaction, we should expect that they will also be among the more conservative strata of the society. The data taken from various public opinion studies in different countries bears out this assumption [Lipset and Linz, 1956, p. 9].

C24.2   The more closely a profession is tied to the business community, the more conservative its political preferences.

For example, engineers and lawyers are high on conservatism, university professors low.

C24.2a   The "free," self-employed, creative professions are particularly likely to hold extreme political preferences.

For example, artists, writers, and "intellectuals" tend to support the liberal or radical side—certainly more so than the professions mentioned above. In general, such professionals are opposed to the whole way of life represented by the business community and hence oppose the conservative political positions associated therewith.

C24.2b   Civil servants are unlikely to take extreme political positions, especially in countries with stable forms of government.

Basically the civil servants seem to be among the most moderate elements in the society, a fact which may not only reflect their greater economic security but their identification with and dependence on the existing system of political arrangements, which would be changed by an extremist party [Lipset and Linz, 1956, p. 52].

C24.3   Especially among professionals, the greater the disparity between aspiration and achievement, the more likely are extreme political positions.

For example, members of "second-choice" professions are more likely to hold extreme political positions than are those in "first-choice" professions·

Men who have been forced to enter their "second-choice" occupation will show higher degrees of discontent than those who have reached their original aspirations, and this discontent will in part be directed against the social system, and be revealed in the higher propensity to back political parties which oppose the *status quo* [Lipset and Linz, 1956, p. 9].

During depressions or other circumstances that limit their opportunities, university students (aspiring professionals) also tend to take extreme stands.

BUSINESSMEN

C24.4   Within business, the leaders of industries that deal directly with other business firms (e.g., heavy industry) are more conservative in their political preferences than those who deal directly with the public (lighter industry, the distributional and processing industries, etc.).

C24.5   Within business, big business is more conservative than small business; and being less subject to cross-pressures, it is less changeable.

> **C24.5a**   The smaller the community, the more conservative the political preferences of small business.

In a small community, all businessmen are likely to hold high status (as well as to have personal relations with one another, thus reinforcing themselves); whereas in a large community, the small businessman takes second place to the big businessman.

C24.6   White-collar workers tend to be less committed to a political position than the owners and managers on the one hand or the manual workers on the other.

The organization of industry and commerce in large units has created a "new middle class" of salaried white-collar workers who are more mobile, less integrated in their communities, and who see fewer stakes in political decisions than the old middle class of small rentiers, shop-keepers, and other property owners [Lane, 1959, p. 326].

This can be seen as the operation of cross-pressures on a large scale.

WORKERS

C24.7   The less the contact between manual workers and other groups in the society, and the more among themselves, the more liberal (sometimes radical) their political preferences.

As a specific example:

The longer a worker and his family have been workers, the more likely is he to support labor-oriented political movements [Lipset and Linz, 1956, p. 60].

C24.7a   The earlier, easier, and more successful the organized class action of workers—in securing political rights and representation via their own political party or trade union—the more moderate their political preferences.

C24.7b   Union members are more likely to vote liberal than non-members.

But note that in the United States, for example,

union membership is associated with Democratic voting less through organized or official pressure than through the interaction that the union environment leads to [Berelson *et al.*, 1954, p. 50].

C24.7c   The less the workers are members of broad community organizations, the more liberal are their political preferences.

C24.7d   The larger the place of employment and the place of residence, the more liberal the political preferences.

Not only are large factories characterized by greater impersonality in worker-management relations, and reduction in inter-class communications, but the larger the size of the work unit, the greater the likelihood that *inter-occupational* communication may take place which will have political consequences. That is, the larger the group, the greater the possibility that a politically aware opinion leader will be present who will help channel workers' attitudes into the modal class pattern [Lipset and Linz, 1956, p. 26].

In addition, the more the worker is subject to managerial authority and routine work, the more liberal his political preferences.

For example, employees on mass production lines in large industrial plants are more liberal than artisans with corresponding skills.

C24.7e   The more isolated the workers' community or the more strongly working class it is, the more radical the political preferences.

Thus, such occupations as mining, lumbering, fishing, sailoring, sheepherding, etc.—which combine isolation of the work community with hard physical work, absentee ownership of the plant, and often of the community, instability in employment, and low opportunity for job mobility—are especially likely to develop radical political preferences.

Cut off from cross-pressures flowing from contact with other sections of the community, facing a highly visible economic class opponent and having available easy means of intra-group communication, the isolated workers are better able to express collectively their discontent with their social and economic situation than are workers exposed to a politically more heterogeneous environment [Lipset and Linz, 1956, pp. 58–59].

C24.7f   The less workers are attached to political organizations of their own class, the more variable their political preferences (even from one extreme to the other).

C24.8   The greater the ratio of farm laborers to farm owners, the more liberal the laborers' political preferences.

Where the ratio of farm labor to farm owner is low, the farm laborer's social situation tends to resemble that of the domestic servant. He is in close personal contact with his employer, often lives adjacent to him, and hence is strongly and frequently exposed to the employer's values. Conversely, the farm laborer is isolated from participation in any farm labor class group and will not be reached by leftist parties [Lipset and Linz, 1956, p. 18].

C24.8a   Farm owners who do not employ farm laborers are more likely to hold liberal political preferences than those who do employ them, especially in large numbers.

C24.9   Particularly in agriculture, political preferences are tied to the prosperity of the group.

In the United States, this is due partly to the traditional self-interestedness of farmers in politics and partly to the historical bias of systems of political representation, which have operated in their favor, so that they have been able to exert more pressure per political unit than the urban worker. As a result:

C24.9a   Farmers growing a crop for market (as against subsistence farmers) are more likely to be changeable in political preferences, especially when dependent on a single cash crop (such as wheat).

C25   In most Western countries there is a clear relationship between religion and political preference.

For example, Catholicism is associated in the United States with the liberal (Democratic) position, whereas in European countries with Catholic political parties, it is associated more with the conservative, or at least the antiradical, position. More precisely:

Those religious groups which have occupied or continue to occupy a privileged position in society support the conservative forces, while those which are in a weaker position tend to back the more liberal or leftist parties. . . . Churches which are or have been state churches are more likely to be linked with conservative parties. . . . Churches which are dominant numerically in a given country are more likely to be conservative. . . . Churches which are disproportionately the churches of the well-to-do and those associated with high-status ethnic groups are more likely to be conservative [Lipset and Linz, 1956, pp. 1, 2].

Incidentally, this finding does not necessarily mean that the association between vote and religion is dictated by the latter, or consciously selected for religious reasons. It can also be, and often is, simply a reflection of primary group ties—like living with like and responding alike. In the United States, at least, this relationship between being Catholic and voting Democratic holds (a) regardless of the voter's position on the issues and (b) especially for the devout.

C25.1   Political parties connected with a particular religion are more likely to be supported by women, by rural residents, by the devout, and by the middle and lower classes than by other groups; and they are more likely to be supported if they are associated with a minority religion in the country.

C26   Women are more likely than men to hold conservative political preferences, especially in countries where church-related political parties are active.

C27   Young people tend to hold political preferences opposed to those held by the older members of their own class or ethnic group.

However, the matter is quite complicated and not easily summarized in this way; there are many associated conditions too detailed to go into here. In any case, the differences are not large, since the so-called generational rebels are not many.

C28   The more homogeneous a person's attitudinal, personal, and social background, the more firmly his political preferences are held and the more they conform to the modal position of the group. The less homogeneous the background—that is, the more cross-pressures the individual is subject to—the more changeable his preferences.

The more consistent the attitudes held on subsidiary issues, the more the surrounding people are of like mind, and the more the social characteristics tend toward the same political position, the stronger and more stable is the political preference. In short, the more "appropriate" the preference is to the social location, the less it will change; mutual support provides stability. Here are some examples of the type of cross-pressures involved:

Upper economic groups that have lower social positions are more likely to hold liberal political preferences than those of the same economic position whose social position is of high status.

White-collar people living in working-class districts are more likely to hold liberal political preferences than those living in middle-class districts; the same holds true for workers.

Workers belonging to middle-class organizations are more likely to hold conservative political preferences than those belonging only to working-class organizations. Similarly, white-collar people belonging to unions are more likely to hold liberal political preferences than those who are not members.

Since the dominant climate of opinion in the United States is a "middle-class position," there is more deviance in political preference among the lower classes than among the upper.

Lower-class people belonging to high-status churches are more likely to hold conservative political preferences than those belonging to low-status churches; and vice versa for upper-class people.

C29   The more gradual any major social transition—such as industrialization, depression, gross movement of population, granting of political rights, or legitimation of a reform movement—the more moderate the political preferences, especially among the working class.

> It is precisely in the countries where workers have been able to form strong unions and secure representation in politics that disintegrative forms of political cleavage are least likely to be found. Communist movements have developed in those countries which are most inclined to deny legitimacy to unions and other democratic expressions of working-class aspirations [Lipset, 1959, p. 113].

As a related matter, in the 1930 depression and across nine European countries, the more severe the depression, the more the Communists gained:

> Using the per cent of the labor force unemployed at the time of the first election following the onslaught of the depression as an indicator of the severity of the economic crisis, and the per cent change in the Communist rate over the last pre-depression election as an indicator of the extremist response to the crisis, the correlation . . . is +.85. If the Fascist vote is included along with that of the Communist vote (excluding those countries which had no Fascist parties), the correlation increases to +.93. This suggests that the more severe the crisis the greater the extremist response [Kornhauser, 1959, pp. 160–61].

The same study reports a correlation of −.93 between per capita income in 1949 and the percentage of the Communist vote in the next election, in sixteen Western democracies—that is, the higher the income, the lower the Communist vote.

C30   As a result of their stable social bases and the impact of historical events, there is substantial continuity in the political preferences of major groups and sections, at least in the United States.

As examples, the Catholic vote in New York state in 1844 was "over-whelmingly Democratic" (Benson, 1961, p. 270); the Negro Republicans in Detroit "were born south of the Mason-Dixon line. This indicates rather clearly that such support as the Republican Party currently receives from Negro Protestants is a survival of the Lincoln heritage" (Lenski, 1961, p.

125). The voting behavior in a sample area in Indiana has been remarkably stable for generations (Key and Munger, 1959). Here is one set of data from this last:

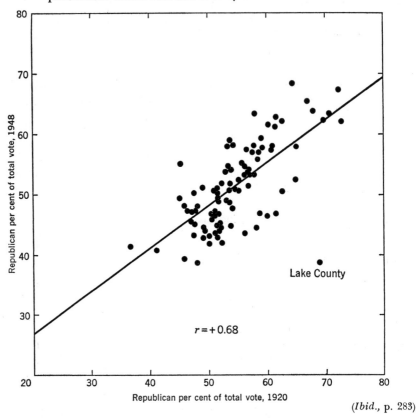

The traditional vote: relation between Republican percentage of total presidential vote in 1920 and 1948 by counties in Indiana

r = +0.68

Lake County

Republican per cent of total vote, 1948

Republican per cent of total vote, 1920

(*Ibid.*, p. 283)

Although most counties were more Democratic in 1948 than in 1920, a substantial correlation, +0.689, existed between the Republican percentages for the two elections. Generally where the Republicans were strong in 1920, they were relatively strong in 1948; where the Democrats were weak in 1920, they were relatively weak in 1948 [*ibid.*, p. 286].

Educational Institutions

Most of the research on educational institutions has been carried out in the United States, so the following findings are based mainly on American experience. In all likelihood, however, they are not all restricted to this country.

D1 Aspiration for and attainment of higher education depend not only on intellectual capacity but also on social class and certain ethnic characteristics (males only).

Accepting the fact that the intelligence of the student is one important determinant of recruitment into the higher educational systems, these studies have shown that when intelligence is controlled, there is still an important variation in recruitment resulting from the effects of the social class and ethnic background of the students. An excellent review of the research on high school dropouts (Allen, 1956) supports this conclusion. With respect to higher education, research by Sibley (1942) shows that both the high school student's intelligence and his father's occupation are related to the amount of education he will obtain [Brim, 1958, p. 37].

A recent analysis of a large sample of American students showed that family status and scholastic ability were about equal in affecting their plans to go to college:

Per cent of high-school seniors planning to attend college, according to scholastic ability (in quartiles) and socioeducational status of the family *

Scholastic-ability quartile	Family-status quintile					All quin-tiles	Total number of cases
	(TOP) 5	4	3	2	(BOTTOM) 1		
(TOP) 4	83	66	53	44	43	61	(8,647)
3	70	53	37	29	29	44	(8,709)
2	65	41	31	20	21	33	(8,696)
(BOTTOM) 1	53	30	22	16	18	24	(8,509)
All quartiles	72	47	35	26	24	40	
Total number of cases	(6,520)	(6,647)	(6,465)	(8,116)	(6,811)		(34,561)

* Students are classified here according to their scholastic aptitude quartile in their own high school. Family status position, however, is constant for all students coming from a given family background, no matter what the social composition of their high school.
The number of cases on which each of the percentages is based ranges from 963 to 2505.

(Rogoff, 1961, p. 246)

Certain ethnic characteristics are also associated with the pursuit of education. Here, for example, are the percentages of high school boys in New Haven who "want" and "expect" to go to college:

Socioeconomic class	Jews (per cent)	Italians (per cent)	Other (per cent)
High	83	(75)	77
Middle	83	45	51
Low	(71) *	38	31

* ( ) refers to small base figures.

(Strodtbeck, 1958, p. 174)

In addition, it is apparent that Negroes in this country have fewer educational opportunities at the higher levels than whites.

In Denmark too, where financial support for university students had been available for some time, the proportion of wage-earners' children at the university was still low (Geiger, 1955). Similarly in France, the proportion of students going beyond the obligatory primary school was tied to the fathers' occupations (Girard, 1953).

D1.1   Lower-class boys who do go on for higher education are more likely to have parents who are dissatisfied with their own class position.

In one study in Boston, involving sons of workers with high I.Q. scores, it was found that

within . . . [this] "common man" group, some parents were satisfied with their own lot in life and did not attempt to push their sons up the status ladder, whereas other parents clearly encouraged their sons to strive for a "better" life. When the parents were rated on this factor on the basis of their interviews, its strong relationship with aspiration was clear [Kahl, 1953, p. 189].

Relation between parental pressure and son's aspiration (twenty-four boys)

Son's aspiration	Parental pressure toward college	
	NO	YES
College	4	8
No college	11	1

$(p < .02)$

(*Ibid.*, p. 190)

Since so many of the top jobs in society require substantial education and training, the educational system is a main channel for allocating personnel, and for doing so on the basis of class and ethnic characteristics as well as on the basis of talent. With the increasing attendance at college, the American system of higher education has become "an avenue of social mobility and an institutional bulwark of ideological equalitarianism" (Lipset and Bendix, 1959, p. 101).

D2   The peer group in educational institutions not only helps to shape the general behavior of the adolescents and young persons outside the classroom but has a strong influence upon the classroom attainment as well.

The climate of a high school or college—do the students consider it primarily as an educational institution? a country club? an athletic site?— has a good deal to do with how well the students do in their classwork, how many go on to further study, etc. According to one intensive analysis of 35,000 high-school seniors in the United States, no matter how privileged or underprivileged the kind of family from which they come, seniors at least double their chances of scoring in the top fourth in aptitude if they attend a school where most of their classmates are from the upper strata. The more well-to-do students there are in a high school, the higher the "college-planning" rates of all students, wealthy and poor alike (Rogoff, 1961).

D2.1   In general, the effect of college attendance upon student values is to homogenize them in the direction of the prevailing environment, with most change occurring at the outset.

For example, some data from three American colleges of different types are shown in the table on page 440. The reviewer of a range of such studies summarizes in this way:

> There is more homogeneity and greater consistency of values among students at the end of their four years [of college] than when they begin. Fewer seniors espouse beliefs that deviate from the going standards than do freshmen [*ibid.*, p. 4].

In addition, the studies seem to show that the influence of college courses themselves upon values is negligible, as compared to the pervasive college atmosphere.

D3   Since the public-school system is operated primarily by adults with middle-class values, the lower-class child is penalized not only on educational grounds but on broadly social grounds as well.

Percentage rejecting beliefs at

	ANTIOCH		COLGATE		MICHIGAN STATE	
	Fresh-men at en-trance	*At end of year*	*As fresh-men*	*As soph-omores*	*As fresh-men*	*As upper class-men*
Anything we do for a good cause is justified	67	80	—	—	41	76
Americans may tend to be materialistic, but at least they aren't cynical and decadent like most Europeans	68	81	54	79	51	68
Europeans criticize the United States for its materialism, but such criticism is only to cover up their realization that American culture is far superior to their own	77	87	67	91	50	78
Our rising divorce rate is a sign that we should return to the values that our grandparents held	—	—	55	77	47	74
People who say they're religious but don't go to church are just hypocrites	74	91	65	82	—	—

(Jacob, 1957, pp. 41–43)

For example, the judgments of predominantly middle-class teachers in Britain about their students are contained in the table on page 441.

D4   As the public educational system grows in size, the recruitment of teachers comes more and more from lower social classes.

Partly this tendency is a natural consequence of the arithmetic: if the system requires a great many teachers, it will have to go farther to get them. In addition, however, teaching careers are a step upward in social mobility for many lower-class people with intellectual interests. In fact:

D4.1   The lower the class origin of college students, the higher the prestige they assign to the teaching career.

D5   The effect of style of teaching or teachers' characteristics on teacher-student relations or on the number of ideas absorbed by the students (i.e., teaching effectiveness) is uncertain.

**Ratings by form masters of certain personality traits
of pupils from different social levels**

School	Form	Indus-triousness	Sense of responsibility	Interest in school affairs	Good behavior	Good manners	Popularity with peers
A	1	MC	MC	MC	MC	MC	MC
	2	—	—	MC	—	MC	MC
	3	WC	WC	MC	MC	WC	WC
B	1	WC	MC	MC	—	—	MC
	2	MC	MC	WC	MC	MC	WC
	3	MC	—	MC	MC	MC	MC
C	1	MC	—	MC	—	MC	MC
	2	WC	MC	MC	MC	MC	MC
	3	—	WC	MC	WC	WC	WC
D	1	MC	MC	MC	—	MC	MC
	2	MC	MC	MC	WC	MC	MC
Total	MC	6	6	10	5	8	8
	WC	3	3	1	2	2	3
	—	2	2	0	4	1	0

MC: Middle class has higher rating.
WC: Working class has higher rating.
—: Social classes have equal rating.

(Himmelweit, 1954, p. 150)

There have been a large number of studies on the effect of the "classroom atmosphere" or the form of teaching, dealing with such matters as the authoritarian or democratic, dominative or integrative approach of the teacher and the relative emphasis on subject or student. But apparently there are no clear conclusions. Here is a recent summary of the summaries:

Even though there is a vast body of research on the relation of teacher characteristics to effectiveness in teaching, the reviews of this research (Domas and Tiedeman, 1950; Barr, Eustice, and Noe, 1955) show no consistent relation between any characteristics, including intelligence, and such teaching effectiveness [Brim, 1958, p. 32].

D6   In periods of crisis, at least in the United States, the better colleges and universities, which usually have faculties that are liberal on matters of academic freedom, are more likely both to come under attack and to respond with a strong stand by teaching staff and administration.

Here are some data from a study of social scientists in American institutions during the McCarthy period, together with the authors' interpretation:

School quality as related to accusations of subversion, threats to academic freedom, and the administration's treatment of accused professors (percentages)

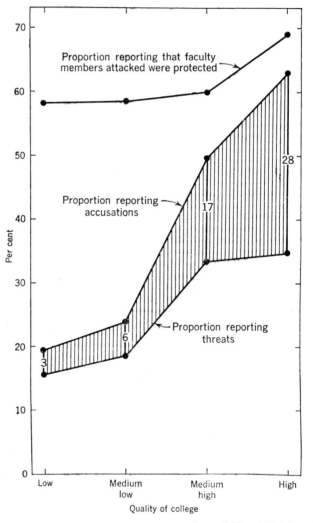

(Lazarsfeld and Thielens, 1958, p. 173)

Threats to academic freedom are reported by an ever larger proportion of respondents, the higher the quality of their college. Our main interest at this point is with the four enclosed percentages inside the shaded area. Representing the difference between accusations and threats, they provide a rough index of administrative absorption. In the low quality colleges there are few accusations, but they seem to be readily converted into actual difficulties for a faculty member; the difference is only 3 per cent. In the best colleges both accusations and difficulties are more frequent, but the difference is 28 per cent; at these schools the administration is much more likely to shield the professor and not to pass on accusations which come to their attention [*ibid.,* p. 174].

Military Institutions

E1   At least in the United States, the professional military career, especially at the lower levels, is held in less prestige by the general population than are civilian occupations of about the same skill.

According to a survey made in 1955, the officer in the armed services ranks just below public-school teacher and above farm owner and carpenter, and the enlisted man just above truck driver (Janowitz, 1960, p. 227).

In a society in which individualism and personal gain are paramount virtues, it is understandable that wide sectors of the civilian population view the military career as a weak choice, as an effort to "sell out" cheaply for economic security and low pay and limited prestige [Janowitz, 1959, p. 47].

As a result, the military may have suffered in the competition with civilian life for the recruitment of able personnel, but that situation is now changing under the impact of shifts in the technology and nature of warfare, as indicated below. Some students believe that such disesteem by the society at large accounts for the unusual ceremonialism within the military establishment; in this respect, the military appears to react much like other minority groups within a society, as we have seen.

E2   The changing technology of warfare (greater firepower, greater mobility, wider arenas of action, more nearly equal dangers to military and civilian personnel)—in conjunction with a world situation based on mutual distrust by the great powers (the cold war)—has had the following effects upon the military establishment in the United States:

a   lessened use of domination to control personnel, increased use of manipulation.

b   lessened centralization of command, increased dispersal of initiative.

c   lessened stress on applying violence, increased stress on deterring violence.

d   lessened conflict with civilian society, increased conflict within services (e.g., regarding who will control the new technology).

    e   lessened separation of the military, increased interdependence with civilian life and personnel (e.g., scientists, engineers, skilled technicians, etc.).

In the Civil War 93.2 per cent of the enlisted personnel in the army had military occupational specialties for which there were no civilian equivalents; by 1954 the rate had dropped to only 28.8 per cent [Janowitz, 1961, p. 522].

    f   lessened reliance on traditional, hereditary, aristocratic military elite, increased reliance on democratic selection of skilled personnel (i.e., less on ascription, more on achievement).

Partly as a result:

E2.1   Organizational and morale tensions arise within the military establishment because of (a) the social heterogeneity of recruits, which tends to break down the existing fraternity among the professional officers; (b) the problem of how to handle personal relations between officers and men when traditional lines of command are changing; (c) the informal cross-pressures that develop between military and civilian life when the two are intermingled; and (d) the disparity that develops between lines of command and levels of skill.

E3   The less the participants in an organization are voluntarily dedicated to the task, the more impersonal and controlled the administration of the organization tends to become—thus accounting for the distinctive character of the military organization in peacetime.

The very nature of military administration and command is predicated on the implicit assumption that the rank and file of soldiers will be either indifferent or non-job oriented. Accordingly we find of all forms of administration the military is most mechanical, most highly structured, and most impersonal and indifferent to personal variability [Dubin, 1958, p. 259].

E4   Making a civilian into a soldier in a short period of time requires an institutional means for bringing the informal, personal pressures of the recruits to bear in reinforcing the formal requirements of the army (and perhaps requires that it be done in a somewhat traumatic way, to emphasize the break between civilian and army life).

The critical problem was to mobilize informal pressures of the soldiers in support of their fellows who conformed and against the non-conformist, and to maximize the internalization of the controls through habituation. . . . The basic training period was, therefore, not one of gradual inculcation of the army *mores,* but one of intensive shock treatment. The new recruit, a lone individual, is helplessly insecure in the bewildering newness and complexity of his environment. Also he is a man; he must show that he is tough enough to "take it." He is an American; the army is a means to winning the war; he must do his best or lose face at home. With personal insecurity on the one hand, and the motivation to "see it through" on the other, he is malleable to the "discipline," which consists of a fatiguing physical ordeal and continued repetition of acts until they become semi-automatic, in an atmosphere dominated by fear. . . . The individual recruit is powerless. He finds solace in the company of his fellows, who are new and bewildered like himself, but who now, with all escapes blocked by fear of formal punishment, further each other's adjustment to the inevitable by applying sanctions of their own to those who "can't take it." The fear of being thought less than a man by one's buddies can be as powerful a control factor as the fear of the guard house. When the former is socially directed to reinforce the latter, the army has begun to succeed in building a soldier—a process which continues until as much as possible is internalized and automatized in the form of "conscience" [Stouffer et al., 1949, I, 411–12].

One study of the period of basic training found that the self-confidence of the recruits as soldiers grew, but that their attitudes toward the army and their leaders became less favorable than they had been (Christie, 1953).

E5   Adjustment to (American) army life (being a "good soldier") is better among recruits who are (a) better educated; (b) sociable and unneurotic in civilian life; (c) from stable homes and with healthy childhoods; (d) in good physical health; (e) young; (f) unmarried; and (g) not continuously in personal contact with their homes.

Here, for example, is the result of a large number of comparisons made in the American army in World War II:

**Number of positive and negative differences in percentages
with favorable attitudes, for a given background
characteristic, holding other variables constant**

	Number of matched comparisons in which differences between percentages favorable in indicated groups are +, −, or 0:										
	High-school graduates—not high-school graduates				*Men 25 and over— men under 25*				*Married— unmarried*		
	+	0	−	*To-tal*	+	0	−	*To-tal*	+	0	−	*To-tal*
Personal esprit	94	4	19	117	51	5	47	103	20	5	63	88
Personal commitment	63	4	13	80	17	3	53	73	5	0	65	70
Satisfaction with status and job	32	9	122	163	80	9	39	128	50	4	44	98

(Stouffer *et al.*, 1949, I, 109)

In some respects—for example, the morale of married men or the army-job satisfaction of the better educated—adjustment is considered a special case of the notion of relative deprivation: the attitude depends on the comparison made. Educated men were more frustrated in ordinary positions than the less educated, hence were less satisfied even though they were promoted more; married men felt they were sacrificing more than the unmarried, hence had less esprit.

E5.1   The better the soldier's attitudes toward the army (i.e., the more personal commitment, spirit, satisfaction), the better are his chances of subsequent promotion.

E6   The more respected and better liked the officer, and the more he shares deprivations with his men (such as unpleasant tasks, poor food and quarters, dangers, etc.), the better the officer-enlisted man relationship, the more cohesive the military group, the better the men's morale, and the more effective the performance.

For example, a study of Air Force crews found that performance on training problems was associated with the equalitarian treatment received from the officers (Adams, 1954).

E6.1   Differences in attitudes between officers and enlisted men are least on the ideological issues involved in the war, and they increase on issues dealing with the status system of the army.

The data were presented in the preceding chapter, finding B5.1 (Speier, 1950).

E7   The stronger the group solidarity of the men fighting together, the better their combat record.

For example:

In a study of some 70 tactical episodes of operation Neptune, the airborne phase of the Normandy invasion, it was found that only a minor fraction was successful if the original unit was disrupted during the drop. If an officer or a noncommissioned officer collected a group of men he had never commanded and tried to lead them into battle, the results were almost uniformly unsatisfactory. The same observations were made from a study of battle stragglers in the Ardennes operation; individual stragglers had little combat value when put into a strange organization. . . .

There are very few psychiatric cases among U.S. submarine crews. To be sure, submarine crews are carefully selected, but since the stress of this service is extreme, social organizational factors, namely, the intimate organization of submarine life, must be operative. A similar pattern held true for bomber crews in World War II, who developed tightly knit primary groups. In the Bomber Command of the RAF, for example, the casualty rate during World War II was reported at 64 per cent, including those who were killed, wounded, missing, and injured. Nevertheless, the psychiatric breakdown rate was only about 5 per cent [Janowitz, 1959, pp. 68–69, 74].

A study of the solidarity of German army units in the last months of World War II similarly concluded:

It appears that a soldier's ability to resist is a function of the capacity of his immediate primary group (his squad or section) to avoid social disintegration. When the individual's immediate group, and its supporting formations, met his basic organic needs, offered him affection and esteem from both officers and comrades, supplied him with a sense of power and adequately regulated his relations with authority, the element of self-concern in battle, which would lead to disruption of the effective functioning of his primary group, was minimized.

The capacity of the primary group to resist disintegration was dependent on the acceptance of political, ideological, and cultural symbols (all secondary symbols) only to the extent that these secondary symbols became directly associated with primary gratifications [Shils and Janowitz, 1948, p. 281].

The conditions of warfare can sometimes narrow the group to a two-man team, but even that is effective in buttressing morale (Janowitz, 1961, p. 547).

E7.1 Recourse to prayer under combat conditions is common among (American) soldiers, especially for those under great stress and with few personal resources for coping with the situation.

Here are some data:

Thoughts which veterans said helped them "When the going was tough," in relation to degree of fear in battle that they report (veteran enlisted infantrymen in one Pacific division, March–April, 1944)

	Percentage saying that having each type of thought helped a lot among men who said:			
	Battle became less frightening or never was frightening; had low fear-symptom score	Battle became less frightening or never was frightening; had high fear-symptom score	Battle became more frightening or was frightening all the time; had low fear-symptom score	Battle became more frightening or was frightening all the time; had high fear-symptom score
Prayer	42	58	61	72
Thinking that you couldn't let other men down	61	62	60	52
Thinking that you had to finish the job in order to get home again	41	37	35	28
Thoughts of hatred for the enemy	43	39	38	34
Thinking of what we are fighting for	34	40	32	29
Total number of cases	(177)	(52)	(317)	(403)

(Stouffer et al., 1949, II, 179)

E7.2   The better a company's attitude toward combat (i.e., the soldiers' willingness to fight and confidence in their ability), the lower its non-battle casualty rates.

E8   In battle, the soldier's ideological commitment—to the objectives of the war or the ideals being fought for—is directly responsible for effectiveness in combat only to a limited degree, except when intimately associated with the primary gratification of political ends (as in a highly ideological conflict, such as a civil war).

For example, the study of the American soldier in World War II concludes:

> Since the feeling of national peril quickly died, and the outcome of the war was a foregone conclusion, there was little to impel men to take the detour [into the army] except external factors, It may be said that except for a very limited number of men, *little feeling of personal commitment to the war emerged*. The war was accepted passively as a national necessity, but this acceptance was not internalized as a sense of personal responsibility [Stouffer *et al.*, 1949, I, 449].

But a study of "fear in battle" showed that ideological convictions were more important in the Spanish Civil War, although even there,

> the soldier in battle is not forever whispering, "My cause, my cause." He is too busy for that. Ideology functions *before* battle, to get the man in, and *after* battle by blocking thoughts of escape. . . . Identification with cause is like a joker in a deck of cards. It can substitute for any other card. The man who has it can better bear inferior material, temporary defeat, weariness or fear [Dollard, 1943, p. 56].

E8.1   The more that men are exposed to actual combat in battle, the less is their conviction that the ideological value of the war is worth the cost.

E8.2   The less the personal, idealistic commitment to the cause of the war, the less the disillusionment among the victors afterward (itself a customary occurrence), but the greater the psychological costs to the individual participant and probably the greater the social cost to the community (in pensions, disgruntlement, claim for special consideration to offset "meaningless" sacrifice, and so on).

E9   Typically, a soldier's combat efficiency reaches a peak after three to five months of combat experience, holds a plateau, and inevitably falls off at some subsequent point.

For the American soldier, "no set of motives or incentives remained permanently effective in indefinite combat" (Stouffer *et al.*, 1949, II, 289). The

soldier's motivations for combat do not increase, and several actually decrease—e.g., his need for prestige or to prove himself. Yet the negative influences do increase: fatigue, fear about survival in continued combat, etc.
Hence there is an increase in nonbattle casualties, in tension and anxiety,
and in psychiatric disabilities. In short, every man has his breaking point.

In addition, combat units disintegrate socially beyond a certain point
in the absence of replacements or relief. That point varies considerably with
the stress and type of battle, the type of soldier, and the administrative
arrangements. For example:

> In North Africa and Italy during World War II, . . . after prolonged exposure
> to combat, the [American] infantryman "wore out, either developing an acute
> incapacitating neurosis or else becoming hypersensitive to shell fire, so overly
> cautious and jittery that he was ineffective and demoralizing to the newer men."
> The point at which this occurred appears to have come somewhere between 200
> and 400 aggregate days of combat. . . . The British command estimated a pe-
> riod twice as long, since it was British policy to afford more brief intervals of
> relief from frontline duty. The nature of the battle also affects the incidence of
> breakdown. In general, the rate of psychoneurotic casualties rises in proportion
> to the rate of those wounded and killed. An important exception occurs during
> full retreat. Under full retreat, psychiatric casualties may not be able to save
> themselves, but it does appear that in such situations the danger to the whole
> group overrides the inclination of the individual soldiers to manifest psycho-
> neurotic behavior. In periods of rapid advance, the rate also drops off
> sharply. . . .
>
> Differences in cultural background and "national character" seem to influence
> the rate and type of psychiatric breakdown in combat. When newly captured
> German prisoners of war and their British captors in North Africa were both sub-
> jected to air attack, it has been reported that the Germans displayed much less
> neurotic behavior. Similarly, Indian units fighting in the Arakan jungles showed
> a lower incidence of neurotic behavior than British units in the same area.
> Yugoslav partisans had a high incidence of hysterical convulsions, a symptom not
> at all common in the American army. In the Japanese army, hysteria was also
> the most common reaction to prolonged stress. Many observers have noted that
> the incidence of psychoneurotic breakdown among American soldiers was not
> only a reaction to the fear of being killed; often anxiety or guilt that was created
> over the fear of killing someone acted as the precipitating factor. Clearly, funda-
> mental social taboos of civilian life were at work here [Janowitz, 1961, pp. 544–
> 45].

SELECTED READINGS

The following titles in each of the institutional spheres will serve, first, to introduce the reader to the behavioral approach to the subject; and, second, to lead him
to numerous other titles in the field. We have included here both summaries of the

literature and instances of empirical work of the sort that produced the findings presented in this chapter.

On Religion:

Michael Argyle. *Religious Behavior*. Free Press, 1959.

Charles Y. Glock. "The Sociology of Religion," in Robert K. Merton *et al.*, eds., *Sociology Today: Problems and Prospects*. Basic Books, 1959, pp. 153–77.

William J. Goode. *Religion Among the Primitives*. Fress Press, 1951.

Gerhard Lenski. *The Religious Factor*. Doubleday, 1961.

Bronislaw Malinowski. *Magic, Science and Religion and Other Essays*. Doubleday, 1954.

Joachim Wach. *Sociology of Religion*. U. of Chicago Press, 1944.

On Economy:

Robert A. Dahl *et al*. *Social Science Research on Business: Product and Potential*. Columbia U. Press, 1959.

Eli Ginzberg *et al*. *Occupational Choice*. Columbia U. Press, 1951.

Frederick Herzberg *et al*. *Job Attitudes: Review of Research and Opinion*. Psychological Service of Pittsburgh, 1957.

Bert F. Hoselitz, ed. *Sociological Aspects of Economic Growth*. Free Press, 1960.

A. J. Jaffe and Charles D. Stewart. *Manpower Resources and Utilization: Principles of Working-Force Analysis*. Wiley, 1951.

Seymour M. Lipset *et al*. *Union Democracy*. Free Press, 1956.

Leonard Sayles. *Behavior of Industrial Work Groups: Prediction and Control*. Wiley, 1958.

William Foote Whyte and Frank B. Miller. "Industrial Sociology," in Joseph B. Gittler, ed., *Review of Sociology: Analysis of a Decade*. Wiley, 1957, pp. 289–345.

On Polity:

Robert E. Lane. *Political Life: Why People Get Involved in Politics*. Free Press, 1959.

Seymour M. Lipset and Juan Linz. *The Social Bases of Political Diversity in Western Democracies*. Forthcoming.

Seymour M. Lipset *et al*. "The Psychology of Voting: An Analysis of Political Behavior," in Gardner Lindzey, ed., *Handbook of Social Psychology*. Addison-Wesley, 1954, pp. 1124–75.

John C. Wahlke and Heinz Eulau. *Legislative Behavior*. Free Press, 1959.

On Education:

Orville G. Brim, Jr. *Sociology and the Field of Education*. Russell Sage Foundation, 1958.

James S. Coleman. *The Adolescent Society: The Social Life of the Teenager and Its Impact on Education*. Free Press, 1961.

A. H. Halsey *et al*., eds. *Education, Economy, and Society*. Free Press, 1961.

Philip E. Jacob. *Changing Values in College*. Harper, 1958.

Paul F. Lazarsfeld and Wagner Thielens, Jr. *The Academic Mind*. Free Press, 1958.

On the Military:

Morris Janowitz. *The Professional Soldier*. Free Press, 1960.

Morris Janowitz. *Sociology and the Military Establishment*. Russell Sage Foundation, 1959.

Samuel Stouffer *et al*. *The American Soldier*. Vol. I: *Adjustment During Army Life*, Vol. II: *Combat and Its Aftermath*. Princeton U. Press, 1949.

"Wait a minute," said the stranger, "fun presently—nobs not come yet—queer place—Dock-yard people of upper rank don't know Dock-yard people of lower rank —Dock-yard people of lower gentry don't know small gentry—small gentry don't know tradespeople—Commissioner don't know anybody. . . ."

While the aristocracy of the place . . . were preserving their dignity at the upper end of the room, the other classes of society were imitating their example in other parts of it.

CHARLES DICKENS
The Pickwick Papers

She knew the latest fashions, the names of the best dressmakers, the days on which the fashionable world drove in the Bois or went to the Opera. She pored over the description of furniture in the works of Eugène Sue. She read Balzac and George Sand, seeking in their pages satisfaction by proxy of all her longings. . . . From all that was close and familiar she turned her thoughts. Her own daily scene—a tedious countryside, a half-witted, middle-class society, an unceasing round of mediocrity—she saw as an exception to some more glorious rule, as something in which, by mere ill-chance, she had been caught and held. Beyond it, stretching as far as eye could see, was a world of joy and passion.

GUSTAVE FLAUBERT
Madame Bovary

Here, before long, Becky received not only "the best" foreigners (as the phrase is in our noble and admirable society slang), but some of the best English people too. I don't mean the most virtuous, or indeed the least virtuous, or the cleverest, or the stupidest, or the richest, or the best born, but "the best"—in a word, people about whom there is no question—such as the great Lady Fitz-Willis, that Patron Saint of Almack's, the great Lady Slowbore, the great Lady Grizzel Macbeth (she was Lady G. Glowry, daughter of Lord Grey of Glowry), and the like. When the Countess of Fitz-Willis (her ladyship is of the King-street family, see *Debrett* and *Burke*) takes up a person, he or she is safe. There is no question about them any more. Not that my Lady Fitz-Willis is any better than anybody else, being, on the contrary, a faded person, fifty-seven years of age, and neither handsome, nor wealthy, nor entertaining; but it is agreed on all sides that she is of the "best People."

WILLIAM MAKEPEACE THACKERAY
Vanity Fair

It gives a million gambits for a mime
On which a social system can be based:
No man is sure he does not need to climb,
A girl can't go on laughing all the time.

WILLIAM EMPSON
Reflection from Anita Loos

Chapter Eleven

SOCIAL STRATIFICATION

Both laymen and scholars commonly characterize people by social class. Some people stand higher in the community than others; some are getting ahead in the world, some are being displaced; some are struggling to make a better life for their children; some emulate, envy, or resent those above them. Stratification deals with who is really who in a society.

As countless novelists have shown, one's position in society has a good deal to do with one's behavior. That it is a central notion in the behavioral sciences is indicated by the extent to which it appears as a descriptive or explanatory factor in other chapters. It also deserves considerable attention in its own right.

DEFINITIONS

In this case, the matter of definition is somewhat extended, and perhaps more hazardous, because behavioral scientists themselves argue a good deal over the proper definition of "class" and the proper bases for stratification. However, the following definitions are reasonably accurate and will serve the purpose of summarizing the findings.

Stratification: The ranking of people in a society, by other members of the society, into higher and lower social positions so as to produce a hierarchy of respect or prestige.

Generally speaking, every society has a conception of what it regards as the ideal type(s) of man—the warrior king, the successful businessman, the small farmer, the scholar, the priest, the aristocrat, and so on. Stratification is the hierarchy that is based on the respect, expressed in both action and speech, that individuals grant to one another in accordance with their conformity to the ideal. The nearer people are to the ideal of the society, the more seriously their views are taken and the more they count in the society as a whole. The respected characteristics can be more or less shared or imitated throughout the society; and they can differ from one part of the society to another (the rugged pioneer on the frontier, the social leader back in Boston) or from one time to another (the military man whose prestige increases during a period of hot or cold war). But the things a society values are unequally distributed—a few people have the most and most people have the rest—and that is what the system of stratification takes into account.

Who and what are class-ified? People are put into classes by other people in the society, but the determination is only seldom made individual by individual, as is true, for example, in the case of purely moral judgments. Instead, the class-ifying judgments are typically based on conventional criteria that distinguish broad social groups (such as immigrants, the rich, the educated), or the holders of certain offices or positions (such as clergy, doctors, truck drivers); or the members of organizations or institutions (such as college faculties, government employees, army officers).

On what bases are people stratified? This is where some of the disagreement over definition enters, with experts arguing over what is the "right" basis on which to class-ify people. Various criteria for stratification have been considered important from time to time and from place to place. The major ones are:

authority
power (political, economic, military)
ownership of property, relation to the means of production, control over land (the feudal estates)
income—amount, type, and sources
consumption patterns and style of life
occupation or skill, and achievement in it
education, learning, wisdom
divinity, "control" over the supernatural
altruism, public service, morality
place in "high society," kinship connections, ancestry (i.e., inherited position)
associational ties and connections
ethnic status, religion, race

Now it should be understood that

these various characteristics are not always evaluated in the same way in all societies. For example, in the United States the significance of kinship connection is less important than it is in China or Great Britain. . . . Ethnic characteristics are more important in the United States than they are in France or Brazil. . . . Education has less significance as a basis of discrimination in the United States than it has in Germany, the Netherlands, or Sweden. Occupation is probably less important as a basis of deference in the United States than it is in Germany [Shils, 1960, p. 766].

Which characteristics become the basis for stratification—or rather, the bases, since the judgment typically combines a number of characteristics and gives differing weights to them—depends on what is considered particularly important by the stratifying society. The values most highly prized in the society tend to be taken as the central bases of the system of stratification:

> The class acquires a dominant position in the degree that the values which it shapes (creates, produces) are highly valued in the body politic. . . . Societies ruled, for example, by a warrior class or priesthood confirm the hypothesis insofar as these classes owe their ruling position to the value put upon the activities characteristic of the class [Lasswell and Kaplan, 1950, p. 207].

Not all important differences among human beings serve as bases for stratification. Only those characteristics ranked in a society as socially better or worse to have than others, those associated with the exercise of power outside the family, and those institutionalized or long range in duration, are used in the system of stratification.

When a person's ranks in different hierarchies are uneven, he is said to be characterized by *status discrepancy*. Thus a person may be high in income but low in occupation (a rich criminal or gambler) or high in occupation and low in ethnic status (a Negro doctor). For example, in twelve metropolitan areas only 23 per cent of the men listed in *Who's Who in America* are also listed in the *Social Register* for the communities (Baltzell, 1953).

In a large, complex society, small discrepancies are numerous and are typically handled by a sort of informal weighting in which one characteristic, or a few, are given precedence. Large discrepancies are often regarded as problems, at least by the persons involved. But on the whole, the various criteria overlap to a substantial extent, especially at the extremes of the distribution. People high on one basis of classification are likely to be high on the others as well: "The rich tend also to be the healthy, respected, informed, and so on, and the poor to be the sickly, despised, ignorant" (Lasswell and Kaplan, 1950, p. 57).

Thus the stratification of people—at least in large, complex societies, where the concept is most useful—is carried out

informally: judgments are made unofficially;
collectively: judgments are made for aggregates of people who themselves never associate together as such;
segmentally: judgments are made on the basis of only a few characteristics, not the "whole man" (unlike personal relations).

Only a small number of classes are generally recognized in a particular society, and they are arbitrarily defined (i.e., there is no set number of classes nor is there a hard-and-fast distinction between, say, upper middle and lower middle). For example:

> With few exceptions, American researchers have been reluctant to accept *a priori* and have been unable to discover empirically the reality of class in the sense of fully developed, sharply defined strata comprised of individuals who are aware of their positions and are capable of corporate action [Broom, 1959, p. 435].

The way sociologists analyze the stratification of American communities is illustrated in these instances:

Middletown (in the Midwest): In this classic inquiry, the community was stratified into six classes: (1) a very small group of the "old" middle class, (2) a larger but still small business and professional group, (3) Middletown's "own middle class in purely locally relative terms," (4) "an aristocracy of local labor," (5) the "numerically overwhelmingly dominant group of the working class," and (6) the "ragged bottom margin" (Lynd and Lynd, 1937, pp. 458–60).

Yankee City (in New England): Six classes were distinguished primarily on the basis of prestige ratings by the residents themselves: from upper upper to lower lower, as in the following distribution:

The hierarchy of Yankee City (percentages)

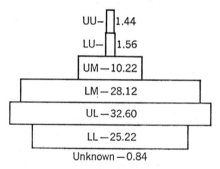

| UU– | 1.44 |
| LU– | 1.56 |
| UM – 10.22 |
| LM – 28.12 |
| UL – 32.60 |
| LL – 25.22 |

Unknown – 0.84   (Warner and Lunt, 1941, p. 88)

That there was a strong overlap between class and occupation in Yankee City is shown by these figures:

	Upper upper (per cent)	Lower upper (per cent)	Upper middle (per cent)	Lower middle (per cent)	Upper lower (per cent)	Lower lower (per cent)
Professionals and proprietors	83.33	85.72	62.16	13.74	2.78	0.73
Wholesale and retail dealers		7.14	15.38	10.87	5.88	2.74
Clerks and kindred workers	16.67	7.14	15.08	28.80	9.19	3.66
Skilled workers			5.23	17.32	12.71	4.57
Semiskilled workers			2.15	27.12	61.53	79.16
Unskilled workers				2.15	7.91	9.14

(*Ibid.*, p. 261)

Old City and *Old County* (in the South): A similar six-fold classification was used, and here is how the various classes described themselves and others:

The social perspectives of the social classes

Upper-upper class		Lower-upper class
'"Old aristocracy"	UU	"Old aristocracy"
"Aristocracy," but not "old"	LU	**"Aristocracy," but not "old"**
"Nice, respectable people"	UM	"Nice, respectable people"
'"Good people, but 'nobody'"	LM	"Good people, but 'nobody'"
"Po' whites"	UL LL	"Po' whites"

Upper-middle class		Lower-middle class
"Society" { "Old families"	UU	"Old aristocracy" (older) | "Broken-down aristocracy" (younger)
"Society" but not "old families"	LU	
"People who should be upper class"	UM	"People who think they are somebody"
"People who don't have much money"	LM	**"We poor folk"**
	UL	"People poorer than us"
"No 'count lot"	LL	"No 'count lot"

Upper-lower class		Lower-lower class
	UU LU	
"Society" or the "folks with money"	UM	"Society" or the "folks with money"
"People who are up because they have a little money"	LM	"Way-high-ups," but not "Society"
"Poor but honest folk"	UL	"Snobs trying to push up"
"Shiftless people"	LL	**"People just as good as anybody"**

(Davis *et al.*, 1941, p. 65)

Plainville (a Midwest village): There are differences between "country people" and "town people," but lineage, wealth, morals, and manners are common to both groups. Here is a diagram of the stratification:

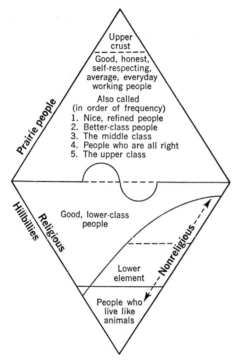

(West, 1945, p. 117)

Bronzeville (the Negro section of Chicago): This caste society within the larger society has its own system of social classes, as illustrated in the following figure:

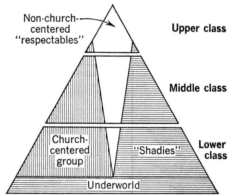

Bronzeville's upper class is oriented around a *secular* pattern of living, with emphasis on "culture" and "refinement" as well as "racial advancement." A smaller group within the upper class is church-centered, and a very small but powerful group earns its living in "shady" pursuits. As we leave the top of society, however, and move toward the bottom, the proportion of "church-minded" people and of "shadies" increases, and the group of "non-church" respectables decreases.

(Drake and Cayton, 1945, p. 525)

Elmtown (a small town in the Midwest): In a study of young people, five classes were distinguished, as follows:

Even though Elmtowners are inconsistent in their designations of a particular class, the systematic analysis of selected cultural traits associated with each of the five classes . . . reveals that the possession of a constellation of differentially evaluated social symbols—functional, pecuniary, religious, educational, reputational, power, lineage, proper associates, memberships in associations—are relied upon by Elmtowners to "hang people on the peg they belong on," to determine "their place in the community" or "their standing in life" [Hollingshead, 1949, pp. 83–84].

The class ratings are symbolized by residential area: Old Residential, the East End, Down by the Mill, North of the Tracks, Below the Canal.

In addition to the arrangements in the society as a whole, systems of stratification can exist locally or institutionally—in a small town, a university, an industry, or a Hollywood studio. All of these tend to follow the principle that ranking is based on what is valued most within the particular community (e.g., distinguished learning in the university community).

Finally, stratification systems are of two kinds—open and closed. In open systems people can move from one ranking to another; in closed systems they cannot, or more precisely, they can do so only to a very limited extent. The former ranks are called classes; the latter, castes. Both can exist at the same time within the same society.

Class: An open aggregate or stratum of people with roughly similar ranking in the particular community or society. In Western industrialized society, and perhaps more generally, the primary basis for classifying has been wealth or some variant of it, such as amount of current income, consumption pattern, or (particularly) occupation. To wealth are often added other criteria for stratification; among them, learning (poor college professors rank higher than their income); service (poor clergymen rank higher than rich wastrels); and inherited status (poor aristocrats rank higher than *nouveaux riches*). As will be seen in what follows, most of the research findings on social stratification have an economic basis for class—sometimes income, sometimes consumption, often occupation.

Caste: A closed or nearly closed aggregate with no or very little intermarriage or movement in or out (examples: the untouchables in India and the Negro in the United States). Caste distinctions are often enhanced by physically visible differences (skin color in the case of U.S. Negroes) and are often embodied in symbolic distinctions such as caste marks or dress. The boundaries of caste are usually sharper than those of class, so that it is especially hard for people to move across the line. In extreme cases, caste boundaries are maintained by legal or religious sanctions (e.g., state laws forbidding miscegenation). Caste membership is hereditary (by ascription), whereas class membership typically starts that way but is subject to shift through achievement. Actually, classes exist within castes: for example, there is a quite elaborate class system among Negroes, based partly on wealth, occupation, and style of life, as in the parent system, but also including such characteristics as respectability and even degree of pigmentation.

Mobility: Movement or shifting of membership between or within social classes. *Horizontal* mobility simply means movement from post to post or place to place within the same class, e.g., a job shift within the professional group. *Vertical* mobility, the more important kind, is movement from one class to another. There are two broad types of mobility: group mobility, or the movement of a class or a caste as a whole; and individual mobility, or the movement of a particular person within the stratification system. For the latter there are two major measures of mobility: generational mobility, the movement between father and son; and career mobility, the movement within an individual's own lifetime.

FINDINGS

We deal first with characteristics of the system of stratification as a whole, then with the placement of individuals and groups and their subsequent mobility, and finally with the behavioral differences among classes (as observed mainly on the American scene).

The Character of Stratification Systems

A1   Every known human society, certainly every known society of any size, is stratified.

The hierarchical evaluation of people in different social positions is apparently inherent in human social organization. Stratification arises with the most rudimentary division of labor and appears to be socially necessary in order to get people to fill different positions and perform adequately in them.

> Looking at the cultures of the world one finds that no society is "classless," that is, unstratified. There are some primitive communities so small that no class strata appear, the social organization resting almost entirely on age, sex, and kinship; but even here chieftainship, individual prowess, and clan or family property introduce an incipient stratification [Davis, 1949, p. 366].

A1.1   The more complex the society, the greater the number of classes or ranks recognized within it.

[It is] the established fact that greater specialization, heterogeneity, and higher division of labor are associated with a greater development of rank orders. . . . Since in the simple societies the degree of differentiation among the adaptive statuses is very low, and in the complex ones differentiation is exceedingly great, the powers of the technology and of the moral and sacred orders are accordingly combined and felt as one in the simple societies, and in the more advanced ones they divide into various political, economic, and religious categories and are felt to be many [Warner, 1957, pp. 245, 246].

For example, there is less stratification within the Negro population in Southern cities than there is in border cities, and less there than in the North—mainly because of the progressively greater occupational specialization (Frazier, 1957). In general, in an open society like the United States, the stratification pyramid, though extremely complex, is relatively flat.

A1.2   If the larger society assigns low status to a visible group that maintains constant internal communication, that group tends to develop status sensitivity within itself and to make a number of internal discriminations in status.

In this respect, says one author, "the military behaves very much like any other minority or low-status group" (Janowitz, 1959, p. 35).

A1.3   The wealthier the country, then the narrower the gap between classes, the larger the middle class, and the greater the consensus on the values of the society.

Enlarging the upper and lower classes, without mediation from the middle, tends to polarize values within the society.

A1.4   Those people who benefit most from the stratification system are most likely to accept it.

As one authority in the field puts it:

Those whom the prevailing system of evaluation relegates to a lower status, even while sharing and acknowledging that status, simultaneously resent and deny it. . . . Ethically radical and politically revolutionary attitudes constitute the extreme form of denial of the claims of the "superior" to their superior status [Shils, 1960, p. 767].

Those on top, on the contrary, tend not only to rationalize the justice of the system but sometimes try to solidify it as something natural or inherent (thus attempting to shift the basis from achievement to ascription). The upper class usually tends to think it is on top because of ability and energy, but the lower class tends to think the ranking is also due to connections and plain luck.

A1.4a The greater the inequities in a society, in the rewards associated with stratification, the more the upper classes stress a style of life or a set of values that sets them apart as particularly deserving.

The greater the inequities in rewards in a society, the more the upper classes have the need to erect or preserve a style of life and value system, which legitimizes their claim to privilege [Lipset and Linz, 1956, p. 18].

A1.5 The size of the community affects the operation of the stratification system in certain ways:

.5a People in small communities are more likely to agree on who ranks where than are city people.

The nearer, the clearer: "More discriminating and sensitive judgments are rendered about the nearby social environment than about those sectors of the society which are more remote" (Shils, 1960, p. 767).

.5b People in small communities, where personal characteristics are more fully visible, are more likely to take into account such nonwealth factors as length of residence and lineage; whereas those in large communities, because of the anonymity of individuals, tend to rely on the common criterion of money and its forms.

"The smaller the community and the higher the social class, the more likely it is that an individual's rank is determined by his personal attributes" (Lipset and Bendix, 1959, p. 275). In the large community, on the other hand, it is difficult to show moral authority or stature to a stranger, and there money is more likely to talk.

.5c The smaller the community, the more responsive and the more influential are the upper classes in general community matters—particularly in setting the "tone" of the community, which all elites seek to do.

A1.6 Across countries, there is substantial agreement on which occupations rank high and low.

Although many people are aware of the occupational hierarchy only dimly and unevenly, although judgments are often vague and differently based, and although disagreements are frequent on the placement of particular persons, positions, and groups—still there is a rough consensus on the ranking of jobs in a variety of societies:

Correlations between prestige scores (or ranks) given to
comparable occupations in six national studies

	U.S.S.R.	Japan	Great Britain	New Zealand	United States	Germany
U.S.S.R.		.74	.83	.83	.90	.90
Japan			.92	.91	.93	.93
Great Britain				.97	.94	.97
New Zealand					.97	.96
United States						.96
Average correlations	.84	.89	.93	.93	.94	.94

(Inkeles and Rossi, 1956, p. 332)

As the authors put it, this result

reveals an extremely high level of agreement, going far beyond chance expectancy, as to the relative prestige of a wide range of specific occupations, despite
the variety of sociocultural settings in which they are found. This strongly suggests that there is a relatively invariable hierarchy of prestige associated with the
industrial system, even when it is placed in the context of larger social systems
which are otherwise differentiated in important respects [*ibid.,* p. 339].

A1.7   Stratifying judgments differ, depending upon the class position
of both the judged and the judger.

As to the former: (a) the extremes of the class distribution are acknowledged more uniformly than are the middle ranks; (b) the better-known
occupations are rated more uniformly; (c) strata close to one's own are
elevated in ranking. This last is another instance of the self-indulging
perception, as referred to in the chapter on perception.

As to the latter: (a) the higher ranks have greater consensus than the
lower (probably the effect of more education); (b) the bases of stratification
are perceived somewhat differently by different classes: "The lower classes
use money as the main criterion; the middle classes, money and morality;
and the upper classes, style of life and ancestry" (Broom and Selznick, 1957,
p. 179).

A2   Some internal strain among classes, due to the competitive pursuit
of objects and values in short supply, is found in every stratified society,
but seldom in a violent form.

The unequal distribution of rewards usually spurs lower-placed individuals and groups to try to increase their share, regardless of the organization

of the system (even in a caste system) and regardless of the recency of any improvement of their status. As we have seen, expectations and demands tend to rise with increments of realization. And:

A2.1   In a class system, conflicts over status differences or mobility are typically seen as individual problems (unless an ethnic group is involved). In a caste system, where ritual is a built-in enforcer of caste solidarity, conflicts tend to be seen as group problems.

A2.2   Class tensions are softened primarily by the appearance or the actuality of opportunities for mobility, but also by the substantial spread of income and higher standards of living, by the "openness" of personal relations among the classes (e.g., intermarriage), by the sharing of basic notions of justice and government, by religious comforts, and by cultural diffusion in general.

Substantial movement upward by individual members of a lower caste will tend to soften the caste system, and even occasionally help to transform it into a class system. For example, a study of a Peruvian town concluded that the achievement of high status occupations and considerable wealth by Indians (the lower caste) has been a definite factor in the shift from a caste to a class system (Adams, 1953).

A3   Through emulation of the values and practices of the upper strata, or through the exercise of political and economic power, the lower strata are able to improve their relative position, even in a caste system.

A3.1   The more open the society, the more likely it is for such improvement to come about as a result of relative power position; the more closed the society, the more likely as a result of emulation.

Consider, as an example of the first, the improved position of lower income groups and Negroes in this country. Actually, the emulation of upper-class behavior is quite general: only those fully resigned to lower-class life avoid it—choosing rather to benefit from the liberties allowed or taken at the bottom. For example,

> evidence that higher-class norms do affect even the radical lower-class leaders may be found in studies [showing] that they take over middle-class norms in non-political areas of behavior [Lipset and Linz, 1956, p. 30].

A3.2   Strong claims for improvement in the standard of living come more from strata above the bottom than from those at the bottom itself (the *lumpenproletariat*).

Those who have advanced even a little begin to appreciate what advancement can mean to them, and thus they press harder for it; they begin to have the energy to do so; they begin to win time to do so from the very battle for existence waged at the bottom; they begin to see what education and literacy can do for them; they begin to develop broader horizons and to grow some leaders of their own. Once the process of improvement gets under way and becomes visible, even the lowest groups are more and more drawn into action.

A3.3   Castes and classes that achieve some upward mobility tend to want more.

This is one reason why such mobility is least likely for the lowest level and more likely for strata above it, as noted above. The members of the strata must have an idea of the desirability and the feasibility of "getting ahead" in order for movement to take place; and often the leadership comes from members of higher classes, particularly intellectuals, motivated by humanitarian or political reasons.

A3.4   The more distinguishable the class or caste in physical appearance, the slower its group mobility (e.g., Negroes as compared with white immigrants in this country).

A3.5   Typically, a class aspires to and struggles for mobility only to the next higher rank(s), the more distant ones being considered too far away for realistic approach.

However, as we have said, the appetite grows by what it feeds on.

A4   The growth and the character of particular systems of stratification are influenced by the following conditions:

.1   *Social change:* The more rapid the social change, usually induced by technological developments, the more open the system of stratification; that is, the weaker the class limitations, the more the shifting in ranks and, as a result, the more the status discrepancies among individuals.

In stable periods, rankings on different bases are more likely to be equivalent. The bases of stratification can and do change through time but not rapidly, not consistently, and not without resistance from above.

.1a   As new groups come to positions of power and wealth in the society, typically over a long period of time, prestige in the system of stratification attaches to them, but only with some lag: power and wealth are attained well before the commensurate prestige.

For example, for most ethnic groups in this country, status and recognition have lagged behind economic success as each group has improved its income position.

.2   *Industrialization:* The more industrialized the society, the more differentiated and open the system of stratification.

When more wealth is created, there are more types of positions to be manned and hence more opportunities for unequal relationships among occupations. At least in Western countries, industrialization tends to shift the basis for stratification from traditional criteria to the technical occupations involved in the industrialization itself; from ascription to achievement, from inherited wealth to earned income. In addition, industrialization creates opportunities for mobility through the creation of upper-level (white-collar) jobs: the richer the society, the greater the opportunities for getting rich. Furthermore, by changing some of the bases for stratification—e.g., by downgrading lineage and the nobility and upgrading production—industrialization also, for a time, makes for increased status discrepancies. At the same time:

.2a   The rate of mobility is apparently affected by the extent of industrialization only up to a certain level.

It is at least doubtful that the rates of mobility and of [economic] expansion are correlated. Since a number of countries for which we have data have had different rates of economic expansion but show comparable rates of social mobility, our tentative interpretation is that the social mobility of societies becomes relatively high once their industrialization, and hence their economic expansion, reaches a certain level [Lipset and Bendix, 1959, p. 13].

.3   *Urbanization:* The more urbanized the society, the more differentiated and open the system.

The city is more class-graded than the country, more differentiated in the types of social positions to be filled, more impersonal (so that family connections count for less), more professionalized, more attractive of talent from small towns and rural areas. In cities, even "the purely caste element in social stratification is minimized. In the great and growing cities of India, for example, the caste system cannot be maintained. In the Middle Ages the budding cities were places where serfs lost their unfree status" (Davis, 1949, pp. 332–33). Some scholars believe, as one puts it, that "the caste system in its full form is possible only in a rural society" (Rose, 1961a, p. 365).

.4   *Ethnic heterogeneity and migration:* The more that new groups become available for stratification, usually at the bottom, the more open the system.

In the United States, for example, almost every generation has had the benefit of rising on top of new groups coming in at the bottom of the system—European immigrants in several waves, urbanized Negroes, migrant farmers. As such groups, usually ethnic in character, themselves become assimilated, they begin moving up the class ladder. New strata need not emerge at the bottom or through migration, but they often do. In addition:

> .4a   The less geographical movement into a society, the more reliance upon traditional bases of stratification.

.5   *Ideology:* The more equalitarian the social philosophy of the society, the more open the system of stratification. And, in turn, an equalitarian ideology is associated with the absence of an hereditary aristocracy, the lack of a feudal past, the presence of a frontier, the presence of deprived groups who are still considered active members of the society, the development of literacy, the growth of political participation by the people generally, and the general improvement of the standard of living across classes.

But at least in industrial societies:

> .5a   The fluidity of the system of stratification is apparently not directly dependent upon religious and cultural differences.

On a broad societal basis, rates of mobility are similar in countries of different religious persuasion (although the rate in Italy, a strong Catholic country, does appear to be lower than other European countries with a similar degree of industrialization).

> .5b   The fluidity of the system of stratification, among occupational strata, is apparently not directly dependent upon the character of the political order.

It is the "social-economic expansion" and not the revolutionary introduction of a socialist order which can be considered a necessary condition of this increase [in Poland]. Increased mobility of this type could have been accomplished also if the capitalist system had persisted [Lipset and Bendix, 1959, p. 282, quoting Ossowski, 1957].

.6   *Popular education:* The more widespread the system of education, the more open the system.

"The frequency of vertical mobility tends to vary with the degree to which access to educational facilities is equalized for all classes" (Freedman *et al.,* 1956, p. 532). And again:

The more a society emphasizes education, without at the same time permitting the right to an education to become the prerogative of any special group, then the more likely it is that the interchange of ranks can go on. For education cannot be inherited [Gross, 1958, p. 190].

.7   *Fertility rates:* The greater the differential in fertility rates among classes, the more open the system.

When the rate of fertility in the upper classes is less than enough for its replacement, and the upper group is hence not filled in by its own members, then there is room for others.

Placement and Movement Within the Class System

Here we deal with the ways in which people get located in one or another class within the system: why are individuals where they are? We cover both the initial allocation of persons to ranks and the degrees and kinds of movement (mobility) that occur thereafter.

B1   The initial placement of an individual in the class system is determined by his parents' position, typically his father's: the child inherits his initial class position and shares the class-ification of the family as a whole.

The individual is not only given his position by the family, he is also trained in the behaviors associated with that position (or associated with the class to which the family aspires). In the bringing-up period, he consciously or unconsciously takes over what goes most appropriately with the status he is being prepared to live in: aspirations and ambitions, attitudes and beliefs, appearance, etiquette and manners, tastes, skills.

> Indeed, the role of the family in creating the occupational outlook of its children is the major device for perpetuation of stratification position through the generations, far more important in the modern world than the amount of money that is inherited [Kahl, 1957, p. 294].

B1.1   The higher the parents' status, the better the child's equipment for retaining his status, but the less his chances of improving it (simply because there is nowhere to go from high status but down).

The high-status child has higher aspirations, wider opportunities open to him, more moral and financial support during periods of preparation and training, and so on.

B1.2   The child's chances for upward mobility are directly influenced by his experience within the family:

> **.2a**   The more stress in early training for independence and responsibility, especially when coupled with the capacity to defer gratifications and to consider people instrumentally, the more desire for upward mobility.

.2b   The parental combination of strong-mother, weak-father is apparently likely to promote upward mobility in the son.

.2c   The more the child is involved with his parents or other adults and the less with his peers, the more likely his upward mobility (assuming the parents are not lower in class than the peers). Hence, the smaller the family, the more likely the mobility of the children.

.2d   The sons of lower-class leaders are especially likely to move up to middle-class positions.

B2   The child typically learns quite early in life, usually by his first years in school, what class he belongs to—not what name to give it but how his beliefs and actions distinguish him from others, who is above and below him, whom to be friends with, and so on.

For example, one investigator found, in a Midwestern community, that first-graders were unaware of class symbols, fourth-graders partially aware, and eighth-graders about as aware as adults themselves (Stendler, 1949). As a result:

B2.a   The child's peer group (the clique) normally reinforces the classifying attributes and tendencies of the parental family.

The peer groups with whom the child associates tend to be of the same class as his own, through residential proximity, school location, family friendships and preferences, etc. Hence, like-classed children are thrown together, with the resultant intensification of the characteristics they hold in common. When children of different classes are occasionally thrown together as, for example, through neighborhood change, the mingling often becomes a source of disturbance not only to both groups of children but to the two groups of parents as well. It also becomes a source of knowledge about "how the other half lives" for each class of children, and hence an important avenue of upward mobility for the lower-placed children. For example:

> The adolescent clique is a crucial medium for maintaining the stratification system. . . . The cultures of the various types of cliques specifically adapt to the activities of teen-agers the general values of the class level of their parents, and thereby teach those values more effectively than the preachments of the parents [Kahl, 1957, p. 135].

B3   Those ethnic groups that value learning, promote early independence of children, and defer gratifications are particularly likely to advance in the class system.

For example Jews and Mormons in this country have higher mobility than Catholics or Protestants; similarly, the Scotch are relatively mobile in Europe. Minority status in itself is a stimulus to advancement in the class system only when combined with such characteristics and with the perceived possibility of advancing. For example, these conditions are satisfied in the case of Jews in America, but traditionally not of Negroes in the rural South.

B3.1   The longer a minority group has been in the society, the more it is assimilated to the values of the larger community, and the less visibly ethnic it is, then the better are its chances at upward mobility.

B4   Working-class youths raised in a big city are more likely to move upward than those raised in a small town: there are more stimuli for mobility in the city, fewer restrictions, more anonymity, and more opportunities (partly because the lesser fertility of the upper-classes, at least until very recently, has provided openings).

For middle- and upper-class youths, however, there is no such effect by size of community, presumably because of the already strong class pressure and motivation for mobility; but even for them the possibility of falling in occupational status is less in the city. As one authority says,

> one important element . . . is the fact that educational opportunities are greater in larger cities and the potential rewards for educational attainment are more visible to those who live in larger cities while attending school [Lipset, 1957b, p. 462].

B5   The farther young people go in the educational system, the better their chances for higher-class positions—especially in the case of lower-class youths.

B5.1   Lower-class children get less encouragement from their families to continue their education, and even downright discouragement.

In the United States, at least until very recently, the decision to go to college has been influenced as much by class position as by intelligence or prior educational achievement or, for that matter, by any other single factor. So by and large it is the particularly intelligent and ambitious youngsters in the lower-class ranks who continue their education—e.g., lower-class youths who are not accepted by their lower-class peers and who themselves accept the values of the schools and their middle-class teachers. Thus such young people are already identifying with middle-class values as they start up the class ranks via the educational system.

B5.2   The further that lower-class youths go in school, then the less vocational their training, the more opportunities open up to them, and the more deliberate and less fortuitous is their choice of a first job.

Typically, the sons of manual workers enter the job market in non-manual positions only on the basis of a college education. With respect to first employment, lower-class youths are more likely, out of necessity, to take the only job they know about when they enter the job market; and "the nature of these early jobs [is] prophetic of the subsequent careers" (Davidson and Anderson, 1937, p. 169).

Although level of intelligence (at least as usually measured) is correlated with the class of the family, there are enough discrepancies both ways to make for both upward and downward mobility. But intelligence is associated with the desire for educational achievement, and usually with the fact as well.

The more the upward mobility in a society, the less the talent available in the lower classes; the less the upward mobility, the more the talent in the lower classes is either underemployed or put into the service of lower-class leadership. This obviously involves a matter of judgment about the use of talent. (For a commentary on the question, see Young, 1959).

B6   In broad terms, class continuity is more constant in a society than interclass mobility, especially historically but even today.

For example, in the United States currently, "sons are more likely to enter their father's occupation than to enter any other single occupation" (Rogoff, 1953, p. 59), although this tendency is often obscured by variations in the relative size of the rate of growth of occupations. The quoted statement is based on the ratio of actual to expected mobility; a more descriptive tabulation, as an instance of intergenerational mobility in the United States, appears on page 472.

B6.1   The farther the distance between classes, the less the movement between them.

For example, generational and career mobility in occupations occurs mainly within manual jobs on the one hand and within nonmanual on the other, rather than between them; and most of it is limited to movements across one or two ranks:

> An unskilled worker may become a semiskilled or skilled worker, and a skilled laborer may become a salesman or a clerical worker, but it is unlikely that an individual who starts his occupational career in the unskilled or semiskilled work group will become an executive or professional [Broom and Selznick, 1957, pp. 437–38].

Movement across the manual-nonmanual line is more common between generations than within a single career.

Occupational mobility, Indianapolis, 1940: proportion of sons
in each occupation according to father's occupation

Father's occupation	Son's occupation (percentages)											Total number of fathers
	Professional	Semiprofessional	Proprietors, managers, officials	Clerks and salesmen	Skilled	Semiskilled	Unskilled	Protective service	Personal service	Farming	All fathers	
Professional	28.3	6.3	7.6	27.9	15.4	9.5	2.5	0.8	1.5	0.2	100.0	(474)
Semiprofessional	15.8	19.3	3.5	17.5	23.7	12.3	2.6	1.8	3.5		100.0	(114)
Proprietors, managers, officials	7.7	3.4	17.6	30.6	14.3	19.8	2.5	1.6	2.1	0.5	100.1	(1203)
Clerks and salesmen	7.7	5.2	7.6	42.2	15.1	16.4	2.4	1.3	1.9	0.2	100.0	(1092)
Skilled	3.3	2.9	4.3	19.1	32.3	26.9	5.6	2.1	3.0	0.6	100.1	(2729)
Semiskilled	2.5	2.1	4.1	17.3	18.4	43.2	5.3	2.2	4.3	0.6	100.1	(1520)
Unskilled	2.4	1.5	2.8	13.1	15.4	30.0	28.6	2.4	3.6	0.3	100.1	(720)
Protective service	2.5	0.8	6.6	22.8	17.0	31.5	8.7	8.3	1.2	0.4	99.8	(241)
Personal service	4.9	4.3	5.5	17.1	22.6	29.9	3.7	1.8	10.4		100.2	(164)
Farming	3.8	1.6	5.9	15.2	23.1	28.7	8.9	3.6	5.1	4.2	100.1	(1635)
Sons of all fathers	5.5	3.1	6.6	22.1	21.9	27.1	6.9	2.3	3.4	1.1	100.0	—
Total number of sons	(548)	(307)	(656)	(2188)	(2163)	(2678)	(684)	(229)	(334)	(105)	(9892)	(9892)

(Rogoff, 1951, p. 410)

B7   The rate of generational mobility is currently about the same in all highly industrialized countries.

"There is relatively little difference in rates of social mobility, as measured by the shift across the manual-nonmanual line, in countries for which sample survey data exist"—the United States, Germany, France, Switzerland, Sweden, Japan, Denmark, Great Britain, and Italy (Lipset and Bendix, 1959, p. 72). From one generation to the next, about 25 per cent of the nonfarm population moves across the line between the working class and the middle class, both ways.

Here is the summary table, plus a sample of detailed figures on individual countries:

Comparative indices of upward and downward mobility (percentages)

Country	Nonfarm populations		
	Upward mobility (nonmanual sons of manual fathers)	Downward mobility (manual sons of nonmanual fathers)	Total vertical mobility (nonfarm population mobile across the line between working and middle class)
United States	33	26	30
Germany	29	32	31
Sweden	31	24	29
Japan	36	22	27
France	39	20	27
Switzerland	45	13	23

Country	Populations with rural and urban occupations classified together		
	High-prestige occupation sons of fathers in low-prestige occupations	Low-prestige occupation sons of fathers in high-prestige occupations	Proportion mobile across high- and low-occupation prestige lines
Denmark	22	44	31
Great Britain	20	49	29
Italy	8	34	16

(Lipset and Bendix, 1959, p. 25)

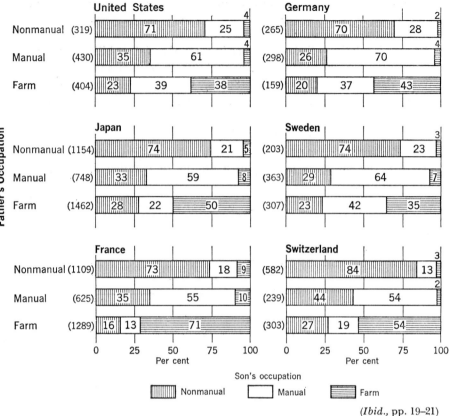

(*Ibid.*, pp. 19–21)

B7.1   In most industrialized countries, the mobility upward is greater than the mobility downward (at a ratio of about 60:40 for the present and recent generations).

B7.2   Whereas actual upward mobility by occupation is as high in Western Europe as in the United States, the belief in it appears to be stronger in the United States.

B7.3   Although the measurements are difficult to make, it appears that there is always a good deal of mobility in societies of some size.

There is much evidence from historians of Western society as well as from contemporary students of basically nonindustrial societies that such societies also have been characterized by considerable mobility [Lipset and Bendix, 1959, p. 75].

As a special case:

The data on Chinese class mobility are more reliable than on the high middle ages in Europe, because each Chinese dynasty accepted the task of compiling

the biographies of important men in the preceding epoch. Given the historio-
graphic customs of China, we know that these were formalized, but they do
contain enough data to make rough guesses about the various dynasties from the
T'ang through the Ching. Each such study has shown that from one-third to
three-quarters of the men of high position in any given generation were new
men, with no apparent family base in the upper stratum. Hsu used local district biographies, and found that only one-fifth of the men had three generations
of higher class position behind them [Goode, 1960, p. 10].

B7.4   At least in the United States and Great Britain, the rate of
upward occupational mobility has been steady over the past few generations (taking into account the changes in the occupational structure).

Here, for example, are the summary mobility measures from one of the
more sophisticated studies of American mobility, comparing the rates of
occupational mobility in 1910 and 1940 for fathers and sons in Marion
County, Indiana (Indianapolis):

Summary mobility measures, 1910 and 1940 *

Measure	1910	1940
Mean mobility rate	.82	.81
Standard deviation	.47	.43
Minimum mobility	.16	.17
Mean minimum mobility	.30	.37

* These measures show that *no significant changes took place in
over-all mobility rates between 1910 and 1940.*

(Rogoff, 1953, p. 49)

And here are similar data for Britain, over a longer span of time:

Relation between status of subjects and fathers

Date of birth of subjects	Percentage of subjects with same status as their fathers	Of subjects differing in status from their fathers, percentage with higher status than their fathers
Before 1890	33.4	31.8
1890–99	33.9	43.1
1900–09	34.4	44.1
1910–19	36.4	42.7
1920–29	37.0	33.7

(Glass and Hall, 1954, p. 188)

B7.5   Migrants, either between or within countries, are more *socially* mobile than those who stay at home.

This was recently documented, e.g., for fathers and sons originating in a small Kentucky town (Scudder and Anderson, 1954).

B7.6   In recent decades, in the United States, access to the business elite has been relatively restricted—more so than access to top positions in labor or the civil service.

> The evidence . . . points strongly to the favored social and economic background of a great majority of those whose later careers placed them in the American business elite. And since the proportion of business leaders coming from middle-class and working-class families has not changed greatly with time, our over-all finding is that the recruitment of the American business elite has remained remarkably stable. We may attempt to allow for the tenuousness of the categories we have had to work with by assuming that between 10 and 20 per cent of the successful businessmen have come from families in which the father was a worker, craftsman, small entrepreneur, lower-white-collar employee, or small farmer. Such a result is still at variance with the popular impression that during the early industrial development opportunities for spectacular upward mobility were readily available to an individual, and that these opportunities have declined markedly with the advance of industrialization. . . . Such a[n equalitarian] doctrine could have carried little conviction if it had been widely known that economic success was greatly facilitated by the influence of a favorable family background [Lipset and Bendix, 1959, pp. 127–28].

Behavioral Differences by Class and Mobility

The members of different classes, or those moving or desiring to move between classes, behave differently on a wide range of matters. Such differences are everywhere fundamental and pervasive; they are among the most important explanatory differences underlying human behavior.

> Sentiments concerning class status and the individual's identification of himself in terms of a particular class status do . . . play a very permeative role in social life. . . . It is seldom the exclusive factor in [life's] choices, but it is also seldom entirely absent [Shils, 1960, p. 768].

In most of what follows we are restricted by the nature of the literature to class differences in the United States, but many of these findings would probably be duplicated elsewhere. Many students, incidentally, are willing to call the following findings "consequences" of stratification or mobility; some, however, prefer simply to call them class differences associated with stratification. A few of the findings also appear in the substantive chapters to which they refer but are included here to give a fuller picture of the behavioral correlates of class membership.

LIFE CHANCES

C1   The higher the class, the lower the morbidity (including severe mental illness and suicide) and the longer the life expectancy—mainly due to the nutritive, hygienic, and medical advantages that money can buy.

For example, here are figures on life expectancy by class, for men in Chicago:

	Lowest economic class	Highest economic class
1920	49.6	60.6
1930	49.5	63.0
1940	56.5	65.4

(Mayer and Hauser, 1953, p. 283)

That life chances in a crisis are sharply related to class is illustrated by the fate of people on the *Titanic*, as reported by Walter Lord in *A Night to Remember*. Only 3 per cent of the female passengers in first class drowned (and most of them remained behind voluntarily), as against 16 per cent of those in second class and 45 per cent of those in third class. Obviously, this had a great deal to do with their locations on the ship: many in third-class were held below deck at gunpoint while others were being evacuated.

As another instance of this finding, it used to be the case that infant mortality was "the most sensitive index we possess of the level of social and economic well-being," but recent data show that this differential is closing rapidly in the modern urban-industrial society like the United States (Stockwell, 1962, p. 110).

And here are figures on the occurrence of schizophrenia by class, in New Haven, Connecticut:

Incidence, re-entry, continuous, and prevalence rates per 100,000 for the schizophrenics—by class (age and sex adjusted)

Class	Type of rate per 100,000			
	Incidence	Re-entry	Continuous	Prevalence
I–II (high)	6	14	97	111
III	8	20	148	168
IV	10	21	269	300
V (low)	20	46	729	895
χ^2	8.50	13.46	355.62	452.68
p	$<.05$	$<.01$	$<.001$	$<.001$

(Hollingshead and Redlich, 1958, p. 236)

This last, however, needs some qualification:

> Perhaps the most impressively consistent correlation found in epidemiological studies is the inverse relationship between social status and rates of schizophrenia, especially in larger cities. . . . One somewhat discordant note in the chorus of findings on socioeconomic status and schizophrenia comes from the research carried out by Kohn and Clausen in Hagerstown, Maryland [Clausen and Kohn, 1956]. We found no evidence of an inverse relationship between rates of schizophrenia and socioeconomic status, regardless of whether ecological or occupational categories were used as the index of status. Moreover, a cursory review of the literature suggests that the correlations between social status and schizophrenia are higher in the largest cities than in medium-sized cities [Clausen, 1959, pp. 488–89].

At the same time, there are some psychosomatic illnesses that are peculiar to certain classes. A large-scale study in New York City found, for example, that the prevalence of colitis, hives and rashes, and hay fever increases from the lower to the higher classes; that asthma and bladder trouble were most prevalent in the higher and lower classes, and least in the middle classes; and that heart conditions were more prevalent in the middle classes than they were in either the higher or the lower classes (Rennie and Srole, 1956).

C2   The higher the class of the family into which he is born, the better the child's chances for high occupational and class position.

For example, in the United States, "The sons of men at the top of the system have from five to eight times more opportunity to succeed their fathers than would be the case if the structure were completely open" (Kahl, 1957, p. 272). As one instance, the job aspirations of young people in a small Midwestern town are given in the chart on page 479.

CHILDBEARING AND REARING

C3   The higher the class, the lower the fertility rate (although this relationship now seems to be softening, for the first time in decades).

C4   Upper-class and especially middle-class children are more likely to be raised according to the latest "expert standards," which are only subsequently adopted by the lower classes.

> From a recent summary of the research literature on this topic:

> Shifts in the pattern of infant care—especially on the part of middle class mothers—show a striking correspondence to the changes in practices advocated in successive editions of U.S. Children's Bureau bulletins and similar sources of expert opinion. . . . Taken together, the findings on changes in infant care lead to the generalization that socialization practices are most likely to be altered in those segments of society which have most ready access to the agencies or agents of change (e.g., books, pamphlets, physicians, and counselors) [Bronfenbrenner, 1958, p. 424].

Vocational choices of adolescents by class and occupational groups (percentages)

Vocational aim	Class II	Class III	Class IV	Class V
Profession or business	77	36	23	7
Farmer	12	11	6	3
Clerical	5	20	20	10
Craftsman	3	12	18	14
Service trades and miscellaneous		8	13	25
Undecided	3	13	20	41

(Hollingshead, 1949, p. 286)

Actually, it appears that the class differences in child-bearing are disappearing or at least narrowing, as "best practices" become generally known. As the reviewer put it:

Either middle-class mothers are beginning to make less use of techniques they previously relied upon, or the working class is starting to adopt them. We are inclined toward the latter hypothesis in the belief that the working class, as a function of increasing income and education, is gradually reducing its "cultural lag" [*ibid.*, p. 420].

Nevertheless, some differences remain:

C4.1   In the United States currently, child-rearing practices appear to differ among the several classes in the following respects: lower-class infants and children are subject to less parental supervision but more parental authority, to more physical punishment and less use of reasoning as a disciplinary measure, to less control of sexual and other impulses, to more freedom to express aggression (except against the parents) and to engage in violence, to earlier sex-typing of behavior (i.e., what males and females are supposed to be and do), to less development of conscience, to less stress toward achievement, to less equalitarian treatment vis-à-vis the parents, and to less permissive upbringing than are their middle-class contemporaries.

For example, on page 481 is the summary tabulation of the "over-all character of parent-child relationship" from a variety of studies:

Furthermore, some scholars believe that there are some differences, within classes, between "entrepreneurial" and "bureaucratic" parents in child-rearing practices concerned with self-control and with adjustment, i.e., roughly speaking, between those "on their own" and those working for large organizations (Miller and Swanson, 1958).

Here is a sample tabulation:

Significance and direction of findings through the use of the internalization indices (dealing with self-control) *

Prediction: Entrepreneurial mothers are more likely than bureaucratic mothers to:	Among upper middles	Among lower middles	Among all middles
	p	p	p
Give delayed attention to crying baby or give no attention	+ <.01	+ <.005	+ <.0005
Wean the baby by the end of twelve months	<.90	<.95	<.90
Feed the baby on a schedule	+ <.05	<.70	+ <.03
Begin bowel training before the baby is ten months old	<.95	+ <.10	+ <.10
Begin urinary training before the baby is eleven months old	<.70	+ <.03	+ <.03
Use symbolic rewards	<.95	<.80	<.70
Use symbolic punishments	<.80	+ <.03	+ <.03

* The notation in this table gives a symbol for the direction of the findings followed by the level of probability. The direction symbols are as follows: a plus (+) sign means the results show the direction predicted; the absence of a symbol indicates that the p value is greater than .50, making hazardous any statement about trends. All p values reaching the .20 level or beyond and having the predicted direction, are presented using one tail of the probability distribution. The degrees of freedom in each χ^2 computation are one.

(*Ibid.*, p. 99)

Sample	Approximate date of practice	Number of cases reported	Age	Middle-class trend	Working-class trend
Berkeley I	1928–32	31	1–3	Grants autonomy Cooperative Equalitarian	Expresses affection Excessive contact Intrusive Irritable Punitive Ignores child
National I	1932	494	0–1		Baby picked up when cries †
National IV	1932	3239	1–12	Higher percentage of children punished †	Nothing done to allay child's fears †
Yellow Springs, Ohio	1940	124	3–12	Acceptant-democratic	Indulgent Active-rejectant
Berkeley II	1939–42	31	9–11	Grants autonomy Cooperative Equalitarian Expresses affection	Excessive contact Intrusive Irritable Punitive Ignores child
Chicago I	1943	100	5		Father plays with child more †
Chicago II	1943–44	433	1–5	"Developmental" conception of "good mother" and "good child"	"Traditional" conception of "good mother" and "good child" †
New Haven I	1949–50	219	1	More necessary discipline to prevent injury or danger †	More prohibitive discipline beyond risk of danger or injury
Boston	1951–52	372	5	Mother warmer toward child † Father warmer toward child * Father exercises more authority * Mother has higher esteem for father † Mother delighted about pregnancy † Both parents more often share authority *	Father demands instant obedience † Child ridiculed † Greater rejection of child † Emphasis on neatness, cleanliness, and order † Parents disagree more on child-rearing policy *
New Haven II	1951–53	48	14–17	Fathers have more power in family decisions † Parents agree in value orientations †	
Palo Alto	1953	73	2½–5½	Baby picked up when cries †	Mother carries through demands rather than dropping the subject †
Eugene	1955–56	206	0–18	Better relationship between father and child †	
Washington, D.C.	1956–57	400	10–11	Desirable qualities are happiness,* considerateness,* curiosity,* self-control *	Desirable qualities are neatness-cleanliness,* obedience *

* Trend significant at 5 per cent level or better.
† The difference between percentages is not significant but the difference between mean ratings is significant at the 5 per cent level or better.

(Bronfenbrenner, 1958, p. 421)

MARITAL AND FAMILY RELATIONS

C5   Marital partners are selected primarily within classes, although there is a sizable amount of intermarriage between neighboring ranks.

C5.1   The closer the class position of the partners, the better the marital adjustment.

Marital adjustment and social class

Social class of husband and wife at time of marriage			
Same class	Good 53.5	Fair 26.0	Poor 20.5
One class apart	Good 35.0	Fair 31.2	Poor 33.8
More than one class apart	Good 14.3	Fair 38.1	Poor 47.6

(Roth and Peck, 1951, p. 481)

C6   The higher the class, the later the age at marriage and the greater the number of unmarried women.

C7   The higher the class, the more companionable the relations between husband and wife—or at least the more that is considered the proper norm.

C8   Family instability (divorce, separation, and abandonment) is greatest in the lower class, then the upper, and least in the middle class.

C9   Upward mobility on the part of only one spouse (especially if it is the woman) makes for poor marital adjustment; and the children tend to identify with the higher-status parent. Similarly, mobility of the children over the parents disrupts the family. Sharp mobility of the family makes for general feelings of insecurity, even among the children (from not knowing how to behave, what is expected, and so on). The more the parents aspire to upward mobility, the less they tend to raise their children in a tension-free atmosphere.

SOCIAL RELATIONS

C10   Voluntary personal relations—friendships, cliques, dating, associations, etc.—are primarily carried on within classes, especially at the extremes.

On page 483, for example, is the dating picture in a Midwestern town.

C10.1   The higher the rank, the more the contact with people of various ranks, and the greater the geographical range of contacts. (Note that this refers only to contact, not to close personal relations.)

Intra- and interclass dating patterns of boys and girls, April, 1942 (percentages) *

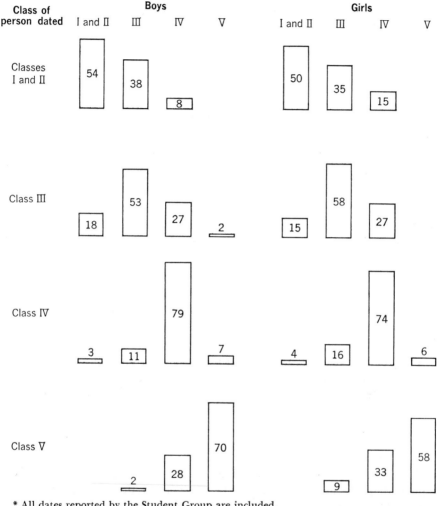

* All dates reported by the Student Group are included.

(Hollingshead, 1949, p. 231)

C10.1a   The more the contact between ranks, the more likely the deviation from class norms on the part of the lower member involved.

And the more such contact occurs, the more reinforced the class system itself becomes:

The high status person reveals, in his mode of communication, his superior position when communicating with a lower status individual. At the same time, the status difference is reinforced by the lower status person confirming his lower position when responding to the person of higher status [Dubin, 1958, p. 345].

C10.2   The farther apart the classes, the fewer the personal relations as "equals."

But it may be easier for the top and the bottom to meet, in the highly regularized forms of a hierarchical society, than the top and the middle or the middle and the bottom.

C11   Organizational memberships are more frequent among the higher classes.

Which organizations are joined also reflects class position—the club for the upper class as against the lodge for the middle and lower-middle class. This applies even to religious affiliation—e.g., among the Protestant sects, typically, the Episcopalian, Presbyterian, Congregational, Quaker, and Unitarian churches are upper and upper-middle, Methodist and Lutheran are middle, and Baptist and evangelical are lower (as indicated in the section on religious institutions).

C12   Those moving up in the class system are less likely than their stationary counterparts to maintain strong personal relations and friendships (partly, though not entirely, due to their greater geographical movement).

> A person who moves up in the social hierarchy will tend to change his friends, join new organizations, move to a new neighborhood; perhaps he will even change his religious affiliation; in some cases he will change his name, often he will alter his political attitudes [Lipset and Bendix, 1959, p. 18].

C13   Sexual behavior differs by social class, especially for men: the members of middle occupational groups (those in semiskilled jobs) who seem to be satisfied with their class position engage in the highest sexual activity —more than the groups above and below them or those middle members who aspire to upward mobility.

To some extent, presumably, this is a matter of expenditure of energy for all concerned: the upper class expends more energy on job and position, the lower on problems of existence, and the aspirants on aspiring. Liberality and experimentation in sexual behavior appear to be greater in the higher (better-educated) classes. There is also some evidence that the potentially mobile or the aspiring take over, in advance, the sexual behavior of the class toward which they are moving—but the validity of the data is not clearly established (see the section on sexual behavior, in the chapter on the family).

VALUES, STANDARDS, MORALITY

C14   The higher the class, the more the value placed on formal education, as both an end and a means, and its correlates—information, knowledge, etc. (at least in the United States and parts of Europe).

> Sociological analyses of the external environment of schools have focused on
> one major problem area, the impact of social class on education. More studies
> have probably been devoted to this problem than to any other in the sociology
> of education. The general conclusion that emerges from most of this literature
> is that nearly every phase of school functioning is influenced by the phenomenon
> of social class. Academic achievement, level of aspiration, participation in extra-
> curricular activities, and the drop-out rate, for example, all tend to be positively
> related to the social-class placement of the child [Gross, 1959, p. 144].

As one instance, here are the grades in Elmtown:

	Per cent with mean grade of		
Class	*85–100*	*70–84*	*50–69*
I and II	51.4	48.6	00.0
III	35.5	63.2	1.3
IV	18.4	69.2	12.4
V	8.3	66.7	25.0
Total	(23.8)	(66.3)	(9.9)

(Hollingshead, 1949, p. 172)

As another, below are the college plans of boys from different classes in 1950
—showing, incidentally, that the low I.Q. sons of upper-class fathers are

**Percentage of boys who expected to go to college,
by I.Q. and father's occupation (percentages) ***

	I.Q. quintile (boys)					
	(LOW)				(HIGH)	*All*
Father's occupation	*1*	*2*	*3*	*4*	*5*	*quintiles*
Major white collar	56	72	79	82	89	80
Middle white collar	28	36	47	53	76	52
Minor white collar	12	20	22	29	55	26
Skilled labor and service	4	15	19	22	40	19
Other labor and service	9	6	10	14	29	12
All occupations	11	17	24	30	52	27

* 3348 second- and third-year male students in Boston area public high schools.

(Kahl, 1953, p. 188)

twice as likely to go to college as the high I.Q. sons of lower class fathers (although the divergence has softened in the years since this study was made). Moreover, the child-rearing practices of lower-class parents are usually not conducive to extended educational application on the part of the children. According to one summary, the children of upper-middle-class parents gradually learn the values and habits of impulse renunciation, deferred gratification, saving, ambition, hard work for future rewards, patience, obedience to legitimate authorities. These values and habits are more conducive to successful adjustment to many years of school and middle-class occupations than are the impulse-following tendencies of lower-class children (Gross, 1958).

C15   Members of the middle class value achievement and prestige more than do members of lower classes; and those middle-class members moving up value them still more.

A study of boys in the northeastern United States showed that while both class and ethnic position affected their scores on a test of motivation for achievement, the differences associated with class were larger (Rosen, 1959a). In short, as a recent summary put it:

> Lower-class people, for example, survey studies have found, participate in fewer voluntary associations and other organized activities. They have less facility in reading and writing. They read fewer magazines and listen to the "less serious" radio and television programs. They know less about political issues and have less expressed interest in them. They are less critical of the sources of the daily news. They are more timid about expressing their opinions to poll interviewers and more often give "don't know" answers. They know less about such matters that concern their economic and social interests as income taxes, price controls, birth control, and consumer's cooperation. They have lower occupational aspirations and tend to go into blind-alley jobs. They have lower expectations for future income and they are much less likely than people in the middle class to say that the future holds good opportunities for them to improve their educational, occupational, or economic position. In brief, as Hyman [1953] has put it, the survey data "show clearly that there is reduced striving for success among the lower classes, an awareness of lack of opportunity, and a lack of valuation of education, normally the major avenue to achievement of high status" [Barber, 1961, p. 108].

C16   The middle class conforms more strictly to the values and standards of conduct of the society as a whole than either the upper or the lower class—for example, there is less alcoholism in the middle class; there is more observance of anti-Negro taboos in the South in the middle class; there is greater observance of sex norms in the middle class.

In a way, this may be simply a statistical artifact: being middle, they are usually more numerous, and hence account for more of "the society as a whole."

There is also some evidence that middle-class people are more deliberate about their purchases of consumer goods than members of the upper or the lower classes (Katona and Mueller, 1954).

C17   Mobile persons identify in norms, standards, values, appearance, and behavior with the upper level to which they aspire.

Those moving up, or wanting to, are more likely to conform to the norms of higher strata ("anticipatory socialization") than to those of their own current class—except in those cases where the individual is clearly rejected socially by the upper class. The upwardly mobile are unlikely to hold strongly to values not associated with mobility, prestige, and achievement. Indeed, many such people are extremely sensitive to status considerations: in England it is said that they have "class on the brain." Those moving down the social ladder tend to retain the values, attitudes, norms, and standards of the class from which they are falling, partly in the aspiration and the hope to return.

C18   Lower-class groups tend toward either a radical political position or a strong religious position.

Such groups are unlikely to be "both moderate in their politics *and* indifferent to religion"; they tend to "have a strong faith either in radical politics or in an emotional religiosity" (Lipset and Bendix, 1959, p. 263).

C19   The greater the rate of social mobility, the more the consensus within the society, because of the spread of the general ideology among those achieving or desiring some mobility (e.g., lower-class sons moving into middle-class jobs); and the less the lower classes adopt a militantly class-conscious ideology or program.

Whereas individual mobility tends to lessen class conflict, group mobility tends to sharpen it. The more changes there are of slight magnitude via individual mobility, the less the chances of sharp or radical or revolutionary changes involving whole strata of people at once.

C20   Sharp mobility (especially downward) tends to produce ethnic prejudices, at least in a country like the United States where ethnic problems exist.

From a study of the subject among American veterans,

the data at hand indicate that while slow upward mobility is closely associated with tolerance, rapid mobility either upward or downward, is positively related to ethnic hostility. . . . [Similarly in Germany] the socially and economically downward-moving lower middle class groups (frequently referred to as the squeezed-out groups) were the followers of Hitler, while the "respectable," relatively secure and static middle classes (those who had not experienced downward mobility) held apart from this extreme form of nationalism (and anti-Semitism) [Bettelheim and Janowitz, 1950, pp. 60–61].

STYLE OF LIFE

C21   Classes differ in their use of leisure and in their tastes: the upper classes, being better educated, are interested in a wider range of life; and by virtue of being upper, they become the arbiters of the "proper" use of money, physical appearance and dress, etiquette, language, and aesthetic taste.

Even their recreational interests are different, from boating and polo through tennis to golf and on down to bowling. Indeed, the exploitation of athletic and entertainment ability is a major avenue of quick mobility for the lower-class youth with talent, at least as far as money is concerned.

Class differences in taste range beyond aesthetic quality in the narrower sense. There are

> variations in the whole experience patterns of different social strata. In a series of Austrian studies I was struck by finding that people of low income prefer sweet chocolate, fabrics with a rubbery touch, and strong-smelling flowers; upper-class consumers favored what one might call more demanding sensory experiences: bitter-dry tastes, irregular weaves, and less pungent fragrances. . . . One can give a more psychological explanation: the lower-class person is starved out for pleasant sense experiences; or a more sociological one: the upper-class individual exhibits his "sensual" wealth by conspicuous non-consumption of strong stimuli. . . . [In addition] we know that, among women of the same actual weight, the tendency to consider themselves overweight shows a high positive correlation with socioeconomic status (Newman, 1957) [Lazarsfeld, in Dahl *et al.*, 1959, pp. 108–09].

C22   The lower classes presumably violate the law more frequently than the upper classes; in any case, they are more likely to be caught and punished.

"Although the data are scanty and unsystematic there is strong evidence of class bias in the administration of justice and legal protection in our society" (Mayer, 1955, p. 39), so it is not altogether clear what the fact is.

> Individuals of the higher economic and occupational levels escape arrest and conviction to a greater extent than lower class persons, even when equally guilty of crimes. Although this may seem a shocking state of affairs, it is not surprising since it costs money to ask for justice. Wealthy persons can employ the best legal talent

and, at times, expert witnesses. They can exercise personal influence to escape arrest or conviction, obtain changes of venue and delays, and if found guilty, they are often fined rather than imprisoned. Poor people, on the other hand, are more likely to be arrested and remanded to jail if they cannot furnish bail. Without financial and political power they cannot defend themselves as effectively when on trial and are more likely to be convicted [*ibid.*, p. 39].

C23   The lower classes are in general more distrustful of authority, as exercised by remote and powerful classes, and more resigned to physical and psychological suffering than are the higher classes.

A deep-seated distrust of authority figures pervades class V persons [lowest class] from childhood to old age. Suspicion is directed toward police, clergymen, teachers, doctors, public officials, public health nurses, and social workers. . . . Politicians are believed to operate a machine designed to exploit poor people. . . . Institutions for care of the disabled and the ill are believed to be run for money and one has to have "pull" to get into them. . . . Hostility against official representatives of society is linked to convictions that they are being exploited. Some believe that they have to live in the slums because the state is taking advantage of them. . . . Class I and II persons are more aware of psychological problems than class IV and V persons. Class I and II persons are also more perceptive of personal frustration, failure, and critical intra-psychic conflicts than class IV and V persons. . . . As a consequence, we believe that far more abnormal behavior is tolerated by the two lower classes, particularly class V, without any awareness that the motivations behind the behavior are pathological, even though the behavior may be disapproved by the class norms [Hollingshead and Redlich, 1958, pp. 130, 172–73].

Furthermore, lower-class people are more likely than are upper-class people to attribute emotional disturbance to "unhappiness, tough luck, laziness, meanness, or physical illness rather than to factors of psychogenic origin" (*ibid.*, p. 175).

PERSONALITY

C24   A person's self-evaluation is strongly influenced by the ranking of his class (that is, by the society's evaluation of the group to which he belongs).

In simplest terms, this means that upper-class people feel individually superior, and lower-class people feel inferior.

C25   Those moving up in class are more subject to mild or moderate emotional and mental disorder (neuroticism) than those who are stationary, partly because of the clash of class values to which they are subject and partly because of their own make-up at the outset.

However, some recent evidence indicates that there are no differences in anxiety between classes: "The tension-anxiety dimension . . . shows almost a zero correlation with socioeconomic status" (**Rennie and Srole**, 1956, p. 455).

C26   The modal personality of the lower class is more limited, restricted, and authoritarian than that of the middle or the upper class.

> Closely linked with economic underprivilege is psychological underprivilege: habits of submission, little access to sources of information, lack of verbal facility. These things appear to produce a lack of self-confidence which increases the unwillingness of the low-status person to participate in many phases of our predominantly middle-class culture [Knupfer, 1947, p. 114].

SELECTED READINGS

Stratification is a central topic in sociology and there is a sizable literature. Two surveys of the field have appeared in recent years:

Bernard Barber. *Social Stratification: A Comparative Analysis of Structure and Process.* Harcourt, Brace & World, 1957.
Joseph A. Kahl. *The American Class Structure.* Holt, Rinehart & Winston, 1957.

In addition, there is an excellent short summary by Edward Shils in the article on class in the *Encyclopaedia Britannica.* For a collection of articles, see:

Reinhard Bendix and Seymour M. Lipset, eds. *Class, Status and Power: A Reader in Social Stratification.* Free Press, 1953.

Among the major empirical studies of stratification in American communities are these titles:

Allison Davis *et al. Deep South: A Social-Anthropological Study of Caste and Class.* U. of Chicago Press, 1941.
Robert S. Lynd and Helen M. Lynd. *Middletown* and *Middletown in Transition.* Harcourt, Brace & World, 1929, 1937.
W. Lloyd Warner and Paul S. Lunt. *The Social Life of a Modern Community* and *The Status System of a Modern Community* (Yankee City). Yale U. Press, 1941, 1942.
James West. *Plainville, U.S.A.* Columbia U. Press, 1945.

On issues of social mobility, see:

David V. Glass, ed. *Social Mobility in Britain.* Free Press, 1954.
Seymour M. Lipset and Reinhard Bendix. *Social Mobility in Industrial Society.* U. of California Press, 1959.
Natalie Rogoff. *Recent Trends in Occupational Mobility.* Free Press, 1953.

Finally, as a sample of the many studies of behavioral differences by class, see:

Urie Bronfenbrenner. "Socialization and Social Class Through Time and Space," in Eleanor E. Maccoby *et al.,* eds., *Readings in Social Psychology.* 3rd ed. Holt, Rinehart & Winston, 1958, pp. 400–25.

Richard Centers. *The Psychology of Social Classes.* Russell Sage Foundation, 1961.

Herbert H. Hyman. "The Value Systems of Different Classes: A Social Psychological Contribution to the Analysis of Stratification," in Reinhard Bendix and Seymour M. Lipset, eds., *Class, Status and Power: A Reader in Social Stratification.* Free Press, 1953.

August B. Hollingshead and Frederick C. Redlich. *Social Class and Mental Illness: A Community Study.* Wiley, 1958.

If the Tiber reaches the walls, if the Nile does not rise to the fields, if the sky doesn't move [i.e., no rain] or the earth does, if there is famine, if there is plague, the cry is at once: "The Christians to the lion!"

TERTULLIAN
Apologeticus

But to minds strongly marked by the positive and negative qualities that create severity—strength of will, conscious rectitude of purpose, narrowness of imagination and intellect, great powers of self-control, and a disposition to exert control over others—prejudices come as the natural food of tendencies which can get no sustenance out of that complex, fragmentary, doubt-provoking knowledge which we call truth. Let a prejudice be bequeathed, carried in the air, adopted by hearsay, caught in through the eye—however it may come, these minds will give it a habituation: it is something to assert strongly and broadly, something to fill up the void of spontaneous ideas, something to impose on others with the authority of conscious right: it is at once a staff and a baton. Every prejudice that will answer these purposes is self-evident.

GEORGE ELIOT
The Mill on the Floss

"Are we likely to be seen on our way?"

"No, unless by native craft," said Schomberg. Ricardo nodded, satisfied. Both these white men looked on native life as a mere play of shadows. A play of shadows the dominant race could walk through unaffected and disregarded in the pursuit of its incomprehensible aims and needs. No. Native craft did not count, of course. It was an empty, solitary part of the sea.

JOSEPH CONRAD
Victory

You've got to be taught
To hate and fear,
You've got to be taught
From year to year. . . .
You've got to be taught before it's too late
Before you are six or seven or eight
To hate all the people your relatives hate,
You've got to be carefully taught.

OSCAR HAMMERSTEIN II
"You've Got To Be Carefully Taught"

Chapter Twelve

ETHNIC RELATIONS

Ethnic identification is, along with class, among the important social differences that affect human behavior. The factor appears throughout this inventory as an independent variable but also requires some concentrated consideration in its own right.

During the course of its history, for example, the United States has been faced with problems of ethnic relations. At the start there was the problem of setting up a unified state with a variety of national stocks. In the middle of the nineteenth century, a civil war was fought around the issue. In the late nineteenth and early twentieth centuries, waves of immigrants affected the social and political life of the country and brought with them religious differences that compounded the impact of national distinctions. Now, in the mid-twentieth century, the country is living through the great social experiment of desegregation that has provided front-page headlines for a number of years and will continue to do so.

With ethnic relations so important on the national front, it is no wonder that behavioral scientists have given a good deal of attention to the matter. A few decades ago they were largely concerned with the assimilation of immigrants; more recently, they have concentrated on the position of important minorities. As a result, our review of what we know about ethnic relations will deal largely with the United States, somewhat with assimilation (which is also included in the chapter on culture), and mainly with attitudes and behavior with regard to Negroes and Jews.*

* Again we issue the reminder that purely descriptive material on the present status of minorities in the United States is omitted in favor of more general findings. We note this here—although the principle applies throughout the volume—because there is a great deal of such material in the behavioral science literature on this topic; for example, the place of the Negro in the labor force, the recent improvement in the Negro's chances of mobility, the shift of Jews to the suburbs, and so on.

DEFINITIONS

Ethnic: This is the generic term commonly used to designate groups characterized by distinctive origin. In a broad way it refers to the "minority groups" of a society—groups whose members are identified as such at birth, groups that have a shared tradition and social life. Ethnic identification stems from what a person *is* when he comes into the world and it is, in the main, irreversible thereafter. In the United States, the major ethnic groups are differentiated in three ways:

Race: People with a common biological heritage involving certain (usually permanent) physical distinctions. The most important racial group in the United States, of course, is the Negro; but in the Western states Orientals have been important too.

In spite of (1) the lack of full genetical data on human beings, (2) the great amount of race mixture, (3) semantic problems, (4) the modifiability of races, and (5) the many difficulties of racial classification, race is not just a figment of the imagination. Scientists can identify major categories of mankind and there is fairly general agreement on smaller groupings [Simpson and Yinger, 1953, p. 63].

Religion: People with a common, and different, system of worship. The most visible American groups are the Jews and in some respects the Catholics. (There can be some question as to whether the Jews should be characterized as a religious or a national community, or both, but that does not matter for our purposes here.)

Nationality: People with a common national origin (short of a racial distinction), usually characterized by a distinctive language or accent. Important national minority groups in the United States have included the Irish, the Italians, the Poles, the Mexicans, the Puerto Ricans.

In short, the underlying idea is that of difference in some fundamental, readily visible, lasting, and socially reinforced way. Ethnic relations refer, then, to interaction with "unlike" people on a "we-and-they" basis. As one authority put it:

A group is a minority group if it is the object of prejudice and discrimination from the dominant groups, and if the members think of themselves as a minority [Rose, 1961, p. 326].

By such a definition, incidentally, a good third of the U.S. population consists of minority groups: about 20 per cent Catholic, 10 per cent Negro, 3–4 per cent Jewish.

Prejudice and discrimination: By *prejudice* we mean essentially a hostile attitude toward an ethnic group, or a member thereof, as such. Some definitions go on to say that prejudice means a hostile attitude that is preconceived or without foundation in fact or knowledge. But such qualifications are often difficult to establish. By *discrimination* is meant disadvantageous treatment of an ethnic group.

The first term refers to feelings (that may or may not be expressed), the second to actions. For example, thinking that Negroes are ignorant or Jews pushy or Mexicans lazy is prejudice. Enforcing residential restrictions against Jews or maintaining school segregation against Negroes or opposing intermarriage with Italians is discrimination. As we shall see, the two are by no means identical.

FINDINGS

Ethnic Differences

A1   With regard to the comparative intelligence of Negroes and whites (in the United States), there are consistent differences in scores on intelligence tests in favor of the whites, but the differences are not large; they are much smaller than the differences within each group, so that there is a great deal of overlap between the groups; differences diminish in size when socioeconomic position or educational opportunity is equated; and they may reflect a bias in the testing instruments themselves. It is probably fair to summarize the matter by saying that most specialists in the subject believe that inherent or genetic differences in intelligence between races have not been established.*

This analysis is an extremely hard one to handle because of the difficulties in the way of proper, controlled measurement presented by differences in social and educational status. To give an idea of the complexity and detail involved in coming to such summary statements, here is only one of twelve double-spreads in only one of the tables summarizing empirical data in Shuey, 1958.

* Because of the policy importance of this point, we wish to add that we personally agree with the resolution passed by the American Anthropological Association at its annual meeting in November, 1961, to the effect that "there is no scientifically established evidence to justify the exclusion of any race from the rights guaranteed by the Constitution of the United States. The basic principles of equality of opportunity and equality before the law are compatible with all that is known about human biology. All races possess the abilities needed to participate fully in the democratic way of life and in modern technological civilization" (*Fellow Newsletter*, AAA, December, 1961, p. 1).

The testing of Negro intelligence, school children: verbal group tests

Author, date	Location	Subjects AGE	Subjects GRADE	N	Method of selection	Results	Comments of author
Long, H. H. (1934)	Washington, D.C.		1A 3A 5A	c-2103 c-1323 c-1258	All 1A, 3A, and 5A c children tested in 1930.	I.Q. SD — 1A 3A 5A — M c: 93.35, 95.71, 92.72 — SD c: 17.10, 15.80, 15.75	Decrease in I.Q. explained by increased inadequacy of community, home environment, and school activities for maturing Negro child.
Charles, C. M. (1936)	St. Louis, Mo.	12-16 12-16		w-172 c-172	W and c boys selected in about equal number for each age-group from schools in different parts of city; schools sought in which social environment of w and c similar. Method of selection within a school's age-group not given.	I.Q. — M, SD, Range — w: 98.31, 12.25, 60-135 — c: 88.60, 11.00, 55-114	Cannot determine whether superiority of w boys is due to inherent factors, to training, to environment, or to possible deficiencies in test used.
Robinson, M. L. and Meenes, M. (1947)	Washington, D.C.		3	c-935	Secured I.Q.'s of pupils in twelve public schools either in 1938-39 or in 1945-46; at least two schools from each section of city. All born in D.C. "for whom I.Q.'s could be obtained." Scores taken from office records.	I.Q. c — M — 1938-39: 97.02 — 1945-46: 99.76	Significant difference between means.
Hess, R. D. (1955)	Chicago, Ill.		6, 7, 8, 9 6, 7, 8, 9	w-high-188 low-178 c-low-179	Sample of 545 elementary-school pupils. High-status w from professional and managerial occupations; low-status w from semiskilled and unskilled; low-status c from unskilled and unemployed. All given a standard test and a new test.*	I.Q. † — M — w High: 108.88, Low 102.83 — c: 90.21	Results suggest that socioeconomic differences between high and low-status samples in this country are exaggerated by standard intelligence tests.

National intelligence tests ‡

Author, date	Location	Subjects AGE	Subjects GRADE	N	Method of selection	Results	Comments of author
Jordan, A. M. (1922)	Fort Smith, Ark.	10-14 10-14	4-8 4-8	w-1502 c-247	Random sampling; 52 per cent of w and 71 per cent of c school children.	MDN SCORES — 10,11,12,13,14 — w: 77, 91.4, 104, 106, 105 — c: 57.5, 66.7, 70.6, 82, 79	Pronounced racial difference found; c were two years behind w at ten years, three to four years behind at thirteen to fourteen years.

c: colored.   w: white.   M: mean   SD: standard deviation.   Mdn: median.
* In a personal communication the author indicated that the standard test used was generally the *Kuhlmann-Anderson* and that the subjects were from six public schools.
For results on the new test, see *Davis-Hess Test*, table 2.
† Author gives mean mental age for each of the twelve CA groups; I.Q.'s calculated by reviewer.
‡ Scale A, Form I was generally employed.

(Shuey, 1958. pp. 92–93)

The present range of scientific opinion can perhaps be fairly illustrated in these quotations from recent reviews of the subject. From a statement by thirty-two social scientists, included as the *Appendix to Appellants' Briefs Filed in the School Segregation Cases in the Supreme Court of the United States, October Term, 1952:*

> The available scientific evidence indicates that much, perhaps all, of the observable differences among various racial and national groups may be adequately explained in terms of environmental differences. It has been found, for instance, that the differences between the average intelligence test scores of Negro and white children decrease, and the overlap of the distribution increases, proportionately to the number of years that the Negro children have lived in the North. . . . Related studies have shown that this change cannot be explained by the hypothesis of selective migration. It seems clear, therefore, that fears based on the assumption of innate racial differences in intelligence are not well founded ["The Effects of Segregation . . . ," 1953, p. 435].

The "concluding statement" of a recent review of about 170 original investigations carried out over the past forty years:

> The remarkable consistency in test results, whether they pertain to school or preschool children, to high school or college students, to drafts of World War I or World War II, to the gifted or the mentally deficient, to the delinquent or criminal; the fact that the colored-white differences are present not only in the rural South and urban South, but in the border and northern areas; the fact that relatively small average differences are found between the IQ's of northern-born and southern-born Negro children in the northern cities; the evidence that the tested differences appear to be greater for abstract than for practical or concrete problems; the evidence that the differences obtained are not due primarily to a lack of language skills, the colored averaging no better on non-verbal tests than on verbal tests; the fact that differences are reported in all studies in which the cultural environment of the whites appeared to be no more complex, rich, or stimulating than the environment of the Negroes; the fact that in many comparisons (including those in which the colored appeared to best advantage) the Negro subjects have been either more representative of their racial group or more highly selected than have the comparable white subjects; all point to the presence of some native differences between Negroes and whites as determined by intelligence tests [Shuey, 1958, p. 318].

From the final summary of another, later review of "comparative psychological studies":

> We are not convinced that genetic differences have been shown; but even if they were so shown . . . the wide overlap between white and Negro distributions of scores should be pointed out so that it is evident that within group differences are far greater than between group differences. It should also be shown that oftimes two groups of white persons differ significantly, and probably in some

if not all cases, partly because of genetic factors. . . . It is clear from the fore-going review that (a) there are still wide differences between Negro and white in many areas of psychological functioning and (b) a number of differences at-tributed in times past to heredity have been shown to be the result of social class determination. It is not clear whether some differences adumbrated here, specifi-cally in the intelligence and temperament realms, are genetically based or not. We agree with Garrett in his Foreword to Shuey's (1958) book, that there are some wholly well-meaning persons who hold that ". . . racial differences ought not to be found; or if found, should immediately be explained away as being somehow immoral and reprehensible." Nevertheless, we are not satisfied that either those who like Garrett believe that genetic differences exist in psychological functions or those who maintain that no such differences can be found have suc-ceeded in establishing their position. Most students in the period of this review have leaned to environmentalist explanations. But this concurrence of judg-ment may be the result of a possibly unjustified extrapolation from Point b above. . . . We frankly are environmentalist in our bias; but we also hope that we are "honest psychologists" enough to recognize that many research results can yet be interpreted from an hereditarian viewpoint without doing violence to them [Dreger and Miller, 1960, pp. 374, 394–95].

It is probably fair to say that many specialists acknowledge a consistent difference in test scores in favor of the whites, but then disagree on how that difference is to be interpreted: whether it is to be assigned to heredi-tary origin or to socioeconomic factors that characterize the disadvantaged position of the Negroes. Certainly the large majority of social scientists, like those signing the first statement quoted above, believes that differences in intelligence scores between Negroes and whites in the United States are directly attributable to such environmental differences as educational op-portunity and class position. It has been demonstrated, to quote one authority in the field, that "as the background improves, so do the scores of the Negroes [in the North] approximate more and more closely the standards set by the Whites" (Klineberg, 1935, p. 59). On another occasion, he con-cluded thus:

Those Negro children who migrated from the South to the North gave no evidence of being superior in "intelligence" (as measured by the tests) when they first came North; rather, they became superior under the influence of the better schooling . . . in the new environment. . . . The most probable interpreta-tion of this finding is that when American Negroes live under relatively favor-able environmental conditions their test scores are correspondingly high, and when whites live under relatively poor conditions their test scores are corre-spondingly low. It is apparently not "race" but environment which is the crucial variable. As for the factors in the environment which are mainly responsible for these and similar results, it is likely that the nature of the available schooling plays a major role [Klineberg, 1957, pp. 46, 47].

National intelligence-test scores and length of residence (combined groups: Lapidus)

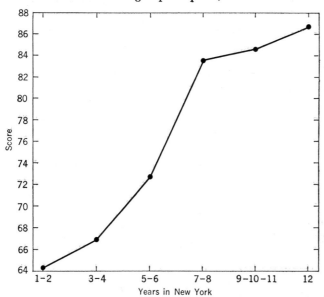

[Reporting on a study of Negro boys in Harlem schools, aged twelve:] There is a very definite tendency for the scores to improve as length of residence [in New York City, for Southern-born] increases.

(Klineberg, 1935, p. 271)

On the same point, here are some data from a carefully controlled study, that show the tendency of Negro children to catch up after a few years in the new environment:

Mean I.Q.'s on Philadelphia tests of mental and verbal ability

Group (Negro children only)	Number of cases	Grade in which test was taken:				
		1A	2B	4B	6B	9A
Philadelphia-born who did not attend kindergarten	424	92.1	93.4	94.7	94.0	93.7
Southern-born entering Philadelphia school system in grades:						
1A	182	86.5	89.3	91.8	93.3	92.8
1B–2B	109		86.7	88.6	90.9	90.5
3A–4B	199			86.3	87.2	89.4
5A–6B	221				88.2	90.2

(Lee, 1951, p. 231)

The investigator's conclusion:

> The migrant [Negro] children, who entered the first grade in Philadelphia, are
> on the first three tests definitely inferior to the Philadelphia-born on the Phil-
> adelphia series of tests, but by the time they have reached the sixth grade there
> is no significant difference in their test ratings and those of the Philadelphia-born
> group, who, like them, had not attended kindergarten [Lee, 1951, p. 233].

Similarly, an investigation of the intelligence of American Indian children
found that those cared for in foster homes, and hence given social opportunities closer to those of white children, scored well above their own
siblings living on the reservation—102 in I.Q. as compared to 87.5 (Garth,
1935).

In this connection, we should add that more inclusive studies (e.g., American Negroes as against African Negroes or American whites as against
native Chinese) or more precise measurements are stymied by the difficulties
in constructing what are called culture-free or culture-fair or culture-con-
trolled tests of intelligence—i.e., tests that do not unduly advantage one
group over another by their very nature. For example, most intelligence
tests favor verbal facility and probably favor middle-class values over lower-
class ones. How can intelligence be measured in a way that is equally fair
to peoples with widely differing experience, background, training, culture?
That is the problem. It is being worked on, but it is certainly difficult (some
think impossible) to surmount. So far, attempts to construct such tests have
not been particularly successful in advancing the matter, and many scholars
believe that the very notion of "culture-free" is inappropriate.

A2   As with comparative intelligence, there is no reason to believe that
there are inherent racial differences in temperament.

> The correlations between traits of intelligence or temperament, on the one hand,
> and anatomical characteristics (stature, skin color, shape of head, size of head,
> height of forehead, and so on), on the other, have almost invariably yielded re-
> sults of no predictive value [Klineberg, 1957, p. 44].

> Until more adequate tests of temperamental characteristics have been constructed
> and the groups studied are equated on the basis of class and other background
> factors, no objective generalizations can be made on the question of race and
> temperament [Simpson and Yinger, 1953, p. 60]

Ethnic Attitudes and Behavior

B1   There is a tendency in most human societies for people to prefer their
own kind and to stereotype ethnic outgroups, especially lower status ones,
in a negative fashion.

In the United States, for example, it is estimated on the basis of various studies that only 20–25 per cent of the adult population could fairly be described as free of hostile attitudes toward one or more minority groups. However, a comment on the research should be noted:

> It has generally been assumed that stereotyped replies to questions on "national characteristics" indicate stereotyped thinking on the part of the respondents; our results suggest per contra that the majority of respondents have no particular views on the subject at all, and are perfectly aware of the fact that any replies they can make are merely the result of cultural and social indoctrination. In other words, the results of studies of this kind are predetermined by the methodology used; when we look for stereotyped views, and give the subject no chance to reply in any non-stereotyped fashion, we should not be surprised that the answer we get is a stereotyped one [Eysenck and Crown, 1948, p. 35].

Ethnic stereotypes serve as a convenient shorthand guide to actual behavior toward members of the ethnic group concerned, and are frequently accepted as such by the minority-group members themselves. Stereotypes condition the kinds of interaction that goes on between the majority and the minority groups and since they are thus reinforced by behavior they have a long life. As Murchison once put it:

> Because they save both time and effort, stereotyped attitudes offer great resistance to change. They resist the inroads of new contradictory experiences and are retained as long as they satisfy and protect the individual.

There is some tentative evidence that

> certain social structural factors [are] associated with prejudice and discrimination against minorities. In a comparative study of 40 societies, it was found that absolute monarchies showed the greatest harshness toward minorities, especially in regard to personal violence and economic exploitation. The same study showed personal violence toward minorities to be associated with feudal economies, with low respect for law, and with well-defined class systems [Rose, 1961, pp. 343–44, referring to Rose, 1960].

Consistent with findings reported earlier on perception and personality:

B1.1   People typically do not appreciate how prejudiced they in fact are.

Prejudiced people ordinarily underestimate the extent of their own prejudices. . . . In general, the prejudiced person is unaware of the influences affecting him, is not accurate in his self-knowledge, is not given to feelings of shame. On the contrary, he is disposed to regard his hostilities as natural and as fully justified by virtue of the misbehavior of the minority groups whom he dislikes [Allport and Kramer, 1946, p. 39].

Percentage of self-ratings on prejudice related to true prejudice score (percentages)

	Less prejudiced	More prejudiced
Much more or a little more than average	3.4	22.4
Average	13.0	38.1
A little less or much less than average	83.7	39.5

(*Ibid.*, p. 35)

B2   People prejudiced against one ethnic group tend to be prejudiced against others.

In other words, prejudice tends to be generalized:

The research results to date indicate that the concept of ethnocentrism is supported in that (1) individuals who display one form of prejudice toward a specific ethnic minority or minorities also tend to display other forms of prejudice, (2) prejudice toward one ethnic minority is usually (although not invariably) accompanied by prejudice toward other ethnic minorities, and (3) the ethnic ingroup is reified to the extent that patriotic and nationalistic sentiments are related to rejection of ethnic minorities [Christie, 1954, p. 154].

That does not mean, of course, that prejudice is directed equally at all ethnic groups; that appears to be true only for the extreme cases.

Here are some illustrative correlations of attitudes toward different minorities, as held by nonminority students at a California college:

	Negro	Japanese	Jewish	Mexican
Japanese	.72			
Jewish	.73	.74		
Mexican	.75	.70	.66	
English	.32	.43	.47	.42

(Campbell and McCandless, 1951, p. 191)

Values indicating relationships among attitudes toward minority groups give ample evidence, were more needed, of the general factor lying behind the attitude toward any one group. Even attitude toward the English (measured by items which because of their systematic nature miss the most potent stereotypes of the Anglophobe) shares to some extent this common factor [*ibid.*, p. 189].

B3   The stereotyping of ethnic groups tends to be quite similar across the society, among various social groups and often even within the stereotyped group itself.

There is a communality in the psychological traits attributed to different ethnic groups by individuals of varying personal experiences, needs, and cultural backgrounds [Harding *et al.*, 1954, p. 1024].

For example, here are the traits frequently assigned by college students, mainly in the 1930's and 1940's, to a number of groups, e.g.:

Jews	shrewd, mercenary, industrious
Negroes	superstitious, lazy, happy-go-lucky
Italians	artistic, impulsive, passionate
English	sportsmanlike, intelligent, conventional
Americans	industrious, intelligent, materialistic
Irish	pugnacious, quick-tempered, witty

(Katz and Braly, 1933)

B3.1   The less contact or experience with the ethnic group in question, the less strongly held the stereotype and the less important it seems to be.

Even so, stereotypes do not always, or even usually, arise from direct experience with the group being stereotyped, but rather from the general social climate in which one lives.

B3.2   Such stereotypes are quite resistant to change, although changing social and economic conditions can lead to shifts over a long period of time.

A dramatic example has been documented in the case of the Chinese in California, in the change from welcomed worker to despised competitor:

In the beginning, race prejudice was subordinated to industrial necessity. The Chinese were among "the most worthy of our new adopted citizens," "our most orderly and industrious citizens," "the best immigrants in California"; they were "thrifty," "sober," "tractable," "inoffensive," "law-abiding"; they showed "an all-round ability" and an "adaptability" beyond praise. As laborers on the ranches they were not competitors, as they had been in the mines. But in the cities, as years passed, as the immigration of whites continued and mining became less profitable, the manifold activities of the Chinese brought them again into competition with white labour in an increasingly large number of occupations. . . . The Chinese were now "a distinct people," "unassimilable," "keeping to their own customs and laws." They "did not settle in America"; "they carried back gold to their homes"; they "went back to China." Their mere presence "lowered the plane of living"; they "shut out the white labour." They were "clannish," "dangerous" because of their secret societies, "criminal," "secretive in their actions," "debased and servile," "deceitful and vicious," inferior from a mental and moral point of view, inmeasurably lower than the Indians, for instance. . . . They were "filthy and loathsome in their habits," and their "unsanitary quarters made the neighborhood uninhabitable." They were "undesirable as workers and as residents of the country" [Schrieke, 1936, pp. 10–12].

B3.3 The stereotype as a whole sets the emotional tone for the several traits within it.

For example, Americans and Jews may both be considered to be "efficient" and "ambitious," but the terms are approved in the one case and disapproved in the other. Here are the data from one study:

The evaluation of traits or stereotypes as a function of the context in which they were rated

Trait or stereotype	Evaluation of trait	Group rated immediately preceding evaluation of traits (percentages)	
		JEWS	SELF
Mercenary	Approving	18	23
	Neutral	22	32
	Disapproving	60	45
Aggressive	Approving	38	54
	Neutral	37	33
	Disapproving	25	13
Emotional	Approving	28	38
	Neutral	55	53
	Disapproving	17	9
Total number of cases		(108)	(100)

(Saenger and Flowerman, 1954, p. 224)

The investigators conclude:

The hypothesis that Jews are disliked because they are ambitious, aggressive, materialistic, to name but a few traits, further rests on the assumption that these traits are considered undesirable no matter to whom they apply. . . . This hypothesis is not borne out by the facts. . . . It is unlikely, therefore, that the characteristics commonly ascribed to Jews are by themselves a main cause of hostility directed toward them. If they were, these traits taken by themselves should have a negative valence [*ibid.*, p. 222].

B3.4 The common stereotypes of the society tend to be copied unconsciously in the mass media of communication.

For example, an analysis of the stories in mass magazines, mainly of the boy-meets-girl type, showed not only that the (100 per cent) Americans appeared more frequently in the cast of characters, but that they received better treatment too:

**The Americans had more desirable occupations
than the other groups (percentages)**

	The Americans	The Anglo-Saxons and Nordics	The others
High occupations	59	29	20
Middle occupations	19	23	20
Low occupations	11	27	36
Illegal and "suspect" occupations	1	2	15
Members of the armed forces	10	19	9
Total number of identifiable characters	(602)	(52)	(66)

(Berelson and Salter, 1946, p. 183)

Whether there is a "kernel of truth" in ethnic stereotypes is still under debate. One study showed, for example, that the "characteristic" gestures attributed to Jews and Italians disappear with their assimilation into the larger society (Efron, 1941), but such information apparently makes little difference to the currency of the stereotype. It is perhaps fair to say that since every ethnic group contains a wide range of behaviors, there is always the opportunity for a prejudiced person to perceive selectively the traits of which he disapproves. Certainly the following seems to be true:

B3.5   Prejudiced people are more likely than others to recognize members of the disapproved ethnic group, and they are more likely to overestimate the proportion of the group in the population.

B4   Discrimination is not simply the result, the acting-out of prejudice: there is discrimination without prejudice and prejudice without discrimination. Over-all, there is a correlation between prejudice and discrimination—such that the more prejudiced are likely also to practice more discrimination against the object of their disapproval—but there are numerous occasions in real life when there is far from a one-to-one relation between them.

In clearly defined situations with a minimum of emotional content—e.g., on the job—members of a disapproved minority group are accepted for the immediate purposes, even though they are discriminated against in another context. A study of workers in a biracial coal mine, for example, concluded that

probably about 20 per cent of the men have favorable attitudes toward Negroes reasonably free from prejudice both within and without the mine. There are another 20 per cent whose attitude both inside and outside the mine is strongly prejudiced and changes little with shift in community relationship. It is the remaining 60 per cent who tend to shift their role and status upon passing from the mine's mouth into the outside world, and who demonstrate very great facility in accepting group expectation as the key to their own assumption of role and status [Minard, 1952, p. 31].

In another study, in New York City, people observed buying from Negro or white clerks in a department store were later queried about their attitudes on the matter, together with a street sample:

Distribution of prejudice ratings (percentages)

Prejudice rating	Observed with Negro clerk	Observed with white clerk	Street sample
Antidiscrimination, no prejudice expressed	38	28	45
Antidiscrimination, but influenced by unfavorable stereotypes	23	34	13
Approves limited employment of Negro sales clerks	18	15	25
Disapproves any employment of Negro sales clerks, but would continue to buy	18	17	12
Would refuse to buy in store employing Negro sales clerks	3	6	5
Mean prejudice rating	2.26	2.38	2.19
Total number of cases	(61)	(53)	(142)

(Saenger and Gilbert, 1950, p. 62)

Finally, in a study of industrial workers in Chicago,

there was no evidence to support the common belief that persons who show a high degree of acceptance of Negroes on the job will necessarily show a low degree of rejection of Negroes in their home communities [Lohman and Reitzes, 1952, p. 244].

Thus, prejudice can be evenly distributed among social groups but discrimination unevenly distributed.

In other words, expressed attitudes and actual behavior are not always in tune, with regard to ethnic or other human relations. Here is how two experts recently summarized the matter:

Specific attitudes shape themselves to behavior. People who actually work with Negroes, especially as equals, develop attitudes favorable towards working with Negroes. People who actually are neighbors of Negroes develop attitudes favorable towards being neighbors of Negroes. . . . Thus, the mass of modern evidence runs counter to the "attitudes-first" fallacy, which holds that prejudice is a lurking state of mind that spills over into overt behavior. It might be more accurate to say that the prejudiced state of mind is typically a function of behavior; except for the danger that *this* formula might be oversimplified into a kind of reverse fallacy. Actually, there emerges an understanding that the key to prejudice must be found *outside* the realm of attitude-behavior relationships. The evidence has demonstrated how both attitudes and behavior are affected by the social frame of reference in which they occur [Raab and Lipset, 1959, p. 22].

The Conditions of Prejudice and Discrimination

The correlates, often causes, of hostility or friendship toward ethnic out-groups have been found in a variety of sources, from broad historical trends to deep psychological forces. They include group characteristics, personal history, contact with ethnic representatives, social position and economic conditions, psychological make-up, and external efforts to reduce prejudice and discrimination, as in informational campaigns. We shall present the complex set of findings in more or less that order.

C1   Prejudice and discrimination are not innate but are learned, usually within the family and often without conscious intent.

Here is a summary of the research evidence:

Prejudices are generally acquired slowly and over a period of time. The child acquires his ethnic values and racial attitudes as he learns other social lessons, from adults, from his peers, and from his life experiences. Groups that are segregated in schools or in the community he assumes are inferior because society treats them as inferiors (Vosk, 1953). Few parents actually teach their children to be prejudiced. However, their own attitudes and behavior, their restrictions on the playmates of their children, and the tendency to stereotype all individuals of a given racial or religious group with certain physical, behavioral, and mental characteristics result in a pattern of prejudice which their children imitate. It is not the parents' attitudes alone, but the whole home influence that is responsible for the development of prejudice [Hurlock, 1956, p. 290].

It appears that prejudiced people tend to recall unpleasant childhood experiences with members of minority groups, but that seems to be more a rationalization after the fact of prejudice than a cause of it.

C1.1   The biographical development of prejudice and discrimination in the United States begins with the recognition of ethnic differences by age five, or even before, coupled with generalized dislike of the minority and a start in accepting ethnic stereotypes, but with inconsistent behavior toward members of ethnic groups. In general, there follows a growth of prejudice until adolescence, coupled with greater complexity, intensity, and organization of the attitudes and with more consistency in behavior.

> Children [aged 9–18] who had had no personal experience with either [Jews or Negroes] were found with strong and definite prejudices toward these minorities. . . . The younger children showed general attitudes of dislike and rejection, but were more or less without specific stereotypes. The older children's responses, in addition to general negative attitudes toward these groups, included specific characterizations and stereotypes [Lippitt and Radke, 1946, pp. 168–69].

C2   People's attitudes and behavior toward ethnic groups typically conform to the norms of the community and of the groups with which they live.

Like most other forms of behavior, prejudice and discrimination follow the going social customs in the community. Here is a summary of how this can come about:

> Social situations may be prejudicial: (1) Where the individual's own behavior is prejudiced as part and parcel of the community's prejudiced pattern of life, e.g., segregated schools, buses, waiting rooms, complete social segregation, habits of deference. (2) Where the models of behavior around the child behave in a prejudiced fashion. . . . (3) Where the unfavorable images of minority groups projected by the social pattern lend themselves to prejudicial behavior. Both the educational and employment status of the Negro, for example, have been artificially depressed. Especially where his contact with minority group members is limited, the child finds it only natural to behave towards Negroes as though they were constitutionally ignorant, and fitted only for menial positions in life. . . . In these several ways, then, it is on the level of actual behavior situations that the normal reproduction of prejudice is effected. . . . It is on the base of these behavior situations that the behavior-attitude spiral of prejudice builds. Attitudes and explicit ideologies are most firmly constructed on the foundation of these existing social situations. [For example], studies of the development of prejudice in children show that young children who have not yet been involved in prejudiced behavior patterns, may pick up prejudiced talk, but this doesn't affect their unprejudiced behavior. Later, after having become involved in prejudiced behavior patterns, they may pick up democratic language in the schools or elsewhere, but this doesn't affect their prejudiced behavior [Raab and Lipset, 1959, pp. 32–33].

As some students of the South have pointed out,

> what is overlooked is that widespread anti-Negro reactions are not necessarily individual personality problems but rather may be institutionalized and culturally expected social patterns [Black and Atkins, 1950, p. 111].

Even in the North, and among young children, the same picture emerges. Here is the conclusion of a study of children in the kindergarten, first, and second grades in Philadelphia:

There is relatively little variation among the neighborhoods in the responses of white children. In all schools but 1 and 6, which have 100 per cent and 94 per cent Negro population respectively, a high proportion of the children express hostility toward Negroes. The presence or absence of Negro children in the three schools appears to have little influence on the attitude of white children. . . . The kinds of stereotypes about [the] Negro do not vary with the neighborhood. One is led to conclude that racial prejudice is so widespread that the sample's differences in neighborhoods do not alter the perception of white as "good" or "bad." Nor do they alter the form of perceived social rejection and exclusion [Radke *et al.*, 1949, p. 410].

In part, this is another specification of the general finding to the effect that people choose to associate with people of like attitudes and behavior.

C2.1   As people move from one social group to another, they tend to take over the attitudes and practices of the new group, in this regard as in others.

A study of attitudes toward the Negro tested three groups of college students: Southern students in a Southern school, Northern students in a Northern school, and Northern students in a Southern school. Here are the data and the conclusion:

Distribution of attitude scores for three populations

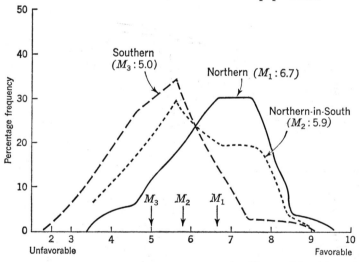

(Sims and Patrick, 1936, p. 194)

The study does suggest that Northern college students are on the average definitely more favorable toward the Negro than are Southern college students; but there are great individual differences within the groups and consequently overlapping between them. As to the causes of these differences our conclusions are only negative. They do not seem to be satisfactorily accounted for by intelligence, sex, degree of maturity, size of home community, or occupational level. Finally, when Northern students are transplanted into the Southern environment their attitude seems to change, gradually becoming more nearly that of the Southern students [*ibid.,* p. 203].

Hence it appears that in cases of conflict over ethnic relations within a group, or conflict between one's prejudice and democratic ideals, the position of the larger community will assert decisive influence over the outcome. This is again a special case of the more general finding to the same effect.

C3   Personal contact with members of ethnic minorities does not automatically increase or reduce tensions: it can do either or neither.

One of the important early studies of prejudice among children found that their attitudes toward Negroes did not vary significantly with their degree of contact with Negroes.

Prejudice in different groups *

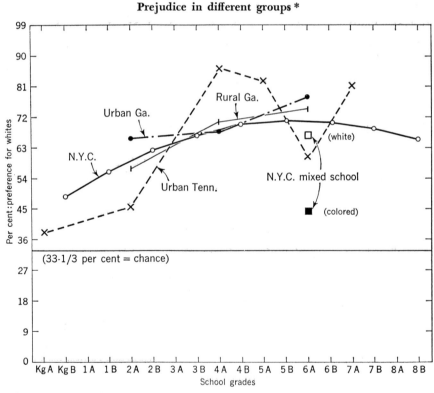

* Graphic comparison of performance on the Show-Me test. Curve for New York City groups is smoothed.

(Horowitz, 1936, p. 20)

The investigator concluded:

> The children in the New York group showed no less prejudice as measured by the tests than did the children in the South. Comparison of the three Southern groups showed no differences among them, in spite of differences in mode of living represented by sampling rural and urban communities. White boys in a mixed school showed as much prejudice as did white boys elsewhere. The colored boys in the mixed school showed a preference for white faces reliably less than did their white classmates (Show Me, $t = 2.93$), yet their mean score was significantly above the "chance" score (Show Me, $t = 2.45$) [Horowitz, 1936, p. 21].

The Show-Me test asked subjects to select, from a set of twelve photographs of white and Negro boys, those preferred for various activities; four of the pictures were of white boys, hence, chance equals one-third.

C3.1 There is a range within discriminatory practice such that there is most discrimination and most prejudice as the the practice comes closer to intimate personal contact.

In this connection, there tends to be considerable difference between what the minority wants and what the majority think the minority wants. In his major study, *An American Dilemma* (1944), Gunnar Myrdal suggested that in the American South the rank order of discriminatory practices is inverse between whites and Negroes: the whites think Negroes want sexual equality most and economic equality least, whereas the Negroes' attitude is the opposite. A study to check this idea was done later in Columbus, Ohio, with this confirming result:

A comparison of Myrdal's Negro rank order of discriminations and the rank order of a sample of Columbus Negroes

Types of discrimination	Myrdal's rank order	Rank order of sample
Economic	1	3
Legal	2	1
Political	3	2
Public services and facilities	4	4
Courtesies and respect	5	6
Sex relations	6	5

Rho = .77

(Banks, 1950, p. 532)

C3.2 In situations of not very high prejudice, the introduction of personal contacts between members of different ethnic groups tends to lead to a lessening of prejudice, and even of discrimination.

Studies to this effect have been carried out in various settings. Here are some data from the army and from a housing project:

**Attitudes toward serving in a company containing Negro and
white platoons among men who have done so and men who
have not (Europe, June, 1945)**

Question: Some army divisions have companies that include Negro platoons and white platoons. How would you feel about it if your outfit was set up like that?

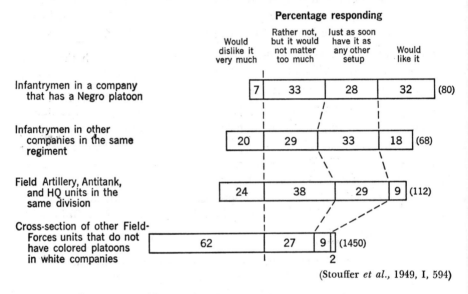

(Stouffer *et al.*, 1949, I, 594)

**Percentage of housewives in the project reporting favorable
change, no change, or unfavorable change in their
attitudes toward negroes (percentages)**

	Integrated interracial projects		Segregated biracial projects	
Present attitude	KOALTOWN	SACKTOWN	BAKERVILLE	FRANKVILLE
Favorable change	59	62	27	18
No change	38	31	66	69
Unfavorable change	3	7	7	13
Total number of cases	(99)	(89)	(99)	(100)

(Deutsch and Collins, 1951, p. 97)

C3.3 The balance is particularly favorable to a lessening of prejudice when the ethnic groups meet on personal terms, on a common task with shared interests or tastes that run across ethnic lines, and on terms of social and economic equality.

For example, dispersion of ethnic members throughout a geographical area or through various social positions will help in time to soften ethnic prejudice. The rationale is to promote their acceptance as individuals, in the fullness of all their characteristics, rather than as examples of a social category that narrows down on a few (disapproved) characteristics.

Here is a summary of the situation in education:

In general, both the acculturation of the subordinate group and its participation with the dominant group in public schools are found to be most successful when:

the minority group of pupils is of approximately the same social-class level as the dominant group of pupils;

the minority is relatively small, constituting at the very most not more than 25 per cent of the school population;

the minority group came from the middle-class in its original home;

it has been in America a relatively long time;

it came from the same kind of community (i.e., rural or urban) as that in which it now lives [Davis, 1957, p. 446].

C4 Prejudice and, perhaps even more, discrimination arise out of the relative social positions of the groups involved and out of changes in relative position, or the threat thereof.

This has already been suggested by the study cited above that dealt with the changing stereotype of the Chinese on the American West Coast. But the finding is important enough to justify more attention and documentation.

Prejudice against the Jews in the United States, for example, grew as they began to compete effectively for middle-class and professional positions.

Anti-Semitism and social mobility (percentages)

	Downward mobility	No mobility	Upward mobility	Total
Tolerant	11	37	50	38
Stereotyped	17	38	18	28
Outpoken and intense	72	25	32	34
Total number of cases	(18)	(68)	(44)	(130)

(Bettelheim and Janowitz, 1950, p. 59)

Again: as cotton prices fell in the South, a few decades ago, lynchings of Negroes increased (Hovland and Sears, 1940). In a study of American veterans of World War II, prejudice against the Jews was found to be highest among those losing occupational and social status. A later study found that the stationary group was more tolerant than either the upward- or the downward-mobile group (Greenblum and Pearlin, 1953).

> Aggressive attitudes, both spontaneous and elicited, were found to be most highly concentrated in the downwardly mobile group, while the pattern was *significantly* reversed for those who had advanced in social status since the period of their previous civilian employment. Those who had experienced no change presented a picture somewhat in the middle [Bettelheim and Janowitz, 1950, p. 58].

On the basis of a review of a number of racial situations, another scholar comes to a similar conclusion:

> Analysis of those racial situations in which prejudice is most pronounced would seem to indicate that of still greater significance is the development of a feeling, on the part of the members of a dominant group, that they are *under threat of displacement from an established social situation;* that is, race prejudice is usually acute in those situations in which members of a dominant group have come to fear that the members of a subordinate group are not keeping to a prescribed place of exclusion and discrimination but instead threaten effectively to claim the privileges and opportunities from which they have been excluded [Pierson, 1950, p. 473].

As a result:

C4.1   People not in direct competition with members of minority groups are less likely to be prejudiced toward them.

For example:

> Retirement from active participation in a competitive society predisposes one to a greater tolerance of outgroup members [Watson, 1950, p. 30].

C4.2   There is somewhat more prejudice and discrimination in hard times than in good ones.

This is so because there is more stress, tension, and strain, some of which gets attached to minorities who are actually competing or can be seen as competing for the scarcer rewards. In a broad historical way, this finding relates the incidence and location of prejudice to the big waves of immigration:

> Prejudice against Negroes and certain other minorities is likely to be especially vigorous and vocal among ethnic groups which have been only recently "Americanized" and which are attempting to move up in the class hierarchy. . . . The cessation of large-scale immigration has thus removed an important element of

flexibility in the balancing system of controlling intergroup hostilities [Williams, 1947, pp. 61, 60].

Thus it might be fair to say that each new wave of immigration helps the earlier one by providing a fresh source at the bottom of society to which prejudice can be attached.

C4.3   Conflict, and especially severe conflict, is more likely when the minority group has secured enough improvement in its situation to appreciate the benefits and want more.

A militant reaction from a minority group is most likely when (a) the group's position is rapidly improving or (b) when it is rapidly deteriorating, especially if it follows a period of improvement. . . . Mass violence (e.g., race riots) is more likely under the following conditions: (a) prolonged frustrations, leading to a high tension level; (b) presence of population elements with a propensity to violence (especially lower class, adolescent males in socially disorganized areas); (c) highly visible and rapid change in intergroup relations; (d) a precipitating incident of intergroup conflict [*ibid.,* pp. 61, 60].

C4.4   There is more discrimination in those areas containing the largest proportions of the minority group, and thus the largest threat to the political, economic, and social position of the majority.

In the current situation of educational desegregation in the American South, for example, the process of desegregation has gone farthest where there are fewest Negroes, proportionately.

C5   The higher the level of education, the less the prejudice and discrimination.

It generally but not always appears from researches that people with college education are slightly less intolerant than people with grade school or high school education (at least they answer questions in a more tolerant way) [Allport, 1954, pp. 79–80].

This last phrase calls attention to the technical problem of assessing "real" attitudes from responses to questionnaire items. Discrimination, e.g., in club memberships, is practiced at the highest educational levels too.

C6   The personality of a prejudiced person tends to be characterized by one or more of the following factors: high frustration and displaced aggression; neuroticism; conservatism, conventionalism, and conformism; authoritarianism and orientation to power; projection of undesirable impulses (notably sexual ones) and sexual repression; rigidity and intolerance of ambiguity; insecurity; cynicism; a "jungle philosophy of life."

Here, for example, are the data from one intensive inquiry:

Variable	Source of data	Degrees of free-dom	Difference in means *	Standard error of difference in means	t-ratio †
Proposition 1. Displacement of aggression	TAT	18	−.70	.63	1.11
	P-F Study	18	−1.85	1.22	1.52
Proposition 2. Outwardly di-rected aggression	TAT	38	+.55	.34	1.62
	P-F Study	38	+.82	.97	.85
Proposition 3. Susceptibility to frustration	Subjective protocols	18	+5.00	2.45	2.04
Proposition 4. Overt disturb-ance	Behavior ratings	18	+1.60	.60	2.67
		18	+.20	.67	.30
Proposition 5. Frustration tol-erance	Behavior ratings and subjective protocols				

TAT: Thematic Apperception Test.   P-F Study: Picture-Frustration Study.

* High in prejudice scored above the low in prejudice on the variable, where the difference is +.

† A *t* of about 1.7 was required for significance at the 5 per cent level.

(Lindzey, 1950, p. 23)

And here is a conclusion from one of the best-known studies of anti-Semitism, *The Authoritarian Personality:*

> The most crucial result of the present study, as it seems to the authors, is the demonstration of close correspondence in the type of approach and outlook a subject is likely to have in a great variety of areas, ranging from the most inti-mate features of family and sex adjustment through relationships to other people in general, to religion and to social and political philosophy. Thus a basically hierarchical, authoritarian, exploitative parent-child relationship is apt to carry over into a power-oriented, exploitively dependent attitude toward one's sex partner and one's God, and may well culminate in a political philosophy and social outlook which has no room for anything but a desperate clinging to what appears to be strong and a disdainful rejection of whatever is relegated to the bottom. The inherent dramatization likewise extends from the parent-child dichotomy to the dichotomous conception of sex roles and of moral values, as well as to a dichotomous handling of social relations as manifested especially in the formation of stereotypes and of ingroup-outgroup cleavages. Conventionality, rigidity, repressive denial, and the ensuing break-through of one's weakness, fear and dependency are but other aspects of the same fundamental personality pattern, and they can be observed in personal life as well as in attitudes toward religion and social issues [Adorno *et al.,* 1950, p. 971].

Although each of these characteristics has been found in one or another study, there are some counter-indications, particularly when social and cultural conditions are taken into account:

> It is quite likely that the "bigot" in certain Deep South communities often may be, in a straightforward sense, less "neurotic" than the racial liberal in that set-

ting. Some evidence consistent with this possibility is already available (Black, 1949). Furthermore, there are fragments of data indicating that the extreme liberal and the extreme bigot may be rather alike in personality characteristics, and quite different from persons holding more moderate positions on racial and cultural issues [Williams, 1953, p. 37].

The study referred to applied measures developed in Massachusetts to a group of Kentucky students and found that

the "average" Kentucky student has a higher prejudice-rating than the average student in Massachusetts, but the "average" Kentucky student does not display . . . correlative personality disturbances as manifested by intensive psychological interviews and projective tests. Only those Kentuckians who had abnormally high prejudice ratings [i.e., in relation to the average rating] displayed personality disturbances [Black, 1949, p. 262].

At the same time, it is probably fair to say that most experts now think that prejudice is not "just another attitude"; that some types of personalities, given the appropriate social circumstances, are prejudice-prone; and that this is a reasonable description of the types:

The general findings indicate that prejudiced individuals tend to manifest: (a) "conventionalized" social conformity with deep ambivalence toward social norms and the authorities enforcing them; (b) a puritanical conscience; (c) repressed hostility toward parents; (d) admiration of power and strength; (e) advocacy of severe punishment; (f) status-anxiety; (g) repressed sexuality; (h) a rigidly dichotomous style of thinking; (i) a tendency to distrust other people; (j) a tendency to view the world as evil and dangerous [Suchman et al., 1958, p. 59].

C7   Getting more information about an ethnic group results in the lessening of prejudice, but not to any great extent.

Here is a specialist's summary of his survey of the research literature on change of attitude toward ethnic groups under different influences designed to bring about a more tolerant attitude:

**Number of studies showing change or lack of change
as a result of specified influences**

	Change	No change	Indefinite
School or college course	8	4	1
Specific propaganda	9	4	1
Personal contacts	3	3	3
Knowledge or acquaintance (correlation)	9	2	1
Time in school	8	6	4

(Rose, 1948, p. 23)

And, as in other cases:

C7.1   The more strongly people feel against ethnic minorities, the less likely they are to be changed in attitudes or behavior by formal communications or propaganda, and especially by the mass media.

They are less likely to see such materials in the first place and less likely to give them credence, interpret them correctly, or accept their validity in the second. In fact, there is some evidence that such "good will" propaganda is mainly seen and appreciated by the various minorities it is designed to support.

It is generally believed in the field that some form of direct or personal communication about prejudice is more effective than indirect or mass communication. An experiment in changing the attitude of Christians toward Jews produced the following results:

Distribution of attitude scores as changed by the indirect and direct group methods (percentages)

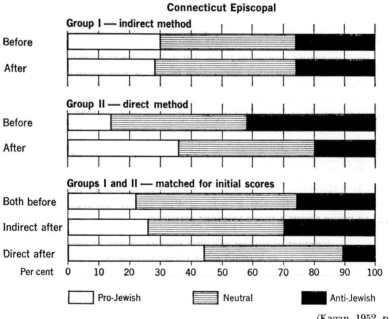

(Kagan, 1952, p. 55)

The Indirect Group Method, which teaches the Jewish origins of and contributions to Christianity and the religio-democratic values of the Bible shared by Christian and Jew alike, does *not* change the attitude of Christian toward the Jew. . . . A significant change in the attitude of Christian toward Jew *is* brought about by the Direct Group Method. A Christian group does lower its mean score in the attitude scale and becomes more favorable toward the Jew, if it is guided to participate in direct discussion of the Christian's personal experiences with and attitudes toward the Jew. The Direct Group Method stimulates group involvement in the Christian-Jewish problem; corrects misinformation about contemporary Jews; affords a group catharsis for hostility; and gives an opportunity for a reorientation of values in relation to the Jew [*ibid.*, pp. 132–33].

At the same time:

C7.2 In an open society, keeping various groups in communication with one another is necessary to maintain social control over prejudice and discrimination.

The more an individual engages in personal interaction with persons of different race, religion, or nationality background, the lower is his general level of prejudice. This result holds not only for majority group prejudices but also for minority prejudices against the majority group and other minorities. It is true of youths as well as their elders. It has been confirmed in 14 different samples, involving about 6000 persons. We find in the communities studied that the more possibilities of cross-group interaction there are, the more interaction actually occurs; the more actual contact there is, the higher the frequency of intergroup friendships; the more intergroup friendships, the less the incidence of stereotyping and categorical antipathy [Williams, 1953, p. 54].

The Impact of Prejudice and Discrimination

D1 As a result of prejudice and discrimination, both the majority and the minority develop a heightened awareness of the minority's distinguishing characteristic(s) that leads to delimited relations and stereotyping on both sides.

The three responses typically open to the minority group are avoidance of contacts, acceptance of the situation, or aggression against it. There are costs in each for both sides, as the following findings make clear.

D1.1 Communication between majority and minority groups tends to be restricted in nature, superficial, or subject to considerable misunderstanding.

In the more serious cases of prejudice or discrimination, contact between the minority group and the majority is likely to be highly patterned, with both sides knowing what is expected of them.

Most Negro-white communication is strongly functional, e.g., it takes place in answer to a specific need rather than a general desire for association. It usually serves a definite purpose and rarely centers about a general exchange of ideas [Suchman *et al.*, 1958, p. 50].

Beyond stylized communication and the quasi-official relations of persons as formal representatives of groups rather than as personal friends, there is actual physical distance, as in segregation or, in the extreme case, the rigid system of caste.

D1.2   The minority group is more likely than the majority to be sensitive to and knowledgeable about intergroup relations.

The reason is that the matter is much more important to the minority group than to the rest of the society, for it is the one that suffers. In addition, of course, there is the arithmetical point that the minority, being smaller, has more contact concentrated on it—or, to describe it differently, that contact with the minority is more diffused across the majority.

D1.3   The ethnic identification becomes centrally important, especially for the minority itself.

For example, minority groups will support "their own kind" in political contests and will oppose others on ethnic grounds. Or individual members of the minority will attribute all their personal shortcomings to the discriminatory situation. One study, for example, showed that Jewish children in the United States are more sensitive about their religion than either Catholic or Protestant children, and the authors conclude that this "intensified group consciousness of Jewish children is, in part, an outcome of anti-Semitism" (Radke *et al.,* 1949, p. 417).

D1.4   The minority group develops hostile, stereotyped attitudes toward other groups in the society, including the majority.

Here is a description of the situation in South Africa, over a decade ago, among educated Bantu:

> The reaction to domination . . . has in this society taken the form of violent resistance or "counter-domination" which finds expression in hostility, aggressiveness, hatred, suspicion, and dislike on the part of the dominated colour-caste group or at any rate in that part of it represented by our sample. . . . Whatever the differences in social and cultural background, in personality make-up or in the vicissitudes of personal experience, the race attitudes of our subjects have all converged upon one final common pathway—with the Afrikaans-speaking South Africans, or "Boers" or "Dutch," as the common object of hostility and aggressiveness [MacCrone, 1947, p. 86].

D1.5   The minority usually aspires to be accepted by the majority and as a consequence imitates the majority's behavior in a quite rigid fashion (including, often, taking over the majority's prejudices toward other minorities).

D1.6   The superior-inferior relations, in situations that allow for intimate personal contacts, often lead to the social dominance of the majority men and the minority women, deriving directly from their own sexual relationships.

It has been said that this is why the American South is run by the white man and the colored woman (who is actually a dominant figure in the Negro society).

> Often, in the relationships between a dominant and an oppressed group, a pattern of sexual contact between the men of the majority and the women of the minority group will develop. . . . Sexual contacts between "superior" and "inferior" influence in many important ways the nature of the relationship between the dominant men and women, the family patterns of the majority and minority groups, the feelings and frustrations of the men of the oppressed group, the status position of the mixed offspring who may result, etc. [Simpson and Yinger, 1953, pp. 235–36].

D2   As a result of prejudice and discrimination, members of the minority group often suffer some deterioration of personality: self-doubt, self-hate, impulsive and superstitious behavior, resigned exploitation of inferior status, deviant behavior, family disturbance, mental illness.

One study, for example, found that among children of nursery-school age, Negroes were more aware of race than the whites and were accordingly subject to strong conflicts in values, to wishful thinking and evasion of reality, and to a sense of threat from their racial status (Goodman, 1952, p. 57). In another inquiry, among public school children in kindergarten, first, and second grade, the children were allowed to assign houses and costumes characteristic of differing status to Negro or white dolls. Even a majority of the Negro children preferred the white doll; and

> in the selection of houses, the great majority of children from both races give the poor house to the Negro doll and the good house to the white doll. These assignments are accompanied by explanations which indicate that the child sees the race represented by the doll as "belonging" to that kind of house. The test responses do not always correspond to what the child experiences in his immediate neighborhood. He responds instead in terms of cultural stereotypes and prejudices [Radke and Trager, 1950, p. 32].

This general finding, incidentally, was taken into account by the Supreme Court in its historic decision on educational segregation ("The Effects of Segregation . . . ," 1953).

The finding holds for foreign minorities as well as for Negroes:

> The Mexican, or Polish, or Italian American, as well as the lower-class white or Negro [often] comes to think of his original culture as inferior, and of the other culture as superior. This general characteristic of "second generation" groups is abundantly illustrated both in scientific studies and in autobiographical accounts [Davis, 1957, p. 448].

D2.1   As a result of prejudice and discrimination, some minority ethnic groups are more likely than the dominant segments of the population to engage in crime and delinquency.

This topic is covered in more detail in the section on social disorganization. Here it is worth noting Myrdal's observation, in *An American Dilemma*, that discrimination prevents the Negro from identifying himself with the society and the law, and thus exacts a heavy social cost.

Something of the same custom prevails between all white employers and Negro employees in the South. This custom has had two effects which operate to raise the Negroes' criminal record: First, it has developed in the Negro a disrespect for the property of others, which sometimes leads him to pilfer things from people to whom he does not stand in the relationship of indulged servant. . . . This feeling is strengthened by the fact that Negroes know that their white employers are exploiting them. . . . Much more deeply based in the caste system than this custom is the Negro's hatred of whites. A not insignificant number of crimes of Negroes against whites are motivated by revenge for discriminatory or insulting treatment. Such a crime may be emotional, as when a Negro suddenly feels that he has stood enough in the way of deprivation and insults and that he only desires to make white people suffer too, even at the cost of his own punishment by law or by a mob. . . . The revenge motive may also lead to a cold and calculating crime: it is said by many Negro social scientists that "mugging"—the robbing and beating of a victim in a certain way by a group of three or four petty professional criminals—was originally practiced only in Negro neighborhoods on white men who were thought to be searching for Negro prostitutes. . . . Caste, especially where it operates to cause legal injustice and insecurity of life and property, prevents the Negro from identifying himself with society and the law. Because the white man regards him as apart from society it is natural for a Negro to regard himself as apart. He does not participate in making the laws in the South, and he has little chance to enforce them. To the average lower class Negro, at least in the South, the police, the courts, and even the law are arbitrary and hostile to Negroes, and thus are to be avoided or fought against. The ever-present hostility to the law and law-enforcement agencies on the part of all Southern Negroes and many Northern Negroes does not often manifest itself in an outbreak against them because the risks are too great. But occasionally this hostility does express itself, and then there is crime. The Negro community tends to be sympathetic toward an individual Negro who commits a crime against whites, since he is only expressing a hostility which is felt generally [Myrdal, 1944, pp. 975–96].

D3   As a result of prejudice and discrimination in severe degree, members of the majority often suffer from feelings of guilt about their treatment of the minority.

For example:

> The prestige gain of belonging to a "superior" group is seldom unambiguous; there are often self-doubts and doubts over the whole-hearted acceptance of his status by the minority-group member—doubts which lead to an almost compulsive need for reassurance in some instances, and thus to a rigid insistence that all the deference forms be followed to the letter [Simpson and Yinger, 1953, p. 237].

D4   Prejudice and discrimination against minority groups are partly maintained by a reinforcing spiral of built-in cause and effect: the disapproved group is deprived, and as a result of the deprivation it is further disapproved.

For example, because they get less and poorer education, Negroes are considered unintelligent by the prejudiced, as a result of which they do not receive educational opportunities. Or again:

> The low family income of Negroes creates a *vicious circle:*
>   Low family income leads to early work for children.
>   Early school leaving restricts later job opportunities and qualifications for job advancement.
>   Limited job opportunities result in low family income.
>   Low family income leads to early work [Broom and Selznick, 1957, p. 487].

D5   Beyond the human costs, there are economic costs of discrimination as well.

In some occupations minorities are not utilized fully, despite their availability and efficiency; not, until recently, even in the armed forces. In addition:

> Prejudice that takes the form of segregated areas in housing and severe limitations on the economic opportunities of minority-group members is an important factor in the development and continuation of slums. Beyond the loss of skills and the loss of purchasing power that such a situation creates, there is the direct financial cost of large expenditures for public health, for fire protection, for police and courts, and for relief [Simpson and Yinger, 1953, p. 248].

Finally, the price of discrimination in the market place must be taken into account. Here is a conclusion from an economic analysis of the matter:

> In 1940, tastes for discrimination in the South appear to have been, on the average, about twice those in the North. . . . A very tentative conclusion . . . would be that neither striking increases nor striking decreases in discrimination against Negroes have occurred during the last four decades [Becker, 1957, p. 125].

SELECTED READINGS

A good deal of empirical work has been done in this field, and there are a number
of summaries of the literature:

Gordon W. Allport. *The Nature of Prejudice*. Beacon, 1954.

John Harding *et al.* "Prejudice and Ethnic Relations," in Gardner Lindzey, ed.,
Handbook of Social Psychology, Vol. II. Addison-Wesley, 1954, pp. 1021–61.

Earl Raab and Seymour M. Lipset. *Prejudice and Society*. Anti-Defamation League
of B'nai B'rith, 1959.

Arnold M. Rose. "Race and Ethnic Relations," in Robert K. Merton and Robert
A. Nisbet, eds., *Contemporary Social Problems*. Harcourt, Brace & World, 1961,
pp. 324–89.

Robin M. Williams, Jr. "Racial and Cultural Relations," in Joseph B. Gittler, ed.,
Review of Sociology. Wiley, 1957, pp. 423–64.

Robin M. Williams, Jr. *The Reduction of Intergroup Tensions: A Survey of Research on Problems of Ethnic, Racial, and Religious Group Relations*. Social
Science Research Council, Bulletin 57, 1947.

On the question of ethnic differences, and particularly the comparative matter of
Negro–white intelligence, here are some central titles:

R. M. Dreger and K. S. Miller. "Comparative Psychological Studies of Negroes and
Whites in the United States," *Psychological Bulletin*, 57, 1960, pp. 361–402.

Otto Klineberg, ed. *Characteristics of the American Negro*. Harper, 1944.

Otto Klineberg. *Negro Intelligence and Selective Migration*. Columbia U. Press,
1935.

Otto Klineberg. *Race Differences*. Harper, 1936.

Audrey M. Shuey. *The Testing of Negro Intelligence*. J. P. Bell, 1958.

As for the nature and conditions of prejudice and discrimination, here are two
of the most important titles in the behavioral sciences in recent decades:

T. W. Adorno *et al. The Authoritarian Personality*. Harper, 1950.

Gunnar Myrdal, with the assistance of Richard Sterner and Arnold M. Rose. *An
American Dilemma*. Harper, 1944.

And following are some major studies in the field:

Morton Deutsch and Mary E. Collins. *Interracial Housing: A Psychological Evaluation of a Social Experiment*. U. of Minnesota Press, 1951.

Eugene Hartley. *Problems in Prejudice*. King's Crown Press, 1946.

Marian Radke *et al.* "Social Perceptions and Attitudes of Children," *Genetic Psychology Monographs*, 40, 1949, pp. 327–447.

Shirley A. Star *et al.* "Negro Soldiers," in Samuel Stouffer *et al., The American
Soldier: Adjustment During Army Life*. Princeton U. Press, 1949, pp. 486–
599.

Finally, on the impact of prejudice and discrimination, see:

Max Deutscher and Isidor Chein. "The Psychological Effects of Enforced Segregation: A Survey of Social Science Opinion," *Journal of Psychology,* 26, 1948, pp. 259–87.
"The Effects of Segregation and the Consequences of Desegregation: A Social Science Statement." *Minnesota Law Review,* 37, 1953, pp. 427–39. (This statement is signed by a number of specialists in the field, and it contains a bibliography of its own.)

And, for an economist's approach to the matter, see:

Gary Becker. *The Economics of Discrimination.* U. of Chicago Press, 1957.

Gorgias. What is there greater than the word which persuades the judges in the courts, or the senators in the council, or the citizens in the assembly, or at any other political meeting?—if you have the power of uttering this word, you will have the physician your slave, and the trainer your slave, and the money-maker of whom you talk will be found to gather treasures, not for himself, but for you who are able to speak and to persuade the multitude.

PLATO
Dialogues

For it is not enough to know *what* we ought to say; we must also say it *as* we ought; much help is thus afforded towards producing the right impression of a speech. . . . These are the three things—volume of sound, modulation of pitch, and rhythm—that a speaker bears in mind. It is those who *do* bear them in mind who usually win prizes in the dramatic contests; and just as in drama the actors now count for more than the poets, so it is in the contests of public life, owing to the defects of our political institutions. . . . Delivery is—very properly—not regarded as an elevated subject of inquiry. Still, the whole business of rhetoric being concerned with appearances, we must pay attention to the subject of delivery, unworthy though it is, because we cannot do without it.

ARISTOTLE
Rhetoric

Communication has just about reached the lowest point, with respect to its importance; and contemporaneously the means of communication have pretty nearly attained the highest point, with respect to quick and overwhelming distribution. For what is in such haste to get out, and on the other hand what has such widespread distribution as . . . twaddle? Oh procure silence!

SOREN KIERKEGAARD

> But when a dream, night after night, is brought
> Throughout a week, and such weeks few or many
> Recur each year for several years, can any
> Discern the dream from real life in aught?

JAMES THOMSON

Chapter Thirteen
MASS COMMUNICATION

Communication is such a natural part of human life that the topic spreads throughout this book. For example, findings on personal communications are not only implicit everywhere but explicit in the sections dealing with learning, socialization, small groups, and complex organizations. In this chapter we restrict ourselves to the literature dealing with the mass media of communication. With the rise of the electronic media in recent decades, a great deal of attention has been paid to the questions: who sees what? from what source? with what effect? *

As the reader will see from what follows, a good deal of the literature deals with the effect of the mass media on people's opinions. Accordingly, it was not always easy to decide whether to enter some findings here or in the section on opinions, attitudes, and beliefs. In some important cases, e.g., that of opinion leadership, we have included material in both sections; for the rest, we simply note the desirability of checking both sections for material in this field. Incidentally, if the following summary seems heavily weighted on the side of mass communications having to do with controversial public issues, that is, we think, a faithful reflection of the state of the literature.

DEFINITIONS

Communication: The transmission of information, ideas, emotions, skills, etc., by the use of symbols—words, pictures, figures, graphs, etc. It is the *act* or *process* of transmission that is usually called communication.

* There is a voluminous and detailed literature of a topical and descriptive nature on the first two of these questions: audience ratings, studies of characteristics of particular audiences, specific comparisons of media coverage, etc. However, we cover here only the findings of sufficient generality from that array.

Mass media: These are usually considered to include newspapers, magazines, books, films, radio, television. Their characteristics are suggested by the terms themselves: their massiveness, or ability to communicate from a single source to large numbers of people; and their mediativeness, or ability to communicate through a mechanical device such as print or a TV screen, making for an impersonal relationship between communicator and audience. Personal conversation is also communication, but by way of contrast it is neither massive nor, normally, mechanically mediated.

Content: What is said in a communication, i.e., the statements or meanings themselves.

Attention or exposure: The generic terms for reading, listening, viewing, and so on—i.e., the act of receiving communications, passively or actively, from the source.

Audience: The generic term for the people who read, listen, see, hear, view. The term can be used to refer to the total audience or to such particular audiences as those for public affairs, sports, soap operas, classical music, etc.

Predispositions: The social or psychological state of the audience, or of a member of the audience, at the beginning of the communication: their information, interests, attitudes, group memberships, personality traits. This includes anything that characterizes the audience insofar as the communication is concerned or that may reasonably be involved in the audience's attention, interpretation, or effect. Some predispositions, e.g., class-related attitudes, may be present at the start of the communication but are not conscious or manifest then; in such cases the communication might "bring them out," i.e., make them visible, felt, and operative.

Effect: Any change in the audience's behavior as a result of communication exposure, whether overt (like voting, enrolling, writing, or buying) or subjective (like becoming better informed or changing one's mind). Such changes in behavior can cover a range of matters: attention, information, knowledge and understanding, wisdom, opinions, attitudes, beliefs, personality traits, skills and aptitudes, or acts. We deal with different kinds of effects below: for example, short- and long-run, reinforcement and conversion.

FINDINGS

Here, perhaps more than elsewhere, the research findings can be organized into one broad generalization, dealing with the importance of audience characteristics in determining what people see, how they interpret it, and what effect it has upon them. As Douglas Waples, an early student of the subject, liked to say: "What reading does to people is not nearly so important as what people do to reading." Now that broad statement perhaps does not say a great deal, but it does say enough to counter the dire alarms of those who feel that the modern media are "pushing people around." In any case, the over-all proposition will now be spelled out and documented in a number of ways. For convenience and ease of presentation, we shall arrange the findings in three main groups: those dealing with attention, those dealing with perception and interpretation, and those dealing with effect.

Attention

A1   People tend to see and hear communications that are favorable or congenial to their predispositions; they are more likely to see and hear congenial communications than neutral or hostile ones. And the more interested they are in the subject, the more likely is such selective attention.

This holds for personal conversation as well as for the mass media: people are more likely to talk about controversial matters with like-minded people than with those who do not share their views.

The more interested people are in the election, the more they tend to expose themselves to propaganda of their own party (percentages) *

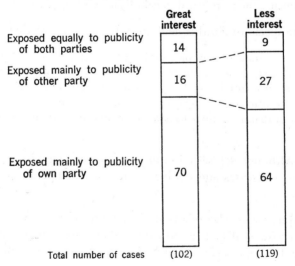

	Great interest	Less interest
Exposed equally to publicity of both parties	14	9
Exposed mainly to publicity of other party	16	27
Exposed mainly to publicity of own party	70	64
Total number of cases	(102)	(119)

* This chart deals only with those with constant vote intention from May to November.

(Lazarsfeld *et al.,* 1948, p. 90)

The evidence for this generalization covers a wide range of audience characteristics: it applies to sex role, educational status, interest and involvement, ethnic status, political attitude, aesthetic position, and, indeed, any way of characterizing people that matters to them. For example, political partisans manage to see their own side more than the opposition side (Lazarsfeld *et al.*, 1948); people already active in a cause are more likely than others to see material intended to recruit additional volunteers (Cartwright, 1949); farmers tend not to listen to radio material with which they disagree (Robinson, 1941); and the college-educated are critical about television in general but full of praise for "their own programs" (Steiner, 1963).

From the evaluation of an intensive campaign to inform the people of Cincinnati about the United Nations, here is a conclusion that exemplifies the typical finding in this connection:

> At the end of the first survey, we made the recommendation that the campaign be addressed in particular to women, the relatively uneducated, the elderly, and the poor—the classes which showed themselves to be most in need of enlightenment. But who, in the end, were the people reached by the campaign? They were the better educated, the younger, and the men—precisely the people most likely to be interested and, being interested, also to be informed. Among those rated as "interested" in September, by virtue of having expressed "keen" interest in two or more of four given international topics, 47 per cent reported exposure to three or more of the media by March; whereas, among those relatively "uninterested," 29 per cent did. . . . The conclusion is that the people reached by the campaign were those least in need of it and that the people missed by it were the new audience the plan hoped to gain [Star and Hughes, 1950, p. 397].

Indeed, some specialists in this field go so far as to assert that

> considering the state of our present knowledge, the reasonable conclusion to reach in any given instance (in the absence of specific information to the contrary) is that any correlation between communications behavior and the personal characteristics of the people involved is a result of *selective exposure,* rather than evidence for the effects of communications [Bauer and Bauer, 1960, p. 29].

> **A1a**   Although self-selection of exposure in line with predispositions is mainly conscious and deliberate, it can also operate nonconsciously as well.

For example, those who report that they are undecided on a controversial political issue still manage to expose themselves predominantly to the side favored by their social predispositions. As a recent summary put it:

> A person, whenever he is free to do so, chooses to read certain messages or listen to certain programs, and not to others. In general, whether he is aware of it or

not, he listens to what he wants to hear and reads messages in support of what he wants to believe [Riley and Riley, 1959, p. 544].

In line with the basic proposition:

A1.1   People are especially likely to seek out congenial communications on a controversial matter just after coming to a decision on the matter.

A1.2   Neutrals on an issue or topic are unlikely to pay much attention to communications on that issue or topic, except when the communications are highly available.

A1.3   The spread of rumors is directly related to audience predispositions: rumors tend to be heard by people to whom they are congenial; they are passed on more by such people; they are changed into more personally satisfactory forms; and they are best countered by the circulation of objective information that is not explicitly tied to the rumor itself.

A1.4   When caught in an inconsistent position (i.e., in group or attitudinal cross-pressures), people will tend either to seek out communications supporting the dominant side or to withdraw interest from the matter. The stronger the cross-pressures, the less the attention, especially among those who are not well informed on the issue or not especially interested in it.

In addition:

Persons under cross-pressures have been found to be peculiarly susceptible to conversion, to be unstable in opinion and thus susceptible to reconversion, and to tend on occasion to lose interest in the issue altogether [Klapper, 1960, p. 96].

But:

A2   Self-selection of communication exposure in line with predispositions is far from complete, even in extreme cases, so that there is usually a sizable minority of people who read and listen to material against or indifferent to their prior position—out of curiosity, accident (e.g., no foreknowledge of what the content will be), lack of predispositional strength or, importantly, simple accessibility of materials.

Interest remains the single most significant determinant of exposure, and the major countering factor to self-selection of communications is sheer accessibility: people tend to see or hear communications to the degree to which they are readily available (Waples, 1932; De Fleur and Larsen, 1958).

A2.1   Under a monopoly of mass communications, many members of the audience can be brought to change their opinions in the desired direction—but even here there are important qualifications: (a) by no means can *all* the members be brought to change their positions; (b) the process takes time; and (c) the monopoly must be complete or nearly complete; if it is not, enough communications will filter through to provide social support for the views of sizable numbers of people previously convinced of positions opposed to the monopolist's position.

A3   Since audience attention is self-selective, exposure to communications in different media tends to be supplementary, not complementary; that is, those who read about a topic also tend to listen, and those who pay attention at one time also tend to pay attention at another.

There is thus a certain concentration of communications exposure, rather than a selective diffusion of exposure among the media. It is generally not the case that some people follow the matter in one of the media and some in another.

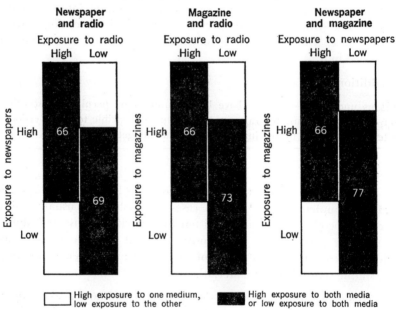

People highly exposed to one medium of communication also tend to be highly exposed to other media (percentages)

(Lazarsfeld *et al.*, 1948, p. 122)

A typical finding, as reported by Lazarsfeld, controverts the popular assumption of a competitive scramble for audiences among the several media. Lazarsfeld found that the audiences in fact overlap to a marked extent: that movie-goers are also radio listeners, magazine readers are also television fans, and nearly all of these at least look at one or more newspapers fairly regularly. Thus a person who has read "Gone with the Wind" is likely to see the motion picture based on the book; and a person who has seen the picture is likely subsequently to read the book [Riley and Riley, 1959, p. 541].

And this finding appears to apply in situations of substitution; thus, the reading supplanted by television seems to be largely that of light novels (Bogart, 1956). Similarly, studies of children's television habits show that the types of programs they prefer on TV are like those they prefer in other media.

A3.1   The smaller and more selective the audience, the more highly concentrated it tends to be.

For example, there are fewer book readers than television viewers, and it takes a smaller proportion of the book readers to account for a given percentage of the total reading done than is the case with television viewing (Berelson, 1949, pp. 96–99).

A3.2   People interested in a topic tend to follow it in the medium that gives it the fullest and most faithful treatment.

Usually that is print, but not always: for example, an exception is telecasts of baseball games for the fan.

A4   The use, and perhaps the effectiveness, of different media varies with the educational level of the audience—the higher the education, the greater the reliance on print; the lower the education, the greater the reliance on aural and picture media. The better educated are more likely than others to pay attention to serious communications dealing with aesthetic or moral or educational issues.

This last—about as well established as any finding in this field (e.g., see Lazarsfeld and Kendall, 1948)—leads to this interesting historical inference: Since the educational level of the population is higher today than ever before, there are not only more book readers per capita today than in earlier times but more readers of "serious books"—even though the average quality of all books read today may be lower than the average quality in earlier periods (which is quite doubtful).

A5   The people most likely to utilize the external opportunities for entertainment furnished by the largest mass media tend to be those least able to rely on their own resources, or the least used to relying on them.

Apart from various social and economic determinants, we found that the first people to buy television were those with the strongest need for ready-made entertainment. In the United States research among adults has shown that the early set buyers were originally more avid cinema-goers and radio listeners. Our work with children [in Britain] also indicates that those from homes which bought television early were more dependent on outside stimulation—they had an unusually high interest in comics, radio, and clubs, and their taste in book reading tended to be narrower. All this suggests a home atmosphere which would seek the stimulation of outside entertainment rather than rely on its own resources [Himmelweit *et al.*, 1958, p. 11].

A5.1   In general, the more recognition that adolescents receive for some personal achievement, the less they use the mass media.

Here, for example, are some recent data:

Influence of value systems rewarding scholarship and athletics on mass media attention of high-school boys

Schools in which:	*Percentage who are frequent users of the mass media*		
	Boys named as best scholars	*Others*	*Difference*
Scholarship very important	16.5	28.0	11.5
Scholarship of average importance	26.7	29.0	2.3
Scholarship of low importance	21.2	26.0	4.8
	Boys named as best atheletes	*Others*	*Difference*
Athletics of high importance	15.9	25.4	9.5
Athletics of medium importance	23.5	29.9	6.4
Athletics of low importance	24.8	22.9	−1.9

(Coleman, 1961a, pp. 238–39)

According to the author:

The general result may be summed up succinctly: when he is in a system that fails to give him status and allow him a positive self-evaluation, the adolescent often escapes to a world where he need not have such a negative self-evaluation: the world of mass media [*ibid.*, p. 243].

A6   Television viewing by children is heaviest among the duller and the emotionally insecure.

Here an addict type emerged who is not exclusive to television; his emotional insecurity and maladjustment seem to impel him toward excessive consumption of any available mass medium. If television is available to such a child, he will view excessively; if not, he will go very often to the cinema, listen a great deal to the radio, or become a heavy reader of comics (but not of books). Such children were characterized by lack of security, by being ill at ease with other children. . . . The active child, socially at ease and with a happy home background, is the least likely to become preoccupied by television. On the other hand, children who view a great deal do so (particularly the intelligent ones) because they have difficulties in making friends or problems in their family relationships. They retreat into viewing or into ready-made entertainment of other types. A vicious circle is then set up whereby the ready access to television aggravates those problems of the children which led them to view heavily in the first instance [Himmelweit *et al.*, 1958, pp. 29, 34].

Following are some data from two large-scale studies of children and television, one in Britain and one in the United States:

**Distribution of moderate to high scores on personality
inventories for matched groups of heavy and occasional
viewers and matched groups of heavy and
occasional cinema-goers (percentages)**

	Viewers		*Cinema-goers*	
Moderate-to-high scores about:	*Heavy*	*Occasional*	*Heavy*	*Occasional*
(1) Feelings of rejection by other children (including, e.g., not getting on with other children, not being popular, feeling left out of things)	58	39	61	48
(2) General feeling of social insecurity (including, e.g., my manners, feeling shy, feeling different from other children)	45	35	40	35
(3) Anxiety about growing up (including, e.g., the thought of marrying, the thought of having to leave school, finding a job when I am older)	48	37	45	35
Total number of cases *	(39)	(39)	(103)	(103)

* The numbers varied slightly from inventory to inventory.

(Himmelweit *et al.*, 1958, p. 389)

Percentage of children who are heavy viewers of television by grade and mental ability *

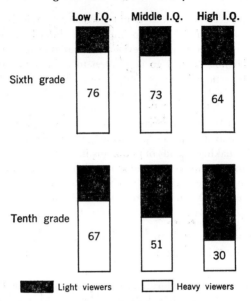

* The chart shows that the percentage of light viewers increases generally between the sixth and the tenth grades, but that the chief increase is in the high I.Q. group.

(Schramm *et al.*, 1961, p. 34)

Perception and Interpretation

B1   People tend to misperceive and misinterpret persuasive communications in accordance with their own predispositions, by evading the message or by distorting it in a favorable direction.

For example, anti-Semites tend to misread the tolerance propaganda put out by Jewish groups; political partisans misinterpret the position of their candidate to bring it more nearly into line with their own position on the issues; partisans on both sides tend to judge neutral speeches as favoring their own points of view; partisans are more likely than others to accept as "fact" those news reports supporting their own position. Here is the summary of a rigorous experimental study:

When the distance between S's [subject's] own stand and the position advocated in communication is small, the communication is judged favorably, as fair and factual. With increasing distance, the favorable reaction is sharply reduced and the communication perceived as propagandistic and unfair. . . . The S's whose own stands diverge widely from the position advocated perceive the communication as further removed from their own stand than it is ("contrast effect"). The present results indicate, though less clearly, that S's whose own stands are close to the position advocated perceive the communication as closer to their own stand than is the case ("assimilation effect") [Hovland *et al.*, 1957a, p. 251].

And here are some results outside the laboratory, from a field study testing the understanding of a cartoon series ridiculing anti-Semitic prejudice:

Number of persons in each prejudice-awareness group who understand and who misunderstand (Mr. Biggott Cartoons)

	Understand	Misunderstand
Group I (most prejudiced)	21	68
Group II (middle group)	28	31
Group III (least prejudiced)	8	3

(Kendall and Wolf, 1949, p. 163)

B1a   Accidental exposure, apparently, is apt to lead to misperception of the message.

Forced or accidental exposure to new information which tends to increase dissonance (within the personality) will frequently result in misinterpretation and misperception of the new information by the person thus exposed in an effort to avoid a dissonance increase [Festinger, 1957, p. 265].

However, accidental or unintended exposure has also been found to be effective, since it can "get around" predispositions more readily when they are not strong and, in view of the accidental occasion, not aroused.

B2   The more trustworthy, credible, or prestigious the communicator is perceived to be, the less manipulative his intent is considered to be and the greater the immediate tendency to accept his conclusions.

However, within reasonable limits, the credibility of the source has little or no influence on the transmission of *factual* information; "information tests reveal equally good learning of what was said regardless of the credibility of the communicator" (Hovland *et al.*, 1953, p. 270). And the effect on opinion of sources perceived differently as to credibility tends to converge after a period of weeks—the effect of sources with high credibility decreases and the effect of those with low credibility increases (in proportion as the audience forgets the sources but retains the content).

B2.1   When the audience has little or no prior knowledge of the communicator's trustworthiness, it tends to decide a question on the basis of the content itself—i.e., the conformity of the content to predispositions.

When the audience does expect or attribute manipulative intent—except perhaps where that is taken as "normal," as in advertising—it develops resistance to acceptance of the message.

B2.2   Communications attributed to sources of low credibility are considered more biased and unfair than identical communications attributed to sources of high credibility. The audience's perception of the source thus tends to influence its interpretation and acceptance of the content.

In summary:

> These results appear to indicate that, under conditions when there is some ambiguity about the credibility of the communicator and when the subject is deeply involved with the issue, the greater the attempt at change the higher the resistance. On the other hand, with highly respected communicators, . . . using issues of lower involvement, the greater the discrepancy the greater the effect. A related study . . . indicates that, when an influence attempt is made by a strongly positive communicator (i.e., a close personal friend), the greater the discrepancy the greater the opinion change, even when the experimenter made a point of stressing the great importance of the subject's opinion [Hovland, 1959, pp. 12–13].

B3   The attribution of a position to "majority opinion" is itself effective in changing attitudes when the audience respects the group from which the majority is taken. Furthermore, such "majority opinion" is typically more effective than "expert opinion."

B4   In cases where the audience approves of the communicator but disapproves of his conclusions, it tends to dissociate the source from the content. In general, there is a tendency to bring source and content into harmony.

Here is the summary of a technical article on this subject:

> Attitude change for a given object of judgment in the direction of the assertion is an approximately linear function of the favorableness of the original attitude toward the other object of judgment with which it is associated. The more favorable the attitude toward a source, the greater the effect of a negative assertion upon lowering attitude toward the concept. Strongly unfavorable sources have just the opposite effects. The same statements hold for changes in attitude toward sources when original attitudes toward concepts are varied [Osgood and Tannenbaum, 1955, p. 54].

B5   In cases of clear incompatibility between what a speaker says and the approval he receives from trusted associates, people tend to misperceive the actual content and distort it in a direction favorable to their own prior position.

For example, in one experiment some subjects from a modern teachers' college heard recordings of a speech purportedly to judge the speaker's logic, presentation, etc. The speaker was identified as a professor of education, and on the recording his speech was interrupted several times by applause. For one group of subjects the applauders were identified as faculty members of the college and for the other group as interested townspeople. The speech was a plea for a return to more authoritarian teaching methods, in strict opposition to the educational philosophy of the subjects' college. All of the subjects tended to attribute to the speaker more modern views than he actually presented, but those who thought faculty members were applauding perceived the speaker as still more modern. Sixty-five per cent of them as compared to 26 per cent of the other group attributed more modern attitudes to the speaker than did the median subject (i.e., the person ranking in the center of the distribution) (Kelley and Woodruff, 1956).

B6 The nature of the source is especially effective in the case of ambiguous or unstructured topics—i.e., those topics on which the content itself is not sufficiently dominant, so that non-content factors can take hold. And vice versa: a firm attitude toward the content will affect attitude toward an ambiguous or neutral source.

B7 The more openly or directly or actively the audience's group identifications are brought into play, the more these identifications determine response.

B7.1 On matters involving group norms, the more attached people are to the group, or the more active they are within it, the more their membership determines their response to communications.

In one experiment, for example, Boy Scouts were exposed to a speaker who criticized their major activities (camping and out-door life). Those Scouts who were most strongly identified with the troop and who particularly valued their membership in it were least likely to change their opinions when expressing their reaction privately (see table on page 540). Integration of membership within a group can even have indirect effects far beyond the sphere of the group itself. For example, a study found that children differed not only in which media materials they liked but in their reasons for liking them. Among young children, 69 per cent of those integrated into peer groups liked the Lone Ranger as compared with 85 per cent of the nonmembers.

While the non-members often described him in subjective terms as "scary," "creepy," "hard to get out of your mind when you go to sleep," the peer group members were more apt to couple their reading of Westerns with "playing guns" in the woods afterward. Thus the peer group members, oriented as they are to

**Positive change and net change for various degrees
of valuation of membership (private
expression of opinion only)**

Degree of valuation of membership	Per cent positive change	Per cent net change *	Number of cases
1 (low)	50.0	+12.5	8
2	41.7	0.0	12
3	41.7	+8.4	24
4	22.2	−38.9	18
5 (high)	22.2	−55.5	9

* Net change is positive change minus negative change.

(Kelley and Volkart, 1952, p. 461)

the need for getting along in the group, appear to judge media in terms of a criterion which we might call *social utility*, to select media materials which will in some way be immediately useful for group living [Riley and Riley, 1951, p. 456].

As a result:

B8   Communications that are thought to represent some particular interest or characteristic of the audience are more influential on opinion than general, undifferentiated sources.

Thus, communications directed to particular audiences are more effective than those directed to "the public at large."

B9   Attitudes toward the mass media seem to transcend their specific content: they grow at least in part out of the physical and social demands the media impose upon the audience.

For example, there seems to be a good deal of guilt or shame associated with "wasting so many hours" watching television, especially among many achievement-oriented people. At least some of it may spill over into criticism of programing and of television in general (Steiner, 1963).

Effect

C1   People respond to persuasive communications in line with their predispositions, and they change or resist change accordingly. Communications will be most effective—that is, will secure the response most in line with the intention of the communicator—when they are in accord with audience predispositions; when they tell people what they (most) want to be told.

As a consequence, people whose opinions are close to the position taken in a communication are more likely to be changed. For example, in a study of wet-dry sentiment,

> when a wet position was espoused, 28% of the middle-of-the-road subjects were changed in the direction of the communicator, as compared with only 4% of the drys. With the dry communication 14% of the middle-of-the-roaders were changed, while only 4% of the wets were changed. Thus, more of the subjects with small discrepancies were changed than were those with large discrepancies [Hovland, 1959, p. 12].

A general statement is this:

> Individuals are more highly persuasible by messages arguing in a direction which increases consistency [within the personality] and are more resistant to those arguing in a direction that increases inconsistency [Rosenberg *et al.*, 1960, p. 204].

Hence, for the three major types of effect:

C1.1   Communications are most likely to reinforce existing positions, then to activate latent positions, and least likely to change or counter existing or latent positions (i.e., to convert).

> Communications research strongly indicates that persuasive mass communication is in general more likely to reinforce the existing opinions of its audience than it is to change such opinions. . . . Regardless of the condition in question—be it the vote intentions of the audience members, their tendency toward or away from delinquent behavior, or their general orientation toward life and its problems—and regardless of whether the effect in question be social or individual, the media are more likely to reinforce than to change [Klapper, 1960, pp. 49–50, 8].

Communications are more effective in canalizing people's existing dispositions than they are in redirecting their responses into directions neutral or counter to their interests, social positions, and group memberships—in which case they encounter a good deal of resistance. As an example, mass communications are more effective in activating a latent taste for cultural values (e.g., good music) than in creating such a taste.

C2   People use their own changes of opinion, however recent or immediate, as blocks against further modification of opinion under the pressure of communications.

> Once a belief is modified by an effective communication there will be a tendency for the newly acquired opinion responses to interfere with the subsequent acquisition of any incompatible opinion responses [Hovland *et al.*, 1953, p. 263].

This will especially be the case if the opinion change was made publicly or if the position was openly advocated to others. Hence:

C3   The fuller the pre-existing information or interest, or the more firmly held the prior attitudes, then the more receptive the audience will be to congenial communications and the more resistant to uncongenial. Similarly, the greater the audience's involvement and interest, the greater will be its acquisition of information and skills.

As we saw above, mass communication can be effective in producing a shift on unfamiliar, lightly felt, peripheral issues—those that do not matter much to the audience or are not tied to audience predispositions. On the others, it is effective in reinforcing opinions but only infrequently changes them.

This series of findings is among the most important in communications research and deserves further summary:

Once seen, communications are most likely to convert or establish opinions for those members of the audience who are neutral on the issue, and least likely to affect those with strong feelings or those whose positions are strongly reinforced by group memberships.

> Mass communication is widely believed to be quite efficient in creating opinions among people who were not previously inclined one way or another on the issue in question. . . . Studies performed both in the laboratory and in the social world indicate that communications are extremely effective in creating opinions on matters about which the audience is *unlikely* to have pre-existing opinions. Communications on such topics have been found capable of "inoculating" audience members, i.e., of rendering them more resistant to later communications or experiences suggesting a contrary view [Klapper, 1960, pp. 60–61].

Another way to put the same general point is to say that people are the more likely to be affected by communications the closer they initially are to the position advocated. To quote from the same experiment referred to above:

> The most frequent result for *S*s whose own stand diverges widely from that advocated in communication is to remain unchanged in their initial attitudes. More *S*s with moderate positions closer to the stand in communication changed in the direction advocated [Hovland *et al.*, 1957a, p. 251].

C3a   The effect of communication programs that try to convert opinions on controversial issues is usually slight.

If the issue matters to the audience, predispositions block the conversion. If the issue does not matter, it gets little attention.

C3b   Conversions are more likely to appear on minor issues, in small amounts, and in the case of audience members cross-pressured on the matter (i.e., with conflicting predispositions).

C4 The communication of facts is typically ineffective in changing opinions in desired directions against the force of audience predispositions: the stronger the predispositions, the less effective the communication of facts.

> Education, or the presentation of information, is relatively ineffective in changing opinions or behavior. The perception and interpretation of "facts" is self-selective and the individual can "protect" himself against facts he does not wish to believe [Suchman *et al.*, 1958, p. 38].

Nevertheless, people are more likely to accept (neutral) factual information from the media than to accept uncongenial editorial positions, interpretations, or evaluations. Thus, because of predispositional resistance, communications affect information and skill more readily than attitudes or motivation. And communications can change the information of the audience, and on occasion even its behavior, without changing the associated attitudes.

> Even in the minds of many professional psychologists there lurks the notion that actions are more "real" than attitudes, and therefore a change in behavior is more difficult to accomplish than is a change of attitude. The opposite is true. One of the generalizations from experimental studies is that "facts" are accepted more readily than "opinions." Looking over a range of the situations in which mass media have been conspicuously effective it appears that they have been effective to the extent that they have capitalized on extant attitudes and, explicitly or implicitly, have fed in "facts" which have suggested an easily available course of action which served those attitudes or values [Bauer and Bauer, 1960, p. 29].

C4.1 Over time, people gradually lose the factual information presented by the media. In the case of evaluational statements, however, there can later be an increased effect (the "sleeper" effect) if predispositions are sufficiently favorable, if the initially unfavorable predispositions fade, or if later experience supports the message.

C5 Over the short run, and on controversial issues, communications are more effective in influencing what is considered salient or important by the audience than in directly influencing uncongenial attitudes.

That is, the media will contribute substantially to determining "what the important issues are" by means of their emphasis, without substantially affecting opinions on the issues.

C6 When opinions do shift under the impact of communications, they tend to regress to the pre-existing position unless they are reinforced by events, other communications, or group pressures.

C7 The more that people read or listen to communications on a given issue, especially in a concentrated fashion, then the less undecided they become, the more interest they develop, the more information they acquire, the more consistent their perceptions are with the messages being communicated, the more strongly partisan they become, the more closely they reflect the media emphasis on the subissues, the more likely they are to act.

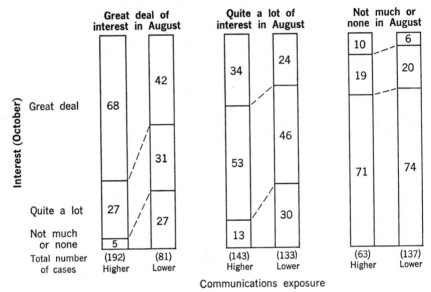

The more media exposure on the campaign, the more political interest and strength of support for the candidate (percentages)

(Berelson *et al.*, 1954, p. 247)

C8   The higher a person's level of intelligence, the more likely it is that he will acquire information from communications.

A possible exception is children and television:

> Children can undoubtedly learn from television; but viewing takes time, some of which might be spent with books or other sources of information. It incurs, therefore, both gain and loss. We found a net profit only for the younger, duller children. . . . For most children in our survey, television proved neither a help nor a hindrance as far as general knowledge was concerned [Himmelweit *et al.*, 1958, pp. 20–21].

But a recent study shows that the better educated the parents, the more likely they are to attribute educational benefits to television (Steiner, 1963).

C9   Particularly during an intensive political campaign or a crisis of public events, exposure to the media of communication increases people's interest in the matter and raises the relevance of the issue for the audience. In addition, such exposure speeds up the trend of opinion within groups and brings inconsistent minor opinions into harmony with major opinions, thus tending to increase both the consistency within groups or strata and the polarization between them; it indirectly intensifies person-to-person influence (by promoting discussion) and it thus heightens social control (since people gain authority over one another).

The campaign increases homogeneity within and polarization between occupational and religious groups

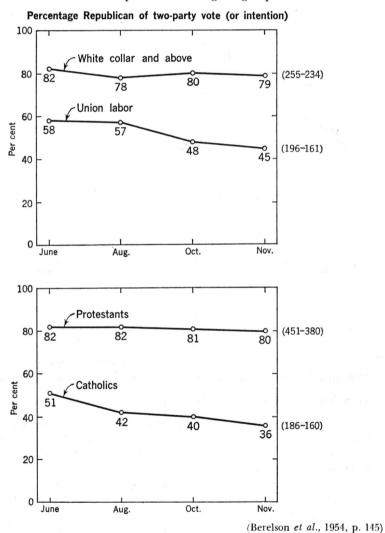

Percentage Republican of two-party vote (or intention)

(Berelson *et al.*, 1954, p. 145)

In this case, as an example, the difference between the class groups was 24 percentage points at the start of the campaign and 34 at the close; and between religious groups, 31 and 44.

C10   With regard to noninformational content, the mass media do not appear to produce substantial amounts of apathy or passivity or reaction to violence. At the least, the evidence is inconclusive.

> Escapist communication has been been held to produce social apathy. No research evidence directly supports or disproves this claim. Related findings *suggest* that such fare probably does not create apathy among the non-apathetic, but probably reinforces the apathy of the already apathetic. . . . Communications research has provided some data relative to the effects of media-depicted crime and violence on values, attitudes, and behavior. Heavy exposure to such fare is apparently not a sufficient or crucial cause of delinquency. In at least five major studies, heavy consumers were found no more likely to be delinquent than were light users or non-users. Two studies do indicate that persons who already have criminal records are likely to be heavy consumers of violent media material, but neither study demonstrates the direction of causation. . . . In combination, these various findings strongly suggest that crime and violence in the media are not likely to be prime movers toward delinquency, but that such fare is likely instead to reinforce the existing behavioral tendencies, *good or ill,* of individual audience members [Klapper, 1960, pp. 205, 164–65].

Furthermore, the alleged inability of the mass media to educate the mass public should be considered in a comparison with the media's disadvantages vis-à-vis the classroom:

> Imagine trying to transmit complex and sophisticated knowledge to students who walk in and out as they please, when some of the most valuable effects might occur among passersby who wander in by chance, when most volunteer students already know what is to be learned, while those who do not already know are not available, when motivation is low, and when neither the subjects nor the teacher have any clear idea about the rewards for learning [McPhee, 1956].

C11   The relative effectiveness of different media depends to a critical extent on *what* and *for whom* (so that generalizations are difficult).

Here is a recent summary of the matter:

> In laboratory experiments, wherein all conditions other than the media are kept constant, formal personal appeal is typically found more effective than radio, which is in turn found more effective than print. Television and films may be hypothesized to fall between personal appeal and radio.
>   In real life situations, informal personal appeal has been consistently found to be more effective than any mass medium, but it is nevertheless not essential to successful persuasion. The relative efficacy of the mass media varies so widely from one topical area to another as to defy generalization. . . . Each of the media

has been ascribed various advantages which are believed, but rarely demonstrated, to be related to that medium's persuasive capabilities. These include such characteristics as the unique ability of print to permit the audience member to govern his rate of exposure, and the ability of the broadcast media to provide the audience member with some sense of personal participation [Klapper, 1960, pp. 129–30].

In general, it appears that the more complex the material, the better print is from the standpoint of comprehension.

With regard to the relative effectiveness of the lecture and the group discussion, a recent summary concluded:

> The majority of these studies find that the lecture and discussion methods . . . are equally effective in terms of information acquired. . . . A number of studies have established clearly that both lecture and discussion methods are capable of effecting changes in attitudes. . . . It appears that discussion methods are superior to lecture methods as a means of changing attitudes and behavior. . . . Discounting possible criticisms of methodology and measurement techniques for the moment, it appears that the discussion method and its variants have a decided advantage over the lecture as a means of developing the several abilities suggested above [ability to evaluate, synthesize, draw inferences, perceive relationships, and apply material learned] [Dietrick, 1960, pp. 92, 94, 95, 99].

An intensive analysis of the effectiveness of the two methods in college classrooms, based on simulated recall of thoughts and feelings at the time, concluded that

> the lecture is especially successful in securing the attention of students to what is being said but that it evokes primarily those thoughts which are appropriate to the following and comprehending of information, while the discussion is more successful in evoking complex problem-solving types of thought [Bloom, 1953, pp. 168–69].

Here is a sampling of the data:

	Lecture (per cent)	Discussion (per cent)
Thoughts about other persons	8	15
Thoughts about the self	5	12
Tangential thoughts about words and phrases used in the lecture or discussion	19	8
Thoughts evidencing simple comprehension of the subject	22	9
Thoughts involving attempts to find solutions to problems and to synthesize the subject	1	8

(*Ibid.*, pp. 165, 166)

There is also evidence on the greater impact-to-action of the discussion method. For example, here is a result from a well-known series of experiments conducted on changing people's food habits during wartime:

Percentage of individuals serving type of food never served before, after lecture and after group decision

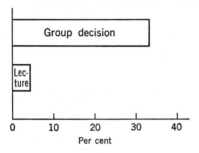

(Lewin, 1953, p. 289)

C12   People with low self-esteem (i.e., those persons high in measures of social inadequacy, inhibition of aggression, and depressive tendencies) are more likely to be influenced by persuasive communications than are those with high self-esteem; but those with acute neurotic symptoms (i.e., neurotic anxiety or obsessional reactions) are more likely to be resistant. Those low in self-esteem are easily persuasible by others because they lack character of their own; the neurotic are too disturbed, too self-concerned, or too negativistic to pay attention or to care.

Some data appear in the chart on page 549. And here is a summary from a study of responses to pressures for conformity:

> [The] more susceptible are more likely to be submissive, low in self-confidence, less intelligent, less original, show less nervous tension, score higher on authoritarian scales, score on the simplicity end of the dimension of the complexity-simplicity scale, show greater dependence on the perceptual field, and comply with requests more frequently [Blake and Mouton, 1961, p. 259].

C13   Active participation in the communicating itself—e.g., passing on the message to someone else, making a speech about it, or simply putting it in one's own words—is more effective for retaining information and for persuading than is passive reception of the communication, especially for people who are low in ability or motivation and for difficult or complex material.

In one experiment, for example, college students were organized into groups of three to prepare talks on a few neutral topics, the talk to be

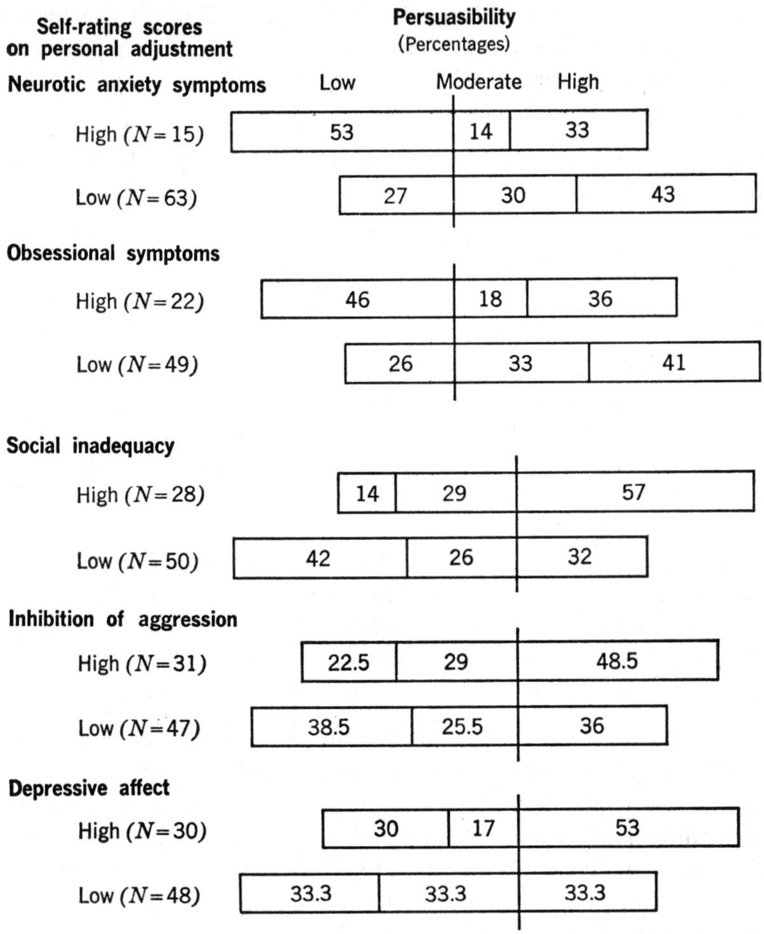

Self-rating scores on personal adjustment	Persuasibility (Percentages)		
Neurotic anxiety symptoms	Low	Moderate	High

Neurotic anxiety symptoms

	Low	Moderate	High
High (N = 15)	53	14	33
Low (N = 63)	27	30	43

Obsessional symptoms

High (N = 22)	46	18	36
Low (N = 49)	26	33	41

Social inadequacy

High (N = 28)	14	29	57
Low (N = 50)	42	26	32

Inhibition of aggression

High (N = 31)	22.5	29	48.5
Low (N = 47)	38.5	25.5	36

Depressive affect

High (N = 30)	30	17	53
Low (N = 48)	33.3	33.3	33.3

(Janis, 1954, as reported in Hovland *et al.*, 1953, pp. 198, 188)

given in each case by one of the three. Opinions were measured before and after, with the following results on two of the topics:

Change in opinion estimates	Future of motion picture industry (percentages)		Future supply of meat (percentages)	
	Speakers	Nonspeakers	Speakers	Nonspeakers
Sizable increase	0	2	0	2
Slight increase	3	9	7	14
No change	23	20	24	16
Slight decrease	29	46	27.5	49
Sizable decrease	45	23	41.5	19

(Janis and King, 1954, p. 213)

The authors' conclusion: "The main findings . . . support the hypothesis that overt verbalization induced by role playing tends to augment the effectiveness of a persuasive communication" (*ibid.*, p. 218). In addition, there is some evidence to the effect that:

> **C13a**   Anticipating a subsequent use increases retention, even of uncongenial material.

For example, college students favoring segregation remembered anti-segregation arguments when they anticipated being involved in a later debate on the issue, but not otherwise (Jones and Aneshansel, 1956). In another case, experimental subjects remembered what would be congenial to the audience they were to report to later: of the people hearing a talk on teachers' salaries, those told they would summarize to a group of teachers tended to recall arguments for increasing salaries, those told they would summarize to a citizen's group interested in economics recalled the opposing arguments (Bauer, 1958).

C14   The mass media exercise an important indirect influence through "opinion leaders"—those trusted and informed people who exist in virtually all primary groups, who are the "models" for opinion within their group, who listen and read in the media, and who then pass on information and influence to their circle of relatives, friends, and acquaintances.

By and large, opinion leaders are like the rank and file of their associates but of slightly higher educational or social status; they give much greater attention to the mass media on the topics of their opinion leadership; they are better informed, more partisan, and more active than their associates. Opinion leaders differ for different topics—sports as against politics, for example—but they have in common their channeling of the impersonal content of mass communications into the personal stream of influence ("the two-step flow of communications"). Opinion leaders are effective, not only because they are personally trusted, but because they can adjust the argument to the individual case, because they can personally and immediately reward agreement, and because they allow for compliance without persuasion. Here, then, is a social mechanism for the group "refraction" of mass communications—important in a large, heterogeneous society.

> **C14.1**   The more communications are directed to the group's opinion leaders rather than to rank-and-file members, the more effective they are likely to be.

> **C14.2**   Word-of-mouth or personal communication from an immediate and trusted source is typically more influential than media communication from a remote and trusted source, despite the prestige of the latter.

In general, use of both together is most effective of all: the media pro-

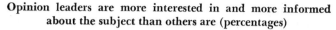

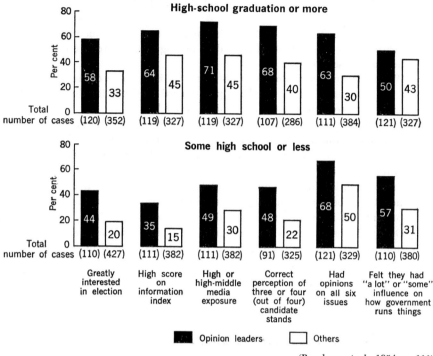

Opinion leaders are more interested in and more informed
about the subject than others are (percentages)

(Berelson *et al.*, 1954, p. 111)

vide the background, the personal contact is more likely to secure acceptance.

C15 Certain characteristics of the content itself are effective in bringing
about acceptance of the message, as follows:

.1 *Order of presentation:* Arousing audience predispositions in favor
of the intended message early in a communication will increase the
likelihood that the message will be accepted and decrease the chances
of later attrition.

For example, preparing the audience early against later counterargu-
ments, securing acceptance and commitment early in the communication,
placing communications congenial to the audience early, arousing audience
needs early—all of these will result in greater acceptance of the message
than their opposites or a neutral order of presentation. But if opposing
views are presented successively, there is little residual effect of primacy.
Here is a summary of the main findings from a series of studies:

(1) When two sides of an issue are presented successively by different communica-
tors, the side presented first does not necessarily have the advantage.

(2) If, after hearing only one side of a controversial issue, a response is made which publicly indicates one's position on the issue, the effectiveness of a subsequent presentation of the second side of the issue is reduced, thus entailing a primacy effect.

(3) The mere act of stating one's opinion anonymously on a questionnaire after hearing only one side of an issue does not significantly reduce the effectiveness of the second side.

(4) When contradictory information is presented in a single communication, by a single communicator, there is a pronounced tendency for those items presented first to dominate the impression received.

(5) The primacy effect found in presenting contradictory information in the same communication was reduced by interpolating other activities between the two blocks of information and by warning the subjects against the fallibility of first impressions.

(6) Presentation of information relevant to the satisfaction of needs after these needs have been aroused brings about greater acceptance than an order which presents the information first and the need-arousal second.

(5) Order of presentation is a more significant factor in influencing opinion for subjects with relatively weak desire for understanding than for those with "high cognitive need."

(8) Placing communications highly desirable to the recipient first, followed by those less desirable, produces more opinion change than the reverse order.

(9) When an authoritative communicator plans to mention pro arguments and also nonsalient con arguments, the pro-first order is superior to the con-first order [Hovland *et al.*, 1957b, pp. 130–37].

.2 *Fear appeals:* Strong appeals to fear, by arousing too much tension in the audience, are less effective in persuasion than minimal appeals.

Effect of different degrees of fear appeal on conformity to dental hygiene recommendations (percentages)

Type of change	Strong fear appeal group (N = 50)	Moderate fear appeal group (N = 50)	Minimal fear appeal group (N = 50)	Control group (N = 50)
Increased conformity	28	44	50	22
Decreased conformity	20	22	14	22
No change	52	34	36	56
Net change in conformity	+8	+22	+36	0

(Janis and Feshbach, 1953, p. 84)

.3 *Conclusion-drawing:* Especially on complex matters, the explicit drawing of conclusions by the communicator is more effective in bringing about audience acceptance than relying upon the audience to draw its own conclusions from the material presented—and presumably this is the more so the less intelligent or the less educated the audience.

.4   One- or two-sided: Presenting only the favored side of a controversial position is more effective than presenting both sides in persuading lesser educated audiences and in reinforcing the already persuaded. Presenting both sides is more effective with the better educated and the opposition, and is also more effective as inoculation against subsequent counter-propaganda.

Before the U.S.S.R. announced its first atomic explosion, two experimental groups and a control group were tested about their estimate of how long it would take that country to produce large numbers of atomic bombs. Then two of the groups heard a program stressing that it would take at least five years for that to occur: one group heard a one-sided argument and the other heard a counterpropaganda program that strongly argued that Russia would be producing quantities of bombs within two years. There was little over-all difference between the effectiveness of the two programs for those who were not exposed to counterpropaganda; but for those who were, the two-sided program was decidedly more effective.

Comparison of a one-sided versus a two-sided presentation for groups exposed and not exposed to subsequent counterpropaganda

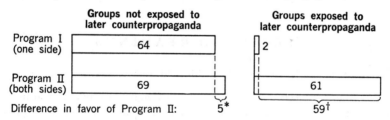

(Hovland *et al.*, 1953, p. 110; data from Lumsdaine and Janis, 1953)

As a general summary on the effects of the mass media, as related to the important matter of economic development in the so-called emerging countries, here is a recent quotation from an expert in the field:

Among the direct and immediate effects which exposure to the media may have upon the individuals are changes in: 1. Attention. 2. Saliency. 3. Information. 4. Skills. 5. Tastes. 6. Images. 7. Attitudes. 8. Actions. . . . Various experimental and survey results suggest that the mass media operate very directly upon attention, information, tastes, and images. Election studies, for example, show that the campaign in the mass media does little to change attitudes in the short run, but does a great deal to focus attention on one topic or another. It also affects the saliency of different issues. Television studies have shown that TV has relatively little direct effect on major attitudes, but it does develop tastes (good or bad) and provides much image material to stock the mind of the viewer. . . .

Changes in skills and attitudes are less apt to be brought about by the mass media operating alone. Here the best we can say is that sometimes they are but often they are not. Often face-to-face relations with a human being toward whom the learner has considerable cathexis is essential for producing changes in those variables. We can, for example, classify attitudes as being of greater or lesser rigidity and saliency. Lightly held attitudes may readily be molded by mass media alone, but not deeply entrenched ones. . . .

Finally, we return to actions, changes in which . . . are almost always checked with reference persons before an individual embarks upon them.

Changes of all of these variables are important in the process of development. But they enter the process in different ways. . . . Changes in actions and in some skills and attitudes will not be effectively produced by mass media alone; rather, the effectiveness of the mass media in influencing them will be a direct function of the effectiveness of political organization to which the mass media are an adjunct.

On the other hand, certain of these changes toward modernization will occur as the mass media develop, whether or not strong political organization exists. Note what these changes are. They are changes in attention, tastes, information, images. That is exactly the revolution of rising expectations! General findings of social psychology based largely upon American experiments and surveys have led us to exactly the same results as area students have formulated from experience with the politics of development: a happy but rare conjunction of observation with theory in the social sciences [Pool, 1963, pp. 250–52].

SELECTED READINGS

For recent summaries of research in this field, see:

Carl I. Hovland. "Effects of the Mass Media of Communication," in Gardner Lindzey, ed., *Handbook of Social Psychology,* Vol. II. Addison-Wesley, 1954, pp. 1062–1103.
Joseph T. Klapper. *The Effects of Mass Communication.* Free Press, 1960.
John W. Riley, Jr., and Matilda White Riley. "Mass Communication and the Social System," in Robert K. Merton *et al.,* eds., *Sociology Today: Problems and Prospects.* Basic Books, 1959, pp. 537–78.

For collections of important studies in this field, see:

Bernard Berelson and Morris Janowitz, eds. *Reader in Public Opinion and Communication.* Rev. ed. Free Press, 1953.
Danial Katz *et al.,* eds. *Public Opinion and Propaganda.* Holt, Rinehart & Winston, 1954.
Wilbur Schramm, ed. *Communications in Modern Society.* U. of Illinois Press, 1948.
Wilbur Schramm, ed. *Mass Communications.* 2nd ed. U. of Illinois Press, 1960.

As examples of the survey approach to communications research there are these titles:

Bernard Berelson *et al. Voting: A Study of Opinion Formation in a Presidential Campaign.* U. of Chicago Press, 1954.
Elihu Katz and Paul F. Lazarsfeld. *Personal Influence.* Free Press, 1955.
Paul F. Lazarsfeld and Patricia L. Kendall. "The Communications Behavior of the Average American," in *Radio Listening in America.* Prentice-Hall, 1948.
Paul F. Lazarsfeld *et al. The People's Choice.* Columbia U. Press, 1948.
Gary A. Steiner. *The People Look at Television.* Knopf, 1963.

As examples of the experimental approach, see:

Carl I. Hovland *et al. The Order of Presentation in Persuasion.* Yale Studies in Attitude and Communication, Vol. I. Yale U. Press, 1957.
Carl I. Hovland *et al. Communication and Persuasion.* Yale U. Press, 1953.
Carl I. Hovland *et al. Experiments on Mass Communications.* Princeton U. Press, 1949.
Milton J. Rosenberg *et al. Attitude Organization and Change: An Analysis of Consistency Among Attitude Components.* Yale Studies in Attitude and Communication, Vol. III. Yale U. Press, 1960.

For two current studies of topical importance, see:

Hilde T. Himmelweit *et al. Television and the Child.* Oxford U. Press, 1958.
Wilbur Schramm *et al. Television in the Lives of Our Children.* Stanford U. Press, 1961.

It is curious to observe the triumph of slight incidents over the mind:—What incredible weight they have in forming and governing our opinions, both of men and things,—that trifles, light as air, shall waft a belief into the soul, and plant it so immovably within it,—that Euclid's demonstrations, could they be brought to batter it in breach, should not all have power to overthrow it.

LAURENCE STERNE
Tristram Shandy

How little solidity and substance there is in the political or social beliefs of nineteen persons out of every twenty. These beliefs, when examined, mostly resolve themselves into two or three prejudices and aversions, two or three prepossessions for a particular party or section of a party, two or three phrases or catch-words suggesting or embodying arguments which the man who repeats them has not analyzed.

JAMES BRYCE
The American Commonwealth

The facts of life do not penetrate to the sphere in which our beliefs are cherished . . . ; as it was not they that engendered those beliefs, so they are powerless to destroy them; they can aim at them continual blows of contradiction and disproof without weakening them.

MARCEL PROUST
Remembrance of Things Past

Although uneducated and ill-informed, I developed immensities of opinion and was not easily convinced of my ignorance or unreason. Invariably I deferred to my own opinions—I still prefer it that way! . . . My opinions served, and were good and proper for me, until they were confuted, and by that time I had generally grown so attached to them that I continued to cherish them privately, as pensioners.

A. E. COPPARD
It's Me, O Lord!

Chapter Fourteen

OPINIONS, ATTITUDES, AND BELIEFS

As we have seen, men differ in many ways: in social class or position, in intelligence, in personality, in group and institutional affiliations. Interwoven with all of these are variations in their opinions, attitudes, and beliefs.

The behavioral sciences have given a great deal of attention to this topic, especially in recent years with the invention of the sample survey and related techniques. Since opinions, attitudes, and beliefs always have to be *about* something—opinions on politics, attitudes toward different occupations, beliefs about God—we have often been faced with the problem of deciding just where in this book to put certain findings. In principle, we have tried to include in this chapter only those generalizations about the formation and change of opinions, attitudes, and beliefs that seem to apply to most spheres of subject matter, and to include in the appropriate sections elsewhere those that apply directly to specific subjects. A little reflection will show, however, that this is by no means an easy or automatic judgment to make, so we simply note here that some related findings, such as those on politics and religion, will be found in other sections.

DEFINITIONS

Opinion, attitude, belief: These terms do not have fixed meanings in the literature, but in general they refer to a person's preference for one or another side of a controversial matter in the public domain—a political issue, a religious idea, a moral position, an aesthetic taste, a certain practice (such as how to rear children). Opinions, attitudes, and beliefs (hereafter, OAB's) are rational and/or emotional judgments on such questions.

They differ from one another in their generality or in the intensity with which they are held. Opinions commonly refer to topical and short-run judgments, usually dealing with questions of public affairs; attitudes are somewhat more enduring and inclusive; beliefs are more basic still, having to do with the central values of life. Thus, people have opinions on the latest economic proposal, attitudes regarding the welfare state, and beliefs about freedom. Or they have opinions on the latest fad in child-rearing, attitudes toward demand feeding, and beliefs about the early development of self-reliance. Opinions and attitudes are presumably adapted to beliefs, which are deep-seated, but are usually more consciously cognitive in their content and are more amenable to change. Opinions are sometimes called impressions or guesses, attitudes are sometimes called views or convictions, and beliefs are sometimes called values or sentiments. There are, however, no hard-and-fast boundaries for the terms, so that one man's opinion may be another man's attitude and still another man's belief.

Most of the research summarized here deals with opinions on political issues, since that is what the bulk of the literature consists of. However, other material is included wherever appropriate.

Reference group: A group to whose standards people refer when considering their OAB's; the actual or imagined set of people one uses as a model, usually those one wants to be approved by. A reference group may be the people one lives with (e.g., family or friends) or one's professional associates, one's political affiliates, the circle one aspires to, and so on. A person normally has different reference groups for different subjects, and he can be an associating member or not. In the broadest sense, a reference group can even be an individual—as when a living or historical figure has sufficient prestige to serve as a guide to conduct.

Cross-pressures: Conflicting influences on a person from the differing positions he takes or from the differing social strata or social groups of which he is a member, whether he is directly conscious of the conflict or not. Thus, a well-to-do Catholic typically experiences cross-pressures on his presidential vote in this country; so does a well-to-do Negro. Similarly, someone who was taught to raise children strictly but who now lives in a community where they are raised permissively is under cross-pressures. The concept extends to attitudinal cross-pressures, as when a person favors part of one side's position and part of the opposition's. The essential element is the pull from two sides, felt or latent.

FINDINGS

Beyond the topic of determining who holds what OAB's, which in the main is dealt with elsewhere in this book, there is the matter of the acquisition of OAB's. This involves two questions: How do they develop?

And how do they change? These questions typically refer to different periods of time. First there is the initial, gradual acquisition of points of view in a particular historical setting and in the early and formative years of life—aesthetic tastes, religious ideas, political preferences, and so on. Once they are acquired there is the question of their subsequent stability or change. Accordingly, we have organized the research findings in this field under two broad headings: (1) the factors determining the initial development of OAB's (the stable, basic, or underlying considerations); and (2) the sources, character, and process of their stability and change over relatively short periods of time.

Initial Development

THE HISTORICAL SETTING

A1   OAB's are more differentiated in more complex societies.

Since OAB's must, by definition, be controversial in character, they can deal only with those subjects on which there is no unanimity (or near-unanimity) within the society. What would be unquestioned custom or dogma in a simple, ecclesiastical, or totalitarian society becomes subject to differences of opinion in a socially heterogeneous, secular society.

> **A1.1**   In the Western world historically and in the East currently, the rise in political importance of the common man's OAB's is associated with the rise of the middle class, the growth of nationalism and industrialism, the expansion of literacy and education, the emergence of democratic institutions, the spread of competing religious dogmas, and the development of the mass media of communication.

Broadly speaking these major historical conditions operate in two ways: first, by increasing the number and intensity of distinctions within a society, as with nationalism or the differentiation of classes; and second, by providing the means for the learning and expression of OAB's, as with the mass media or democratic institutions.

A2   OAB's originating in an earlier period persist to be influential in a later period, both within a single lifetime and over generations.

For example, the generations that came of voting age during the depression and early New Deal period not only were likely to consider economic issues as the basis for their political opinions at the time; they also were more likely than other generations to stress economic issues in later and more prosperous times, when such other matters as international affairs had grown in objective importance. Similarly, members of national and religious minority groups, of the generation that came of political age in the 1920's (when immigration and assimilation were major problems), were more likely to base their political opinions on nationality and religious considerations, and this basis for opinions also persisted despite changing social circumstances. Hence, a certain amount of opinion current at any particular time is dominated, or at least conditioned, by historical issues and events of a much earlier time (Berelson *et al.*, 1954).

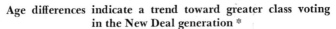

Age differences indicate a trend toward greater class voting in the New Deal generation *

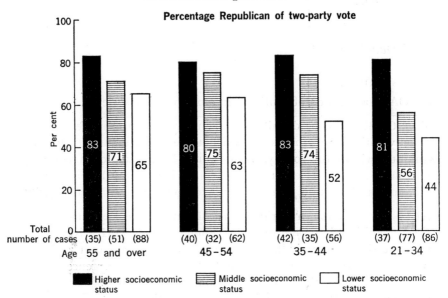

* This study, done on the 1948 presidential election, shows a greater spread among the classes for those age groups that came of voting age in the depression and New Deal years.

(Berelson *et al.*, 1954, p. 60)

In public affairs, this persistence is usually embodied in the image of a political party that tends to retain its position relative to another political party over long periods of time, despite changes in the pattern of events, circumstances, and each party's absolute position. In some cases of "traditional" opinions, as in the South or in New England in this country, voting patterns can be traced back almost a century; for example, Southern counties with high proportions of Negroes (the reinforcing factor) maintain the attitudes assumed during Reconstruction and have continuously voted more Democratic than counties with low proportions of Negroes. Thus, the opinions held by earlier generations are effective in determining the opinions of later generations with whom they are in direct or indirect contact, each generation influencing the one that follows. In short, the political temper at the time a generation is learning its OAB's will shape such dispositions initially; once shaped, they have a self-maintaining capacity (in ways to be explained below).

All this does not mean, of course, that OAB's do not change with time. Even the most basic values are affected by events and shifts in the conditions of life. For example, here is a summary statement of those changes in values (beliefs) currently under way in the United States that are "documented by some empirical data":

1. Decline of the Puritan Ethic as the core of the dominant middle-class value system. . . .
   (a) Rise in value upon "being" or "being and becoming" as opposed to "doing." . . .
   (b) Trend toward "present time" in contrast to "future time" value-orientation. . . .
   (c) Increase of aesthetic and recreational values. . . .
2. Increase in "otherdirectedness." . . . I see the "return to religion" as an aspect of this shift and of the following one.
3. Emergence of explicit value placed upon "psychological health." . . .
4. More prizing of some kinds of tolerance and of some kinds of diversity. . . .
5. Drift toward equalization of the roles of the sexes [Kluckhohn, 1958, p. 207].

The same effect can be seen across societies as well as within them. A series of studies of the Ways of Life preferred by college students in several countries found a

> contrast . . . between the more self-centered orientation of the Western students and the more society-centered orientation of the Asiatic students . . . especially when the contrast is made to the United States results. But it cannot be expanded into a distinguishing characteristic of East and West in general. Historically there have been times when the emphasis has been reversed. The present contrast may be due largely to the fact that the social problems facing the Asiatic nations were at the time of the ratings much more serious than those facing the Western nations. This may also help explain why the stress on action . . . is so much stronger and the stress on detachment . . . so much weaker than would be expected in terms of the traditional conceptions of the Orient. . . . If we turn from contrasts to a search for similarities, it may be noted that in spite of important cultural differences there is still considerable agreement in the overall liking of many of the Ways [Morris, 1956, pp. 64–65].

And such values typically stay close to home. For example, when people of different countries are asked about their personal aspirations and fears, it is such matters as the health and living standard of the family that score at the top rather than national or international political matters, even war and peace. Here are some recent data from the United States and Brazil, countries differing widely in socioeconomic development:

	Leading personal aspirations (percentages)	
	Mentioned by Americans	Mentioned by Brazilians
Good health of self or family	56	43
Decent or improved standard of living for self or family	38	43
Have own house, land, etc.	24	30
Peace; no war; no threat of war	9	(—)

(Cantril and Free, 1962, p. 11)

THE PARENTAL FAMILY

A3   OAB's are "inherited" from one's parents: people learn them early in life and the learning persists into adulthood.

The matter is summarized in the table on page 563.

Political interest and political preference begin to show themselves clearly by about the time children are ten years old, and throughout the teens such concerns become increasingly developed. By the early teens interest is high and by the late teens it is the equivalent of that in adult life. As for sex differences, boys learn at a very early age that they are supposed to be more interested in public affairs than girls are—just as their fathers are more interested in politics than are their mothers, on the average—and they become so: they are better informed, they read and listen more, they talk politics more. "Thus already at early ages, boys are directed toward politics and here lie the seeds of the adult differentiations everywhere found in studies of political participation" [Hyman, 1959, p. 31].

In short, the learning of OAB's begins when people are very young— religious affiliation quite early, political beliefs a little later—and persists into enduring differences among adults. The OAB's of children and youths usually correspond to those of their parents. Even in later adult life, in the United States, from two-thirds to three-fourths of the voters vote for the party their fathers normally voted for, and the statistical correlation with the father's vote is usually as strong as that with one's own current class or occupation. As a result:

A3a   Children's interest in and attitudes on public affairs correspond closely to strata differences among adults: upper-class children are more interested than lower-class children, ethnic differences in political preferences appear early in life.

Past studies of the agreement in politically relevant views among parents and children

Study	Sample	Dimension	Findings
Bassett	87 high-school children and their parents in a small city in 1948	Likelihood of war	Negative, no significant difference between agreement observed and that to be expected among random pairs of individuals.
Duffy	Freshmen in 1935 at Sarah Lawrence and their parents	Attitude toward war	Correlations were negligible. Author concludes little or no correspondence within family.
Hirschberg and Gilliland	200 college undergraduates and their parents	Attitude toward New Deal, "Fascist Attitudes"	R * ranges from .4 to .7, depending on family pair and attitude.
Peterson	Children from grades 7 to 12. Depending on family pair involved, N's vary between 45 and 89	Attitude toward New Deal, government ownership	R ranges from .3 to .8, depending on family pair and attitude studied.
Newcomb and Svehla	Children were fourteen years or older, N was 548 families	Attitude toward Communism	R ranges from .5 to .6, depending on family pair studied.
Fisher	College students. About 150 pairs of parents and children	Economic attitudes	Correlations range from .1 to .6, depending on dimension and family pair studied.
Remmers and Weltman	High-school youth in rural Indiana and Illinois, 200 families	Political items and party preference	Poll items have correlations of about .7. Party preference varies between .8 and .9.
Helfant	166 high-school seniors and their parents in Teaneck, N.J., around 1950	Attitude toward war, Russia, and international affairs	On war, correlation with father not significantly different from zero, with mother .16; on Russia correlations were respectively .18 and .28; on international affairs, correlations were respectively .11 and .27.
Stagner	100 college students and their parents in 1936	Ten questions on liberalism and conservatism; political party preference	Correlations were not presented. Plurality of offspring more liberal than parents; considerable number more conservative; daughters much more likely to deviate in liberal direction from mothers than sons from fathers. On party preference, agreement with parents is exceedingly high.
Himelhoch	68 Jewish undergraduates at N.Y.U. and their parents	California "E" and "F" scales	On ethnocentrism, C * was .57. Correlation between parents and offspring on F (Authoritarianism) was not significant.
Morgan and Remmers	Purdue undergraduates and their parents; depending upon pair, N varies from 12 to 17 pairs	Liberalism as measured by Harper's "Social Study" questionnaire	Children are more liberal than their mothers, who are more liberal than fathers. Father/child and mother/child correlations are between .6 and .7, while father/mother correlation is less than .4.
Harris, Remmers, and Ellison	Over 300 Purdue undergraduates	Party preference	46 per cent of the men and 54 per cent of the women have same party preference as parents; in 4 out of 5 families the mother and father have the same party preference.

* R and C are correlational measures.

(Hyman, 1959, pp. 70–71)

For example, the proportions of high school students who were *not* following the presidential campaign in 1952 (Hyman, 1959, p. 35) are as follows:

Family income low	42 per cent
Family income medium	25 per cent
Family income high	14 per cent

Such differences among children from different social backgrounds appear in the early school years and grow throughout the school period, although the increments decrease over time, since the initial variations are large.

A3.1   The early indoctrination or incorporation of parental views itself makes for the stability of OAB's in later life.

This is so because of the child's strong identification with his parents and, occasionally, his later but often equally strong rebellion against their position; partly because the parent has a priority in time and the child originally has no conflicting OAB's to be overcome; and partly because the child also has a long time in which to become habituated to the OAB's as his own.

A3.2   As for political affairs, what is typically learned or passed on, from father (usually) to child, is not so much an ideology as a party affiliation.

The broad effect of this is to provide a stable means of easy adjustment to newly arising political issues and events over a long period of years.

A3.3   The parental influence on the politics of the child is heightened for the political majority in a community and attenuated for the minority.

As we have seen in other connections, the larger community can take some toll, through counterinfluence against the family itself. Although this effect has been documented primarily for political opinions, it probably holds for attitudes and beliefs as well.

A3.4   Between generations, the weaker the parents' feelings on a matter, the less influence they exert on their children.

If the parents are split in their attitudes, or if they are caught in cross-pressures, or if they are just not interested in political affairs—under such conditions, the children are likely to take an independent position. For example, see the data in the table on page 565.

A3.5   As a child grows up, he grows away from the original parental influence to the extent that he comes into contact with new ways of life, new social groups, new community environments, and so on.

In particular, children who are better educated than their parents tend to shift their attitudes away from those of their parents, and the younger members of large minority groups tend to deviate from their elders. A

Relation of parents' party identification
to that of offspring (percentages)

Question: While you were growing up, did your parents think of themselves as Democrats or Republicans? Or did they shift around from one party to another?

	Both parents Democrats	Both parents Republicans	Parents split, shifting, nonvoters, or vote unknown
Democrats	72	16	36
Republicans	12	63	21
Independents, those with no party connections, affiliations with minor parties, or politics not ascertained	16	21	43
Total number of cases	(657)	(387)	(445)

(Campbell *et al.,* 1954, p. 99)

large study of the values of American college students found, for example, that those leaving their fathers' political allegiance tended to be in schools where the students were predominantly affiliated with the opposition party (Goldsen *et al.,* 1960, pp. 102–03).

> Even where political loyalties are strong among the parents, the second genera- tion's repudiation of immigrant parents and middle-class children's repudiation of working-class parents makes the transmission of these loyalties more tenuous in America than in many other countries [Lane, 1959, p. 208].

A3.6   The notion that political attitudes are formed in rebellion against the parents is true for only a small proportion of people.

Here is the summary of a large-scale study of college students in the United States:

> The present-day college student, then, is not even in political revolt against his parents. If there is any "rebelliousness" it runs the gamut from A to B, culmi- nating in the adoption of an "independent" political position. And where this mild rebellion does occur, it is more likely to be in the conservative (Republican) direction.
>
> But what about the small group of students who *did* rebel—students who sup- ported a political party different from that of their parents. Perhaps in this group, at least, we might encounter a hard core of youthful rebels—a group of angry, or at least irritated, young men who, in liberating themselves from the political traditions of their parents, have likewise declared their independence from the traditional thinking of their sociological status-groups. But no: analysis of the

factors related to "rebellion" against father's vote indicates quite an opposite tendency. It turns out that students who go contrary to the political views of their fathers are finding a way of adjusting their own political views more nearly to the accepted norms of certain sociological groups to which they feel an allegiance [Goldsen *et al.*, 1960, p. 101].

In a few cases, however, the feelings involved are so intense and their psychological meaning so strong that they do tend to persist in active form. Furthermore, such rebellious counterformation of attitudes and beliefs seems to occur most frequently among those children who were subject to the strictest parental control and least frequently where control was moderate. For example, some scholars believe that the strongest political movements among youth occur in countries like Germany, where a period of psychological stress is coupled with an authoritarian father.

A3.7   Among young people, the more important the subject of the OAB is to them, the more likely they are to go along with their peers rather than their parents.

In the United States, for example, this finding would differentiate the political sphere from the sphere of popular music, courting practices, hot-rod cars, and other staples of adolescent culture. At the same time,

the most conspicuous factor in the development of an individual's social values appears to be his home and family life. . . . Children were found to resemble their parents in moral knowledge, but were not significantly like their club leaders, school teachers, or Sunday School teachers [Dukes, 1955, p. 37, citing Hartshorne *et al.*, 1930].

GROUP MEMBERSHIP

A4   People hold OAB's in harmony with their group memberships and identifications.

A basic finding in social psychology is that the attitudes a person holds depend in part upon his social contacts and particularly upon the groups in which he holds membership [Kelley, 1955, p. 275].

There is strong agreement on OAB's within the most personal and intimate circles—within the family, among friends, and even among co-workers. People tend to join organizations that are congenial to their existing attitudes; such membership not only supports existing judgments but also crystallizes latent judgments.

It becomes apparent that the consumer faced with a baffling array of brands, the voter choosing between political courses with unknown consequences, and the entertainment-seeker with untold possibilities on his television dial makes choices which are not based primarily on the inherent merits of the object chosen—no matter how persuasively these merits may have been advertised to them. It further appears that these choices are widely affected, not alone by the choice object itself or by advertising and propaganda about it, but also by other people. . . . Thus his reactions are not random relative to the reactions of these others. His perceptions and his responses form part of a pattern of interaction and mutual orientations among all the members of the group [Riley and Riley, 1959, p. 552].

A4.1   The more homogeneous the social environment of the individual, the more intensely he holds his OAB's and the more likely he is to act on them.

Homogeneity in characteristics normally makes for cohesiveness within the group and for agreement on controversial matters. For example, the longer people live in a community, the more likely they are to hold opinions in agreement with the majority of the community. As for action as a consequence of group cohesiveness, the homogeneity of the class-conscious environment of Berlin and Viennese workers before World War II led to a higher turnout at the polls among them than among the middle class, whereas, for example, that would be reversed in the typical American middle-class community. Here is the relation between vote in a presidential election and the votes of one's three best friends:

The voter's strength of conviction is related to the political homogeneity of his associates

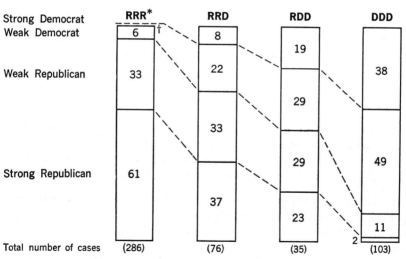

* RRR: Three closest friends all Republicans. RRD: Two Republican, one Democrat; and so on.
† Less than 1 per cent.

(Berelson *et al.*, 1954, p. 99)

A4.2   The more the personal contact among members of a group, the more likely that they will agree on OAB's.

This is a matter not only of sharing information and interpretation on what is appropriate and "correct" but also of prestige and support mutually given and taken. Among the Viennese workers just mentioned, for example, politics was considered so important that other aspects of life were given a political complexion through the administration of social, educational, cultural, and athletic affairs, thus increasing opportunities for mutual reinforcement through constant contact.

> **A4.2a**   When the OAB's of one's active associates differ from those of respected groups with whom one is not in direct or continuous contact, the former are more likely to win out.

> **A4.2b**   Opinions and attitudes, and even on occasion beliefs, are changed temporarily to fit in with the position of a new group with which one is temporarily in contact.

For example, Southern students have been found to soften their racial attitudes when in conferences where they are outnumbered by Northerners holding different attitudes. In fact there is even evidence to indicate that simply acting out a different position (role-playing) will affect attitudes (King and Janis, 1956). And it has been shown that people tend to remember what they think a reference group will want to hear (Zimmerman and Bauer, 1956).

A4.3   The more salient or important an issue is to a group, the more closely its members will agree in their OAB's.

An opinion aggregate is the more likely to attain solidarity the more highly controversial the opinion, and the more the aggregate is in a minority. . . . Intense conflict with other opinions enhances mutual identification of those sharing the given opinion [Lasswell and Kaplan, 1950, pp. 38–39].

> **A4.3a**   Over a period of time the less interested members of a social group respond to group changes only slowly, since the conditions making for shifts among the interested members tend to affect them less and come to their attention later.

It takes a heavy campaign to reach the less interested, i.e., to bring them up to date on their group's stand. But even they will nevertheless usually take over the opinions of the group, since loyalty to their fellows means more to them than the "right" position on a matter they care little about, and the "rightness" of which, in any case, they can hardly judge.

A4.4   The more complex or ambiguous or unpredictable the consequences of the OAB, the more people rely on group ties as a basis for decision.

For many people this is the case in a presidential election, since the outcome is hard to evaluate against its alternative. The power of such group ties, incidentally, can persist even when they are no longer directly relevant to or "rational" for the issue.

A4.5   When people fall out with an initial group over an OAB that is important for them, they tend to seek out social support from people congenial to their new position.

This is a matter of choosing whether the group or the OAB is the more important. As an example:

> The radical tends to cut himself off from the rest of the community and depends more on his political associates for love and friendship. The radical organization is likely to lose members who fail to find satisfying primary relations within the group or find them elsewhere [Broom and Selznick, 1957, p. 575, citing Kornhauser, 1953].

A5   When people develop an OAB, their evaluation of an objective situation depends on whom they compare themselves with: different groups, different evaluations.

This involves the concept of "relative deprivation." For instance, the opinions of many soldiers in World War II about the draft or their promotion or assignment were best explained by examining their relations with other groups like themselves but subject to different conditions: drafted married men felt deprived relative to both married civilians and unmarried soldiers (Stouffer *et al.*, Vol. 1, 1949). And:

A5.1   The more firmly anchored an OAB is in the perception of relative deprivation, the less changeable it is.

A6   OAB's within a group are particularly subject to influence by the most respected and prestigious member(s) of the group, the opinion leader(s).

In most families, for example, the father is the opinion leader on most subjects (besides care of the house and child-rearing). Virtually every group has its opinion leaders on various topics: they know more about the topic, are the touchstone for the group's position, and are looked to for information and guidance.

In a major study of opinion leadership among women in a middle-sized American community, it was found that such leadership was exercised mainly within a given social class and that in the spheres of marketing and fashion older women led younger women. Only in the sphere of politics was there much vertical leadership, from a higher class; and even there, the leadership was primarily exercised by the men in the immediate circle—husbands and fathers (Katz and Lazarsfeld, 1955).

A6a   The opinion leaders within a group tend to be a little better educated than the other members—but only "a little," so that they are not out of touch with the core sentiment of the group.

This notion of the opinion leader is given fuller treatment in the chapter on Mass Communication.

SOCIAL STRATA

A7   There are differences in OAB's that derive from the social strata in which people find themselves or from the social characteristics that they have: whether they live in the city or the country, whether they live in one geographic region or another, whether they are white or colored, Protestant, Catholic, or Jewish, rich or poor, young or old, men or women, educated or uneducated.

Partly, membership in a given social stratum limits or conditions a person's view of the world, simply as a matter of experience: if one is poor, economic issues are important to him; if one is Negro, racial issues are. Moreover, such membership inevitably carries with it society's pressures and expectations that people act in ways appropriate to their stations: males are supposed to "be a man" and everybody is expected to "act his age." In the case of both conditioning and pressure, the prescribed behaviors, as we have already noted, are passed on from generation to generation—primarily through the influence of the parents—and are supported by personal relations in closely knit social groups. Such groups, of course, operate mainly within rather than between strata, and they interpret and reinforce the leanings that experience gives to different strata.

At present, at least in the United States, differences in OAB's stem from three major factors and two minor ones. The major factors are residence, ethnic status, and class; the minor ones are age and sex.

A7.1   *Residence:* There are two conditions of residence that affect the development of OAB's: geographical region and urban-rural location.

In this country, people born and raised in the South traditionally support one political party and people born and raised in upper New England traditionally support the other. There are equally sharp regional differences in other countries: in Italy (with the exception of Rome) there is a regular increase in conservative votes and religious loyalties from the North to the South.

The urban-rural difference partly derives from agricultural as against industrial employment, but it can also be traced to the greater sophistication of the city (at least before the automobile and the mass media blurred such a difference). Even now there are clear differences between country and city in political preference, in moral temper, in the sense of control over one's fate, and probably in religious affiliation.

A7.2   *Ethnic status:* There are important and enduring differences in secular OAB's among different nationality, racial, and religious groups.

Partly they persist from historical situations in which such groups found themselves: nationality groups and their immigration and assimilation; the Jews and the rise of Hitler or the establishment of Israel; the Negroes and civil rights. In the political sphere, for example,

> the plain fact is that the two-party vote in the U.S., at least in national elections, can be closely tied to the ethnic identification of the voters. . . . Indeed, there is good reason to believe that the influence of religion on vote—simply in the sense of religious membership or identification—is stronger than the class or socioeconomic difference. . . . If there is a "class vote" in the U.S. there is a "religious vote" as well [Berelson, 1961, p. 259a].

Here are the attitudes on an important political issue in the early 1950's in the United States:

Relation of party identification to attitude toward Senator Joseph McCarthy among Protestants and Catholics (percentages)

	Protestants					Catholics				
	SD	WD	Ind	WR	SR	SD	WD	Ind	WR	SR
Pro-McCarthy	7	6	7	11	23	18	19	23	20	39
Neutral	34	44	47	48	44	47	53	53	48	33
Anti-McCarthy	55	45	35	33	28	33	21	20	28	23
Other responses	4	5	11	8	5	2	7	4	4	5
Total number of cases	(184)	(213)	(173)	(128)	(123)	(51)	(58)	(55)	(25)	(18)

SD and WD: Strong and weak Democrats.
Ind: Independents.
SR and WR: Strong and weak Republicans.

(Campbell and Cooper, 1956, p. 149)

With regard to religious beliefs themselves, a recent study of the values of American college students concluded that the Catholics were most strongly committed to religion, the Jews least, and the Protestants in between.

> The Catholics are most agreed on the necessity for a religious or ethical belief system to be based on absolute and traditional values. . . . The Jewish students approach religion, apparently, in virtually the opposite way. These young people are most likely to agree that absolute or ritualistic values are *not* important in a religious or ethical belief system. They tend to stress the individual and societal values that a belief system can bulwark. They seem to stress ethical and

social content rather than absolute or Divine sanction. The Protestants appear to be somewhere in between. . . . With the exception of the Catholic students, the kinds of beliefs which most of these young people accept as legitimate religious values seem to center around the personal and individual approach to religion. "Personal adjustment," an "anchor for family life," "intellectual clarity"—these are the kinds of criteria which most of the students agree are important. These are also the kinds of approaches which can be expected to appeal to everyone, which everyone can share—perhaps a least common denominator of religious belief and religious feeling; secular values rather than sacred ones [Goldsen *et al.*, 1960, pp. 164–68].

A7.3   *Class:* The third important characteristic is class—whether measured by income, occupation, education, inherited status, or some combination thereof.

In all modern industrial countries, the upper class is in general not only more interested and more informed about public affairs but also more likely to support what is usually regarded as the conservative or "rightist" position on political affairs than are the lower classes, which tend to side with the liberal or "leftist" position. Matters of aesthetic taste are most highly correlated with education. Even religious beliefs are strongly affected by class position, as we have seen.

Another important, and perhaps less apparent, instance of class differences has to do with what is a more basic attitude or even a belief, namely, the tendency toward a so-called authoritarian position, i.e., intolerance on civil liberties, prejudice against minorities, skepticism toward the motives of others, and pessimism on humanity's chances generally. It is the lower classes that are the more authoritarian, in this sense, and the class differences begin to appear in children at a quite early age. So the radical political position that rests on the libertarian sentiments of the working class must come to terms with this central fact. To demonstrate the correlation between authoritarianism and schooling, here are the proportions of Americans with differing education who score high on a scale of tolerance toward various minority positions in politics (e.g., respecting the rights of Socialists, atheists, Communists, etc.):

	Per cent of cases	Total number of cases
College graduates	66	308
Some college	53	319
High school graduates	42	768
Some high school	29	576
Grade school	16	792

(Stouffer, 1955, p. 90)

A7.3a The more strongly people identify themselves with a given stratum, the more sharply their OAB's are defined by its boundaries.

That is, those people who not only live in a region but are devoted to it are more likely to take extreme positions on the norms associated with that region; those people who are Catholic not only by birth but by personal dedication are more likely to take a strong "Catholic position" on political matters too; and so on. In other words, differences in OAB's by residence, ethnic identification and class—though clear and consistent on the basis of an objective classification of people—are increased somewhat when the people's own feelings about their identifications are taken into account.

A7.4 *Age:* At least in recent years, younger people seem to follow the class lead more and the religious lead less in determining their political opinions.

In addition, age appears to bring with it not only a developing conservatism, in the usual sense, but also a higher degree of authoritarianism. With respect to the latter consequence, the effect of age is countered by the effect of education. As each new generation in this country is better educated than the one before, it is more tolerant; but as it grows older it becomes less so. "Although [the youth of today] is likely to be more tolerant when he reaches 60 than were his own parents at 60, he may at the same time be less tolerant than he was in his own younger days" (Stouffer, 1955, p. 94). With aging, then, the differences produced by education become less pronounced.

Age differences are also involved in the movement of generational OAB's through time (see A2, p. 559).

A7.5 *Sex:* Social pressures and expectations everywhere lead men to take a more active political role than women, and everywhere women tend to be more religious and to take a more "conservative" political position than men, i.e., to follow the class lead less and the religious lead more.

For example, here are how men and women split their votes between the two major parties in West Germany in the mid-1950's:

	Men (per cent)	Women (per cent)
Social Democrats (SPD)	58	40
Christian Democrats (CDN)	25	39

(Linz, 1959, p. 235)

In surveys of American students, men consistently score higher on tests of theoretical, economic, and political values, and women score higher on the aesthetic, religious, and social values (Dukes, 1955, p. 19).

A7a   On the whole, there seems to be no relation between intelligence and values; that is, between the scores made on an intelligence test and those made on a test measuring various kinds of values, of the sort illustrated above.

A review of the empirical literature is contained in Dukes, 1955. A few studies have shown correlations between intelligence and social values, but others have been inconclusive.

Stability of OAB's

B1   For a population as a whole, there appears to be little lasting development of OAB's that is independent of parental, group, or strata predispositions and is based mainly on "objective" or "rational" analysis of information and ideas.

In the political sphere, for example, the so-called independent voters—those persons who shift relatively frequently between political parties—turn out to be the people with the least information and the least interest in the matter.

B1.1   Especially among the less interested and the less involved, and on peripheral or unclear topics, once authoritative action is taken, opinion tends to crystallize in support of the action and the pre-existing indecision or doubt tends to dissipate.

This is termed the *"fait accompli* effect." The best example, perhaps, is the way marginal opinion becomes favorable when Congress or the President acts on a debated matter. There is some confirmation from experimental evidence on a related subject:

A disliked event outside the individual's control (a *fait accompli*) will result in positive change toward that event when the individual feels he could have avoided it or when he feels he did have prior choice [Rosenberg *et al.,* 1960, p. 213].

B2   The more interested people are in an issue, the more likely they are to hold consistent positions on that issue.

A sense of concern—emotional investment in the election outcome—tends to reinforce a more general "strain towards consistency." The more concerned a person is about the outcome of an election, the more likely he is to bring in line all his attitudes toward the candidates and issues so that none of them push him toward a different voting decision. Presumably, this is also true if one of the issues becomes invested with great emotion, in which case other emotions will then be brought into line so that the decision can be made with a minimum of conflict [Lane, 1959, p. 145].

B2.1   The more a person is emotionally involved in his beliefs, the harder it is to change him by argument or propaganda—that is, through an appeal to intelligence—to the point of virtual impossibility (as in cases of deeply felt matters based on strata and reinforced by primary group support).

Indeed, it is even the case that:

B2.1a   Once a person commits himself to a position, that commitment itself becomes a barrier against change, however immediately counterinfluences are brought to bear.

B3   Given consistent support from historical, parental, group, and strata characteristics, OAB's are unlikely to change at all.

If, for example, historical conditions remain the same; if the parents have felt strongly and harmoniously about a particular matter and instilled the appropriate belief early and thoroughly; if strata characteristics in later life are consistent with the position; if the primary groups surrounding the person agree on the matter—then it is hardly too much to say that the OAB simply will not change. Too much is going for it and too little against it. But life being as complicated and variable as it is, the underlying factors are not often in such harmony, and hence there are numerous opportunities for short-run changes in OAB's, especially under the impact of unanticipated events.

This finding, incidentally, has been given dramatic and poignant confirmation in the modern world by the so-called brainwashing experiences of military and political captives. Men placed in situations in which they received no emotional support from their fellows were especially likely to give in (Schein, 1957).

Generally, however, the effect of "brainwashing" has been greatly exaggerated, in the view of a recent summary of the scholarly writings:

1. No special or novel scientific "gimmick" for influencing behavior was involved in Chinese or Russian Communist practice. Hypnotism and drugs were not involved. . . .

2. The Communist practices of indoctrination, interrogation, and confession elicitation did not rest upon a deliberate application of a scientific theory of behavioral influence, Pavlovian or any other. Rather, they represented a blend of (a) traditional lore of interrogators, Communist proselytizers, and prosecutors, (b) common sense and not uncommon nonsense about the human personality, (c)

Communist dogma, and (d) cultural conceptions of the person who offends authority in the traditions of Russia and China.

3. The practices of the Chinese Communists did not involve a new and unprecedented epitome of the arts of influence. Applications of coercion, persuasion, and radical changes of social environment have been used frequently in history to produce changes on belief and behavior as extreme and as ego-alien as those produced in recent times by Communist "brainwashers." Cries of "I am a wretched sinner but am beginning to see the light" have always been with us, along with self-abnegating and self-destructive confessions, opportunistic or delusory, to all manner of crimes and diabolic alliances [Biderman, 1962, p. 550].

In any case:

B4   OAB's, and particularly beliefs, change more slowly than actual behavior.

Behavior, being visible, is more responsive to extreme pressures and accommodations. OAB's, being private until expressed, can be maintained without even being subject to question or argument. And there is no necessary reason for OAB's and behavior to be in harmony: we are polite to acquaintances we really don't like, we go along with the majority in a committee action rather than make a fuss, we go to the polls even though we really don't care about the outcome.

A considerable body of common sense observation, clinical data, and, more recently, experimental findings indicates that in many instances attitude change follows after behavioral change. Such common phrases as "rationalization," "sour grapes," etc., are adequate labels for the process at work. . . .

Research under the direction of Leon Festinger has shown that precisely this sort of attitude change follows after a commitment to action. Confirmed cigarette smokers are more likely to deny that any relationship has been established between cigarette smoking and lung cancer. Recent car buyers read advertisements that confirm them in the wisdom of their decisions, etc. Kelman, working independently of Festinger, has affected children's attitudes toward comic books by "bribing" them to make statements in favor of one or another type of comic. Kelman's findings make it possible to specify conditions under which a private change of opinion will and will not accompany the coerced change of public position [Bauer and Bauer, 1960, pp. 30–31].

This last is, of course, an instance of the effect of role-playing on change of attitude, as noted elsewhere.

B4a   With regard to the sphere of personal morality, there is a clear discrepancy between values and behavior.

People may know what is right and profess to believe in it and yet do what is wrong. Here is the conclusion of a recent survey of the literature:

Experimental studies have revealed that discrepancies between moral concepts and moral behavior are greater than is popularly believed. Abstract knowledge of what is wrong does not keep children from cheating when a particular situation arises in which they are tempted to cheat (Hartshorne and May, 1928a). Children who say it is "wrong" to be aggressive with their classmates are not consistent in their behavior when playing with them (Fite, 1940). Delinquent children rarely are ignorant of the wrongs they do. Their ethical knowledge is very similar to that of nondelinquents (Bartlett and Harris, 1935; Hill, 1935; Glueck and Glueck, 1950). . . . The relationship between intelligence and morality is important, but it is not so important as was previously believed. . . . Hartshorne and May (1928b), for example, found a correlation of .50 between intelligence and honesty scores in the case of school children. . . . Studies of honesty have revealed correlations of approximately .25 between moral knowledge and conduct (Hartshorne and May, 1928b; V. Jones, 1936). Thus, one can predict with only a small degree of accuracy from a child's moral knowledge what his conduct will be [Hurlock, 1956, pp. 411, 438, 406].

B5   People less interested in a matter hold weaker OAB's and are more likely to change their minds.

They get little reinforcement on the matter from the mass media because they pay little attention to them. They get little support from their social groups because they tend not to discuss the matter. The internal connections between a particular position and others they may hold more strongly are tenuous, and so OAB's are not shored up from within. Hence, such people are altogether less subject to influences "keeping them in line," and the influences mean less to them when encountered. Since interest is low, other factors—such as following a friend's advice—take precedence.

The uninvolved member of the electorate is, as might be expected, the most likely to change his views. He is more likely to shift away from his sociologically "natural" position between elections, when the pressure is off, and to shift back again when campaign pressures mount and his political group alignments are again brought into focus. More than the involved voter, he is likely to vote with his economic or ethnic group and to adopt whatever views are communicated to him through these sources. He is, so to speak, more at the mercy of social pressures because of the lack of inner convictions to give him a steady orientation in the face of conflicting influences [Lane, 1959, p. 145].

B5.1   The less interested take longer to make up their minds, being under less self- or group-pressure to do so.

In fact, they are quite likely not to come to a conclusion at all, particularly—and this is usually the case—in the absence of a definite *terminus ad quem* that "forces" a decision, e.g., Election Day. Here are some illustrative data:

People greatly interested in the election make their final vote decision earlier than less interested people (percentages)

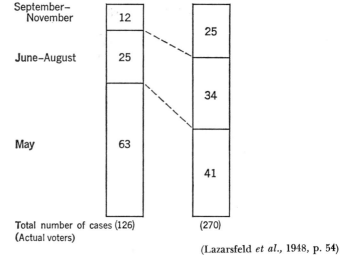

Total number of cases (126)   (270)
(Actual voters)

(Lazarsfeld *et al.*, 1948, p. 54)

B6   When people's OAB's do not hang together harmoniously, they are more likely to change some of them.

Disparity among attitudes, recognized by the holder, is by no means uncommon, since all but the most highly interested (the "fanatics" or the "true believers") are likely to have some doubts, reservations, indecisions, or simple gaps in their attitudes on any big set of issues or subjects. In many cases such inconsistency presents no problem at all; life is not usually seen as a black-and-white matter, so a certain amount of self-contradiction is considered natural and is easily tolerated. But when the inconsistency is brought home frequently or forcibly, then it does tend to become uncomfortable and something has to be done about reducing it. There seems to be, at least in Western culture, a "strain toward consistency" or, as it is currently phrased, a reaction against "cognitive dissonance" (Festinger, 1957).

B6.1   When OAB's are in conflict, they are often brought into consistency through guided perception or interpretation.

For example, the person plays down the differences between his own attitudes and the positions taken by "his side" (his candidate, strata, social group, party, or organization) and plays up the differences with the opposition; or he agrees with the opposition on ends, but disagrees on means; or, as in this case, he tends not to notice the difference:

Partisans tend not to perceive differences with their own candidate or similarities to the opposition candidate (percentage who don't know their own candidate's stand)

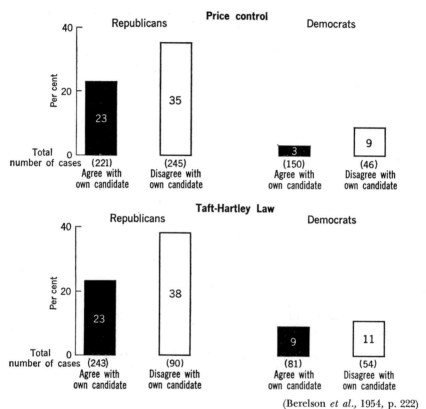

(Berelson *et al.*, 1954, p. 222)

B6.2   OAB's are more likely to be brought into consistency:

(a) by the more interested and involved. They more often manage to avoid unfavorable realities or to deny their existence or their importance in order to avoid feeling that they hold conflicting positions.

(b) on vague or ambiguous issues. Such issues, similar to a projective test, leave more room for perceptual maneuvers, particularly for the stronger partisans. The side with an "objective" advantage tends to play it up, and the other side tends to play it down—in perception and interpretation as well as in propaganda.

Any situation, then, which is ambiguous for the individual is likely to produce attitude change. His need for cognitive structure is such that he will either modify his beliefs to impose structure or accept some new formula presented by others. He seeks a meaningful picture of his universe, and when there is ambiguity he will reach for a ready solution. Rumors abound when information is unavailable [Katz, 1960, p. 191].

(c) the more isolated the judgment, i.e., the less it ties into a whole system of judgments. OAB's are themselves interrelated and hence mutually supporting, so that a change in one will require changes in others. And it is harder to change one aspect of a system of attitudes than to change an isolated position.

(d) when the emotional loading of the issue is changed.

When the affective component of an individual's attitude is altered, there occurs a corresponding and consistent reorganization of his beliefs about the object of that affect [Rosenberg et al., 1960, p. 200].

Hence:

B6.3   The effect of a campaign—a period of intensified communication and discussion on a topic—is to reduce personal inconsistency in OAB's and bring them into greater harmony with one another through resolving conflicts, establishing a priority of loyalties, harmonizing minor issues in line with major ones, etc.

There is more homogeneity in opinions *within* strata and groups after a campaign than before and, hence, sharper differences *between* strata and groups, as we have seen.

The political process which finds its climax in the campaign is a system by which disagreements are reduced, simplified, and generalized into one big residual difference of opinion [Berelson et al., 1954, p. 183].

B7   The more that people are subject to social inconsistency, that is, when their group attachments are at variance with one another (conflict among multiple roles, memberships, loyalties, identifications, associations, etc.), the more likely they are to change their OAB's. In other words, OAB's are more subject to change when people are subject to cross-pressures.

For example, the less homogeneity in OAB's within a person's family or his circle of friends, the less stable his own OAB's. Or, as another example: the relatively equal support given to different political positions by people in the middle of the socioeconomic distribution, as compared with those at the extremes, can be seen as an effect of cross-pressures. Here is one of the early evidences of the effect of cross-pressures (and interest) upon stability of political attitudes:

The less interest people have and the more cross-pressures to which they are subject, the more variable are their vote intentions (percentages)

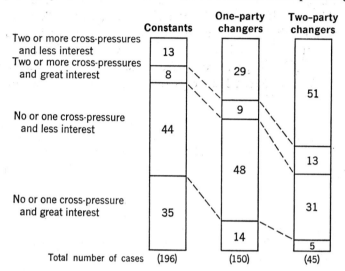

(Lazarsfeld *et al.*, 1948, p. 68)

Research on voting has shown that cross-pressures resulting from multiple-group affiliations or loyalties account for much of the "deviation" from the modal pattern of a given group. Individuals who are subject to pressures driving them in different political directions must either deviate from the modal pattern of one or "escape into apathy." But since most people with multiple and politically inconsistent loyalties are not non-voters, multiple-group identification has the perhaps more important effect of reducing the emotion in their political choices. German data indicate that Catholics voting Socialist are much less hostile to Adenauer than are Protestants. In the United States and Great Britain, manual workers who vote Republican or Conservative are less liberal on economic issues than workers who opt for the Democratic or Labor Parties, but more liberal than middle-class supporters of their own party. The fact that a significant segment of the voters of each major party identifies with values associated with other parties forces the leaders of each party to make concessions to retain such voters, when they have a majority, and offers hope that they may gain needed support when they are in opposition [Lipset, 1959, pp. 94–95].

Such cross-pressures are particularly likely to affect people who change their social environment in one way or another. As examples:

Consider first the move from home to college. If the "distance" in attitudes between the two is not great, then little cross-pressure exists for the young man or woman who makes the move; in such cases, the two environments reinforce one another and attitudes are only strengthened. But often the new environment differs markedly from the old and then it can make a real difference, especially at the impressionable college age: the new student tends to take over the predominant and prestigious OAB's of the upper classmen, the faculty, and the college community in general. This is what happened to many well-to-do girls from conservative homes who went to a progressive, liberal college, as compared to college men from similar backgrounds but in a different kind of campus atmosphere (Newcomb, 1943). Here are some of the data:

Per cent of conservative replies to eight items by freshmen and seniors at Williams and Bennington Colleges

Item number	Freshmen		Seniors	
	WILLIAMS ($N = 250$)	BENNINGTON ($N = 55$)	WILLIAMS ($N = 164$)	BENNINGTON ($N = 40$)
6	34	29	19	5
10	37	22	41	0
11	35	26	29	8
12	52	48	36	5
14	22	21	22	0
18	50	37	27	5
21	35	24	24	5
24	80	62	61	27

(*Ibid.*, p. 32)

Such changes are only hastened by the fact that most others in the situation are going through the same process; this makes for a minimum of resistance and conflict. It is not clear, though, how lasting such changes are once the person returns to the original environment; presumably the veneer wears off and the initial opinions re-emerge under support from the initial sources.

Or take social mobility. Persons moving upward in social class are likely to take on the OAB's of the groups into which they are moving, or toward which they aspire. Those moving downward, however, typically hold to the position taken by their former, more prestigious group. In each case, it is the upper reference group that counts, not the current membership group.

Note, for example, these data from a recent study of young people:

Social mobility related to choice of party and candidate (percentages)

Party preference	Up-wardly mobile	Nonmobile, in class where upward mobiles originated	Nonmobile, in class to which upward mobiles moved	Down-ward mobile	Nonmobile, in class where downward mobiles originated	Nonmobile, in class to which downward mobiles moved
Republican	23	8	21	31	21	11
Independent	9	18	28	8	28	17
Democratic	68	74	51	61	51	72
Total number of cases	(82)	(73)	(73)	(75)	(73)	(73)

(Maccoby *et al.*, 1954, p. 35)

The same picture emerges for groups changing their life situations and thus developing cross-pressures slowly and over a long period of time. For example, the longer that immigrant groups are in this country, the closer they come to taking on typically American OAB's as against their native ones—partly because of their lowered nationalistic and ethnic identifications but also because of a rise in income and status that puts them into new communities and gives them new contacts. And, finally, there is the change that a social crisis such as a depression brings to the whole community, particularly to that part of the community most subject to cross-pressures on that issue. To the extent that the crisis changes social positions relatively as well as absolutely, there will be further changes in OAB's.

B7a   By and large, a cross-pressured person tends to change toward the prevailing attitude of his most favored reference group. And the greater the divergence between his attitude and that of the congenial group, the more likely the change toward the group.

Thus the cross-pressured tend finally to decide less on substance than on the salience of the matter and on the importance of group memberships. The net effect, again, is increased homogeneity of attitudes within particular strata and groups.

B7.1   The more cross-pressured a person is or feels on a given issue, the less interest he maintains in it, as a way of escaping from a situation that threatens actual or potential tension.

In effect, such escape says that the person considers his peace of mind or the smooth maintenance of friendships as more important than the issue in question.

B7.2   The more cross-pressured a person is or feels, the later he decides on his OAB.

When loyalties pull in different directions, it is harder to decide what is right than when all pressures go in the same direction. And if it is possible, the person finds it easy and even justifiable to put the matter off altogether, since there is so much to be said on each side.

B7.3   The more cross-pressured a person is or feels, the less stable his opinions are between campaigns (when he is not particularly subject to communications recalling him to the "correct" line) and the more susceptible they are during campaigns (when he is subject to such communications).

SELECTED READINGS

OAB's are of such importance to human behavior that, on a variety of subjects, they are constantly under study by behavioral scientists. Here are some important titles of recent years:

By an anthropologist:
Clyde Kluckhohn. "Have There Been Discernible Shifts in American Values During the Past Generation?" in Elting Morison, ed., *The American Style.* Harper, 1958, pp. 145–217.

By a psychologist:
William F. Dukes. "Psychological Studies of Values," *Psychological Bulletin,* 52, 1955, pp. 24–50.

By a philosopher:
Charles Morris. *Varieties of Human Value.* U. of Chicago Press, 1956.

By a team of sociologists:
Rose K. Goldsen *et al. What College Students Think.* Van Nostrand, 1960.

On the development of political opinions:

Herbert Hyman. *Political Socialization: A Study in the Psychology of Political Behavior.* Free Press, 1959.

On change in OAB's:

Theodore Newcomb. *Personality and Social Change.* Holt, Rinehart & Winston, 1957.

See also parts of the studies of voting by Lazarsfeld, Berelson, Campbell, and their associates cited in the section on political institutions.

On opinion leadership:

Elihu Katz and Paul F. Lazarsfeld. *Personal Influence*. Free Press, 1955.

On the operation of OAB's in the armed forces during wartime:

Samuel A. Stouffer *et al. The American Soldier*. Princeton U. Press, 1949. Vols. I, II.

For a topical analysis of some important attitudinal issues:

Herbert H. Hyman and Paul B. Sheatsley. "The Current Status of American Public Opinion," *National Council for the Social Studies Yearbook*, 21, 1950, pp. 11–34.

Samuel A. Stouffer. *Communism, Conformity, and Civil Liberties: A Cross-Section of the Nation Speaks Its Mind*. Doubleday, 1955.

And for the current literature, see the *Public Opinion Quarterly*.

Hellas had in ancient times no settled population; on the contrary migrations were of frequent occurrence, the several tribes readily abandoning their homes under the pressure of superior numbers. . . . Destitute of capital, never planting their land (for they could not tell when an invader might not come and take it all away, and when he did come they had no walls to stop him), thinking that the necessities of daily life could be supplied at one place as well as another, they cared little for shifting their habitation, and consequently neither built large cities nor attained to any other form of greatness.

THUCYDIDES
The Peloponnesian War

It is evident that men are by nature in contact with and tied to each other, even where kinship is absent. . . . Such contact may produce a solidarity nearly as powerful as that produced by kinship.

IBN-KHALDUN
Prolegomena

Above all, one thought
Baffled my understanding; how men lived
Even next-door neighbours, as we say, yet still
Strangers, not knowing each the other's name. . . .
Among the close and overcrowded haunts
Of cities where the human heart is sick.

WILLIAM WORDSWORTH
The Prelude

It would be rash to affirm that Don Calogero drew an immediate profit from what he had learned; he did try to shave a little better and complain a little less about the waste of laundry soap; but from that moment there began, for him and his family, that process of continual refining which in the course of three generations transforms innocent peasants into defenseless gentry.

GIUSEPPE DI LAMPEDUSA
The Leopard

Chapter Fifteen
THE SOCIETY

In the broad sweep from the individual through the family, the small group, the organization, the institution, strata and publics, we now reach the level of the society. We might say that whereas we dealt earlier with various parts of the society, we deal here with matters that characterize the society as a whole. But that may not be precisely so, and in any case would be subject to a good deal of conceptual and definitional argument. So all we are inclined to claim is that for our purposes this chapter is a reasonable way to handle five remaining fields in which the behavioral sciences have done a substantial amount of work:

> Social Demography
> Social Geography
> Social Change
> Social Conflict
> Social Disorganization

At least the last three of these are usually characterized in the literature by the adjective "social," and the others seem appropriately included here as well.

DEFINITIONS

Society: By *society* is usually meant an aggregate of people that is self-sustaining, that has a definite location and a long duration, and that shares a way of life. Thus we use the term to speak of a small, primitive society as well as of a large, complex one. An isolated tribe in New Guinea is a society; so is the United States.

Social demography: This term has to do with the growth and the character of populations and with their distribution as it is affected by birth and death rates, by emigration and immigration.

Social geography: Although this term is not particularly current in the literature, we use it here to refer to two classes of material: urban-rural differences and climatic or environmental effects on behavior. In both cases, human behavior is influenced by physical location.

Social change: Although everything in life is constantly changing, this term refers only to broad and basic changes in the nature of a society: the organization of the family, the arrangements for earning a living, the character of religious observances, the values held by the population, the technology employed, and so on. It refers primarily to shifts in the fundamental institutions and organizations of the society.

Social conflict: This term refers to the pursuit of incompatible, or at least seemingly incompatible, goals, such that gains to one side come about at the expense of the other. Conflicts can go on between societies or nations (the Cold War); between groups or strata or institutions within a society (the "class war," labor-management relations, disputes between or within communities); or between individuals (a lawsuit or a marital separation). In this last case, the conflict would have to involve large numbers of people before it would typically be called *social* conflict.

Social disorganization: This term has been used for broader purposes, but as employed here it refers primarily to behavior at variance with the general norms of the society, such as crime, alcoholism, mental illness,* or suicide. This is often called deviant behavior—deviant, that is, from what people in a society are generally expected or entitled to do. What is considered deviant behavior in one society may of course be thought quite appropriate in another. In addition, we include here a brief section on behavior under disaster conditions, since that involves a certain degree of social disorganization.

FINDINGS

Social Demography

As a preliminary to this section, we think it appropriate to make two points that probably apply more directly here than elsewhere. The first is that in the nature of the case the field of demography is heavily historical

---

* By including some findings on psychotic behavior, incidentally, we do not wish to suggest that severe mental illness necessarily is socially caused or that organic causes are absent: not at all. We are only trying to set down what is known from the social point of view. The biological and medical material is simply outside our scope here, though we are persuaded that constitutional factors are of great importance in such illness.

and descriptive; there is a large and impressive literature reporting population size, composition, and movement for much of the world over much of its history. The second is that by virtue of the availability of national censuses the field is particularly rich in data. Both circumstances mean that the following generalizations can be enriched by numerous particular instances but, in many cases, qualified as well. So varied and plentiful are the data, across countries and historical periods, that exceptions can be cited for many of the following findings. On the whole, however, we believe that they hold, as broad generalizations from the evidence.

GROWTH AND CHARACTER

A1   Major industrialization makes for shifts in the rate of growth and the distribution of the population, through such means as the growth of metropolitan centers, the opening up of new areas, the indirect effects upon the organization of the family and the standard of living, and the increased secularization that tends to open the class structure.

For example, in industrialized countries, larger proportions of the population are in cities than in nonindustrialized countries; and larger proportions are in the working ages (although the proportion of the older population is increasing), whereas in nonindustrialized regions there are larger proportions of children.

A1.1   In general (although not always), a rise in the standard of living is accompanied sooner or later by a drop in the rate of growth of the population.

This comes about largely through the greater use of methods of birth control. It also appears that:

A1.1a   During a period of general decline in the birth rate, the later the decline begins in a particular country, the faster its pace.

A1.2   In the current era the poorer, less-developed countries and regions of the world are increasing in population more rapidly than the better-off ones. Death rates fall earlier and faster than birth rates; and before the latter can catch up, there is a period of substantial growth.

Here is a recent summary:

Among the industrialized countries, Japan and most of the countries of Europe are now growing relatively slowly—doubling their populations in 50 to 100 years. Another group of industrialized countries—the United States, the Soviet Union, Australia, New Zealand, Canada, and Argentina—are doubling their populations in 30 to 40 years, approximately the world average. The pre-industrial, low-income, and less-developed areas of the world, with two thirds of the world's population—including Asia (except Japan and the Asiatic part of the Soviet

Union), the southwestern Pacific islands (principally the Philippines and Indonesia), Africa (with the exception of European minorities), the Caribbean Islands, and Latin America (with the exception of Argentina and Uruguay)—are growing at rates ranging from moderate to very fast. Annual growth rates in all these areas range from one and one-half to three and one-half per cent, doubling in 20 to 40 years [Coale, 1963, p. 9].

The reduction of fertility and mortality *

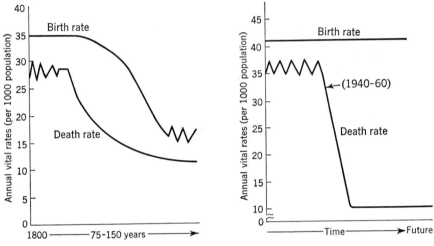

* The figure on the left is a schematic presentation of birth and death rates in western Europe after 1800. (The time span varies roughly from 75 to 150 years.) The figure on the right is a schematic presentation of birth and death rates in less-developed countries, mid-twentieth century. (The steep drop in the death rate from approximately 35 per thousand began at times varying roughly between 1940 and 1960 from country to country.)

(*Ibid.*, pp. 10, 15)

As one authority puts it:

The theory of modern population change revolves around the idea of a "demographic transition"—a cycle in which there are three phases: First, a regime of *slow* population growth characterized by *high* birth and death rates; second, a period of *rapid* population growth characterized by *high* fertility but *low* death rates, due to the lag of fertility decline behind mortality decline (the "demographic gap"); and third, a regime of *slow* population growth characterized by *low* birth and death rates [Davis, 1959a, p. 208].

What happens is that mortality comes under control faster and earlier, through public health measures, than does fertility, via contraceptive measures. And the decline of the death rate in the underdeveloped countries has been especially sharp since World War II, sharper than the corresponding rates in the Western world: "The recent trends (in mortality) approach or exceed the most rapid ever encountered among the nations with lowest mortality today" (Stolnitz, 1956, pp. 26–27). The result is that, on the average, populations are increasing fastest today in those areas already at a low standard of living. Such growth has serious economic consequences:

> The Report on the World Social Situation [U.N., 1957] spells out the three major ways in which rapid population growth in the underdeveloped countries adversely affects their social and economic development: "First, it can increase the pressure of population on land that is already densely settled and so retard increases in the productivity of agricultural labour. . . . Second, accelerating population growth can aggravate the problem of capital shortage, which is one of the most important obstacles to economic development of nearly all underdeveloped countries. . . . Third, the high birth-rates of the underdeveloped countries create a heavy load of dependent children for the working population" [Cook, 1960, p. 386].

A2 So far as can be determined, the "quality" of a population is at least maintained over time.

> There is at present no sufficient scientific basis for believing that the higher birth rates of the people in the lower-income groups (but not including the socially inadequate) are causing a genetic deterioration from one generation to another [Osborn, 1960, p. 416].

More than that, it seems clear that throughout a population a higher standard of living, with attendant improvements in nutrition, makes for better health, physical stature, and so on; and it probably makes for slightly higher (tested) intellectual capacities as well.

MIGRATION

First, as to migration within a country:

A3 Population movement tends to be concentrated: people who move once are more likely to move again; places into which people are moving are also places from which people are moving; people are much more likely to move short distances than long ones.

Furthermore, there is evidence to the effect that:

A4 Migration is proportional to the number of opportunities at a given distance and inversely proportional to the number of intervening opportunities.

Here are the key data from the first development of this generalization, showing a remarkably close correspondence between the predicted and actual moves within Cleveland, Ohio:

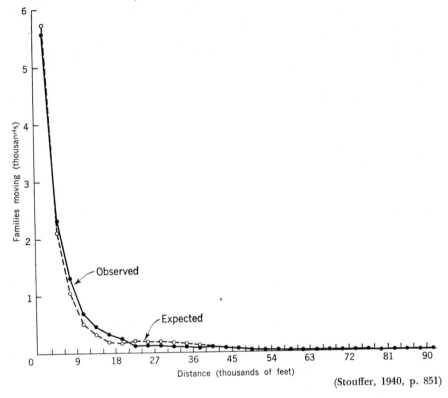

Number of families moving from locations within twelve white census tracts, by intervals of distance, Cleveland, Ohio, 1933–35

Distance (thousands of feet)

(Stouffer, 1940, p. 851)

A5   In general, within most countries (especially the industrialized ones), the major streams of free migration are between communities of the same type (e.g., urban to urban or suburban); from rural to urban areas; from the less prosperous areas to the more prosperous; among the young; among men; and among the better educated and the better-off.

The major consequence of internal migration is to redistribute the available manpower, although some scholars add that "by siphoning off excess population into areas of greater opportunity, internal migration becomes a mechanism of personal adjustment for the citizen" (Bogue, 1959, p. 487).

As to international migration:

A6   Over the centuries, forced emigration—through the displacement of territory as a result of war, through flight before the aggressor, through political repression (e.g., the Jews in Germany), through capture (e.g., the African slave trade), through partition (e.g., India-Pakistan)—has been an important form of population movement; and although the records are unclear, it may well be as large as, or even larger than, free emigration.

In the past, geography was a chief barrier to free international migration —which, incidentally, received a major impetus from the development of the steamship; now political and ethnic barriers are more important (Kirk, 1958).

A7   Over the long run, free international migration is tied to differential economic opportunity: sending countries have a high rate of population growth relative to economic growth; receiving countries have a need for human talent to exploit resources.

> With regard to the stage of population growth, immigration is regarded as desirable in the early stages of a country's development when a rapidly growing population will hasten the most profitable development and use of resources. . . . Favorable to immigration are conditions: (1) Where the native population is insufficient for full economic development or defense; (2) Where there is a seasonal or continuing labor shortage; (3) Where there is a specialized need for certain skills and technology; (4) Where there are the twin phenomena of an aging population and a declining rate of natural increase. Conversely, where there is already full occupation of land and resources, where labor supply is adequate or in surplus, and where the population is growing through natural increase as fast as productive capacity can be expanded, immigration may frankly be regarded as contrary to national interest on purely demographic grounds. . . . Immigration delivers free on board a capable and able-bodied labor supply whose very expenses of transportation, education, and rearing are prepaid by the sending country. In the case of the United States, the stream of immigration after 1820 must have aided in advancing economic maturity and military security by something like half a century [Vance, 1958, pp. 83–84].

This generalization is illustrated in the historical movements from Eastern Europe to Western Europe, and from Western Europe to the United States. Actually, international migration in the modern world "has been a vast secular process of rural-urban transference, which is itself a necessary condition of economic growth" (Thomas, 1959, pp. 524–25). Again:

> Rural-urban migration is one of the most powerful and consistent forces in the world today. In numbers this movement is vastly more than international migration, and international migration itself is more often than not to the cities of the receiving countries [Kirk, 1958, p. 25].

Moreover, there is some evidence to the effect that:

A7.1   At least over the short run, the state of the economy in the receiving country is more influential in stimulating free migration than is that of the sending country.

That is, the "pull" is stronger than the "push." . . . In sending countries industrialization inhibits emigration; in receiving countries industrialization stimulates immigration [Thomas, 1959, pp. 527, 531].

A7.2   With regard to personal characteristics, free international migration is particularly likely to consist of young adults and of men.

But during periods of reduced migration, women are more numerous:
they are joining the men who migrated earlier. As for age:

A country experiencing a high and sustained volume of emigration always has a
relatively large number of teen-agers. A self-generating mechanism is at work;
fifteen years after the original thinning-out of the 15–35 age group, the number
passing into the 15–20 group is abnormally large in relation to the population
as a whole [*ibid.*, pp. 528–30].

Finally, with regard to the question of differential migration by "quality"
of population, "we are not in a position to say anything definite about the
intelligence differential in international migration" (*ibid.*, p. 526).

FERTILITY *

A8   The major differentials in human fertility are social in character: all
human societies control fertility to some extent.

No population has all the babies it could have. Naturally, fertility (the
rate of having children) is ultimately dependent on fecundity (the capacity
to have children), which in turn depends on the general state of health as
well as on the conditions specifically associated with childbearing.

A high frequency of infertility has been noted among impoverished populations.
Societies probably differ in fecundity because of differences in knowledge about
fecundity and because of differences in care of the woman during pregnancy and
parturition [Ryder, 1959, p. 417].

There have been unsuccessful attempts to attribute group differences in
fecundity to group differences in activity patterns, diet, and nervous tension. While some of these relationships may be true of specific individuals,
it has not yet been shown that they can account for large group differences
in fecundity.

The deliberate control of fertility, however, is far stronger in limiting
childbirth than any impairment in fecundity. Societies have controlled
fertility in widely different ways: by postponing marriage, enforcing celibacy,
providing frequent occasions for sexual abstinence, delaying or preventing
remarriage, and practicing contraception, abortion, sterilization, or even
infanticide. For one example, as we have seen, the proportion of never-

* A full review of the literature that would have contributed to this section but
appeared too late for inclusion is Freedman, 1963.

married women ranges from less than 1 per cent in India and about 3 per cent in Ceylon to 21 per cent in Sweden and 26 per cent in Ireland.

Historically, despite common belief to the contrary, the major contraceptive control of fertility has come from male rather than female methods—and in the first instance, before devices were available, by *coitus interruptus* (still an important folk method throughout the world). And fertility, like other aspects of behavior, is responsive to shifts in cultural and social influence. For example:

> Whatever may be true of the foreign-born themselves, the second and third generations tend to adopt the family-building pattern of their country of adoption [Thomas, 1959, p. 530].

In general:

> **A8a**   Fertility controls are less likely to be accepted in most societies than are techniques for controlling mortality, as each becomes available, largely because the former is more likely to be inconsistent with existing values and requires individual decisions.

Mortality can be reduced through the application of modern public health measures on a mass scale, and individual motivations are not involved beyond the general desire to live longer. But individuals must themselves take action to reduce fertility, in a sphere of behavior strongly invested with values of a religious, political, moral, and social character.

As a general rule, societies with high mortality rates tend to look with favor on early marriages, for the obvious reason.

> **A8b**   Throughout the world, a large proportion of people say they are favorable to the idea of limiting family size, especially after the third or fourth child; but information about family planning is uneven in the underdeveloped areas, and practice is limited, primitive, and erratic. In every population the urban, the better educated, and the more modernized groups accept and use contraception earliest, most frequently, and most effectively.

This finding takes on particular importance in view of the present interest in the "population problem," a result of the combination of continuing high fertility rates and decreased mortality rates in the underdeveloped areas of the world. Concerted efforts to bring down the birth rate in such populations are just beginning, and some experimental programs in limited areas have succeeded in lowering the birth rate by five to seven points over five years or so. It now appears that such efforts may be more successful than were earlier national efforts to increase the birth rate.

Actually,

> the norm of the small family and the practice of family limitation has been
> established across a wide range of societies: across religious affiliations (e.g.,
> Catholic Southern Europe and Protestant Northern Europe); political ideologies
> (e.g., the U.S. and the U.S.S.R.); industrial and agricultural economies, and rich
> and poor ones (e.g., within Europe); better-educated societies and poorer-edu-
> cated ones (again, within Europe); the West and Asia (e.g., Japan); and, just
> beginning, perhaps, the tropical countries as well as the temperate ones [Berelson,
> 1962, p. 3].

A9   The major differentials in human fertility are the following, most
of them for modern Western nations.

By Historical Period

.1   higher fertility in stable times than in periods of sharp social change.

.2   higher fertility (in the United States) in the late summer-early fall,
lower in the spring.

**Adjusted monthly variations in births of white males and
white females in the United States, 1955**

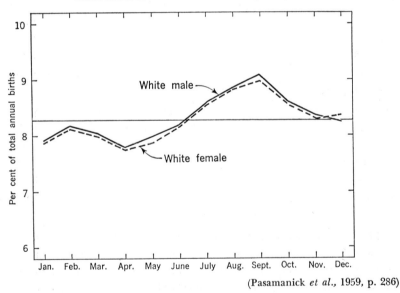

(Pasamanick *et al.*, 1959, p. 286)

And quite possibly for a behavioral reason:

> The August-September peak has traditionally and more or less facetiously been
> attributed to the longer and colder winter months. The explanation for the con-
> sistent spring dip in births has been more difficult to formulate. We believe that
> the annual spring decline in births may be attributed . . . primarily to the
> discomforts of high summer temperatures and high humidity. This discomfort

. . . probably reduces the frequency of coition and consequently of conceptions [*ibid.,* pp. 285–86].

.3   higher fertility in underdeveloped or preindustrialized countries.

Indeed, some scholars believe that satisfactory control of fertility cannot be achieved in preindustrial societies. Furthermore:

> [Industrial societies] have undertaken to lower fertility, not primarily by extending further the negative effect of the variables by which fertility was lowered in the pre-industrial stage, but by using readily available institutional mechanisms with respect to marriage and by employing the possibilities of their advanced technology for conception control [Davis and Blake, 1956, pp. 234–35].

.4   higher fertility in times of prosperity.

In industrial countries, such as the United States, the birth rate is tied somewhat to the business cycle (allowing for a nine- to twelve-month lag).

Real per capita personal income, nuptiality, fertility, and respective trends, 1920–58

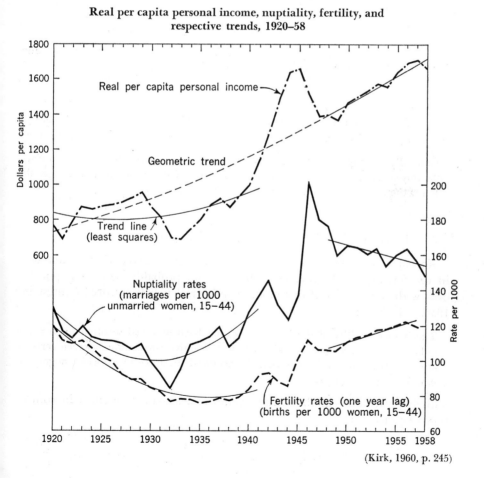

(Kirk, 1960, p. 245)

However, the cycle is by no means controlling:

> While fertility responds sensitively to business cycles in its trend deviations, changes in economic conditions are not accompanied by changes in fertility of comparable magnitude. Thus over the whole period studied a trend deviation of 4 per cent in real per capita income produced a trend deviation of only 1 per cent in fertility [Kirk and Nortman, 1958, p. 160].

The finding also holds for nonindustrial countries, on the whole:

> For northern European agrarian communities of the eighteenth century, it has been shown that abundant harvests were followed by years with high birth rates, and years with crop failures were followed by years with low birth rates. Among other things, variations in physical stamina which might influence the ability to carry pregnancies to successful completion seem to have operated to produce the rather close correlation between food conditions and both legitimate and illegitimate fertility [U.N., 1953, p. 84].

By Cultural Patterns

.5   higher fertility among descendants of large families.

> In a number of studies positive correlations have been found between the number of children born to a family and the number of children within the husband's and/or wife's family. In other words it would appear that family size has a tendency to run in families [ibid., p. 90].

.6   higher fertility in societies in which women have not been "emancipated" and, in the emancipated societies, among nonworking women.

> Gainfully employed wives have fewer children than those who are not gainfully employed. And the longer such wives are employed during their marriage, the fewer the number of children they bear [ibid., pp. 88–89].

By Social Position

.7   higher fertility in lower socioeconomic groups.

An early, and classical, review of the subject observed that "differences in the fertility of the social-economic classes probably became important only with the growth of our modern industrial urban culture" (Notestein, 1936, p. 1). Now:

> The higher fertility of the lower classes has been observed so often in so many different countries that the existence of a negative correlation between fertility and socioeconomic status has virtually acquired the force of a sociodemographic law [Wrong, 1956, p. 72].

This is partly due—in the United States at least—to differences in contraceptive practices:

> Among the couples whose fertility was entirely planned, the ones with a higher income, better education, etc., were the ones with the higher fertility. The find-

ings suggest that the ordinary class differentials in fertility, long observed in Western society, are a function of failure to plan the number and spacing of pregnancies in the more disadvantaged strata rather than a function of a desire for large families [Davis, 1953, pp. 19–20].

Educational level is an important factor in this connection, and not only in the earlier spread of contraceptive practice among the better informed and more sophisticated, but also because "they tend to marry later, to postpone remarriage longer, to have higher aspiration levels for their children, and to seek medical advice more freely" (Davis, 1959a, p. 225). In short:

In emphasizing the role of education, we are emphasizing the fact that a high educational level is a necessary, if not sufficient, condition for reducing the birth rate. Peoples living in underdeveloped areas live in cultures in which high fertility is an integral part. In order to reduce fertility, the entire outlook on life, including attitudes towards fertility, must undergo change. Education is a necessary part of such changes; without increased education, economic development alone, as evinced by increases in real product, for example, will not affect the birth rate [Jaffe, 1960, p. 524].

In recent years, this differential seems to be flattening out in the United States, and elsewhere as well.

In the recent rise of the birth rate, it is known that the classes that had the lowest birth rate during the depression showed the greatest gain, while those experiencing the highest rates showed the least gain. This has meant a narrowing of differential fertility as between income groups [Davis, 1953, p. 21].

.7a   The topmost socioeconomic groups have higher fertility rates than the middle or middle-high groups in many Western countries.

.8   higher fertility among stable families than among those who move either geographically or socially.

For example, from a study of people listed in *Who's Who in America:*

Military and foreign service officers on the one hand and literary and artistic men on the other report much below average numbers of children. Musicians, painters, actors, and entertainers have exceptionally high proportions of childlessness. Among these extremely unlike groups the common denominator would seem to be unusually frequent changes in places of residence and employment aggravated for the last named occupations by irregularity and insecurity of income. . . . Those who have an inherited status appear to have more than average numbers of children. This is evidenced by the higher fertility of those reporting attendance in private secondary schools and the premium universities and the lower family size of those lacking higher education. It would seem that the "self-made" man who fought his way up from the ranks may often have sacrificed having children in order to get ahead [Kirk, 1957a, p. 97].

In general:

> Whereas formerly most men took their social position for granted, concern with improving one's own position or that of one's children became an ever-pressing preoccupation in those countries where family limitation spread. The effect of social mobility on fertility appears to be attributed in general to the fact that rearing children absorbs money, time, and effort which could otherwise be used to rise in the social scale. Social mobility is thus more feasible with one or two children than with a large number [U.N., 1953, p. 79].

This is often taken to be the explanation for the lesser fertility of the middle groups, as noted above: they are still aspiring, and hence are devoting energy and money to that end. However, a recent study showed no relation between social stability and fertility in the United States (Westoff *et al.*, 1961), although the relation does seem to hold in Europe.

.9   higher fertility in rural than in urban settings, and higher in rural farm than rural nonfarm; higher in small cities than in large ones.

> Many factors believed to promote family limitation in cities to a greater extent than in the country have been suggested. First, it has been pointed out that family life in the city is less cohesive, because family members participate in other institutions and have a broader range of contacts outside the family. Second, children are not regarded as an economic asset in the city, as they are in the country. A smaller proportion of children, especially young children, generally contribute to the family income in the city, and those who contribute do so on a smaller scale. Third, status aspirations, the achievement of which may be handicapped where support of a large family is mandatory, are probably more prominent in cities, as are the opportunities to gratify such ambitions. Further, the importance of the spirit of "rationality" and "independence of tradition" prevailing in cities has also been emphasized [U.N., 1953, p. 78].

In addition, of course, it may be easier to take care of children in the country, and contraceptive information and materials are more available in the city. In any case, rural residents are on the average lower on the socioeconomic scale, and thus there is an important overlap here with that characteristic.

.10   higher fertility among Catholics than among Protestants, higher among Protestants than among Jews.

There are differences by religion in a number of non-Western societies as well. In general, the greater the religious interest and identification of married people, the larger the number of children. But at the same time, at least in the United States:

> Coreligionists differing in residential and socioeconomic status do not resemble one another as closely in their fertility behavior as much as they resemble persons of the same status who differ in religious affiliation [Wrong, 1956, pp. 69–70].

This quotation, incidentally, serves to remind us of the other-things-equal character of these differences.

.11   higher fertility, in the United States—and perhaps in other countries as well—among national and racial minorities low in socioeconomic status (e.g., Negroes and Puerto Ricans).

A10   The sex ratio at birth (i.e., the number of males born per one hundred females) is not constant: there are slightly more males for U.S. whites as compared with Negroes, for younger as compared with older mothers, and for first-born as compared with later-born children.

However, these differences are not large: for example, the white-Negro difference is about 106 (males per one hundred females) to 103; the average sex ratio for white mothers under thirty is only about one point above that for mothers thirty and over, and similarly for first- as against later-order births (McMahan, 1951). Incidentally, the belief that the sex ratio at birth increases during a war or immediately thereafter is apparently not valid:

Based on the sex ratio, by race and for the registration area of the United States, the data support the hypothesis that the sex ratio at birth does not consistently change as a direct influence of war either during the war years or immediately thereafter [*ibid.,* p. 283].

MORTALITY

A11   The major differentials in human mortality are social in character, except that between men and women.

To be sure, the span of life is biologically fixed. But within this span there is overwhelming evidence that most of the variation in mortality rates among large population groups, except that between the sexes, has its origin in environmental factors. . . . As age-specific death rates become smaller and smaller, genetic influence will assume increasing importance as a determinant of variation in longevity, but for most of the population of the world, environmental factors will long remain the major determinant [Dorn, 1959, p. 461].

Here are the central differences:

.1   lower mortality with economic growth, prosperity, and a rise in standard of living.

It is clear . . . that the general improvement in the mortality experience of the Western nations during the eighteenth and the first part of the nineteenth centuries was due more to a rising level of living, better working conditions, and broad social reforms than to the development of scientific methods for the control of individual diseases. Some death rates due to particular illnesses declined after economic improvement but before the specific cures for those illnesses were developed [U.N., 1953, p. 60].

.2   lower mortality with rise of modern medicine and public health practices.

.3   lower mortality within industrialized countries, but with this qualification:

One must differentiate between the contrast among countries and that within a single country. Agricultural populations usually have a shorter average length of life than the populations of highly industrialized nations, but within a given country the rural population historically has experienced lower death rates than the urban population. Advances in medicine, public health, and sanitation combined with the concentration of hospital and medical facilities in cities have resulted in a remarkable improvement in the health of urban populations; today the rural-urban differential in mortality that has been so marked in the past has sharply diminished and in some instances has disappeared [Dorn, 1959, pp. 459–60].

.4   lower mortality among the upper classes.

Even the causes of death vary by social class:

In a recent analysis of mortality by cause of death in England and Wales, it was found that while pulmonary tuberculosis was causing about twice as high a death rate among semi-skilled and unskilled workers as among professional and white-collar workers, the mortality from diabetes mellitus, angina pectoris and appendicitis was three or more times as high in the latter group as the former (Sutherland, "Variations in Occupation Mortality Between and Within Social Classes," 1947) [U.N., 1953, p. 63].

Because the mortality of wives is correlated with the husband's occupation, it is believed that

the influence of occupational hazards on mortality must be very small compared with the influence of the different social and economic situations of the various occupational groups [ibid., p. 63].

.5   lower mortality for the white race than the yellow; lower for the yellow than the black.

This relative standing appears to reflect social, economic, and environmental rather than biological differences. . . . It is true that there is some evidence for differences in racial susceptibility to specific diseases, but the extent to which these differences have their origin in biological traits, in contrast to environmental conditions, remains undetermined [Dorn, 1959, pp. 458–59].

.6   lower mortality among women.

Undoubtedly, part of the higher mortality among men arises from their greater exposure to occupational and industrial hazards and from differences in manner of living between males and females. The available evidence suggests, though, that much of the sex difference is biological in origin. It has been observed among deaths *in utero* and continues throughout the remainder of the life span with minor exceptions [*ibid.*, p. 458].

An ingenious test of the matter was recently done by studying the mortality differentials among teachers and administrative personnel of Roman Catholic Brotherhoods and Sisterhoods engaged in educational work, thus eliminating "five highly significant sources of differential stress between the sexes: (1) male service in the armed forces; (2) greater male liberty to dissipate; (3) the dissimilar roles of husband and wife; (4) male employment in hazardous and life-shortening occupations; and (5) the employment of men and women in diverse occupations." The study clearly showed greater mortality among the Brothers and thus, in the view of the investigator,

indicate (1) that biological factors are more important than sociocultural pressures and strains in relation to the differential sex death rates; and (2) that the greater sociocultural stresses associated with the male role in our society play only a small and unimportant part in producing the differentials between male and female death rates [Madigan, 1957, pp. 205, 209].

Expectations of life in years at age fifteen

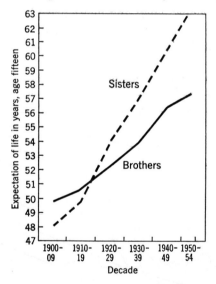

(*Ibid.*, p. 211)

Actually, it appears that female mortality is higher, relative to male, in the underdeveloped countries.

.7   lower mortality among the married than among the unmarried or divorced, especially among men.

Why this is so is not clear. Again, is it selection (the healthier marry) or is it effect (the married lead more regular lives, are better adjusted to life, get better care when ill?) The differences are not large for women, but they are substantial for men.

Social Geography

CITY AND COUNTRY

B1   Although there are and have always been large cities in preindustrial countries, industrialization brings a sharp increase in the degree of urbanization.

> The degree of urbanization increases sharply as industrialism increases. It follows that those parts of the world still mainly in the peasant agrarian stage of economic development manifest the least urbanization. . . . As of 1950, the (Pearsonian) correlation between degree of industrialization and degree of urbanization, as measured by our indices, was .86, taking the countries and territories of the world as our units [Davis and Golden, 1954, p. 8].

Similarly, there is a correlation across countries between wealth and urbanization. In the modern world, the so-called emerging countries are urbanizing at a faster rate than the developed ones; and hence urbanization is tending to even out throughout the world, under the impact of industrialization. Here are some trends in urbanization:

Growth of the proportion of population in cities of 100,000
plus, for the world and for selected countries, 1800–1951

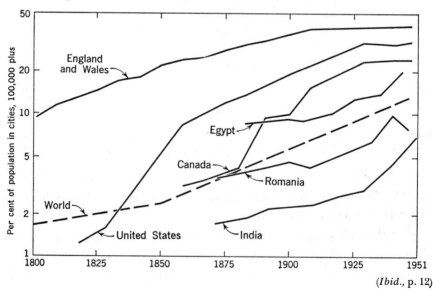

(*Ibid.*, p. 12)

As for the situation within the United States,

> there is no clear-cut relationship between degree of industrialization and current rate of growth; many of the more rapidly growing communities are those specialized in so-called tertiary industries. The well-known association of industrial and urban growth in the past contrasts with the comparatively static sizes of present-day manufacturing centers [Duncan, 1959, p. 696, citing Reiss, 1956].

In early times and in preindustrial societies, the city was likely to be "a religious or cult center, or a political-administrative center, or a central place of protection," rather than an economic center (Hoselitz, 1960, p. 219).

B1.1   The greater the urbanization and industrialization, the smaller the agricultural population (per unit of land), because of the concomitant increase in agricultural efficiency.

B1.2   Urbanization in the less developed countries is accompanied by increased literacy and education, more use of the formal media of communication, and increased rates of voting. Rapid urbanization there, at the outset, tends to sharpen the strata differences among the population.

Here are some data on the interrelationships of such factors:

Dependent variable	Multiple-correlation coefficient	Standard error
Urbanization	.61	.09
Media participation	.84	.04
Literacy	.91	.03
Political participation	.82	.05

(Lerner, 1957, p. 272)

Both the size of these coefficients and their ascending order are relevant. Their consistent significance demonstrates that the relationship between these four series of independent events is *systemic*—that rates of growth in these four sectors of the participant society have in fact "gone together" in most extant societies [*ibid.*, p. 272].

And here is a broad view of the impact on stratification:

> [In underdeveloped countries the] stable population . . . [including] professional people, intellectuals, and members of the middle and wealthier strata . . . differ more from the common man in the countryside, the recent immigrant, and even the ordinary worker in the city than in Western countries. Above all, the economic differences between the two groups are usually greater. Next, differences in political power and social status are usually greater. . . . If the urban

elite is tradition-oriented . . . , it is made up of literate priests and aristocrats; if it is a "modernizing" elite . . . , its members are western-educated persons who often are far removed in their thinking and action from the less "secularized" and frequently still profoundly tradition-oriented rural masses. This cultural difference causes the greatest divergence between city and country in Asia and Africa; and the recent rapid growth of Asian cities which has brought so many rural people into the few metropolitan primate centers has tended to enhance this difference, especially as between social groups within the city [Hoselitz, 1960, pp. 225–26].

B1.3   In time, urbanization tends to even out various aspects of behavior within the city, as a result of the interdependence and mutual visibility that builds up there.

With the absorption of formerly disparate units of population into an inclusive organization—that is, the urban community—goes a generalization of culture. A common denominator is necessarily sought in all things. Means of exchange and value schemes, language, production processes, modes of transportation and communication, charity, religious practices, recreation, and so forth, all tend to submit to the leveling influence of the sustained interaction involved in mutual dependence. It is obvious that there cannot be a monetary system adapted to the preferences of each individual; the monetary system must be adapted to the average requirement. The same is true of language, means of transportation, and, in the long run, of less concrete manifestations of behavior [Freedman *et al.*, 1956, p. 369].

B1.4   Urbanization in the modern world is associated with political stability.

[The list of] those nations having less than 10 per cent of their populations in large cities . . . generally includes countries that have not been characterized by great political stability: Bulgaria, Burma, Ceylon, Colombia, Dominican Republic, El Salvador, Haiti, India, Iran, Rumania, Turkey, and Yugoslavia. . . . It is fair to say that in the modern world internal political stability is more likely to be found with a high degree of urbanization than in a peasant economy and society [Kirk, 1957b, p. 308].

B2   The major behavioral differences between urban and rural residents appear to be these (mainly from American studies):

    a   more foreign immigrants in the cities than in rural areas.

    b   more political and religious tolerance in the cities than in rural areas.

    c   less religious observance in the cities than in rural areas, especially in the form of church attendance by men.

    d   more change in the cities, more stability in the country.

e   higher level of education in the cities than in rural areas.

f   more severe mental illness in the cities than in rural areas (not conclusive).

g   more illegitimate births in the cities than in rural areas (not conclusive).

h   fewer married people in the cities than in rural areas.

i   lower birth rate in the cities than in rural areas.

j   more divorce in the cities than in rural areas.

k   more crime in the cities than in rural areas (not conclusive), although probably more crimes of violence, proportionately, in rural areas.

l   more suicide in the cities than in rural areas.

Note that this list does not include one item that was long thought to distinguish urban from rural life, especially among earlier generations of sociologists—namely, the relative absence of close personal relations in the city. Indeed, in the United States, the spread of machinery to the farm, the automobile, and the mass media of communication are diminishing the traditional social differences between city and country.

B3   Migration from rural to urban areas occurs particularly among young people (more opportunities in the city); among women (less work for them on the farm); and among the more intelligent (greater opportunities; however, this last item is not conclusive). The more capable migrants from rural areas are more likely to travel longer distances and to larger centers than the less capable, who settle in nearby cities.

B4   The location of cities appears to be determined by "breaks in transportation" (ports, railroad junctions), with regard to commercial functions; by geographical resources, with regard to specialized functions; and by uniform placement, with regard to central-service functions.

> Since most cities combine varying proportions of each of these three functions, it is too much to expect that a simple three-category scheme can be directly applied in empirical work with definitive results. Nonetheless, there is abundant unsystematic evidence illustrating the plausibility of this account of urban locational patterns [Duncan, 1959, p. 689, citing Harris and Ullman, 1945].

B5   Within the city, the density of population is highest near the central business district and along the radial thoroughfares, although the automobile has meant a great deal of branching out from these areas of concentration.

> The distribution of urban residents in terms of intensity of land occupance varies considerably according to type and size of cities, but characteristically the areas of highest density are near the central business district. . . . The declining density, however, is not uniform in all parts of the city. Along or near radial transportation routes density is usually higher than in sections removed from the major thoroughfares. . . . Within the limits of topographic conditions, the city thus tended to assume a star-shaped pattern, the points of the star being outlying settlements along the outer reaches of urban transportation lines. Widespread use of the automobile and passenger bus has somewhat modified this star-shaped pattern of expansion [Gist and Halbert, 1956, pp. 119, 121, 122–23].

B5.1   From the center of the city to the periphery, home ownership increases, the proportion of foreign-born decreases, and the proportion of lower-status groups decreases.

> [This] concentric zone theory is most useful in interpreting data for great cities of rather rapid growth which (1) were not impeded unduly in their orderly expansion by hills or other peculiarities of the topography, (2) were not greatly influenced by the automobile, and (3) developed during the period of mass European immigration [Broom and Selznick, 1957, p. 451].

B5.2   Within the cities, the slum areas have the highest incidence of criminal and deviant behavior of various kinds: juvenile delinquency, prostitution, severe mental illness, alcoholism and drug addiction, physical and mental disabilities, crimes of violence.

> Changing land-use patterns, high residential mobility, excessive density, physical blight, and poverty in the midst of plenty all contribute to the creation of problem areas. Such areas in time develop a social character that distinguishes them from other areas. If they attract impoverished people, they may also attract social misfits and pariahs. Their social climate may be such as to encourage and foster unconventional behavior, or at least to tolerate it. Slum codes and standards are often at variance with those of other residential districts [Gist and Halbert, 1956, p. 144].

B6   Within the city, the several classes or ethnic groups tend to live together; and as people move up the class ladder, they typically seek to signalize their advance by moving their residences into the "better" parts of town or into the "better" suburbs.

As a result, upward mobile members of the minority group tend to become residentially diffused throughout the city, and residential diffusion is greatest for those who can be assimilated into the host society most easily. For example, in America northern Europeans (and their descendants) have greater residential diffusion in the host city than Negroes—i.e., the former (and their descendants) travel farthest away from the original home neighborhood when securing new housing and become spread throughout the city to a greater extent. Ecological segregation is greatest for those races and nationalities which can be assimilated least easily (*ibid.*, pp. 185–90, 195).

B6.1   Residential segregation within a city is greater for the extreme groups (the highest and the lowest classes) than for the middle groups.

The indexes of residential segregation form a U-shaped pattern. The highest values are observed for the professionals and the laborers and the lowest value for the clerical workers. The degree of residential segregation varies only slightly among the professional, managerial, and sales groups; however, it declines markedly for the clerical workers and then increases regularly for each successive group [Duncan and Duncan, 1955, p. 497].

Index of residential segregation of each major occupation group, for employed males in the Chicago metropolitan district, 1950

Major occupation group *	By census	By zone sector segments
Professional, technical, and kindred workers	30	21
Managers, officials, and proprietors, except farm	29	20
Sales workers	29	20
Clerical and kindred workers	13	9
Craftsmen, foremen, and kindred workers	19	14
Operatives and kindred workers	22	16
Service workers, except private household	24	20
Laborers, except farm and mine	35	29

* Does not include farmers and farm managers, private household workers, farm laborers, and occupation not reported.

(*Ibid.*, p. 497)

The corollary is that the greater the class differences, the greater the residential distinctions.

B7   The less the ethnic heterogeneity and the less the migration, the greater the moral integration of the large American city.

"Moral integration" is based upon the (inverted) crime rate and the welfare effort in the community. Here are the figures for some cities (over 100,000 population) that have high and low rates of integration:

City	Adjusted crime index	Adjusted welfare effort index	Integration index
Rochester	17.3	22.4	19.0
Syracuse	17.1	16.9	17.0
Worcester	14.8	19.6	16.4
Erie	15.0	18.6	16.2
Milwaukee	18.4	10.5	15.8
Bridgeport	15.6	14.8	15.3
Buffalo	17.8	9.9	15.2
Louisville	4.1	15.0	7.7
Portland (Oregon)	6.7	8.1	7.2
Jacksonville	6.2	5.5	6.0
Memphis	3.8	8.7	5.4
Tulsa	3.7	8.5	5.3
Miami	5.8	3.6	5.1
Atlanta	2.5	7.6	4.2

(Angell, 1951, p. 14)

B8   The more physical mobility within the city, the less social intimacy within the neighborhood.

At the same time:

B8.1   New residents in a community associate with their neighbors more than do old residents (who know more people in other parts of town).

In all newly formed communities studied, a large proportion of the associations are with families living close by—the more homogeneous the new community, the larger the proportions of associates who live adjacent will be, and the longer the propinquous relationships will tend to persist. Desires to associate with persons of similar religion, social class, former acquaintanceship, and many other factors result in the scattering of members of informal groups in modern mobile society [Loomis and Beegle, 1957, pp. 110–11].

B9   Technological innovations (inventions) tend to be developed and perfected in the cities and then to spread to rural areas.

This appears to be the case for all kinds of innovations, including those dealing directly with rural concerns, such as agricultural equipment.

NATURAL ENVIRONMENT

The effect upon human behavior of such geographical conditions as terrain and climate is a fascinating subject; but because the literature in this field is especially unfamiliar to us, we cannot claim to represent it fully here. In any case the subject is highly complex, and our impression is that relatively few findings are generally accepted by scholars in this field. Some years ago, a position of "environmentalism" was put forward (usually identified with the geographer Ellsworth Huntington) that most specialists consider far too extreme. As a result, the field has reacted against such generalizations so that it is difficult, at least for outsiders like us, to say at this point just what is considered definitive about natural-environmental effects on human behavior. We present here only a few propositions in order to illustrate the subject, with no claim to completeness or to scholarly consensus. Accordingly we do not number them in the usual way.

. . .   The natural environment affects the distribution of human populations, but less so as societies move from an agricultural to an industrial base.

> Since the Industrial Revolution, the location of economic activities and the distribution of population have come to depend less on physical resources than they formerly did. The diminishing proportion of the population engaged in agriculture and technological improvements within agriculture have freed man, to a large extent, from his dependence on those qualities of land and climate which formerly confined his settlements within a rather narrow range. The development of transportation facilities has also made it less important than formerly to locate industrial establishments near sources of energy and raw materials. Thus the geographic factors in general have played a decreasing part in the determination of population distribution. Man has been able to exert an increasing measure of individual or social control in the choice of his habitats, within the broad limits set by nature [U.N., 1953, pp. 176–77].

At the same time, some scholars believe that "the level to which a culture can develop is dependent upon the agricultural potentiality of the environment it occupies" (Meggers, 1954, p. 822). This conclusion is based upon an analysis of the diffusion of cultural traits among societies with high and low "agricultural potential," the idea being that traits diffuse within the high areas, even distant ones, more readily than from them to the low areas, even adjacent ones.

. . .   The more demanding the natural environment, from the standpoint of physical survival, the less the attention devoted to supernatural matters.

One authority advances the Eskimos as an instance:

> They retain of course a share of the taboos and the supernatural beliefs of all primitive cultures; but their primary and dominant orientation is realistic. They differ from the Samoans in that they have a minimum of social mechanisms and statuses to distract their attention. Their relations are personal, man to man, with little in the way of institutions as a framework. . . . The cause for this [realistic] orientation can perhaps be sought in the extraordinarily trying circumstances of survival in the Arctic. The Eskimo must be mechanical-minded,

able-bodied, manually skillful, and practical. Too many taboos or rituals would tie his hands, limit his resourcefulness, take up time that must be given to survival activities to a visibly greater extent than among almost any other people. Supernaturalism thus tends to drop into the background, relatively [Kroeber, 1948, p. 603].

. . .   Mental vigor is stimulated by moderate climates.

Huntington [1915] concluded, and no one has refuted the evidence, that for mental vigour, an average outdoor temperature of 50 to 60° is better than one above 70°. Much of the tropical half of the world has an average temperature well above 70°, with the result that intellectual activity is handicapped. Conversely, in the cooler parts of middle latitudes, man's intellectual activity has been comparatively great. . . .

A northward shift during the last 3,000 years of "Civilization" has occurred as man has been able to partly overcome by buildings, clothing, and more adequate diet some of the ill effects of relatively low temperatures. As civilization has spread into cooler latitudes it has risen to higher average levels, intellectually. . . . Where the precipitation is distributed fairly evenly throughout the year, man is able to carry on successfully many more activities than are feasible in regions having chiefly winter or summer precipitation. As a partial result, the more advanced modern civilizations are largely in such regions [Visher, 1957, pp. 203–04, 210].

Here is the result, for example, of an analysis of achievement motivation in the folk stories of primitive societies with different mean temperatures:

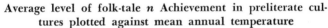

Average level of folk-tale *n* Achievement in preliterate cultures plotted against mean annual temperature

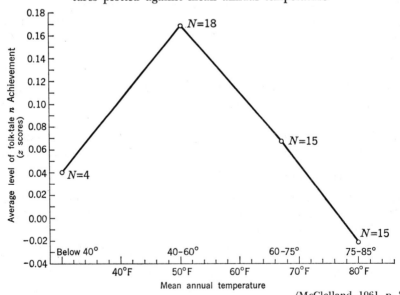

(McClelland, 1961, p. 385)

In addition, the association of high *n* Achievement with daily or monthly temperature variation is, if anything, even greater. The measure of temperature variation was computed as either the maximum difference between mean temperatures at different seasons of the year or the median variation of the mean daily ranges in temperatures at different times of the year, whichever was larger. Temperature variation can occur either daily or seasonally, and either one would provide the kind of "stimulating" environment that Huntington considers desirable for producing an energetic response. Of the 26 cultures classified as high in *n* Achievement, only two—the Yoruba in Africa and the Ifaluk in the South Pacific—did not have at least 15° F of daily or seasonal variation in temperature, whereas, one-half of the cultures classified as low in *n* Achievement did not have even this much temperature variation [*ibid.*, p. 385].

And other students have remarked on the generally low level of activity, including mental activity, in tropical environments. For example:

Apart from a reduced desire for activity, there seem to be no permanent deleterious *direct* climatic effects in healthy persons living under natural conditions in the tropics. . . . Some loss of mental initiative is probably the most important single direct result of exposure to tropical environment. . . . Certainly, the usual pattern of life in tropical countries is more leisurely and less productive of material goods than that which is found in most temperate latitudes, and a case can be made for at least some influence of climate in this respect. Man in the temperate zones has built up his civilizations around the important demands created by cold weather for securing food and shelter in advance. In so doing, he has developed a culture in which activity and making provision for the future have high social values. In tropical populations, on the other hand, climate provides neither the social nor the physiological drive for activity and saving beyond the needs of the more or less immediate future. This difference in "spontaneous" activity marks one of the most important conflicts at the personal level between temperate and tropical modes of behavior [Lee, 1957, pp. 99–100].

. . .   Environmental changes that are favorable to human health conditions, from the standpoint of climate, altitude, and diet, tend to increase body dimensions and perhaps to increase mental energy as well.

In all of the comparable studies, dimensions of stature and those which vary with stature increase considerably as between sedente (remain in native country) and immigrant, and immigrant and American-born [Kaplan, 1954, p. 795].

There is even some evidence that American babies born in the North in the summer months have slightly higher I.Q. scores in later life than those born at other times, presumably because of the healthier start in life they receive in that favorable season.

Social Change

C1   Social changes, however large, that are desired by the people involved can be assimilated with little social disruption. Changes that are not desired,

even quite small ones, can be put into effect only at considerable social and
personal cost.

> We have learned the pleasing truth, that society talks back. Even the small-scale,
> technologically inferior peoples of the world have tremendous powers to resist
> changes they do not want, and to adhere, often at great cost, to their valued and
> distinct way of life. At the same time, we have learned that changes which peo-
> ple desire, radical or not, can be made swiftly, without great cost, and that a
> society may nearly redo itself—in a generation—if it wants to (Mead, 1956) [Nash,
> 1959, p. 79].

As one example, there is the case of the Japanese village of Suye Mura,
studied in 1935–36 and again in 1952–53, after a great war, an occupation,
unsettled economic conditions, a new constitution and civil code, and deliberate efforts to realize a great deal of social change. The young people
have changed their ideas and style of life, or sought to, but the village
leaders still follow the old ways (Yoshino, 1956). As a corollary:

> **C1a**   Social changes imposed on a society from outside are especially
> likely not to be accepted. Forced change from the outside tends to
> result in overt compliance but covert resistance.

> **C1.1**   The more a social change threatens or appears to threaten the
> traditional values of the society, the greater the resistance to that change
> and the greater its attendant cost in social and personal disorganization.

> In relation to ideological and value systems . . . the thesis seems inherent in
> recent work by a number of students that if, under conditions of change, the
> basic cultural rationale retains its validity, even extensive behavioral changes
> can take place without threat to group or individual integrity and morale. . . .
> But if these basic elements are threatened or undermined, the group or individ-
> ual concerned is likely to lapse into states of disorganization, insecurity, anxiety,
> self-depreciation, and low morale, though usually accompanied by attempts to
> establish a new rationale. . . . Several theorists have suggested that, so long as
> the basic value system stands reasonably firm, selective change can proceed with
> minimum strain and stress. At the other extreme, some groups and individuals
> have undergone, or are in process of undergoing, the experience of having their
> value systems in jeopardy or shattered, catastrophically or through a prolonged
> series of crisis episodes [Keesing, 1953, pp. 85, 80].

A topical application can be seen currently with regard to the so-called
emerging nations:

> Historical experience indicates that no society ever simply abandons its tradi-
> tional culture. On the contrary, the old culture almost always leaves permanent
> and significant marks of continuity on the fully modernized society. Neverthe-
> less, the traditional culture must undergo drastic alteration. It is thus of the very
> nature of the modernizing process that at every step of the way the impulses mak-
> ing for modernization are in active contention with powerful forces tending to

retard and to frustrate the transformation of the traditional society into full constructive modernity [Millikan and Blackmer, 1961, p. 19].

C1.2   The more integrated the society, with regard to both values and institutions, the more successfully it can respond to social change, by resisting, facilitating, incorporating, or adjusting.

C1.3   The slower the introduction of social changes, with attendant discussion and persuasion, or the more they are introduced through existing institutions, the less the disruption of the prevailing way of life (that is, the more time and pressure there will be for adjustment to the change, including rationalizing it to present practice).

An abrupt shift from traditional social ties makes people particularly susceptible to new identifications, opinions, practices, institutions, political practices, ways of life; as, for example, currently in the emerging countries of the Middle East, Southeast Asia, and Africa.

C1.4   Social change is more likely to occur in heterogeneous societies than in homogeneous ones.

There are simply more different points of view available in a heterogeneous society, more ideas, more conflicts in interest, more groups and organizations of different persuasions—plus a greater secularism and tolerance that tend to promote social change by opening more areas of life to decision rather than subjecting them to authority.

> Where stability is the dominant note, it may relate variously to long identity and exclusiveness, adaptation to a highly specialized habitat, rigidly institutionalized social structure favorable to homeostasis, the unifying stamp of a single religion, or similar determinants. By contrast, mobility may be basic in a society where populations and ethnic traditions have been diversified and on the move, and frequent adjustment has been historically occurring in the face of technological, political, or other factors of mobility. Change in the sense of "progress" and "advancement" can even become a pervasive value for a group during a given period, as in the contemporary American milieu [Keesing, 1953, p. 83].

C2   Within a society, social change is likely to occur more frequently or more readily:

.1   in the material aspects of the culture (e.g., technology) than in the nonmaterial (e.g., values).

.2   in the aspects close to the society's "cultural focus" than in those at the periphery.

.3   in the less basic, less emotionally charged, less sacred, more instrumental or technical aspects (e.g., tools, tactics, competitive goals, impersonal means) than in the opposite (e.g., primary group relations, territorial and religious stability, systems of prestige).

.4   in the simple elements of the society than in the complex ones.

.5   in the nonsymbolic elements of the society than in the symbolic ones.

.6   in form than in substance.

.7   in matters arranged on a scale with narrow intervals than in those arranged in a sharp dichotomy.

For example, with regard to extending the political franchise to the Negro (but with application to other aspects of ethnic relations as well, such as educational desegregation):

> The abrupt character of the division between white and Negro, with no such intermediate groups as are present in economic gradations to shift their support now to one side and now to another, has reduced the possibility of gradual change [Lane, 1959, p. 15].

.8   in elements for which roughly equivalent substitutes are available or provided in the society than otherwise.

.9   in elements congenial to the given culture than in strange elements.

.10   in periods of crisis and stress than in normal or quiescent periods.

.11   the larger the cultural base, as a stimulant to further invention and innovation.

> In the long historical view, the rate of growth of culture is sometimes described as following the *exponential* or *compound-interest curve,* since each new invention increases with "snowball effect" the possibilities of further invention [Freedman *et al.,* 1956, p. 330].

.12   via the cities than via the countryside.

> Cities are focal points of change. Most social and economic change begins among the upper classes and then spreads downward to the traditionally inarticulate lower classes and outward to the countryside. The cultural innovations of urban areas have prestige attached to them [Foster, 1962, p. 29].

C3   There is always a tendency in society to achieve stability after a period of sharp social change, either by directly adjusting to the change itself or by accommodating it to the parent culture.

So social disruptions are followed by social reorganizations aimed to re-establish some security. As in the case of personal conflict, so with social change: most men do not like to live indefinitely under conditions of insecurity, anxiety, uncertainty, and disorder. Actually, some scholars believe that "the initial survival value of any innovation is conservative in that it makes possible the maintenance of a largely traditional way of life in the face of changed circumstances" (Hockett, 1960, p. 96).

C3.1 After changes making for greater interdependence of social units, the reorganization works to establish broader norms to encompass the new groups.

Historically, whenever the area of functional interdependence has been expanded, there has been a period of disorganization during which more comprehensive norms and forms of organization slowly developed. For example, such a period accompanied the growth of modern nation-states in the last four centuries. In short, much of the so-called disorganization of modern urban society may be connected with this kind of transition [Freedman *et al.*, 1956, p. 448].

C4 Within a society, social change is unlikely to be based on the lowest social stratum.

It requires some improvement to perceive of the possibility of improvement, and to be willing to devote the necessary energy and take the necessary risks.

A person must have a certain amount of security to fight for a larger share. Those who have nothing to lose but their chains are too closely chained, psychologically, to the desperation of their lot to generalize their predicament, face the consequences of a malcontent position, or otherwise add to their suffering by striving for social change [Lipset and Linz, 1956, p. 28].

C5 Social changes of some scope in one part of a society affect other parts not directly involved in the change itself.

For example, changes in the economic organization of a small town, specifically the growth of absentee-owned industries within the town, have been shown to shift the political and social leadership of the community. In communities highly dependent upon a single industry or plant, the community itself can become socially disorganized as a result of tension within the industry or plant (Warner and Low, 1947; Walker, 1950) or can be held together by harmonious relations there (Harbison and Dubin, 1947). On a larger scale:

Industrialized farming breaks down socially unified and homogeneous rural communities and fosters the development of urban social relations and urban values. Land no longer is valued as the *place* of residence, work, and identity; it is evaluated as *property* to be bought and sold. Although American rural society remains more locality-oriented than the urban society, the basis for local autonomy is rapidly disappearing [Broom and Selznick, 1957, p. 427].

On the broad historical front:

It is quite true that the materialism of industrial societies has destroyed many cultural values and that the reliance on self-interest and on individualism has jeopardized many ideals and institutions tending to safeguard the unity and solidarity of societies. And it is certainly *possible* that the resulting changes may eventuate in a "decline of civilization," although, contrary to the conservative perspective, this is again less probable as industrialization is developed successfully, because in that case new ideals and institutions arise in place of the old, and different forms of social cohesion may therefore become viable. The decline of civilization envisaged by the conservatives is only the *extreme* form which the transformation of values and institutions may take under very special conditions [Bendix and Lipset, 1957, pp. 89–90].

And changes can have reciprocal effects that work back on the initial shifts. For example:

> While the growth of secular groups increases the impersonality of social relationships, the impersonality makes it possible for secular groups to function effectively. Similarly, while social change increases secularism, secularism reduces resistance to social change [Freedman *et al.*, 1956, p. 452].

Since different aspects of the society do not change at the same rate—artifacts usually change faster than attitudes—some students have considered the resultant "imbalance" an instance of "cultural lag" (Ogburn, 1927).

C6   The leaders of major social changes in a society are unlikely to come from the group traditionally in control; they are more apt to come from deviant, marginal, disaffected groups.

Here are some historical instances:

> In England far more leaders of the world's first industrial revolution came from among the religious nonconformists than from any other single group, even though the nonconformists formed only seven or eight per cent of the population of England. Many other leaders came from the lowland Scots, who had come under the political and social domination of the English.
>
> In Japan disaffected social groups led the way in modernization. In about 1600 one group of clans, the Tokugawa, gained dominance over the entire country and subjected other clans, the "outer clans," to political and social subordination. Under the Tokugawa a national peace was imposed; the warrior class, the Samurai, lost their traditional social position and also steadily declined in wealth. The move toward modernization, which fermented under the surface, led to the overthrow of the Tokugawa in 1868 and thereafter proceeded rapidly, led by Samurai and individuals from the outer clans.
>
> In Colombia the Spanish conquerors inhabited three high valleys which are the sites of the four main present cities of Colombia. In two of these valleys they developed landed estates and became landed gentry or cattlemen. In the third, Antioquia, because the land was less suitable and because other activities were more attractive, they did not. During the eighteenth and nineteenth centuries, as the historical literature of the time shows, the gentry of the other two valleys looked down on the Antioqueños because they too had not become gentry, and the Antioqueños resented this attitude. Today it is the Antioqueños who are spearheading economic and political modernization throughout Colombia.

In India successive waves of migration over several millennia have resulted in the existence of a number of social groups who even today are very conscious of their historical differences from each other. It is probably significant that much of the effective modern business activity to date in India has been initiated by several of the minority social groups—the Parsis, the Marwari, and others. . . .

It appears that a traditional society turned the more readily to modernization if there was any articulate group of men in it with reason to be unhappy about their position. Feeling aggrieved, already questioning the values and attitudes of the traditional society, they were psychologically prepared to accept new ways of life as a means of proving their worth and gaining self-satisfaction, status, and prestige. Put another way, the traditional society, despite its surface of coherence and stability, was often marked by inner conflicts; and one of the effects of intrusion from without was often to permit those conflicts to take forms that contributed significantly to modernization [Millikan and Blackmer, 1961, pp. 9–10].

C6.1   As agents of major social changes in countries emerging from traditional into modern industrial culture, the intellectuals sooner or later join forces with one or another of the power groups in the society.

The men of the secular intelligentsia become individually impatient and as a group extremist in their views of what must be done. They may form alliances of various sorts—with each other, with foreign agents, even with "deviants" among the traditionalist sectors of landowners and sacred intelligentsia. But ultimately, if they are to make more than a quick splash, the secular intelligentsia ally themselves with the military sector, the bureaucracy, or the business elite.

The historical logic is clear. The other elites have the coercive power and organization needed to maintain stability; the secular intelligentsia have the knowledge needed to effect change. Military, bureaucratic, or business leadership alone usually has foundered because its perspective is too narrow to cope with the variety of problems that arise in modernizing societies; the secular intelligentsia alone usually have failed because their ideas outrun their capacity to develop institutions that are operational. Neither can manage the transition without the other, and so forms the "unholy alliance," which Western social scientists have described (and decried) [Millikan and Blackmer, 1961, p. 36].

C6.2   Innovators within a society are more likely to be younger than the resisters of change, of higher social status, and more oriented to the outside world; moreover, they take less time to adopt the new idea or practice and they discontinue less often.

For a full summary on the diffusion of (mainly agricultural) innovations, published too late for detailed inclusion here, see Rogers, 1962.

Social Conflict

D1   The more substantial or encompassing the social conflict (that is, the more central to the society's values or the more people are involved), the greater the pressures for its solution.

In other words, the greater the conflict, the more people will feel they have to do something, rather than simply withdraw from the matter. In the long run, human societies are probably characterized by what Sumner called the "strain toward consistency." Men generally do not like to live long in a state of dispute and recrimination, or even uncertainty, especially over important matters.

D2   Social conflict is more intense:

.1   the less adjustable the goals or the more fixed the rewards being sought by the disputants (e.g., the economic returns under dispute in a labor-management conflict).

.2   the less the contact or openness between disputants.

> In a society where movement from a lower to a higher class occurs to a great extent and where the workers are not politically subordinated, class conflicts are attenuated and the ideology of the class struggle finds it difficult to gain a foothold [Lasswell and Kaplan, 1950, p. 36].

Thus, the more multiple the loyalties and identifications within a society, or even the more the cross-pressures, the less the likelihood of serious conflict, because of the mediating influence of the men in the middle. As a student of community conflicts puts it:

> Particularly revealing is the community dominated by one group, with a separate, subjugated minority. In such a case, the subjugated minority, with no chance to win a dispute, may erupt in unorganized outbursts of violence. For example, Zimmerman (1938) finds such behavior in the lower class in two rigidly dominated communities, one in Mississippi and one in Siam; and Hughes (1946a) finds this behavior among the English minority in French Canadian towns. In cases where the sides are more evenly split, hostility may lead to a real conflict and perhaps a realignment of community power. . . .
>
> In short, the mass-society form of local community that is arising through locality specialization generates a special kind of community conflict, a "revolt of the masses" against the administrative elite who have been making decisions. These revolts sometimes explode into real conflicts, because the intermediary associations, through which opinions are both expressed and compromised, are largely missing [Coleman, 1961b, pp. 569, 604].

.2a   The sharper the conflict, the greater the tendency for participants to associate only with those of like mind; and thus, in turn, the sharper the conflict becomes, because of hardening of antagonistic positions.

One premonitory sign of approaching war between North and South was the territorial segregation of opinion holders on hotly contested issues in large sectional regions. Since 1865, on the contrary, there has been a long attrition of the "solid South." . . . Especially familiar are the political cleavages between those who dwell in cities and the farmers, and, inside cities, the typical contrast in the political attitudes and perspectives of the residents of poor and of rich wards.

During noncrisis periods, persons of conflicting attitudes can live side by side. As antagonisms intensify, however, the dispersed pattern is broken up as fellow believers seek safety in segregation (the Loyalist families in the American colonies, for instance, sought refuge during the secession from the Empire by fleeing to the strongholds of imperial authority in New York and Canada) [Lasswell and Kaplan, 1950, p. 253].

.3   the less integrated the community involved in the conflict.

The extremes are clear: the integration of the small, primitive community as against the diversity of the large industrial and urban society—although even here, note, there can be and are real strains in the former and real consensus in the latter.

.3a   In the case of community conflict, the poorly integrated members of the community are the most likely to aggravate the conflict beyond the bounds of normal disagreement.

When community members are highly involved with the community per se, identifying their own future with that of the community, that identification . . . appears to modify and constrain the disagreement. People who feel apart, and *unidentified,* are quickest to overstep the bounds of legitimate methods and carry the dispute into disruptive channels. When there are few or none who are identified, then there are essentially no norms to restrain the opposing sides. Conversely, if most people and organizations in the community are identified with community as a whole, then the potentially disruptive effects of the dispute are felt by all; there are conscious attempts at reconciliation [Coleman, 1957, p. 21].

.4   the more that ideology is involved.

Conflicts over ideologies are less easily resolved than conflicts over power. Conflict over power can usually be compromised more readily, partly because the disputants still agree on enough of the rules and partly because they tend to act like "reasonable" men (and divide the power). In conflicts over ideologies, however, the very rules are often in dispute as well as the substance, and men are likely to be more emotionally involved.

.5   the more committed the participants to the organizations involved in the controversy.

For example, there appears to be less involvement in the general population in large cities than in small towns; or in voluntary associations toward which the members give only segmental or partial allegiance.

.6   the more uncertain or unstable the rules by which the conflict is supposed to be resolved.

This situation typically occurs under conditions of crisis, and it makes for more recurrent conflict and for greater likelihood of panic or other socially uncontrolled behavior.

D3 Human conflicts cannot usually be settled by removing the original source of conflict.

If it takes time for that to happen, each side typically has so much "face" invested in the dispute that that in itself becomes a barrier to resolution.

D3.1 As more people beyond the initial disputants become involved in a conflict, even on a matter capable of rational solution, its resolution becomes more difficult.

Again this is so because personalities become central to the disagreement, beyond the original principles. It is much easier even for professors, dedicated to the search for truth, to resolve or clarify their differences in private than to do so in front of a seminar or a session of a professional convention, let alone a TV camera.

In general, it also appears that human conflicts are typically settled short of the destruction of one of the parties to the dispute.

D4 In the face of a threat from the outside, a human group, unit, or society subordinates its internal conflicts to the common good (survival). When the external threat is removed, the internal conflicts return to action.

A conflict, in short, tends to dichotomize the participants into clear "we's" and "they's." This principle can be seen in operation in a boys' gang, a family, a primitive tribe, a country subject to a national disaster, or a modern society going to war.

> If a tribe's customary outlet for aggression in war is blocked, one may predict an increase in intratribal hostility (perhaps in the form of witchcraft) or in pathological states of melancholy resultant upon anger being turned inward against the self [Kluckhohn, 1949, p. 267].

> The history of warfare has proved repeatedly that as long as there is an outside threat to a group or a collective goal to be achieved, internal antagonisms and individualist concerns are subordinated to the safety and interests of the whole group. But when the outer threats are removed or the collective goal achieved or abandoned, the individual concerns and the individual antagonisms come to the surface. Then the unity of the group may become seriously weakened [Stouffer *et al.*, 1949, II, 552].

D5 The natural history of a community conflict includes these features: (a) the polarization of personal relations around the issue under controversy and the increasing of personal contacts within each camp; (b) the emergence of partisan leaders and organizations, usually new ones that are more extremist than the existing ones; (c) the increasing use of word-of-mouth as more adaptable to partisan purposes than the media of mass communications; (d) the broadening of the dispute from specific to general issues, from old to new ones, and from disagreement over issues to personal antagonisms.

> The processes may be said to create a "Gresham's Law of Conflict": the harmful and dangerous elements drive out those which would keep the conflict within bounds [Coleman, 1957, p. 14].

D6 Crisis hastens and intensifies the going trend in social relations: if the community is integrated, crisis will increase the integration; if the community is poorly integrated, crisis will disrupt it.

This can be seen both in the large and the small: in the nation-state (e.g., a depression) and within the family (e.g., the addition of a child dissolving some families but increasing the solidarity of others).

Social Disorganization

DISASTERS

E1 The response of people to a peacetime disaster, such as a tornado or a flood or a large explosion, typically takes the following form:

(a) People who have previously experienced a disaster tend to respond appropriately to an advance warning; people who have not had such experience tend to respond to the warning by seeking other cues that allow them, in effect, to disregard the warning. Just as there is a tendency to underplay the likelihood of the event's occurring at all, so there is a tendency to underestimate its destructiveness afterwards.

> Many people tend to deny or disbelieve information that danger is near at hand. They seize on any vagueness, ambiguity, or incompatibility in the warning message enabling them to interpret the situation optimistically. They search for more information that will confirm, deny, or clarify the warning message, and often they continue to interpret signs of danger as signs of familiar, normal events until it is too late to take effective precautions [Fritz, 1961, p. 665].

(b) There is very little panic during and immediately after the disaster.

> The notion that people typically "panic," become "hysterical," or "go to pieces" in the presence of danger is not supported by disaster research findings. . . . Although some cases of individual or small-group panic have occurred in disasters, its frequency and significance in disaster have been grossly exaggerated. It is a rare response rather than a typical one [*ibid.*, p. 671].

Usually, there is much more traffic *to* the scene of disaster than *from* it.

(c) An informal but effective and highly solidary social organization arises soon after the disaster to deal with the consequences, even in isolated communities, and the leadership is more likely to come from those with most stake in the community—heads of families, for instance, rather than single men. At this time the normal social distinctions are sharply lessened, but gradually reappear with the passage of time. Only later do conflicts arise over alleged inequities in handling the consequences.

The widespread sharing of danger, loss, and deprivation produces an intimate, primary group solidarity among the survivors, which overcomes social isolation and provides a channel for intimate communication and expression and a major source of physical and emotional support and reassurance. . . . The social disorganization that occurs in disaster is essentially a social disorganization of secondary group life. . . . Except momentarily, it does not disorganize primary-group life. On the contrary, this is strengthened, and this in turn constitutes the nucleus out of which the society can once again reconstitute itself and develop a new complexity of organization [*ibid.,* pp. 689–90].

(d) The first reaction is typically concern for the safety of one's family and other intimates and then for the larger community—even on the part of those with community responsibilities, who often feel caught in this cross-pressured situation. In general, there is less feeling of self-interest and more concern for the community than exists in normal times.

The net result of most disasters is a dramatic increase in social solidarity among the affected populace during the emergency and immediate postemergency periods. The sharing of a common threat to survival and the common suffering engendered by the disaster tend to produce a breakdown of social distinctions and a great outpouring of love, generosity, and altruism. During the first days and weeks following a major community-wide disaster, people tend to act toward one another spontaneously, sympathetically, and sentimentally, on the basis of common human needs rather than in terms of pre-disaster differences in social and economic status [National Research Council, 1958, pp. 18–19].

(e) Most people experiencing a severe disaster soon suffer some kind of emotional or physical upset—nausea, diarrhea, "nerves," or the like—that continues to some degree for days or even weeks. But such transitory reactions do not incapacitate most of the sufferers from responding realistically to the event and its aftermath; moreover, they rarely arrive at chronic states of severe mental disturbance.

(f) The farther people are from the scene of disaster, the less accurate their information about it and the less their concern for the victims.

(g) For the victims themselves, the disaster remains for years a major event in their lives.

A re-study of a midwestern river town conducted more than 15 years after a severe flood in 1937 showed that the disaster was still a salient fact in the life of the community. People tended to date events in terms of the disaster; their memories of the happenings in the flood remained vivid; and they still identified many of their fellow inhabitants in terms of the kind of social role (rescue worker, helper, etc.) that they played in the disaster.

The continuing public recognition of the disaster as an important juncture in human experience also provides a form of social absolution: people are permitted to make a clean break with the past and take a fresh start in reorganizing their lives [Fritz, 1961, p. 692].

In general, then, many of the commonly held notions about behavior under disaster conditions turn out to be incorrect. Here is a summary from a recent summary:

(1) Mass panic is a phenomenon that occurs rarely and only under certain circumstances; (2) Few actual cases of looting can be discovered; (3) Stricken populations are not a "dazed, helpless mass," but help themselves and perform rescue and welfare tasks; (4) The social group organization does not break down but is strengthened; (5) There are only isolated examples of breakdown of moral codes; (6) There is no significant increase in psychoses and psychoneuroses; (7) Emotional aftereffects are widespread but relatively mild and transitory; (8) Morale and optimism soon rebound and are abnormally high in some respects; and (9) The big problem of crowd control is not flight of the victims from the disaster area, but a convergence of people to the disaster area from the outside [National Research Council, 1958, p. 2].

CRIME AND DELINQUENCY

Here as elsewhere, the best available data are not always good data, because of the great difficulty in securing valid statistics on crime rates. The data collected officially are often incomplete, and incomplete in a biased manner, and they vary in definition from one time to another and from one jurisdiction to another. As one authority recently put it: "Statistical data on the true crime rate cannot be compiled, for the simple reason that it is impossible to determine the amount of crime in any given locality at any particular time" (Cressey, 1961, p. 26). Again, popular notions to the contrary notwithstanding, "it is impossible to state unequivocally how much delinquency there is in the United States or whether it has been increasing or decreasing over the past several decades" (Cohen and Short, 1961, p. 83). Although we believe the following findings to be among the better established ones in the field, it is well to keep this caveat in mind.

E2   As compared in each case with their counterparts, criminal behavior is more likely:

.1   among those people not closely tied to their own social groups or to the society as a whole through the sharing of behavioral norms.

The weaker the social controls, the more deviation from them; hence, the more social disorganization, the more crime. Relatively more criminals and delinquents come from broken homes, from broken marriages, from families that have moved around (and thus loosened social ties) than come from unified, socially integrated families. There is some evidence that the delinquency rate is higher for "those whose parents are separated or divorced than it is for those who have lost a parent by death" (Goode, 1961, p. 455). In fact, some students of the matter believe that this is a, or even *the,* fundamental factor in causing juvenile delinquency: "It is the social-control approach that can best explain the rise or fall of delinquency rates" (Raab and Selznick, 1959, p. 62).

.1a   The closer the tie to groups themselves deviant from the general social norms, the more criminal behavior there is.

That is, some groups provide their own support for deviant behavior, and thus the criminal is complying with his own group's social norms—he is, so to speak, conforming to his own subculture. In short:

> The potential reaction of the individual's primary group plays a major role in determining whether or not the individual will engage in deviant behavior; and if the individual lacks primary groups which support such adherence to the norms or identifies himself with others who place a positive value on violating the laws of society, the likelihood of crime increases [Sykes, 1956, p. 74].

Thus criminal behavior sometimes is learned behavior—learned from the deviant groups themselves.

> One criminologist has pointed out that the gang influences individuals toward delinquency and crime in a number of ways: by promoting attitudes of hostility toward community agencies of social control, by teaching techniques of crime and a general pattern of destructiveness, by enforcing its system of assigning highest prestige to the most daring or skilled criminals, and by serving as a medium of contact between beginners, more experienced juvenile delinquents, and older professional criminals [Broom and Selznick, 1957, p. 622, citing Taft, 1950].

.2   among men.

"Sex status is of greater statistical significance in differentiating criminals from noncriminals than any other trait" (Cressey, 1961, p. 33). Furthermore:

> Compared with females, males have a great excess of crimes in all nations, all communities within nations, all age groups, all periods of history for which we have statistics, and all types of crime except those related to the female sex, such as abortion. In the United States, males are arrested approximately ten times as frequently as females, and they are committed to prisons and reformatories approximately twenty times as frequently as females. Of the cases coming before juvenile courts, about 85 per cent are boys. The official statistics are probably biased in favor of females, but even if correction could be made for the statistical

bias, the criminal sex ratio probably would be well over 600 or 700. . . . Criminal sex ratios are highest in countries where females are rigidly supervised, and lowest in the countries in which females have the greatest freedom and the closest approximation to equality with males. . . . There is some evidence that the sex ratio has been decreasing in the last few centuries and especially in the last fifty years, as women have acquired statuses more nearly equal to those of men [Broom and Selznick, 1957, p. 639].

The difference in crime rate between men and women is smaller in larger cities and among such ethnic groups as the Negroes.

.3   among lower-class groups.

At least such groups are more heavily represented in official statistics. It is likely that a good deal of white-collar and upper-class crime goes undiscovered or unpunished—the employer allowing an embezzling employee to resign quietly instead of prosecuting, the upper-class parent getting his son out from under a delinquency charge—but it is still probable that proportionately more crimes are committed by the lower classes. In addition:

Types of crime are significantly related to social status. One's position in the class structure determines the opportunities, facilities, and the requisite skills for specialized crimes. Lower-class persons cannot ordinarily violate laws prohibiting embezzlement, for they are seldom in positions of financial trust. On the other hand, a person trained to carry on the routine duties of trust has at the same time been trained in whatever technical skills are necessary for the violation of that position. But he may have no training or skill in how to steal an automobile. Furthermore, persons of different social classes have different conceptions of the kinds of crimes which are appropriate to their statuses. An upper-class person who would not think of burglarizing his neighbor's house, because such a crime is "beneath him," might take some of his neighbor's money by misrepresentations in a business negotiation [Broom and Selznick, 1957, p. 624].

.4   among younger people.

The crime rate is highest in the late teens. It goes down gradually thereafter: from about age twenty for males and a few years older for females.

The concentration of certain crimes, such as burglary and robbery, in the young-adult group, has been observed for several centuries. English statistics indicate that burglars and robbers of the fifteenth and sixteenth centuries were approximately the same age as present-day burglars and robbers [Broom and Selznick, 1957, p. 640].

Certain types of crime are associated in the United States with different ages: car theft with the teens; robbery and rape with the twenties; gambling and drug addiction with the thirties; drunkenness, embezzlement, and fraud later on.

.5   among certain minority groups.

For example, even taking account of lower socioeconomic status, Negroes appear to have a higher crime rate in the United States than whites. But there is no simple uniformity:

> Racial and ethnic groups have been shown by many studies to have widely varying delinquency rates. The Negro delinquency rate, for example, is exceptionally high. Estimates of the number of delinquents among Negroes range from about twice to about five times as high as would be expected on the basis of the proportion of Negroes in the total population. Puerto Ricans, Mexicans, and American Indians likewise have been found to have especially high delinquency rates. Orientals have usually been found to comprise a lower portion of all delinquents than their proportion in the total population [Cohen and Short, 1961, p. 86].

Here too there seems to be some bias at work. In one study of delinquent boys, for instance:

> The case records of 300 institutionalized delinquents—179 Negro, 121 white—were analyzed to determine whether the courts were committing Negro and white children on the same bases. . . . The study discloses that Negro children are committed younger, for less serious offenses, with fewer previous court appearances, and with less prior institutionalization. . . . [In addition] there appears to be a tendency for the white delinquent to be afforded a larger number of probationary periods prior to institutionalization than is the case with the Negro delinquent [Axelrad, 1952, pp. 570, 574].

.6   in urban areas.

However, with the leveling out resulting from modern transportation and communication, the urban-rural difference is lessening. Within the city, there is relatively more criminal and delinquent behavior in the deteriorated areas, in the areas housing transitory populations, and in the areas housing people of mixed origins. Here is a sociological explanation:

> In general, these areas are characterized by one or more of the basic conditions that lead to a low degree of normative integration. In some of these areas there are substantial numbers of people living in relative isolation from primary groups. The hypothesis has been advanced that social isolation leads to deviant behavior, since the isolated individual lacks the direction sanctions of the group. The individual is not expected to conform closely to the norms of groups of which he is not a communicating member. This hypothesis has been used to "explain" certain types of suicide and mental disorder. The areas with high rates of deviant behavior are also frequently characterized by the existence of groups with norms deviant from those of the larger community. Many persons whose behavior is deviant in terms of the norms of the larger community or society are conforming to the norms of such deviant subgroups. . . . The areas with high deviant rates are also likely to be those in which cultural conflict is high. They contain many persons who are members of several groups with conflicting group

norms. Immigrants and their children have often been concentrated in those areas. Children born to such culturally marginal persons acquire ambiguous definitions of the norms in the process of socialization [Freedman *et al.*, 1956, pp. 455–56].

.7   among the less religious.

The rate of crime is lower for people who actually go to church regularly; it is not lower for people who merely hold orthodox beliefs. The rate is higher for Catholics and lower for Protestants and Jews in all countries, though this is partly due to class differences. Catholics have a particularly high rate for crimes of violence, while Protestants have a slightly above-average rate for sexual offences and Jews for fraud. Suicide is lowest for Catholics, highest for Protestants [Argyle, 1958, p. 100].

.8   in "normal" times rather than in times of war or disaster.

In time of war, disaster, and physical calamity, as has often been noted, crimes, suicides, divorces, and community conflicts tend to diminish in number. Within a military organization itself there is a sudden reduction of tensions and delinquencies when war comes [Nisbet, 1961, p. 5].

In addition, there is evidence to the effect that there are fewer burglaries and robberies in times of prosperity.

However,

> **E2a**   So far as personality or intelligence or physique are concerned, there does not seem to be a "criminal type"—but the evidence is by no means clear-cut.

Here is a summary of an intensive review of the empirical evidence:

During the last twenty-five years objective personality tests have been widely used to investigate differences between criminals and noncriminals. Of 113 such comparisons [in thirty tests], 42 per cent showed differences in favor of the noncriminals, while the remainder were indeterminate. The doubtful validity of many of the obtained differences, as well as the lack of consistency in the combined results, makes it impossible to conclude from these data that criminality and personality elements are associated [Schuessler and Cressey, 1950, abstract, p. 476].

The authors go on to point out various technical deficiencies of the studies that make it difficult to draw positive conclusions from them: e.g., doubtful causal relations, inadequate sampling, questions as to validity of the measures, noncomparability, and so on. At the same time, several experts believe that personality—in the form, say, of weak character or conscience—is a predisposing factor, given the appropriate social environment. As for intelligence:

E. H. Sutherland (1931) analyzed about 350 reports on mental tests of criminals and . . . concluded that the delinquent population closely resembles the general population in intelligence scores and that feebleminded persons in the community at large do not show excessive rates of delinquency. These conclusions are consistent with Carl Murchison's statistical analysis in 1926, and with Simon H. Tulchin's analysis in 1939. They represent an almost complete retraction of the early conclusion that mentally defective persons are overrepresented in groups having high crime rates [Cressey, 1961, pp. 50–51].

Some students believe that somatotype (body build) matters: a tendency toward delinquency among mesomorphs (muscle and bone predominating) as against endomorphs (soft roundness), ectomorphs (linearity and fragility), or balanced physiques (Glueck and Glueck, 1956).

A number of prediction studies have been done in the field of criminology, with regard not only to the prediction of criminal or delinquent behavior but of the observance of parole regulations as well. For a detailed review of them, see Glueck and Glueck, 1959, Appendix A. Here is one of the better-known prediction efforts:

Extent of agreement among social, Rorschach, and psychiatric prediction tables in placing 424 boys (205 delinquents and 219 nondelinquents) in their proper predictive category

Description	Number	Per cent
Three tables correctly identify boy as delinquent	86	20.2
Three tables correctly identify boy as nondelinquent	122	28.8
Two of the three tables correctly identify boy as delinquent	80	18.9
Two of the three tables correctly identify boy as nondelinquent	80	18.9
Two of the three tables incorrectly identify boy as delinquent	31	7.3
Two of the three tables incorrectly identify boy as nondelinquent	15	3.5
Three tables incorrectly identify boy as delinquent	8	1.9
Three tables incorrectly identify boy as nondelinquent	2	0.5
Total	424	100.0

(Glueck and Glueck, 1950, p. 268)

E3   The fact that several of the disposing characteristics (listed in E2) are constant, combined with the fact of reinforcing experience for convicted criminals while in jail, results in high rates of recidivism: about three-fourths of those entering jail have been there before. And the younger the person at the time of first offense, the higher the rate of recidivism and the sooner it occurs.

E4   The efficacy of various treatments for the control of delinquency has not been established.

In a large-scale test of the effectiveness of psychological counselors over a period of years, with matched samples of treated and nontreated boys, it was found that despite the strong belief of the counselors that they were effective, there were essentially no differences in terminal adjustment or in delinquent or, subsequently, in criminal behavior between the two groups (Powers and Witmer, 1951; follow-up study by McCord and McCord, 1959). For example, here are the terminal ratings:

**Distribution of T-boys and their C-twins by
terminal adjustment ratings**

Terminal adjustment	Treated	Control
1. Good adjustment	46	52
2a. Fairly good	38	42
2b. Fairly good; neurotic type	21	16
3a. Rather poor	11	9
3b. Rather poor; neurotic type	12	10
4a. Definitely poor	4	4
4b. Definitely poor; neurotic, psychotic, neurological disorder	7	4
4c. Definitely poor; chronic delinquent	9	11
Total number of cases	148	148

(Powers and Witmer, 1951, p. 414)

Even granted a certain amount of inaccuracy in the ratings (an inaccuracy that obtained to some extent in the treated series as well as in the control), it would appear difficult to maintain that the presence of Study services made any great difference in the terminal adjustment of the T-boys [*ibid.*, p. 414].

With regard to extensive interview therapy as well as area projects and so-called progressive programs within detention institutions, here are the conclusions of a recent review:

[There is] little evidence that interview therapy significantly affects delinquent behavior. . . . It is the impression of those who have dedicated themselves to the promotion and guidance of these projects that they have reduced delinquency in high rate areas . . . but the fact remains that the effectiveness of these programs has yet to be demonstrated. . . . *All* institutions have fairly high rates of recidivism, and it is still not definitely known how much more effective *any* of them is than the available alternatives, including the alternative of "doing nothing" [Cohen and Short, 1961, pp. 121, 124, 123].

E5   The death penalty does not appear to influence the rate of homicide.

Here are some data and the conclusions from a careful and thorough analysis of the matter:

Rates of police homicide (per 100,000 population)

Capital punishment states		Abolition states	
Connecticut	0.5	Maine	0.0
Illinois	1.1	Michigan	1.3
Indiana	2.3	Minnesota	1.5
Iowa	2.0	North Dakota	1.9
Massachusetts	0.8	Rhode Island	0.6
Montana	5.7	Wisconsin	1.2
New Hampshire	0.5		
New York	0.9		
Ohio	2.2		
South Dakota	0.0		
Vermont	0.0		
Total (182 cities)	1.3	Total (82 cities)	1.2

(Sellin, 1959, p. 56)

We have examined comparatively . . . rates in selected states that do and those that do not have the death penalty; we have compared the rates of capital crimes in specific states or countries that have experimented with abolition in order to observe the effect of the abolition or the introduction of capital punishment on such rates; we have noted the specific effect of highly publicized executions on homicides in a metropolitan city; and we have tried to learn if the claim of the police is true, when they say that their lives are safer in states that have the death penalty. Anyone who carefully examines the above data is bound to arrive at the conclusion that the death penalty, as we use it, exercises no influence on the extent or fluctuating rates of capital crimes. It has failed as a deterrent [*ibid.*, p. 63].

PROSTITUTION, ADDICTION, SUICIDE

E6   Prostitution occurs in almost every human society.

Prostitution is virtually universal, found everywhere except perhaps in some of the very simplest primitive communities [Davis, 1961a, p. 272].

E6.1   The greater the sexual freedom of women, the less prostitution.

There can be little doubt that during the present century in industrial societies a rise in feminine sex freedom has occurred, especially among the single, widowed, and divorced. . . . With the greater availability of ordinary women for sexual companionship, we should expect the role of the prostitute, in both volume and status, to decline. This is what the available evidence seems to show. . . . Kinsey finds that what the male has lost in frequency of intercourse with prostitutes he has gained in frequency with non-prostitutes [*ibid.,* pp. 282–83].

E7   Drug addiction in the United States occurs particularly among men, among those in the personal service and entertainment occupations, among those in the socially disorganized sections of a very few of the largest cities (where deviants from conventional morality tend to cluster), and among Negroes and Puerto Ricans.

This represents a shift from the pre-World War II picture, when drug addicts were older, less resident in metropolitan areas, and more native-white than is now the case.

The areas of highest rates of drug use tend to be inhabited by the most disadvantaged minority groups and by the least successful or most deviant members of other population groups. These are the areas with the highest rates of adult crime, the highest rates of prostitution and illegitimacy, the highest prevalence of infant mortality and of tuberculosis, the highest proportion of broken families and of non-family living arrangements. They have high population density and high population turnover. . . . A high proportion of the families lacks a stable male head [Clausen, 1961a, pp. 194–95].

E8   There is more drinking in societies caught in a struggle for subsistence; in societies generally more permissive (e.g., those with fewer sexual restrictions); by members of deprived minority groups (e.g., Negroes and Indians in the United States); by people from broken marriages; and by members of certain religious groups.

With regard to this last:

The religious orientation of the family seems to have some bearing on whether and how their offspring will drink. The incidence of drinkers is greater in the more permissive religious groups (e.g., Jews and Catholics as opposed to, say, Mormons), but when those who belong to the less permissive groups take up drinking, Straus and Bacon (1953) say that they are less apt to be temperate about it [Winch, 1957, p. 365].

With regard to the behavioral correlates of alcoholism in individuals, there is some evidence to the effect that sons who reject harsh fathers are more inclined to become alcoholics (McCord and McCord, 1960).

E9   The greater the integration of a human group (and the less that conflict is believed to be normal within it), the less the amount of suicide or attempted suicide within that group.

Thus, the stronger the ties of family or of other groups important to the individual, the less the tendency to suicide. For example, children of broken homes are more disposed to attempt suicide; so are rural males living in the urban-rural fringe and employed in urban occupations; so are residents of the central, socially disorganized sections of large cities. There is some evidence that suicide is more frequent among those social categories with few people in them, thus making personal interaction difficult; for example, among Orientals in the United States or among those older people who are not married and among the very young who are.

This tendency to suicide in cases of social disorganization (illustrated further in the list below) is especially marked, apparently, if no socially approved alternative ways of life are available with supporting groups. "Nadel (1951) has argued that the less tolerant a culture is of misfits and the fewer the socially approved ways of living offered, the greater the predisposition to suicide" (Kluckhohn, 1954, p. 945).

E10   As compared in each case with their counterparts, suicide is more likely (mainly in the United States):

.1   among men.

.2   among the older.

.3   among whites.

.4   among the secular, and among Protestants as against Catholics or Jews.

This was first documented and explained by a great pioneer on this subject:

> If religion protects man against the desire for self-destruction, it is not that it preaches the respect for his own person to him with arguments *sui generis;* but because it is a society. What constitutes this society is the existence of a certain number of beliefs and practices common to all the faithful, traditional and thus obligatory. The more numerous and strong these collective states of mind are, the stronger the integration of the religious community, and also the greater its preservative value. The details of dogmas and rites are secondary. The essential thing is that they be capable of supporting a sufficiently intense collective life. And because the Protestant church has less consistency than the others it has less moderating effect upon suicide. . . . [And this is a special case of] the general conclusion: suicide varies inversely with the degree of integration of the social groups of which the individual forms a part [Durkheim, 1958 edition, pp. 170, 209].

.5   in the city (although this difference is also flattening out with the leveling influences of recent decades).

.6   among the single, divorced, and widowed.

.7 among the extremes in occupational status: the very high and the very low.

.8 in times of economic depression, especially for people of higher socioeconomic status; in addition, there is less suicide during wartime.

As for level of civilization:

Until such time as we have something other than impressionistic accounts of suicide in nonliterate and other non-European societies any cross-cultural generalization is suspect. For the time being one tentative conclusion is that the suicide rates of nonliterate peoples are probably low on the average, but also that the rates for some of them now exceed or have exceeded those of several European countries [Gibbs, 1961, pp. 233–34].

E11 Suicide and homicide appear to be inversely related, by cities and other regions.

There is some evidence that this relationship holds across countries:

If we assume that the Scandinavian culture is relatively introvert, there should be a high rate of self-destructive acts such as suicide and alcoholism in Scandinavian countries. If we assume that the Mediterranean culture is relatively extrovert, there should be a high rate of other-destructive acts as homicide and assaults in Mediterranean countries. (The evidence supports these presumptions.) What is suggested is that the high rate of suicide in the three Scandinavian countries is partly due to the tendency for social conflicts to be expressed as personal conflicts, and vice versa for Latin countries [Galtung, 1958, p. 40].

This inverse relationship was recently explained in this way:

When behavior is required to conform rigidly to the demands and expectations of other persons, the probability of suicide as a response to frustration is low and the probability of homicide as a response to frustration is high. When behavior is freed from the requirement for conformity to the demands and expectations of others, the probability of suicide is high and the probability of homicide is low [Henry and Short, 1954, pp. 101–02].

As a corollary of the main finding: whereas suicide rates are low in times of prosperity and high in times of depression, the opposite is the case for homicide rates.

MENTAL ILLNESS

E12 Mental illness occurs in all societies, but what is defined as mental illness ranges considerably from one society to another and even from one segment of a society to another, and so do the symptoms and the duration of the episodes of mental illness. In most societies there is a stigma attached to mental illness that is not present in the case of physical illness.

A recent critical review of this literature suggested that the one conclusion warranted was that "the mental disorders known to Western psychiatry do occur among primitive peoples throughout the world" [Clausen, 1961b, p. 160, citing Benedict and Jacks, 1954].

As for differences in symptoms,

The hostility of the "primitive" psychotic is much more likely to be directed outward, that of the individual from the Jewish-Christian tradition inward. Paranoid schizophrenia and paranoid forms of mental illness in general appear to be relatively infrequent in nonliterate societies—or at any rate, they are less frequently recognized. Depression is extremely rare in some "primitive" groups, notably the African Negroes [Kluckhohn, 1954, p. 947, citing Benedict and Jacks, 1954].

With regard to the stigmatizing character of severe mental illness:

The tendency toward normalizing deviant behavior and denying the existence of mental illness is . . . clearly illustrated in a study of the interpretations made by wives confronted by the mental illness of the husband. Grossly psychotic symptoms are often interpreted as reflections of physical illness, as "understandable" reactions to situational stress or as indications of meanness or weakness in the spouse. Communications of the wife to relatives and friends frequently conceal the nature of the husband's illness or minimize its severity. Many of these wives deny that they regard mental illness as a stigma; but their communications clearly reflect their belief that others so regard it [Clausen, 1956, p. 14].

Although some work has recently been done, and is being done, on the incidence and prevalence of mental disorders in the general population, it is still a little hazardous to cite specific figures. However, a recent survey reported that, for the United States, "the prevalence of psychoneuroses is variously estimated at from 5 per cent of the population on up to perhaps 25 per cent" (Clausen, 1961b, p. 137).

And a large-scale, intensive survey of Midtown Manhattan, a section of New York City, published too late for full inclusion in this inventory, found that about 20–25 per cent of the adult residents of the district had an array of symptoms similar to those accepted for treatment, across the range from private practitioners to mental hospitals. About 3 per cent were fully or severely "incapacitated" in their daily life by mental disturbance and another 7.5 per cent showed "severe symptom formation" (Srole et al., 1962).

E12.1   At least some psychotic disorders are associated with, or even caused by, hereditary factors.

The data accumulated from the research of geneticists and genetically-oriented psychiatrists suggest that heredity definitely plays a part in the etiology of some schizophrenic disorders. . . . The incidence of the disease over a lifetime is about 1 per cent for the general population, but for children who have a schizophrenic parent it is 10–12 per cent and for brothers or sisters of a schizo-

phrenic it is 10–15 per cent. Since, however, the effects of heredity and environment are both operative in family lines, the most impressive evidence of a genetic
factor in schizophrenia is that which rests upon comparisons of fraternal and
identical twins. . . . If one of two identical twins develops schizophrenia, the
chances that his co-twin will also become schizophrenic are at least two in three
(different studies indicate from 65–85 per cent concordance for schizophrenia)
[Clausen, 1961b, p. 162].

E13   Over the past century in the United States—during a period of great
industrialization and urbanization—there has been no increase in the incidence of psychotic behavior by age group, up to age fifty, at least as indicated by rates of hospitalization.

Here are some of the data and conclusions from a pioneering study in
the field:

**Male and female age-specific first-admission rates, Massachusetts,
1885, and age-specific first-admission (with mental disorder)
rates, Massachusetts, 1917–40**

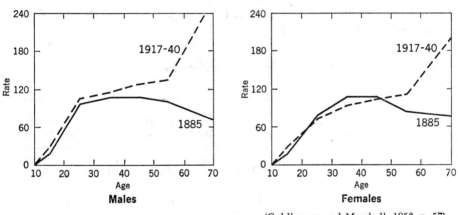

(Goldhamer and Marshall, 1953, p. 57)

When appropriate comparisons are made which equate the class of patients received and the conditions affecting hospitalization of the mentally ill, age-specific first-admission rates for ages under 50 are revealed to be just as high during
the last half of the 19th century as they are today.
   There has been a very marked increase in the age-specific admission rates in
the older age groups. The greater part of this increase seems almost certainly to
be due to an increased tendency to hospitalize persons suffering from the mental
diseases of the senium. However, there is a possibility that some of the increase
may be due to an actual increase in the incidence of arteriosclerosis [*ibid.*, p. 91].

E13.1   If the stress of wartime has any effect on the rate of mental disorder, it is to lower it.

Furthermore:

E14   There is probably as much mental illness in highly integrated, homogeneous communities as in those with diverse or conflicting values.

A critical study here dealt with the amount and kind of mental illness among the Hutterites, "a society whose members share over four centuries of common history, tradition, and faith, and are bound together by many close kinship ties" (Eaton, 1955, p. 208). As a result of a thorough enumeration of the entire community, the study concludes that

> our findings do not confirm the hypothesis that a simple and relatively uncomplicated way of life provides virtual immunity from mental disorders. . . . Psychoses and other forms of mental disorder were found to occur with regularity in the Hutterite population [*ibid.,* p. 209].

Incidentally, the authors suggest that their results support the idea of organic, genetic factors predisposing toward mental illness. The tabulation below shows the Hutterite psychosis rate as third highest,

> but the true rank order is probably much lower, when allowance was made for known methodological shortcomings of the enumeration procedures of the different studies [*ibid.,* p. 211].

Comparison of ten lifetime morbidity surveys of psychoses by the standard expectancy method

Survey	Total population	Actual number of cases found (a)	Expected number of cases (e)		Expectancy ratios (a/e)	
			Hutterite norms	New York State norms	Hutterite norms	New York State norms
Arctic Norwegian village	1,325	38	19	26	1.97	1.43
North Swedish area	8,651	107	94	141	1.14	.76
Ethnic Hutterites	8,542	53	53	85	1.00	.62
Bornholm Island	45,694	481	773	1,049	.62	.46
Baltimore Eastern Health District	55,129	507	822	1,144	.62	.44
Williamson County, Tennessee	24,804	156	271	502	.58	.31
West Swedish island	8,735	94	186	260	.51	.36
Bavarian villages, Rosenheim area	3,203	21	49	84	.43	.25
Formosa area	19,913	76	194	273	.39	.28
Thuringia villages	37,546	200	617	841	.32	.24

(*Ibid.,* p. 75)

The notion that social isolation, especially in childhood and youth, pre-disposes to severe mental illness is not clearly supported by the available evidence (but see pp. 66 ff.).

E15   Mental illness is perhaps slightly higher in urban than in rural areas—although this difference may be due simply to reporting differences and to differences in the way of handling such behavior (for example, more inclination in rural areas to keep a grandparent with senile psychosis at home than to hospitalize him).

E15.1   Within the city, the rates of hospitalization for mental disorder are highest in the central area of high population movement, low status, and mixed population, and least in the high status residential areas.

E16   At least in the United States, mental illness is more prevalent in the lower classes than the upper; more severe there; less likely to be treated; and, when treated, more likely to receive custodial or organic therapy than psychotherapy.

For example, here are some data on treatment received, from a study in New Haven, Connecticut:

Principal type of psychiatric therapy received by neurotic patients, by class (percentages)

	Class			
Type of treatment	I–II (*high*)	III	IV	V (*low*)
Classical analysis and analytic psychotherapy	46.9	20.9	5.1	4.1
Directive psychotherapy	50.0	62.6	69.7	54.1
Group psychotherapy	1.0	2.6	2.9	8.2
Organic therapy (shock, drugs, operations)	2.0	9.6	16.6	9.8
Custodial care	0.0	4.3	5.7	23.0
Total number of cases	(98)	(115)	(175)	(61)

$x^2 = 128.72$, 9 df, $p = .001$ *

* Directive and group psychotherapy combined for x^2 analysis.

(Hollingshead and Redlich, 1958, p. 267)

In addition, there is a tendency for the psychiatrist to see lower-class people as sicker than middle- or upper-class members, largely because of the divergence from his own background and values, and to give them less time and attention.

We may indulge ourselves in the following generalizations as viewed by the psychiatrist: the class V neurotic behaves badly, the class IV neurotic aches physically, the class III patient defends fearfully, and the class I–II patient is dissatisfied with himself [*ibid.*, p. 240].

Indeed, this finding can be applied to the field of health generally:

Recent studies in intracultural situations, both in this country and in other societies, indicate a tendency for extrinsic class considerations to overshadow intrinsic therapeutic considerations in the relation between professional and patient. Preliminary findings suggest that the degree to which the qualities considered essential to the therapeutic relationship, namely, mutual trust, respect, and cooperation, are present in a given professional-patient relationship varies inversely with the social distance between the participants. Conversely, the greater the social distance, the less likely the participants will be to perceive each other in terms of the ideal roles of professional and patient, and the more likely to perceive each other in terms of their class status in the larger society [Simmons, 1958, pp. 17–18].

There is also some evidence to the effect that the type of psychosis or neurosis, as diagnosed by the psychiatrist, tends to vary by socioeconomic class in the following ways:

Psychosis	*Neurosis*
Affective psychoses more frequent in upper class	Character neuroses, obsessive-compulsives and depressives more frequent in upper class
Organic psychoses and schizophrenia greater in lower class	Antisocial and immature reactions, phobia and anxiety, psychosomatic and hysterical reactions more frequent in lower class

E16.1   Sharp social mobility does seem to produce neurotic reactions, but the evidence with regard to more severe disturbance is unclear.

E16.2   Mental illness appears to be more prevalent in deprived minority groups than in the population at large, but that relationship is overlaid with differences in social class. (There do not appear to be differences by generation in the United States, from immigrant to third generation.)

SELECTED READINGS

Since this topic includes a collection of fields that have their own separate literatures, it might be best to begin with some recent reviews in rather brief form and work out from there. All of the following have bibliographies that reach far into the literature.

From Joseph B. Gittler, ed. *Review of Sociology: Analysis of a Decade.* Wiley, 1957:

Howard W. Beers. "The Rural Community," pp. 186–220.
Marshall B. Clinard. "The Sociology of Delinquency and Crime," pp. 465–99.
Noel P. Gist. "The Urban Community," pp. 159–85.
Clyde V. Kiser. "Population Research," pp. 56–86.

From Robert K. Merton *et al.,* eds. *Sociology Today: Problems and Prospects.* Basic Books, 1959:

C. Arnold Anderson. "Trends in Rural Sociology," pp. 360–75.
John A. Clausen. "The Sociology of Mental Illness," pp. 485–508.
Marshall B. Clinard. "Criminological Research," pp. 509–36.
Albert K. Cohen. "The Study of Social Disorganization and Deviant Behavior," pp. 461–84.
Kingsley Davis. "The Sociology of Demographic Behavior," pp. 309–33.
Gideon Sjoberg. "Comparative Urban Sociology," pp. 334–59.

From Robert K. Merton and Robert A. Nisbet, eds. *Contemporary Social Problems.* Harcourt, Brace & World, 1961:

John A. Clausen. "Drug Addiction," pp. 181–221.
John A. Clausen. "Mental Disorders," pp. 127–80.
Albert K. Cohen and James F. Short, Jr. "Juvenile Delinquency," pp. 77–126.
James S. Coleman. "Community Disorganization," pp. 553–604.
Donald R. Cressey. "Crime," pp. 21–76.
Kingsley Davis. "Prostitution," pp. 262–90.
Kingsley Davis. "The World's Population Crisis," pp. 291–323.
Charles E. Fritz. "Disaster," pp. 651–94.
Jack P. Gibbs. "Suicide," pp. 222–61.

In addition, a recent, thoroughgoing review of the whole field of population, with articles on all the demographic matters included here, should be mentioned, together with another survey of that field:

Philip Hauser and Otis Dudley Duncan, eds. *The Study of Population: An Inventory and Appraisal.* U. of Chicago Press, 1959.
United Nations. Department of Social Affairs, Population Division. *The Determinants and Consequences of Population Trends: A Summary of the Findings of Studies on the Relationships Between Population Changes and Economic and Social Conditions.* United Nations, 1953.

Finally, a recent review of the literature on social change:

Gilbert Kushner *et al. What Accounts for Sociocultural Change? A Propositional Inventory.* Institute for Research in Social Science, U. of North Carolina, 1962.

As for specific studies, a number of major titles are cited in this section and can be located through the bibliography.

It is true, that what is settled by custom, though it be not good, yet at least it is fit, and those things which have long gone together, are, as it were, confederate within themselves; whereas new things piece not so well; but, though they help by their utility, yet they trouble by their inconformity: besides, they are like strangers, more admired, and less favored.

FRANCIS BACON
Of Innovations

Laws are coldly reasoned out and established upon what the lawmakers believe to be a basis of right. But customs are not. Customs are not enacted, they grow gradually up, imperceptibly and unconsciously, like an oak from its seed. In the fullness of their strength they can stand up straight in front of a world of argument and reasoning, and yield not an inch. We do not know how or when it became custom for women to wear long hair, we only know that in this country it *is* custom, and that settles it. Maybe it is right, maybe it is wrong—that has nothing to do with the matter; customs do not concern themselves with right or wrong or reason. But they have to be obeyed; one may reason all around them until he is tired, but he must not transgress them, it is sternly forbidden. Women may shave their heads elsewhere, but here they must refrain or take the uncomfortable consequences. Laws are sand, customs are rock. Laws can be evaded and punishment escaped, but an openly transgressed custom brings sure punishment. The penalty may be unfair, unrighteous, illogical, and a cruelty; no matter, it will be inflicted, just the same. Certainly, then, there can be but one wise thing for a visiting stranger to do— find out what the country's customs are, and refrain from offending against them. . . . Custom is custom; it is built of brass, boiler iron, granite; facts, reasonings, arguments have no more effect upon it than the idle winds have upon Gibraltar.

SAMUEL L. CLEMENS
Letters from the Earth

In their working, and in much of their emotional life, their attitudes are closer to other scientists than to non-scientists who in religion or politics or class have the same labels as themselves. If I were to risk a piece of shorthand, I should say that naturally they had the future in their bones.

They may or may not like it, but they have it. That was as true of the conservatives J. J. Thomson and Lindemann as of the radicals Einstein or Blackett: as true of the Christian A. J. Compton as of the materialist Bernal: of the aristocrats Broglie or Russell as of the proletarian Faraday: of those born rich, like Thomas Merton or Victor Rothschild, as of Rutherford, who was the son of an odd-job handyman. Without thinking about it, they respond alike. That is what a culture means.

C. P. SNOW
The Two Cultures and the Scientific Revolution

Chapter Sixteen
CULTURE

Almost everything discussed in this book is conditioned by culture: ways of learning, types of personality, the organization of the family or the economy, the distribution of classes, the relations among ethnic groups. Since almost everything human is conditioned by culture, it follows that the preceding chapters have been dealing with culture in one way or another. Hence, what remains here is to treat the topic in a residual fashion.

What is left to present about culture are those findings which deal with culture per se—with the nature of culture, with certain cultural processes, and with relations among cultures. It is important to stress this limitation in order to make quite clear what is being attempted here, namely, to put forward the residual findings that deal with the global character of culture. And it is almost needless to add that we do not try to present here, as such, the numerous ethnographic reports on individual societies or cultures. (It is only fair to the field to note here that neither of us is an anthropologist, so we may not have come as close to the target here as in other chapters.)

DEFINITIONS

Culture: It is perhaps more presumptuous here than elsewhere in this book for us to attempt a brief definition of an important term. About a decade ago, two distinguished anthropologists, A. L. Kroeber and Clyde Kluckhohn, put forward a 223-page paper, "Culture: A Critical Review of Concepts and Definitions," in which they analyzed in great detail a total of 164 definitions. It would be appropriate to quote here their summary definition, but they did not offer one:

We do not propose to add a one hundred and sixty-fifth formal definition. . . . We think it is premature to attempt encapsulation in a brief abstract statement

643

which would include or imply all of the elements that seem to us to be involved. . . . Without pretending to "define," however, we think it proper to say at the end of this summary discussion of definitions that we believe each of our principal groups of definitions points to something legitimate and important. In other words, we think culture is a product; is historical; includes ideas, patterns, and values; is selective; is learned; is based upon symbols; and is an abstraction from behavior and the products of behavior [Kroeber and Kluckhohn, 1952, p. 157].

Expressed in that statement is the general idea of culture: the abstracted nonbiological conditions of human life—"artifacts, sociofacts, mentifacts." A man is immersed in a culture, or in cultures, from birth to death. The human organism becomes a human being through participation in culture. (The anthropological use of the term, of course, is not at all equivalent to the aesthetic meaning of the term. Shakespeare's plays and Beethoven's symphonies are manifestations of culture in both senses, but the anthropological meaning also includes the ways of making the stone ax and the turbine, the idea of justice and tolerance of cross-cousin marriage, primitive language and the behavioral sciences.)

This notion is so central to the behavioral sciences that something more must be said, by way of emphasis. Human culture is made up both of conscious and nonconscious elements—the latter being the so-called implicit or covert culture that is so much taken for granted as to be considered natural and not appreciated until broken. As Kroeber and Kluckhohn say:

All cultures are largely made up of overt, patterned ways of behaving, feeling, and reacting. But cultures likewise include a characteristic set of unstated premises and categories ("implicit culture") which vary greatly between societies. Thus one group unconsciously and habitually assumes that every chain of actions has a goal and that when this goal is reached tension will be reduced or disappear. To another group, thinking based upon this assumption is by no means automatic. They see life not primarily as a series of purposive sequences but more as made up of disparate experiences which may be satisfying in and of themselves, rather than as means to ends [ibid., p. 157].

Culture is shared with other people. It influences not only how one behaves but how one expects others to behave toward him: "What kinds of behavior the individual anticipates being rewarded or punished for; what constitutes rewards and punishments; what types of activity are held to be inherently gratifying or frustrating" (ibid., p. 157).

Culture is learned behavior. For the most part, it is learned early in life and invested with a good deal of emotion: "The individual is seldom emotionally neutral to those sectors of his culture which touch him directly. Culture patterns are felt, emotionally adhered to or rejected" (ibid., p. 157). Deviations from the going culture usually cost something in comfort, status, peace of mind, safety, or some other value.

Culture is built "on top" of man's biological equipment—although, as we shall see, it can affect physiological matters as well as social and psychological ones.

Heredity gives us at birth certain generic human faculties. How we shall use these, and therefore how we shall mainly live, the culture in which we are launched thereupon decides. But it leaves us, theoretically at least, certain choices between alternatives in its total scheme; and it leaves us also a degree of freedom of departure from its norms in personal mannerisms, innovations, and successes [Kroeber, 1948, p. 290].

Man has to eat to live, but whether he eats steak or snails will be determined by his culture. He has to sleep, but there are cultural patterns for that too: *we* typically sleep eight hours a day, all at one time, at night. He has to engage in sexual relations for reproductive purposes, but sexual practice varies widely by culture. Even some of his physical reactions are given meaning by culture: a lump in the throat becomes sorrow, a tightening of the skin fear, a certain feeling in the stomach fright, a certain movement of the mouth a smile.

A culture hangs together; the parts fit one another, at least roughly.

Cultures are constantly and automatically acquiring or reacquiring a sort of integration. But this is a very different thing from the organic integration that holds together, say, a grasshopper or a rabbit. This organic integration involves a pattern of finished animal that is essentially predetermined when two germ cells unite to start a new individual. Cultural integration—or for that matter human social integration—is invariably of a much looser sort. It is an accommodation of discrete parts, largely inflowing parts, into a more or less workable fit. It is not a growth of parts unfolding from a germ in accord with a pre-existing harmonious master plan [*ibid.*, p. 287].

Culture can refer to a scope both broader and narrower than a single society. Thus, on the broader basis we can speak of the elements of Western culture that are shared beyond the boundaries of the United States or of Italy or of any other society in the Western world. On the narrower basis, it has become fashionable in the behavioral sciences recently to speak of *subcultures:* the ways of behaving peculiar to a particular group within a larger one. Thus, there are subcultures for longshoremen, professional baseball players, university professors, members of the beat generation, inmates of a prison, Texas oilmen, a boys' gang, the world of fashion, jazz musicians, behavioral scientists, and any other group of some size. An individual can simultaneously live in and be affected by more than one culture.

In short, it is fair to say that whereas all of human behavior is in some sense physiologically or biologically based, only a small part of it is physiologically or biologically determined. For the rest, there are the perceptions, the definitions of the situation, the interpretations, the values, the responses, the manners, the language, the religions, and the philosophies that are "given" at any moment by the culture.

> In the whole gamut of social relations human beings behave as they do not just by virtue of their properties as unique biological organisms and not just in terms of inevitably human response to their situations, but because they have learned and accepted certain artificial conventions current in a particular culture [Kluckhohn, 1953, p. 31].

By way of summary, here is the original and classical definition of the term: "That complex whole which includes knowledge, belief, art, morals, law, custom, and any other capabilities and habits acquired by man as a member of society" (Tylor, 1891, p. 1).

Acculturation and assimilation: The process of learning a culture different from the one in which a person was originally raised is called acculturation. Thus, an immigrant leaving a peasant life in Poland and moving to New York City has to face acculturation in the new land. So, perhaps to a lesser extent, does a Southern Negro farmer or a Kentucky mountaineer when he gets a job on a Detroit assembly line. So does a lower-class child when he enters a middle-class school. Learning the first culture is sometimes called socialization, sometimes enculturation. Learning other cultures is called acculturation, and the term is usually used for movement across widely different cultures rather than for movement from one subculture to another within a parent society.

The process of an outsider's being accepted as a genuine member of a new social group is called assimilation. One is acculturated to a culture, assimilated into a society. As we shall see, one process can occur without the other.

FINDINGS

A1 Despite their great differences in other respects, all cultures have a number of characteristics in common—the so-called cultural universals.

Partly, of course, this depends on the generality of the system of classification used. But here are some important characteristics, as examples: marriage and the family, systems of counting, incest taboos, deference to parents, use of all three personal pronouns, such psychological states as "happiness" or "sadness," general prohibitions on murder or lying or stealing (at least so far as comembers are concerned). Some years ago, an American anthropologist presented

> a partial list of [73] items, arranged in alphabetical order to emphasize their variety, which occur, so far as the author's knowledge goes, in every culture

known to history or ethnography: age-grading, athletic sports, bodily adornment, calendar, cleanliness training, community organization, cooking, cooperative labor, cosmology, courtship, dancing, decorative art, divination, division of labor, dream interpretation, education, eschatology, ethics, ethnobotany, etiquette, faith healing, family, feasting, fire making, folklore, food taboos, funeral rites, games, gestures, gift giving, government, greetings, hair styles, hospitality, housing, hygiene, incest taboos, inheritance rules, joking, kin-groups, kinship nomenclature, language, law, luck superstitions, magic, marriage, mealtimes, medicine, modesty concerning natural functions, mourning, music, mythology, numerals, obstetrics, penal sanctions, personal names, population policy, postnatal care, pregnancy usages, property rights, propitiation of supernatural beings, puberty customs, religious ritual, residence rules, sexual restrictions, soul concepts, status differentiation, surgery, tool making, trade, visiting, weaning, and weather control [Murdock, 1945, p. 124].

Now it is apparent that many of these so-called universals are quite general in character. For example, marriage exists in all cultures, but takes many different forms, and so does housing or hygiene or tool-making or deference given to parents or many of the others on the list. Some of them are closely related to biological requirements: weaning, obstetrics, postnatal care, natural functions. Some are quite formal: no known human languages "lack 'words' beginning with consonants, although there are some that do not permit 'words' beginning with vowels" (Kluckhohn, 1954, p. 952). Some items are still in dispute: there are scholars who believe that the stress toward closure is present in all cultures, but others do not agree. Many of the cultural universals are there because they help to provide for human survival:

Each human language . . . must be one which every normal member of the group can learn to speak; each culturally patterned dietary must provide for human growth; each family and community system must provide for the care of human children during their long dependency and for their education, must regulate the patterns of mating and of competition, and must pattern the behavior of members of the social group [Mead, 1958, p. 482].

Some people like to define such cultural universals as making up "true" human nature, since they appear as part of the human condition everywhere. But again their generality in most cases argues against placing much weight on this notion. It is probably closer to the scholar's view of the matter to think of "human nature," if one wishes to go beyond the biological base, as being extremely plastic in character and capable of taking a large number of forms under the pressure of the culture learned in infancy and childhood.

Among the most important cultural universals is language. Although anthropologists have done a good deal of impressive work on historical and structural linguistics, we have considered that field too specialized and technical for inclusion in this inventory.

A2   Marked differences in cultural prescriptions, and hence in human behavior, are found not only for clearly social or psychological matters such as etiquette or religious values or social organization, but also for behaviors closely tied to the physiological equipment of man.

Fatigue, tolerance to physical pain, conditions affecting nausea, appetite, the rhythm of evacuation, the means for sexual arousal, fineness in perceiving colors, motor gestures—all of these vary markedly among cultures. In addition, there are some interesting borderline cases, such as speech disability:

> The fact that I have been unable to find a single unequivocal case of complete absence of stuttering among a people suggests that biological or idiosyncratic life history factors can be productive of stuttering in all cultures. On the other hand, impressive differences in degree of incidence suggest that cultural influences are operative [Kluckhohn, 1954, p. 944].

Another is the production of dreams: whereas the dreams of Americans derive a good deal of their content from the sexual frustration believed to mark that society, those of a South American Indian tribe living on the edge of subsistence are filled with material based on hunger frustration.

> If dreams are an unconscious expression of desires, then those of the Siriono clearly reflect their preoccupation with the quest for food. While I was only able to record data on some 50 dreams, more than 25 of these are related directly to the eating of food, the hunting of game, and the collecting of edible products from the forest [Holmberg, 1950, p. 91].

A3   Culture is not directly associated with race: men of different biological stocks participate in the same culture, men of the same biological stock have different cultures.

> The research of the last hundred years, especially studies of the diffusion of cultural traits and detailed studies of the behavior of living primitive peoples, has established the independence of patterned cultural behavior from the racial constitution of the particular carriers. . . . Extensive efforts to demonstrate the genetic superiority of one racial group of man over another have so far failed, so that the present working assumption is that, as far as their capacity to learn, maintain, transmit, and transform culture is concerned, different groups of *Homo sapiens* must be regarded as equally competent [Mead, 1958, p. 481].

Babies of any parentage can be taught the language of the family rearing them. Orientals or Africans can become acculturated to Western practices, and vice versa.

A4   The smaller and more primitive the society, the more homogeneous (nonpluralistic) its culture tends to be.

This point has been put in these dramatic terms: the primitive society is more "we," the advanced society more "I." In any case, it is clear that the large society, simply by virtue of its level of organization, is more subject to division of labor and specialization, with all that that implies. But:

> As the total culture is thereby varied and enriched, it also becomes more difficult for each member of the society really to participate in most of its activities. He begins to be an onlooker at most of it, then a bystander, and may end up with indifference to the welfare of his society and the values of his culture. He falls back upon the immediate problems of his livelihood and the narrowing range of enjoyments still open to him, because he senses that his society and his culture have become indifferent to him [Kroeber, 1948, p. 291].

A4.1   The more complex the culture or the society, with regard to its organization and division of labor, the more complex its artistic products.

Thus upper-class culture, in the *aesthetic* sense, is more complex than lower-class culture.

Culture Change and Contact *

B1   Particular cultures do not inevitably pass through a series of parallel developments—the evolutionary idea applied to the individual culture—but in a broad way it can be said that human culture as a whole has gone through certain stages of development.

Here is a summary statement by a specialist in the field of cultural change:

> Twentieth-century research has accumulated a mass of evidence which overwhelmingly supports the contention that particular cultures diverge significantly from one another and do not pass through unilinear stages. Since this basic fact of cultural history is no longer a matter of major controversy, those who have sought to keep the tradition of nineteenth-century evolution alive have been forced to shift their frame of reference from the particular to the general. . . . Their reconstruction of world culture history, therefore, is made in such general terms as to be quite acceptable to everyone. No one doubts that hunting and gathering preceded farming and herding and that the last two were preconditions of "civilization," which is broadly characterized by dense and stable populations, metallurgy, intellectual achievements, social heterogeneity and internal specialization, and other features [Steward, 1953, p. 324].

B1.1   By and large, cultural elements tend to grow in number and, through progressive differentiation, in complexity.

There is a central difference between cultural development and organic evolution:

* A good deal of similar material is contained in the section on social change in the preceding chapter.

Broadly speaking, the process of cultural development is an additive and there-fore accumulative one, whereas the process of organic evolution is primarily a substitutive one. When men acquire flight, they add it to their former faculties; when birds acquired it, they converted a pair of legs into wings. One might thus fairly enough suspect that new culture tended to be incremental and not re-placing; and that therefore the total stock of culture of any society, and of humanity as a whole, would show a normal inclination to grow. All in all, the verdict of history confirms such a judgment. There may have been occasional periods of stress for this or that society in which its total inventory of cultural items diminished. There is nothing to show that such hard times and shrinkages ever extended simultaneously to all the societies on earth. While one particular form of civilization is undergoing atrophy or decay, neighboring ones are usually coming into vigor [Kroeber, 1948, p. 297].

B2   The closer or the more closely related the cultures, the more artifacts and cultural traits they hold in common—but they do not share, to the same degree, characteristics of social organization, such as forms of marriage, forms of the family, rules of descent, or kinship groupings.

Distributions conforming to such historical hypotheses [having to do with dif-fusion of cultural traits among related peoples] have been established for com-plex artifacts (e.g., the loom, the outrigger canoe, the spear thrower, the syringe, the wheel), for food crops (e.g., maize, manioc, wheat, rice, taro), for ceremonials (e.g., circumcision, the couvade, increase rites, the potlatch, the sun dance), and for numerous other aspects of culture. That they represent the normal in culture history can no longer be questioned.

One of the most extraordinary conclusions of the present study is that traits of social organization show practically no tendency to yield distributions of this type. Intertribal similarities are, to be sure, found in very restricted areas, where historical connections are indubitable, but rarely indeed do they extend to an entire culture area or to more than a minority of the tribes of a linguistic stock. Nor are they distributed in a few non-contiguous areas, as is characteristic in most instances of independent invention. On the contrary, they tend to occur widely over the entire earth in many disconnected areas almost as though their appearance were due to sheer chance. Their extraordinarily scattering distri-bution is revealed [in the following table] which indicates the incidence of . . . important traits in each of the five major continental or insular areas of the world [Murdock, 1949, pp. 192–93].

The diffusion of cultural elements is an extremely complicated matter; here is the view of a leading authority:

Specific elements of culture, or groups of such elements, diffuse very widely at times and may be said to be always tending to diffuse: the wheel, for in-stance, smelting of metals, the crown as a symbol of royalty, battleships, Bud-dhism. The relations of elements among themselves, on the other hand, tend to change by internal growth rather than by external imitation. Of this sort are the relations of the classes and members of societies, the fervor with which religion

Traits of Social Organization	Africa	Eurasia	North America	Oceania	South America
FORMS OF MARRIAGE					
Monogamy	1	16	13	8	5
Limited polygyny	5	7	18	21	10
Preferential sororal polygyny	11	4	23	13	5
Nonsororal polygyny	45	6	13	11	1
Polyandry	0	1	0	1	0
FORMS OF THE FAMILY					
Independent nuclear	1	12	16	13	5
Independent polygynous	14	4	16	13	4
Independent polyandrous	0	1	0	1	0
Bilocal extended	1	1	3	3	1
Matrilocal extended	1	2	8	4	8
Avunculocal extended	2	0	4	1	0
Patrilocal extended	21	11	12	7	2
RULES OF DESCENT					
Bilateral	4	8	36	13	14
Matrilineal	11	2	20	15	3
Patrilineal	45	23	13	21	4
Double	5	1	1	11	0

(*Ibid.*, pp. 193–94)

is felt, the esteem accorded to learning or wealth or tradition, the inclination toward this or that avenue of subsistence or economic development. By conquest or peaceful pressure or penetration one people may shatter the political structure or social fabric of another, may undermine its conservatism, may swerve its economic habits. But it is more difficult to find cases of the people voluntarily adopting such tendencies or schemes of cultural organization in mere imitation of the example of another than of its adopting specific culture content—the wheel or the crown or Buddhism—from outside. The result is that culture relations or patterns develop spontaneously or from within probably more frequently than as a result of direct taking-over. Also, the types of culture forms being limited in number, the same type is frequently evolved independently. Thus monarchical and democratic societies, feudal or caste-divided ones, priest-ridden and relatively irreligious ones, expansive and mercantile or self-sufficient and agricultural nations, evolve over and over again [Kroeber, 1948, p. 241].

Again, as between the Old and New Worlds:

The parallels are striking and undeniable. They include the independent development—independent, that is, according to most but not all anthropologists—of an impressive list of basic features: domesticated plants and animals, irrigation, large towns and cities, metallurgy, social classes, states and empires, priesthoods, writing, calendars, and mathematics [Steward, 1953, p. 323].

B2.1   As a general rule, in consequence of contact between cultures, material objects (artifacts) are taken over earlier than nonmaterial characteristics.

That is, for example, tools and clothing are adopted before religious ideas or social organization.

B2.2   If the contact of cultures is prolonged, and especially if it involves a degree of interdependence, some mutual adaptation almost always results.

According to one authority:

> In conclusion it may be said that the only constant phenomenon in situations of continuous first-hand contact, i.e., acculturation under our definition, is the establishment, in the two cultures involved, of mutual modifications and adaptations which will enable the two groups to live together. Even this is not absolutely constant, for one of the groups may not succeed in making such adaptations and become extinct in consequence. However, if both groups survive, the adaptations will be made. It also seems that the more stable the conditions of contact and environment which the two groups have to adapt to, the more readily the adaptations can be made. . . . Lastly, everything indicates that the ultimate end of situations of close and continuous first-hand contact is the amalgamation of the societies and cultures involved, although this conclusion may be postponed almost indefinitely if there is opposition to it on both sides [Linton, 1940, p. 519].

B2.3   The major single source of cultural change is not independent discovery or invention but borrowing through cultural contact. And the more the contact with other cultures, especially with a variety of them, the more complex a society becomes.

The United States is a good example for this finding, with regard to the "melting pot" character of the country, since waves of immigrants have been assimilated and in the process their own cultures have influenced the parent brand. Among simple societies, trading peoples are believed to be more sophisticated than nontrading peoples. Here is an authoritative summary:

> Members of the group appropriate forms of behavior they first encounter in alien societies. Consequently it logically follows that societies that afford their members ample contact with other societies may be expected to change more rapidly and to become more complex than societies whose members have little contact outside their local groupings. The greater the range of novelty to which people are exposed, the greater the likelihood that they will adopt new forms. Contact between societies is the single greatest determinant of culture change [Foster, 1962, p. 25].

B2.4   The greater the contact among cultures, the more the diffusion of common traits and the more alike the societies tend to become.

This is not to say that they become exactly alike—only more alike. Japan is like the West in technology, but not in a lot of other cultural traits.

B2.5   In general, cultural traits diffuse outward from the point of origin along the most-used lines of communication and contact; and those traits that are objectively superior or that come from a more powerful or prestigious source are especially likely to be taken over.

As an example:

> Besides those cultural behaviors which may be said to be permanent, there are those which show some intrinsic and humanly recognizable superiority among existing forms and which can be communicated without intensive apprenticeship learning (Kroeber, 1948). The idea of the wheel, the arch, pottery, the domestication of animals, and so on, may be grasped in its essentials by people of such very different levels of sophistication that at any time in history the diffusion of these ideas can be much wider than their actual use [Mead, 1958, p. 485].

And the traits that come from a prestigious source are particularly likely to be taken over by the upper-status groups of the receiving society. For example, in the United States,

> a steady penetration of white American patterns into Negro life has been under way ever since the Negroes first came to this country, and is at present accelerating. As in any acculturation process, the manner and degree of acceptance vary with different patterns. . . . It is the upper class that has to the greatest degree taken over both form and meaning. The middle class has adopted fewer white patterns, and it is in most cases the form rather than the meaning that has been accepted. The lower class follows the fewest, and most of these in form merely [Powdermaker, 1939, p. 61].

B2.6   As a result of culture contact, whatever was learned early in life tends to resist change and whatever was learned late in life changes most readily.

> That which was traditionally learned and internalized in infancy and early childhood tends to be most resistant to change in contact situations. . . . [In a study of an American Indian tribe:] that which persists, i.e., kinship, role conceptions and values, was learned early, and the primary agents of cultural transmission were members of ego's lineage. The age-grade society system and the religious complex, which no longer exist, were learned late, from agents of transmission who were not members of ego's lineage and who were all respect-relatives. . . .
>
> Partial support for the universality of the early learning hypothesis is provided by two frequently stated anthropological findings as to which aspects of culture tend to persist longest in contact situations. One group of students has found that core culture, implicit values, cultural orientations, and personality are most resistant to change. . . . Another group of students interested in social structure suggests that family and kinship institutions tend to persist [Bruner, 1956, pp. 194, 197].

Perhaps another way to put this is to say that the cultural traits inconsistent with the core culture will be most resisted and that the core culture is typically learned early and firmly. Here is an example dealing with sports:

> Though there is a great demand in our society for exciting spectator sports, bullfighting has never been imported from neighboring Mexico. The reason seems to be that bullfighting is inconsistent with our culture's traditional rejection of activities involving unnecessary cruelty to living things [Freedman *et al.*, 1956, p. 114].

B3   People can be acculturated without being assimilated into a society, and they can be assimilated without being acculturated; the latter is more difficult and less frequent than the former; and the process is usually costly to those being assimilated, psychologically and socially.

For example, in the United States it is probably fair to say that the Amish are more assimilated than they are acculturated, whereas the Northern Negro is more acculturated than he is assimilated. Note that

> migration is an instrument of cultural diffusion and social integration. The person who migrates from one community to another unites in himself two cultures. Temporarily, he tends to be a disruptive force in the community into which he enters. If members of one culture invade a community of another culture in large numbers, they tend to form a "community within a community" and to create cultural diversity and ethnic tension. Only by a slow process of assimilation, which sometimes requires a generation or more, the migrant group and the receiving community are finally adjusted to each other [Bogue, 1959, p. 487].

And the assimilation itself leads, of course, to changes in style of life. For example:

> The observation has been made repeatedly that the children of immigrants to the United States are relatively immune from the influence of authoritarian parents, owing in large measure to more complete assimilation of the children and their economic importance to the family unit [Loomis and Beegle, 1957, pp. 87–88].

Assimilation can also lead to a shift in the type of gestures used during speech. A study of the gestures used by "traditional" Eastern Jews and Southern Italians in New York City and by their assimilated counterparts concluded that "both from the standpoint of number of people gesturing and manner of gesticulation in those people who do gesture, the assimilated . . . (a) appear to differ greatly from their respective traditional groups, and (b) appear to resemble each other" (Efron, 1941, p. 136). In general, the newcomer, marginal between two cultures, can seek out the new, hold to the old, or escape into a kind of generalized apathy—a large-scale, continuing response to a cross-pressured situation (Child, 1943).

On a broader scale, here are two summarizing paragraphs from a famous study of the assimilation of immigrants into the United States, in this case the demoralizing and disorganizing assimilation of the Polish peasant:

> The peasant was adapted to the life of a permanent agricultural community, settled for many hundreds of years in the same locality and changing so slowly that each generation adapted itself to the changes with very little effort or abstract reflection. . . . The peasant was not accustomed to expect unfamiliar happenings in the course of his life within his community, and if they came relied upon his group, which not only gave him assistance . . . but helped him regain his mental balance. . . . The peasant drew all his social stimulations, checks and suggestions from direct social contact with his milieu. . . . He was until quite recently a member of a politically and culturally passive class. . . .
>
> . . . It is not strange that in the different conditions which he finds in this country he becomes more or less disorganized. . . . Scattered and isolated within a practically unknown, usually indifferent, often contemptuous, sometimes even hostile society, in poor and insecure economic conditions, with very insufficient leadership, and a partly pretentious, selfish [and] nationalistic . . . formulation of ideals by this leadership, these small groups of people whose higher interests were indissolubly bound up with their old milieu and who, separated from this milieu, have lost the only real foundation of their cultural life, have already almost succeeded in uniting themselves into one cultural body and in creating institutions which are indubitably factors of progress. These institutions have not prevented a rapid demoralization of those who remain outside of their influence, the new system is neither as rich nor as efficient in controlling the individual as was the old organization, doomed to decay in the new conditions, but this task is beyond the powers of Polish-American society as isolated from American society [Thomas and Znaniecki, 1918, pp. 1824–25].

B3.1   The more the contact, across a broad representation of age and sex groups (as against merely the specialized contact of, e.g., traders), the faster the acculturation.

In the United States, the Japanese on the West Coast acculturated faster than the Mexicans because their occupations brought them into more contact with the larger society; because they were less numerous and hence had less reinforcing contact within their own group; because they experienced less educational segregation (on religious grounds); and because they had fewer migratory ties to the "old country," since it was farther away (Broom and Selznick, 1957, p. 470). As a related proposition:

> As two populations approach equality in the degree of their participation in the various noneconomic institutions of a given society, their distribution in the labor force and in the occupational structure as well will also approach uniformity [Freedman et al., 1956, pp. 404–05].

B3.2   Upwardly mobile people and those of higher socioeconomic status tend to acculturate faster than their nonmobile counterparts. Even within deprived ethnic groups, the middle-class members are more acculturated to the larger society than are the lower.

The results confirm the widely reported finding showing a strong positive relationship between acculturation, higher social status and social mobility. . . . Even when the entire ethnic group is predominantly of the lower class, as in the case of Puerto Ricans, . . . the middle class among them is more acculturated than the lower class. . . . The reason why high social status in Hungary is related to acculturation in the United States is due to the similarity of status ascriptions of the two systems [Weinstock, 1963].

SELECTED READINGS

The definitional work with which we began this chapter will introduce some of the issues and complexities residing in the concept of culture:

Alfred L. Kroeber and Clyde Kluckhohn. "Culture," *Papers of the Peabody Museum,* 47, 1952.

The following are introductions to the subject of culture and behavior:

Clyde Kluckhohn. "Culture and Behavior," in Gardner Lindzey, ed., *Handbook of Social Psychology,* Vol. II. Addison-Wesley, 1954, pp. 921–76.
Clyde Kluckhohn. *Mirror for Man.* McGraw-Hill, 1949.
Alfred L. Kroeber. *Anthropology.* Rev. ed. Harcourt, Brace & World, 1948.
Alfred L. Kroeber. *Configurations of Culture Growth.* U. of California Press, 1944.
Alfred L. Kroeber, ed. *Anthropology Today: An Encyclopedic Inventory.* U. of Chicago Press, 1953. (See especially the articles by Joseph Greenberg and Harry Hoijer on language, Meyer Shapiro on style, Julian H. Steward on process, Clyde Kluckhohn on the universal categories of culture, Claude Levi-Strauss on social structure, A. Irving Hallowell on culture and personality, Ralph Beals on acculturation.)
George P. Murdock. *Social Structure.* Macmillan, 1949.

Although they are not covered individually here, it is worth calling attention to some of the important anthropological investigations of different cultures throughout the world:

Ruth Benedict. *Patterns of Culture.* Houghton-Mifflin, 1934.
Fred Eggan. *Social Organization of the Western Pueblos.* U. of Chicago Press, 1950.
E. E. Evans-Pritchard. *The Nuer.* Oxford U. Press, 1940.
Raymond Firth. *Elements of Social Organization.* Philosophical Library, 1951.
Meyer Fortes. *The Web of Kinship Among the Tallensi.* Oxford U. Press, 1949.
Max Gluckman. *Judicial Process Among the Barotse of Northern Rhodesia.* Free Press, 1955.
Clyde Kluckhohn. "Navajo Witchcraft," *Papers of the Peabody Museum,* 22, No. 2, 1944.
Margaret Mead. *Coming of Age in Samoa.* Morrow, 1928.
A. R. Radcliffe-Brown. *Social Organization of Australian Tribes.* Macmillan, 1931.
Robert Redfield. *The Folk Culture of Yucatan.* U. of Chicago Press, 1941.

The unexamined life is not worth living.

PLATO
Apology

'Tis all in pieces, all coherence gone,
All just supply and all relation.

JOHN DONNE

It is more important to study men than books.

FRANÇOIS DE LA ROCHEFOUCAULD

Happiness is a perpetual possession of being well deceived.

JONATHAN SWIFT
Tale of the Tub

The rapid progress true science now makes, occasions my regretting sometimes that I was born so soon. It is impossible to imagine the height to which may be carried, in a thousand years, the power of man over matter. We may perhaps learn to deprive large masses of their gravity, and give them absolute levity, for the sake of easy transport. Agriculture may diminish its labor and double its produce; all diseases may by sure means be prevented or cured, not excepting even that of old age, and our lives lengthened at pleasure even beyond the antediluvian standard. O that moral science were in as fair a way of improvement, that men would cease to be wolves to one another, and that human beings would at length learn what they now improperly call humanity!

BENJAMIN FRANKLIN
Letter to Joseph Priestley

The nightly moonshine interwove itself with the morning mist, and enveloped him as in a role, which he hugged about his person, and seldom let realities pierce through.

NATHANIEL HAWTHORNE
The House of the Seven Gables

The actions of men are so various and uncertain, that the best statement of tendencies, which we can make in a science of human conduct, must needs be inexact and faulty. This might be urged as a reason against making any statements at all on the subject; but that would be almost to abandon life. Life is human conduct, and the thoughts and emotions that grow up around it. By the fundamental impulses of our nature we all—high and low, learned and unlearned—are in our several degrees constantly striving to understand the courses of human action, and to shape them for our purposes, whether selfish or unselfish, whether noble or ignoble. And since we *must* form to ourselves some notions of the tendencies of human action, our choice is between forming those notions carelessly and forming them carefully. The harder the task, the greater the need for steady patient inquiry; for turning to account the experience, that has been reaped by the more advanced physical sciences; and for framing as best we can well thought-out estimates, or provisional laws, of the tendencies of human action.

ALFRED MARSHALL
Principles of Economics

Most of life is so dull that there is nothing to be said about it, and the books and talk that would describe it as interesting are obliged to exaggerate, in the hope of justifying their own existence. Inside its cocoon of work or social obligation, the human spirit slumbers for the most part, registering the distinction between pleasure and pain, but not nearly as alert as we pretend.

E. M. FORSTER
A Passage to India

We have experienced a great age of rationalism, marked by scientific advances beyond anything that earlier times had thought possible, and confronting mankind with the prospect of a society more open than any it has ever known. And in the last forty years we have also experienced something else—the unmistakable symptoms of a recoil from that prospect. . . . What is the meaning of this recoil, this doubt? Is it the hesitation before the jump, or the beginning of a panic flight? . . . Once before a civilised people rode to this jump—rode to it and refused it.

Was it the horse that refused, or the rider? That is really the crucial question. Personally, I believe it was the horse—in other words, those irrational elements in human nature which govern without our knowledge so much of our behavior and so much of what we think is our thinking. And if I am right about this, I can see in it grounds for hope. . . . The men who created the first European rationalism were deeply and imaginatively aware of the power, the wonder and the peril of the Irrational. But they could describe what went on below the threshold of consciousness only in mythological or symbolic language; they had no instrument for understanding it, still less for controlling it; and in the Hellenistic Age too many of them made the fatal mistake of thinking they could ignore it. Modern man, on the other hand, is beginning to acquire such an instrument. It is still very far from perfect, nor is it always skillfully handled; in many fields, including that of history, its possibilities and its limitations have still to be tested. Yet it seems to offer the hope that if we use it wisely we shall eventually understand our horse better; that, understanding him better, we shall be able by better training to overcome his fears; and that through the over-coming of fear, horse and rider will one day take that decisive jump, and take it successfully.

E. R. DODDS
The Greeks and the Irrational

Chapter Seventeen
CONCLUSION

There they are: 1045 numbered findings from the scientific study of human behavior. Not all absolutely true, not all final or definitive—but certainly among the best-established generalizations of this scope. Taken together, these findings reveal a good deal about the subjects studied in the behavioral sciences, the ways in which they are studied, and the kind of knowledge that emerges.

Now that we are hundreds of pages removed from the Introduction, it seems only fair to the behavioral sciences, and to this book, to repeat a few points made there that have to do with our criteria for inclusion. First, it is important for the reader to appreciate that these 1045 could have been one fifth as many or five times as many, depending on the criteria. If we made our requirements for evidence more stringent, we would have fewer findings; if we relaxed them considerably, so that any plausible hypothesis could qualify, we would have many, many more. If we had stipulated greater generality, we would have had many fewer findings (although they would have suffered, in our view, from a lack of content); if we had moved in the other direction, toward concreteness, we would have collected a wealth of highly specific findings of limited application. So this selection is arbitrary, though we hope not unreasonably so. In any case, to repeat what was said at the outset, what is contained here is not "all there is" to the behavioral sciences.

It should also be clear by now that we have been unable to apply our criteria fully, precisely, and uniformly over the great range of materials reported on here. That task, if not inherently impossible, is at any rate beyond our powers. The findings vary in almost every possible way: in subject, in depth, in relevance, in coverage, in evidence, in applicability, in sophistication. As a result, to say the least, the borderline decisions are extremely difficult to make with full consistency. In the end, the reader

should understand that this is a "more or less" collection, a first approximation and not an absolute reproduction.

Nor, finally, do we claim completeness for our effort. But again, as we
said at the start, we do claim that this book illustrates what the behavioral
sciences do, and we believe that it is quite representative of the empirical
generalizations presently validated in the field—the propositions about
human behavior for which the behavioral sciences of the twentieth century
can put forward some amount of hard evidence.

What is the utility of such an inventory? In the first place, of course, it
consists of knowledge—for its own sake and for its application to human
affairs. Man is curious about nature, not least human nature, and scientific
investigation is one good way to satisfy that curiosity. Anyone will note
here—we do too—findings that interest him and findings that do not; findings that surprise him and findings that do not; findings that enlighten
him and findings that do not; findings that he believes and findings that
he does not. To any single observer some findings will appear obvious,
some trivial, some simply wrong; we trust that at the same time others will
seem instructive, important, and right.

In any case, the findings reported here do have the support of evidence
scientifically gathered—and that is the justification for their inclusion. Indeed, we are inclined to think that this support is a distinctive contribution
of the behavioral sciences, perhaps *the* distinctive contribution, beyond the
other ways of "knowing" about human behavior. The behavioral sciences
certainly have no monopoly on insight into human behavior—there are few
"discoveries" in this book—nor even on concepts or systems. But they are
unique in putting ideas and observations, sooner or later, to the test of
scientific evidence. For the scholar, the implication is that the question,
"What generalizations did he establish?" is a central one; for the layman,
the implication is that here is a method for learning something both valid
and worth knowing.

As for "theory"—the term has several meanings in the behavioral sciences
—these findings are the stuff of theory: the material of which theories are
built. Taken together, just as they are, the findings provide an impressive
range of prediction, itself a test of theory in science. Beyond that, there
is raw material here in which synthesizing minds may see higher-order
principles; for example, here is an instance in which findings from two
fields seem readily to come together:

In the psychological material on level of adaptation, we noted that any
judgment of a stimulus is made with respect to some series, spatial or
temporal, that it can be compared with. The series not only establishes
boundaries within which the judgment is made but also establishes the

values to be used in judging: the reader will recall the experiments on heavy and light weights. What we later called the reference group partakes of the same character: men tend not only to judge whether someone is old or young, intelligent or not intelligent, with respect to the series of people within which he is being judged; but also to make normative judgments by referring them to the standards of the approved groups of people.

And here is an instance that we came to call "the spiral finding":

Deprived children tend to become poor parents, whose own children then tend to be deprived (Chap. 3, C2); the unpopular child, feeling rejected, withdraws, becomes more ingrown and, as a result, more unpopular (Chap. 3, C10); a deteriorating area of the city attracts social delinquency, as a result of which it deteriorates further (Chap. 15, B5.2); the official leadership of a formal organization, when opposed by the informal channels of personal relations within it, will tend to tighten up bureaucratic controls, and as a result the informal channels become more cohesive still (Chap. 9, B5.1); a deprived group such as Negroes in the United States are restricted in such social opportunities as education, as a result of which they are thought to be less educable and hence deprived further (Chap. 12, D4). . . .

The appetite does indeed seem to grow on what it feeds on—so much so that one scholar (p. 291) has referred to "the virtuous circle" when the mutual effect runs in a positive direction. Whether or not there is a tide in the affairs of men, there does seem to be a spiral. And, illustratively, working with such convergences may be one way to build a more summary, economic, coherent architecture of findings than is offered here—that is, to build better theories in the behavioral sciences.

Further as to theory, the reader will have noticed that there are surprisingly few references in this inventory to several of the great names in the field—to Freud, Wundt, or William James in psychology; to Weber, Durkheim, or Simmel in sociology. It seems to us that the genius of such men lies in their revolutionary reformulating of human problems, their striking (at the time) redirection of lines of inquiry. Such men typically do not provide us with the type of empirical documentation required in this inventory—the systematically collected and carefully measured bits and pieces of scientific evidence. But in overturning the old ground, they point the way to new inquiries and hitherto unappreciated problems. So while a Freud or a Weber rarely appears in person, such men stand behind a large number of important findings throughout the book, as pioneering guides for later explorers of the terrain. In the long-term division of labor in an intellectual field, after a great intuitive thinker has upset common conceptions, it falls to others—to lesser men individually but perhaps greater collectively—to take up the challenge of verifying, disproving, and eventually reformulating the original insights.

Finally, such an inventory helps to reveal gaps in knowledge and perhaps suggests how to fill them. We are impressed with the value of such inventories in showing where inquiry is particularly needed in a given field; and we believe that it might be possible to develop such inquiry in a quite systematic way, across cultures and societies, on the basis of much more detailed, much more technical inventorying than we have attempted here, done by specialists within each field. There is a model for such an enterprise: the International Geophysical Year (IGY), in which teams of scientists from many countries collaborated in investigating the physical world. One might even think of an International Behavioral Science Year (IBSY), to investigate the mind and the heart of man, his ways of life and his social institutions. If so, inventories of where we now are and where we would like to be could well serve as starting point.

The Findings and the Image of Man

It remains to say a few words about a Big Question: the nature of man. This is, of course, the most fundamental question of all, and we approach it with due diffidence. Since it is the kind of collective question that is everyone's business in the behavioral sciences, it turns out to be no one's in particular. Hence it is all the more necessary to give it some attention from time to time, and as compilers of this inventory we take this opportunity to start a discourse.

If this were all we knew about man, what would he appear to be? How does the image of man that emerges from the behavioral sciences compare with other images developed in the Western world over the ages?

Most of the great systems of human thought have contained within them some concept of what man is. They are great because the conceptions have been rich ones and have illumined some facets of man's complex nature that earlier ages left in shadow. What have been some of the key terms? The philosophical image of man in the ancient world centered on virtue and reason: man apprehending virtue through the use of reason and following its demands. The Christian image added sin and love: the control of sinful impulses, the redemption of evil human nature by transfiguring love. The political image of the Renaissance introduced power and will: the control of the social environment, the common man's sharing in the glory of the leader, energy liberated to affect political ends, the rise of the state and the national ideal to take its place alongside the religious one. The economic image of the eighteenth and nineteenth centuries rationalized man's interest in property, things, money: the invisible hand automatically transforming the individual good into the common good, and at the same time sharpening the third basic political division, class. The psychoanalytic image of the early twentieth century dealt with another form of love: with ego and self; with instinctual impulses and their indirect, often incomplete, gratification; with the determination of man's estate in childhood, and largely through nonconscious controls; with libido and sex. Over the years, such images live and cumulate, with varying emphases and interpretations in different eras. The behavioral science image may be the latest contribution to this great stream of thought; it certainly is not the last.

How, in a similar way, might we characterize the man of the behavioral sciences? He is a creature far removed from his animal origins, even in such instinctual matters as sexual or maternal behavior; a creature of enormous plasticity, able to live in a wide range of physical environments and an even wider range of cultural or social ones; at the same time, a creature who needs to simplify reality in order to cope with it effectively; a creature subject to the influence of complex "forces," whether from the outside or the inside, such that almost nothing is caused by any other single thing, not even by the critical event (there are always "cultural, economic, political, social, psychological, and situational determinants," "it all depends," "some do, some don't," and everything is always "more complicated than that"); a creature who is subject to the probabilities of influence; to whom everything is natural that he is familiar with, and most other things unnatural; who can, however, adapt to a variety of experience if given time and social support.

Perhaps the character of behavioral science man can best be grasped through his orientation to reality. He is a creature who adapts reality to his own ends, who transforms reality into a congenial form, who makes his own reality. And he does this in two ways.

First, he is extremely good at adaptive behavior—at doing or learning to do things that increase his chances for survival or for satisfaction. He has learned to manipulate and modify his environment for his own purposes; and he has achieved, through accumulation, a degree of control and mastery in which present generations surpass not only the power but even the fantasies of recent ones. Man's ability to make bridges or bombs or vaccines, his skill at recruiting armies or selling insurance or educating his offspring—these were not newly discovered by the behavioral sciences. But the underlying capacities and processes—perceiving, learning, thinking, communicating—have been analyzed and systematized, and their potentials and limitations clarified, in the findings we have reported.

But there is another way in which man comes to terms with reality when it is inconsistent with his needs or preferences; and it is here that the behavioral-science model departs most noticeably from the others. In his quest for satisfaction, man is not just a seeker of truth, but of deceptions, of himself as well as others. (As La Rochefoucauld said, "Social life would not last long if men were not taken in by each other.") When man can come to grips with his needs by actually changing the environment, he does so. But when he cannot achieve such "realistic" satisfaction, he tends to take the other path: to modify what he sees to be the case, what he thinks he wants, what he thinks others want.

Thus, he adjusts his social perception to fit not only the objective reality but also what suits his wishes and his needs (Chap. 4, B3, B9); he tends to remember what fits his needs and expectations (Chap. 5, B12.2), or what he thinks others will want to hear (Chap. 13, C13a); he not only works for what he wants but wants what he has to work for (Chap. 5, A11.4); his need for psychological protection is so great that he has become expert in the "defense mechanisms" (Chap. 6, D1.2); in the mass media he tends to hear and see not simply what is there but what he prefers to be told (Chap. 13, A1), and he will misinterpret rather than face up to an opposing set of facts or point of view (Chap. 13, B1, B5); he avoids the conflicts of issues and ideals whenever he can by changing the people around him rather than his mind (Chap. 14, A4, A4.5, B7a), and when he cannot, private fantasies can lighten the load and carry him through (Chap. 6, D2, D3); he thinks that his own organization ranks higher than it actually does (Chap. 9, B9) and that his own group agrees with him more fully than it does (Chap. 8, B1.5); and if it does not, he finds a way to escape to a less un- congenial world (Chap. 13, A5.1). In the "strain toward consistency," it is often reality that pays the price. "Did we know what our intimates and dear relations thought of us," observed Thackeray in *Vanity Fair,* "we should live in a world that we should be glad to quit, and in a frame of mind and a constant terror, that would be perfectly unbearable."

For the truth is, apparently, that no matter how successful man becomes in dealing with his problems, he still finds it hard to live in the real world, undiluted: to see what one really is, to hear what others really think of one, to face the conflicts and threats really present, or, for that matter, the bare human feelings. Animals adjust to their environment more or less on its terms; man maneuvers his world to suit himself, within far broader limits.

What makes him able to do this, largely, is his symbolic capacity and the language that goes with it. Not only can things be named, manipulated, studied, preserved, and communicated all without any physical contact; but things can be called by other than their real names, and names can be devised to suit occasions, thus adding innumerable (and inexpensive) op- portunities for gratification as well as control. Deference, respect, affection, virtue, justice, status, honor—these and other desirable qualities are be- stowed largely through words, and hence are far more available than ma- terial objects. More often than not, in social life, the word can be applied to fit occasions more easily than the occasion modified to fit the word. In the end, as well as in the beginning, is the word.

This distinctively human quality—can it be called a form of manipulation?—is apparently what makes life tolerable, livable, bearable against all the burdens: against lack of talent, loss of position, pressure of demands, compromise of integrity, the whips and scorns of time, the oppressor's wrong, the proud man's contumely, the pangs of despised love, the law's delay, the insolence of office and the spurns that patient merit of the unworthy takes. In short, man lives not only with the reality that confronts him but with the reality he makes. As a poet of our time saw:

> Go, go, go, said the bird: human kind
> Cannot bear very much reality.
>
> (T. S. Eliot, *Burnt Norton*)

If this means that the scientist has found what the artist has always known about the place of illusions in life, so much the better for both—and for the continuity between them.

For the burden and the benefit come from the same source: life, and reality, is other people. (So, as Sartre said in *No Exit,* is hell.) Nearly all of these findings, all except a few that deal with near-physiological aspects of behavior, lead the individual directly to other people—not only for facts and beliefs about the nature of the world, but also for what he has learned to want, to value, to consider right and good, to worship. The actions and reactions of others are not only his primary source of information but they determine his primary goals beyond those physical things he requires for survival. In an open, fast-changing society, this makes for strains for the individual; said one sociological commentator recently:

> The problem of reality in our time . . . arises because individuals have left old anchorages, no longer follow inherited ways, are constantly faced with the problems of choice (the ability to choose—to choose careers, styles of life, friends, political representatives—is for the mass of people, something new in social history), and find no longer authoritative standards or critics to guide them [Bell, 1963].

In maintaining man's morale, the small group around him is often more important than the large issues involved (Chap. 8, B2, and Chap. 9, A7); in political affairs, he votes with his friends as well as for the candidate (Chap. 14, A14.1); in the search for rationality and for the good, it is the surrounding group that sets the standard: the right, from religion to etiquette, is what one's peers agree is right (Chap. 8, B1, and Chap. 14, B1); in psychotherapy, even a "Hmm" can get positive results (Chap. 5, A9); when immediate evidence from his own senses clearly contradicts the statements of others, he may not only agree overtly but actually be convinced of his "error" (Chap. 8, B1.3b); and his very picture of himself stems in large part from how others regard him (Chap. 11, C24, and Chap. 12, D2).

So behavioral science man is social man—social product, social producer, and social seeker—to a greater degree than philosophical man or religious man or political man or economic man or psychoanalytic man—or the man of common observation and common sense, for that matter. Our man seeks virtue through reason far less than he seeks approval through the people around him; his evil comes from frustration, not from inherent nature; he is less concerned with the exercise of power than with his relations with those who are powerful, and he has learned ways to limit the power they seek to exercise over him; he seeks acceptance and the good view of the community more than he seeks political power or economic riches, and he can even control his strongest instincts, the libidinous side of his nature, to this end. The traditional images of man have stressed, as prime motivating agents, reason or faith or impulse or self-interest; the behavioral science image stresses the social definition of all of these. Here, the individual appears less "on his own," less as a creature of the natural environment, more as a creature making others and made by others.

Or so it seems from much of the inventory. But this image is as yet incomplete, just as the behavioral sciences themselves, from any historical perspective, are still near their starting point. So far as man is concerned, this inventory is incomplete historically, incomplete geographically, incomplete culturally. Most of the findings, the large majority, are based on modern Western man, particularly on Americans, perhaps not even a representative sample of them. Does the general burden of these findings hold for Indians, Arabs, Africans, the peasants of Eastern Europe, the villagers of Turkey, Londoners of the eighteenth century, Japanese in the modernizing era?

Indeed, as one reviews this set of findings, he may well be impressed by another omission perhaps more striking still. As one lives life or observes it around him (or within himself) or finds it in a work of art, he sees a richness that somehow has fallen through the present screen of the behavioral sciences. This book, for example, has rather little to say about central human concerns: nobility, moral courage, ethical torments, the delicate relation of father and son or of the marriage state, life's way of corrupting innocence, the rightness and wrongness of acts, evil, happiness, love and hate, death, even sex. (On such matters, the behavioral sciences, with a focus on evidence, and psychoanalysis, with attention to the human stuff itself, should learn to make common cause more successfully than heretofore.)

Why the lacunae? Partly because of the youth of the field: it takes time to accumulate the scientific means to study such subtle matters. Partly, perhaps, this is the price paid for method, for system, for abstraction: the concern of science for concepts, for replicability, for objectivity, for rates and patterns.

> The scientific method (whatever that may be) has achieved its successes by reducing the subjective individual component of experience to a minimum. In its unremitting effort to produce as wide agreement as possible, it is most successful when it has reduced natural phenomena to "pointer readings." Most of what makes life worth living, its warmth, its color, its love and joy, as well as its pain and its tragedy—indeed all its immediately subjective presentations to consciousness—is deliberately circumvented or simply omitted. The world science presents to us is in a very real sense alien to immediate experience with its wave lengths in place of our tones and colors, its tropisms, drives or conditioned responses in place of our loves, hates, and free will [Morison, 1963].

But whatever the reasons, between the image of life that appears in the world of the behavioral sciences and the image in the world of art, there are differences worthy of reflection. Not yet, anyway, do the behavioral sciences see life steadily and see it whole.

What becomes of "human nature" in all this? Once we get much beyond the physiological or neurological base of behavior, human nature spreads out as far as one can see. For human beings around the world behave in the greatest variety of ways—each natural in its own community, each an expression of human nature, each equally so. And as Terence said, long ago, "Difference from me is not the measure of absurdity."

Is this, then, the way man really is? Certainly this is part of the story. Is it the whole story? Certainly not, but then the behavioral sciences are still in early process, and this image will change as our knowledge changes and advances.

As we say, there they are: a large number of scientific findings about the behavior of human beings. Taken together, they represent a milestone on the developing path of the behavioral sciences, and, more important, on the way to man's understanding of himself. The findings should be judged not only against the contribution of other ways of knowing about man— from literature, from religion, from philosophy, from introspection and observation—but by their own criteria, as part of science.

In the end, the behavioral sciences will make a distinctive, indeed an indispensable, contribution to the naturalistic description of human nature —the contribution of hard knowledge tested by the methods of science. To that outcome, we offer this inventory.

BIBLIOGRAPHICAL INDEX

Boldface numbers following each entry identify the pages of this book
on which the reference is cited.

Adams, Richard N. "A Change from Caste to Class in a Peruvian Sierra Town," *Soc. Forces,* 31, 1953, pp. 238–44. **464**

Adams, Stuart. "Social Climate and Productivity in Small Military Groups," *Amer. Sociol. Rev.,* 19, 1954, pp. 421–25. **446**

Adamson, Robert E. "Functional Fixedness as Related to Problem-Solving: A Repetition of Three Experiments," *J. Exper. Psychol.,* 44, 1952, pp. 288–91. **203**

Adamson, Robert E., and Donald W. Taylor. "Functional Fixedness as Related to Elapsed Time and to Set," *J. Exper. Psychol.,* 47, 1954, pp. 122–26. **204**

Adorno, Theodore W., Else Frenkel-Brunswik, Daniel J. Levinson, and R. Nevitt Sanford. *The Authoritarian Personality: Studies in Prejudice.* Ed. by Max Horkheimer and Samuel H. Flowerman. Harper & Row, 1950. **516, 524**

Aiken, E. G. "The Effort Variable in the Acquisition, Extinction, and Spontaneous Recovery of an Instrumental Response," *J. Exper. Psychol.,* 53, 1957, pp. 47–51. **154**

Alexander, F. "Five Year Report of the Chicago Institute for Psychoanalysis: 1932–1937." 1937. **288**

Allen, Charles M. *Combating the Dropout Problem.* Science Research Associates, 1956. **437**

Allport, Floyd H. *Theories of Perception and the Concept of Structure.* Wiley, 1955. **131**

Allport, Gordon W. *The Nature of Prejudice.* Beacon, 1954. **515, 523**

Allport, Gordon W., and Bernard M. Kramer. "Some Roots of Prejudice," *J. Psychol.,* 22, 1946, pp. 9–39. **501, 502**

Allport, Gordon W., and Leo J. Postman. "The Basic Psychology of Rumor," *Trans. N.Y. Acad. Sci.* (Series 2), 8, 1945, pp. 61–81. **185**

Allport, Gordon W., and Leo J. Postman. "The Basic Psychology of Rumor," in Eleanor E. Maccoby *et al.,* eds., *Readings in Social Psychology.* 3rd ed. Holt, Rinehart & Winston, 1958, pp. 54–65. **186**

Anastasi, A. *Differential Psychology.* 3rd ed. Macmillan, 1958. **236**

Anderson, C. Arnold. "Trends in Rural Sociology," in Robert K. Merton *et al.,* eds., *Sociology Today: Problems and Prospects.* Basic Books, 1954, pp. 360–75. **641**

Angell, Robert Cooley. "The Moral Integration of American Cities," *Amer. J. Sociol.,* 57, part 2, 1951. **610**

Argyle, Michael. *Religious Behavior.* Routledge & Kegan Paul, 1958. **392–93, 395, 629.** Free Press, 1959. **450**

Argyle, Michael. *The Scientific Study of Social Behavior.* Methuen, 1957. **340, 351, 355, 370**

Aronson, Elliot, and Judson Mills. "The Effect of Severity of Initiation on Liking for a Group," *J. Abnorm. Soc. Psychol.,* 59, 1959, pp. 177–81. **154**

Asch, S. E. "Effects of Group Pressure Upon the Modification and Distortion of Judgments," in Eleanor E. Maccoby *et al.,* eds., *Readings in Social Psychology.* 3rd ed. Holt, Rinehart & Winston, 1958, pp. 174–83. **335, 336**

Asch, S. E. "Forming Impressions of Personality," *J. Abnorm. Soc. Psychol.,* 41, 1946, pp. 258–90. **114**

Atkinson, John W., and George H. Litwin. "Achievement Motive and Test Anxiety

Conceived as Motive To Approach Success and Motive To Avoid Failure," *J. Abnorm. Soc. Psychol.*, 60, 1960, pp. 52–63. **275**

Austin, George A., Jerome S. Bruner, and Robert V. Seymour. "Fixed-Choice Strategies in Concept Attainment," *Amer. Psychologist*, 8, 1953, p. 314 (abstract). **199**

Axelrad, Sidney. "Negro and White Male Institutionalized Delinquents," *Amer. J. Sociol.*, 57, 1952, pp. 569–74. **628**

Babchuk, N., and William J. Goode. "Work Incentives in a Self-Determined Group," *Amer. Sociol. Rev.*, 16, 1951, pp. 679–87. **409**

Baldwin, George B. *Beyond Nationalization: The Labor Problems of British Coal.* Harvard U. Press, 1955. **413**

Bales, Robert F. "The Equilibrium Problem in Small Groups," in Talcott Parsons, Robert F. Bales, and Edward A. Shils, *Working Papers in the Theory of Action.* Free Press, 1953, pp. 111–61. **346, 350, 351**

Bales, Robert F. *Interaction Process Analysis: A Method for the Study of Small Groups.* Addison-Wesley, 1950. **35, 361**

Bales, Robert F. "Small Group Theory and Research," in Robert K. Merton *et al.*, eds., *Sociology Today: Problems and Prospects.* Basic Books, 1959, pp. 293–305. **341, 361**

Bales, Robert F., and Edgar F. Borgatta. "Size of Group as a Factor in the Interaction Profile," in A. Paul Hare *et al.*, eds., *Small Groups: Studies in Social Interaction.* Knopf, 1955, pp. 396–413. **359–60**

Bales, Robert F., A. Paul Hare, and Edgar F. Borgatta. "Structure and Dynamics of Small Groups: A Review of Four Variables," in Joseph B. Gittler, ed., *Review of Sociology: Analysis of a Decade.* Wiley, 1957, pp. 391–422. **356, 359, 361**

Bales, Robert F., Fred L. Strodtbeck, Theodore M. Mills, and Mary E. Roseborough. "Channels of Communication in Small Groups," *Amer. Sociol. Rev.*, 16, 1951, pp. 461–68. **349**

Ball, R. S. "Reinforcement Conditioning of Verbal Behavior by Verbal and Nonverbal Stimuli in a Situation Resembling a Clinical Interview." Unpublished doctoral dissertation, Indiana U., 1952. **144**

Baltzell, E. Digby. " 'Who's Who in America' and 'The Social Register': Elite and Upper Class Indexes in Metropolitan America," in Reinhard Bendix and Seymour M. Lipset, eds., *Class, Status and Power: A Reader in Social Stratification.* Free Press, 1953, pp. 172–84. **455**

Banks, W. S. M., II. "Rank Order of Sensitivity to Discrimination of Negroes in Columbus, Ohio," *Amer. Sociol. Rev.*, 15, 1950, pp. 529–34. **511**

Barber, Bernard. "Social-Class Differences in Educational Life-Chances," *Teachers College Record*, 63, 1961, pp. 102–13. **486**

Barber, Bernard. *Social Stratification: A Comparative Analysis of Structure and Process.* Harcourt, Brace & World, 1957. **490**

Barker, Roger G. "An Experimental Study of the Resolution of Conflict by Children," in Quinn McNemar and Maud A. Merrill, eds., *Studies in Personality.* McGraw-Hill, 1942, pp. 13–34. **272**

Barker, Roger G., T. Dembo, and Kurt Lewin. "Frustration and Regression: An Experiment with Young Children," *University of Iowa Studies in Child Welfare*, 18, No. 386, 1941. **270**

Barker, Roger G., Jacob S. Kounin, and Herbert F. Wright, eds. *Child Behavior and Development.* McGraw-Hill, 1943. **85**

Barker, Roger G., and Herbert F. Wright. *One Boy's Day: A Specimen Record of Behavior.* Harper & Row, 1951. **35**

Barnard, Chester. *The Functions of the Executive.* Harvard U. Press, 1950. **371**

Barr, Arvil S., Daniel E. Eustice, and Edward J. Noe. "The Measurement and Prediction of Teacher Efficiency," *Rev. Educ. Res.*, 25, 1955, pp. 261–69. **441**

Barron, Frank. "Creative Vision and Expression in Writing and Painting," in Institute of Personality Assessment and Research, *The Creative Person.* U. of California and University Extension, Liberal Arts Dept., 1961, pp. II-1–II-19. **228, 229**

Barron, Frank, Dorwin Cartwright, and Richard S. Crutchfield. *Creativity and Conformity.* Foundation for Research on Human Behavior, 1958. **230**

Barron, Milton L. *People Who Intermarry.* Syracuse U. Press, 1946. **306**

Bartlett, E. R., and D. B. Harris, "Personality Factors in Delinquency," *School and Society*, 43, 1935, pp. 653–56. **577**

Bartlett, Frederick C. *Remembering.* Cambridge U. Press, 1932. **186–87, 236**

Barton, Allen H. *Organizational Measurement and Its Bearing on the Study of College Environments.* College Entrance Examination Board, 1961. **380**

Bass, Bernard M. *Leadership, Psychology, and Organizational Behavior.* Harper & Row, 1959. **361**

Bauer, Raymond A. "The Communicator and the Audience." *J. Conflict Resolution* 2, 1958, pp. 67–77. **550**

Bauer, Raymond A., and Alice H. Bauer. "America, Mass Society and Mass Media," *J. Soc. Issues*, 16, 1960, pp. 3–66. **530, 543, 576**

Bavelas, Alex. "Communication Patterns in Task-Oriented Groups," *J. Acoustical Soc. Amer.*, 22, 1950, pp. 725–30. **356**

Bayley, Nancy. "Consistency and Variability in the Growth of Intelligence from Birth to Eighteen," *J. Genet. Psychol.*, 75, 1949, pp. 165–96. **215**

Bayley, Nancy. "On the Growth of Intelligence," *Amer. Psychologist*, 10, 1955, pp. 805–18. **62**

Bayley, Nancy, and M. H. Oden. "The Maintenance of Intellectual Ability in Gifted Adults," *J. Gerontol.*, 10, 1955, pp. 91–107. **222**

Beach, Frank A. "Characteristics of Masculine 'Sex Drive,'" in Marshall R. Jones, ed., *Nebraska Symposium on Motivation.* U. of Nebraska Press, 1956, pp. 1–32. **49**

Beach, Frank A. "Experimental Investigations of Species-Specific Behavior," *Amer. Psychologist*, 15, 1960, pp. 1–18. **45–46**

Beach, Frank A., and J. Jaynes. "The Effects of Early Experience upon the Behavior of Animals," *Psychol. Bull.*, 54, 1951, pp. 239–63. **85**

Becker, Gary. *The Economics of Discrimination.* U. of Chicago Press, 1957. **523, 525**

Becker, Selwyn W., and Jean Carroll. "Ordinal Position and Conformity," *J. Abnorm. Soc. Psychol.*, 65, 1962, pp. 129–31. **255**

Beckham, A. A. "Minimal Intelligence Levels for Several Occupations," *Personnel J.*, 9, 1930, pp. 309–13. **211**

Beers, Howard W. "The Rural Community," in Joseph B. Gittler, ed., *Review of Sociology: Analysis of a Decade.* Wiley, 1957, pp. 186–220. **641**

Bell, Daniel. "The Disjunction of Culture and Social Structure." Unpublished paper read at American Academy of Arts and Sciences conference, "Toward a Redefinition of Culture," May, 1963. **665**

Beloff, H. "Two Forms of Social Conformity: Acquiescence and Conventionality," *J. Abnorm. Soc. Psychol.*, 56, 1958, pp. 99–104. **259**

Bendix, Reinhard, and Seymour M. Lipset, eds. *Class, Status and Power: A Reader in Social Stratification.* Free Press, 1953. **490**

Bendix, Reinhard, and Seymour M. Lipset. "Political Sociology: An Essay and Bibliography," *Current Sociology*, 6, 1957, pp. 79–169. **426–27, 617–18**

Benedict, Paul K., and Irving Jacks. "Mental Illness in Primitive Societies," *Psychiatry*, 17, 1954, p. 389. **636**

Benedict, Ruth. *Patterns of Culture.* Houghton Mifflin, 1934. **656**

Benson, Lee. *The Concept of Jacksonian Democracy.* Princeton U. Press, 1961. **435**

Berelson, Bernard. *Content Analysis in Communications Research.* Free Press, 1952. **35**

Berelson, Bernard, with the assistance of Lester Asheim. *The Library's Public.* Columbia U. Press, 1949. **533**

Berelson, Bernard. "Population Control: Social Factors." Unpublished ms., 1962. **596**

Berelson, Bernard. "Voting Behavior," in *Encyclopaedia Britannica*, 23, 1961, pp. 259a–60b. **571**

Berelson, Bernard, and Morris Janowitz, eds. *Reader in Public Opinion and Communication.* Rev. ed. Free Press, 1953. **554**

Berelson, Bernard, Paul F. Lazarsfeld, and William N. McPhee. *Voting: A Study of Opinion Formation in a Presidential Campaign.* U. of Chicago Press, 1954. **418, 419, 423, 432, 544, 545, 551, 555, 560, 567, 579, 580**

Berelson, Bernard, and Patricia J. Salter. "Majority and Minority Americans: An Analysis of Magazine Fiction," *Pub. Opin. Quart.*, 10, 1946, pp. 168–90. **505**

Berenda, Ruth W. *The Influence of the Group on the Judgments of Children.* King's Crown Press, 1950. **336**

Berlyne, Daniel E. "The Arousal and Satiation of Perceptual Curiosity in the Rat," *J. Comp. Physiol. Psychol.*, 48, 1955, pp. 328–46. **294**

Berlyne, Daniel E. "The Influence of Complexity and Novelty in Visual Figures on Orienting Responses," *J. Exper. Psychol.*, 55, 1958(a), pp. 289–96. **246**

Berlyne, Daniel E. "The Influence of the Albedo and Complexity of Stimuli on Visual Fixation in the Human Infant," *Brit. J. Psychol.*, 49, 1958(b), pp. 315–18. **246**

Bettelheim, Bruno. "Individual and Mass Behavior in Extreme Situations," in Eleanor E. Maccoby *et al.*, eds. *Readings in Social Psychology.* 3rd ed. Holt, Rinehart & Winston, 1958, pp. 300–10. **276**

Bettelheim, Bruno, and Morris Janowitz. *Dynamics of Prejudice: A Psychological and Sociological Study of Veterans.* Harper & Row, 1950. **487–88, 513, 514**

Biderman, Albert D. "The Image of 'Brainwashing,'" *Pub. Opin. Quart.*, 26, 1962, pp. 547–63. **575–76**

Binder, A., D. McConnell, and Nancy A. Sjoholm. "Verbal Conditioning as a Function of Experimenter Characteristics," *J. Abnorm. Soc. Psychol.*, 55, 1957, pp. 309–14. **144**

Birch, Herbert G. "The Role of Motivational Factors in Insightful Problem-Solving," *J. Comp. Psychol.*, 38, 1945, pp. 295–317. **264–65**

Bitterman, M. E. "Toward a Comparative Psychology of Learning," *Amer. Psychologist*, 15, 1960, pp. 704–12. **133**

Black, Percy. "White-Negro Relations: A Different Slant," ed. by Robin M.

Williams, Jr., ed., *Rural Sociol.*, 14, 1949, pp. 261–62. **516–17, 517**

Black, Percy, and Ruth Davidson Atkins. "Conformity Versus Prejudice as Exemplified in White-Negro Relations in the South: Some Methodological Considerations," *J. Psychol.*, 30, 1950, pp. 109–21. **508**

Blake, Robert R., and Jane S. Mouton. "The Experimental Investigation of Interpersonal Influence," in Albert D. Biderman and Herbert Zimmer, eds., *The Manipulation of Human Behavior*. Wiley, 1961, pp. 216–76. **335, 548**

Blake, Robert R., and Jane S. Mouton. "Personality," *Annu. Rev. Psychol.*, 10, 1959, pp. 203–32. **63, 260–61**

Blankenship, A. B., and P. L. Whitely. "Proactive Inhibition and the Recall of Advertising Material," *J. Soc. Psychol.*, 13, 1941, pp. 311–22. **165**

Blau, Peter M. *Bureaucracy in Modern Society*. Random House, 1956. **365–66, 367**

Blau, Peter M. *The Dynamics of Bureaucracy*. U. of Chicago Press, 1955. **368, 370, 380**

Blauner, Robert. "Work Satisfaction and Industrial Trends in Modern Society," in Walter Galenson and Seymour M. Lipset, eds., *Labor and Trade Unionism: An Interdisciplinary Reader*. Wiley, 1960, pp. 339–60. **409**

Bloom, B. S. "Thought-Processes in Lectures and Discussions," *J. Gen. Educ.*, 7, 1953, pp. 160–69. **547**

Blum, Gerald S. "An Experimental Reunion of Psychoanalytic Theory with Perceptual Vigilance and Defense," *J. Abnorm. Soc. Psychol.*, 49, 1954, pp. 94–98. **102**

Blum, Gerald S. "Perceptual Defense Revisited," *J. Abnorm. Soc. Psychol.*, 51, 1955, pp. 24–29. **102–03**

Bogart, Leo. *The Age of Television*. Frederick Ungar, 1956. **533**

Bogue, Donald J. "Internal Migration," in Philip M. Hauser and Otis Dudley Duncan, eds., *The Study of Population: An Inventory and Appraisal*. U. of Chicago Press, 1959, pp. 486–509. **592, 654**

Boland, J. L. "Type of Birth as Related to Stuttering," *J. Speech Hear. Dis.*, 16, 1951, pp. 40–43. **73**

Bond, Elden A. *Tenth-Grade Abilities and Achievements*. Teachers College, Columbia U., 1940. **212**

Bordeaux, Jean, Review of J. G. Watkins. "A Case of Hypnotic Trance Induced in Resistant Subject in Spite of Active Opposition" (*Brit. J. Medical Hypnotism*, Summer, 1951), in *Annu. Rev. Hypnosis Literature*, 1–2, 1953, p. 49. **125**

Borgatta, Edgar F., Arthur S. Couch, and Robert F. Bales. "Some Findings Relevant to the Great Man Theory of Leadership," in A. Paul Hare *et al.*, eds., *Small Groups: Studies in Social Interaction*. Knopf, 1955, pp. 568–74. **346**

Bowlby, John. *Maternal Care and Mental Health*. World Health Organization, Monograph Series, No. 2, 1952. **66, 67, 68**

Bram, Joseph. *Language and Society*. Doubleday, 1955. **329**

Brayfield, Arthur H., and Walter H. Crockett. "Employee Attitudes and Employee Performance," *Psychol. Bull.*, 52, 1955, pp. 396–424. **411**

Bridges, Kathrine M. Banhan. "Emotional Development in Early Infancy," *Child Development*, 3, 1932, pp. 324–41. **54**

Briggs, Leslie J., and Homer B. Reed. "The Curve of Retention for Substance Material," *J. Exper. Psychol.*, 32, 1943, pp. 513–17. **167**

Brim, Orville G., Jr. *Sociology and the Field of Education*. Russell Sage Foundation, 1958. **437, 441, 450**

Bromiley, Reginald B. "Conditioned Responses in a Dog After Removal of Neocortex," *J. Comp. Physiol. Psychol.*, 41, 1948, pp. 102–10. **138**

Bronfenbrenner, Urie. "Socialization and Social Class Through Time and Space," in Eleanor E. Maccoby *et al*, eds., *Readings in Social Psychology*. 3rd ed. Holt, Rinehart & Winston, 1958, pp. 400–25. **478, 481, 491**

Broom, Leonard. "Social Differentiation and Stratification," in Robert K. Merton *et al.*, eds., *Sociology Today: Problems and Prospects*. Basic Books, 1959, pp. 429–41. **456**

Broom, Leonard, and Philip Selznick. *Sociology: A Text with Adapted Readings*. Harper & Row, 1957. **310, 316, 331, 463, 471, 523, 569, 608, 617, 626–27, 655**

Brotz, Howard. Personal communication, 1959. **331**

Brown, Andrew W. "The Change in Intelligence Quotients in Behavior Problem Children," *J. Educ. Psychol.*, 21, 1930, pp. 341–50. **216**

Brown, Judson S. "Gradients of Approach and Avoidance Responses and Their Relation to Level of Motivation," *J. Comp. Physiol. Psychol.*, 41, 1948, pp. 450–65. **273, 274**

Brown, Roger W. Appendix, in Jerome S. Bruner *et al.*, *A Study of Thinking*. Wiley, 1956, pp. 247–312. **190**

Brown, Roger W., and E. H. Lenneberg. "A Study in Language and Cognition," *J. Abnorm. Soc. Psychol.*, 49, 1954, pp. 454–62. **190**

Bruner, Edward M. "Cultural Transmission and Cultural Change," *Southwestern J. Anthropology*, 12, 1956, pp. 191–99. **653**

Bruner, Jerome S., and Cecile C. Goodman. "Value and Need as Organizing Factors in Perception," *J. Abnorm. Soc. Psychol.*, 42, 1947, pp. 33–44. **117**

Bruner, Jerome S., Jacqueline J. Goodnow, and George A. Austin. *A Study of Thinking.* Wiley, 1956. **192, 199, 236**

Bruner, Jerome S., and Leo J. Postman. "On the Perception of Incongruity: A Paradigm," *J. Pers.*, 18, 1949, pp. 206–23. **113**

Bryan, William L., and Noble Harter. "Studies in the Physiology and Psychology of the Telegraphic Language," *Psychol. Rev.*, 4, 1897, pp. 27–53. **157, 158**

Bugelski, B. R. "Interference with Recall of Original Responses After Learning New Responses to Old Stimuli," *J. Exper. Psychol.*, 30, 1942, pp. 368–79. **165**

Burgess, Ernest W., and Harvey J. Locke. *The Family: From Institution to Companionship.* 2nd ed. American Book Co., 1953. **315, 323**

Burt, Cyril, and Margaret Howard. "The Multifactorial Theory of Inheritance and Its Application to Intelligence," *Brit. J. Stat. Psychol.*, 9, 1956, pp. 95–131. **219**

Butt, Harold E. "An Experimental Study of Early Childhood Memory: Final Report." *J. Genet. Psychol.*, 58, 1941, pp. 435–39. **181**

Bush, R. R., and W. K. Estes, eds. *Studies in Mathematical Learning Theory.* Stanford U. Press, 1959. **235**

Butler, John M., and Gerard V. Haigh. "Changes in the Relation Between Self-Concepts and Ideal Concepts Consequent upon Client-Centered Counseling," in Carl R. Rogers and Rosalind F. Dymond, eds., *Psychotherapy and Personality Change.* U. of Chicago Press, 1954. pp. 55–75. **292**

Campbell, Angus, and Homer C. Cooper. *Group Differences in Attitudes and Votes: A Study of the 1954 Congressional Election.* Survey Research Center, U. of Michigan, 1956. **571**

Campbell, Angus, Gerald Gurin, and Warren E. Miller. *The Voter Decides.* Harper & Row, 1954. **565**

Campbell, Donald T., and Boyd R. McCandless. "Ethnocentrism, Xenophobia, and Personality," *Hum. Relat.*, 4, 1951, pp. 185–92. **502**

Cantril, Hadley, and Lloyd A. Free. "Hopes and Fears for Self and Country," *Amer. Behavioral Scientist*, 6, 1962 (October Supplement), pp. 1–32. **562**

Caplow, Theodore, and Reece J. McGee. *The Academic Marketplace.* Basic Books, 1958. **379**

Carmichael, H. T., and T. H. Masserman. "Results of Treatment in a Psychiatric Outpatients' Department," *J. Amer. Med. Assoc.*, 113, 1939, pp. 2292–98. **288**

Carmichael, Leonard. "A Further Study of the Development of Behavior in Vertebrates Experimentally Removed from the Influence of the Environmental Stimulation," *J. Comp. Psychol.*, 34, 1942, pp. 285–92. **58**

Carmichael, Leonard, ed. *Manual of Child Psychology.* 2nd ed., Wiley, 1954. **85**

Carmichael, Leonard, H. P. Hogan, and A. A. Walter. "An Experimental Study of the Effect of Language on the Reproduction of Visually Perceived Form," *J. Exper. Psychol.*, 15, 1932, pp. 73–86. **184, 185**

Cartwright, Dorwin. "Some Principles of Mass Persuasion: Selected Findings of Research on the Sale of United States War Bonds," *Hum. Relat.*, 2, 1949, pp. 253–67. **530**

Cartwright, Dorwin, and Alvin Zander, eds. *Group Dynamics: Research and Theory.* 2nd ed. Harper & Row, 1960. **361**

Caudill, William. *Effects of Social and Cultural Systems in Reactions to Stress.* Social Science Research Council, Pamphlet 14, 1958. **318**

Centers, Richard. *The Psychology of Social Classes.* Russell Sage Foundation, 1961. **491**

Chapin, F. Stuart. "Social Institutions and Voluntary Associations," in Joseph B. Gittler, ed., *Review of Sociology: Analysis of a Decade.* Wiley, 1957, pp. 259–88. **315, 334, 353, 366**

Child, Irvin L. *Italian or American? The Second Generation in Conflict.* Yale U. Press, 1943. **654**

Child, Irvin L. "Socialization," in Gardner Lindzey, ed., *Handbook of Social Psychology*, Vol. 2. Addison-Wesley, 1954, pp. 655–92. **64, 75, 85**

Christie, Richard. "Authoritarianism Re-examined," in Richard Christie and Marie Jahoda, eds., *Studies in the Scope and Method of the Authoritarian Personality.* Free Press, 1954, pp. 123–96. **502**

Christie, Richard. "An Experimental Study of Modification in Factors Influencing Recruits' Adjustment to the Army." Unpublished ms., Research Center for Human Relations, New York U., 1953. **445**

Clausen, John A. "Drug Addiction," in Robert K. Merton and Robert A. Nisbet, eds., *Contemporary Social Problems.* Harcourt, Brace & World, 1961(a), pp. 181–221. **633, 641**

Clausen, John A. "Mental Disorders," in Robert K. Merton and Robert A. Nisbet, eds., *Contemporary Social Problems.* Harcourt, Brace & World, 1961(b), pp. 127–80. **636–37, 641**

Clausen, John A. *Sociology and the Field of Mental Health.* Russell Sage Foundation, 1956. **636**

Clausen, John A. "The Sociology of Mental Illness," in Robert K. Merton *et al.*, eds., *Sociology Today: Problems and Prospects.* Basic Books, 1959, pp. 485–508. **478**

Clausen, John A., and M. L. Kohn. "The Relation of Schizophrenia to the Social Structure of a Small City." Unpublished paper presented at the annual meeting of the American Assoc. for the Advancement of Science, December, 1956. **478**

Clinard, Marshall B. "Criminological Research," in Robert K. Merton *et al.*, eds., *Sociology Today: Problems and Prospects.* Basic Books, 1959, pp. 509–36. **641**

Clinard, Marshall B. "The Sociology of Delinquency and Crime," in Joseph B. Gittler, ed., *Review of Sociology: Analysis of a Decade.* Wiley, 1957, pp. 465–99. **641**

Coale, Ansley. "World Population Problems," in *The Growth of World Population.* National Academy of Sciences, 1963, pp. 8–19. **589–90**

Coch, Lester, and John R. P. French, Jr. "Overcoming Resistance to Change," *Hum. Relat.*, 1, 1948, pp. 512–32. **354**

Cochran, W. G., and Gertrude M. Cox. *Experimental Designs.* 2nd ed. Wiley, 1950. **35**

Cohen, Albert K. "The Study of Social Disorganization and Deviant Behavior," in Robert K. Merton *et al.*, eds., *Sociology Today: Problems and Prospects.* Basic Books, 1959, pp. 461–84. **641**

Cohen, Albert K., and James F. Short, Jr. "Juvenile Delinquency," in Robert K. Merton and Robert A. Nisbet, eds., *Contemporary Social Problems.* Harcourt, Brace & World, 1961, pp. 77–126. **625, 628, 631, 641**

Cohen, B. D., H. I. Kalish, J. R. Thurston, and E. Cohen. "Experimental Manipulation of Verbal Behavior," *J. Exper. Psychol.*, 47, 1954, pp. 106–10. **144**

Coleman, James S. *The Adolescent Society: The Social Life of the Teenager and Its Impact on Education.* Free Press, 1961(a). **450, 534**

Coleman, James S. *Community Conflict.* Free Press, 1957. **621, 623**

Coleman, James S. "Community Disorganization," in Robert K. Merton and Robert A. Nisbet, eds., *Contemporary Social Problems.* Harcourt, Brace & World, 1961(b), pp. 553–604. **620, 641**

Coleman, James S. Unpublished memorandum, 1958. **307**

Cook, Robert C. "World Population Growth," *Law and Contemporary Problems*, 25, 1960, pp. 379–88. **591**

Courts, F. A. "Relation Between Experimentally Induced Muscular Tension and Memorization," *J. Exper. Psychol.*, 25, 1939, pp. 235–56. **170**

Cressey, Donald R. "Crime," in Robert K. Merton and Robert A. Nisbet, eds., *Con-temporary Social Problems.* Harcourt, Brace & World, 1961, pp. 21–76. **625, 626, 629–30, 641**

Cronbach, Lee J. *Educational Psychology.* Harcourt, Brace & World, 1954. **217** 2nd ed. Harcourt, Brace & World, 1963. **235**

Cronbach, Lee J. *Essentials of Psychological Testing.* 2nd ed. Harper & Row, 1960. **35, 211, 213–14, 215**

Crutchfield, Richard S., D. G. Woodworth, and R. A. Albrecht. *Perceptual Performance and the Effective Person.* U.S. Air Force Personnel and Training Research Center, 1955. **116**

Curran, D. "The Problem of Assessing Psychiatric Treatment," *Lancet*, 2, 1937, pp. 1005–09. **288**

Cushing, M. C. "Affective Components of the Response Class as a Factor in Verbal Conditioning," *Dissertation Abstr.*, 17, 1957, p. 2313. **144**

Dahl, Robert A., Mason Haire, and Paul F. Lazarsfeld. *Social Science Research on Business: Product and Potential.* Columbia U. Press, 1959. **410, 450**

Daily, J. M. "Verbal Conditioning Without Awareness," *Dissertation Abstr.*, 13, 1953, pp. 1247–48. **144**

Dauer, Manning J. *The Adams Federalists.* Johns Hopkins Press, 1953. **417**

Davidson, Percy Erwin, and H. Dewey Anderson. *Occupational Mobility in an American Community.* Stanford U. Press, 1937. **471**

Davis, Allison. "Acculturation in Schools," in Milton L. Barron, ed., *American Minorities.* Knopf, 1957, pp. 446–49. **513, 521**

Davis, Allison, Burleigh B. Gardner, and Mary R. Gardner. *Deep South: A Social-Anthropological Study of Caste and Class.* U. of Chicago Press, 1941. **457, 490**

Davis, Arthur K. "Bureaucratic Patterns in the Navy Officers Corps," in Robert K. Merton *et al.*, eds., *Reader in Bureaucracy.* Free Press, 1952, pp. 380–95. **366**

Davis, Clara M. "Choice of Formulas Made by Three Infants During the Nursing Period," *Amer. J. Diseases in Children*, 50, 1935, pp. 385–94. **48**

Davis, Clara M. "A Practical Application of Some Lessons of the Self-Selection Diet and Feeding of Children in Hospitals," *Amer. J. Diseases in Children*, 46, 1943, pp. 743–50. **48**

Davis, Clara M. "Self-Selection of Diet by Newly Weaned Infants," *Amer. J. Diseases in Children*, 36, 1928, pp. 651–79. **48**

Davis, Kingsley. "The Demographic Consequences of Changes in Productive Technology: An Essay on the Problem of Measurement," in G. Balandier *et al.*, *Social, Economic and Technological Change: A Theoretical Approach.* International Bureau for Research in the Social Implications of Technical Progress. Presses Universitaires de France, 1959(a), pp. 193–227. **590, 599**

Davis, Kingsley. *Human Society.* Macmillan, 1949. **65, 385, 388, 460, 466**

Davis, Kingsley. "Population Analysis and Social Behavior." Unpublished paper presented to the Conference on Research in Human Relations, Rockefeller Foundation, February-March, 1953. **598–99**

Davis, Kingsley. "Prostitution," in Robert K. Merton and Robert A. Nisbet, eds., *Contemporary Social Problems.* Harcourt, Brace & World, 1961(a), pp. 262–90. **632–33, 641**

Davis, Kingsley. "The Sociology of Demographic Behavior," in Robert K. Merton et al., eds., *Sociology Today: Problems and Prospects.* Basic Books, 1959(b), pp. 309–33. **641**

Davis, Kingsley. "The World's Population Crisis," in Robert K. Merton and Robert A. Nisbet, eds., *Contemporary Social Problems.* Harcourt, Brace & World, 1961(b), pp. 291–323. **641**

Davis, Kingsley, and Judith Blake. "Social Structure and Fertility: An Analytic Framework," *Economic Development and Cultural Change,* 4, April, 1956, pp. 211–35. **304, 305, 597**

Davis, Kingsley, and Hilda H. Golden. "Urbanization and the Development of Pre-Industrial Areas," *Economic Development and Cultural Change,* 3, October, 1954, pp. 6–26. **604**

De Charms, Richard, Jerome Levy, and Michael Wertheimer. "A Note on Attempted Evaluations of Psychotherapy," *J. Clin. Psychol.,* 10, 1954, pp. 233–35. **289**

De Fleur, Melvin L., and Otto N. Larsen. *The Flow of Information: An Experiment in Mass Communication.* Harper & Row, 1958. **531**

Dement, William. "The Effect of Dream Deprivation," *Science,* 131, 1960, pp. 1705–07. **175, 176**

Dement, William, and Nathaniel Kleitman. "The Relation of Eye Movements During Sleep to Dream Activity: An Objective Method for the Study of Dreaming," *J. Exper. Psychol.,* 53, 1957, pp. 339–46. **175**

Dempsey, Edward W. "Homeostasis," in S. S. Stevens, ed., *Handbook of Experimental Psychology.* Wiley, 1951, pp. 209–35. **294**

Dennis, Wayne. "Infant Development Under Conditions of Restricted Practice and of Minimum Social Stimulation: A Preliminary Report," *J. Genet. Psychol.,* 53, 1938, pp. 149–57. **70**

Dennis, Wayne. "Variations in Productivity Among Creative Workers," *Scientific Monthly,* 80, 1955, pp. 277–78. **235**

Dennis, Wayne, and Marsena G. Dennis. "The Effect of Cradling Practices upon the Onset of Walking in Hopi Children," *J. Genet. Psychol.,* 56, 1940, pp. 77–86. **57**

Despert, J. L. "Anxieties, Phobias, and Fears in Young Children with Special Reference to Prenatal and Neo-natal Factors," *Nervous Child,* 5, 1946, pp. 8–24. **73**

Deutsch, Morton, and Mary E. Collins. *Interracial Housing: A Psychological Evaluation of a Social Experiment.* U. of Minnesota Press, 1951. **512, 524**

Deutscher, Max, and Isidor Chein. "The Psychological Effects of Enforced Segregation: A Survey of Social Science Opinion," *J. Psychol.,* 26, 1948, pp. 259–87. **524**

Dewey, John. *How We Think.* Heath, 1933. **202**

Dietrick, David C. "Review of Research," Appendix A, in Richard J. Hill, *A Comparative Study of Lecture and Discussion Methods.* Fund for Adult Education, 1960, pp. 90–118. **547**

Dietze, A. G., and G. E. Jones. "Factual Memory of Secondary School Pupils for a Short Article Which They Read a Single Time," *J. Educ. Psychol.,* 22, 1931, pp. 586–98, 667–76. **167**

Ditchburn, R. W., D. H. Fender, and Stella Mayne. "Vision with Controlled Movements of the Retinal Image," *J. Physiol.,* 145, 1959, pp. 98–107. **89**

Dixon, N. F. "The Effect of Subliminal Stimulation upon Autonomic and Verbal Behavior," *J. Abnorm. Soc. Psychol.,* 57, 1958, pp. 29–36. **94, 131**

Dollard, John. *Criteria for the Life History.* Yale U. Press, 1935. **35**

Dollard, John, with the assistance of Donald Horton. *Fear in Battle.* Institute of Human Relations, Yale U., 1943. **448**

Dollard, John, Leonard W. Doob, Neal E. Miller, O. H. Mowrer, and Robert R. Sears. *Frustration and Aggression.* Yale U. Press, 1939. **269, 270, 295**

Dollard, John, and Neal E. Miller. *Personality and Psychotherapy: An Analysis in Terms of Learning, Thinking, and Culture.* McGraw-Hill, 1950. **147, 279**

Domas, Simeon J., and David Tiedeman. "Teacher Competence: An Annotated Bibliography," *J. Exper. Educ.,* 19, 1950, pp. 101–218. **441**

Dorn, Harold F. "Mortality," in Philip M. Hauser and Otis Dudley Duncan, eds., *The Study of Population: An Inventory and Appraisal.* U. of Chicago Press, 1959, pp. 437–71. **601, 602–03**

Drake, St. Clair, and H. R. Clayton. *Black Metropolis.* Harcourt, Brace & World, 1945. **458**

Dreger, Ralph M., and Kent S. Miller. "Comparative Psychological Studies of Negroes and Whites in the United States," *Psychol. Bull.,* 57, 1960, pp. 361–402. **497–98, 524**

Dubin, Robert. *The World of Work: In-*

dustrial Society and Human Relations. Prentice-Hall, 1958. **400, 444, 483–84**

Dukes, William F. "Psychological Studies of Values," *Psychol. Bull.,* 52, 1955, pp. 24–50. **566, 574, 584**

Dulany, Don E., Jr. "The Place of Hypotheses and Intentions: An Analysis of Verbal Control in Verbal Conditioning," in Charles W. Eriksen, ed., *Behavior and Awareness.* Duke U. Press, 1962, pp. 102–29. **147**

Duncan, Otis Dudley. "Human Ecology and Population Studies," in Philip M. Hauser and Otis Dudley Duncan, eds., *The Study of Population: An Inventory and Appraisal.* U. of Chicago Press, 1959, pp. 678–716. **605, 607**

Duncan, Otis Dudley, and Beverly Duncan. "Residential Distribution and Occupational Stratification," *Amer. J. Sociol.,* 60, 1955, pp. 493–503. **609**

Duncker, Karl. "On Problem Solving," trans. by Lynne S. Lees, *Psychol. Monogr.,* 58, No. 5, 1945. **201, 202, 204, 236**

Durkheim, Emile. *Suicide.* Trans. by John A. Spaulding and George Simpson. Free Press, 1958. **634**

Duverger, Maurice. *Political Parties: Their Organization and Activity in the Modern State.* Trans. by Barbara and Robert North. 2nd English ed., rev. Methuen, 1959. **423**

Eaton, Joseph W., in collaboration with Robert J. Weil. *Culture and Mental Disorders.* Free Press, 1955. **638**

Ebbinghaus, H. *Das Gedächtnis.* Duncker & Humbolt, 1885. **167**

Ebbinghaus, H. *Memory.* Trans. (of *Das Gedächtnis*) by H. A. Ruger and C. E. Bussenius. Teachers College, Columbia U., 1913. **235**

Edfeldt, Ake W. *Silent Speech and Silent Reading.* U. of Chicago Press, 1960. **172, 173, 174**

Edwards, A. L. *Experimental Design in Psychological Research.* Rev. ed. Holt, Rinehart & Winston, 1960. **35**

"The Effects of Segregation and the Consequences of Desegregation: A Social Science Statement." *Minnesota Law Rev.,* 37, 1953, pp. 427–39. **497, 521, 525**

Efron, David. *Gesture and Environment.* King's Crown Press, 1941. **505, 654**

Eggan, Fred. *Social Organization of the Western Pueblos.* U. of Chicago Press, 1950. **656**

Eisenstadt, Shmuel N. *The Absorption of Immigrants.* Free Press, 1955. **71**

Eisenstadt, Shmuel N. *From Generation to Generation: Age Groups and Social Structure.* Free Press, 1956. **82**

Ekman, P. "A Comparison of Verbal and Nonverbal Behavior as Reinforcing Stimuli of Opinion Responses." Unpublished

doctoral dissertation, Adelphi College, 1958. **144**

Ellis, Willis D. *A Source Book of Gestalt Psychology.* Harcourt, Brace & World, 1938. **109, 130**

English, H. B., E. L. Welborn, and C. D. Killian. "Studies in Substance Memorization," *J. Gen. Psychol.,* 11, 1934, pp. 233–59. **167**

Erickson, Milton H. "Experimental Demonstrations of the Psychopathology of Everyday Life," *Psychoanal. Quart.,* 8, 1939(a), pp. 338–53. **280–81**

Erickson, Milton H. "An Experimental Investigation of the Possible Anti-Social Use of Hypnosis," *Psychiatry,* 2, 1939(b), pp. 391–414. **123–24**

Erickson, Milton H., and Elizabeth M. Erickson. "Concerning the Nature and Character of Post-Hypnotic Behavior," *J. Gen. Psychol.,* 24, 1941, pp. 95–133. **124**

Estes, William K. "An Experimental Study of Punishment." *Psychol. Monogr.,* 57, No. 3, 1944. **152**

Etzioni, Amitai. *A Comparative Analysis of Complex Organizations: On Power, Involvement, and Their Correlates.* Free Press, 1961(a). **377, 380**

Etzioni, Amitai, ed. *Complex Organizations: A Sociological Reader.* Holt, Rinehart & Winston, 1961(b). **380**

Evans-Pritchard, E. E. *The Nuer.* Oxford U. Press, 1940. **656**

Eysenck, H. J. "The Effects of Psychotherapy: An Evaluation." *J. Consult. Psychol.,* 16, 1952, pp. 319–24. **287, 288, 299**

Eysenck, H. J., and S. Crown. "National Stereotypes: An Experimental and Methodological Study," *International J. Opin. Attitude Res.,* 2, 1948, pp. 26–39. **501**

Fahmy, Sumaya A. "Conditioning and Extinction of a Referential Verbal Response Class in a Situation Resembling a Clinical Diagnostic Interview," *Dissertation Abstr.,* 13, 1953, pp. 873–74. **144**

Farber, Bernard. "Effects of a Severely Mentally Retarded Child on Family Integration," *Monogr. Soc. Res. Child Development,* 24, No. 2, 1959. **380**

Fenichel, O. "Ten Years of the Berlin Psychoanalytic Institute: 1920–1930." **288**

Ferster, C. B., and B. F. Skinner. *Schedules of Reinforcement.* Appleton-Century-Crofts, 1957. **155**

Festinger, Leon. "Informal Social Communication," *Psychol. Rev.* 57, 1950, pp. 271–92. **361**

Festinger, Leon. "The Psychological Effects of Insufficient Rewards," *Amer. Psychologist,* 16, 1961, pp. 1–11. **153, 154**

Festinger, Leon. *A Theory of Cognitive Dissonance.* Harper & Row, 1957. **266, 295, 537, 578**

Festinger, Leon, and Daniel Katz, eds. *Research Methods in the Behavioral Sciences.* Holt, Rinehart & Winston, 1953. **35**

Festinger, Leon, Stanley Schachter, and Kurt Back. *Social Pressures in Informal Groups.* Harper & Row, 1950. **328, 332, 334**

Festinger, Leon, and John Thibaut. "Interpersonal Communication in Small Groups," *J. Abnorm. Soc. Psychol.,* 46, 1951, 92–99. **347**

Filby, Yasuko. "Teaching Machines," *Nordisk Psykologi,* 13, 1961, pp. 209–56. **149**

Firth, Raymond. *Elements of Social Organization.* Philosophical Library, 1951. **656**

Firth, Raymond, F. J. Fisher, and D. G. MacRae. "Social Implications of Technological Change as Regards Patterns and Models," in G. Balandier *et al., Social, Economic and Technological Change: A Theoretical Approach.* International Bureau for Research in the Social Implications of Technical Progress. Presses Universitaires de France, 1959, pp. 261–93. **397, 401**

Fischer, S., and H. Hirschberg. "Die Verbreitung der eidetischen Anlage im Jugendalter und ihre Beziehungen zu körperlichen Merkmalen," *Zeitschrift für die gesamte Neurologie und Psychiatrie,* 88, 1924, pp. 241–95. **188**

Fisher, R. A. *The Design of Experiments.* 4th ed. Oliver & Boyd, 1947. **35**

Fite, M. D. "Aggressive Behavior in Young Children and Children's Attitudes Toward Aggression," *Genet. Psychol. Monogr.* 22, 1940, pp. 151–319. **577**

Fleishman, Edwin A., Edwin F. Harris, and Harold E. Burtt. *Leadership and Supervision in Industry: An Evaluation of a Supervisory Training Program.* Ohio State U., 1955. **372**

Ford, Clellan S., and Frank A. Beach. *Patterns of Sexual Behavior.* Harper & Row, 1951. **294, 298, 299, 301, 303, 314, 322**

Forlano, G. *School Learning with Various Methods of Practice and Rewards.* Teachers College, Columbia U., 1936. **166**

Fortes, Meyer. "Introduction," in Jack Goody, ed., *The Developmental Cycle in Domestic Groups.* Cambridge Papers in Social Anthropology, No. 1. Cambridge U. Press for the Dept. of Archaeology and Anthropology, 1958, pp. 1–14. **82–83**

Fortes, Meyer. *The Web of Kinship Among the Tallensi.* International African Institute. Oxford U. Press, 1949. **656**

Foster, George M. *Traditional Cultures, and the Impact of Technological Change.* Harper & Row, 1962. **616, 652**

Frazier, Franklin. *The Negro in the United States.* Rev. ed. Macmillan, 1957. **461**

Freedman, Ronald. *The Sociology of Human Fertility: A Trend Report and Bibliography.* Prepared for the International Sociological Association, with the support of UNESCO. Blackwell, 1963. **594**

Freedman, Ronald, Amos H. Hawley, Werner S. Landecker, Gerhard E. Lenski, and Horace M. Miner. *Principles of Sociology.* Rev. ed. Holt, Rinehart & Winston, 1956. **307, 329, 467, 606, 616, 617, 618, 628–29, 654, 655**

Freeman, Frank N., and Charles D. Flory. "Growth in Intellectual Ability as Measured by Repeated Tests," *Monogr. Soc. Res. Child Development,* 2, No. 2, 1937. **63**

Freeman, G. L. "Changes in Tonus During Completed and Interrupted Mental Work," *J. Gen. Psychol.,* 4, 1930, pp. 309–34. **170**

French, E. G., and F. H. Thomas. "The Relation of Achievement Motivation to Problem Solving Effectiveness," *J. Abnorm. Soc. Psychol.,* 56, 1958, pp. 45–48. **260**

Frenkel-Brunswik, Else. "Intolerance of Ambiguity as an Educational and Perceptual Personality Variable," *J. Pers.,* 18, 1949, pp. 108–43. **116**

Frenkel-Brunswik, Else, and R. Nevitt Sanford. "Some Personality Factors in Anti-Semitism," *J. Psychol.,* 20, 1945, pp. 271–91. **282–83**

Freud, Sigmund. *The Interpretation of Dreams.* Trans. by A. A. Brill. Macmillan, 1933. **295**

Freud, Sigmund. "Psycho-analytic Notes upon an Autobiographical Account of a Case of Paranoia (Dementia Paranoides)," in *Collected Papers,* Vol. III. Hogarth, 1911, pp. 387–470. **285**

Freud, Sigmund. *The Psychopathology of Everyday Life.* Macmillan, 1913. **280** 1917. **295**

Friedrich, Ernst. "Jugend in Gefangenschaft: Bericht eines aus Russland Heimgekehrten Studenten" ("Youth in Captivity: A Report of a Student Returned from Russia"), *Deutsche Universitäts-Zeitung,* 5, 1950, pp. 13–25. **242**

Fries, Margaret E. "Mental Hygiene in Pregnancy, Delivery, and Puerperium," *Mental Hygiene,* 25, 1941, pp. 221–36. **73**

Fritz, Charles E. "Disaster," in Robert K. Merton and Robert A. Nisbet, eds., *Contemporary Social Problems.* Harcourt, Brace & World, 1961, pp. 651–94. **623, 624–25, 641**

Galtung, Johan. "A Framework for the Analysis of Social Conflict." Unpublished ms., 1958. **635**

Gardner, B. B. *Human Relations in Industry.* Irwin, 1944. **370**

Gardner, G. E. "Evidences of Homosexuality in 120 Unanalyzed Cases with Paranoid Content," *Psychoanal. Rev.*, 18, 1931, pp. 57–62. **285**

Garth, Thomas R. "A Study of the Foster Indian Child in the White Home." Unpublished paper read at the 43rd annual meeting of the American Psychological Assoc., Ann Arbor, Mich., September, 1935. Abstract in *Psychol. Bull.*, 32, 1935, pp. 708–09. **500**

Gates, Arthur I. "Recitation as a Function in Memorizing," *Arch. Psychol.*, 6, No. 40, 1917. **166**

Geiger, Theodor. "Recruitment of University Students," *Acta Sociologia*, 1, 1955, pp. 39–48. **438**

Geldard, Frank A. *The Human Senses.* Wiley, 1953. **130**

Gerwitz, Jacob L., and Donald M. Baer. "Deprivation and Satiation of Social Reinforcers as Drive Conditions," *J. Abnorm. Soc. Psychol.*, 57, 1958, pp. 165–72. **253**

Gesell, Arnold. *Infancy and Human Growth.* Macmillan, 1928. **56–57**

Gesell, Arnold. *The Mental Growth of the Pre-school Child.* Macmillan, 1925. **56–57**

Gesell, Arnold, and Frances L. Ilg, with Louise B. Ames and Glenna E. Bullis. *The Child from Five to Ten.* Harper & Row, 1946. **85**

Gesell, Arnold, and Helen Thompson. "Learning and Maturation in Identical Twins: An Experimental Analysis by the Method of Co-twin Control," in R. G. Barker, J. S. Kounin, and H. F. Wright, eds., *Child Behavior and Development.* McGraw-Hill, 1943, pp. 209–27. **57**

Gesell, Arnold, *et al. The First Five Years of Life.* Harper & Row, 1940. **85**

Getzels, Jacob W., and Philip W. Jackson. *Creativity and Intelligence: Explorations with Gifted Students.* Wiley, 1962, **228, 231, 232, 233, 234**

Gibb, Cecil A. "Leadership," in Gardner Lindzey, ed., *Handbook of Social Psychology*, Vol. II. Addison-Wesley, 1954, pp. 877–920. **342, 344, 373**

Gibbs, Jack P. "Suicide," in Robert K. Merton and Robert A. Nisbet, eds., *Contemporary Social Problems.* Harcourt, Brace & World, 1961, pp. 222–61. **635, 641**

Gibson, James J. "The Reproduction of Visually Perceived Forms," *J. Exper. Psychol.*, 12, 1929, pp. 1–39. **183**

Ginzberg, Eli, Sol W. Ginsburg, Sidney Axelrad, and John L. Herma. *Occupational Choice: An Approach to a General Theory.* Columbia U. Press, 1951. **404, 450**

Girard, Alain. "L'Orientation et la Selection des Enfants d'Age Scolaire dans le Département de la Seine," *Population*, 8, 1953, pp. 649–72. **438**

Girden, Edward. "A Review of Psychokinesis (PK)," *Psychol. Bull.*, 59, 1962, pp. 353–88. **128**

Gist, Noel P. "The Urban Community," in Joseph B. Gittler, ed., *Review of Sociology: Analysis of a Decade.* Wiley, 1957, pp. 159–85. **641**

Gist, Noel P., and L. A. Halbert. *Urban Society.* 4th ed. Crowell, 1956. **608–09**

Gittler, Joseph B., ed. *Review of Sociology: Analysis of a Decade.* Wiley, 1957. **641**

Glass, David V., ed. *Social Mobility in Britain.* Free Press. 1954. **490**

Glass, David V., and J. R. Hall. "Social Mobility in Great Britain: A Study of Inter-Generation Changes in Status," in David V. Glass, ed., *Social Mobility in Britain.* Free Press, 1954, pp. 177–265. **475**

Glick, Paul C., and Emanuel Landau. "Age as a Factor in Marriage," *Amer. Sociol. Rev.*, 15, 1950, pp. 517–29. **308**

Glock, Charles Y. "The Sociology of Religion," in Robert K. Merton *et al.*, eds., *Sociology Today: Problems and Prospects.* Basic Books, 1959, pp. 153–77. **389, 392, 450**

Gluckman, Max. *Judicial Process Among the Barotse of Northern Rhodesia.* Free Press, 1955. **656**

Glueck, Sheldon, and Eleanor Glueck. *Physique and Delinquency.* Harper & Row, 1956. **630**

Glueck, Sheldon, and Eleanor Glueck. *Predicting Delinquency and Crime.* Harvard U. Press, 1959. **630**

Glueck, Sheldon, and Eleanor Glueck. *Unraveling Juvenile Delinquency.* Harvard U. Press for the Commonwealth Fund, 1950. **83, 577, 630**

Goldfarb, William. "The Effects of Early Institutional Care on Adolescent Personality," *J. Exper. Educ.*, 12, 1943, pp. 106–29. **67**

Goldhamer, Herbert, and Andrew W. Marshall. *Psychosis and Civilization.* Free Press, 1953. **637**

Goldiamond, Israel. "Indicators of Perception: Subliminal Perception, Subception, Unconscious Perception: An Analysis in Terms of Psychophysical Indicator Methodology," *Psychol. Bull.*, 55, 1958, pp. 373–407. **131**

Goldsen, Rose K., Morris Rosenberg, Robin M. Williams, Jr., and Edward A. Suchman. *What College Students Think.* Van Nostrand, 1960. **393, 404–05, 565–66, 571–72, 584**

Goode, William J. "Contemporary Thinking About Primitive Religion," *Sociologus*, 5, 1955, pp. 122–31. **385, 388, 389**

Goode, William J. "Family Disorganization," in Robert K. Merton and Robert A. Nisbet, eds., *Contemporary Social Problems.* Harcourt, Brace & World,

1961, pp. 390–458. **307, 311, 312, 313, 322, 395, 626**

Goode, William J. *Industrialization and Family Change.* Paper presented at the North American Conference on the Social Implications of Industrialization and Technological Change, sponsored by UNESCO, Canadian National Commission for UNESCO, United States National Commission for UNESCO, U. of Chicago, 1960. **397–98, 399, 474–75**

Goode, William J. *Religion Among the Primitives.* Free Press, 1951. **450**

Goode, William J. "The Sociology of the Family," in Robert K. Merton *et al.*, eds., *Sociology Today: Problems and Prospects.* Basic Books, 1959, pp. 178–96. **314**

Goode, William J. *World Revolution and Family Patterns.* Free Press, 1963. **323**

Goode, William J., and Paul Hatt. *Methods in Social Research.* McGraw-Hill, 1952. **35**

Goodman, Mary Ellen. *Race Awareness in Young Children.* Addison-Wesley, 1952. **521**

Gordon, Hans C., and Benjamin J. Novak. "I.Q. and Month of Birth," *Science,* 112, 1950, pp. 62–63. **226**

Gottheil, E. "Über das latente Sinnengedächtnis der Jugendlichen und seine Aufdeckung," *Zeitschrift für Psychologie,* 87, 1921, p. 73. **188**

Gough, E. Kathleen. "Changing Kinship Usages in the Setting of Political and Economic Change Among the Nayars of Malabar," *Journal of the Royal Anthropological Institute of Great Britain and Ireland,* 82, part 1, 1952, pp. 71–88. **398**

Gough, H. G. "Techniques for Identifying the Creative Research Scientist," in Institute of Personality Assessment and Research, *The Creative Person.* U. of California and University Extension, Liberal Arts Dept., 1961, pp. III-1–III-27. **228**

Gouldner, Alvin W. *Patterns of Industrial Bureaucracy.* Free Press, 1954. **377, 380**

Graham, Stanley R. "The Effects of Psychoanalytically Oriented Psychotherapy on Levels of Frequency and Satisfaction in Sexual Activity," *J. Clin. Psychol.,* 16, 1960, pp. 94–98. **291**

Gray, Philip H. "Theory and Evidence of Imprinting in Human Infants," *J. Psychol.,* 46, 1958, pp. 155–66. **70, 85**

Greenblum, Joseph, and Leonard I. Pearlin. "Vertical Mobility and Prejudice: A Socio-Psychological Analysis," in Reinhard Bendix and Seymour M. Lipset, eds., *Class, Status and Power: A Reader in Social Stratification.* Free Press, 1953, pp. 480–91. **514**

Greenspoon, J. "The Effect of Two Nonverbal Stimuli on the Frequency of Members of Two Verbal Response Classes,"

Amer. Psychologist, 9, 1954, p. 384 (Abstract). **144**

Greenspoon, J. "The Reinforcing Effect of Two Spoken Sounds on the Frequency of Two Responses," *Amer. J. Psychol.,* 68, 1955, pp. 409–16. **144**

Gross, Edward. *Work and Society.* Crowell, 1958. **467, 486**

Gross, Neal. "The Sociology of Education," in Robert K. Merton *et al.*, eds., *Sociology Today: Problems and Prospects.* Basic Books, 1959, pp. 128–52. **485**

Grossberg, John M. "The Effect of Reinforcement Schedule and Response Class on Verbal Conditioning," *Dissertation Abstr.,* 16, 1956, p. 2211. **144**

Guide to the Use of the General Aptitude Test. U.S. Gov't. Printing Office, 1958. **211**

Gusfield, Joseph R. "Social Structure and Moral Reform: A Study of the Women's Christian Temperance Union," *Amer. J. Sociol.,* 61, 1955, pp. 221–32. **366**

Haggerty, A. D. Review of Milton V. Kline, "Hypnotic Age Regression and Intelligence" (*J. Genet. Psychol.,* 77, 1950), in *Annu. Rev. Hypnosis Literature,* 1–2, 1953, pp. 34–35. **122**

Haire, Mason. "Psychology and the Study of Business: Joint Behavioral Sciences," in Robert A. Dahl *et al.*, *Social Science Research on Business: Product and Potential.* Columbia U. Press, 1959, pp. 45–98. **410**

Hall, Calvin S., and Gardner Lindzey. "Psychoanalytic Theory and Its Applications in the Social Sciences," in Gardner Lindzey, ed., *Handbook of Social Psychology,* Vol. I. Addison-Wesley, 1954, pp. 143–80. **78**

Hall, Robert A., Jr. *Linguistics and Your Language.* Doubleday, 1960. **191**

Halsey, A. H., Jean Floud, and C. Arnold Anderson, eds. *Education, Economy, and Society.* Free Press, 1961. **450**

Halverson, Henry M. "The Development of Prehension in Infants," in R. G. Barker, J. S. Kounin, and H. F. Wright, eds., *Child Behavior and Development.* McGraw-Hill, 1943, pp. 49–66. **55**

Hamilton, D. M., I. H. Vanney, and T. H. Wall. "Hospital Treatment of Patients with Psychoneurotic Disorder," *Amer. J. Psychiat.,* 99, 1942, pp. 243–74. **288**

Hamilton, D. M., and T. H. Wall. "Hospital Treatment of Patients with Psychoneurotic Disorder," *Amer. J. Psychiat.,* 98, 1941, pp. 551–57. **288**

Hamilton, G. V. *A Research in Marriage.* Boni, 1929. **286**

Harbison, Frederick H., and Robert Dubin. *Patterns of Union-Management Relations.* Science Research Associates, 1947. **617**

Harding, John, Bernard Kutner, Harold Proshansky, and Isidor Chein. "Prejudice and Ethnic Relations," in Gardner Lindzey, ed., *Handbook of Social Psychology*, Vol. II. Addison-Wesley, 1954, pp. 1021–61. **503, 523**

Hare, A. Paul, Edgar F. Borgatta, and Robert F. Bales. *Small Groups: Studies in Social Interaction*. Knopf, 1955. **361**

Harlow, Harry F. "The Nature of Love," *Amer. Psychologist*, 13, 1958, pp. 673–85. **294**

Harlow, Harry F., and Margaret K. Harlow. "The Effect of Rearing Conditions on Behavior." *Bull. Menninger Clin.*, 26, 1962(a), pp. 213–24. **68, 69–70**

Harlow, Harry F., and Margaret K. Harlow. "Social Deprivation in Monkeys," *Scientific American*, 207, No. 5, 1962(b), pp. 136–46. **69**

Harlow, Harry F., Margaret K. Harlow, and Donald R. Meyer. "Learning Motivated by a Manipulation Drive," *J. Exper. Psychol.*, 40, 1950, pp. 228–34. **249**

Harlow, Harry F., and Robert R. Zimmermann. "Affectional Responses in the Infant Monkey," *Science*, 130, 1959, pp. 421–32. **247**

Harrell, Thomas W., and Margaret S. Harrell. "Army General Classification Test Scores for Civilian Occupations," *Educ. Psychol. Measmt.*, 5, 1945, pp. 229–39. **223–24**

Harris, Chauncy D., and Edward L. Ullman. "The Nature of Cities," *Annals of the American Academy of Political and Social Science*, No. 242, 1945, pp. 7–17. **607**

Hartley, Eugene L. *Problems in Prejudice*. King's Crown Press, 1946. **524**

Hartman, C. H. "Verbal Behavior of Schizophrenic and Normal Subjects as a Function of Types of Social Reinforcement," *Dissertation Abstr.*, 15, 1955, pp. 1652–53. **144**

Hartshorne, Hugh, and Mark A. May. *Studies in Deceit*. Macmillan, 1928(a). **577**

Hartshorne, Hugh, and Mark A. May. *Studies in the Nature of Character*. Macmillan, 1928(b). **577**

Hartshorne, Hugh, Mark A. May, and Frank K. Shuttleworth. *Studies in the Organization of Character*. Macmillan, 1930. **566**

Haskell, Raymond I. "A Statistical Study of the Comparative Results Produced by Teaching Derivation in the Ninth Grade Latin Classes and in the Ninth Grade English Classes of Non-Latin Pupils in Four Philadelphia High Schools." Unpublished doctoral dissertation, U. of Pennsylvania, 1923. **162**

Hauser, Philip, and Otis Dudley Duncan, eds. *The Study of Population: An Inventory and Appraisal*. U. of Chicago Press, 1959. **641**

Havighurst, R. J., and Leota L. Janke. "Relations Between Ability and Social Status in a Midwestern Community," *J. Educ. Psychol.*, 35, 1944, pp. 357–68. **211**

Hebb, D. O. "The American Revolution," *Amer. Psychologist*, 15, 1960, pp. 735–45. **91**

Hebb, D. O. "Drives and the C. N. S. (Conceptual Nervous System)," *Psychol. Rev.*, 62, 1955, p. 243. **91**

Hebb, D. O. "The Motivating Effects of Exteroceptive Stimulation," *Amer. Psychologist*, 13, 1958, p. 109. **91**

Hecht, Selig, and Simon Shlaer. "An Adaptometer for Measuring Human Dark Adaption," *J. Optical Soc. Amer.*, 28, 1938, pp. 269–75. **93**

Heidbreder, Edna. "An Experimental Study of Thinking," *Arch. Psychol.*, 11, No. 73, 1924. **194**

Heidbreder, Edna, Mary L. Bensley, and Margaret Ivy. "The Attainment of Concepts: IV. Regularities and Levels," *J. Psychol.*, 25, 1948, pp. 229–329. **193, 197**

Heise, George A., and George A. Miller. "Problem Solving by Small Groups Using Various Communication Nets," *J. Abnorm. Soc. Psychol.*, 46, 1951, pp. 327–35. **357**

Hendrickson, G., and W. H. Schroeder. "Transfer of Training in Learning To Hit a Submerged Target," *J. Educ. Psychol.*, 32, 1941, pp. 205–13. **162**

Henry, Andrew F., and James F. Short, Jr. *Suicide and Homicide: Some Economic, Sociological and Psychological Aspects of Aggression*. Free Press, 1954. **635**

Heron, Woodburn. "Cognitive and Physiological Effects of Perceptual Isolation," in Philip Solomon et al., eds., *Sensory Deprivation*, a symposium at the Harvard Medical School. Harvard U. Press, 1961, pp. 6–33. **90–91**

Herzberg, Frederick, Bernard Mausner, Richard O. Peterson, and Dora F. Capwell. *Job Attitudes: Review of Research and Opinion*. Psychological Service of Pittsburgh, 1957. **410–11, 450**

Hess, Eckhard H. "Imprinting." *Science*, 130, 1959, pp. 133–41. **42, 43**

Hess, Eckhard H. Personal communication, 1963. **103–04**

Hess, Eckhard H., and James Polt. "Pupil Size as Related to Interest Value of Visual Stimuli," *Science*, 132, 1960, pp. 349–50. **103**

Hildum, D. C., and R. W. Brown. "Verbal Reinforcement and Interviewer Bias," *J. Abnorm. Soc. Psychol.*, 53, 1956, pp. 108–11. **144, 146**

Change. Yale U. Press, 1953. **537, 541, 549, 553, 555**

Hovland, Carl I., Arthur A. Lumsdaine, and Fred D. Sheffield. *Experiments on Mass Communication.* Princeton U. Press, 1949. **555**

Hovland, Carl I., Wallace Mandell, Enid H. Campbell *et al. The Order of Presentation in Persuasion.* Yale Studies in Attitude and Communication, Vol. I, ed. by Carl I. Hovland. Yale U. Press, 1957(b). **551–52, 555**

Hovland, Carl I., and Robert R. Sears. "Minor Studies of Aggression: VI. Correlations of Lynchings with Economic Indices," *J. Psychol.,* 9, 1940, pp. 301–10. **268–69, 514**

Huddleson, J. H. "Psychotherapy in 200 Cases of Psychoneurosis," *Mil. Surgeon,* 60, 1927, pp. 161–70. **288**

Hughes, Everett C. *French Canada in Transition.* Routledge & Kegan Paul, 1946(a). **620**

Hughes, Everett C. "The Knitting of Racial Groups in Industry," *Amer. Sociol. Rev.,* 11, 1946(b), pp. 512–19. **332**

Hull, Clark L. *A Behavior System.* Yale U. Press, 1952. **235**

Hull, Clark L. *Hypnosis and Suggestibility.* Appleton-Century-Crofts, 1933. **121, 122**

Hull, Clark L. "Quantitative Aspects of the Evolution of Concepts: An Experimental Study," *Psychol. Monogr.,* 28, No. 123, 1920. **193**

Hull, Clark L., Carl I. Hovland, Robert T. Ross, *et al. Mathematico-deductive Theory of Rote Learning.* Yale U. Press, 1940. **160**

Humphrey, George. *Thinking: An Introduction to Its Experimental Psychology.* Wiley, 1951. **174**

Hunt, J. McV. "The Effects of Infant Feeding Frustration upon Adult Hoarding in the Albino Rat," *J. Abnorm. Soc. Psychol.,* 36, 1941, pp. 338–60. **76**

Huntington, Ellsworth. *Civilization and Climate.* Yale U. Press, 1915. **612**

Hurlock, Elizabeth B. *Child Development.* 3rd ed. McGraw-Hill, 1956. **59, 85, 507, 577**

Hyman, Herbert H. *Political Socialization: A Study in the Psychology of Political Behavior.* Free Press, 1959. **562, 563–64, 584**

Hyman, Herbert H. *Survey Design and Analysis.* Free Press, 1955. **35**

Hyman, Herbert H. "The Value Systems of Different Classes: A Social Psychological Contribution to the Analysis of Stratification," in Reinhard Bendix and Seymour M. Lipset, eds., *Class, Status and Power: A Reader in Social Stratification.* Free Press, 1953, pp. 426–42. **486, 491**

Hyman, Herbert H., with William J. Cobb *et al. Interviewing in Social Research.* U. of Chicago Press, 1954. **35**

Hyman, Herbert H., and Paul B. Sheatsley. "The Current Status of American Public Opinion," *National Council for the Social Studies Yearbook,* 21, 1950, pp. 11–34. **585**

Hymes, Dell H. "Lexicostatistics So Far," *Current Anthropology,* 1, 1960, pp. 3–44. **190**

Inhelder, B., and Jean Piaget. *The Growth of Logical Thinking from Childhood to Adolescence.* Basic Books, 1958. **198**

Inkeles, Alex, and Peter H. Rossi. "National Comparisons of Occupational Prestige," *Amer. J. Sociol.,* 61, 1956, pp. 329–39. **463**

Irwin, Orvis C. "The Distribution of the Amount of Motility in Young Infants Between Two Nursing Periods," *J. Comp. Psychol.,* 14, 1932, pp. 429–45. **263**

Isaacs, Wayne, James Thomas, and Israel Goldiamond. "Application of Operant Conditioning To Reinstate Verbal Behavior in Psychotics," *J. Speech Hear. Dis.,* 25, 1960, pp. 8–12. **149**

Jacob, Philip E. *Changing Values in College: An Exploratory Study of the Impact of College Teaching.* Harper & Row, 1957. **440** 1958. **450**

Jacobson, Edmund. "Electrophysiology of Mental Activities," *Amer. J. Psychol.,* 44, 1932, pp. 677–94. **171**

Jacobson, Edmund. *Progressive Relaxation.* 2nd ed. U. of Chicago Press, 1938. **169, 171**

Jacobson, Paul H. *American Marriage and Divorce.* Holt, Rinehart & Winston, 1959. **311, 323**

Jaffe, A. J. "Population Trends and Controls in Underdeveloped Countries." *Law and Contemporary Problems,* 25, 1960, pp. 508–35. **599**

Jaffe, A. J., and Charles D. Stewart. *Manpower Resources and Utilization: Principles of Working-Force Analysis.* Wiley, 1951. **450**

James, William. *Principles of Psychology.* Holt, Rinehart & Winston, 1890. **53**

Janis, Irving L. "Personality Correlates of Susceptibility to Persuasion," *J. Pers.,* 22, 1954, pp. 504–18. **549**

Janis, Irving L., and Seymour Feshbach. "Effects of Fear-Arousing Communications," *J. Abnorm. Soc. Psychol.,* 48, 1953, pp. 78–92. **552**

Janis, Irving L., and Bert T. King. "The Influence of Role Playing on Opinion Change," *J. Abnorm. Soc. Psychol.,* 49, 1954, pp. 211–18. **549, 550**

Janowitz, Morris. "The Military Establishment: Organization and Disorganization," in Robert K. Merton and Robert A. Nisbet, eds., *Contemporary Social Problems.* Harcourt, Brace & World, 1961, pp. 515–52. **444, 447, 449**

Janowitz, Morris. *The Professional Soldier: A Social and Political Portrait.* Free Press, 1960. **443, 451**

Janowitz, Morris. *Sociology and the Military Establishment.* Russell Sage Foundation, 1959. **370, 443, 446, 451, 461**

Jasper, Herbert H. "Electroencephalography," in Wilder Penfield and Theodore C. Erickson, eds., *Epilepsy and Cerebral Localization.* Thomas, 1941, pp. 380–454. **177**

Jasper, Herbert H., and C. Shagass. "Conditioning of the Occipital Alpha Rhythm in Man," *J. Exper. Psychol.,* 28, 1941, pp. 373–88. **178**

Jenkins, William O., and Julian C. Stanley, Jr. "Partial Reinforcement: A Review and Critique," *Psychol. Bull.,* 47, 1950, pp. 193–234. **151**

Jersild, Arthur T. *Child Psychology.* 4th ed. Prentice-Hall, 1954. **61–62**

Johnson, Daniel M. *The Psychology of Thought and Judgment.* Harper & Row, 1955. **356**

Johnstone, John, and Elihu Katz. "Youth and Popular Music: A Study in the Sociology of Taste," *Amer. J. Sociol.,* 62, 1957, pp. 563–68. **340**

Jones, Edward E., and Jane Aneshansel. "The Learning and Utilization of Contravaluant Material," *J. Abnorm. Soc. Psychol.,* 53, 1956, pp. 27–33. **550**

Jones, Ernest. "Decennial Report of the London Clinic of Psychoanalysis: 1926–1936." **288**

Jones, G. M. Personal communication to D. O. Hebb, in "The American Revolution," *Amer. Psychologist,* 15, 1960, pp. 735–45. **91**

Jones, Marshall R., ed. *Nebraska Symposium on Motivation.* U. of Nebraska Press, 1953– . **295**

Jones, V. *Character and Citizenship Training in the Public School.* U. of Chicago Press, 1936. **577**

Kagan, Henry E. *Changing the Attitude of Christian Toward Jew: A Psychological Approach Through Religion.* Columbia U. Press, 1952. **518–19**

Kahl, Joseph A. *The American Class Structure.* Holt, Rinehart & Winston, 1957. **468, 469, 478, 490**

Kahl, Joseph A. "Educational and Occupational Aspirations of 'Common Man' Boys," *Harvard Educ. Rev.,* 23, 1953, pp. 186–203. **438, 485**

Kahn, Robert, and Daniel Katz. "Leadership Practices in Relation to Productivity and Morale," in Dorwin Cartwright and

Alvin Zander, eds., *Group Dynamics: Research and Theory.* Harper & Row, 1953, pp. 612–28. **375**

Kahn, Robert, Arnold Tannenbaum, Robert Weiss, *et al. A Study of the League of Women Voters of the United States.* U. of Michigan, Survey Research Center, 1956. **380**

Kanfer, F. H. "The Effect of Partial Reinforcement on Acquisition and Extinction of a Class of Verbal Response," *J. Exper. Psychol.,* 48, 1954, pp. 424–32. **144**

Kaplan, Bernice A. "Environment and Human Plasticity," *Amer. Anthropologist,* 56, 1954, pp. 780–800. **613**

Katona, George, and Eva Mueller. "A Study of Purchase Decisions," in L. H. Clark, ed., *Consumer Behavior,* 1, 1954, pp. 30–87. **487**

Katz, Daniel. "The Functional Approach to the Study of Attitudes," *Pub. Opin. Quart.,* 24, 1960, pp. 163–204. **580**

Katz, Daniel, and K. W. Braly. "Racial Stereotypes of 100 College Students," *J. Abnorm. Soc. Psychol.,* 28, 1933, pp. 280–90. **503**

Katz, Daniel, Dorwin Cartwright, Samuel Eldersveld, and Alfred McClung Lee, eds. *Public Opinion and Propaganda.* Holt, Rinehart & Winston, 1954. **554**

Katz, Elihu, and Paul F. Lazarsfeld. *Personal Influence.* Free Press, 1955. **555, 569, 585**

Keesing, Felix M. *Culture Change: An Analysis and Bibliography of Anthropological Sources to 1952.* Stanford U. Press, 1953. **614, 615**

Kelley, Harold H. "Communication in Experimentally Created Hierarchies," *Hum. Relat.,* 4, 1951, pp. 39–56. **370**

Kelley, Harold H. "Salience of Membership and Resistance to Change of Group-Anchored Attitudes," *Hum. Relat.,* 8, 1955, pp. 275–89. **566**

Kelley, Harold H. "The Warm-Cold Variable in First Impressions of Persons." *J. Pers.,* 18, 1950, pp. 431–39. **114**

Kelley, Harold H., and John W. Thibaut. "Experimental Studies of Group Problem Solving and Process," in Gardner Lindzey, ed., *Handbook of Social Psychology,* Vol. II. Addison-Wesley, 1954, pp. 735–85. **336, 337, 361**

Kelley, Harold H., and Edmund H. Volkart. "The Resistance to Change of Group-Anchored Attitudes," *Amer. Sociol. Rev.,* 17, 1952, pp. 453–65. **540**

Kelley, Harold H., and Christine L. Woodruff. "Members' Reaction to Apparent Group Approval of a Counternorm Communication," *J. Abnorm. Soc. Psychol.,* 52, 1956, pp. 67–74. **539**

Kendall, Patricia L., and Katherine M. Wolf. "Deviant Case Analysis in the Mr.

Kluckhohn, Clyde. "Culture and Behavior," in Gardner Lindzey, ed., *Handbook of Social Psychology*, Vol. II. Addison-Wesley, 1954, pp. 921–76. **634, 636, 647, 648, 656**

Kluckhohn, Clyde. "Have There Been Discernible Shifts in American Values During the Past Generation?" in Elting E. Morison, ed., *The American Style: Essays in Value and Performance*. Harper & Row, 1958, pp. 145–217, **561, 584**

Kluckhohn, Clyde. *Mirror for Man*. McGraw-Hill, 1949. **622, 656**

Kluckhohn, Clyde. "Navajo Witchcraft," *Papers of the Peabody Museum*, 22, No. 2, 1944. **656**

Kluckhohn, Clyde. "The Present State of American Anthropology: Future Needs and Emphases." Unpublished ms. prepared for the Educational Survey of the U. of Pennsylvania, 1957. **4**

Klüver, Heinrich. "An Experimental Study of the Eidetic Type," *Genet. Psychol. Monogr.*, 1, 1926, pp. 71–230. **187–88**

Knapp, Robert H., and H. B. Goodrich. *Origins of American Scientists*. U. of Chicago Press, 1952. **392**

Knight, R. O. "Evaluation of the Results of Psychoanalytic Therapy," *Amer. J. Psychiat.*, 98, 1941, pp. 434–46. **288**

Knupfer, Genevieve. "Portrait of the Underdog," *Pub. Opin. Quart.*, 11, 1947, pp. 103–14. **490**

Koffka, Kurt. *Principles of Gestalt Psychology*. Harcourt, Brace & World, 1935. **109, 130**

Köhler, Wolfgang. *Gestalt Psychology*. Liveright, 1920. **130**

Köhler, Wolfgang. *The Mentality of Apes*. Harcourt, Brace & World, 1926. **237**

Komarovsky, Mirra. *The Unemployed Man and His Family*. Dryden, 1940. **403–04**

Kornhauser, William. "Liberal and Radical Political Careers." Unpublished doctoral dissertation, U. of Chicago, 1953. **569**

Kornhauser, William. *The Politics of Mass Society*. Free Press, 1959. **404, 421, 435**

Krasner, Leonard. "Studies of the Conditioning of Verbal Behavior," *Psychol. Bull.*, 55, 1958(a), pp. 148–70. **143, 144**

Krasner, Leonard. "A Technique for Investigating the Relationship Between the Behavior Cues of the Examiner and the Verbal Behavior of the Patient," *J. Consult. Psychol.*, 22, 1958(b), pp. 364–66. **144**

Krebs, A. M. "Two Determinants of Conformity: Age of Independence and Training in *n* Achievement," *J. Abnorm. Soc. Psychol.*, 56, 1958, pp. 130–31. **260**

Krech, David, and Richard S. Crutchfield. *Elements of Psychology*. Knopf, 1958. **92, 108, 118, 171, 218, 219**

Krechevsky, I. "The Genesis of 'Hypotheses' in Rats," *University of California Publications in Psychology*, 6, 1932, pp. 45–64. **194, 195**

Kroeber, Alfred L. *Anthropology*. Rev. ed. Harcourt, Brace & World, 1948. **192, 387, 611–12, 645, 649, 650–51, 653, 656**

Kroeber, Alfred L., ed. *Anthropology Today: An Encyclopedic Inventory*. U. of Chicago Press, 1953. **656**

Kroeber, Alfred L. *Configurations of Culture Growth*. U. of California Press, 1944. **656**

Kroeber, Alfred L., and Clyde Kluckhohn. "Culture: A Critical Review of Concepts and Definitions," *Papers of the Peabody Museum*, 47, No. 1a, 1952. **643–44, 656**

Kroger, William S., and S. T. DeLee. "The Use of the Hypnoidal State as an Amnesic, Analgesic and Anesthetic in Obstetrics," *Amer. J. Obstetrics & Gynecology*, 44, 1943, p. 655. **121**

Kroh, O. "Subjektive optische Anschauungsbilder bei Jugendlichen," *Zeitschrift für pädagogische Psychologie*, 23, 1922, pp. 40–50. **188**

Krumboltz, J. D., and W. W. Farquhar. "Reliability and Validity of *n* Achievement," *J. Consult. Psychol.*, 21, 1957, pp. 226–31. **260**

Kubala, Albert L., and Martin M. Katz. "Nutritional Factors in Psychological Test Behavior," *J. Genet. Psychol.*, 96, 1960, pp. 343–52. **218**

Kubie, Lawrence S. "Problems and Techniques of Psychoanalytic Validation and Progress," in E. Pumpian-Mindlin, ed., *Psychoanalysis as Science*. Stanford U. Press, 1952, pp. 46–124. **280**

Kubzansky, Philip E., and P. Herbert Leiderman. "Sensory Deprivation: An Overview," in Philip Solomon *et al.*, eds., *Sensory Deprivation*, a symposium at the Harvard Medical School. Harvard U. Press, 1961, pp. 221–38. **91**

Kushner, Gilbert, Mickey Gibson, John Gulick, John J. Honigmann, and Richard Nonas. *What Accounts for Sociocultural Change? A Propositional Inventory*. Institute for Research in Social Science, U. of North Carolina, 1962. **641**

Lack, David L. *The Life of the Robin*. Penguin, 1943. **40**

Lambert, W. W., R. L. Solomon, and P. D. Watson. "Reinforcement and Extinction as Factors in Size Estimation," *J. Exper. Psychol.*, 39, 1949, pp. 637–41. **117**

Landis, C. "Statistical Evaluation of Psychotherapeutic Methods," in S. E. Hinsie, ed., *Concepts and Problems of Psychotherapy*. Heineman, 1938, pp. 155–65. **288**

Landis, Judson T. "Marriages of Mixed and Non-Mixed Religious Faith," *Amer. Sociol. Rev.*, 14, 1949, pp. 401–07. **310**

Landis, Paul H., and Katherine H. Day. "Education as a Factor in Mate Selection," *Amer. Sociol. Rev.*, 10, 1945, pp. 558–60. **306**

Lane, Robert E. *Political Life: Why People Get Involved in Politics.* Free Press, 1959. **424, 425–26, 431, 450, 565, 574–75, 577, 616**

Lantz, Beatrice. "Some Dynamic Aspects of Success and Failure," *Psychol. Monogr.*, 59, No. 1, 1945, **270**

Lashley, K. S. *Brain Mechanisms and Intelligence.* U. of Chicago Press, 1929. **169**

Lasswell, Harold D., and Abraham Kaplan. *Power and Society: A Framework for Political Inquiry.* Yale U. Press, 1950. **330, 455, 568, 620–21**

Laughlin, William, and Gordon Marsh. "A New View of the History of the Aleutians," *Arctic*, 4, 1951, pp. 75–88. **192**

Lazarsfeld, Paul F. "Sociological Reflections on Business: Consumers and Managers," in Robert A. Dahl *et al. Social Science Research on Business: Product and Potential.* Columbia U. Press, 1959, pp. 99–155. **488**

Lazarsfeld, Paul F. "Youth and Occupation." Unpublished ms., no date. **404**

Lazarsfeld, Paul F., Bernard Berelson, and Hazel Gaudet. *The People's Choice.* Columbia U. Press, 1948. **332, 426, 529, 530, 532, 555, 578, 581**

Lazarsfeld, Paul F., and Patricia L. Kendall. "The Communications Behavior of the Average American," in *Radio Listening in America.* Prentice-Hall, 1948, pp. 1–17. **533, 555**

Lazarsfeld, Paul F., and Morris Rosenberg, eds. *The Language of Social Research: A Reader in the Methodology of Social Research.* Free Press, 1955. **35**

Lazarsfeld, Paul F., and Wagner Thielens, Jr. *The Academic Mind.* Free Press, 1958. **327, 442–43, 450**

Lazarsfeld-Jahoda, Marie, and Hans Zeisel. *Die Arbeitlosen von Marienthal.* Psychologische Monographien, 1933. **403**

Lazarus, Richard S., and Robert A. McCleary. "Autonomic Discrimination Without Awareness: A Study of Subception," *Psychol. Rev.*, 58, 1951, pp. 113–22. **94**

Leavitt, Harold J. *Managerial Psychology.* U. of Chicago Press, 1958. **358**

Leavitt, Harold J. "Some Effects of Certain Communication Patterns on Group Performance." Unpublished doctoral dissertation, Massachusetts Institute of Technology, 1949. **356**

Lee, Douglas H. K. *Climate and Economic Development in the Tropics.* Harper & Row, 1957. **613**

Lee, Everett S. "Negro Intelligence and Selective Migration: A Philadelphia Test of the Klineberg Hypothesis," *Amer. Sociol.*

Rev., 16, 1951, pp. 227–33. **219, 499, 500**

Leeper, Robert. "Cognitive Processes," in S. S. Stevens, ed., *Handbook of Experimental Psychology.* Wiley, 1951, pp. 730–57. **193**

Lehman, Harvey C. *Age and Achievement.* Princeton U. Press, 1953. **234**

Leighton, Alexander H. *The Governing of Men.* Princeton U. Press, 1945. **371**

Lennard, Henry L., and Arnold Bernstein. *The Anatomy of Psychotherapy: Systems of Communication and Expectation.* Columbia U. Press, 1960. **351, 352**

Lenski, Gerhard. *The Religious Factor.* Doubleday, 1961. **306, 395–96, 435–36, 450**

Lerner, Daniel. "Communication Systems and Social Systems: A Statistical Exploration in History and Policy," *Behavioral Science*, 2, 1957, pp. 266–75. **605**

Levine, Jerome M., and Gardner Murphy. "The Learning and Forgetting of Controversial Material," *J. Abnorm. Soc. Psychol.*, 38, 1943, pp. 507–17. **182**

Lévi-Strauss, Claude. "Social Structure," in Alfred Kroeber, ed., *Anthropology Today.* U. of Chicago Press, 1953, pp. 524–53. **319**

Lewin, Kurt. *A Dynamic Theory of Personality.* Trans. by Donald K. Adams and Karl E. Zener. McGraw-Hill, 1935. **250, 251, 295**

Lewin, Kurt. *Resolving Social Conflicts: Selected Papers on Group Dynamics.* Ed. by Gertrude Weiss Lewin. Harper & Row, 1948. **361**

Lewin, Kurt. "Studies in Group Decision," in Dorwin Cartwright and Alvin Zander, eds., *Group Dynamics: Research and Theory.* Harper & Row, 1953, pp. 287–301. **548**

Liddell, H. Personal communication to John Bowlby, in *Maternal Care and Mental Health.* World Health Organization, Monograph Series, No. 2, 1952. **58**

Lindley, Richard H., and K. E. Moyer. "Effects of Instructions on the Extinction of Conditioned Finger-Withdrawal Response," *J. Exper. Psychol.*, 61, 1961, pp. 82–88. **138**

Lindzey, Gardner. "Differences Between the High and Low in Prejudice and Their Implications for a Theory of Prejudice," *J. Pers.*, 19, 1950, pp. 16–40. **516**

Lindzey, Gardner, ed. "Part 3. Research Methods," in *Handbook of Social Psychology*, Vol. I: *Theory and Method.* Addison-Wesley, 1954. **35**

Linton, Ralph. "The Distinctive Aspects of Acculturation," in Ralph Linton, ed., *Acculturation in Seven American Indian Tribes.* Appleton-Century-Crofts, 1940, pp. 501–20. **652**

Linz, Juan J. "The Social Bases of West German Politics." Unpublished doctoral dissertation, Columbia U., 1959, **427, 573**

Lippitt, Ronald, and Marian Radke. "New Trends in the Investigation of Prejudice," *Annals of the American Academy of Political and Social Science*, No. 244, *Controlling Group Prejudice*, March, 1946, pp. 167–76. **508**

Lipset, Seymour M. *Agrarian Socialism: The Cooperative Commonwealth Federation in Saskatchewan*. U. of California Press, 1950. **366, 380, 420, 425**

Lipset, Seymour M. *Political Man: The Social Bases of Politics*. Doubleday, 1960. **394, 422**

Lipset, Seymour M. "Political Sociology," in Robert K. Merton *et al.*, eds., *Sociology Today: Problems and Prospects*. Basic Books, 1959, pp. 81–114. **420, 435, 581**

Lipset, Seymour M. "Political Sociology, 1945–55," in *Sociology in the United States*. UNESCO, 1957(a), pp. 1–13. **417**

Lipset, Seymour M. "Social Mobility and Urbanization," in Paul K. Hatt and Albert J. Reiss, Jr., eds., *Cities and Society: The Revised Reader in Urban Sociology*. Free Press, 1957(b), pp. 458–66. **470**

Lipset, Seymour M. "Trade Unions and Social Structure: I," *Industrial Relations*, 1, 1961, pp. 75–89. **412**

Lipset, Seymour M., and Reinhard Bendix. *Social Mobility in Industrial Society*. U. of California, Institute of Industrial Relations. U. of California Press, 1959. **439, 462, 466, 467, 473, 474, 476, 484, 487, 490**

Lipset, Seymour M., Paul F. Lazarsfeld, Allen H. Barton, and Juan J. Linz. "The Psychology of Voting: An Analysis of Political Behavior," in Gardner Lindzey, ed., *Handbook of Social Psychology*, Vol. II. Addison-Wesley, 1954, pp. 1124–75. **450**

Lipset, Seymour M., and Juan J. Linz. "The Social Bases of Political Diversity in Western Democracies." Unpublished ms., 1956, forthcoming. **424, 427, 428, 430, 431, 432, 433, 450, 462, 464, 617**

Lipset, Seymour M., Martin A. Trow, and James S. Coleman. *Union Democracy*. Free Press, 1956. **412, 417, 450**

Lohman, Joseph D., and Dietrick C. Reitzes. "Note on Race Relations in Mass Society," *Amer. J. Sociol.*, 58, 1952, pp. 240–46. **506**

Long, L., and L. Welch. "Influence of Levels of Abstractness on Reasoning Ability," *J. Psychol.*, 13, 1942, pp. 41–59. **198**

Loomis, Charles P., and J. Allan Beegle. *Rural Sociology: The Strategy of Change*. Prentice-Hall, 1957. **610, 654**

Lorenz, K., and Nikolaas Tinbergen. "Taxis und Instinkthandlung in der Eirollbewegung der Graugans I," *Zeitschrift für Tierpsychologie*, 2, 1938, pp. 1–29. **41**

Lorge, Irving. *Influence of Regularly Interpolated Time Intervals on Subsequent Learning*. Teachers College, Columbia U., 1930. **159**

Lorge, Irving, David Fox, Joel Davitz, and Marlin Brenner. "A Survey of Studies Contrasting the Quality of Group Performance and Individual Performance, 1920–1957," *Psychol. Bull.*, 55, 1958, pp. 337–72. **355**

Luby, Elliot D., Charles E. Frohman, James L. Grisell, Joseph E. Lenzo, and Jacques S. Gottlieb. "Sleep Deprivation: Effects on Behavior, Thinking, Motor Performance, and Biological Energy Transfer Systems," *Psychosom. Med.*, 22, 1960, pp. 182–92. **243**

Luchins, Abraham S. "Mechanization in Problem Solving: The Effect of *Einstellung.*" *Psychol. Monogr.*, 54, No. 6, 1942. **205, 208**

Luff, M. C., and M. Garrod. "The After-Results of Psychotherapy in 500 Adult Cases," *Brit. Med. J.*, 2, 1935, pp. 54–59. **288**

Lumsdaine, Arthur A., and Irving L. Janis. "Resistance to 'Counterpropaganda' Produced by a One-Sided Versus a Two-Sided 'Propaganda' Presentation," *Pub. Opin. Quart.*, 17, 1953, pp. 311–18. **553**

Lynd, Robert S., and Helen M. Lynd. *Middletown*. Harcourt, Brace & World, 1929. **490**

Lynd, Robert S., and Helen M. Lynd. *Middletown in Transition: A Study in Cultural Conflicts*. Harcourt, Brace & World, 1937. **456, 490**

Lyon, D. O. "The Relation of Length of Material to Time Taken for Learning." *J. Educ. Psychol.*, 5, 1914, pp. 85–91. **160**

McCarthy, Dorothea. "Language Development in Children," in Leonard Carmichael, ed., *Manual of Child Psychology*. Wiley, 1946, pp. 476–581. **59**

McClelland, David C. *The Achieving Society*. Van Nostrand, 1961. **401, 402, 403, 612–13**

McClelland, David C., ed. *Studies in Motivation*. Appleton-Century-Crofts, 1955. **295**

McClelland, David C., and John W. Atkinson. "The Projective Expression of Needs: I. The Effect of Different Intensities of the Hunger Drive on Perception," *J. Psychol.*, 25, 1948, pp. 205–22. **115**

McClelland, David C., John W. Atkinson, Russell A. Clark, and Edgar L. Lowell. *The Achievement Motive*. Appleton-Century-Crofts, 1953. **80, 81, 85, 260, 295**

Maccoby, Eleanor E., Richard E. Matthews, and Anton S. Morton. "Youth and Political Change," *Pub. Opin. Quart.*, 18, 1954, pp. 23–39. **583**

McConnell, James V., Richard L. Cutler, and Elton B. McNeil. "Subliminal Stimulation: An Overview." *Amer. Psychologist*, 13, 1958, pp. 229–42. **95**

McCord, William, and Joan McCord, with Jon Gudeman. *Origins of Alcoholism.* Stanford U. Press, 1960. **633**

McCord, William, and Joan McCord, with Irving K. Zola. *Origins of Crime: A New Evaluation of the Cambridge-Somerville Youth Study.* Columbia U. Press, 1959. **631**

MacCrone, I. D. "Reaction to Domination in a Color-Caste Society: A Preliminary Study of the Race Attitudes of a Dominated Group," *J. Soc. Psychol.*, 26, 1947, pp. 69–98. **520**

McDowell, M. "Juvenile Warts Removed with the Use of Hypnotic Suggestion," *Bull. Menninger Clin.*, 13, 1949, pp. 124–26. **123**

McGaugh, J. L., and R. C. Hostetter. "Retention as a Function of the Temporal Position of Sleep and Activity Following Waking." Unpublished ms., 1961. **165**

McGeoch, John A. "The Influence of Associative Value upon the Difficulty of Nonsense-Syllable Lists," *J. Genet. Psychol.*, 37, 1930, pp. 421–26. **166**

McGeoch, John A., and Arthur L. Irion. *The Psychology of Human Learning.* 2nd ed. Longmans, Green, 1952. **164–65** McKay, 1958. **235**

McKinnon, Donald W. "Creativity in Architects," in Institute of Personality Assessment and Research, *The Creative Person.* U. of California and University Extension, Liberal Arts Dept., 1961, pp. V-1–V-24. **227, 229, 230**

McMahan, C. A. "An Empirical Test of Three Hypotheses Concerning the Human Sex Ratio at Birth in the United States, 1915–1948," *Milbank Memorial Fund Quart.*, 29, 1951, pp. 273–93. **601**

McNair, D. M. "Reinforcement of Verbal Behavior," *J. Exper. Psychol.*, 53, 1957, pp. 40–46. **144**

McNemar, Quinn. *The Revision of the Stanford-Binet Scale: An Analysis of the Standardization Data.* Houghton Mifflin, 1942. **209, 219, 225**

McPhee, William. Unpublished memorandum on Mass Dynamics, 1956. **546**

McQueen-Williams, M. "Maternal Behavior in Male Rats," *Science*, 82, 1935, pp. 67–68. **49**

MacRae, Duncan, Jr. "The Relation Between Roll Call Votes and Constituencies in the Massachusetts House of Representatives," *Amer. Political Science Rev.*, 46, 1952, 1046–55. **420, 421**

Madigan, Francis C. "Are Sex Mortality Differentials Biologically Caused?" *Milbank Memorial Fund Quart.*, 35, 1957, pp. 202–23. **603**

Maier, Norman R. F. "An Aspect of Human Reasoning," *Brit. J. Psychol.*, 24, 1933, pp. 144–55. **236**

Maier, Norman R. F. *Frustration: A Study of Behavior Without a Goal.* McGraw-Hill, 1949. **269, 270, 295**

Maier, Norman R. F. "Reasoning in Humans: II. The Solution of a Problem and Its Appearance in Consciousness," *J. Comp. Psychol.*, 12, 1931, pp. 181–94. **206**

Malinowski, Bronislaw. *Magic, Science and Religion and Other Essays.* Free Press, 1948. **385, 387, 388** Doubleday, 1954. **450**

Mandler, G., and W. K. Kaplan. "Subjective Evaluation and Reinforcing Effect of Verbal Stimulus," *Science*, 124, 1956, pp. 582–83. **144**

March, James G., and Herbert A. Simon, with Harold Guetzkow. *Organizations.* Wiley, 1958. **363–64, 380, 414**

Marion, A. J. "The Influence of Experimenter Status upon Verbal Conditioning." Unpublished doctoral dissertation, U. of California, 1956. **144**

Marquart, Dorothy I., and Lois L. Bailey. "An Evaluation of the Culture Free Test of Intelligence," *J. Genet. Psychol.*, 86, 1955, pp. 353–58. **222**

Marshall, Alfred. *Principles of Economics.* Macmillan, 1890. **7–8**

Martin, William E., and Celia B. Stendler. *Child Behavior and Development.* Rev. ed. Harcourt, Brace & World, 1954. **85**

Masland, Richard L., Seymour B. Sarason, and Thomas Gladwyn. *Mental Subnormality: Biological, Psychological, and Cultural Factors.* Basic Books, 1958. **216**

Maslow, A. H. *Motivation and Personality.* Harper & Row, 1954. **295**

Masserman, Jules H. *Principles of Dynamic Psychiatry.* 2nd ed. Saunders, 1961. **269–70, 278, 284**

Masserman, Jules H., and H. T. Carmichael. "Diagnosis and Prognosis in Psychiatry," *J. Mental Science*, 84, 1938, pp. 893–946. **288**

Masserman, Jules H., and K. S. Yum. "An Analysis of the Influence of Alcohol on Experimental Neuroses in Cats," *Psychosom. Med.*, 8, 1946, p. 36. **278**

Matz, P. B. "Outcome of Hospital Treatment of Ex-Service Patients with Nervous and Mental Disease in the U.S. Veterans' Bureau," *U.S. Vet. Bur. Med. Bull.*, 5, 1929, pp. 829–42. **288**

Max, Louis W. "An Experimental Study of the Motor Theory of Consciousness: III. Action-Current Responses in Deaf-mutes During Sleep, Sensory Stimulation, and Dreams," *J. Comp. Psychol.*, 19, 1935, pp. 469–86. **172**

Mayer, Albert J., and Philip M. Hauser. "Class Differences in Expectation of Life at Birth," in Reinhard Bendix and Seymour M. Lipset, eds., *Class, Status and Power: A Reader in Social Stratification.* Free Press, 1953, pp. 281–84. **477**

Mayer, Kurt B. *Class and Society.* Doubleday, 1955. **488–89**

Mayo, Elton. *The Human Problems of an Industrial Organization.* Macmillan, 1933. **371**

Mayo, Elton, and George F. Lombard. *Teamwork and Labor Turnover in the Aircraft Industry of Southern California.* Harvard U., Graduate School of Business Administration, Business Research Studies, No. 32, 1944. **410**

Mead, Margaret. *Coming of Age in Samoa.* Morrow, 1928. **84–85, 656**

Mead, Margaret. "Cultural Determinants of Behavior," in Anne Roe and George G. Simpson, eds., *Behavior and Evolution.* Yale U. Press, 1958, pp. 480–503. **647, 648, 653**

Mead, Margaret. *New Lives for Old.* Morrow, 1956. **614**

Mednick, Martha T., and Ogden R. Lindsley. "Some Clinical Correlates of Operant Behavior," *J. Abnorm. Soc. Psychol.,* 57, 1958, pp. 13–16. **149**

Meehl, Paul. *Clinical vs. Statistical Prediction: A Theoretical Analysis and Review of the Evidence.* U. of Minnesota Press, 1954. **35**

Meggers, Betty J. "Environmental Limitation on the Development of Culture." *Amer. Anthropologist,* 56, 1954, pp. 801–24. **611**

Melton, Arthur W. "Motivation and Learning," in Walter S. Monroe, ed., *Encyclopedia of Educational Research.* American Educational Research Assoc. Rev. ed. Macmillan, 1950, pp. 672–73. **261–62**

Melton, Arthur W., and W. J. Von Lackum. "Retroactive and Proactive Inhibition in Retention: Evidence for a Two-Factor Theory of Retroactive Inhibition," *Amer. J. Psychol.,* 54, 1941, pp. 157–73. **165**

Melzack, Ronald, and T. H. Scott. "The Effects of Early Experience on the Response to Pain," *J. Comp. Physiol. Psychol.,* 50, 1957, 155–61. **64**

Merei, Ferenc. "Group Leadership and Institutionalization," in Eleanor E. Maccoby *et al.,* eds., *Readings in Social Psychology.* 3rd ed. Holt, Rinehart & Winston, 1958, pp. 522–32. **343**

Merton, Robert K. "Puritanism, Pietism, and Science," in *Social Theory and Social Structure.* Rev. ed. Free Press, 1957, pp. 574–606. **391–92**

Merton, Robert K., Leonard Broom, and Leonard S. Cottrell, Jr., eds. *Sociology Today: Problems and Prospects.* Basic Books, 1959. **641**

Merton, Robert K., Ailsa P. Gray, Barbara Hockey, and Hanan C. Selvin, eds. *Reader in Bureaucracy.* Free Press, 1952. **380**

Merton, Robert K., and Robert A. Nisbet, eds. *Contemporary Social Problems.* Harcourt, Brace & World, 1961. **641**

Miles, H. H. W., E. L. Barrabee, and J. E. Finesinger. "Evaluation of Psychotherapy," *Psychosom. Med.,* 13, 1951, pp. 83–105. **288**

Miller, Daniel R., and Guy E. Swanson. *The Changing American Parent: A Study in the Detroit Area.* Wiley, 1958. **72, 480**

Miller, Neal E. "Experimental Studies of Conflict," in J. McV. Hunt, ed., *Personality and the Behavior Disorders,* Vol. I. Ronald Press, 1944, pp. 431–65. **273**

Miller, Neal E. "Theory and Experiment Relating Psychoanalytic Displacement to Stimulus-Response Generalization," *J. Abnorm. Soc. Psychol.,* 43, 1948, pp. 155–78. **252, 295**

Miller, Neal E., and Richard Bugelski. "Minor Studies of Aggression: II. The Influence of Frustrations Imposed by the In-Group on Attitudes Expressed Toward Out-Groups," *J. Psychol.,* 25, 1948, pp. 437–42. **267–68**

Millikan, Max F., and Donald L. M. Backmer, eds. *The Emerging Nations: Their Growth and United States Policy.* Massachusetts Institute of Technology, Center for International Studies. Little, Brown, 1961. **399, 614–15, 618–19**

Millikan, Robert Andrews. "Essay IV," in Albert Einstein, John Dewey *et al., Living Philosophies.* Simon & Schuster, 1931. **391**

Mills, Theodore M. "Power Relations in Three-Person Groups," *Amer. Sociol. Rev.,* 18, 1953, pp. 351–57. **360**

Milton, T. "Authoritarianism, Intolerance of Ambiguity, and Rigidity, Under Ego- and Risk-Involved Conditions," *J. Abnorm. Soc. Psychol.,* 55, 1957, pp. 29–33. **259**

Minard, Ralph D. "Race Relationships in the Pocahontas Coal Field." *J. Soc. Issues,* 8, 1952, pp. 29–44. **505–06**

Mock, J. F. "The Influence of Verbal and Behavioral Cues of a Listener on the Verbal Productions of the Speaker." Unpublished doctoral dissertation, U. of Kentucky, 1957. **144**

Monahan, Thomas P., and William M. Kephart. "Divorce and Desertion by Religious and Mixed-Religious Groups," *Amer. J. Sociol.,* 59, 1954, pp. 454–65. **312**

Moreno, J. L. *Sociometry, Experimental Method and the Science of Society.* Beacon House, 1951. **361**

Morgan, Clifford T. *Introduction to Psychology*. 2nd ed. McGraw-Hill, 1961. **151**

Morgan, Clifford T., and E. Stellar. *Physiological Psychology*. McGraw-Hill, 1950. **294**

Morgan, J. B., and J. T. Morton. "The Distortion of Syllogistic Reasoning Produced by Personal Convictions," *J. Soc. Psychol.*, 20, 1944, pp. 39–59. **205**

Morison, Robert S. "Toward a Redefinition of Culture." Unpublished paper presented to the American Academy of Arts and Sciences Conference, May, 1963. **666**

Morris, Charles. *Varieties of Human Value*. U. of Chicago Press, 1956. **561, 584**

Morse, Nancy, and E. Reimer. "The Experimental Change of a Major Organizational Variable," *J. Abnorm. Soc. Psychol.*, 52, 1956, pp. 120–29. **369**

Mowrer, Orval H. "A Stimulus-Response Analysis of Anxiety and Its Role as a Reinforcing Agent," *Psychol. Rev.*, 46, 1939, pp. 553–66. **295**

Murchison, Carl. *Criminal Intelligence*. Clark U. Press, 1926. **630**

Murdock, George P. "The Common Denominator of Cultures," in Ralph Linton, ed., *The Science of Man in the World Crisis*. Columbia U. Press, 1945, pp. 123–42. **646–47**

Murdock, George P. "Family Stability in Non-European Cultures," *Annals of the American Academy of Political and Social Science*, No. 272, November, 1950, pp. 195–201. **311**

Murdock, George P. *Our Primitive Contemporaries*. Macmillan, 1934. **391**

Murdock, George P. *Social Structure*. Macmillan, 1949. **35, 300, 313, 316–17, 318, 319, 321–22, 323, 650–51, 656**

Murray, Henry A., ed. *Explorations in Personality: A Clinical Experimental Study of Fifty Men of College Age*. Oxford U. Press, 1938. **35, 257–58**

Myrdal, Gunnar, with the assistance of Richard Sterner and Arnold M. Rose. *An American Dilemma*. Harper & Row, 1944. **511, 522, 524**

Nadel, S. F. *The Foundations of Social Anthropology*. Cohen & West, 1951. **634**

Nagel, Ernest. "Methodological Problems of the Social Sciences," in *The Structure of Science: Problems in the Logic of Scientific Explanation*. Harcourt, Brace & World, 1961, pp. 447–502. **8–9**

Nash, Manning. "Applied and Action Anthropology in the Understanding of Man," *Anthrop. Quart.*, 32, 1959, pp. 67–81. **614**

National Research Council. "A Brief Review of Salient Specific Findings on Morale and Human Behavior Under Disaster Conditions." Unpublished memorandum, April 18, 1958. **624, 625**

Naylor, J. C., and C. H. Lawshe. "An Analytical Review of the Experimental Basis of Subception," *J. Psychol.*, 46, 1958, pp. 75–96. **131**

Neustatter, W. L. "The Results of Fifty Cases Treated by Psychotherapy," *Lancet*, 1, 1935, pp. 796–99. **288**

Newcomb, Theodore M. *Personality and Social Change: Attitude Formation in a Student Community*. Dryden, 1943. **332, 582** Holt, Rinehart & Winston, 1957. **584**

Newcomb, Theodore M. "The Study of Consensus," in Robert K. Merton *et al.*, eds., *Sociology Today: Problems and Prospects*. Basic Books, 1959, pp. 277–92. **329**

Newman, Edwin B. "Perception," in Edwin G. Boring, Herbert S. Langfeld and Harry P. Weld, eds., *Foundations of Psychology*. Wiley, 1948, pp. 215–49. **105**

Newman, Horatio, Frank N. Freeman, and Karl J. Holzinger. *Twins: A Study of Heredity and Environment*. U. of Chicago Press, 1937. **217–18**

Newman, Joseph. *Motivation Research and Marketing Management*. Harvard U., Graduate School of Business Administration, Division of Research, 1957. **488**

Nisbet, Robert A. "The Study of Social Problems," in Robert K. Merton and Robert A. Nisbet, eds., *Contemporary Social Problems*. Harcourt, Brace & World, 1961, pp. 3–18. **629**

Notestein, Frank W. "Class Differences in Fertility," *Annals of the American Academy of Political and Social Science*. November, 1936, pp. 1–11. **598**

Nottingham, Elizabeth K. *Religion and Society*. Doubleday, 1954. **385–86, 387**

Nuthmann, Anne M. "Conditioning of a Response Class on a Personality Test," *J. Abnorm. Soc. Psychol.*, 54, 1957, pp. 19–23. **144**

Ogburn, William F. *Social Change*. Viking, 1927. **618**

Olds, James S. "Hypothalamic Substrates of Reward," *Physiol. Rev.*, 42, 1962, pp. 554–604. **249**

Olds, James S. "Self-Stimulation of the Brain," *Science*, 127, 1958, pp. 315–24. **248–49**

Olds, James S., and Peter Milner. "Positive Reinforcement Produced by Electrical Stimulation of Septal Area and Other Regions of Rat Brain," *J. Comp. Physiol. Psychol.*, 47, 1954, pp. 419–27. **294**

Orlansky, Harold. "Infant Care and Personality," *Psychol. Bull.*, 46, 1949, pp. 1–48. **76–77, 85**

Osborn, Frederick. "Qualitative Aspects of Population Control: Eugenics and Euthenics," *Law and Contemporary Problems*, 25, 1960, pp. 406–25. **591**

Osborne, M. F. "Brownian Motion in the Stock Market," *Operations Research*, 7, 1959, pp. 145–73. **97**

Osgood, Charles E. *Method and Theory in Experimental Psychology*. Oxford U. Press, 1953. **109, 235**

Osgood, Charles E. "The Nature and Measurement of Meaning," *Psychol. Bull.*, 49, 1952, pp. 197–237. **200**

Osgood, Charles E., and Percy H. Tannenbaum. "The Principle of Congruity in the Prediction of Attitude Change," *Psychol. Rev.*, 62, 1955, pp. 42–55. **538**

Ossowski, Stanislaw. "Social Mobility Brought About by Social Revolution." Working paper presented at 4th Working Conference on Social Stratification and Social Mobility, International Sociological Assoc., 1957. **467**

Palmer, Gladys L., with the assistance of Carol P. Brainerd. *Labor Mobility in Six Cities: A Report on the Survey of Patterns and Factors in Labor Mobility, 1940–1950*. Committee on Labor Market Research, Social Science Research Council, 1954. **404**

Pasamanick, Benjamin, Simon Dinitz, and Hilda Knobloch. "Geographic and Seasonal Variations in Births," *Public Health Reports*, 74, 1959, pp. 285–88. **596–97**

Pavlov, I. P. *Conditioned Reflexes*. Trans. and ed. by G. V. Anrep, Oxford U. Press, 1927. **136, 236, 245, 277**

Peak, Helen. "Psychological Structure and Psychological Activity," *Psychol. Rev.*, 65, 1958, pp. 325–47. **119**

Peierls, R. E. *The Laws of Nature*. Scribner's, 1956. **4**

Penfield, Wilder, and Theodore Rasmussen. *The Cerebral Cortex of Man: A Clinical Study of Localization of Function*. Macmillan, 1950. **170**

Piaget, Jean. *The Construction of Reality in the Child*. Basic Books, 1954. **198**

Piaget, Jean. *The Moral Judgment of the Child*. Harcourt, Brace & World, 1932. **78**

Piaget, Jean. *The Origins of Intelligence in Children*. International Universities Press, 1952. **198**

Pierson, D. "Race Prejudice as Revealed in the Study of Racial Situations," *Int. Soc. Sci. Bull.*, 2, 1950, pp. 467–78. **514**

Plant, Walter T., and Harold Richardson. "The I.Q. of the Average College Student," *J. Counsel. Psychol.*, 5, 1958, pp. 229–31. **211**

Poincaré, Henri. "Mathematical Creation," in *The Foundations of Science*, trans. by George Bruce Halsted. Science Press, 1946, pp. 383–94. **201**

Pool, Ithiel de Sola. "The Mass Media and Politics in the Modernization Process," in Lucien W. Pye, ed., *Communications and Political Development*. Princeton U. Press, 1963, pp. 234–53. **553–54**

Pope, Liston. *Millhands and Preachers*. Yale U. Press, 1942. **389**

Pope, Liston. "Religion and the Class Structure," *Annals of the American Academy of Political and Social Science*, No. 256, March, 1948, pp. 84–91. **394**

Porter, D. "Some Effects of Year Long Teaching Machine Instruction," in E. Galanter, ed., *Automatic Teaching: The State of the Art*. Wiley, 1959, pp. 85–90. **149**

Postman, Leo J., and Lucy Rau. "Retention as a Function of the Method of Measurement," *University of California Publications in Psychology*, 8, No. 3, 1957. **164**

Potter, Stephen. *The Theory and Practice of Gamesmanship: The Art of Winning Games Without Actually Cheating*. Holt, Rinehart & Winston, 1948. **101**

Powdermaker, Hortense. *After Freedom: A Cultural Study in the Deep South*. Viking, 1939. **653**

Powers, Edwin, and Helen Witmer. *An Experiment in the Prevention of Delinquency: The Cambridge-Somerville Youth Study*. Columbia U. Press, 1951. **631**

Purcell, Theodore V. *The Worker Speaks His Mind on Company and Union*. Harvard U. Press, 1953. **414**

Quay, Herbert C. "The Effect of Verbal Reinforcement on the Recall of Early Memories," *J. Abnorm. Soc. Psychol.*, 59, 1959, pp. 254–57. **146, 147**

Raab, Earl, and Seymour M. Lipset. *Prejudice and Society*. Anti-Defamation League of B'nai B'rith, 1959. **506–07, 508, 523**

Raab, Earl, and Gertrude J. Selznick. *Major Social Problems*. Harper & Row, 1959. **626**

Räber, Hans. "Analysis of the Courtship of a Domesticated Turkey-Cock (Meleagris)," *Behavior*, 1, 1948, pp. 237–66. **43**

Radcliffe-Brown, A. R. *Social Organization of Australian Tribes*. Macmillan, 1931. **656**

Radke, Marian, and Helen Trager. "Children's Perceptions of the Social Roles of Negroes and Whites," *J. Psychol.*, 29, 1950, pp. 3–33. **521**

Radke, Marian, Helen Trager, and Hadassah Davis. "Social Perceptions and Attitudes of Children," *Genet. Psychol. Monogr.*, 40, 1949, pp. 327–447. **509, 520, 524**

Radke-Yarrow, Marian, and Leon J. Yarrow. "Child Psychology," *Annu. Rev. Psychol.*, 6, 1955, pp. 1–28. **70–71**

Raginsky, B. B. "Mental Suggestion as an Aid in Anesthesia," *Anaesthesiology*, 9, 1948, p. 472. **122**

Redfield, Robert. *The Folk Culture of Yucatan*. U. of Chicago Press, 1941. **656**

Reiff, Robert, and Martin Scheerer. *Memory and Hypnotic Age Regression*. International Universities Press, 1959. **180**

Reiss, Albert J., Jr. "Research Problems in Metropolitan Population Redistribution," *Amer. Sociol. Rev.*, 21, 1956, pp. 571–77. **605**

Rennie, Thomas, and Leo Srole. "Social Class Prevalence and Distribution of Psychosomatic Conditions in an Urban Population," *Psychosom. Med.*, 18, 1956, pp. 449–56. **478, 489–90**

Reynolds, B. "The Acquisition of a Trace Conditioned Response as a Function of the Magnitude of the Stimulus Trace," *J. Exper. Psychol.*, 35, 1945, pp. 15–30. **137**

Rhine, J. B., and J. G. Pratt. *Parapsychology: Frontier Science of the Mind.* Thomas, 1957. **126, 131**

Rhine, Louisa E., and J. B. Rhine. "The Psychokenetic Effect: I. The First Experiment," *J. Parapsychol.*, 7, 1943, pp. 20–43. **130**

Rhodes, Raphael H. "Hypnosis: What It Is and What It Does," in Raphael H. Rhodes, ed., *Therapy Through Hypnosis.* Citadel Press, 1952. **124–25**

Rickers-Ovsiankina, Maria A. "Studies in the Personality Structures of Schizophrenic Individuals: II. Reaction to Interrupted Tasks," *J. Genet. Psychol.*, 16, 1937, pp. 179–96. **250**

Ridde, O. R., R. W. Bates, and E. L. Lahr. "Maternal Behavior in Rats Induced by Prolactin," *Proceedings of the Society of Experimental Biology*, 32, 1935, pp. 730–34. **49**

Rieken, Henry W., and George C. Homans. "Psychological Aspects of Social Structure," in Gardner Lindzey, ed., *Handbook of Social Psychology*, Vol. II. Addison-Wesley, 1954, pp. 786–832. **341, 346, 348, 351, 352, 354, 361**

Riley, John W., Jr., and Matilda White Riley. "Mass Communication and the Social System," in Robert K. Merton *et al.*, eds., *Sociology Today: Problems and Prospects.* Basic Books, 1959, pp. 537–78. **530–31, 532–33, 554, 566–67**

Riley, Matilda White, and Richard Cohn. "Control Networks in Informal Groups," *Sociometry*, 21, 1958, pp. 30–49. **337**

Riley, Matilda White, and John W. Riley, Jr. "A Sociological Approach to Communications Research," *Pub. Opin. Quart.*, 15, 1951, pp. 445–60. **539–40**

Riley, Matilda White, John W. Riley, Jr., and Mary E. Moore. "Adolescent Values

and the Riesman Typology," in Seymour M. Lipset and Leo Lowenthal, eds., *Culture and Social Character*. Free Press, 1961, pp. 370–86. **71**

Ringer, Benjamin B. "The Parishioner and His Church: A Study in the Sociology of Religion." Unpublished doctoral dissertation, Columbia U., 1956. **392, 393**

Robinson, William S. "Radio Comes to the Farmer," in Paul F. Lazarsfeld and Frank N. Stanton, eds., *Radio Research 1941*. Duell, Sloan & Pearce, 1941, pp. 224–94. **530**

Rock, Irvin. "The Role of Repetition in Associative Learning," *Amer. J. Psychol.*, 70, 1957, pp. 186–93. **167–68**

Roe, Anne. "Personal Problems and Science," in Calvin Taylor and Frank Barron, eds., *Scientific Creativity*. Wiley, 1963. **234**

Rogers, Carl R. "An Overview of the Research and Some Questions for the Future," in Carl R. Rogers and Rosalind F. Dymond, eds., *Psychotherapy and Personality Change*. U. of Chicago Press, 1954, pp. 413–34. **291–92**

Rogers, Everett M. *Diffusion of Innovations.* Free Press, 1962. **619**

Rogoff, Natalie. "Local Social Structure and Educational Selection," in A. H. Halsey *et al.*, eds., *Education, Economy, and Society*. Free Press, 1961, pp. 241–51. **437, 439**

Rogoff, Natalie. *Recent Trends in Occupational Mobility.* Free Press, 1953. **471, 475, 490**

Rogoff, Natalie. "Recent Trends in Urban Occupational Mobility," in Paul K. Hatt and Albert J. Reiss, Jr., eds., *Reader in Urban Sociology*. Free Press, 1951, pp. 406–20. **472**

Rokeach, Milton. *The Open and Closed Mind.* Basic Books, 1960. **236**

Rose, Arnold M. "The Comparative Study of Intergroup Conflict," *Sociol. Quart.*, 1, 1960, pp. 57–66. **501**

Rose, Arnold M. "Race and Ethnic Relations," in Robert K. Merton and Robert A. Nisbet, eds., *Contemporary Social Problems*. Harcourt, Brace & World, 1961, pp. 324–89. **466, 494, 501, 523**

Rose, Arnold M. *Studies in Reduction of Prejudice*. 2nd ed. American Council on Race Relations, 1948. **517**

Rose, Arnold M. *Union Solidarity: The Internal Cohesion of a Labor Union.* U. of Minnesota Press, 1952. **414**

Rosen, Bernard C. "Race, Ethnicity, and the Achievement Syndrome," *Amer. Sociol. Rev.*, 24, 1959(a), pp. 47–60. **486**

Rosen, Harold. "Hypnosis in Surgery," in Jerome M. Schneck, ed., *Hypnosis in Modern Medicine*. 2nd ed. Thomas, 1959(b), pp. 61–88. **121–22**

Rosenberg, B. G., and Carl N. Zimet. "Authoritarianism and Aesthetic Choice," *J. Soc. Psychol.*, 46, 1957, pp. 293–97. **259**

Rosenberg, Milton J., Carl I. Hovland, William J. McGuire, Robert P. Abelson, and Jack Brehm. *Attitude Organization and Change: An Analysis of Consistency Among Attitude Components*, Yale Studies in Attitude and Communication, Vol. III, ed. by Carl I. Hovland and Milton J. Rosenberg. Yale U. Press, 1960. **541, 555, 574, 580**

Rosenow, Curt. "The Incidence of First-Born Among Problem Children," *J. Genet. Psychol.*, 37, 1930, pp. 145–51. **73**

Ross, Arthur M., and Paul T. Hartman. *Changing Patterns of Industrial Conflict.* Wiley, 1960. **413, 415**

Ross, T. A. *An Enquiry into Prognosis in the Neuroses.* Cambridge U. Press, 1936. **288**

Roth, Julius, and R. F. Peck. "Social Class and Social Mobility Factors Related to Marital Adjustment," *Amer. Sociol. Rev.*, 16, 1951, pp. 478–87. **482**

Rotter, Julian B. "Psychotherapy," *Annu. Rev. Psychol.*, 11, 1960, pp. 381–414. **143, 290**

Rowland, Lloyd W. "Will Hypnotized Persons Try To Harm Themselves or Others?" in Lesley Kuhn and Salvatore Russo, eds., *Modern Hypnosis.* Psychological Library, 1947, pp. 39–44. **123**

Rubinstein, E. A., and M. B. Parloff. "Research Problems in Psychotherapy," in *Research in Psychotherapy.* American Psychological Assoc., 1959, pp. 276–92. **289–90**

Ryder, N. B. "Fertility," in Philip M. Hauser and Otis Dudley Duncan, eds., *The Study of Population: An Inventory and Appraisal.* U. of Chicago Press, 1959, pp. 400–36. **594**

Saenger, Gerhart H. "Social Status and Political Behavior," *Amer. J. Sociol.*, 51, 1945, pp. 103–13. **422**

Saenger, Gerhart H., and Samuel Flowerman. "Stereotypes and Prejudicial Attitudes," *Hum. Relat.*, 7, 1954, pp. 217–38. **504**

Saenger, Gerhart H., and Emily Gilbert. "Customer Reactions to the Integration of Negro Sales Personnel," *International J. Opin. Attitude Res.*, 4, 1950, pp. 57–76. **506**

Salzinger, K., and Stephanie Pisoni. "Reinforcement of Affect Responses of Schizophrenics During the Clinical Interview." Paper read at Eastern Psychological Assoc., New York, April, 1957(a). **144**

Salzinger, K., and Stephanie Pisoni. "Reinforcement of Verbal Affect Responses of Schizophrenics During the Clinical Interview: The Effect on Conditioning of Placement of the Period of Reinforcement." Paper read at American Psychological Assoc., New York, August, 1957(b). **144**

Sanford, Fillmore H. "Research on Military Leadership," in John C. Flanagan *et al.*, *Psychology in the World Emergency.* U. of Pittsburgh Press, 1952, pp. 17–74. **342**

Sanford, R. N., Margaret M. Adkins, R. B. Miller, and Elizabeth Cobb. "Physique, Personality and Scholarship," *Monogr. Soc. Res. Child Development*, 8, No. 1, 1943. **75**

Sapir, Edward. *Language: An Introduction to the Study of Speech.* Harcourt, Brace & World, 1921, pp. 21–22. **189**

Sapir, Edward. "The Status of Linguistics as a Science," *Language*, 5, 1929, pp. 207–14. **190**

Sarason, Barbara R. "The Effects of Verbally Conditioned Response Classes on Post-Conditioning Tasks," *Dissertation Abstr.*, 12, 1957, p. 679. **144**

Sarason, I. G. "Interrelations Among Individual Difference Variable, Behavior in Psychotherapy, and Verbal Conditioning." Paper read at Western Psychological Assoc., Eugene, Ore., May, 1957. **144**

Sayles, Leonard R. *Behavior of Industrial Work Groups: Prediction and Control.* Wiley, 1958. **371, 400, 413, 450**

Sayles, Leonard R., and George Strauss. *The Local Union.* Harper & Row, 1953. **413, 414**

Schachter, Stanley. *Psychology of Affiliation: Experimental Studies of the Sources of Gregariousness.* Stanford U. Press, 1959. **74, 252, 254, 255, 295**

Scheerer, Martin, Eva Rothmann, and Kurt Goldstein. "A Case of 'Idiot Savant': An Experimental Study of Personality Organization," *Psychol. Monogr.*, 58, No. 4, 1945. **216**

Schein, Edgar H. "Reaction Patterns to Severe, Chronic Stress in American Army Prisoners of War of the Chinese," *J. Soc. Issues*, 13, 1957, pp. 21–30. **575**

Schilder, P. "Results and Problems of Group Psychotherapy in Severe Neuroses," *Mental Hygiene*, 23, 1939, pp. 87–98. **288**

Schilling, Rudolf. "Über 'Inneres Sprechen'," *Zeitschrift für Psychologie*, 111, 1929, pp. 204–46. **172**

Schjelderup-Ebbe, T. "Social Behavior of Birds." In Carl Murchinson, ed., *Handbook of Social Psychology.* Clark U. Press, 1935, pp. 947–72. **253**

Schmeidler, Gertrude R., and R. A. McConnell. *ESP and Personality Patterns.* Yale U. Press, 1958. **129**

Schramm, Wilbur, ed. *Communications in Modern Society.* U. of Illinois Press, 1948. **554**

Schramm, Wilbur, ed. *Mass Communications.* Rev. ed. U. of Illinois Press, 1960. **554**

Schramm, Wilbur, Jack Lyle, and Edwin B. Parker. *Television in the Lives of Our Children.* Stanford U. Press, 1961. **536, 555**

Schrieke, B. *Alien Americans: A Study of Race Relations.* Viking Press, 1936. **503**

Schuessler, Karl F., and Donald R. Cressey. "Personality Characteristics of Criminals," *Amer. J. Sociol.,* 55, 1950, pp. 476–84. **629**

Scodel, Alvin, and Harvey Austrin. "The Perception of Jewish Photographs by Non-Jews and Jews," *J. Abnorm. Soc. Psychol.,* 54, 1957, pp. 278–80. **115–16**

Scudder, Richard, and C. Arnold Anderson. "Migration and Vertical Occupational Mobility," *Amer. Sociol. Rev.,* 19, 1954, pp. 329–34. **476**

Sears, Robert R. "Experimental Studies of Projection: I. Attribution of Traits," *J. Soc. Psychol.,* 7, 1936, pp. 151–63. **283, 286**

Sears, Robert R. *Survey of Objective Studies of Psychoanalytic Concepts.* Committee on Social Adjustment, Social Science Research Council, Bulletin 51, 1943. **285, 286**

Sears, Robert R., Eleanor E. Maccoby, and Harry Levin. *Patterns of Child Rearing.* Harper & Row, 1957. **72, 77, 79**

Sears, Robert R., John W. M. Whiting, Vincent Nowlis, and Pauline S. Sears. "Some Child-Rearing Antecedents of Aggression and Dependency in Young Children," *Genet. Psychol. Monogr.,* 47, 1953, pp. 135–236. **73, 79, 85**

Seashore, Stanley E. "Administrative Leadership and Organizational Effectiveness," in Rensis Likert and Samuel P. Hayes, Jr., eds., *Some Applications of Behavioral Research.* UNESCO, 1957, pp. 44–80. **372**

Seashore, Stanley E. *Group Cohesiveness in the Industrial Group.* Institute of Social Research, 1954. **372**

Secord, Paul F. "Facial Features and Inference Processes in Interpersonal Perception," in Renato Tagiuri and Luigi Petrullo, eds., *Person Perception and Interpersonal Behavior.* Stanford U. Press, 1958, pp. 300–15. **113**

Seeman, Julius. "Psychotherapy," *Annu. Rev. Psychol.,* 12, 1961, pp. 157–94. **146**

Seibert, L. C. *A Series of Experiments on the Learning of French Vocabulary.* Johns Hopkins U., Studies in Education, No. 18, 1932. **166**

Sellin, Thorsten. *The Death Penalty.* American Law Institute, 1959. **632**

Sells, Saul B. "The Atmosphere Effect: An Experimental Study of Reasoning," *Arch. Psychol.,* 29, No. 200, 1936. **205**

Selltiz, Claire *et al. Research Methods in Social Relations.* Rev. ed. Holt, Rinehart & Winston, 1959. **35**

Selznick, Philip. *Leadership in Administration.* Harper & Row, 1957. **377**

Selznick, Philip. *TVA and the Grass Roots: A Study in the Sociology of Formal Organization.* U. of California Press, 1953. **366, 368, 380**

von Senden, Marius. *Raum- und Gestaltauffassung bei operierten Blindgeborenen vor und nach der Operation. (Space and Sight: The Perception of Space and Shape in the Congenitally Blind Before and After Operation.* Trans. by Peter Heath. Methuen, 1960.) Barth, 1932. **106**

Sewell, William H., and Paul H. Mussen. "The Effects of Feeding, Weaning, and Scheduling Procedures on Childhood Adjustment and the Formation of Oral Symptoms," *Child Development,* 23, 1952, pp. 185–91. **76**

Shaffer, Laurance F. "Fear and Courage in Aerial Combat," *J. Consult. Psychol.,* 11, 1957, pp. 137–43. **276**

Sharp, Walter R. *The French Civil Service.* Macmillan, 1931. **366**

Sherif, Muzafer. "The Formation of a Norm in a Group Situation," in Muzafer Sherif, *The Psychology of Social Norms.* Harper & Row, 1936, pp. 89–112. **333**

Sherif, Muzafer. "Group Influences upon the Formation of Norms and Attitudes," in G. E. Swanson *et al.,* eds., *Readings in Social Psychology.* Rev. ed. Holt, Rinehart & Winston, 1952, pp. 249–62. **332**

Shils, Edward A. "Class," in *Encyclopaedia Britannica,* 5, 1960, pp. 766–68. **454–55, 461, 462, 476, 490**

Shils, Edward A. *The Present State of American Sociology.* Free Press, 1948. **4**

Shils, Edward A. "Primary Groups in the American Army," in Robert K. Merton and Paul F. Lazarsfeld, eds., *Continuities in Social Research.* Free Press, 1950, pp. 16–39. **330**

Shils, Edward A. "The Study of the Primary Group," in Daniel Lerner and Harold D. Lasswell, eds., *The Policy Sciences: Recent Developments in Scope and Method.* Stanford U. Press, 1951, pp. 44–69. **361, 371**

Shils, Edward A., and Morris Janowitz. "Cohesion and Disintegration in the Wehrmacht in World War II." *Pub. Opin. Quart.,* 12, 1948, pp. 280–315. **372, 447**

Shlien, John M., Harold H. Mosak, and Rudolf Dreikurs. "Effects of Time Limits: A Comparison of Two Psychotherapies," *J. Counsel. Psychol.,* 9, 1962, pp. 31–34. **293**

Shuey, Audrey M. *The Testing of Negro Intelligence.* J. P. Bell, 1958. **495, 496, 497, 498, 524**

Shuttleworth, Frank K. "The Nature Versus Nurture Problem: II. The Contributions of Nature and Nurture to Individual Differences in Intelligence," *J. Educ. Psychol.*, 26, 1935, pp. 655–81. **217**

Sibley, Elbridge. "Some Demographic Clues to Stratification," *Amer. Sociol. Rev.*, 7, 1942, pp. 322–30. **437**

Sidowski, J. B. "Influence of Awareness of Reinforcement on Verbal Conditioning," *J. Exper. Psychol.*, 48, 1954, pp. 355–60. **144**

Siipola, Elsa M. "A Group Study of Some Effects of Preparatory Set," *Psychol. Monogr.*, 46, No. 6, 1935, pp. 27–38. **114**

Sills, David L. Personal communication, 1962. **364**

Sills, David L. "A Sociologist Looks at Motivation," in Nathan E. Cohen, ed., *The Citizen Volunteer*. Harper & Row, 1960, pp. 70–93. **365**

Sills, David L. *The Volunteers: Means and Ends in a National Organization*. A report of the Bureau of Applied Social Research, Columbia U. Free Press, 1957. **366, 368, 370, 380**

Simmons, Leo W. *The Role of the Aged in Primitive Society*. Yale U. Press, 1945. **320–21**

Simmons, Ozzie G. *Social Status and Public Health*. Social Science Research Council, pamphlet No. 13, 1958. **640**

Simon, Charles W., and William H. Emmons. "Responses to Material Presented During Various Levels of Sleep," *J. Exper. Psychol.*, 51, 1956, pp. 89–97. **179**

Simpson, George E., and J. Milton Yinger. *Racial and Cultural Minorities*. Harper & Row, 1953. **400, 494, 500, 521, 522, 523**

Sims, Verner M., and James R. Patrick. "Attitude Toward the Negro of Northern and Southern College Students," *J. Soc. Psychol.*, 7, 1936, pp. 192–204. **509–10**

Sjoberg, Gideon. "Comparative Urban Sociology," in Robert K. Merton *et al.*, eds., *Sociology Today: Problems and Prospects*. Basic Books, 1959, pp. 334–59. **641**

Skinner, B. F. *The Behavior of Organisms: An Experimental Analysis*. Appleton-Century-Crofts, 1938. **141, 153, 237**

Skinner, B. F. "A Case History in Scientific Method," *Amer. Psychologist*, 11, 1956, pp. 221–33. **133–34**

Skinner, B. F. "Pigeons in a Pelican," *Amer. Psychologist*, 15, 1960, pp. 28–37. **148**

Skinner, B. F. *Science and Human Behavior*. Macmillan, 1953. **156**

Skodak, Marie, and Harold M. Skeels. "A Final Follow-Up Study of One Hundred Adopted Children," *J. Genet. Psychol.*, 75, 1949, pp. 85–125. **217**

Slater, Philip E. "Role Differentiation in Small Groups," in A. Paul Hare *et al.*, eds., *Small Groups: Studies in Social In-teraction*. Knopf, 1955, pp. 498–515. **346**

Smith, Donald E., and Julian E. Hochberg. "The Effect of 'Punishment' (Electric Shock) on Figure-Ground Perception," *J. Psychol.*, 38, 1954, pp. 83–87. **111**

Smoke, K. L. "An Objective Study of Concept Formation," *Psychol. Monogr.*, 42, No. 4, 1932. **199**

Smoke, K. L. "Negative Instances in Concept Learning," *J. Exper. Psychol.*, 16, 1933, pp. 583–88. **199**

Snyder, William. "Psychotherapy," *Annu. Rev. Psychol.*, 9, 1958, pp. 353–74. **289**

Soal, Samuel G., and F. Bateman. *Modern Experiments in Telepathy*. Yale U. Press, 1954. **131**

Sorokin, Pitirim A. *Man and Society in Calamity*. Dutton, 1942. **244**

Spearman, C. *The Abilities of Man: Their Nature and Measurement*. Macmillan, 1927. **212**

Speier, Hans. "The American Soldier and the Sociology of Military Organization," in Robert K. Merton and Paul F. Lazarsfeld, eds., *Continuities in Social Research*. Free Press, 1950, pp. 106–32. **378, 446**

Spelt, David K. "The Conditioning of the Human Fetus *in Utero*," *J. Exper. Psychol.*, 38, 1948, pp. 338–46. **138**

Spielberger, Charles D. "The Role of Awareness in Verbal Conditioning," in Charles W. Eriksen, ed., *Behavior and Awareness*. Duke U. Press, 1962, pp. 73–101. **146**

Spivak, M., and J. Papajohn. "The Effect of the Schedule of Reinforcement on Operant Conditioning of a Verbal Response in the Autokinetic Situation," *J. Abnorm. Soc. Psychol.*, 54, 1957, pp. 213–17. **144**

Spragg, S. D. S. "Morphine Addiction in Chimpanzees," *Comp. Psychol. Monogr.*, 15, No. 7, 1940. **242**

Spuhler, J. N. "Physical Anthropology and Demography," in Philip M. Hauser and Otis Dudley Duncan, eds., *The Study of Population: An Inventory and Appraisal*. U. of Chicago Press, 1959, pp. 728–58. **309**

Srole, Leo, Thomas Langner, Stanley Michael, Marvin Opler, and Thomas Rennie. *Mental Health in the Metropolis: The Midtown Manhattan Study*. McGraw-Hill, 1962. **636**

Star, Shirley A., and Helen MacGill Hughes. "Report on an Educational Campaign: The Cincinnati Plan for the United Nations," *Amer. J. Sociol.*, 55, 1950, pp. 389–400. **530**

Star, Shirley A., Robin M. Williams, Jr., and Samuel A. Stouffer. "Negro Soldiers," in Samuel A. Stouffer *et al.*, *The American Soldier: Adjustment During Army Life, Studies in Social Psychology in World War II*, Vol. I. Princeton U.

Press, 1949, pp. 486–599. **524**

Stein, Morris I. "Social and Psychological Factors Affecting Creativity of Industrial Research Chemists." Unpublished ms., presented at Fall meeting of the Industrial Research Institute, Pittsburgh, Pa., October, 1957. **227**

Stein, Morris I., and Shirley J. Heinze. *Creativity and the Individual.* Free Press, 1960. **236**

Steiner, Gary A. *The People Look at Television.* Knopf, 1963. **530, 540, 544, 555**

Stendler, Celia B. *Children of Brasstown.* U. of Illinois Press, 1949. **469**

Stephens, J. M. *Educational Psychology.* Rev. ed. Holt, Rinehart & Winston, 1956. **235**

Stevens, S. S. "Sensation and Psychological Measurement," in Edwin G. Boring, Herbert S. Langfeld, and Harry P. Weld, eds., *Foundations of Psychology.* Wiley, 1948, pp. 250–68. **96**

Stevens, S. S. "The Surprising Simplicity of Sensory Matrics," *Amer. Psychologist,* 17, 1962, pp. 29–39. **97, 98**

Stevens, S. S., ed. *Handbook of Experimental Psychology.* Wiley, 1951. **130, 235**

Steward, Julian H. "Evolution and Process," in Alfred L. Kroeber, ed., *Anthropology Today.* U. of Chicago Press, 1953, pp. 313–26. **649, 651, 656**

Stigler, George J. "The Development of Utility Theory, II," *J. Political Economy,* 58, 1950, p. 373. **97**

Stockwell, Edward G. "Infant Mortality and Socio-Economic Status: A Changing Relationship," *Milbank Memorial Fund Quart.,* 40, 1962, pp. 101–11. **477**

Stogdill, Ralph M. "Personal Factors Associated with Leadership: A Survey of the Literature," *J. Psychol.,* 25, 1948, pp. 35–71. **342**

Stolnitz, George J. "Comparison Between Some Recent Mortality Trends in Underdeveloped Areas and Historical Trends in the West," in *Trends and Differentials in Mortality.* Milbank Memorial Fund, 1956, pp. 26–34. **590–91**

Stouffer, Samuel A. *Communism, Conformity, and Civil Liberties: A Cross-Section of the Nation Speaks Its Mind.* Doubleday, 1955. **429, 572–73, 585**

Stouffer, Samuel A. "Intervening Opportunities: A Theory Relating Mobility and Distance," *Amer. Sociol. Rev.,* 5, 1940, pp. 845–67. **592**

Stouffer, Samuel A., *et al. The American Soldier: Adjustment During Army Life. Studies in Social Psychology in World War II,* Vol. I. Princeton U. Press, 1949. **371, 372, 373, 376, 380, 444–45, 448, 451, 512, 569, 585**

Stouffer, Samuel A., *et al. The American Soldier: Combat and Its Aftermath. Studies in Social Psychology in World War II,* Vol. II. Princeton U. Press, 1949. **337, 380, 447, 448, 451, 585, 622**

Stouffer, Samuel A., *et al. Measurement and Prediction. Studies in Social Psychology in World War II,* Vol. IV. Princeton U. Press, 1950. **35**

Strakosch, Frances Marie. *Factors in the Sex Life of Seven Hundred Psychopathic Women.* Utica, N.Y.: State Hospitals Press, 1934. **285**

Straus, Robert, and Selden D. Bacon. *Drinking in College.* Yale U. Press, 1953. **633**

Strauss, George, and Leonard R. Sayles. *Personnel: The Human Problems of Management.* Prentice-Hall, 1960. **408**

Street, Roy F. *A Gestalt Completion Test: A Study of a Cross Section of Intellect.* Teachers College, Columbia U., 1931. **107**

Strodtbeck, Fred L. "Family Interaction, Values, and Achievement," in David C. McClelland, Alfred L. Baldwin, Urie Bronfenbrenner, and Fred L. Strodtbeck, *Talent and Society.* Van Nostrand, 1958, pp. 135–94. **438**

Strodtbeck, Fred L. "Husband-Wife Interaction over Revealed Differences," *Amer. Sociol. Rev.,* 16, 1951, pp. 468–73. **315**

Strodtbeck, Fred L. Item in *Report for the Five Years 1946–1951.* Harvard U., Laboratory of Social Relations, 1952. **315**

Strupp, Hans H. "Psychotherapy," *Annu. Rev. Psychol.,* 13, 1962, pp. 445–78. **290, 293, 294**

Suchman, Edward A., *et al. Desegregation: Some Propositions and Research Suggestions.* Anti-Defamation League of B'nai B'rith, 1958. **517, 519, 543**

Sundal, A. Philip, and Thomas C. McCormick. "Age at Marriage and Mate Selection: Madison, Wisconsin, 1937–1943," *Amer. Sociol. Rev.,* 16, 1951, pp. 37–48. **306–07**

Sussman, Marvin B. "The Help Pattern in the Middle-Class Family," *Amer. Sociol. Rev.,* 18, 1953, pp. 22–28. **320**

Sutherland, E. H. "Mental Deficiency and Crime," in Kimball Young, ed., *Social Attitudes.* Holt, Rinehart & Winston, 1931, pp. 357–75. **629–30**

Sutherland, I. "Variations in Occupational Mortality Between and Within Social Classes," *Brit. J. Soc. Med.,* 1, 1947, pp. 126–34. **602**

Sutter, J., and L. Tabah. "Les Nations d'Isolat et de Population Minimum," *Population,* 6, 1951, pp. 481–89. **307**

Swadesh, Morris. "Lexico-statistic Dating of Prehistoric Ethnic Contacts," *Proceedings of the American Philosophical Society,* 96, 1952, pp. 452–63. **191, 192**

Sykes, Gresham M. *Crime and Society.* Random House, 1956. **626**

Taffel, C. "Anxiety and the Conditioning of Verbal Behavior," *J. Abnorm. Soc. Psychol.*, 51, 1955, pp. 496–501. **144**

Taft, Donald R. *Criminology.* Macmillan, 1950. **626**

Tagiuri, Renato, and Luigi Petrullo, eds. *Person Perception and Interpersonal Behavior.* Stanford U. Press, 1958. **131**

Tatz, S. J. "Symbolic Mediation in 'Learning Without Awareness.' " Paper read at Eastern Psychological Assoc., Atlantic City, March, 1956. **144**

Terman, Lewis M. "Mental and Physical Traits of a Thousand Gifted Children," in Roger G. Barker, Jacob S. Kounin, and Herbert F. Wright, eds. *Child Behavior and Development.* McGraw-Hill, 1943, pp. 279–306. **52–53**

Terman, Lewis M. *Psychological Factors in Marital Happiness.* McGraw-Hill, 1938. **75**

Terman, Lewis M., and Maud A. Merrill. *Measuring Intelligence.* Houghton Mifflin, 1937. **210**

Terman, Lewis M., and Maud A. Merrill. *Stanford-Binet Intelligence Scale: Manual for the Third Revision Form L-M.* Houghton Mifflin, 1960. **210, 236**

Terman, Lewis M., and M. H. Oden. *The Gifted Child Grows Up. Genetic Studies of Genius,* Vol. IV. Stanford U. Press, 1947. **216**

Terman, Lewis M., and M. H. Oden. *The Gifted Group at Mid-Life. Genetic Studies of Genius,* Vol. V. Stanford U. Press, 1959. **216**

Terman, Lewis M., *et al. Mental and Physical Traits of a Thousand Gifted Children. Genetic Studies of Genius,* Vol. I. Stanford U. Press, 1925. **52**

ter Pelkwijk, J. J., and Nikolaas Tinbergen. "Eine Reizbiologische Analyse einiger Verhaltensweisen von *Gasterosteus Aculeatus L,*" *Zeitschrift für Tierpsychologie,* 1, 1937, pp. 193–204. **40**

Thomas, Brinley. "International Migration," in Philip M. Hauser and Otis Dudley Duncan, eds., *The Study of Population: An Inventory and Appraisal.* U. of Chicago Press, 1959, pp. 510–43. **593–94, 595**

Thomas, John L. *The American Catholic Family.* Prentice-Hall, 1956. **306**

Thomas, William I. *The Unadjusted Girl.* Little, Brown, 1923. **257**

Thomas, William I., and Florian Znaniecki. *The Polish Peasant in Europe and America,* Vol. II. Knopf, 1918. **655**

Thompson, George G. "Developmental Psychology," *Annu. Rev. Psychol.,* 10, 1959, pp. 1–42. **58**

Thorndike, E. L. "Mental Discipline in High School Studies," *J. Educ. Psychol.,*
15, 1924, pp. 1–22, 83–98. **162**

Thurstone, L. L., and Richard L. Jenkins. *Order of Birth, Parent-Age, and Intelligence.* U. of Chicago Press, 1931. **226**

Thurstone, L. L., and T. G. Thurstone. *Factorial Studies of Intelligence.* U. of Chicago Press, 1941. **212, 213–14**

Tinbergen, Nikolaas. *The Study of Instinct.* Oxford U. Press, 1951. **40, 41, 236**

Titus, H. Edwin, and E. P. Hollander. "The California F Scale in Psychological Research, 1950–1955," *Psychol. Bull.,* 54, 1957, pp. 47–64. **260**

Trist, Eric, and K. W. Bamforth. "Some Social and Psychological Consequences of the Longwall Method of Coal-Getting," *Hum. Relat.,* 4, 1951, pp. 3–38. **410**

Tryon, Robert C. "Genetic Differences in Maze-Learning Ability in Rats," in National Society for the Study of Education Yearbook, *Intelligence: Its Nature and Nurture: I. Comparative and Critical Exposition.* Public School Publication Co., 1940, pp. 111–19. **218**

Tulchin, Simon H. *Intelligence and Crime.* U. of Chicago Press, 1939. **630**

Tyler, Leona E. *The Psychology of Human Differences.* 2nd ed. Appleton-Century-Crofts, 1956. **222, 236**

Tylor, Edward B. *Primitive Culture.* 3rd English ed. Murray, 1891. **646**

Underwood, B. J. "Associative Inhibition in the Learning of Successive Paired-Associate Lists," *J. Exper. Psychol.,* 34, 1944, pp. 127–35. **165**

Underwood, Frances W., and Irma Honigmann. "A Comparison of Socialization and Personality in Two Simple Societies," *Amer. Anthropologist,* 49, 1947, pp. 557–77. **76**

United Nations, Department of Economic and Social Affairs. *Demographic Aspects of Manpower: I. Sex and Age Patterns of Participation in Economic Activities.* U.N., 1962. **406, 407–08**

United Nations, Department of Economic and Social Affairs. *Report on World Social Situation,* No. 24. U.N. Pub. Sales. 1957. **591**

United Nations, Department of Social Affairs, Population Division. *The Determinants and Consequences of Population Trends: A Summary of the Findings of Studies on the Relationships Between Population Changes and Economic and Social Conditions.* Population Studies, No. 17. U.N., 1953. **598, 600, 601, 602, 611, 641**

Vance, Rupert B. "Prerequisites to Immigration: Elements of National Policy," in Proceedings of the 1957 Annual Conference of the Milbank Memorial Fund, *Selected Studies of Migration Since World War II*. Milbank Memorial Fund, 1958, pp. 75–88. **593**

Verplanck, William S. "The Control of the Content of Conversation: Reinforcement of Statements of Opinion," *J. Abnorm. Soc. Psychol.*, 51, 1955, pp. 668–76. **144, 145**

Vinacke, William Edgar. "The Investigation of Concept Formation," *Psychol. Bull.*, 48, 1951, pp. 1–31. **198, 236**

Vinacke, William Edgar. *The Psychology of Thinking*. McGraw-Hill, 1952. **44**

Visher, Stephen S. "Climatic Influences," in Griffith Taylor, ed., *Geography in the Twentieth Century*. Rev. ed. Philosophical Library, 1957, pp. 196–220. **612**

Vogel, W., R. W. Baker, and R. S. Lazarus. "The Roles of Motivation in Psychological States," *J. Abnorm. Soc. Psychol.*, 56, 1958, pp. 105–12. **260**

Vosk, M. "Correlates of Prejudice," *Rev. Educ. Res.*, 23, 1953, pp. 353–61. **507**

Wach, Joachim. *The Comparative Study of Religions*. Ed. by Joseph M. Kitagawa. Columbia U. Press, 1958. **386–87**

Wach, Joachim. *Sociology of Religion*. U. of Chicago Press, 1944. **389, 450**

Wahlke, John C., and Heinz Eulau. *Legislative Behavior*. Free Press, 1959. **450**

Walker, Charles R. *Steeltown: An Industrial Case History of the Conflict Between Progress and Security*. Yale Labor and Management Center Series. Harper & Row, 1950. **617**

Walker, Charles R., and Robert H. Guest. *The Man on the Assembly Line*. Harvard U. Press, 1952. **410**

Wallas, Graham. *The Art of Thought*. Harcourt, Brace & World, 1921. **202**

Wallis, Allen, and Harry J. Roberts. *Statistics: A New Approach*. Free Press, 1956. **35**

Wang, G. H. "The Relation Between 'Spontaneous' Activity and Oestrous Cycle in the White Rat," *Comp. Psychol. Monogr.*, 2, No. 6, 1923. **262**

Waples, Douglas. "The Relation of Subject Interests to Actual Reading," *Library Quart.*, 2, 1932, pp. 42–70. **531**

Ward, Lewis B. "Reminiscence and Rote Learning," *Psychol. Monogr.*, 49, No. 4, 1937. **163**

Warden, C. J. *Animal Motivation Studies: The Albino Rat*. Columbia U. Press, 1931. **246**

Warner, Lucien. "What the Younger Psychologists Think About ESP," *J. Parapsychol.*, 19, 1955, pp. 228–35. **127**

Warner, W. Lloyd. "The Study of Social Stratification," in Joseph B. Gittler, ed.,

Review of Sociology: Analysis of a Decade. Wiley, 1957, pp. 221–58. **315–16**

Warner, W. Lloyd, and J. O. Low. *The Social System of the Modern Factory*. Yankee City Series, Vol. IV. Yale U. Press, 1947. **617**

Warner, W. Lloyd, and Paul S. Lunt. *The Social Life of a Modern Community*. Yankee City Series, Vol. I. Yale U. Press, 1941. **456, 490**

Warner, W. Lloyd, and Paul S. Lunt. *The Status System of a Modern Community*. Yankee City Series, Vol. II. Yale U. Press, 1942. **490**

Washburn, Sherwood. Personal communication, 1961. **83**

Washburn, Sherwood, and Irven DeVore. "The Social Life of Baboons," *Scient. Amer.*, 204, No. 6, 1961, pp. 62–71. **50**

Watkins, J. G. "A Case of Hypnotic Trance Induced in Resistant Subject in Spite of Active Opposition," *Brit. J. Med. Hypnotism*, 2, 1951, pp. 26–31. **125**

Watson, Goodwin. "A Comparison of the Effects of Lax Versus Strict Home Training," *J. Soc. Psychol.*, 5, 1934, pp. 102–05. **269**

Watson, Jeanne. "Some Social and Psychological Situations Related to Change in Attitude," *Hum. Relat.*, 3, 1950, pp. 15–56. **514**

Webb, Eugene. "Weber's Law and Consumer Prices," *Amer. Psychologist*, 63, 1961, p. 450. **97**

Weber, Max. *The Protestant Ethic and the Spirit of Capitalism*. Trans. by Talcott Parsons. Scribner's, 1958. **391**

Weber, Max. *The Theory of Social and Economic Organization*. Trans. by A. M. Henderson and Talcott Parsons. Free Press, 1947. **376–77**

Wechsler, David. *The Measurement and Appraisal of Adult Intelligence*. 4th ed. Williams & Wilkins, 1958. **211, 220, 221, 236**

Wechsler, David. *The Wechsler Adult Intelligence Scale Manual*. Psychological Corp., 1955. **215, 221**

Weinstock, S. Alexander. "Some Factors that Retard or Accelerate the Rate of Acculturation," *Hum. Relat.*, 1963 (in press). **656**

Weissberg, A. *The Accused*. Simon & Schuster, 1951. **252**

Weitzenhoffer, André M. *Hypnotism: An Objective Study in Suggestibility*. Wiley, 1953(a). **122, 123, 125, 126**

Weitzenhoffer, André M. Abstract of "The Production of Antisocial Acts Under Hypnosis," (*J. Abnorm. Soc. Psychol.*, 44, 1949, p. 420), in *Annu. Rev. Hypnosis Literature*, 1–2, 1953(b), pp. 49–50. **124**

Welch, L. "A Preliminary Investigation of Some Aspects of the Hierarchical Development of Concepts," *J. Gen. Psychol.*, 22, 1940, pp. 359–78. **198**

Welch, L., and L. Long. "A Further Investigation of the Higher Structural Phases of Concept Formation," *J. Psychol.*, 10, 1940(a), pp. 211–20. **198**

Welch, L., and L. Long. "The Higher Structural Phases of Concept Formation of Children," *J. Psychol.*, 9, 1940(b), pp. 59–95. **198**

Wells, Wesley Raymond. "Expectancy Versus Performance in Hypnosis," in Lesley Kuhn and Salvatore Russo, eds., *Modern Hypnosis.* Psychological Library, 1947, pp. 292–310. **123**

Wendt, Hans-Werner. "Motivation, Effort, and Performance," in David C. McClelland, ed., *Studies in Motivation.* Appleton-Century-Crofts, 1955, pp. 448–59. **260, 263**

Wertheim, J., and S. A. Mednick. "The Achievement Motive and Field Independence," *J. Consult. Psychol.*, 22, 1958, p. 38. **260**

Wertheimer, Max. *Productive Thinking.* Rev. by Michael Wertheimer. Harper & Row, 1959. **206, 207, 208, 236**

Wertheimer, Michael. "Principles of Perceptual Organization," in David C. Beardslee and Michael Wertheimer, eds., *Readings in Perception.* Van Nostrand, 1958, pp. 115–35. **106, 107, 108, 110**

West, James. *Plainville, U.S.A.* Columbia U. Press, 1945. **458, 490**

Westoff, Charles F., Robert G. Potter, Jr., Philip C. Sagi, and Elliot G. Mishler. *Family Growth in Metropolitan America.* Princeton U. Press, 1961. **600**

White, Leslie A. "Ikhnaton: The Great Man vs. the Culture Process," *J. Amer. Oriental Soc.*, 68, 1948, pp. 91–114. **391**

White, Ralph K., and Ronald O. Lippitt. *Autocracy and Democracy.* Harper & Row, 1960. **344, 345**

Whiting, John W. M. "The Cross-Cultural Method," in Gardner Lindzey, ed., *Handbook of Social Psychology*, Vol. I. Addison-Wesley, 1954, pp. 523–31. **300**

Whiting, John W. M., and Irvin L. Child. *Child Training and Personality: A Cross-Cultural Study.* Yale U. Press, 1953. **71, 72, 77, 78, 85**

Whorf, B. L. *Language, Thought, and Reality.* Ed. by John Carroll. Wiley, 1956. **190**

Whyte, William Foote. *Street Corner Society.* U. of Chicago Press, 1943. **341**

Whyte, William Foote, and Frank B. Miller. "Industrial Sociology," in Joseph B. Gittler, ed., *Review of Sociology: Analysis of a Decade.* Wiley, 1957, pp. 289–345.

408–09, 414, 450

Wickes, T. A., Jr. "Examiner Influence in a Testing Situation," *J. Consult. Psychol.*, 20, 1956, pp. 23–26. **144**

Wiener, Morton. "Word Frequency or Motivation in Perceptual Defense," *J. Abnorm. Soc. Psychol.*, 51, 1955, pp. 214–18. **101**

Wilder, J. "Facts and Figures on Psychotherapy," *J. Clin. Psychopath.*, 7, 1945, pp. 311–47. **288**

Wile, I. S., and R. David. "The Relation of Birth to Behavior," *Amer. J. Orthopsychiat.*, 11, 1941, pp. 320–34. **73**

Williams, Carl D. "Case Report: Elimination of Tantrum Behavior by Extinction Procedures," *J. Abnorm. Soc. Psychol.*, 59, 1959, p. 269. **142**

Williams, Robin M., Jr. "Racial and Cultural Relations," in Joseph B. Gittler, ed., *Review of Sociology: Analysis of a Decade.* Wiley, 1957, pp. 423–64. **524**

Williams, Robin M., Jr. *The Reduction of Intergroup Tensions: A Survey of Research on Problems of Ethnic, Racial, and Religious Group Relations.* Social Science Research Council, Bulletin 57, 1947. **514–15, 524**

Williams, Robin M., Jr. "Review and Assessment of Research on Race and Culture Conflict." Unpublished paper presented to Conference on Research in Human Relations, Rockefeller Foundation, February–March 1953. **516–17, 519**

Wilner, Daniel M., Rosabelle P. Walkley, and Stuart W. Cook. "Residential Proximity and Intergroup Relations in Public Housing Projects," *J. Soc. Issues*, 8, 1952, pp. 45–69. **349**

Wilson, W. C., and W. S. Verplanck. "Some Observations on the Reinforcement of Verbal Operants," *Amer. J. Psychol.*, 69, 1956, pp. 448–51. **144**

Winch, Robert F. "Marriage and the Family," in Joseph B. Gittler, ed. *Review of Sociology: Analysis of a Decade.* Wiley, 1957, pp. 346–90. **71, 307, 309, 633**

Winch, Robert F. *Mate Selection: A Study of Complementary Needs.* Harper & Row, 1958. **309, 323**

Witkin, H. A. " 'Hypotheses' in Rats: An Experimental Critique: I. The Genesis of Systematic Behavior in Linear Situations," *J. Comp. Psychol.*, 30, 1940, pp. 457–82. **195–96.**

Wolfe, John B. "Effectiveness of Token-Rewards for Chimpanzees," *Comp. Psychol. Monogr.*, 12, No. 5, 1936. **256**

Wolfle, Dael. *America's Resources of Specialized Talent.* Harper & Row, 1954. **211**

Wolpe, Joseph. *Psychotherapy by Reciprocal Inhibition.* Stanford U. Press, 1958. **277–78, 290–91**

Woodworth, Robert S. *Experimental Psychology*. Holt, Rinehart & Winston, 1938. **194**

Wrong, Dennis H. *Population*. Random House, 1956. **598, 600**

Yarrow, Leon J. "Maternal Deprivation: Toward an Empirical and Conceptual Reevaluation," *Psychol. Bull.*, 58, 1961, pp. 459–90. **85**

Yaskin, J. C. "The Psychoneuroses and Neuroses: A Review of 100 Cases with Special Reference to Treatment and Results," *Amer. J. Psychiat.*, 93, 1936, pp. 107–25. **288**

Yerkes, Robert M., and James H. Elder. "Oestrus, Receptivity, and Mating in Chimpanzee," *Comp. Psychol. Monogr.*, 13, No. 5, 1936. **301**

Yinger, J. Milton. *Religion, Society, and the Individual*. Macmillan, 1957. **394**

Yoshino, I. Roger. "A Re-study of Suye Mura: An Investigation of Social Change," *Proceedings of the Pacific Sociological Society*, 1956. **614**

Yoshioka, J. G. "Weber's Law in the Discrimination of Maze Distance by the White Rat," *U. of California Publications in Psychology*, 4, 1929, pp. 155–84. **97**

Young, Michael. *The Rise of the Meritocracy, 1870–2033*. Random House, 1959. **223, 471**

Young, Michael, and Peter Willmott. *Family and Kinship in East London*. Free Press, 1957. **320**

Young, Paul Thomas. *Motivation of Behavior*. Wiley, 1936. **48**

Young, Paul Thomas. "Reversal of Food Preferences of the White Rat Through Controlled Prefeeding," *J. Genet. Psychol.*, 22, 1940, pp. 33–66. **48**

Zawadski, Bohan, and Paul F. Lazarsfeld. "The Psychological Consequences of Unemployment," *J. Soc. Psychol.*, 6, 1935, pp. 224–51. **404**

Zeigarnik, B. "Das Behalten erledigter und unerledigter Handlungen" ("On the Retention of Completed and Uncompleted Activities"), *Psychologische Forschung*, 9, 1927, pp. 1–85. **251**

Zelditch, Morris, Jr. "Role Differentiation in the Nuclear Family: A Comparative Study," in Talcott Parsons, Robert F. Bales, *et al.*, *Family, Socialization and Interaction Process*. Free Press, 1955, pp. 307–51. **314**

Zeman, Hans. "Verbreitung und Grad der eidetischen Anlage," *Zeitschrift für Psychologie*, 96, 1925, pp. 208–73. **188**

Zetterberg, Hans. "Theorie, Forschung und Praxis in der Soziologie," *Handbuch der empirischen Sozialforschung*, 1, 1961, pp. 64–104. **409**

Zimmerman, Carle C. *The Changing Community*. Harper & Row, 1938. **620**

Zimmerman, Claire, and Raymond A. Bauer. "The Effect of an Audience upon What Is Remembered," *Pub. Opin. Quart.*, 20, 1956, pp. 238–48. **568**

SUBJECT INDEX

Absenteeism, 371, 374, 408–11
Absolute threshold, 91, 92–95
Academic freedom, 441–42
Acculturation: of minority groups, 512–13; and assimilation, 646, 654, 655–56
Achievement motive (need achievement), 80–81, 257; and creativity, 227; measurement of, 260–61; correlates of, 263–64; and anxiety, 275; and economic development, 399, 401–03; and political preferences, 430–31; and social mobility, 464–65, 468–71, 485–86, 600; and fertility, 599–600; effect of climate on, 612–13
Achievement-ascription, 444, 459–63
Action potentials, 170–71
Adaptation, see Sensory adaptation
Adaptive behavior, 38, 44, 88
Adjustment in marriage, 310
Adlerian psychotherapy, 293
Aesthetic judgments, 97, 488
Affection: age at first appearance of, 54; and personality development, 75
Affiliation: as aspect of socialization, 44, 75, 252; as motive (need affiliation), 252, 254–55; and anxiety, 254–55; see also Dependency and Identification
Africa, see Underdeveloped countries
Age: and I.Q. score, 62, 220–22; and hypnotizability, 125; and prognosis in psychotherapy, 293–94; and sexual behavior, 299, 302, 303–04; and divorce, 313; and church involvement, 392–93; and political activity, 421–24; and political opinions, 560, 573; and mental illness, 637
Aged, 319–20
Age-differential: for marriage partners, 307–08, 309; in migrations, 607; in criminal behavior, 627; in suicide rates, 634
Age-grading, 82–84
Age-structure of population, 594
Aggrandizement effect, 379
Aggression: effect of punishment on, 72–73; factors in development of, 81–82; frustra-

tion of, 82, 267–70; as motive (need aggression), 258; repression of, 281; displacement of, on minority groups, 514, 515–16
Agrarian communities: fertility in, 597–98, 600; mortality in, 602; see also Underdeveloped countries and Urban-rural differences
Agrarian political parties, 418
"Aha!" phenomenon: in thinking, 168; in problem-solving, 201
Alcoholism: posthypnotic suggestion in treatment of, 124–25; in cats, as relief for experimental neurosis, 278; class differences in, 486; correlates of, 633
Ambition, see Achievement motive
Anal personality, 285–86
Anger, age at first appearance of, 54
Animal behavior and human behavior, 50, 156–57
"Anticipatory socialization," 330–31, 428, 464, 469–70, 487, 520
Anti-Semitism, 282–83, 488, 513–14, 516; and perception of Jews, 115–16
Anxiety: and severity of socialization, 75; alleviated by posthypnotic suggestion, 124–25, 126; as conditioned response, 138; arising from dream deprivation, 176; and creativity, 227; and affiliative needs, 254–55; and authoritarian personality, 260; as result of avoidance-avoidance conflict, 276; and marital adjustment, 310
Apathy and mass media, 546
Apes, 50, 64
Aphasia, 169
Approach-approach conflict, 271–72
Approach-avoidance conflict, 272–75, 278–79
Approval as motivational factor, 253, 255
Aspiration level, 275
Assimilation: in perceptual organization, 109; and contrast, 118–19; in attitude

B 4
C 5
D 6
E 7
F 8
G 9
H 0
I 1
J 2